Disaster in Korea

Number Eleven: Williams-Ford
Texas A&M University Military History Series

DISASTER IN ☆ KOREA

THE CHINESE CONFRONT MACARTHUR

By Lt. Col. Roy E. Appleman (Ret)

TEXAS A&M UNIVERSITY PRESS
COLLEGE STATION

Copyright © 1989 by Roy E. Appleman
Manufactured in the United States of America
All rights reserved
Second Printing, 2009

The paper used in this book meets the minimum
requirements of the American National Standard for
Permanence of Paper for Printed Library Materials,
Z39.48-1984. Binding materials have been chosen
for durability.

LIBRARY OF CONGRESS CATALOGING-IN-PUBLICATION DATA

Appleman, Roy Edgar.
　　Disaster in Korea : the Chinese confront MacArthur /
by Roy E. Appleman.—1st ed.
　　　　p.　　cm.—(Texas A&M University military
history series ; no. 11)
　　Bibliography: p.
　　Includes index.
　　ISBN 0-89096-344-4 (alk. paper)
　　1. Korean War, 1950–1953—Campaigns.　2. China.
Chung-kuo jen min chih yüan chün.　I. Title.
II. Series: Texas A&M University military history
series ; 11.
DS918.A79　　1989
951.9′042—dc19　　　　　　　　　　　　　88-28133
　　CIP
　　ISBN 13: 978-1-60344-128-5 (pbk.)
　　ISBN 10: 1-60344-128-X (pbk.)

First published as Number Eleven:
Texas A&M University Military History Series

Contents

List of Illustrations		*page* vii
List of Tables		ix
List of Maps		xi
Preface		xiii
Chapter 1.	Prelude to MacArthur's Attack to End the War	3
2.	Uncertainty on the Eve of the UN Advance	23
3.	UN and CCF Positions and Orders of Battle	34
4.	The First Day of Eighth Army's Attack	49
5.	The Second Day of Eighth Army's Attack	60
6.	The CCF 2nd Phase Offensive	74
7.	The CCF Armies' Rout of the ROK II Corps	77
8.	Defeat of the US 25th Infantry Division	102
9.	Withdrawal of Eighth Army Left Flank to the Chongchon River	143
10.	The CCF 40th Army Attack on the US 2nd Infantry Division	154
11.	The US 2nd Infantry Division Retreats to Kunu-ri	193
12.	MacArthur Calls a Commanders' Conference	212
13.	Withdrawal of Eighth Army South of the Chongchon River	220
14.	Withdrawal of the 2nd Infantry Division from Kunu-ri	227
15.	Back to Pyongyang	294
16.	Evacuation of Pyongyang	313
17.	The Waist of Korea	341
18.	Big Bugout or Skillful Retreat?	354
19.	The Death of General Walker	390
Notes		398
Bibliographical Note		438
Index		441

Illustrations

Gen. Douglas MacArthur and Lt. Gen. Walton Walker	*page* 4
Bridges over the Yalu River	25
Maj. Gen. John Coulter serving Thanksgiving dinner	36
Gen. Douglas MacArthur and Maj. Gen. John Coulter	38
Maj. Gen. William Kean and Lt. Gen. Walton Walker	39
Maj. Gen. John Church	41
Maj. Gen. Laurence B. Keiser	42
2nd Infantry Division squad advancing down a hill	66
Carrying supplies on a packboard to 9th Infantry	67
The 8076th MASH at Kunu-ri	195
11th Engineer Battalion constructing floating bridge	204
Eighth Army troops withdrawing past refugees	301
8th Kings Royal Irish Hussars covering withdrawal from Pyongyang	302
North Koreans fleeing across Taedong River	319
ROK 2nd Division withdrawing ten miles south of Pyongyang	322

Tables

1. Eighth Army strength, 24 November 1950 — *page* 40
2. Chinese XIII Army Group order of battle, 24 November 1950 — 44
3. Alignment of Eighth Army and CCF forces, 25 November 1950 — 76
4. Casualties for US 2nd Division as of 30 November 1950 — 286
5. Strength of US 2nd Division units, 30 November 1950 — 287
6. US 2nd Division artillery losses at Kunu-ri — 289
7. ROK II Corps strength, 3 December 1950 — 312

Maps

1. Eighth Army area of combat, 25 November–2 December 1950   *page* 6
2. Eighth Army attack plan, 24 November 1950   35
3. CCF XIII Army Group deployment, 24 November 1950   46
4. CCF 38th and 42nd armies' attacks on ROK II Corps, 25–30 November 1950   78
5. US 25th Division attack and CCF counterattack, 24–29 November 1950   103
6. Task Force Dolvin, 25–27 November 1950   105
7. CCF attack on 9th Infantry, 2nd Division, 25 November 1950   157
8. CCF 40th Army attack on 9th and 23rd infantries and crossing of Chongchon River, 25–26 November 1950   170
9. 2nd Division front line, 2 A.M., 28 November 1950   194
10. Withdrawal of I Corps, 25–29 November 1950   221
11. 2nd Division positions in Kunu-ri and vicinity, 29–30 November 1950   228
12. 2nd Division at Kunu-ri, 30 November 1950   239
13. Eighth Army withdrawal positions, 30 November–12 December 1950   295
14. The waist of Korea   342
15. Plan for withdrawal defense lines given in Operational Plan 12, 11 December 1950   357
16. Eighth Army front line, 31 December 1950   396

Preface

Flushed with the victory of Inchon and Seoul in the late summer of 1950, Gen. Douglas MacArthur ignored many warnings and forged ahead in the autumn, determined to complete the victory for all of Korea. To this end, he ordered what he thought would be the last campaign: his Eighth Army would advance to the north and his X Corps to the northeast. From the Korean side of the Yalu River border they would be able to see China's desolate Manchuria province and the Soviet Union's Siberian wasteland. Korea would be unified once again, the Korean War won.

This volume tells the story of Eighth Army's misfortunes in the west in that campaign, so optimistically launched in late November 1950. The results dimmed forever MacArthur's aura of military might and led directly to his eclipse and downfall in the early spring of 1951.

It is a story of a sophisticated modern army being overwhelmed by a Chinese army group of light infantry that carried small arms and grenades and that emerged from its mountain hideouts to strike at night with stunning speed against a surprised American and United Nations army. The ancient Chinese weapons of noise and strange calls at night (bugle, shepherd's horn, and an assortment of whistles) together with colored flares worked effectively for them as a communications system in attack and at the same time frayed the nerves of their adversaries, often to the point of paralysis.

The Chinese onslaught in late November and early December in the hills south of the Yalu was not that of an ignorant command system; it was well planned and showed the influence of deep study of Antoine Henri Jomini's theory of warfare. It was characterized by surprise and frontal attack to hold an enemy while other formations attacked one or both flanks and still other parts executed forced marches to reach the rear of the enemy and cut off his retreat. These tactics created great confusion in the separated UN ranks and frequently led to panic and unit disintegration. From the Chinese point of view the campaign against Eighth Army in the west was also a classic example of using night fighting to demoralize an adversary not accustomed to such action.

The campaign was fought with the UN forces, including the Americans, believing that the legendary Chinese soldier Gen. Lin Piao, famous in the Long March and afterward in the Communists' ranks, commanded his veterans of the Fourth Field Army in the battles against Eighth Army. Such was not the case. Lin Piao was not in Korea during the fighting, nor did he command the troops of the Chinese XIII Army Group of his Fourth Field Army. Even now, one comes upon statements in writings on the Korean War that Lin Piao was the adversary commander.

Another myth widely circulated at the time (and still repeated), apparently believed by commanders in Korea and Western military analysts, is that the Chinese exploited the physical gap between Eighth Army and the X Corps—that they attacked through it and around the right flank of Eighth Army to destroy the ROK II Corps on the army's flank, gain the exposed rear of Eighth Army, and then roll up the army line westward, thus causing the quick defeat of the UN forces and threatening their destruction. Nothing could be more misleading. The Chinese never operated in a military way in the gap, any more than the UN did. It simply was not feasible to do so. Neither side made use of the gap in the high Northern Taebaek Mountains. The fact is that the Chinese attacked the ROK II Corps frontally and broke through its center. The deep penetration through the *center* of its *front* and the exploitation of that breakthrough to pour waiting columns of troops through it to the *rear* of the ROK corps on the army right flank is what caused the rapid disintegration of Eighth Army's right flank and the enemy's subsequent enveloping movement behind the army's center.

It has seemed that no one then or later who has written on the subject has done any independent study of the military positions and movements of both sides in this action or plotted their locations on a tactical map. If this had been done, the readily accepted explanation that the Chinese gained a great victory by exploiting a gap between the Eighth Army and the X Corps could not have survived. It simply did not happen that way. I believe that this book will lay that myth to rest.

I began studies and interviews as early as 1951, when I was in Korea attached to Eighth Army and wanted to learn what had happened the preceding winter. At that time I centered my studies on Kunu-ri, which seemed to have been the critical event. Over the years I continued interviews and carried on correspondence with individuals who survived the fighting in November and December 1950. In 1961 the Department of the Army published my *South to the Naktong, North to the Yalu* as its official combat history of the Korean War from its beginning on 25 June 1950 to 24 November 1950. The latter date marks the beginning of General MacArthur's campaign to drive to the border and to end the war. It is also the date at which this volume picks up the combat story in the west. My *East of Chosin: Entrapment and Breakout in Korea, 1950* tells the story of Army troops east of Chosin Reservoir in MacArthur's resumption of his efforts to end the war.

The writing of this volume was long delayed because not until after I retired could I find the time necessary to study properly the existing archival records. All the unit reports of the Eighth Army engaged in ground combat in Korea are preserved in the National Archives, Federal Records Center, Record Group 407, in Federal Building 1, Suitland, Maryland. I spent two years there, going through the official records of Eighth Army units and the intelligence reports of prisoner interrogations and translated enemy documents. I also spent nearly two months at the Army History Research Center, at Carlisle Barracks, Pennsylvania, studying the Matthew B. Ridgway Papers.

Preface

This book is based on my study of the actual records of the units involved, supplemented by interviews and correspondence with participants, as the notes and documentation will disclose, together with in-depth map study of the terrain involved. My purpose was to present as precisely as possible just what did happen on the ground at the combat level.

Perhaps the most difficult part of the work was to understand what happened at Kunu-ri on 29–30 November and 1 December 1950 that resulted in the virtual destruction of the US 2nd Infantry Division as a combat-effective force. The records are wholly inadequate to describe the events. Most of them were lost in the action. It was only by interviews, and principally through correspondence, with survivors over a period of nearly thirty years that I was eventually able to synthesize at least an approximation of what happened.

A few comments about military terminology may be helpful. The United States Army uses arabic numerals to signify squads, platoons, battalions, regiments, and divisions. It uses capital letters to signify companies. Roman numerals are used to designate corps, and spelled-out numbers to designate armies. Thus, "IX Corps" and "Eighth Army."

Throughout, I use several abbreviations common in discussions of the Korean War and in US military parlance generally, the most common of which are the following:

AAA AW	Antiaircraft Artillery, Automatic Weapons
ASP	Ammunition Supply Point
ATIS	Allied Translation and Interrogation Service
BAR	Browning Automatic Rifle
CCF	Chinese Communist Forces
CG	Commanding General
CO	Commanding Officer
CP	Command Post
DA	Department of the Army
EUSAK	Eighth US Army in Korea
FA	Field Artillery
FEC	Far East Command
GHQ	General Headquarters
HQ	Headquarters
I&R	Intelligence and Reconnaissance
JCS	Joint Chiefs of Staff
KMAG	Korean Military Advisor Group
MSR	Main Supply Road
NK	North Korea
QM	Quartermaster
RCT	Regimental Combat Team
RFP	Relative Fire Power
ROK	Republic of Korea (South Korea)
RTO	Rail Transportation Officer
TACP	Tactical Air Control Party
UN	United Nations

For those who are not well acquainted with military usage, it will be helpful to clarify what may seem the bewildering nomenclature of companies within battalions of an infantry regiment. There are three infantry battalions in a regiment—the 1st, 2nd, and 3rd. Each battalion has four companies—three rifle companies and one weapons company. A regiment thus comprises twelve companies. Each company has a capital letter as its name, and the lettering progresses through the battalions from A Company through M Company. (J is not used, because of possible ambiguity in telephone or radio communication.) One familiar with the company nomenclature would know at a glance that D, H, and M are the weapons companies of the three battalions in a regiment and that the others are the rifle companies.

The period of time covered in this volume is from 24 November to 26 December 1950. In that short time the CCF had not only defeated but routed the UN forces under General Walker in the west of North Korea to such an extent that the evacuation of Pyongyang and the frantic retreat south toward the Han River and Seoul, below the 38th Parallel, often seemed a "bugout." This volume recounts one of the worst defeats an American Army has ever suffered. It also reveals astonishing military-command failures that are possibly unique in our history.

General Walker was killed in a jeep accident on 23 December 1950. His replacement in command was Lt. Gen. Matthew B. Ridgway, who arrived in Korea directly from Washington to assume command of Eighth Army and the UN forces on 26 December. By that time the Chinese had moved south from the Pyongyang area and had established contact with the new Eighth Army defense line just north of Seoul and the Han River. Reorganized North Korean divisions had also moved south from the border to form an assault line east of the North Koreans who had remained in the mountains of central Korea. Together they were ready to launch a major attack across the breadth of Korea when General Ridgway assumed command. This volume's narrative ends at that point.

The Chinese and North Korean attack, beginning on New Year's Eve 1950, marks the beginning of a new phase of the war. That story, with the UN forces under General Ridgway's command, will be told in another volume.

Finally, I would like to acknowledge the contributions of Don Bufkin, who prepared the maps based on sketches I provided, and of M. L. Creamer, who prepared the index.

Disaster in Korea

1. Prelude to MacArthur's Attack to End the War

The half year that had passed since the North Korean army swept across the 38th Parallel on 25 June 1950, and in a matter of days nearly destroyed the American-trained South Korean army, had seen many unexpected and untoward changes in the uncertain fortunes of war. The American and UN entry into the conflict had changed the course of events only gradually. The victory that had seemed so certain in the first week for the Soviet-supported North Korean attack faded, and their attack stalled three months later along the Naktong River and the Pusan perimeter in the southern part of the Korean peninsula.

At that critical moment, Gen. Douglas A. MacArthur launched his seaborne invasion behind the enemy lines at Inchon, captured Seoul, and cut off the North Koreans to the south from their base of supply and lines of communication. Quickly, the US Eighth Army and ROK soldiers drove north against a disintegrating and demoralized enemy force and joined the American seaborne troops that had landed at Inchon. The fortunes of war had reversed suddenly in the brilliant maneuver of Inchon. By the end of September 1950 the invaders had been driven out of South Korea. Lt. Gen. Walton H. Walker's Eighth Army and Maj. Gen. Edward M. Almond's X Corps again controlled all of Korea south of the 38th Parallel.

In October 1950 the decision was made to drive on north across the parallel and to reunify Korea by completing the destruction of the fleeing North Koreans. This objective seemed within grasp. But in late October, Chinese Communist forces suddenly appeared in North Korea in the area south of the Yalu River. They entered the battle only a day's march or two from the Manchurian border. Their surprise onslaught all but destroyed two South Korean divisions and cut to pieces a regiment of the American 1st Cavalry Division. All the UN forces on the west side of the peninsula beat a retreat to a line generally south of the Chongchon River, about fifty miles south of the Manchurian border. On 6 November, as silently and as quickly as they had appeared in attack, the Chinese forces broke contact and withdrew into the cold, northern hills. Just where they were or what their intention for the future was, no one knew.

With this disappearance of the Chinese troops, confidence quickly returned to the American and UN forces, and General MacArthur ordered an advance to the northern boundary of Korea. The Eighth Army advance in the west began on 24 November. It was to be joined three days later by the X Corps attack

Gen. Douglas MacArthur (*left*) and Lt. Gen. Walton H. Walker, commanding general of Eighth Army (*right*), after the conference at Kimpo Airfield, Seoul, 11 December 1950. US Army photograph SC 354108

on the east side of Korea. But then disaster struck. Chinese troops in massive formations sprang up out of the snow-covered mountains and in the west sent the US Eighth Army and the ROK Army reeling southward.

The sudden blow stunned Eighth Army, as if a phantom force had unnerved it. Its only desire, seemingly, was to flee the ghastly, dreaded scene. In the days that followed, Eighth Army never got hold of itself. It did not try to face about and never really fought the Chinese forces in the west in a unified, holding, defensive battle. For the next month it was simply a case of breaking contact with the enemy and of outrunning them southward.

In the east, the X Corps never was able to launch the attack that was planned for 27 November. The X Corps, centering on the 1st Marine Division, was itself attacked just as it assembled for its planned attack north and northwest to help Eighth Army. The tide never turned, and there was no sign that it would turn, until Lt. Gen. Matthew B. Ridgway assumed command of Eighth Army and the UN command in Korea at Christmastime, 1950. His presence in Korea was a direct result of General Walker's death in a jeep accident on 23 December.

The Korean War was thus six months old when General Ridgway came to the Korean peninsula to take command of the US Eighth Army and the United Nations forces. The Chinese Communist troops were jubilant because of their great victory over the American and UN troops—a victory of such proportions that it must have surprised them exceedingly. After all, they were a peasant light-infantry force, poorly and unevenly armed, short of hand and shoulder arms, without artillery, armor, or air power, and possessed of only a primitive supply system. Electronic communication equipment was all but nonexistent among them. A year after they had seized control of China from Chiang Kai-shek, the Chinese Communist leaders in Peking had committed their army in 1950 to a war south of the Yalu River against the strongest military power in the world. It was against a field force equipped with sophisticated weapons and having uncontested control of the skies and an unchecked naval power in the seas around the peninsula. It must have seemed a rash act indeed, a gamble, but one that the Soviet leaders had urged the Chinese to take.

In the period from 24 November to 25 December 1950—one month—a series of disasters unequaled in our country's history overwhelmed American arms. The events seemed to spell utter and total defeat. When Chinese troops entered the Korean War and confronted Americans, it marked the first time the United States found itself in military conflict with a Communist force. From 25 October 1950, which the Chinese themselves give as the beginning of their military action in Korea, until the end of May 1951, the fighting was essentially a war of movement, with both sides maneuvering and avoiding static lines and both sides alternately hoping for victory. Only in midyear, 1951, after the large-scale Chinese attack in the middle of the peninsula collapsed and the American pursuit slowed in the rugged mountains of north-central Korea, did truce talks start and the war gradually become one of position, of heavily fortified main lines of resistance on both sides.

In the six months' war of movement, the Chinese held the initiative most of the time. During this period they mounted what they called phase attacks, or campaigns. Their captured documents and orders list five different campaigns against the UN forces in Korea. One can do no better than to adopt their nomenclature to divide the war during this period into its principal phases, as listed below. The abbreviation "CCF" will be used generally throughout this work for the UN term "Chinese Communist Forces." The Chinese referred to their troops in Korea as Chinese Volunteers. The official Chinese name for its armed forces was the "People's Liberation Army," or PLA, as it is often referred to in documents.

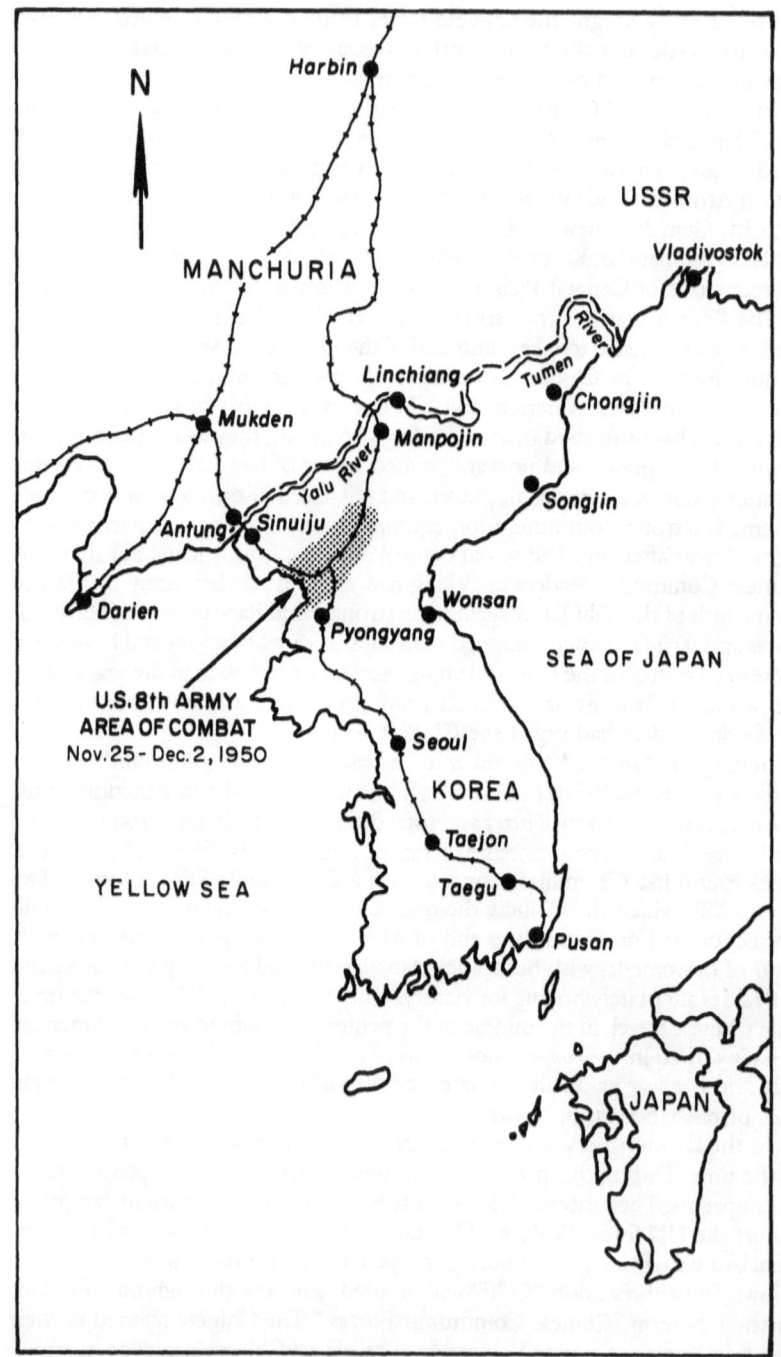

Map 1. Eighth Army's area of combat in Korea, 25 November–2 December 1950.

The CCF Phase Attacks

1st Phase	25 October–8 November 1950
2nd Phase	24 November–25 December 1950
3rd Phase	31 December 1950–7 January 1951
4th Phase (1st Impulse)	11 February–14 March 1951
(2nd Impulse)	15 March–21 April 1951
5th Phase (1st Impulse)	22–29 April 1951
(2nd Impulse)	16–21 May 1951

The 1st Phase Campaign must be considered a Chinese victory, in that it accomplished its purpose. It stopped the UN advance toward the Yalu in October 1950.[1]

The 2nd Phase Campaign was a massive attack across the breadth of Korea against all the advancing UN forces. This volume takes up the combat story of that phase with Eighth Army's projected attack to the border, beginning on 24 November 1950, and the resulting CCF 2nd Phase attack. The 2nd Phase Campaign succeeded brilliantly in the west, but in the east against the X Corps it must be considered a limited success. Even though X Corps withdrew from northeast Korea, actually it defeated the CCF IX Army Group and largely destroyed it.

Then followed the Chinese 3rd Phase Campaign, which was successful. It drove the Eighth Army and the UN command out of Seoul and south of the Han River. The Chinese and the revived North Korean forces were now penetrating once more into South Korea.

The 4th Phase Campaign tried to open a way down the central part of the peninsula behind the main part of Eighth Army to Pusan. It failed.

The 5th Phase Campaign, 1st Impulse, was a major effort in the west; the 2nd Impulse concentrated its strength in the central part of Korea. Both parts of the 5th Phase Campaign were disastrous defeats for the Chinese.

Why Did Chinese "Volunteers" Enter Korea?

The true story of why the Chinese government decided to intervene in the Korean War and just when that decision was made cannot be known with certainty until the Chinese, and possibly the Soviet, archives are opened to researchers.

The Chinese involvement in the initial North Korean attack is less clear, but according to Nikita Khrushchev, China approved it in advance. Once the war had begun, Chinese authorities started moving strong combat forces from central and south China toward its Manchurian border with Korea. After the Inchon landing in September and the subsequent disintegration of the North Korean Army following the fall of Seoul, the Chinese government became intensely interested in the future actions of the UN forces.

This concern was clear when, on 3 October 1950, Chou En-lai, the Chinese foreign minister, called Ambassador Sardar K. M. Panikkar of India to his office. He told him that, if the United States or United Nations forces crossed the 38th Parallel, China would send troops to defend North Korea. He said that this action would not be taken if only South Korean troops crossed the parallel. The

Indian goverment quickly spread this message to all the world. On 10 October, a week later, Peiping radio broadcast a declaration of Chinese intentions that repeated this warning. Five days later a reliable source reported that Moscow would have a surprise awaiting the American force it if approached the northern border of Korea. The net result, however, in the high councils of the United States, and particularly in General MacArthur's Far East Command Headquarters in Tokyo, was general disbelief and an underestimation of the seriousness of these declarations.[2]

Two reasonably reliable sources now available to us clarify the contemporaneous Chinese attitude toward the Korean War. Edgar Snow, in his *Red China Today: The Other Side of the River,* published in 1962, records a conversation he had with Chou En-lai in China. This conversation, according to Snow, was on 30 August 1960. Chou En-lai said that, after the Korean War broke out and American troops entered South Korea, the United States adopted a policy of aggression toward Communist China. It sent the Seventh Fleet to the Taiwan Strait and exercised military control over Taiwan and the waters separating it from the mainland. Communist China deeply resented this presence. When the United States showed intentions of crossing the 38th Parallel and pushing on up to the Chinese border at the Yalu River, China issued its warning through the Indian ambassador. Snow quoted Chou En-lai as saying of that period: "The Chinese people could only take the action of volunteering support to Korea in its war of resistance against the United States. But this action was not taken until four months after the United States stationed its forces in the Taiwan Straits and exercised military control over Taiwan, and not until the United States troops had crossed the Thirty-eighth Parallel and approached the Yalu River."[3]

There can be only speculation, even today, as to details of the story behind Chinese intervention in the Korean War and of a possible Soviet role in starting the war. But one account known to us since 1970 seems highly credible in its general outline. In that year Nikita Khrushchev published a portion of his memoirs in English under the title *Khrushchev Remembers*. He told what he knew of the North Korean, Chinese, and Soviet roles in starting and then continuing the Korean War.

Khrushchev said that North Korean Premier Kim Il Sung originated the idea. Near the end of 1949, he headed a North Korean delegation to Moscow. At that time he proposed to Joseph Stalin that North Korea invade South Korea. Stalin was sympathetic to the idea of extending Communist control over South Korea. Kim Il Sung assured Stalin that, as soon as his troops invaded the South, there would be a civilian uprising that would overthrow Syngman Rhee. He felt that the war would be short.

Stalin, however, did not approve the plan at that time but asked Kim Il Sung to consider the matter further and then come back with a definite plan. The North Korean premier returned home but soon came back to Moscow with his plan. According to Khrushchev, Stalin was still concerned that the United States might intervene. Kim Il Sung argued that the war would be won so quickly that the United States would have no chance to interfere.

At this point, Stalin decided to ask for Mao Tse-tung's opinion of Kim Il Sung's proposal. The Chinese leader approved it. Mao thought that the United States would not intervene but would treat the matter as an internal affair for the Koreans to decide themselves. Khrushchev tells of a big dinner at Stalin's dacha at this time where the Soviet leaders gave Kim Il Sung their blessing and toasted him success.

Just before Kim Il Sung launched his surprise attack across the 38th Parallel on 25 June 1950, Stalin ordered all the Soviet military advisors with the North Korean regiments, divisions, and army headquarters, as well as other Soviet consultants who for years had been helping to organize the North Korean Army, back to Soviet territory. Khrushchev asked Stalin why he was doing this, as they could be of great assistance to North Korea. Stalin snapped back, "It's too dangerous to keep our advisors there. They might be taken prisoner. We don't want there to be evidence for accusing us of taking part in this business. It's Kim Il Sung's affair."

Later, when things started going bad for North Korea, Khrushchev suggested to Stalin that perhaps they should send a qualified Soviet military commander, such as Malinovsky, commander of the Russian Far Eastern Military District, to help Kim Il Sung wage the war. He said Stalin reacted to this suggestion with extreme hostility.

American troops crossed the 38th Parallel in force on 9 October and moved rapidly northward. At this point, Chou En-lai arrived in Moscow. Stalin had gone to Sochi, the Black Sea resort, and Chou flew directly there to see him. On his return to Moscow, Stalin told Khrushchev what transpired at Sochi. He said Mao Tse-tung had sent Chou to see him. Mao wanted to know if Stalin thought the Chinese should move troops into North Korean territory to stop the American and South Korean forces. In their discussions on this subject at Sochi, Stalin and Chou concluded it would be fruitless for China to intervene. But before Chou started back to China, either Stalin or Chou (at Mao's instructions) reopened the discussion. This further discussion ended with a reversal of the earlier decision. It was now decided that China should help North Korea. Chinese troops were already massed along the border and in nearby areas of Manchuria. Stalin and Chou believed these troops were numerous enough to stop the United Nations forces.

From Chinese sources we learn that the question of whether Communist China would enter the Korean War was debated in a meeting of the Political Bureau of the Central Committee of the Communist Party in China, held 3–7 October 1950 in Peking. The decision of the group, and of Mao Tse-tung (Mao Zedong), was to establish the Chinese People's Liberation Army of Volunteers (CPV) to aid North Korea. The decision was taken by Mao Tse-tung on 8 October, and Peng Dehuai, commander of the Northwest Military Region, was appointed CPV commander and concurrent political commissar in orders signed in the early-morning hours of 8 October by Mao as chairman of the Chinese People's Revolutionary Military Commission. This meeting is mentioned in the English edition of *Memoirs of a Chinese Marshal.*

In chapter 14, "The War to Resist U.S. Aggression and Aid Korea," Marshal Peng states: "At noon on October 4, 1950, three days after National Day, an airplane arrived in Xi'an City. I was told to leave for a meeting in Beijing without the slightest delay.

"The Party Central Committee was holding a meeting to discuss the dispatch of troops to aid Korea when I arrived at Zhongnanhai [part of the former imperial palace used as the premises of the Party Central Committee and the State Council] at 4 P.M. . . .

"The Central Committee meeting resumed in the Yiniantang Hall . . . the next afternoon (5 October). After listening to other comrades, I said, 'It is necessary to dispatch troops to aid Korea. If China is devastated by war, it only means that the Liberation War will last a few years longer. The U.S. will find a pretext at any time to invade China if its troops are poised on the bank of the Yalu River and in Taiwan.'

"Chairman Mao made the decision to send me to Korea. I did not decline the offer. . . .

"At dusk on October 18, 1950 I crossed the Yalu River with vanguard units of the Chinese People's Volunteers."[4]

Peng established his first headquarters in Korea in an old mine at the village of Taeyu-dong, a few miles northwest of Onjong and Huichon. He remained there during the Chinese 1st and 2nd Phase campaigns, after which he removed to a different headquarters near Pyongyang. Of the 2nd Phase Campaign, Peng states: "The enemy fled south in panic, abandoning Pyongyang and falling back on the 38th Parallel.

"This campaign laid the foundation of victory in the War to resist U.S. Aggression and Aid Korea. The Democratic People's Republic of Korea recovered all its lost territory by the end of the campaign. In the wake of the Second Campaign, our forces pursued the enemy and by mid-December made a sneak approach to the 38th Parallel. After making a thorough reconnaissance of enemy positions, our forces got everything ready for an offensive."[5]

The UN forces and MacArthur's headquarters believed all this time that Marshal Lin Piao, commander of the Chinese Fourth Field Army, commanded the Chinese Volunteers in Korea. That belief is still held by nearly all American and British writers on the Korean War. Clay Blair in his book *The Forgotten War: Americans in Korea 1950–1953*, published in late 1987, places Lin Piao as the Chinese commander of the Chinese Volunteers in Korea in 1950–51. The truth is that Lin Piao was never in Korea and never was associated with the Chinese Volunteers in Korea.

According to Chinese writer Wei Wei, in his historical novel *East* and supplements to it entitled "Chief Peng," in seven chapters published in the July–August 1984 issue of *Kunlun* magazine, a bimonthly magazine put out by the Chinese Liberation Army, Peng had an extensive conversation with Mao Tsetung on the afternoon of 5 October in which Mao told him of a meeting with Lin Piao the previous night. In that meeting Mao broached the subject of Lin leading the Volunteers in Korea. He told Lin that "we've assembled some armies in south Manchuria. They used to be units of the Fourth Field Army. If they fight, they will have to depend on the northeast for support at first. We felt that sending Comrade Lin Biao would be pretty good. When I sounded him out on this last night though, he was obviously very nervous and said right away that his health was very poor and that he was only able to sleep two or three hours a night. . . ." Lin had previously commented that he was dubious about China sending Volunteers against American forces in Korea.

At his first headquarters in Korea, Mao Anying, the oldest son of Mao Tse-tung, was killed by a napalm burst during an American air attack on 25 October 1950.

Gen. Han Xianchu was deputy commander of the Chinese People's Volunteers, and second to Marshal Peng in command of the Korea Volunteers. He had a very active role in the Korean War. In the 2nd Phase Campaign he commanded forces in the Tokchon and Yongwon areas, destroying a large part of two South Korean divisions, making the campaign's breakthrough there and continuing on to cut off and destroy US forces and their allies in the Samso-ri and Kunu-ri areas. In the 3rd Phase Campaign he commanded units that crossed the 38th Parallel and captured Seoul.[6]

At this time, Khrushchev was in Moscow, an important member of the politburo. He was allowed to read the numerous documents and reports that flowed regularly into Moscow from Peiping on the Korean War. He wrote of this period:

> In the archives you can find documents in which P'eng Te-huai gave his situation reports to Mao Tse-tung. P'eng composed lengthy telegrams expounding elaborate battle plans against the Americans. He declared categorically that the enemy would be surrounded and finished off by decisive flanking strikes. The American troops were crushed and the war ended many times in these battle reports which P'eng sent to Mao, who then sent them along to Stalin.[7]

It would appear that neither the Soviet Union nor China contemplated intervening in the worsening state of affairs for North Korea after the Inchon landing and the collapse of Kim Il Sung's plan for winning in the South, until the UN troops crossed the 38th Parallel. The UN crossing of the 38th Parallel seems to have surprised the Soviets, the Chinese, and even the North Koreans themselves. In an order to the North Korea People's Army, dated 14 October 1950, Kim Il Sung said in part, "Many of us felt that the 38th Parallel would be as far as the US Forces would attack."[8]

The outbreak of the Korean War directly affected Communist China's plans for an invasion of Taiwan, where Chiang Kai-shek's remnant Nationalist forces had taken refuge. The victorious Chinese Communists had concentrated their best troops, the Fourth and Third field armies, along the coast of the East China Sea, opposite Taiwan (Formosa), where they had been undergoing amphibious training. At the same time, all kinds of watercraft, big and small, were being assembled along the mainland coast for the projected crossing.[9]

We have noted that Mao Tse-tung approved Kim Il Sung's idea of an invasion of South Korea, but we do not know the date of that approval or when Kim received the final approval of both the Soviet Union and China. The date may be suggested by the fact that in June, before the North Korean crossing of the 38th Parallel on 25 June, elements of Lin Piao's Fourth Field Army, considered the best in the People's Liberation Army, suddenly left their positions opposite Taiwan and marched to Canton. There they entrained for Antung, Manchuria, on the Yalu River, bordering Korea. Other parts of the Fourth Field Army from different parts of China also moved to the Korean border. Just what motives and intentions prompted these moves are unknown. It would seem that they were precautionary against any eventualities that might develop, since the Chinese leaders knew that Kim Il Sung was about to launch his invasion of the south. Once the war began and the United States intervened, the United States Seventh Fleet immediately took position in the Taiwan Strait, and a Chinese Communist crossing from the mainland to Taiwan then became impossible.

In the late summer and early autumn of 1950, as the military situation worsened for the North Koreans, the Chinese Third Field Army began moving from South China to Manchuria, adding greatly to the buildup of Chinese Communist strength there. By mid-October the CCF Third and Fourth field armies had concentrated about 400,000 troops in Manchuria just across the Yalu River from North Korea. It was elements of Lin Piao's Fourth Field Army, but not under the command of Lin Piao, that first intervened in the Korean War near the end of October.[10]

On 25 October 1950 the ROK 1st Division captured three Chinese prisoners near Unsan in North Korea, the first to be taken by UN forces in Korea. On the other side of the peninsula in the X Corps zone of action, the 26th Regiment of the ROK 3rd Division captured 16 Chinese prisoners four days later, on 29 October. Although these Chinese troops had not entered combat until the last week of October, they had crossed from Manchuria into Korea two weeks earlier. Within a few days after United States troops crossed the 38th Parallel at Kaesong on 9 October, Chinese troops of the Fourth Field Army began crossing the Yalu. The first crossed on 13–14 October, or possibly on 12 October. The evidence on this point is conflicting. By 20 October, four CCF armies of three divisions each had crossed into Korea. All were from Lin Piao's Fourth Field Army.

Two of these armies, the 39th and 40th, crossed the Yalu from Antung in Manchuria to Sinuiju, North Korea. Two other armies, the 38th and 42nd, crossed farther east, from Chian, Manchuria, to Manpojin, Korea. Three of the four armies, the 39th, 40th, and 38th, marched south and southwest to face the Eighth Army in northwest Korea. The 42nd Army moved southeast to guard the left (east) flank of the other three armies and, if necessary, to confront elements of the X Corps that might advance toward the Chosin Reservoir from the Hungnam area on the east coast. The 124th Division of this army started down the road from Chosin, and it was this division that the ROK 26th Regiment, moving north from Hamhung, met near the end of November.

Two more armies, the 50th and 66th, crossed the border about two weeks after the first four. They both crossed the Yalu from Antung to Sinuiju, completing the crossing by 31 October. The six CCF armies now in Korea constituted the CCF XIII Army Group of the Fourth Field Army. They totaled 18 divisions (or possibly 19, since the 50th Army may have had four divisions). Not all these divisions were involved in combat during the last week of October and the first week of November. Some remained hidden in reserve. Five of the six armies were concentrated in front of Eighth Army in northwest Korea. Troops from three of these armies fought the CCF 1st Phase Offensive, which lasted from 25 October to 8 November.

There then took place a new and important movement of CCF troops into Korea that set the stage for the great 2nd Phase Offensive, which the CCF launched near the end of November. The IX Army Group of the Third Field Army moved by rail from Shantung Province in China, just west across the Yellow Sea from

Korea, to the Korean border. Upon arrival there in the first half of November, two-thirds of it crossed immediately into Korea. The IX Army Group was composed of three armies—the 20th, 26th, and 27th—of three divisions each. Actually, each had four divisions, as all were reinforced from the 30th Army by a division. The IX Army Group, therefore, had a total of 12 divisions.

One army, the 20th, crossed the Yalu at Chian-Manpojin. Another, the 27th, crossed at Linchiang, 65 miles upstream from Manpojin. Linchiang was the farthest upstream crossing of the Yalu during the war. Both Chinese armies started at once for the Chosin Reservoir. The 26th Army remained in reserve at Linchiang on the north side of the border in Manchuria.

The 20th Army arrived in the vicinity of the Chosin Reservoir on 13 November and at once relieved the 42nd Army there. That army then started westward to join its parent organization, the XIII Army Group, in front of the Eighth Army.

Thus, by mid-November 1950, with a temporary lull settled over most of the front, there were a total of 30 or 31 Chinese divisions in Korea, together with supporting troops.

Much had happened in the course of a month. Starting with an estimate of only a few Chinese "Volunteers," mixed in with North Korean units that had escaped to far northern Korea toward the end of October, the UN command estimate of Chinese troops in North Korea had risen by 24 November to a total of 60,000 to 70,000. The heavy blows the Chinese had delivered north of the Chongchon in late October and in early November had forced this revised estimate. At the same time, the delaying action of the Chinese 124th Division against the ROK 26th Regiment, and subsequently against the US 7th Marine Regiment, on the road to the Chosin Reservoir, reinforced the conclusion that substantial Chinese forces had entered the war.

But suddenly the Chinese soldiers in front of Eighth Army in the west disappeared northward into the hills—out of contact with the UN forces everywhere. With their disappearance from the battlefield, confidence quickly returned to the UN command. General MacArthur reactivated plans for a resumption of the drive to the Yalu to end the war. At this juncture, there were in fact about 210,000 Chinese soldiers at predetermined points in the mountainous country north of the UN forces, waiting to assault them in surprise attack on their two main lines of advance. Another 30,000 Chinese soldiers were at the border ready to cross into Korea and join in the battle if they were needed.[11]

The strangest and most ominous fact in the situation was the inability of United States intelligence, including UN air cover over the skies of North Korea, to discover the movement of any of the Chinese troops that had crossed from Manchuria and taken their battle positions. Their presence was not known until they revealed it in surprise attack.

The Chinese Army and Its Leaders

Why had not American intelligence, with complete command of the skies over the terrain where the Chinese concentrated south of the Yalu, discovered their movement and presence? A fundamental factor in the situation was that the

Chinese troop movements during this period were nearly always made at night and therefore were not subject to aerial observation. Before dawn the troops were carefully hidden and camouflaged, and they remained undisclosed during the day. Troop discipline was complete, and harsh if necessary. But even so, by 24 November, when Eighth Army resumed its attack toward the Yalu, it had taken 96 CCF prisoners. These prisoners talked freely and disclosed extensive information, later proved generally correct, about the Chinese forces then in Korea. They identified six Chinese armies in Korea.[12]

Korean civilian reports of heavy Chinese troop movements in front of the UN forces were not taken seriously, because they could not be confirmed from other sources, even though they supported the evidence given by Chinese prisoners. The UN military authorities had a strong inclination to believe what they wanted to, and they concluded that conditions were favorable for a quick ending of the war. The intelligence material for a different assessment of the situation was at hand, but it was erroneously interpreted. The strongest sentiment for what proved to be a faulty evaluation of the enemy situation was in the Far East Command in Tokyo, and especially in the Far East commander, Gen. Douglas MacArthur.

CCF march discipline and capabilities were not generally understood in the American forces at this time. It was to be a critical factor not only in the events that unfolded at the end of November 1950 in Korea but also in those that continued on into the first months of 1951. The march performance of the Chinese infantry equaled the best of antiquity. Xenophon describes the retreat of 10,000 Greeks from Persia in 401 B.C. It is one of the classic military movements of all time, averaging a little under 24 miles a day. Roman legions set records seldom surpassed for disciplined and speedy marches. The routine Roman military pace covered 20 miles in five hours, the usual day's march for a legion. Normal training exercises required a legion to perform such marches at least three times a month. In one of Caesar's notable campaigns in Gaul, his troops marched 50 miles in 24 hours to begin the siege of Gergovia.[13]

The CCF performance in the Korean War compares favorably with these classic military performances of antiquity. A well-documented episode discloses that a Chinese army of three divisions in the winter of 1950–51 marched from Antung, in Manchuria, across the Yalu to its assigned combat assembly area 286 miles away in a period of between 16 and 19 days. One of the divisions, following a circuitous route over mountainous roads and trails, averaged 18 miles daily for 18 days in a march of 324 miles. For Chinese infantry in Korea, the day's march began in darkness after 7 P.M. and ended by 3 A.M. the next morning, a time period of between seven and eight hours of night march. Camouflage and defense measures against airplanes had to be completed before daylight. Every man, animal, and piece of equipment had to be concealed. During daylight hours only small scouting parties moved ahead to select the next night's bivouac area. If emergency factors required daylight movement, all CCF units were under standing orders to become immobile if aircraft approached. Officers were enpowered to shoot at once any man who disobeyed. It was this kind of march capability and discipline that put at least 210,000 Chinese soldiers into place in front of the UN forces in November, and they lay perfectly concealed while hostile aircraft overhead searched the ground below for signs of life. Aerial observers did not see the Chinese soldiers, nor did aerial photographs reveal their presence.[14]

The Chinese political and military leaders who launched and directed the massive offensive against American and UN forces in Korea at the end of 1950 and in 1951 were all experienced veterans of the Long March to Shensi Province, where they arrived 20 October 1935, one year and four days after breakout from Kiangsi Province in southeastern China. They had also witnessed the subsequent patient and persistent development of Communist military doctrine, power, and successes in the 15 years that followed.

At the head of the Chinese Communist government stood Mao Tse-tung, with Chou En-lai as his foreign minister. The top military command consisted of old-time leaders, nearly all of whom had been young men when they led the Long March from Kiangsi Province in southeast China to Yenan in Shensi Province in northwest China. At their head stood Chu Teh, commander in chief of the People's Liberation Army. This army was divided into four field armies, in which the might of the Chinese Communist armed forces was concentrated. There was also the North China Field Forces.

Peng Te-huai commanded the First Field Army, Lin Po-cheng the Second, Ch'en Yi the Third, and Lin Piao the Fourth. Peng Te-huai's First Field Army normally was garrisoned in and responsible for northwestern China, a critical area adjacent to the Soviet border. Lin Piao's Fourth Field Army had been based in Manchuria and northeastern China, adjacent to Korea and eastern Siberia, until it moved south in the final phases of the Chinese civil war and came to rest on the East China Sea coast, opposite Formosa. But it had now moved back to its old base—Manchuria—and was concentrated along the Yalu River boundary with Korea.

In the Chinese intervention in Korea, overall military command of Korean operations was under Peng Te-huai. The first Chinese "Volunteers" that entered Korea were presumably under Kim Il-Sung's command in the west, opposite the Eighth Army. The Chinese troops of the Third Field Army that conducted the 2nd Phase Campaign in northeast Korea against the X Corps at Chosin Reservoir were under Chinese command exclusively. Since Peng Te-huai was the dominant commander in the Korean War for the Chinese and North Korean forces after late October 1950, a word about him is appropriate.

Peng Te-huai in youth had been a Hunan peasant. Poverty had led him into banditry. Later he became a soldier. He had his own guerrilla band in 1928 when he joined Mao Tse-tung in the Chinese Communist movement. In the 1930s he was second after Chu Teh as deputy commander in chief of the Chinese Communist forces. He helped to organize the First and Second field armies and took over personal command of the First Field Army. When China intervened in the Korean War, he became commander of the so-called Chinese "Volunteers." Peng was a heavily built man "with a body like a bull and the face of a bulldog," said one observer. He never overcame his peasant upbringing and even later in life read only haltingly. His military talent was not universally admitted, but he was impulsive and very aggressive by nature and thus had the potential for leadership. He was also quarrelsome and did not hesitate to dispute with Mao Tse-tung. Within the Chinese forces he was considered a soldier's soldier. He was stubborn and a rugged fighter, fully capable of enduring any battlefield hardship. He was popular with his troops. He favored modernization of the Chinese army, with sophisticated weapons and tactics, a position that eventually brought him into conflict with Mao. He fell from grace in 1959, accused of collusion with the Soviets.

During the heavy fighting of the Korean War in the 1st, 2nd, and 3rd phases of the Chinese Communist offensives in late 1950 and early 1951, no Chinese military leader figured larger in the American and UN intelligence reports and speculations as the mastermind of Chinese tactics than Lin Piao, commander of the famed Fourth Field Army. It was generally believed on the American side that he commanded the Chinese "Volunteers." There is frequent mention of his name in UN intelligence reports from November 1950 to March 1951, most of it speculative, but always with the assumption that, under Peng Te-huai, he in fact was the field commander of the Chinese troops in Korea. The fact that choice divisions of his Fourth Field Army fought the major part of the early campaigns in the intervention no doubt was a factor in establishing this belief in the minds of American and UN commanders. When General Ridgway arrived in the Far East to take command of Eighth Army, he was told that his opposite number in Korea was Lin Piao.[15] And during the course of the MacArthur hearings before the Joint Military Affairs Committees of Congress in 1951, Pentagon officials made several references to Lin Piao as the Chinese commander.

The evidence is convincing not only that Lin Piao was not connected in any way with command of troops in Korea, but also that he was never in Korea during the several major Chinese offensives from November 1950 through June 1951. But since the American commanders thought at the time that he was the enemy commander, and since the crack troops of his Fourth Field Army, who reflected his tactics and training, did drive the Eighth Army out of North Korea, it is perhaps in order to say something about this man.

Lin Piao was one of the authentic heroes of the Long March, having led the advance guard of that historic fighting march. Lin Piao was born about 1908 in the north of Hupei Province. His real name was Lin Yu-jung, and he was the son of a textile manufacturer. The name that he carried through adult life – Lin Piao – means "Tiger Cat." He was an early enrollee in the Whampoa Military Academy at Canton, then under Chiang Kai-shek's Chinese Nationalists. When civil war broke out between the Nationalists and the Communists, Lin joined Chu Teh. Subsequently both joined Mao Tse-tung. Lin was a gifted military leader. Following the fame he gained as leader of the Advance Guard in the Long March, at age 28 in Yenan he became the commanding general of the 115th Division of the Chinese Communist Eighth Route Army. He was both courageous and daring. He was seriously wounded fighting the Japanese in Shensi Province in 1938 and went to Moscow for medical attention. A rumor, never fully documented, has him joining the Soviets in the defense of Leningrad in 1941–42.

At the end of the civil war in China, Lin returned to Moscow, possibly because of another wound, after the campaign that carried his Fourth Field Army from Manchuria to the Formosa Strait. His health from this time on was spotty (there is evidence he may have had tuberculosis), and poor health, as well as recent or old wounds, may have been a factor in his not taking a leading role in the Korean War. He was a rival of Peng Te-huai for military preferment. Some years after the end of the Korean War, he became for a period the publicly named heir to Mao Tse-tung. The importance of Lin Piao for us in the Korean War lies in the fact that the American military and political leaders thought that he commanded the best troops of the Chinese Liberation Army that struck the US Eighth Army in northwest Korea in late November 1950 and sent it southward in a massive retreat, without parallel in United States military history.

Intelligence gained later from documents and prisoner interrogations indicates that the XIII Army Group command staff crossed the Manchurian border into Korea on or about 19 November 1950 and arrived that night at what they called Sheng Fang Tung, about 15 miles south of Kanggye. There, in an old mine, the Chinese command staff in Korea, supposedly working under Kim Il Sung, directed the operations of the Chinese forces in Korea.[16] This is the same place where Peng established his first headquarters in Korea, as stated earlier.

A few words are needed at this point to describe the nature of the weapons the Chinese "volunteer" forces carried when they intervened in the Korean War. These Chinese soldiers were the same army that had won the Chinese civil war. It was essentially a guerrilla army trained to endure long marches on small amounts of plain food and to fight with light infantry weapons—submachine guns, rifles, grenades, machine guns, and light mortars. Its weapons were not standardized. They were of Japanese, Soviet, and American manufacture. After they won the civil war in 1949, the Chinese Communists added to their arsenal a vast number of American weapons—M-1 rifles, Browning Automatic Rifles (BARs), Thompson submachine guns, light and heavy machine guns, and 60-mm and 81-mm mortars—taken from Chiang Kai-shek's two million Nationalist soldiers who surrendered to them. They also had some American 105-mm howitzers, but these were not at first brought to Korea. Great numbers of former Chinese Nationalist soldiers—sometimes entire divisions—were taken into the Communist armies. These former Nationalist soldiers were used in Korea, integrated into the Communist ranks and kept under the watchful eye of the Communist officers.

Transport and communication in the Chinese forces were primitive. Yet, their prowess as fast-moving light infantry, their numbers, and their use of classic tactics of combining frontal attack to fix the enemy and then sending equal or stronger forces in enveloping moves to attack the enemy flanks and to cut off a retreat route were formidable. These tactics proved almost totally effective against the South Koreans at first and often were equally effective against American units. These tactics were constant features of Chinese Communist operations in Korea.

The fear that a nation of 450 million people might throw into battle increasing numbers of readily available light infantry, even though poorly armed and supplied, was one of the imponderables that influenced the battle in Korea after the Chinese soldiers first appeared. The Chinese peasant was used to political indoctrination and accepted death as a matter of course. He was usually illiterate and therefore could not be trained quickly in the use of technical weapons and equipment, had they been available. His main strengths were superb abilities as a night fighter possessed of raw courage to do as ordered, great physical endurance on the march, and tenacity in attack. The Chinese soldier was ordinarily conscripted from the age of 15 years on up, on the basis of a quota given to each geographic area. Generally, conscription was camouflaged as a method of obtaining "volunteers."

The great variety of small-arms models, calibers, and diversity of manufacturers made for a shortage of ammunition for the Chinese army, except for those instances when large amounts of it had been captured along with the weapons. Perhaps not more than one-third of the Chinese infantry had shoulder arms and handguns; the rest were armed with grenades. The grenadiers often formed the first wave of attackers. They moved into enemy positions throwing grenades and often overran outposts and frequently the first main line of resistance. Other Chinese soldiers armed with automatic weapons (the familiar tommy gun or burp gun) and rifles followed them.

At the time of their intervention, the Chinese forces in Korea had no artillery with them. As a result, they seldom used anything larger than mortar fire in their assaults. Nearly all the larger weapons, such as a few antitank guns, were drawn by animal. Although there was artillery in the Chinese army tables of organization, those units that had any left it behind in China or Manchuria at first, since they then had no way of moving it rapidly and secretly to the Korean battle front. The Chinese also had no antiaircraft guns in Korea at first. They had to rely on infantry machine guns for what little defense they could improvise against air attack. Their best defense was concealment and camouflage, which they did use extensively. The Chinese possessed some Soviet truck-mounted rocket launchers.

The Chinese field army was organized in units called (in descending order) army groups, armies, divisions, regiments, battalions, companies, platoons, and squads, and often fire teams. Their organization below army level was triangular, similar to that of American forces below division level. A Chinese army usually had three divisions, a division had three regiments, a regiment had three battalions, a battalion had three companies (although sometimes companies seemed to be numbered on a regimental basis), a company had three platoons, and a platoon had three squads. A Chinese army would compare roughly in size with an American corps. A typical infantry company had a weapons platoon, which possessed light 60-mm mortars, 3.5-inch rocket launchers, and three light machine-gun squads. Great variation in the number and type of weapons existed among the Chinese units.

A typical regiment would have about 2,500 officers and men. But in such a regiment there might be no more than 400 rifles and carbines, 180 pistols, 200 submachine guns, 60 light machine guns, 18 heavy machine guns, 27 light 60-mm mortars, 12 medium 81-mm (or 82-mm) mortars, 4 heavy 120-mm mortars, 18 rocket launchers, a few small 70-mm howitzers, a few 57-mm recoilless rifles, probably no trucks, perhaps 150 horses and 30 carts, a few field telephones, and probably no radios. One must keep in mind that, in the initial campaigns in Korea, when the Chinese achieved their greatest successes, only one in three or four soldiers, on average, had a rifle, carbine, burp gun, or pistol. Most of the Chinese soldiers were simply grenade throwers.[17]

The first four Chinese armies to cross into Korea were the 38th, 39th, 40th, and 42nd. They crossed the Yalu River between 14 and 20 October. The 50th and 66th armies crossed into Korea about ten days later, so that by the end of the month, the CCF XIII Army Group had six of its armies, with 19 divisions, in North Korea.

Of the five Chinese armies in northwestern Korea facing Eighth Army and the UN allies in the west, only three—the 38th, 39th, and 40th—took part in the fighting in the 1st Phase Offensive. Two others, the 50th and the 66th, were hidden in the hills to the west of the combat area and held in reserve. They were not committed.

The one army that had moved eastward to the Chosin Reservoir area—the 42nd—did not engage in heavy combat except for its 124th Division. That division fought the delaying battles on the road leading up to the reservoir, first against the 26th Regiment of the ROK 3rd Division in late October and early November, and subsequently against the 7th Marine Regiment of the 1st Marine Division. The Chinese 126th Division remained in position around the Chosin Reservoir except for reconnaissance eastward to and beyond Fusen Reservoir. There, one of its regiments had some minor engagements and patrol actions with the 3rd Battalion of the US 31st Infantry Regiment of the 7th Infantry Division. The Chinese 125th Division took up a blocking position on the road leading south from Yudam-ni at the Chosin Reservoir and was not in action.

On 13 November, the 20th Army of the Chinese IX Army Group, Third Field Army, relieved the 125th Division in the vicinity of Yudam-ni. That division then started west and southwest, followed by the 124th and 126th divisions, to join their parent organization, the XIII Army Group of the Fourth Field Army, in front of the US Eighth Army. By the end of the third week of November, these three divisions of the 42nd Army were on the Chinese left (eastern) flank of the CCF XIII Army Group, in the vicinity of Huichon-Tokchon.[18]

The Chinese 1st Phase Offensive

A short summary of the results of the Chinese 1st Phase Offensive between 25 October and 8 November 1950 will give the picture of the situation in Korea at the time General MacArthur opened his general attack on 24 November to reach the northern border of Korea. As the last week of October opened, the ROK II Corps, under Eighth Army control, advanced up the valley of the Chongchon River as far as Huichon. There the 7th Regiment of the ROK 6th Division turned northwest over cart tracks toward Chosan on the Yalu. Other parts of the division proceeded west toward Onjong. The Reconnaissance Platoon of the ROK 7th Regiment entered Chosan on 26 October. There they saw scurrying North Koreans cross the bridge into Manchuria. This ROK reconnaissance platoon was the only element of Eighth Army ever to reach the Yalu River and the border. Maj. Harry Fleming, Korean Military Advisor (KMAG) with the ROK 7th Regiment, who accompanied the reconnaissance platoon, was the only American (other than later prisoners of war) to see the Yalu from the ground in the Eighth Army sector during the Korean War.

On the same day that this reconnaissance platoon moved into Chosan unopposed, 26 October, Chinese forces sprang a trap on the ROK 7th Regiment at Onjong and, during fighting that continued into the night, destroyed or dispersed it. At the same time, the battalion of the ROK 6th Division that had stopped just short of the Yalu below Chosan, while the reconnaissance platoon entered the town, was cut off and destroyed. Two more ROK regiments that hastened toward the scene from Huichon were similarly destroyed or dispersed on 29 October by the Chinese near Onjong. At the end of the month, therefore, the Chinese had destroyed four regiments of the ROK 6th and 8th divisions—the bulk of the ROK II Corps—as effective fighting units. The ROK 7th Division hurried into blocking positions in the valley of the Chongchon River above Kunu-ri and Won-ni to hold in check two Chinese divisions that now poured southwest down the valley from the Huichon area.

Farther west, the ROK 1st Division had advanced northward from the Chongchon valley at the same time the ROK II Corps advanced to its near destruction in the Huichon-Onjong area. It reached Unsan on 25 October. There, on that day, it was the first UN unit to meet Chinese in battle in the Korean War.

The ROK 1st Division commander, Gen. Paik Sun Yup, who had served with Japanese troops many years earlier in Manchuria and had often fought against Chinese, went forward and identified enemy dead and a few prisoners as Chinese. He was certain of it. That day the Chinese pushed back his 11th Regiment. The rest of his division held positions just north and east of Unsan.

At this juncture, the Eighth Army sent the 1st Cavalry Division toward Unsan to help the ROK 1st Division. The 8th Cavalry Regiment led the way. It arrived at Unsan on 30 October, behind the ROK troops, and there relieved two battalions of the ROK 12th Regiment in the line north of Unsan. As the newly arrived troops of the 8th Cavalry Regiment settled into their positions on 1 November just north of Unsan, great smoke clouds darkened the sky in all directions.

Under cover of the smoke haze, large elements of a Chinese division moved into positions to the north, west, and south of the 8th Cavalry. These Chinese cut the road six miles south of Unsan. They stubbornly held their roadblock positions against attacks by the 5th Cavalry Regiment, which came up behind the lead regiment, and prevented all assistance from reaching the latter. Only on the east, where the ROK 1st Division fought desperately to hold its ground, could the 8th Cavalry look for any help.

The night of 1–2 November was a dark and grim one for the American 8th Cavalry troops. The Chinese cut all escape roads and infiltrated the American positions, and organized resistance evaporated. Many of the 8th Cavalry escaped through the hills. On the regimental southern sector, however, the 3rd Battalion was surrounded, without hope of rescue, late in the afternoon of 2 November. Eastward from it, the ROK 1st Division took heavy casualties from Chinese attack and fell back.

Thus, by 4 November at Unsan, elements of the Chinese 115th and 116th divisions of the 39th Army, aided by some units of two other divisions of the Fourth Field Army near Onjong, about ten miles northeast of Unsan, had all but destroyed two ROK divisions and badly crippled another, and ominously for the Americans, Chinese soldiers from the 39th Army had effectively destroyed the 8th Cavalry Regiment. American tank and artillery losses were also heavy at Unsan.

By pulling back all of Eighth Army on the western flank, regrouping parts of I Corps, and rushing up its reserves, General Walker and his Eighth Army were able to hold the lower Chongchon valley from Won-ni and Kunu-ri westward to the Yellow Sea. The Chinese, following up their surprising victories at Onjong and Unsan, attacked Eighth Army in its bridgehead on the north side of the Chongchon River, from Anju on the west to Kunu-ri on the east, in a series of bloody battles from 3 to 6 November. Driven back everywhere almost to the riverbank, Eighth Army held there. The Chinese troops at this point suddenly faded away northward into the hills.[19]

Coinciding with this 1st Phase Offensive, a new element entered the war—in the air. On 31 October the first Soviet-built MiG-15 entered combat over Korean territory. From then on, the part of Korea bordering the lower Yalu and Manchurian territory near Antung and Sinuiju was to be contested by these planes when American bombers and fighter planes approached. On 8 November the first battle in aerial warfare between jets took place near the Yalu at Sinuiju. Lt. Russell Brown, piloting an American F-80, shot down in flames a MiG-15. F-80s flew escort cover for the first bomber strike against the Yalu River bridges at Sinuiju. Previously, these bridges had been forbidden targets to the bombers.

While the above-mentioned events were taking place on the Eighth Army front in northwestern Korea, the 1st Phase Offensive eastward in the X Corps area was primarily to protect the east flank of the Chinese attack against Eighth Army. It was of a reconnaissance-in-force type, and if necessary it could become a delaying action if enemy forces were encountered. Such an encounter was most likely to occur on the road leading north from Hungnam toward the Chosin Reservoir.

The first solid evidence the X Corps had that Chinese troops were in front of it below the Chosin Reservoir came on 29 October. On that day the ROK 26th Regiment of the 3rd Division, which was advancing toward the reservoir from Hungnam, captured 16 prisoners from the 370th Regiment of the Chinese 124th Division, 42nd Army. Maj. Gen. Edward M. Almond, the X Corps commander, went to the ROK I Corps headquarters in Hungnam to interview these prisoners. He was convinced from their story that large units of Chinese were in Korea. He reported this information immediately to General MacArthur in Tokyo.

The 7th Marine Regiment of the 1st Marine Division relieved the ROK troops and took over the advance toward Chosin Reservoir. They were from the start opposed by the same Chinese troops the ROKs had encountered. In a series of sharp engagements the Marines learned that at least a Chinese regiment blocked their advance. Elsewhere, the 3rd Battalion, 31st Infantry, of the 7th Infantry Division discovered that elements of another Chinese division, the 126th, had penetrated to the east side of the Fusen Reservoir, some 20 miles east of Chosin Reservoir, in the X Corps zone. Prisoners from the 124th Division revealed that a third Chinese division, the 125th, was in the Chosin area.

Thus, three Chinese divisions, constituting the 42nd Army of the XIII Army Group of Lin Piao's Fourth Field Army, had moved to the Chosin Reservoir region from the main body of the army group, which was in front of Eighth Army in the west. The 125th Division engaged in no combat at this time, its mission being to guard the approaches to Yudam-ni and the reservoir area from the west and southwest.

The CCF 20th Army of the IX Army Group relieved the 125th Division and the 42nd Army on 13 November near Yudam-ni. The 125th Division thereupon started west and southwest to join, together with its two sister divisions that followed it, their parent organization, the XIII Army Group. They arrived before the Eighth Army resumed its advance toward the border on 24 November and took their position in the Tokchon-Huichon area on the left flank of the Chinese army group. Thus, by the beginning of the last week of November, the XIII Army Group was concentrated in front of Eighth Army in the west, and the larger part of the IX Army Group of the Third Field Army had entered Korea and was in position near the Chosin Reservoir to confront X Corps.

Through the 1st Phase Offensive and up to 24 November 1950, United States battle casualties in the Korean War had been 27,827–21,529 in Eighth Army and 6,298 in X Corps. Of the Eighth Army casualties, 4,157 had been killed in action, 391 more had died of wounds, and 4,834 were missing in action. As both sides prepared for a new offensive in late November 1950, neither Eighth Army nor X Corps knew the size and extent of the Chinese forces in their front. They were so poorly informed and simultaneously so confident of their capability to overcome the Chinese who might oppose them that, on 24 November, when the Eighth Army advance began in the west, and on 27 November, when the X Corps began its advance, the UN command expected a quick victory that would give them control of all Korea to the Chinese border —and end the war.

2. Uncertainty on the Eve of the UN Advance

When President Truman questioned General MacArthur at their meeting on Wake Island on 15 October 1950 about the possibility of Chinese intervention, the general dismissed it as unlikely and said that, if the Chinese tried it, he could destroy them with his air force. In any event, he said, not more than 60,000 would ever get south of the Yalu. But when, a little more than a week later, Chinese in fact did spring out of the Korean hills in surprise attacks and drive the Eighth Army back to the Chongchon River, both MacArthur in Tokyo and the Joint Chiefs of Staff in Washington were surprised. What no one had believed would happen had happened.

Confidence in Tokyo, however, quickly reasserted itself after the Chinese suddenly withdrew from contact on 6 November, and faded away northward into the hills. The Far East Command resumed plans to continue the Eighth Army drive to the Yalu and end the war.

The scare in Washington was not so easily dissipated. There was a running argument in telecommunications between MacArthur's headquarters and the Joint Chiefs of Staff as to the true state of affairs concerning Chinese intervention. What did the future hold? How far should the UN forces try to go northward? The United Nations allies of the United States and South Korea, particularly Great Britain, viewed with alarm and profound skepticism MacArthur's desire to resume the offensive to reach the border. They unflinchingly opposed his desire to bomb Chinese bases in Manchuria and to knock out the Yalu River bridges.

On 6 November MacArthur notified the Joint Chiefs that he intended to have B-29s knock out the bridges over the Yalu at Sinuiju and Antung to stop or slow Chinese reinforcements from entering Korea. American officials in Washington had promised the British government there would be no action that might involve Manchuria without informing them. The Joint Chiefs, acting on President Truman's orders, promptly directed MacArthur to call off these proposed bomber strikes. And they asked him to explain why he found the situation suddenly so dangerous, when previously he had not reported it to be so. He was directed not to bomb any targets within five miles of the Manchurian border. This order went to MacArthur only an hour and 20 minutes before the B-29s were to take off. This directive stung MacArthur to reply vehemently that his command was threatened with destruction. He asked for an immediate reconsideration of the order and that the president be informed of his request.[1]

This message surprised Washington officials. Gen. Omar N. Bradley, chairman of the Joint Chiefs of Staff, read MacArthur's message to the president over the telephone. After much debate among officials of the administration, Washington gave in to MacArthur in part. They told him he could bomb targets up to the border and that he could bomb the *Korean end* of the bridges. In these exchanges on 6 and 7 November, MacArthur estimated for the Joint Chiefs of Staff that there were between 30,000 and 40,000 Chinese troops in Korea but that as many as 350,000 CCF ground troops could be sent into Korea to join the battle. MacArthur assured the Joint Chiefs that he would not violate Manchurian or Siberian territory and that he would not destroy the hydroelectric installations along the Yalu.

The rail and highway connections between China and Korea across the Yalu River were necessarily important in any major Chinese intervention. They would dictate the nature and volume of troop movements and of logistic supply of those troops once they were in Korea. In all, there were 12 railroad and highway bridges across the Yalu and Tumen rivers that separated Korea from Manchuria and Siberia. The most important were those between Antung in Manchuria and Sinuiju in Korea, near the mouth of the Yalu and the west coast of the peninsula. The bridges here were 3,000 feet long and very strong. The American Bridge Company had built the Sinuiju highway bridge in 1900. It was reputed to be as strong as any in the world. The Japanese had built a sturdy double-track railroad bridge of 12 trusses across the Yalu at Sinuiju in 1934, only 350 yards north of the highway bridge. It was the largest rail bridge ever built by the Japanese. Upstream at Sakchu, a double-track railroad bridge crossed the Yalu, and still farther upstream at Manpojin both a rail bridge and a combination highway and footbridge crossed the river. There were six highway bridges at other locations on the Yalu—Ongondong, Chongsongjin, Linchiang, Hyesanjin, Samanko, and Hoeryong.

Argument over the question of "hot pursuit" was a related issue at this time. MacArthur ardently wanted to have his fighter planes follow the Chinese planes across the Yalu to their bases just north of the river, where they might be destroyed. Washington decided it would be too risky and denied MacArthur this authority.

The Joint Chiefs reacted with increasing caution to the Chinese intervention as November advanced. They suggested to MacArthur on 9 November that his mission, as stated in their previous instructions to him on 27 September—to destroy the North Korean forces—might have to be altered. The Joint Chiefs thought that it might be advisable to abandon his plan to drive to the Yalu and that his forces should go on the defensive and strive to hold what they already had gained.[2]

MacArthur strongly opposed this proposal on the same day he received it. He insisted the attack should continue to the border. He reaffirmed his faith in the ability of his air force to limit the number of Chinese able to reach the south side of the Yalu. He said he meant to launch his attack on 15 November. MacArthur spoke bitterly of British influence in opposition to his plans. The Joint Chiefs on this same day, 9 November, sent to Defense Secretary George C. Marshall an analysis for the National Security Council, which was scheduled to consider the matter. The Joint Chiefs' basic thought was that the Chinese

Highway and railroad bridges over the Yalu River between Sinuiju, Korea (*foreground*), and Antung, Manchuria, 14 November 1950. The *Leyte* strike that month dropped three spans of the highway bridge but left the railroad bridge intact. National Archives 80-G-423495

could not drive the United Nations force from Korea without "material assistance by Soviet naval and airpower." If that happened, World War III would have begun, and the United States would have had to evacuate Korea at once.

In the National Security Council meeting, General Bradley said he thought the UN forces could hold their present positions generally, but he did not agree with MacArthur that bombing the Yalu River bridges would stop Chinese forces from entering Korea in strength. He pointed out that, in two to four weeks, the Yalu would be frozen over, and then bombing the bridges would be academic. General Marshall questioned the X Corps troop dispositions, but General Bradley defended MacArthur's deployment of the X Corps as necessary to occupy all of Korea. Pressed on this point, Bradley admitted that, from a military point of view, better defensive lines for the UN forces would be found as the line increasingly moved south of the Yalu.

Earlier, the Joint Chiefs had several times indicated in cables to MacArthur that they thought the "waist of Korea," the narrow section of the peninsula on a line between Pyongyang on the west and Wonsan on the east, would offer the best defensive line for the UN forces. MacArthur had accepted this reasoning at the end of September, but once his X Corps had landed at Wonsan on the east coast, he found reasons to alter his position and persuaded the Joint Chiefs to allow him to proceed farther north. That change in objectives, approved by the Joint Chiefs, may have been their most serious mistake of the Korean War.

In the end, they decided not to change MacArthur's plans to resume the offensive. Thus, the final decision was made in Washington on 9 November. That there were misgivings about the outcome was evident.[3]

The Gap between Eighth Army and X Corps

When Secretary of Defense George C. Marshall in the National Security Council meeting of 9 November spoke disapprovingly of the disposition of the X Corps in Korea, he was referring to the separate commands of Eighth Army in the west and of X Corps in the east and northeast. The two commands were not in physical contact with each other. They were separated by the so-called gap. It was widely feared by many, including Maj. Gen. Oliver P. Smith, commander of the 1st Marine Division, in X Corps, that strong enemy forces would penetrate this gap and operate against the flanks of both Eighth Army and of X Corps and possibly gain the rear areas of either separated commands. Critics saw this situation as an invitation for military disaster. Many highly placed military analysts and political leaders in the United States and abroad, principally in England, charged that such a penetration took place in the subsequent Chinese 2nd Phase Offensive of late November and early December 1950. General MacArthur caught the brunt of these charges.

There has been no greater misunderstanding, and resulting explosions of rhetoric pro and con, during the entire course of the Korean War than the controversy over the so-called gap between Eighth Army and X Corps. The critics who leveled the charge of gross tactical error in separating the two commands included military men involved in the actual fighting, war correspondents cabling their dispatches back to the United States or other countries, members of the Joint Chiefs of Staff in Washington, editorial and military writers in the American press, foreign military writers, and foreign offices. The critics charged that it was in and through this gap that the Chinese moved to turn the right flank of Eighth Army and brought about the defeat of the UN forces at the end of 1950.

An interesting example of reference to the gap occurred in Gen. Omar N. Bradley's testimony as chairman of the Joint Chiefs of Staff in the MacArthur hearings on 24 May 1951, when he cited it as a serious cause of UN (he meant MacArthur's) failure in the Chinese 2nd Phase Offensive (see p. 1143 and following in the MacArthur hearings transcripts). Yet, in the 9 November 1950 meeting of the National Security Council on the military situation in Korea, he had upheld MacArthur's separation of commands. An example of how writers and historians of the Korean War continued to be misled on the subject is the position of Robert Leckie, in his *Conflict: The History of the Korean War, 1950–53* (New York: G. P. Putnam's Sons, 1962). He wrote of the gap as "that wide open left flank" (p. 199). He admitted it could not be closed, but he said, "it could be penetrated, and the Chinese were already poised for this purpose." He was wrong. They were not poised to penetrate the gap, and they never penetrated it in their attacks against the UN forces.

MacArthur at the time, and later, defended his decision to separate the two commands temporarily, because of geographic and logistic considerations, and to coordinate their actions himself from Tokyo. The operations plan called for the two forces to meet in the vicinity of Kanggye. They would then be united under the command of Gen. Walton H. Walker, commander of Eighth Army. Both General MacArthur and General Almond of X Corps have denied that the Chinese ever used the so-called gap to effect flanking movements against either the army or the corps for the defeat of those forces.[4]

On the basis of research into the "gap" question, using the Eighth Army and X Corps unit G-3 operational journals and message files of units adjacent to the gap, and plotting on a scale-50,000 map overlay the movements of Chinese forces in the 2nd Phase Offensive, there is no reason not to support MacArthur's and Almond's views. Neither the UN Forces nor the Chinese used the gap for important military movement.

Those who wrote and talked about the disastrous results of the gap simply never understood the detailed topography of the area or the military movements and subsequent actions that took place on the right flank of Eighth Army and the left flank of X Corps on the two sides of the gap. It seems important to discuss this misunderstood subject briefly.

The high, almost trackless, Taebaek Range of mountains in northern Korea made it almost impossible to form a continuous line across the peninsula. To the northeast of the Taebaek Range, the Yangnim Range rose even higher, to 8,000 feet, and extended to the Manchurian border and beyond it and was almost devoid of human habitation. The ridges of the Taebaek Range trended mostly north-south, but valleys ran in all directions. The whole area was rugged, partly forested, well drained, but unfavorable to lateral (east-west) cross-country movement. The hills generally rose to 6,500 feet elevation, and their slopes were steep. Valleys were narrow, winding, and gorgelike. In the upper regions of the gap area that have been discussed, the westward-flowing major streams, such as the Taedong, the Yesong, and the Imjin, flow in narrow, steep-sided valleys or gorges. There are no routes across this region for rapid, large-scale military movement. The existing roads or tracks, all dirt and gravel, were narrow and winding and crossed the cut-up and rugged terrain in steep 2,000- to 3,500-feet-high passes.[5] These mountains are really a continuation southward of the mountains of southern Manchuria.

The Northern Taebaek Range and the Yangnim Range effectively cut off a great expanse of north and northeastern Korea from the more highly developed and more accessible western and northwestern parts of the peninsula along and inland from the Yellow Sea. If all of Korea were to be reunited, then this northeastern part could not be ignored. Troops operating there for the purpose of establishing administrative and civil control could not be supported logistically from the Pusan-Seoul west-coast rail and roadnet available above Pyongyang and the Taedong River. MacArthur felt there was no alternative to using the east-coast ports of Wonsan and Hungnam and various minor ports and beaches to support the X Corps if it were to be used in that part of Korea.

An inescapable logistic fact at this time was the knowledge that UN airpower had rather thoroughly destroyed all the bridges and rail track north of Seoul, that the harbor facilities of Inchon had been badly damaged, and that the long and narrow channel to the port of Chinnampo had not been swept of mines. In November 1950 there was still no usable rail bridge across the Taedong River at Pyongyang. All military supplies carried northward from the ports of Pusan and Inchon had to be unloaded on the south side of the Taedong, ferried to the north side, and there reloaded on railcars to go on northward toward the front. Chinnampo, the port for the North Korean capital, Pyongyang, 30 air miles downstream from it on the Taedong, had not yet been reopened to shipping.

As we shall see, the date for the Eighth Army advance had to be postponed from 15 November to 24 November because supplies for it could not be accumulated by the earlier date. Only by utilizing all available means—airlift, rail, truck—could Eighth Army get the supplies forward to the Chongchon front to allow it to begin its advance on 24 November.

With the supply situation for Eighth Army in the west such a hard reality, there can be no question that the X Corps in the northeast could not have been supplied from the Eighth Army zone for a military operation at the end of November. The logistics for X Corps operations were dependent on east-coast facilities. Considering that the X Corps was separated physically from the Eighth Army by approximately 50 air miles of almost trackless, snow-covered mountains between their closest flank positions, it seemed to General MacArthur that he could coordinate the two forces from Tokyo better than they could be coordinated from any point in Korea.

The hue and cry about the gap between the two UN forces in Korea at the time the Chinese struck at the end of November 1950 seems to be without merit. It is without merit because neither side ever operated tactically in any force in this gap. It was a sterile, trackless waste, as negative for the Chinese as it was for the UN.

Instead of using a gap of any kind to outflank either of the two UN forces, the Chinese pattern of attack against the X Corps in the east was a strong frontal holding attack and a simultaneous movement around the immediate flanks on both sides to cut the roads behind the main forward elements. In the west against Eighth Army, the Chinese simultaneously attacked the center and the right flank frontally. On the right flank they penetrated the ROK II Corps at once and then rolled it up to the rear, which exposed the rest of Eighth Army from that flank. Once the Chinese had penetrated the ROK Corps, they sent strong forces to the ROK rear and cut off its line of retreat.

Furthermore, in their attacks against the Eighth Army and the X Corps, the Chinese command used two separate and distinct forces that could not cooperate with each other. These operations, in effect, constituted two different fronts in North Korea. It was a geographic necessity. The two fields of combat were tactically independent of each other, except in the matter of timing. In this respect both sides made an attempt to coordinate their efforts on both fronts. The CCF succeeded better in this than did the UN.

In northeastern Korea, X Corps units were far north of the line of Eighth Army in the west. A straight line drawn east from the Eighth Army front after the battles along the Chongchon in late October and early November would have passed through the rear areas of X Corps, far south of its front positions. Thus, the X Corps front was not only far north of that of the Eighth Army, but it was also separated from it by the wide lateral terrain gap. All of North Korea west and northwest of the X Corps front in November was either in enemy hands or unoccupied. On any line projected westward, north of the X Corps bases of Hungnam and Hamhung, and the axis of advance north from them to the Chosin Reservoir, there were no UN forces all the way to the Yellow Sea, except a few X Corps outposts to the northwest of Hamhung and north of Wonsan. These disparate troop deployments meant that any physical contact between the two UN forces would have to be between units in the southern part of the X Corps zone and units in the northeastern part of the Eighth Army zone.

The extent of the lateral gap differed from time to time as one or both commands tried to bring their patrol bases closer to each other. In early November the gap extended a minimum distance of 20 air miles between the northernmost right-flank position of Eighth Army to the nearest left-flank position of X Corps. The distance from the 23rd Infantry position on Eighth Army's right flank west of Tokchon to that of the 3rd Battalion, 1st Marines, in the X Corps zone at Majon-ni was 50 air miles. After the South Korean Marine Corps's 3rd Battalion established a blocking position at Tongyang on 14 November, the distance between the edges of the gap had shortened to about 35 air miles on a line drawn from Pyongyang eastward to Wonsan. Road and trail distances were much farther. While the air-mile distance between Maengsan, Eighth Army's easternmost position beyond Tokchon, to X Corps's westernmost position at Kwangchon, just across the X Corps boundary, was 20 miles; by road and trail it was nearly 50 miles.

General MacArthur never expected firm and continuous physical contact between the Eighth Army and the X Corps in North Korea. But he did expect and did have communication between them by radio and liaison plane. There was a daily air flight by an Eighth Army liaison officer to X Corps and back. Each command had radio communication with the other. And there was constant radio and telecon communication between MacArthur's headquarters in Tokyo and both the Eighth Army and X Corps headquarters. Beginning on 25 October, the US Fifth Air Force made two reconnaissance flights daily between the ROK II Corps, at Eighth Army's extreme right flank, to the X Corps's left flank. These daily flights were to report on any enemy movements that might be taking place in the area between the two commands.[6]

In addition to the means of communication available, the two separate commands made many efforts in November to establish physical contact by means of patrols, nearly all of them motorized, to designated meeting points. Eighth Army made the first of these efforts on 6 November when it sent a patrol from K Company, 23rd Infantry, 2nd Division, to Songsin-ni, an agreed-upon meeting point on the boundary between the two command zones, five miles east of Yangdok. The K Company patrol arrived there on 7 November, but no X

Corps unit was there to meet it. This patrol, however, did find and destroy 16 boxcars of enemy ammunition, including 80-mm and 47-mm shells and an assortment of weapons, including six self-propelled guns, 47-mm antitank guns, antitank rifles, heavy machine guns, and one heavy mortar. Petroleum supplies found on the train were handed over to ROK troops.[7] Yangdok stood in the mountains, near the middle of the peninsula, on the railroad that crossed laterally from Wonsan and Hungnam to Sunchon and Pyongyang. Why this trainload of enemy military supplies had been temporarily abandoned there is not known.

Eighth Army now received a message from X Corps saying that, because of the 30-mile distance from Majon-ni and guerrilla action in its vicinity, the 3rd Battalion, 1st Marines, could not get a patrol through to the meeting point. X Corps suggested a meeting point farther north, perhaps at Hadongsan-ni or Sachang-ni. Eighth Army thereupon withdrew the 23rd Infantry patrol and prepared to send one from the 38th Infantry of the 2nd Division on the route proposed by X Corps. General Almond then ordered the US 3rd Infantry Division to establish a patrol base from which the two commands could effect a meeting near their boundary. As a result, the 1st Battalion, 65th Infantry, established a patrol base on 10 November at Kwangchon, four air miles, but eight road miles, east of the boundary.

The day before, on 9 November, the 38th Infantry had sent the motorized 2nd Reconnaissance Company eastward for the purpose of reaching Hadongsan-ni. It could not get there because of cratered roads and huge boulders blocking the way. Other patrols tried other tracks through the mountains but found all of them impassable for motorized units.

On 11 and 12 November, X Corps patrols from the 1st Battalion, 65th Infantry, reached the boundary meeting place but found no contact unit there from Eighth Army. On 12 November however, a liaison plane scouting over this no-man's-land discovered a ROK patrol from the Eighth Army zone and dropped a message to it, arranging a meeting the next day at the boundary. The next day a patrol from the 1st Battalion, 65th Infantry, went nine miles beyond the boundary in an effort to contact this ROK patrol but failed to make contact with it.

At the same time, a patrol from E Company, 38th Infantry, got no farther than ten miles east of Maengsan, where the track it was following became impassable. It seemed there was no route passable to a motorized patrol through the gap area. Some of the narrow dirt roads and tracks had craters 15 feet deep and spread to as much as 35 feet in diameter. The North Korean guerrilla bands operating in the area apparently were under orders to make all routes impassable to vehicles of any kind – and this would mean from their own side as well as from the UN side.

The effort now turned to a foot patrol from Eighth Army. On 13 November, an Eighth Army liaison plane dropped two messages to a X Corps patrol, informing it that a South Korean foot patrol from the 10th Regiment, ROK 8th Division, was trying to get to the boundary by another route. The next day at 10 A.M., 14 November, a platoon of the 2nd Battalion, 10th ROK Regiment, met a patrol from the 1st Battalion, 65th Infantry, near the village of Songhadong, just west of the boundary between Eighth Army and X Corps. This ROK patrol had come 45 miles from its base at Maengsan in the Eighth Army zone.

En route it had encountered several North Korean bands, some recruited recently with one or more Chinese among them, and had fought several skirmishes with them. The ROK patrol estimated the total strength of the guerrilla bands it met numbered about 400 men. This ROK patrol required ten days to make the round trip of about 90 miles from Maengsan to the meeting place and back.[8]

Again, on 18 November, an Eighth Army patrol from the 3rd Battalion, 38th Infantry, reached the boundary at Hadongsan-ni. This motorized patrol could go no farther, as a blown bridge stopped it. There was no X Corps unit there to meet it.[9]

Only once, then, on 14 November 1950 was there any physical contact between ground troops of Eighth Army and X Corps, although there had been persistent, repeated efforts to establish such contact. Such was the nature of the gap between Eighth Army and X Corps.

To deny the myth of the military importance of the gap between Eighth Army and the X Corps is not to justify the existence of the two separate commands or to approve the separate missions assigned to them. These are separate and different matters. In them lay the fundamental military errors of judgment.

The decision to try to pacify all of Korea south of the border and to unify the country again was unsound, given the UN forces available to do it. Even if there had been no Chinese crossing of the Yalu, it is hard to see how the UN forces could have secured the border and have handed it over to the South Korean government and expected the latter to administer this land. For one thing, the X Corps in northeast Korea was scattered too thin and its units too distant from each other to accomplish the objective of truly gaining control of the long border there, for any length of time. At that time hostile remnants of the defeated North Korean Army were being reorganized and rehabilitated just south of the border in the Kanggye area, and they were anxious to resume the conflict. In the west, Eighth Army would face the same prospect of renewed North Korean hostilities.

Sound analysis and common sense would have resulted in a unified Korean command over the Eighth Army and the X Corps, deployed to defend and hold a line from Wonsan on the east to Chinnampo on the west, including a defense position above Pyongyang. This line would have passed through or north of Yangdok, Kangdong, and Pyongyang. It would have been anchored on its east and west ends on good ports for logistic and supply purposes, with a railnet south of the defense line—at the waist of Korea. This line would have utilized the best available lateral road running east-west across a narrow part of the peninsula, which could have been improved with engineering work. The rail- and roadnet north of this line was poor or nonexistent, except along either coast, and would not have offered the enemy an adequate communication and transport system for promising military operations.

Logistic Problems Delay Army Attack

General MacArthur notified the Joint Chiefs of Staff in Washington on 9 November that General Walker planned to launch the Eighth Army attack toward the border on 15 November. Both X Corps, under Almond, and Eighth Army, under Walker, were still operating under MacArthur's 24 October order to advance to the North Korean border and, once it had been reached, to turn over its defense to the South Koreans. Pursuant to this continuing order, General Walker on 6 November issued his Eighth Army Operational Plan for a renewal of the offensive—just about the time the CCF broke off their 1st Phase Offensive at the Chongchon River line and faded away into the timbered northern hills. The date for resumption of the attack was set for 15 November, nine days away.

Walker would have three corps in the attack: the US I Corps, the US IX Corps, and the ROK II Corps. It had been estimated that 3,000 tons of supplies would be needed daily by these forces for passive defense but that a minimum of 4,000 tons daily would be required for offensive combat. Before the Eighth Army attack could begin, this level of supply would have to be achieved at the Chongchon front. It had not been reached when Walker issued his order of 6 November, nor had it been reached by 15 November. Therefore, D-day had to be postponed. On 14 November, Walker issued a supplementary order that the attack would be started on a day and hour to be announced later.

The Far East Command and Eighth Army had to use sea, air, and all forms of land transportation to accumulate the necessary supplies at the Chongchon front to support a resumption of the advance. The daily requirement of 4,000 tons of supplies was achieved finally by bringing 2,000 tons by rail up to the south side of the Taedong River at Pyongyang from Pusan; by unloading another 1,000 tons at the newly reopened port of Chinnampo, which was to Pyongyang what Inchon was to Seoul; and by bringing in another 1,000 tons daily by emergency airlift.

Chinnampo was situated ten miles upstream from the mouth of the tidal Taedong River, on the north side of its estuary, and more than 30 miles by rail and highway southwest of Pyongyang. The entire Yellow Sea approach was mineable. The approach through to the Taedong River had to be swept for mines for 30 miles, and then another 40 miles to the Chinnampo docks. Because the US minesweeper force had been wholly occupied in clearing Wonsan harbor on the east coast, it was not until 29 October that the first ships arrived to begin the Chinnampo sweep. By 2 November the Navy had learned the pattern of the minefield. It comprised 217 moored and 25 magnetic mines. Five lines of mines had been laid across the main channel north of Sok To Island, and one line south of it. Large jellyfish, more than four feet in diameter, floating a few feet beneath the surface, added to the difficulty of locating the mines, as they often created false alarms.

A small South Korean craft made a safe passage through the cleared channel to Chinnampo on 3 November. Some tugs and barges made it up the Taedong channel on succeeding days, and when an LST reached the Chinnampo docks on 10 November, the western approach and southern channel were considered cleared. By 17 November, 14 ships had reached Chinnampo, and by 20 November 40,000 tons of supplies had been unloaded there. That same day the hospital ship *Repose* arrived. The clearing of the channel to Chinnampo and the use of that port greatly improved the logistic situation for General Walker's Eighth Army during the third week of November. In contrast to Wonsan, no lives or ships had been lost in clearing the minefields from the long, twisting approach to Chinnampo.[10]

All elements of Eighth Army were either short of, or entirely without, winter clothing on the eve of the advance. The temperatures were already freezing or below in North Korea. On 13 November the 27th Regiment of the 25th Division made its first issue of shoepacs, but only about two-thirds of the regiment received them. The remainder of the regiment could not be fitted—the shoes were too large. Six pairs of wool ski socks were issued for each pair of the shoepacs. As late as 17 November, the 2nd Infantry Division had been out of petroleum products for two days, and half its vehicles were "deadlined" (inoperative) for lack of spare parts. On 19 November, 17 planeloads of 33,000 field jackets arrived from Japan for the 1st Cavalry and 24th Infantry divisions, and six more planes brought 40,000 pairs of mittens and 33,000 mufflers.[11] The overseas supplies division of the Quartermaster Corps in the United States was already understocked, and it was not prepared for the large amount of winter clothing needed for fighting the Korean campaign in subarctic weather.

By 17 November however, the supply situation at the front had improved enough for General Walker to instruct the Eighth Army to begin its attack on 24 November. MacArthur then notified the Joint Chiefs of Staff of the new date. In the same message, MacArthur optimistically reported that, in the past ten days, intensified air attacks had isolated the battlefield from enemy reinforcements. On 21 November, Eighth Army advised its three corps that H hour for the attack was 10 A.M. on 24 November. Word of this had filtered to front-line units by 23 November—Thanksgiving Day.

3. UN and CCF Positions and Orders of Battle

By 22 November, Eighth Army units in jump-off positions were nearly all in place for the 24 November attack. On the army right, the ROK II Corps had reached its lines of departure on 21 November. On the same day, the 25th Infantry Division of the US IX Corps established its CP at Kunu-ri, and the next day it relieved the 1st Cavalry Division in the center of the line north of the Chongchon River in the area of Yongbyon known as the Walled City. The 1st Cavalry Division thereupon went into army reserve.

The 25th Division CP had one of the longest moves of any Eighth Army unit to reach its frontline position. It left Kaesong on the morning of 19 November and arrived in Kunu-ri on 21 November, after a journey of 187 miles. The Turkish Brigade, newly arrived in Korea, was detached from the 25th Division at this time, and on 20 November became part of the US IX Corps reserve. The 24th Infantry Division and the ROK 1st Division on the army left had only slight adjustments to make in their dispositions to be ready for the jump-off.

During preparations for the army attack, the Eighth Army CP had remained at Pyongyang. But General Walker was seldom there. It was vaguely understood by many that he had established a small forward CP in the vicinity of Sinanju or Anju on the Chongchon River at the western end of the front. According to Brig. Gen. William A. Collier (a senior colonel and Eighth Army deputy chief of staff in November 1950), General Walker, near the end of October, when the British 27th Brigade and the US 24th Infantry Division had first crossed the Chongchon River, made plans to establish his forward CP at Anju for the drive to the border. General Milburn, US I Corps commander, had his headquarters at Anju during the CCF 1st Phase Offensive. The army records generally are silent as to where General Walker was during the attack toward the border, but when he was not on the go, he was probably at the army advance headquarters on the Chongchon River with a very small staff. Probably the best authority on this subject is General Collier, who wrote, "Between the 15th–20th of November the Advance Headquarters actually moved to Anju and set up for operations adjacent to General Milburn's I Corps–this Advance Hq actually remained there until I Corps withdrew and just did manage to get the radio and various trucks etc. out."[1]

Kunu-ri became something of a magnet for Eighth Army activity in the days before the army attack toward the border on 24 November. On 18 November,

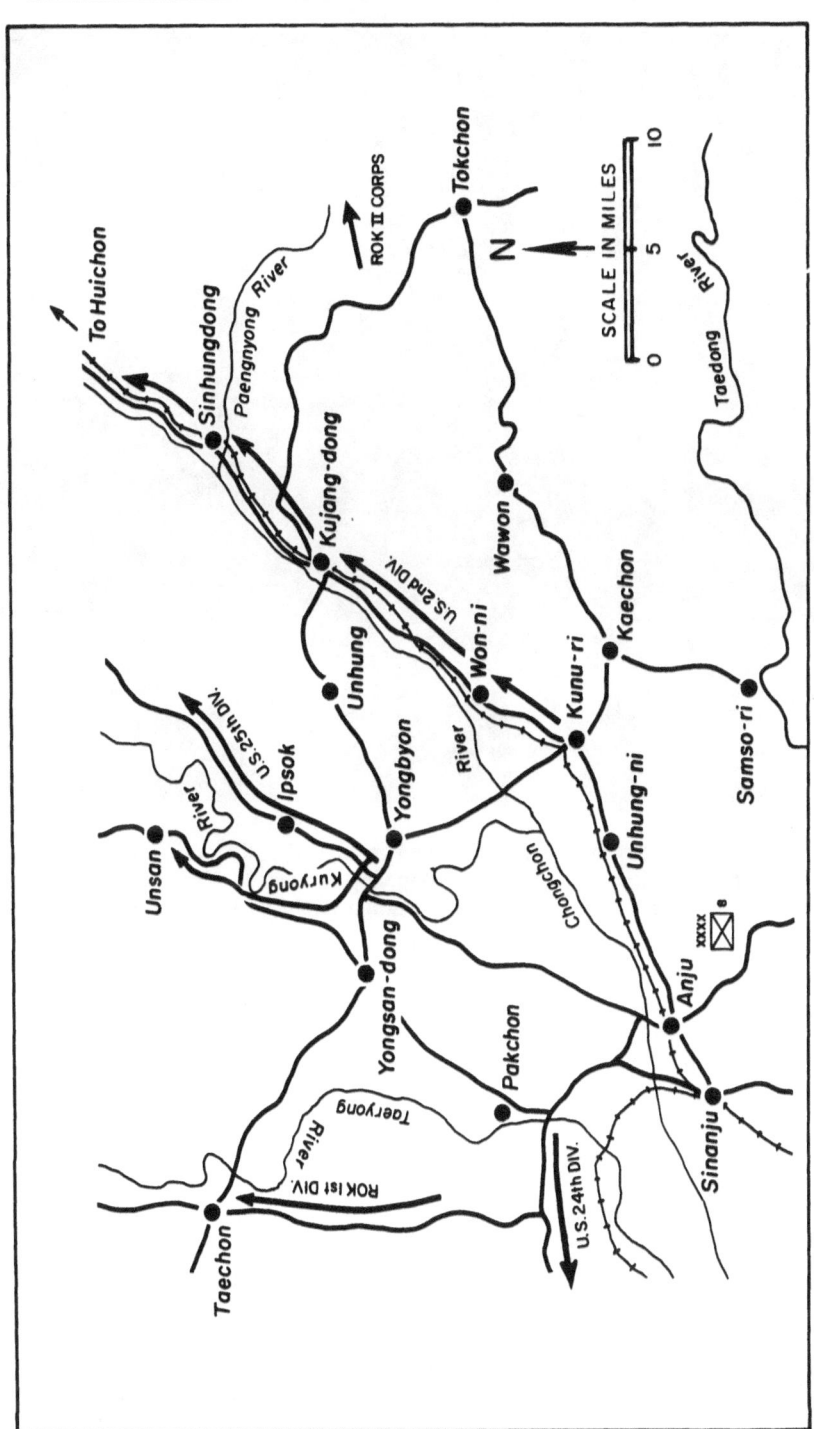

Map 2. Eighth Army's attack plan, 24 November 1950.

Maj. Gen. John B. Coulter, commanding general, US IX Corps, Eighth Army, serves the first piece of meat at Thanksgiving dinner, 23 November 1950, in the enlisted men's mess at Kunu-ri. National Archives 111-SC 355612

the US 2nd Infantry Division established its CP in a draw about a mile northeast of the town. At the same time, the 2nd Division's regiments moved to their assigned jump-off positions north and northeast of Kunu-ri. On 22 November, the US IX Corps moved its CP from Chasan to Unhung-ni, which was a few miles west of Kunu-ri on the road to Anju.

Thanksgiving Day fell on 23 November in 1950 – right in the midst of Eighth Army's final preparations for its attack to end the war. Thousands of frozen turkeys were moved to the Chongchon River front. Everyone was to have the traditional feast – from those who had it served on a white tablecloth in rear headquarters areas to those who took it from a container and ate it standing beside their tank or sitting just outside their foxhole. But many did not get their turkey on the date planned. Some units did not get the turkey thawed out in time to roast it for Thanksgiving Day dinner. They had to wait until the next day for it. Many soldiers said it was the best meal they had had in Korea.

On Thanksgiving Day the Australian Battalion, in slit trenches north of Pakchon on the west side of the army line, was on the point of going into an army reserve position. One of its members spoke admiringly of the dinner and recorded what the battalion menu was for that day. He said they had "roast turkey and cranberry sauce, shrimp cocktail, asparagus, fresh tomatoes, stuffed olives, tinned pineapple, nuts, sweets, fruitcake, fruit cocktail."[2]

Pfc. Arthur J. Cohen of Headquarters Company, 2nd Infantry Division, on the Chongchon River near Kunu-ri, wrote in his diary for 23 November that the army had furnished "the best meal we had in Korea up to that time." He also added that he and the others had been informed that the division was jumping off the next morning in the offensive to "end the war." He said, "Home by Christmas and Germany by spring was on all our minds and morale was high."[3]

Maj. Gen. John B. Coulter, commander of the US IX Corps, and Maj. Gen. John Kean, commander of the US 25th Division, visited Col. Henry K. Fisher's 35th Infantry Regimental CP for turkey on 23 November. While there, Coulter gave Fisher the impression that he was overly optimistic about ending the war in a few days. Coulter, who had just visited Maj. Gen. Laurence B. Keiser, commander of the US 2nd Infantry Division, added that "Dutch" Keiser was "raring to go." Fisher did not share this degree of optimism. He said that, when his regiment relieved the 19th Infantry of the 24th Division in the front lines for the big push, Colonel Moore of the 19th Infantry told him that his patrols had had trouble in going beyond a certain point—enemy turned them back. Thanksgiving Day had perhaps special omens for K Company, 35th Infantry. One of its patrols that day found a wounded Chinese soldier, the 25th Division's first Chinese prisoner in the war.[4]

Although Eighth Army reported on 20 November that there had been a noticeable increase in enemy reconnaissance patrols, the lack of enemy contact, except in the ROK II Corps area on the army right flank, led to a general feeling that things were going to be easy. The Far East Command Daily Intelligence Summary covering 24 November reflected something of this euphoria in saying, "There are some indications which point to the possibility of a withdrawal of CCF to the Yalu River or across the border into Manchuria."[5]

Eighth Army Order of Battle, 24 November

A comparison of the front lines as they existed from 26 October to 24 November across all of Korea indicated that they had changed least in the area immediately around Tokchon. Here the ROK II Corps held the right flank of Eighth Army, and here the enemy had shown the least inclination to yield ground.

Eighth Army was drawn up for its big attack on a line running a few miles north of the Chongchon River from Anju eastward for about 35 air miles. There the line crossed to the south side of the Chongchon River and held generally eastward to Tokchon. From there it continued on southeasterly into the ever-higher mountains, with the extreme eastern flank at Maengsan.[6] At that point began the much talked about "gap" between Eighth Army and the X Corps.

On 24 November, Eighth Army consisted of four US infantry divisions, the

Gen. Douglas MacArthur talking with Maj. Gen. John B. Coulter, commanding general, US IX Corps, Eighth Army, Korea, 1950. National Archives SC 352940

US 187th Airborne Regimental Combat Team (RCT), four ROK infantry divisions, the British 27th and 29th brigades (the latter replacing the former a week or two later), the Turkish Brigade, and smaller battalion-sized contingents from Belgium, Thailand, and the Philippines. Not all the UN contingents were at the front. The British 29th Brigade, for instance, had just arrived at Pusan and

Maj. Gen. William B. Kean, commanding general, 25th Infantry Division, Eighth Army, talking with Lt. Gen. Walton H. Walker, commanding general, Eighth Army, in his jeep at a forward headquarters, Korea, 1950. US Army photograph SC 345544

was in the act of moving north to join the army. In the army line, the US I Corps was on the left, the US IX Corps was in the center, and the ROK II Corps was on the right (see table 1).

On the left, or western, flank, I Corps had only the 5th RCT on line, at the army's extreme left flank, with the 21st Infantry Regiment scheduled to take the lead in an advance up the west coastal road. The 19th Regiment was in division reserve. I Corps's second division, the ROK 1st Division, had its 12th and 11th regiments on line, with the 15th Regiment in reserve, to the east of the 24th Division. The I Corps line was entirely north of the Chongchon River.

To the east of I Corps, in the center of the army line, IX Corps had the 25th Division on its left next to the I Corps boundary and the ROK 1st Division. It had the 35th Infantry Regiment next to the ROKs at the division boundary;

in the center it placed a special task force, known as Task Force Dolvin, and on the 25th Division right was the 24th Infantry Regiment. This division, like all of I Corps, was north of the Chongchon River. The IX Corps's second division, the US 2nd Infantry Division, was the right-flank division, and at its right-flank boundary met the ROK II Corps near Tokchon. The 2nd Division was mostly along the Chongchon River road, but the 9th Infantry Regiment slanted to the north of the river near Won-ni, although one battalion remained on the river road. The 38th Regiment entered the hills south of the river and extended the army line southeastward toward the ROK II Corps. The 23rd Regiment at first was in reserve.

The ROK II Corps picked up the Eighth Army line near Tokchon, southeast of the 2nd Division. Its ROK 7th Division was on its left flank adjoining the 2nd Division boundary, and near Tokchon; its ROK 8th Division was on its right flank and held the easternmost positions of the Eighth Army line. The ROK 6th Division was in corps reserve. The ROK 7th Division CP was at Tokchon; the ROK 8th Division CP was at Maengsan; and the ROK II Corps CP was at Pukchang-ni, about 15 miles south of Tokchon on the main road leading south.

With regard to this army line for the 24 November attack, mention must be made of a special situation at the boundary of the IX Corps with the ROK II Corps near Tokchon. When the 38th Infantry Regiment, on the 2nd Division's right flank, took its jump-off positions, it relieved four battalions of ROK troops from the 3rd, 5th, and 19th regiments. These ROK troops shifted to new positions farther east. In its new positions northwest of Tokchon, the US 38th Regiment was not comfortable tactically. On 23 November, it asked for authority to move to other positions, in attack if necessary, that were north

Table 1. **Eighth Army Strength, 24 November 1950**

Major Contingents	No. of Personnel
Ground Forces	
US Eighth Army	111,085
KATUSA[a]	9,736
British Army units	11,181
Turkish Brigade	5,055
ROK Army[b]	102,000
ROK Marines attached to Eighth Army	2,212
Subtotal	241,267
US Air Force in Korea[c]	13,204
Total	254,571

SOURCE: EUSAK, War Diary, 23 Nov. 1950, G-4 Sec., Annex A to PLR No. 133.
NOTE: This table does not include US naval units actively engaged along the west coast of Korea in support of Eighth Army. It also does not include infantry battalions recently arrived in Korea from Belgium, Thailand, and the Philippines but not involved in the November fighting.
[a] South Korean troops attached to Eighth Army.
[b] The entire ROK Army at this time numbered 203,807, approximately half of which was attached to Eighth Army.
[c] Most of the Air Force personnel was for the support of Eighth Army.

Maj. Gen. John H. Church, commanding general, 24th Infantry Division, Eighth Army, Korea, 1950. US Army photograph SC 349842

of the Tokchon–Kujang-dong road. The authority was granted. Col. George B. Peploe then moved hastily to the newly authorized positions, where he thought he had a better chance to secure the Tokchon-Kujang lateral road. This road ran from the Chongchon River southeast through the mountains to the ROK II Corps front in the vicinity of Tokchon. On the IX Corps's right flank, the 38th Regiment placed its 1st Battalion on its left flank, east of the river road, and its 3rd Battalion in the hills around Somin-dong and extending toward

Maj. Gen. Laurence B. Keiser, commanding general, 2nd Infantry Division, Eighth Army, Korea, 1950. US Army photograph SC 347647

the ROK II Corps boundary. The 2nd Battalion was in regimental reserve.

In taking its positions on the 38th Regimental right flank, I Company of the 3rd Battalion discovered an abandoned mine. In it the company found more than 500 tons of American-made mortar shells and small-arms ammunition—a large enemy ammunition dump in the mountains.[7]

It should be mentioned that the British 27th Brigade, at Pakchon in I Corps reserve, had been ordered to move to Kunu-ri to become part of IX Corps for the ensuing operations.[8]

The Eighth Army artillery officer calculated Eighth Army had considerable superiority over the Chinese and North Korean forces in artillery firepower. He evaluated the enemy artillery firepower at about three-tenths that of the Eighth Army command. He concluded: "The artillery personnel of the North Korean and Chinese Communist Forces are poorly trained with techniques inferior to our own. It is further believed that the enemy's signal and motor equipment are inadequate and of poor quality and that their ammunition resupply capabilities are much less than our own."[9] He also believed that American air forces had inflicted a crippling loss on CCF motor transport during November. The CCF supporting artillery was thought to be mostly of 75-mm and 76-mm howitzers of varied manufacture, originating in the United States, Soviet Union, Japan, and China, together with a considerable number of 45-mm and 57-mm antitank guns.

Of the total 789 artillery-support weapons listed in Eighth Army on the eve of the attack, 257 were in the US I Corps, 478 in the US IX Corps, and only 54 in the ROK II Corps. Each of the four American infantry divisions had 52 105-mm howitzers and 18 155-mm howitzers. The 2nd Infantry Division had in addition 12 8-inch howitzers attached to it, the only weapons of this caliber then in Korea. In assessing American and South Korean combat capabilities, it must be kept in mind that the ROK forces' artillery and tank support was always far less than that enjoyed by the American units. The ROK II Corps artillery support at this time consisted of 42 105-mm howitzers and 12 75-mm pack howitzers. The ROK 1st Division in the US I Corps had more artillery support than any other ROK division—at least double that of the others—and it also had a greater variety and range of weapons. Overall, the Eighth Army and attached troops were rated a RFP of 18,735, as against a RFP of 5,500 for the enemy. This was a superiority of nearly 3½ to 1. Eighth Army estimated it had sufficient artillery ammunition on hand to support an attack for five days and, with normal resupply, to sustain the attack for at least ten days.[10]

Eighth Army issued its Operational Plan No. 16 on 23 November. It called for the army to resume the offensive, destroy the enemy, and seize the ground within an established phase line and to be prepared then to resume the attack to the northern border of Korea.

From right to left along the line (from east to west), the missions were assigned as follows: the ROK II Corps mission was to advance through Huichon to Kanggye and hence to Manpojin on the Yalu. The US IX Corps would be in the center on the ROK II Corps's left as far as Huichon. Both US IX Corps and the ROK II Corps would use the main supply road (MSR) northeastward up the Chongchon River to Huichon and then cross the divide over the mountains to Kanggye. After the initial advance, this road was to be the main supply road for the ROK II Corps. If everything went according to plan, the ROK II Corps would meet elements of the US X Corps at or near Kanggye in its attack toward Manpojin from Yudam-ni and the Chosin Reservoir. The US I Corps on the west was to drive north to the border in its sector. No troops were to go beyond the south bank of the Yalu River, nor would fire be exchanged with enemy troops on the north bank. Rigid control of troops was to be exercised so that they did not damage or disrupt power plants or their operation near or at the border.[11]

The Eighth Army plan of operations called for a general advance that would reach the border at the Yalu from its mouth in the west where it emptied into the Yellow Sea and extend eastward as far as Manpojin on the river. The US X Corps attack from the Chosin Reservoir toward Kanggye with the 1st Marine Division and an RCT from the 7th Division was designed to help Eighth Army and to protect its right flank as it neared the border.

General Walker's plan called for a closely coordinated attack so that he would have the army under control at all times. There was to be no wild dash in a race for the border. His plan reflects a respect for the way the Chinese executed their 1st Phase Offensive. He did not want to be caught off guard again.

The CCF Order of Battle on 24 November

In front of Eighth Army in northwest Korea on 24 November 1950 were six Chinese armies with 19 divisions (see table 2). On the west flank and north of

Table 2. **Chinese XIII Army Group Order of Battle, 24 November 1950**

Army	Divisions	Regiments
38th	112th	334th, 335th, 336th
	113th	337th, 338th, 339th
	114th	340th, 341st, 342nd
39th	115th	343rd, 344th, 345th
	116th	346th, 347th, 348th
	117th	349th, 350th, 351st
40th	118th	352nd, 353rd, 354th
	119th	355th, 356th, 357th
	120th	358th, 359th, 360th
42nd	124th	370th, 371st, 372nd
	125th	373rd, 374th, 375th
	126th	376th, 377th, 378th
50th	148th	442nd, 443rd, 444th
	149th	445th, 446th, 447th
	150th	448th, 449th, 450th
	167th[a]	499th, 500th, 501st
66th	196th	586th, 587th, 588th
	197th	589th, 590th, 591st
	198th	592nd, 593rd, 594th
Total: 6 armies	19 divisions	57 regiments

SOURCE: FEC, Daily Intelligence Summary No. 3207, 21 June 1951.
[a]The 167th Division came originally from the 56th Army.

the Chongchon River—generally opposite the US I Corps—were the Chinese 50th and 66th armies; the 50th with four divisions, the 66th with three divisions. In the center, directly opposite the main UN concentration of the US IX Corps, were the Chinese 39th and 40th armies, each with three divisions. On the Chinese left flank, and opposite the ROK II Corps, east of the Chongchon generally and south of Huichon, were the Chinese 38th and 42nd armies, each with three divisions. These last two armies were poised to strike the ROK II Corps at Eighth Army's right, or east, flank.

The Chinese tactical plan, as it later developed, was to penetrate the ROK II Corps front, then get into its rear areas, turn westward and roll up that corps, and at the same time attack the IX Corps frontally all along its front, including the eastern part of the US I Corps front in this same attack. The 50th and 66th armies on the western end of the line, in front of I Corps, were to assist the frontal attack against the UN center as needed. The plan was designed to turn the UN right flank and then roll up the Eighth Army from east to west and pin it against the west coast or force it to retreat southward.

The Chinese forces, then, all 19 divisions, were in place on 24 November, ready to meet and then counterattack the Eighth Army. They comprised about 150,000 light-infantry troops, virtually all of them available as front-line fighters. The Chinese divisions had very little tail (logistic and support service units) in contrast to what the American and UN units had.[12]

On 24 November, the day Eighth Army launched its troops northward once more, MacArthur's intelligence officer, Maj. Gen. Charles Willoughby, in communications to the Department of the Army, said the UN forces were opposed by 82,799 North Koreans and between 40,000 and 70,935 Chinese soldiers.[13] This estimate was grossly in error. In the Chinese 2nd Phase Offensive there were no North Korean forces in the attack. Only relatively small groups of North Korean soldiers, cut off behind the lines and acting as guerrillas, contributed anything to the Chinese attack. The remnants of the decimated and disorganized North Korean divisions that survived the fighting of the Inchon landing and the battle for the possession of Seoul had retreated to the vicinity of Kanggye and the Manchurian border. At the time of the Chinese 2nd Phase Offensive, they were still there in late November, taking in replacements and reorganizing. The North Korean guerrillas behind Eighth Army were a threat only in the vicinity of Chorwon, where their activities seem to have been coordinated with the Chinese attacks.[14]

The Scene of Battle

The Chongchon River drainage was the arena where military events of far-reaching importance took place in the last week of November 1950—events totally unexpected by Eighth Army and the Far East Command—and so devastating in their results as to constitute one of the great surprises of military history. This arena encompassed the valley of the Chongchon River, its tributaries, and the finger ridges that ran down between them from the high ground on both sides. The Chinese troops lay in hidden assembly areas, carefully camouflaged, generally about 10 to 12 miles north of, and out of contact with, the bulk of

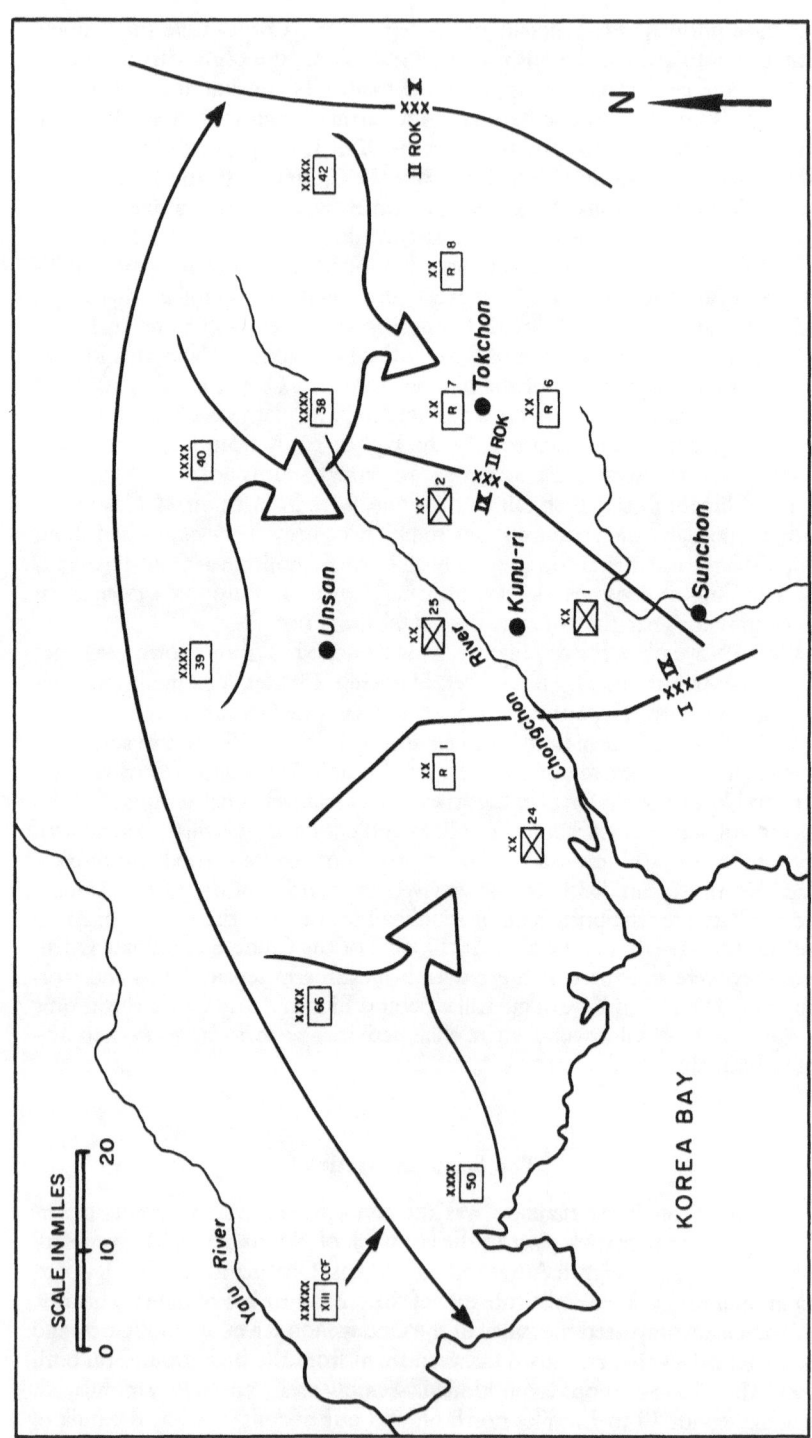

Map 3. The CCF XIII Army Group's deployment against Eighth Army, 24 November 1950.

Eighth Army when the latter began its movement north on the morning of 24 November. For this reason, the initial advance of the UN forces was unopposed. Because of their importance in controlling the tactical movements of both forces, the physical features of the terrain should be described.

Korea is a land of unending hills and valleys, and nowhere is this feature more pronounced than in the northern part of the peninsula. In the northwestern part, where Eighth Army stood poised to begin its attack, the Chongchon River and its tributaries, with their interlocking hills and mountains, constituted the last remaining major physical barrier between Eighth Army and the Manchurian border. The Chongchon River and its two major tributaries, the Kuryong and the Taeryong, all flow from the north. These rivers drain the western face of the high mountains that rise in the almost trackless highlands south of the Yalu in the north-central part of Korea. South of the Chongchon River, the Taedong River, also running from northeast to southwest, parallels it generally at an air-mile distance of from 20 to 25 miles, with an irregular divide separating their respective drainages. The Taedong River runs through Yongwon and Tokchon at the northeast of the Eighth Army sector and flows southwest through Sunchon to Pyongyang and on to the Yellow Sea below Chinnampo. Beyond the Chongchon drainage to the northeast, the Northern Taebaek Range gives way to the high, cold Yangnim Range, which borders the Yalu River and continues on northward across the trough of the river into Manchuria.[15]

A railroad and a highway bridge cross the Chongchon River at Sinanju, and five miles upstream from these another highway bridge crosses the river at Anju. In the valley of the Chongchon a railroad and a vehicular road follow along the south bank of the river within the area of operations. At Huichon, 65 air miles upstream from the mouth of the Chongchon, the river breaks up into a number of tributaries that fan out in a semicircle where they drain down from the high mountain mass of a divide. The Chongchon River runs generally parallel to the Yalu, about 65 miles south of it. Both flow southwest into the Yellow Sea. The main railroad and highway on the west coast run from Seoul to Pyongyang and northward, crossing the Chongchon at Sinanju. From there they continue west and northwest to Sinuiju at the Chinese border and cross the Yalu to Antung.

Inland from the west coast, mountainous spines extend southward from the Yalu to the valley of the Chongchon, and as the distance inland eastward increases, they become ever higher, rougher, and more forbidding. These mountains reach their greatest heights and become almost trackless wastes between the Chosin Reservoir and the Yalu, where the Yangnim Range continues on into Manchuria. The Yalu itself, except for its lower coastal reaches, runs through a gorgelike channel rimmed by high mountains on both sides. The large Suiho hydroelectric dam on the middle Yalu impounds a reservoir of the same name that extends upstream for 60 miles, pushing water into scores of little lateral fjordlike valleys.

Above the Suiho Reservoir there is a major highway crossing of the Yalu River from Chian in Manchuria. Eight miles farther upstream in Manpojin on the Korean side, there are both railroad and highway crossings. Twenty-five air miles southeast of Manpojin, on a major road from it, lies Kanggye, situated in the very heart of a mountain fastness. There both North Korean government officials and ranking military commanders had assembled during the long retreat northward after the Inchon landing. From Kanggye a quick withdrawal could be made across the boundary into a Manchurian sanctuary if it became necessary.

About 20 air miles east and upstream from Sinanju, on the south bank of the Chongchon, lies the town of Kaechon and a village on its northern edge called Kunu-ri. Kaechon absorbed Kunu-ri after World War II, and newer maps do not show the latter. But in this narrative the name Kunu-ri will be used for this Korean town because that is how it was shown on the old maps used by the American soldiers who became so familiar with the place. That name is repeated a thousand times in the United States Army records of those last days of November 1950.

From Kunu-ri an important secondary roadnet ran northward beyond the Chongchon River through the ancient walled town of Yongbyon to Ipsok and Unsan and on to the Yalu River. From Kujang-dong on the Chongchon, 15 air miles northeast of Kunu-ri, a road ran southeasterly across mountainous terrain to Tokchon, 18 air miles away. From Kunu-ri still another dirt road ran almost due east to Tokchon, a distance of 25 air miles, but farther by road. Tokchon was deep in the mountains, situated on the north side of a bend in the Taedong River. Much was to happen in the Kunu-ri–Kujang-dong–Tokchon triangle of land. Also from Kunu-ri, and destined to be of unusual military importance, was another dirt road that went south through hill country across a divide between the Chongchon and Taedong rivers to Sunchon, 30 miles away.

The configuration of the valley of the lower Chongchon in relation to the mountain ridges that approach it from the Yalu should be noted. On the north side of the lower Chongchon for a distance of some miles, the ground varies from flat to low hills, with shallow valleys between the hills. Beginning about 15 air miles north of the Chongchon, the ground rises more sharply into rough, mountainous terrain. A road ran northeastward and generally parallel to the Chongchon River from Taechon on the west through Unsan and Onjong, and from there curved in a loop east to Huichon, following this topographical cleavage along the base of the higher hills.

The towns of Taechon, Unsan, Onjong, and Huichon stand at the entrances to the narrow valleys in the mountain ranges that extend northward to the Yalu. These limited corridors of advance form a natural defensive barrier to any military movement from the valley of the Chongchon to the Yalu border. Here, along this topographical cleavage line connected by the Taechon-Huichon road, the Chinese had established their major troop assemblies, unknown to Eighth Army. They used this terrain in a masterly way, first to draw the Eighth Army into a dispersed advance, and then to launch a surprise attack upon it.[16]

4. The First Day of Eighth Army's Attack

Friday morning, 24 November 1950, broke clear, with near freezing temperatures along the Eighth Army line at the Chongchon. By midafternoon the temperature had risen to 57 degrees—a warm day for that time of year. The sky was clear in the west, but scattered clouds hung over the central and eastern parts of the army front.[1]

Troop movements were everywhere in evidence as the sun rose. The British 27th Brigade moved southward across the Chongchon, where it found ice floes drifting sluggishly. After crossing, the brigade turned eastward on the south side toward Kunu-ri, where it would pass from I Corps to IX Corps control in reserve. A north wind blew clouds of yellow dust from the crowded road. The journey was uncomfortable.[2] As anyone who has been on Korean roads knows, they are mud when it rains, rough and slippery when frozen, and thick with choking dust at other times.

Some of the thousands who moved out of their bivouac areas that morning could reflect on changes the past month had brought. Before the Chinese 1st Phase Offensive near the end of October, the Department of Defense had planned a cutback in the number of troops scheduled to go to Korea. It had also taken steps to reduce reinforcements from UN allies. Prior to 6 November more than 8,000 South Korean troops attached to Eighth Army (KATUSA) had been released. It was all part of the prevailing opinion that the war was about over and that the attached South Koreans would no longer be needed. On 6 November Eighth Army hastily canceled the order for release of KATUSA troops.

In one of the last-minute shuffles of troops in preparation for advance, Eighth Army on 24 November, placed the Turkish Brigade under IX Corps control, with its 2nd and 3rd battalions ordered to move north from Kaesong to join the brigade at Kunu-ri the next day. The Turkish Brigade had not yet seen action in Korea.

Eighth Army also seemed optimistic that the war would end soon. But in a conversation with General Walker, Colonel Fisher of the 35th Infantry said that General Walker did not seem to have the overoptimism that most did. In commenting on the impending attack toward the Yalu, Walker said to Fisher, "I have been there once before; this time we are going to take it easy."[3] Col. Albert K. Stebbins, the Eighth Army G-4 and a close friend of Walker, told the author that Walker did not really want to make the attack to the border but reluctantly carried out orders.

Walker's order for the attack reflected caution and the intention to proceed with a closely coordinated advance so that he would have the army under control at all times. While there is no documentary evidence that Walker was wildly optimistic about the impending attack, it would seem on balance that he did not officially oppose it. He expected opposition but seemed to think Eighth Army could drive to the border. His chief of staff, Maj. Gen. Leven C. Allen, shared this view.[4]

On the army's extreme left, the 21st Regiment of the US 24th Division passed through the 5th RCT and struck out north on the morning of 24 November along the coastal road leading from Sinanju toward Chongju. In the late afternoon I and K companies received a few rounds of small-arms fire. From Chongju the regiment was to continue northwest along the coastal road toward Sinuiju at the mouth of the Yalu. On this first day, it met virtually no opposition. Civilians along its line of advance, however, reported that enemy were in front of it but constantly withdrawing before contact was made.[5]

East of the 21st Infantry, the ROK 11th Regiment of the ROK 1st Division relieved the 5th RCT of the 24th Division and attacked north across the Taeryong River toward Taechon. The 5th RCT then relieved the 2nd Battalion of the ROK 12th Regiment of the ROK 1st Division, whereupon the ROK 12th Regiment moved up on the left of the ROK 11th Regiment, both receiving enemy small-arms fire in the afternoon, but no real opposition. Up ahead of the advancing ROK 1st Division, the Air Force bombed and napalmed Taechon and vicinity. At dark the two ROK regiments stood three to four miles southwest and southeast of Taechon. During the day both regiments had encountered several undefended enemy roadblocks. Again, there were many signs that enemy forces were withdrawing in front of them.[6] It had been an easy day for I Corps.

East of I Corps and the ROK 1st Division, the 25th Infantry Division on the left flank of IX Corps began its advance northward, following generally the course of the Kuryong River, a tributary of the Chongchon. The division headed for its first objectives of Unsan and Ipsok. The former was west of the Kuryong; the latter was east of it. The division expected to encounter a center of enemy troop concentration and hard fighting. The Kuryong River split the division's ten-mile front, which necessitated some special tactical dispositions. Because of expected heavy enemy opposition to its advance, the 25th Division's firepower was reinforced by three field artillery battalions, two of them, the 77th and 82nd, taken from the 1st Cavalry Division, which was now in Eighth Army reserve. The third artillery battalion, the 90th, was borrowed from the Turkish Brigade, which had just arrived at the front and was not expected to be committed to action immediately.

Col. Henry K. Fisher's 35th Infantry, minus B Company, advanced along the west side of the Kuryong about four miles toward Unsan without meeting enemy resistance.

Maj. Gen. William B. Kean, the division commander, formed a special task force to advance on the east side of the Kuryong River, opposite Colonel Fisher's 35th Infantry. This special task force was expected to meet enemy on its axis of advance, the road north from Yongbyon, one of the few remaining walled towns of medieval Korea. The road ran west from Yongbyon a few miles to the Kuryong River and then turned north along its east bank toward Ipsok. Beyond Ipsok, the road curved slightly eastward around the so-called Turtle's Head and Camel's Head bends of the Kuryong River. The special task force was known as Task Force Dolvin and took its name from its commander, Lt. Col. Weldon G. Dolvin, commanding officer of the 89th Tank Battalion.

To the right, or east, of Task Force Dolvin, the 24th Infantry Regiment, popularly known among its members as the Deuce-Four, commanded by Col. John T. Corley, completed the 25th Division deployment. This regiment was the only all-black infantry regiment in Eighth Army. Its officers, however, were white and were handpicked from among the top performers in the US Army. The 24th Infantry's line of advance on the right of Task Force Dolvin led it into hilly country with poor roads.[7]

The 25th Division's third regiment, Col. John "Mike" Michaelis's 27th (Wolfhound) Regiment, was held in division reserve.

General Kean had little worry about his left flank, with Colonel Fisher, an experienced, middle-aged officer, in command there. Fisher was a professional in the best sense of the term—wise and judicious in the use of weapons, calm and decisive under battle stress. He did not spend his time having energetic public-relations personnel meet incoming planes to snatch away to his CP feature writers for US national magazines and newspapers. Fisher was a quiet, thinking commander, not glamorous; he never sought headlines.

Task Force Dolvin left its line of departure just north of the walled city of Yongbyon. It was one of the few major units that met enemy fire on the 24th—Chinese small-arms fire in the afternoon. Its composition was a mixed one from three different battalions together with several special support units, all chosen for their combat capabilities:

Task Force Dolvin
B Company (less one platoon), 89th Medium Tank Battalion (8213th
    Ranger Company, attached)
E Company, 27th Infantry Regiment (Assault Gun Platoon, 89th Tank
    Battalion, attached)
B Company, 35th Infantry Regiment (1st Platoon, B Company, 89th
    Medium Tank Battalion, attached)
25th Reconnaissance Company
C Company, 65th Engineer Combat Battalion
Reconnaissance Platoon, 89th Medium Tank Battalion

The 105-mm howitzer artillery support units (two or three battalions, varying because of changing circumstances) are not given as constant units of the task force.[8] The Ranger Company in the task force was the first and only one of that type then in Eighth Army. B Company, 35th Infantry, and E Company, 27th Infantry, were two handpicked infantry units and formed the backbone of the task force.

Advance elements of Task Force Dolvin had barely crossed their line of departure at 10 A.M. when two American prisoners of the Chinese came into the task force south of Ipsok. They said Chinese had brought them to within three miles of the American lines and told them to go on down the road and they would meet American soldiers. They said there were 28 more American prisoners, unable to walk because of wounds, waiting up the road. The prisoners were members of the 8th Cavalry Regiment who had been captured near Unsan (now directly in the path of the 35th Regiment) a month earlier in the CCF 1st Phase Offensive. Colonel Dolvin refused to send ambulances for the waiting Americans. He said his force would attack toward them. His advance reached the group just north of Ipsok about 1:30 P.M. and found them to number 24 instead of the stated 28. The battalion aid station, with the help of ambulances from the 25th Division, evacuated all the former prisoners to the rear and turned them over to medical authorities.[9] Brig. Gen. George Barth, commanding the division artillery, brought back three of the prisoners in his jeep. These men reported they had been well treated but had suffered from wounds, intense cold, and meager rations.

It is not clear why the Chinese released these prisoners. An enemy document captured more than two months later but apparently issued in late November 1950 (since it covered information obtained by interrogating American prisoners of war between 13 and 23 November) said the Chinese commander of the prisoner-of-war stockade at Pyoktong on the Yalu River selected and investigated 27 American prisoners who were to be released. On the night of 19 November, interpreter Yun Ki Bok started with them toward the front, and at a point four kilometers from the American lines, he released them. This document said those released were slightly wounded and of below-average intelligence.[10] Information obtained from some of the released prisoners indicated they were told on 21 November that they would be released. On the night of 23 November they were placed in houses a few miles in front of the American positions and told to send two of their number the next morning through the Chinese positions to contact American soldiers. The next morning local Chinese screening forces apparently withdrew north of Ipsok.[11]

Of interest was the statement of one of the released men that, as they traveled south from the Yalu, they encountered a roadblock about every 20 miles. As they neared the front, there were roadblocks about every quarter of a mile.

When Task Force Dolvin got under way on 24 November, B Company, 35th Infantry, was deployed on the left; B Company, 89th Tank Battalion, was in the center; and E Company, 27th Infantry, was on the right. In the early afternoon the force passed through and around Ipsok, a small village situated in a shallow east-west valley, south of a low range of hills. In the afternoon about 4 P.M., a group of Chinese in the hills east of the road rose up in groups of three or four and fired rifles at B Company, which returned their fire. This drove off the Chinese screening force. The tanks in the center of the road helped by firing a few rounds at the Chinese. The task force went into positions late in the afternoon three to four miles north of Ipsok.

Meanwhile, the 24th Infantry Regiment was supposed to be advancing on the right, or east, of Task Force Dolvin. A meeting of contact patrols between the two forces had been arranged for that evening. First Lt. Robert K. Sawyer, 3rd Platoon leader of the 25th Reconnaissance Company, took his platoon eastward up a shallow valley to the designated meeting point on the regimental boundary. He and his men waited several hours during the frigid night, while a full moon lighted the frosty landscape. Eventually the 24th Infantry patrol arrived, reported it had seen nothing, and continued on its way.[12]

That morning, Col. John Corley's 24th Infantry had moved up on the right of Task Force Dolvin, relieved the 8th Cavalry Regiment, and with its 1st Battalion on the left and its 2nd Battalion on the right, started its main advance east of Yongbyon toward Unhang. It had no opposition during the day.

The other US division in IX Corps, the 2nd Infantry Division, put its 9th Infantry Regiment in the lead as it started from Kunu-ri north up the Chongchon River valley. Nothing eventful happened to it during the day, except that its 3rd Battalion found seven self-propelled guns and three T-34 (Soviet-built) tanks on flatcars in a railroad tunnel south of Won-ni (Pugwon). All were in good condition. Ahead of the troops, the Air Force bombed and napalmed every village along the way. Elements of the 9th Infantry were nearly two miles north of Kujang-dong by evening.[13]

On the right, or east, of the 9th Infantry, the 38th Infantry Regiment was on higher ground east of and away from the river. There, Col. George Peploe's regiment held the vital right flank of the IX Corps, inland from Kujang-dong and next to the left flank of the ROK II Corps, 15 miles northwest of Tokchon. On 24 November Peploe's men met Chinese patrols that quickly withdrew and disappeared. By evening the 38th Regiment was in the high hills east of the Chongchon River but not in contact with the ROK II Corps. The 23rd Regiment of the division, at first in reserve, had left Sunchon on 23 November and the next day reached Kunu-ri, poised to follow the rest of the division northward up the Chongchon.

During the day, aerial observers studied high and massive Hill 1229, seven to eight air miles northward in the center of the 38th Infantry zone of advance. They discovered freshly dug positions on it and estimated that there were at least 500 enemy troops on the mountain. Air strikes were directed on these positions, killing an estimated 150 enemy.[14]

The only place on the Eighth Army line where there was hard fighting on 24 November was on its right flank, in the area of the ROK II Corps, near Tokchon. Actually, the Eighth Army attack there on 24 November was only a continuation of fighting that had been in progress for many days. Chinese had opposed ROK troops there from the very first attempt of the South Koreans to occupy Tokchon. When the ROKs made a determined effort on 24 November to move ahead, the Chinese again fought them to a standstill. At the end of the day the South Koreans were no more than 1,000 yards from where they had started in the morning. The situation at Tokchon and eastward from it in the ROK Corps zone of operation requires some explanation, in view of what was to happen there in the next 48 hours.

The Special Situation at Tokchon

The Chinese 1st Phase Offensive in late October had caught the Eighth Army by surprise north of the Chongchon River in a series of major ambushes. The ROK II Corps, then also on the army right flank, suffered serious losses at that time. The 2nd and 19th regiments of the ROK 6th Division were hit hard, and its 7th Regiment had been cut off just below Chosan on the Yalu – only about 300 men from it ever escaped back to friendly lines. The ROK 6th Division at this time had been rendered combat ineffective. At the same time, the 10th Regiment of the ROK 8th Division suffered heavy losses.

In the Eighth Army withdrawal after this first meeting with the CCF, the ROK II Corps moved south and east. It was still on the army line on the right, extending its line to the vicinity of Tokchon. Some of its elements took up blocking positions farther east near Maengsan on the army's extreme right, or eastern, flank.

Tokchon is situated on the north bank of the Taedong River. A sharp, cone-shaped hill, rising from the flat, although narrow, valley of the Taedong, about a mile west of Tokchon, dominated the town. This hill was studded with caves. In the fighting there in the first part of November, it became known as the Honey Comb. The 16th and 21st regiments of the ROK 8th Division had the mission of capturing Tokchon and Honey Comb Hill that dominated it. When the ROK troops arrived, they found that Chinese were in Tokchon and had occupied the area in force.

For eight consecutive days, the ROK regiments fought to capture their Tokchon objectives. They would blast their way to the crest of Honey Comb by day, and each night the Chinese would drive them off. After the eighth day of this see-saw fighting, the Chinese in mid-November suddenly withdrew from Tokchon.

After 14 November, the 10th Regiment of the ROK 8th Division held the extreme right flank blocking position at Maengsan, about 15 air miles southeast of Tokchon, but many more miles by a narrow, twisting mountain road. Its patrols into the gap eastward toward the US X Corps found North Korean guerrilla bands of recently conscripted personnel, but no Chinese units.

On 18 November the ROK II Corps boundary was shifted eastward again, and the US IX Corps took over the positions west of Tokchon then held by the ROK 6th and 7th divisions. The ROK 7th Division now moved to the ROK 8th Division positions north and east of Tokchon, and the ROK 8th Division was ordered to new positions north and east of Yongwon, about 15 air miles northeast of Tokchon. The ROK 6th Division, still far understrength and in the process of taking in replacements and reorganizing because of its earlier heavy losses, went into corps reserve. The ROK 7th and 8th divisions occupied their new positions without great difficulty. The Chinese in front of them gave only token resistance but maintained contact with the ROK troops. On 24 November the 2nd Regiment of the ROK 6th Division assembled at Tokchon as part of the ROK II Corps reserve.[15]

The ROK 7th Division, now next to the US IX Corps boundary, had had only limited operational experience since its reorganization. The ROK 8th Division was the only major unit of the ROK II Corps that was in relatively good condition. A ROK division at full strength had about 12,000 men. But it must be remembered that, at whatever strength, the ROK divisions in the ROK II Corps were supported by only one battalion of light artillery – 105-mm howitzers – and they had no armor. The ROK II Corps headquarters itself had no additional artillery or support weapons. The ROK II Corps on 24 November occupied by far the most rugged terrain of the Eighth Army front.

In one respect the UN Command had by now given improved support to the ROK units. In the early months of the war there was only a haphazard attempt to supply a balanced and suitable food ration to the South Korean troops. The command was wholly preoccupied with other more pressing matters. But in the late summer and early autumn, a ROK Army ration was developed, known as the 12-in-1 ration. It was first issued to ROK troops in November 1950 and was airlifted from Kimpo airfield, near Seoul, to Pyongyang and then forwarded by truck to the ROK units.[16]

The ROK II Corps positions on 24 November had the 3rd and 8th regiments of the ROK 7th Division, in that order, extending the line eastward from the US 2nd Division boundary northwest of Tokchon, with the 5th Regiment in division reserve. The 10th and 21st regiments of the ROK 8th Division were on the extreme right in the direction of Maengsan and Yongwon. The 16th Regiment of the division was in a blocking position at Maengsan and patrolling daily eastward into the gap toward X Corps. The ROK 6th Division was in corps reserve, with its 2nd Regiment assembled at Tokchon. The 7th Regiment had a strength of only 119 officers and 1,443 enlisted men and was at Kunu-ri. The division's third regiment, the 19th, was far to the rear, just moving to Hwachang, Songchon, and Yangdok, 45 to 50 air miles south of Tokchon. It could be of no immediate use in any crisis at the front. The ROK II Corps headquarters on 24 November moved to Pukchang-ni, 15 air miles south of Tokchon.[17]

There was a damaging incident in the ROK II Corps rear just before the 24 November attack that also adversely affected the corps's combat effectiveness. In a well-planned and equally well-timed move on 23 November, a large North Korean guerrilla force of about 1,500 men attacked the town of Songchon, about 50 miles south of Tokchon. Songchon was on the ROK II Corps MSR. The attack was unusually successful. It blocked the corps's supply road at a critical moment, and in addition it destroyed ammunition dumps and field hospitals the ROKs had established there. The ROK II Corps immediately started the 19th Regiment of its 6th Division to Songchon to reopen the road. This left only the 2nd and 7th regiments of the 6th Division in corps reserve. Only the 2nd Regiment was combat effective.

This was the situation when Chinese stopped in their tracks the three ROK regiments in the II Corps center and right, the 8th Regiment of the 7th Division and the 10th and 21st regiments of the 8th Division, on the morning of 24 November after they had climbed less than half a mile into the hills in their attacks. Heavy fire from Chinese positions, protected by sheer cliffs, formed a steel and rock wall that repeated ROK assaults failed to dent. The ROK II Corps advance stopped. It was the one place on the Eighth Army front where no appreciable gain was made that first day.[18]

Aside from these actions at the front on 24 November, the 25th Infantry Division airlifted truck drivers from Pyongyang to Pusan to drive back 101 vehicles that were badly needed; the 1st Cavalry Division quartermaster was able to issue winter shoepacs and pile-lined jackets to division troops; two new UN units arrived at Pusan for duty in Korea (the Netherlands Battalion and the British 29th Brigade), and Eighth Army ordered the 5th Cavalry Regiment to assume responsibility for the Sunchon–Kunu-ri MSR to the US IX Corps.[19]

MacArthur Goes to Korea on 24 November

Gen. Douglas MacArthur planned to go to Korea on 24 November to see the attack start. In a sense, he meant to launch the Eighth Army attack by his presence on the Chongchon River front. Prior to 24 November, the last General Headquarters FEC communiqué MacArthur had issued was no. 11, on 6 November. This summed up the situation as he saw it at the end of the Chinese 1st Phase Offensive. In that communiqué he spoke of Eighth Army's escaping from "a possible trap . . . surreptitiously laid [and] calculated to encompass the destruction of the United Nations Forces. . . ."[20] In the days that followed, MacArthur carried on an argument with the Joint Chiefs of Staff, as already noted, that he should be allowed to renew his attack toward the border, despite the "trap" from which the Eighth Army had so recently escaped.[21]

On 24 November MacArthur issued his Communiqué No. 12. It reflected his views at the outset of the UN offensive on 24 November, or at least the view he wished to present to the world, and it is therefore of great interest and importance. It is quoted in full below:

> The United Nations massive compression envelopment in North Korea against the new Red Armies cooperating there is now approaching its decisive effort. The isolating component of the pincer, our Air Forces of all types, have for the past three weeks, in a sustained attack of model coordination and effectiveness, successfully interdicted enemy lines of support from the North so that further reinforcement therefrom has been sharply curtailed and essential supplies markedly limited. The eastern sector of the pincer [X Corps], with noteworthy and effective Naval support, has steadily advanced in a brilliant tactical movement and has now reached a commanding enveloping position, cutting in two the northern reaches of the enemy's geographical potential. This morning the western sector of the pincer moves forward in general assault in an effort to complete the compression and close the vise. If successful this should for all practical purposes end the war, restore peace and unity to Korea, enable the prompt withdrawal of United Nations military forces, and permit the complete assumption by the Korean people and nation of full sovereignty and international equality. It is that for which we fight.
>
> (Signed) Douglas MacArthur,
> Gen. of the Army,
> United States Army,
> Commander-in-Chief.[22]

This is an amazing document. It was wrong on many different aspects of the real situation, as revealed disastrously in the next few days. It reflects a colossal misjudgment of the military situation in Korea. One British correspondent with the British 27th Brigade wrote later that "this document filled us with alarm and despondency."[23]

On the heels of this communiqué, General MacArthur arrived in Korea. He had just obtained a new Constellation airplane, the only one in the Far East Command. His party, flying from Tokyo on the morning of 24 November, included key members of his staff—Gen. Courtney Whitney; General Wright, his G-3; General Willoughby, his G-2; General Stratemeyer, commander of the Fifth Air Force; and several chiefs of US news bureaus in Tokyo. The Constellation landed at the Sinanju airstrip near Gen. Frank Milburn's I Corps headquarters on the lower Chongchon River. General Walker was there to meet MacArthur's party. There was the customary round of visits to the Eighth Army higher and subordinate headquarters and briefings there. These told him and his party that the attack was already under way and that nothing unusual had happened. But Milburn told the group of officers he thought the Unsan area at the right side of I Corps was heavily defended and would be a tough place for the IX Corps, on his immediate right. The party went next to Maj. Gen. John Church's 24th Division Headquarters at Anju, where there was another briefing. Church told MacArthur and the others present that the attack was going well in his division zone, on the army left, and that there had been no opposition. Optimism and enthusiasm prevailed.[24] MacArthur's group then went to General Coulter's IX Corps CP at Unhung-ni, near Kunu-ri. The MacArthur party left there at 1 P.M. for Sinanju and the flight back to Japan.

While the party was at Anju, an incident took place that the news media took full advantage of and essentially falsely reported. At the 24th Division CP, Generals MacArthur, Church, and Coulter and some other ranking officers were engaged in general conversation while standing alongside a jeep. Church had just told MacArthur that he thought the troops could go all the way to the border. MacArthur replied in a light vein, "Well, if they go fast enough, maybe some of them can be home by Christmas."

The journalists standing a little distance away heard part of the conversation — MacArthur's remark about troops being home by Christmas. On the basis of that fragment, they filed reports that were printed in nearly every important newspaper in the United States the next day. Many newspapers attributed their version to either the UP or the AP dispatches from Korea on 24 November. These dispatches said that General MacArthur had told Generals Church and Coulter that the soldiers would be home by Christmas. The *New York Times* on its front page for 24 November (a day behind Far East time) quoted the Associated Press as alleging that MacArthur said, "I hope to keep my promise to the GI's to have them home by Christmas." The *New York Herald Tribune* on its front page for 25 November, citing a United Press dispatch from the northwestern front on 24 November, reported MacArthur as having said to General Coulter, "You tell them when we get up to the Yalu River they can all come home. I want to make good my statement that they will eat Christmas dinner at home." This widely circulated story is a good example of inexact and exaggerated news dispatches. One Pentagon official, when he read the press accounts of the remarks attributed to General MacArthur, let forth with the witticism that "General MacArthur has been in the Far East so long he's come to think of Japan as home." The storm of comment on the inaccurate quotation led MacArthur a few days later to assert that his alleged "home by Christmas" was a misquote. And indeed it was.[25]

By midafternoon General MacArthur and his party were back at the Sinanju airstrip and aboard the Constellation for the three-hour flight back to Tokyo. When Lt. Col. Anthony F. Story, MacArthur's personal pilot, was ready to take off, MacArthur surprised everyone by telling "Toney" Story to head for the mouth of the Yalu River. The Constellation was unarmed and would be an easy target at the border for the MiG fighter planes just across the border in Manchuria. MacArthur said he wanted to reconnoiter behind the enemy's lines. He would not don a parachute, and he would not be diverted from his intention to fly to the border (though no one tried very hard to change his mind).

Fortunately, no MiGs rose to meet the Constellation as it approached the Yalu. Once there, MacArthur ordered Story to turn east and follow the river at an altitude of 5,000 feet. MacArthur later described the scene that spread out below them:

> At this height we could observe in detail the entire area of international No-Man's Land all the way to the Siberian border. All that spread before our eyes was an endless expanse of utterly barren countryside, jagged hills, yawning crevices, and the black waters of the Yalu locked in the silent death grip of snow and ice. It was a merciless wasteland. If a large force or massive supply train had passed over the border, the imprints had already been well covered by the intermittent snowstorms of the Yalu Valley.[26]

The next day, 25 November, MacArthur sent a long and persuasive-argumentative message to the Joint Chiefs of Staff about their continuing concern of driving to the border and the possibility of spreading the conflict by such action. In this message MacArthur alluded to his flight over the Yalu basin the preceding day. He said in part:

> ... from a mil standpoint my personal rcn of the Yalu River line yesterday demonstrated conclusively that it would be utterly impossible for us to stop upon commanding terrain south of the river as suggested and there be in a position to hold under effective control its lines of approach to North Korea. The terrain ranging from the lowlands in the west to the rugged central and eastern sectors is not adaptable to such a system of defense were we, for any reason, to sacrifice the natural def features of the river line itself, features to be found in no other natural def line in all of Korea. . . .
>
> Moreover any failure on our part to prosecute the mil campaign thru to the achievement of its public and oft repeated obj of destroying all en forces south of Korea's northern boundary as essential to the restoration of unity and peace to all of Korea would be fraught with most disastrous consequences. It would be regarded by the Korean people as a betrayal of their sovereign and territorial integrity and of the solemn undertaking entered into in their behalf. . . .
>
> The entry of CC into the Korean conflict was a risk we knowingly took at the time we committed our forces. Had they entered at the time we were beleaguered behind our Pusan perimeter beachhead, the hazard would have been far more grave than it is now that we hold the initiative and have a much smaller area within which to interdict their hostile moves. Our forces are committed to seize the entire border area, and indeed in the east have already occupied a sector of the Yalu River with no noticeable political or mi. Soviet or Chinese reaction. . . . It is my plan just as soon as we are able to consolidate psns along the Yalu River to replace as far as possible American forces with those of the ROK and publicly announce orders affecting:
> (1) the return of American forces to Japan;
> (2) the parole of all prisoners of war to their homes;
> (3) the leaving of the unification of Korea and the restoration of the civil processes of govt to the people, with the advice and assistance of the UN authorities.[27]

After he had returned to Tokyo from his visit to Korea, MacArthur issued a further and special communiqué to the United Nations, which recorded his optimism. He said in part:

> The giant U.N. pincer moved according to schedule today. The air forces, in full strength completely interdicted the rear areas and air reconnaissance behind the enemy line, and along the entire length of the Yalu River border, showed little sign of hostile military activity. . . .
>
> Our losses were extraordinarily light. The logistics situation is fully geared to sustain offensive operations. The justice of our course and promise of early completion of our mission is reflected in the morale of troops and commanders alike.[28]

The Far East commander was living in a dream world. Rarely in warfare was the reality on the "other side of the hill" so different from that contemplated by an opponent. Rarely in military history has a commander made so erroneous a mistake of the capability of the enemy he expected to encounter.

5. The Second Day of Eighth Army's Attack

Saturday, 25 November was a day of brilliant sunshine after a cold night that left streams frozen along their edges. The movement of men and transports and of artillery and their trains on the Chongchon valley road and tributary roads leading northward into the hills had crumbled road shoulders to a powder. Murky dust palls hung in the air. They were particularly noticeable where heavy movements up the Chongchon River road supported the advance of the 9th and 38th regiments of the 2nd Infantry Division northeast of Kunu-ri.

On the army's left, the US 21st Infantry Regiment of the 24th Division had easy going. Just before noon it reached the southern outskirts of Chongju on the west coastal road. It had secured the town by 2:25 P.M. without enemy contact. During the afternoon, however, it captured 60 North Korean soldiers in the vicinity of the town. Elements of the 52nd Field Artillery Battalion, which was supporting the 21st Infantry, captured two Chinese soldiers. In the late afternoon, K Company sent out a patrol that encountered an enemy force on Hill 192. In the ensuing fight the patrol lost one man killed. The patrol estimated an enemy company held the hill. During the day the regiment had traveled almost due west from its starting point before the coastal road turned north toward the Manchurian border.[1]

The condition of the 24th Division troops at this time was similar to that of most American troops in Eighth Army. They had not received their winter clothing of parkas, shoepacs, ski socks, pile liners, and pile caps, although the temperature was often near or below freezing. The situation was so desperate that the division kept trucks at the Pyongyang airstrip to bring forward as fast as possible any winter clothing that arrived there by airlift. If no clothing came, then the trucks would haul rations. The division had exhausted its B ration by 18 November, and after that it had to use combat rations, which it had been hoarding for the expected advance. Some unit messes also had to drain gasoline from vehicles to cook food.[2]

The 5th RCT, 24th Division, moved to the right of the 21st Infantry to protect the 24th Division's east flank and to maintain contact there with the ROK 1st Division. Intelligence gained from civilians indicated strong CCF forces were to its northeast in the Taechon area, squarely in the line of advance of the ROK 1st Division, just eastward across the division boundary. I Corps, as a precaution, moved the 19th Infantry Regiment to Pakchon to protect the 24th Division rear.³

On line immediately east of the 5th RCT were two regiments of the ROK 1st Division. They followed the axis of the main road leading north to Taechon, with the 12th Regiment on the left and the 11th Regiment on the right. Both regiments halted for the night just below Taechon. The 12th Regiment, south of the town, had a quiet night, but CCF strongly attacked the 11th Regiment after midnight. The story of the enemy attacks at Taechon will be told in a later chapter. The ROK 1st Division was well aware by evening of 25 November, on the basis of its own observations, aerial reports, and civilian reports obtained during 24–25 November, that there was a very heavy enemy concentration just north of Taechon, directly in its path.

Although the ROK 1st Division had no important action during the day, it did figure in an important event on the twenty-fifth – it captured a Chinese captain early in the morning about two miles south of Taechon. It was the most revealing, and at the same time the most ominous, event of the day for the ROK 1st Division, and for Eighth Army as well.

Capt. Lui Ping Chang was the operations officer of the 590th Regiment, 197th Division, of the Chinese 66th Army. His regiment and division had crossed the Yalu from Antung to Sinuiju on 24 October. Since that time they had not been in combat but had moved south by mountain trails, never far from the front. On the morning of 25 November the 66th Army had concentrated in the area north of Taechon, and it was then that Capt. Lui Ping Chang had deserted. He had a wealth of information and was interrogated all the way back up the echelon of Eighth Army command. There exist in the official records many translations of his interrogations. They are generally consistent throughout, and later events proved them remarkably accurate.

Chang (as the interrogation reports refer to him) revealed that the entire 66th Army, with its three divisions – the 196th, 197th, and 198th – was in position north and northeast of Taechon, from three to five miles above the town. He gave the 66th Army's strength as being about 26,600 men, division strength as 6,600, regimental strength as about 2,000, and battalion strength as about 600 men. The 66th Army's plan, he said, was to wait in its position above Taechon until UN forces walked into its trap, then cut them off, surround them, and annihilate them. Chinese troops were entrenched on both sides of the road north of Taechon, he said, with demolitions and bangalore torpedoes ready for use against tanks. Antitank guns had been emplaced at favorable places, and some artillery in the hills overlooked terrain corridors, ready to place interdicting fire on them.

Chang said rifle companies in the 197th Division were armed with nine light machine guns, two 60-mm mortars, and ten submachine guns. The rifle companies of 160 to 170 men were well equipped with small arms, most of them being American-made weapons taken from Chiang Kai-shek's Nationalist soldiers when they surrendered or were captured in 1949 or earlier. The Heavy Machine Gun Company had six heavy machine guns, two 82-mm mortars, and four antitank rifles.

In addition to describing the strength and positions of the 66th Army, Chang gave a rather complete order of battle and the general locations of the entire CCF XIII Army Group that faced Eighth Army. He said the 39th Army was behind and north of the 66th Army, that the 38th and 40th armies were spread out for an unknown distance west of the railroad running from Kujang-dong toward Kanggye, but that many of their units were concentrated in the Kunu-ri area. He did not know where the 50th Army was, nor did he know that the 42nd Army had arrived on the east flank of the XIII Army Group. Otherwise, his information was correct, except he was unaware that the 39th Army had moved from behind the 66th Army to southeast of it. He also described in great detail the manner of CCF night marches.[4] Chang's information, speedily borne out by developing events, must have had a stunning effect on those of the Eighth Army staff who learned of it in the days immediately following his defection to the ROK 1st Division.

At the same time that Capt. Lui Ping Chang was undergoing his first interrogation, Col. Henry G. Fisher's 35th Infantry Regiment, minus B Company, which had been attached to Task Force Dolvin, was advancing along the west side of the Kuryong River straight toward Unsan, known to have been one of the CCF assembly areas. On the way, some of his troops came upon the bodies of members of the US 8th Cavalry, some still in their sleeping bags. They had been killed when a CCF force overran a battalion of the 8th Cavalry a month earlier, during the CCF 1st Phase Offensive.

During the day, Fisher's troops passed through Yongsan-dong, a major road center on the west side of the Kuryong River, connecting Taechon with Unsan and Yongbyon. The regiment stopped for the night a few miles north of Yongsan-dong. Fisher expected to reach Unsan the next day. He expected to encounter Chinese in its vicinity. But throughout 25 November, the 35th Infantry had almost no opposition.[5] Thus far the western side of Eighth Army's advance had been singularly free of enemy resistance.

When Task Force Dolvin moved out on the morning of 25 November from its overnight positions just north of Ipsok, the 25th Reconnaissance Company relieved E Company, 27th Infantry, in its position along the Kuryong River. E Company now took the lead on the left (west) side of the road, while B Company, 35th Infantry, led off on the right side. The 1st Platoon of the 25th Reconnaissance Company then relieved the 8213th Ranger Company and B Company, 89th Tank Battalion, on Hill 222 on the west side of the road close to the Kuryong River. Supporting division artillery and ammunition trains were grouped around Ipsok.

The road slanted east of north, pushed in that direction by the course of the Kuryong River, which meandered mightily in this area. The Camel's Head bend of the river was just ahead to the west. The road tried to find the easiest course through the hills and avoided following the tortuous course of the river, but it was never far from it. The hills eastward gave little room for passage.

The Ranger Company, freed from Hill 222, joined E Company in leading the advance northward between the road and the river. The two units encountered delaying, screening Chinese forces most of the day and were under long-range small-arms fire at intervals, which caused no damage. Task Force Dolvin's advance units made slow but steady gains during the day, reaching a point about nine road miles north of Ipsok by dusk. E Company, 27th Infantry, occupied Hill 201 west of the road, which overlooked the Kuryong River. The Ranger Company was immediately west of the road on Hill 205, a little farther north than E Company. It was the most advanced unit of Task Force Dolvin. Hill 205 was northeast a distance of about one mile and across a flat valley from E Company on Hill 201.

While E Company occupied Hill 201 without trouble, the Ranger Company had come to a point the Chinese meant to hold. The Ranger Company attacked the hill late in the afternoon and just barely managed to seize it, engaging in hand-to-hand fighting. The scale was weighted in favor of the Rangers by the heavy supporting fire of the 77th Field Artillery Battalion firing from its positions just north of Ipsok.[6]

At dark, Task Force Dolvin had thus made a good advance. Evidence accumulated during the day, however, that CCF screening forces were watching it carefully, and then just before dark the Ranger Company had a very hard battle, suffering many casualties, in taking Hill 205, the northernmost point of advance. Task Force Dolvin never got any farther.

Lieutenant Colonel Dolvin established his CP for the night in a little valley just south of Hill 222 and close to the Kuryong River. It was about midway between Ipsok and the Ranger Company's hill—perhaps five road miles south of the latter. The 77th and 90th field artillery battalions went into firing positions just north of Ipsok and were prepared to support the task force ahead of them.[7]

Aerial reconnaissance during the afternoon north of Ipsok and in front of Task Force Dolvin reported heavy enemy troop movement, presumably Chinese. Most of this enemy movement slanted laterally southeast across the front of Task Force Dolvin. Dolvin's advance at the same time slanted northeast because of the general constricting course of the looping bends of the Kuryong River on his west side. Events during the late afternoon and intelligence coming in during the day suggested there might be enemy action against the task force during the night.

The situation for Task Force Dolvin was not improved by the fact that, across its boundary to the east, or right, the 1st Battalion, 24th Infantry Regiment, had failed to establish contact with it. Its position was unknown. This left the right flank of Task Force Dolvin open. It offered an opportunity for Chinese forces reported moving to the southeast in front of it to come around that flank and get into Dolvin's rear.[8]

That morning the 24th Infantry had lined up again on the right side of Task Force Dolvin and formed the right flank of the 25th Division. Its 1st Battalion was on the left, the 3rd Battalion was in the center, and the 2nd Battalion was on the right of the regimental line. The main 24th Infantry advance initially was east along the Yongbyon-Unhung road, toward Kujang-dong on the Chongchon River, with D Company, 89th Tank Battalion, attached to the regiment. The 3rd Battalion led the column down this road, reaching a point about three miles southwest of Unhung by evening. During the day, the 2nd and 3rd battalions had some slight contact with enemy groups. By accident of geography the 24th Regiment was advancing toward enemy-held territory, and by accident of time it was at the moment the Chinese were moving into the valleys and draws to follow corridors of approach to the main forces of Eighth Army. The 24th Regiment, in the main, was on the high ground of the divide between the Kuryong and the Chongchon Rivers and away from the principal enemy movements. There the roadnet was very poor. So poor was it that E and G companies of the 2nd Battalion tried to move by motor column through the left flank of the 2nd Division zone along the Chongchon River to join F Company, 24th Infantry, on the 25th Division's right flank. The 2nd Division canceled this move through it while it was in progress because of enemy roadblocks on the route. E and G companies then took to mountain trails on foot to reach F Company. They sent all tanks, artillery, and heavy mortars back to the battalion CP.[9]

The 2nd Infantry Division along the Chongchon

During 25 November, the 9th Infantry Regiment, commanded by Col. Charles C. Sloane, Jr., on the 2nd Division's left flank and adjoining the boundary with the 24th Infantry, 25th Division, moved up the jammed Chongchon River road. North of Kujang-dong, the 3rd Battalion and the 2nd Battalion (the latter minus E Company) and the battalion advance headquarters group crossed to the west side of the Chongchon River, where they adjoined the zone of the 25th Division. There they advanced into the hills lining that side of the river. The 3rd Battalion sent K Company across and north of a dry wash to occupy Hill 180, less than a mile west of the Chongchon River, and it sent L Company to occupy Hill 153, on the south side of the dry wash, somewhat closer to the river. The 2nd Battalion, less its command group and E Company, also west of the river, assembled and dug in on the south side of a hill, in an irregular line, opposite the village of Sinhung-dong on the east side of the river. In this position the 2nd Battalion (–) faced both the Chongchon River to the east of it and the dry wash to the south of it. The units of the 2nd and 3rd battalions, 9th Infantry, occupied these positions without opposition.

In the meantime, the 1st Battalion, 9th Infantry, E Company, of the 2nd Battalion, and the 2nd Battalion's forward command group continued north along the main road on the east side of the Chongchon, past Hill 329, later known as Chinaman's Hat, crossed the Paengnyong River, and entered the village of Sinhung-dong on its north bank. About one mile north of Sinhung-dong, crowded close to the river and the road, was Hill 219.[10]

During the morning of 25 November, B Company, 9th Infantry, received orders to seize Hill 219. There had been thus far no indication the 1st Battalion would have any trouble in doing so. The hill appeared to be unoccupied. According to one source B Company had a strength of 116 men when it started for Hill 219; another source gave its strength as 129 able-bodied men. Capt. William C. Wallace commanded the company. He had four medium tanks and two quad-50 M16 antiaircraft gun carriages to give him supporting fire, if needed.

An aspect of the state of mind of the troops and their morale and discipline, widespread in Eighth Army at this time, is revealed by the fact that most of the men in B Company had thrown away their helmets. In the increasingly cold weather, pile caps were much more comfortable. Bayonets also had been discarded. Only two men, both new in the company, had them. There was less than one grenade on average to a man. Most of the men carried fewer than 50 rounds of small-arms ammunition for their personal weapon.

Hill 219 was a ridge with three knobs, each increasing in height from the lower one at the south end to the peak at the north end. Captain Wallace thought the easiest route to the top was from the western, river side of the hill. A little after 10 A.M., his 2nd and 3rd platoons started from the road at the western base of the hill. The point group was within 25 yards of the crest of the middle knob when a shower of grenades suddenly came down upon it. Enemy rifle fire followed. The men scrambled for cover. Pfc. Lawrence E. Smith, Jr., leading the point squad, glanced up and saw five Chinese running from the knob toward the higher one to the north. The 3rd Platoon at the northern base of the hill now began climbing up. In attempting to lead the 2nd Platoon closer to the crest, Captain Wallace was hit by a grenade explosion close to his face and shoulder. The tanks and quad-50s on the road were of no help, as they were so close to the lower slope that intervening folds of ground prevented their fire from reaching the crest of Hill 219.

Command passed to 1st Lt. Ellison C. Wynn when Wallace was wounded. Wynn continued the attack on the high knob. Enemy fire, however, knocked out the machine-gun section, killing both the gunner and assistant gunner. For a short time thereafter, Wynn was on the forward position alone, throwing hand grenades. A few men joined him, and they held out for a time. Once a group got to within 50 feet of the top, only to find that they had four bullets left among them as they prepared for a rush to the top.

The 1st Battalion commander realized it was an impossible situation and ordered Wynn to withdraw. Bleeding from wounds, he led his remaining men back down the hill. The survivors of B Company took positions around the bottom of the hill at dark. Wallace and Wynn both received the Distinguished Service Cross for their leadership and courage in combat on Hill 219 during the day.

The fight for the hill was not over, but it is to be noted here that the 3rd Platoon's positions on the north slope of Hill 219 during 25 November constituted the farthest northern advance any element of Eighth Army gained in its ill-fated offensive. This was another point the Chinese had marked as a no-pass line.[11]

Chinaman's Hat – Hill 329

A place-name destined to be better known than Hill 219 to the men of the 2nd Division who fought at the northern tip of the Eighth Army advance was Chinaman's Hat. It was a mile and a half south of Hill 219 and named for its resemblance to the traditional conical hat of a Chinese peasant. The name was well chosen, because many former Chinese peasants fought around and occupied it at this time. Officially, however, it was marked on the maps as Hill 329 (that is, its elevation is 329 meters). The hill's lower end was a sharp cone rising steeply from the bank of the Chongchon River, just south of a large tributary, the Paengnyong River, flowing from the east. Sinhung-dong was

Sgt. Elijah McLaughlin (*left front*) leads his 2nd Infantry Division squad in an advance down a hill northwest of the Chongchon River, late November 1950. The squad is composed of black, white, and South Korean troops. National Archives 111-SC 353466

half a mile north of Chinaman's Hat on the opposite, or north, side of the Paengnyong.

Kujang-dong, about three and a half miles south of Chinaman's Hat, was a larger settlement than Sinhung-dong and also on the east side of the Chongchon River and astride the MSR of the 2nd Division up the Chongchon valley. There the 2nd Division had concentrated a mass of artillery to support all its infantry farther north.

Three battalions of 105-mm howitzers (the 15th, 37th, and 99th) and the 17th Battalion of 8-inch howitzers, the largest artillery in Korea at the time and the only battalion of it, were in battery firing positions about 3,000 yards south of Kujang-dong. The 15th Battalion was the normal support artillery for the 23rd Infantry Regiment; the 37th was the normal support for the 9th Infantry Regiment. The 99th Battalion was borrowed from the 1st Cavalry Division, which was then in Eighth Army reserve.

Two more artillery battalions, the 61st and the 503rd (155-mm), minus A Battery, moved on up the valley of the Chongchon, past Kujang-dong, to posi-

Pfc. Ernest Tidwell carries rations on a Korean packboard to his platoon of the 9th Infantry Regiment, 2nd Infantry Division, in Kunu-ri section, November 1950. Pfc. John Adams is his guard. National Archives 111-SC 354128

tions a little south of Chinaman's Hat. Their positions there were crowded, but they were the best available that close to the front in the narrow river valley. The 61st Battalion emplaced its howitzers near the river and farther north than the 155-mm howitzers of the 503rd Battalion. Altogether, then, there were six battalions of artillery in the valley of the Chongchon to support the 2nd Division advance. Another battalion, the 38th, the normal support for the 38th Infantry Regiment, accompanied it into the hills east of the valley.

The four battalions of artillery emplaced south of Kujang-dong were about four miles distant from the 9th Infantry front, about five to six miles from B Company at Hill 219, and from three to five miles from the spread-out 38th Infantry in the hills east of the Chongchon River and Kujang-dong. This was a very large artillery concentration within a distance of four miles of Chinaman's Hat on the evening of 25 November.[12]

According to the 2nd Division plan, Col. Paul L. Freeman's 23rd Infantry Regiment was to take over the point of the 2nd Division advance up the Chongchon on 26 November. With that purpose in mind, Lt. Col. Claire E. Hutchins, Jr., led his 1st Battalion out of Kunu-ri and proceeded northward along the river road. It was expected that Hill 219, where Chinese forces had held up B Company, 9th Infantry, all during the day on 25 November, would be reduced by morning of 26 November. The 23rd Infantry would then pass through the 9th Infantry and continue the division attack toward Huichon, which was the division's immediate objective.

Hutchins's battalion arrived at the 503rd Field Artillery Battalion position south of Chinaman's Hat about 4 P.M. on 25 November, while B Company, 9th Infantry, was still trying to take Hill 219, two miles to the north. Colonel Freeman's 23rd Infantry Regimental headquarters, the 23rd Tank Company, and the Heavy Mortar Company were with the 1st Battalion. Hutchins placed his 1st Battalion near the 503rd Artillery Battalion, west and north of it, thus giving it close-in protection. Both the 503rd Artillery and the 1st Battalion, 23rd Infantry, were in a slight widening of the Chongchon River floodplain southwest of Chinaman's Hat.

Hutchins placed two rifle companies on line: he put A Company in the rice-paddy land close to and facing westward to the 50-yard-wide Chongchon River, with a refused flank on the north, bent to the east. The river was only three to four feet deep in front of A Company. Troops could wade it easily. Hutchins placed B Company eastward from the river, where A Company's line ended on the north, to the road. There he established a roadblock.

After the two rifle companies of the 1st Battalion had gone into their positions, the 61st Field Artillery Battalion, already mentioned, came up, passed through B Company's line, and went into a separate perimeter for the night a little more than half a mile farther north. It was the closest of all army units to Chinaman's Hat.

Six tanks came up and took interspersed positions among the A Company infantry. Most of them faced north toward the area the 61st Field Artillery Battalion had occupied. The rest of the 23rd Tank Company was behind A Company's left flank. Capt. Melvin R. Stai commanded A Company.

Meanwhile, Colonel Freeman established his 23rd Regimental Headquarters, together with Headquarters Company, on a small hill east of the road and railroad tracks, at the southern base of Chinaman's Hat. Had he expected enemy action that night, Freeman most certainly would not have placed his headquarters in this vulnerable position.

The 2nd and 3rd battalions of the 23rd Infantry were not then under Colonel Freeman's control and were not present that night at Chinaman's Hat. The 2nd Battalion was still south of Kujang-dong under 2nd Division control, and the 3rd Battalion was under 38th Infantry control in a blocking position on its MSR, which ran from Kujang-dong eastward into the high hills.[13]

The movement of the 23rd Infantry to Chinaman's Hat in the late afternoon of 25 November was to have important consequences in the next 24 hours. Chinese reconnaissance patrols, unseen, had left the area to make their reports on the vulnerability of the artillery from Kujang-dong northward before the 23rd Infantry units arrived at Chinaman's Hat. As seen by the Chinese patrols, the artillery was without infantry protection. CCF plans for attack on the artillery that night were thus made hastily, without knowledge of the infantry arrival and intelligence on developments at Chinaman's Hat late in the afternoon.

As stated earlier, Col. George B. Peploe, commander of the 38th Infantry Regiment, had previously moved his regiment to the area east of Kujang-dong, into the hill country back from the Chongchon. He had with him the 38th Artillery Battalion of 105-mm howitzers and A Battery, 503rd Artillery Battalion, of 155-mm howitzers attached. He felt he would need this artillery with him, as most of his regiment would be out of range of the artillery to be massed in the Kujang-dong area in the Chongchon valley. Peploe established his CP at Unbong-dong.

His line of departure for the 38th Infantry part of the division attack would be essentially the Paengnyong River, three to five miles east of Chinaman's Hat, from the Kujang-dong–Somin-dong–Tokchon road. That road was the only feasible axis of advance into the mountainous country where Peploe's regiment's assignment lay. There was a short connecting road to the Paengnyong-chon valley road north of it, near the point where the two roads converged and went southeast to Tokchon. This connecting road lay just east of Somin-dong. Peploe's 38th Regiment had its 1st Battalion, Lt. Col. William Kelleher commanding, on the regimental left, facing north. It was the regimental battalion closest to the Chongchon River. The 3rd Battalion, Lt. Col. Harold V. Maixner commanding, extended the line eastward into the hills. Lt. Col. James H. Skeldon's 2nd Battalion was in reserve, but it was scheduled to relieve the 1st Battalion on the line on the morning of 25 November.[14]

The 38th Infantry had forbidding terrain in front of it and on its right flank, next to the ROK 3rd Regiment of the ROK 7th Division. Its area of action in the attack was destined to be the Paengnyong River valley and the hills on either side of it. The Paengnyong River flowed almost due west from its origin on the west side of the divide between the Taedong and Chongchon rivers and joined the Chongchon at the northern base of Chinaman's Hat, just south of the village of Sinhung-dong. The key town of Tokchon on the Taedong River lay about ten air miles southeast of the right flank of the 38th Regiment's position on 25 November.

The highest ground in front of the 38th Regiment was Hill 1229, a massive mountain five air miles to the northeast but 16 miles by mountain foot trails. Aerial reports indicated enemy groups were on the mountain, as well as mortar positions and several ammunition dumps. The 38th Regiment had captured three North Korean prisoners who said that in the past week they had seen several thousand Chinese troops on Hill 1229. US aerial reports placed as many as 2,000 Chinese troops there.

Then, on 25 November, a Joint Operations Center aerial report revealed that a trail from the vicinity of Huichon, running to the southeast toward the Tokchon area, formerly considered impassable to vehicles, had been improved during the past 36 hours so as to permit vehicular traffic. It stated also that a bridge on this trail was under construction. Improving this trail to road status was interpreted at once as a means of speeding movement of enemy troops, weapons, and supplies to enemy forces acting against Eighth Army's right flank.[15] As soon as Maj. Gen. Laurence Keiser, commander of the 2nd Division, received this information, he said his division and the adjacent ROK troops would be heavily attacked.

So much intelligence had been reported about the huge enemy concentration on Hill 1229 that higher command decided a ground reconnaissance of the situation there was in order. Colonel Peploe, however, does not recall that the 38th Infantry at the time had much information about an enemy concentration on and in the vicinity of Hill 1229. According to him, this information must have been held mostly by division and higher headquarters. In any event, the 38th Regiment had to send a strong infantry patrol to the hill. This task fell to A Company, 1st Battalion.

On the morning of 25 November, the 2nd Battalion, 38th Infantry, relieved the 1st Battalion and a company of the 9th Infantry that held the left flank of the 38th Regimental line. Already, however, A Company of the 1st Battalion had started on its hazardous patrol toward Hill 1229, and it was not included in the 1st Battalion's reverting to regimental reserve.[16]

Lieutenant Colonel Kelleher had ordered Capt. Jack W. Rodarm at 1:30 A.M., 25 November, to take his A Company to Hill 1229 to find out what was there. Rodarm was to be ready to move at 4 A.M. Trucks carried A Company up the valley two and a half miles to its point of departure. There were 125 men in A Company, and a few more men were attached to it for special functions. Capt. Leonard Lowery, 1st Battalion executive officer, went along with 20 Korean carriers with rations. Each man in the company carried two grenades and a good supply of small-arms ammunition. There were 14 BARs, two light machine guns, one 60-mm mortar, and one 57-mm recoilless rifle included in the company's weapons.

The 2nd Battalion was supposed to occupy ridges on both sides of the Paengnyong River when it relieved the 1st Battalion that morning. Of particular importance to the A Company patrol was F Company's position on a hill on the north side of the valley. From its point of departure in the valley, the patrol took four hours to climb one and a half miles. By then it was daylight. A burst of machine-gun fire suddenly cut across the front of Cpl. Renaldo Acosta, the lead scout. He and others behind him dropped to the ground. Immediately all of A Company sought cover as enemy automatic and rifle fire ripped the ground around them. From its sound, Rodarm thought it came from American-made weapons. It did—from American weapons taken by the CCF from Nationalist Chinese forces. A Company's support platoon in the rear worked its way to the ridge top, and the Chinese soldiers there fled. F Company of the 2nd Battalion now came up the ridgeline from its hill position on the north side of the valley and occupied the knob formerly held by the Chinese. A Company continued its patrol toward Hill 1229. It was now about noon.

While the fight for the Chinese-held hilltop had been in progress, the Korean carriers scattered. Rodarm by radio had informed Lieutenant Colonel Kelleher at the 1st Battalion CP of what had happened. He now came up the trail to join A Company. The company was way behind schedule on its way to Hill 1229. Kelleher and Captain Lowery set a faster pace. By late afternoon, the company reached Hill 453, considerably less than halfway to Hill 1229. The men had been climbing since early in the morning, and the firefight had tired them more. Many were near exhaustion, and the company was scattered down the trail from the point squad, as many lagged behind. Kelleher stopped the point frequently to let those in the rear catch up.

Near Hill 453, an unseen enemy soldier threw a grenade from a clump of bushes along the trail. It exploded close to Lt. John O. Crockett of the 1st Platoon and Captain Rodarm, who was with him. This incident, together with the knowledge that the enemy had a screening force watching the patrol's progress and the near exhaustion of the men, caused Kelleher and Rodarm to stop for the night when they reached Hill 453. It was nearly dark when A Company stopped and began establishing a defense perimeter on top the hill. At this point, Lieutenant Colonel Kelleher took the trail back to his 1st Battalion CP. It was apparent from the day's events that A Company's approach to Hill 1229 from the south was covered almost from its beginning by an enemy screening force and that Chinese in force were ahead of it on higher ground.[17]

While A Company headed north on its arduous patrol, another rifle company from the 2nd Battalion started southeast from the valley of the Paengnyong on what was thought to be a routine mission. About noon of 25 November, Lt. Robert H. Rivet led G Company from Sinhung-dong to relieve C Company of the 1st Battalion at its position on Hill 291, about two air miles southeast of Chinaman's Hat. Rivet's company had a better-than-average strength of 164 men in the then understrength rifle companies of Eighth Army. The two air miles converted into many more miles by the twisting and exceedingly rough and steep trails the company followed to reach Hill 291.

When G Company arrived at the hill past midafternoon, the men were tired. It took over C Company's badly chosen positions but made no change in them, even though it inherited platoon positions on three different hills, none of them in sight of the others or of the company CP. The latter was a mile behind the nearest platoon-held hill. And C Company had not dug in. When G Company started to do so, it found that shale and slate lay just beneath the surface. After their exhausting climb into the hills, the men quickly gave up trying to dig holes, and the officers did not try to force them to do it. From the northern crest of Hill 219, it was about one-half air mile due north to the Paengnyong River; from its most distant southern tip it was about one air mile to the stream. A small trail came south up a draw from the Paengnyong to the east side of the hill.[18]

At twilight on 25 November, Col. George B. Peploe's 38th Infantry held scattered positions for about five miles in the terrain on both sides of the Paengnyong northeast of Kujang-dong and Sinhung-dong. Its right flank had a boundary with the ROK 3rd Regiment of the ROK 7th Division.[19]

In summarizing Eighth Army's situation at twilight on 25 November, the second day of its attack, one may say its west flank in the area of the 21st Infantry, 24th Division, had met almost no opposition, but contact had been made with enemy reconnaissance parties that had withdrawn in front of the 21st Infantry. The ROK 1st Division, adjacent to it on the east, had also advanced without opposition, but as evening approached it had intelligence that large bodies of Chinese troops were just ahead of it near Taechon. Next on the right, just west of the Kuryong River, the 35th Infantry of the US 25th Division had advanced without opposition to a point just south of Unsan. Across the Kuryong River on its east side, Task Force Dolvin had had light skirmishes with a Chinese screening force nearly all day north of Ipsok on the hills bordering the Kuryong River, and late in the afternoon its Ranger Company had had a hard fight, suffering many casualties, in capturing Hill 205 on the left side of the road leading north. To the east of Task Force Dolvin, in rough terrain, the 24th Regiment of the 25th Division had had no important resistance – the area seemed to be strangely free of enemy forces.

Farther east, in the valley of the Chongchon River, the 2nd and 3rd battalions of the 9th Infantry had crossed to the west side of the stream near Kujang-dong and then continued north into hills bordering the river on that side. By dark they had reached a point approximately opposite Sinhung-dong and Chinaman's Hat and had gone into position there on a series of three hills. Meanwhile, the 1st Battalion of the 9th Infantry had advanced along the Chongchon valley road east of the river to Sinhung-dong, where its B Company had attacked Hill 219, just north of the village. Chinese troops on the hill resolutely turned back all efforts during the day to drive them from it.

Previously, the 38th Regiment of the 2nd Division had turned east from the Chongchon valley at Kujang-dong, where it followed a poor secondary dirt road into increasingly rough terrain eastward toward Somin-dong and Tokchon. Its 2nd and 3rd battalions were on line from left to right on hills lining the Paengnyong-gang, its 3rd Battalion having a boundary with the ROK 3rd Regiment of the ROK 7th Division of the ROK II Corps. Before daylight that morning, A Company of the 1st Battalion started on a patrol toward Hill 1229, a dominating height north of the 38th Regiment, where aerial reconnaissance and prisoner intelligence had reported large numbers of Chinese troops and mortar emplacements to have been concentrated.

The ROK II Corps front on 25 November remained much as it was on 24 November. On its left flank, in the area of the ROK 3rd Regiment, there had been little enemy opposition, and the 3rd Regiment had advanced northward short distances. Elsewhere, the ROK II Corps had made no gains. Accordingly, by evening of 25 November a gap had developed between the ROK 3rd Regiment on the corps left and the rest of the II Corps. Just before dark the Chinese launched a precision attack with a massed assault force against the ROK II Corps.

Thus stood Eighth Army's advance toward the border at dark on 25 November. B Company, 9th Infantry, at Hill 219 was the farthest northern point gained by the army in the valley of the Chongchon. In the center, Task Force Dolvin's most advanced position at dark was Hill 205, some miles north of Ipsok, held by the Ranger Company. Eighth Army troops were to go no farther. In the vicinity of Taechon, Unsan, Ipsok, Sinhung-dong, and eastward into the ROK II Corps area, Eighth Army had run out of easy going. By dark on 25 November it had reached the positions where the Chinese concentrations were waiting for them.

But let us see how the Far East Command intelligence in Tokyo interpreted these events: "Pressure of the current UN offensive showed the enemy willing to withdraw north to the point of abandoning field guns, tanks and self-propelled artillery. It is now considered unlikely that the enemy will operate extensively on the flank of the Eighth Army. His alignment is not expected to remain roughly West to East but rather an oblique disposition west of the Chongchon River, in the direction of Huichon."[20] It would appear that the Far East Command intelligence officer believed the Eighth Army advance would continue without serious difficulty.

Underscoring the situation at the Eighth Army front at dusk on 25 November was an unusual incident that had occurred before dawn that morning, 45 air miles behind the front. The 187th Airborne Regiment was in Eighth Army reserve near Kangdong, about 20 miles northeast of Pyongyang, on the main lateral road from the North Korean capital to Wonsan on the east coast. The 2nd Platoon of B Company of the airborne regiment occupied Hill 171 near the town. Before daylight on 25 November, an enemy force tried to seize the hill. After a two-hour fight, the 2nd Platoon, less its 3rd Squad, which had been held in reserve, had expended nearly all its ammunition. With the attacking enemy within 25 yards of the platoon position, the platoon leader had to commit the 3rd Squad. Cpl. Joe R. Baldonado, machine gunner of that squad, put his weapon in an exposed position in a hurry, having no time to dig in, where he could place heavy fire on the assaulting enemy. His stream of machine-gun fire caused these troops to fall back. Several times enemy assault squads attacked Baldonado's gun position with grenades, but by good luck none of them put Baldonado out of action. Near daylight, however, about 7 A.M. in a final assault, an enemy grenade explosion killed Baldonado. But with daylight at hand, the enemy withdrew after this last attack.[21]

This fierce fight on a platoon position nearly 50 air miles south of the army battle front was undoubtedly carried out by a North Korean guerrilla force and is one of many episodes that occurred deep behind the Eighth Army front that showed to what an extent bypassed North Korean army groups in guerrilla-type action tried to coordinate their action with Chinese attack plans to disrupt UN rear areas at this time.

6. The CCF 2nd Phase Offensive

As soon as it began to grow dark, Chinese troops were in movement against specific American and ROK positions all across the front, except at the extreme left flank, held by the 24th Infantry Division. This was not an attack through any gap. Nor was it only an attack against the UN or Eighth Army's right flank and a turning movement there. It was a head-on attack against Eighth Army, stretching all the way from Taechon, in front of the ROK 1st Division in the west, right on eastward against the US 25th and 2nd infantry divisions in the army center, before culminating in the ROK II Corps zone on the right flank. The Chinese were intent on making penetrations anywhere they could find them and then encircling small or large portions of Eighth Army as circumstances permitted.

As events turned out, and probably as the CCF anticipated, their earliest important penetration came in the ROK II Corps. They exploited it well, and thus began a turning movement through the Eighth Army's right flank and around it when that flank collapsed. But this effort succeeded only because their frontal attacks across the Eighth Army succeeded at the same time – the entire Eighth Army front was pressed back. The CCF 50th Army, on the American left flank, held back at first to permit the other Chinese forces at the center and at the right flank to accomplish their initial objectives and then to press and swing the Eighth Army westward toward the coast. The Chinese plan was an example of classic military tactics as stated by such theorists as Antoine Henri Jomini and Karl von Clausewitz.

As the Eighth Army troops stopped in late afternoon and evening of 25 November to dig in for the night, activity in the Chinese assembly areas just ahead of them became frenzied but orderly. As was to be learned later so well, the typical CCF method of preparing for a major attack was to withdraw from immediate contact, leaving only light screening and reconnaissance forces behind to observe the enemy. Then, out of sight and beyond light artillery range, the main force rested, reorganized, resupplied, and reassembled in preparation for another major effort. Nearly every major Chinese attack in the Korean War followed this pattern. When ready to renew combat, Chinese soldiers left their assembly areas in approach-march formations, beginning at dusk or soon after dark, and by a rapid night march approached their previously determined points of contact and assault. Normally, the attack formations would reach their points of departure within three or four hours after leaving their assembly areas. In these hours of approach the Chinese soldiers often went at a dogtrot and usually silently. They covered a lot of distance in a short time. Well rested, and perfectly disciplined in such marches, they were ready to rush the enemy's positions by midnight or earlier. So it was this time.

A day-to-day recounting of events along the Eighth Army front would make difficult reading. Events will therefore be recounted by considering one definable sector of the front (ordinarily a UN corps sector) at a time. Each battle is followed through to a conclusion, if the outcome was clear. In nearly all cases during the Chinese 2nd Phase Offensive, a conclusion was reached, or its outcome evident, after three days and three nights. By that time the Eighth Army was in retreat everywhere.

It seems best to start with the CCF assault against the ROK II Corps on the Eighth Army right flank because it was there that the enemy breakthrough first was decisive and complete. The effect of enemy victory spread westward to all other sectors. Next came the defeat of the American troops in the UN line's center in the area of Taechon, Unsan, Ipsok, and Yongbyon. And following closely that series of triumphs, the enemy overcame the US 2nd Division in its holding actions, and that division fought a rear-guard action in withdrawing to the Kunu-ri area, at the same time covering the crossing of the Chongchon River to the south side by many other units of the IX Corps. And finally, there was the effort of the 2nd Infantry Division to escape, at the rear of the Eighth Army retreat, through a long and heavily gunned Chinese gauntlet that stretched along the road south from Kunu-ri to Sunchon on 30 November.

By the end of November and the first day of December, the Chinese 2nd Phase Offensive had decisively defeated the Eighth Army, and the latter was gathering speed in a headlong retreat southward. The days and nights from the evening of 25 November to 1 December 1950 are crowded with a churning, hectic, often bizarre, series of battles, large and small, clear across the Eighth Army front. Taken together at any one moment, they render difficult any attempt to hold up a mirror and present them in a narrative form that would give an overall view of the ever-changing scene. (See table 3 for a lineup of forces involved across the battlefront.) Just how the Chinese XIII Army Group accomplished their amazing victory will unfold in the following chapters.

Table 3. **Alignment of Eighth Army and CCF Forces, 25 November 1950**

Battle Locations (west to east)	Attacking CCF Forces	Defending UN Forces[a]
		US I Corps
West coastal area; Chongju	50th Army[b]–148th, 149th 150th (167th?) divs.	US 24th Div.–5th RCT, 19th Inf., *21st Inf.*
Taechon, Yongbyon	66th Army[c]–196th, 197th, 198th divs.	ROK 1st Div.–*11th, 12th,* 15th regts.
		US IX Corps
Ipsok, Unsan	39th Army[d]–115th, 116th, 117th divs.	US 25th Div.–24th Inf., 27th Inf., 35th Inf. (includes TF *Dolvin*)
Kujang-dong, Sinhung-dong	40th Army[e]–118th, 119th, 120th divs.	US 2nd Div.–*9th, 23rd, 38th inf.*
		ROK II Corps
Tokchon	38th Army[f]–112th, 113th, 114th divs.	ROK 7th Div.–*3rd,* 5th, *8th* regts.
Yongwon, Maengsan	42nd Army[g]–124th, 125th, 126th divs.	ROK 8th Div.–*10th,* 16th, *21st* regts.

SOURCE: FEC, Daily Intelligence Summary No. 3207, 21 June 1951, Box 473.

NOTE: This FEC summary is a translation of a captured Chinese document, which gives this XIII Army Group order of battle about the latter part of Feb. 1951. It is probably the most important enemy document the UN forces captured prior to July 1951. The date, place, and circumstances of capture are unknown, but it was acquired probably in the latter part of Feb. 1951. Many additional enemy sources support its accuracy.

The 38th and 42nd armies crossed the Yalu at Manpojin, and the 42nd Army initially moved to the Chosin Reservoir area to block the advance of the US X Corps there and to protect the XIII Army Group's left (east) flank. When the Chinese IX Army Group later arrived at the Chosin Reservoir area prior to the 2nd Phase Offensive and relieved the 42nd Army, the latter moved west to join its parent organization, the XIII Army Group for the 2nd Phase Offensive. The 39th, 40th, 50th, and 66th armies crossed the Yalu River at Sinuiju. Some elements of the CCF 1st and 8th artillery divisions were also engaged with Eighth Army during the Chinese 2nd Phase Offensive.

[a] Front-line units appear in italics.

[b] Originated from three Nationalist Chinese divisions and other Nationalist units that defected in Manchuria in 1945.

[c] Part of XX Army Group until it entered Korea; included one Nationalist division; initial contact with US forces on 1 Nov. 1950, but then in reserve until 25 Nov.

[d] Integrated old 269th Nationalist Division; seized Kuryong River area and Yongbyon.

[e] Foremost combat organization of CCF Army; attacked along Chongchon River.

[f] Integrated one or more Nationalist divisions; penetrated ROK II Corps front; turned back Turkish Brigade; formed massive roadblock that trapped US 2nd Division at Kunu-ri.

[g] Integrated one Nationalist division in 1949; 124th Division at low strength because of combat in X Corps area against ROK 23rd Regt. and 7th Marines along Hamhung–Hagaru-ri road; after defeating ROK 8th Div., turned the Eighth Army flank and drove on Sunchon, in army rear; met by 1st Cav. Div. and halted in the vicinity of Sinchang-ni.

7. The CCF Armies' Rout of the ROK II Corps

Two ROK divisions, the 7th and 8th, of the ROK II Corps were on line at dark 25 November. The boundary between them, with the 7th Division on the left, or west, ran on a generally north-south line about eight miles east of Tokchon. The ROK 7th Division had brought up its 5th Regiment late in the afternoon of 25 November to fill the gap in its lines, as its 3rd Regiment had advanced to the northwest on the ROK II Corps left flank against little or no opposition, while its 8th Regiment on the boundary with the ROK 8th Division made no progress. The ROK 7th Division thus had its three regiments, the 3rd, 5th, and 8th, in that order, on line from left to right by evening.

Across the ROK division boundary to the east, the ROK 8th Division had its 10th Regiment bordering the ROK 7th Division. The ROK 8th Division's 21st Regiment was on line at the right flank near Yongwon. The third regiment, the 16th, was south of and behind the 21st Regiment, in the vicinity of Maengsan. The ROK II Corps's third division, the 6th, was in rear areas reorganizing after its near destruction three weeks earlier northwest of Huichon by Chinese forces in the 1st Phase Offensive. Only its 2nd Regiment, at Tokchon, was considered combat effective.

The CCF 38th Army, with its 112th, 113th, and 114th divisions, stood in front of the ROK II Corps, ready to launch its devastating attacks. As early as 21 November two CCF soldiers from the 112th Division were captured near Yongwon on the right flank. They confirmed that the 38th Army had shifted east from the Kujang-dong area along the Chongchon and that its 112th Division would confront the ROK II Corps in a frontal holding action until the 2nd Phase Offensive began. Then the other divisions of the 38th Army would make an enveloping movement after the army achieved a penetration of the ROK line. Their immediate objective was the capture of Tokchon. The Chinese plan then called for the recently arrived CCF 42nd Army to assume the right flank position and make an enveloping move south and southwest toward Sunchon, while the 38th Army drove west from Tokchon. Prisoners taken later during the actions at Yongwon, Maengsan, and Tokchon confirmed that this is precisely what happened.[1]

A Chinese soldier from the 374th Regiment, 125th Division, 42nd Army, captured in the fighting on the ROK right flank at this time, criticized the ROKs they had faced. He said the ROKs were guilty of many weaknesses in combating

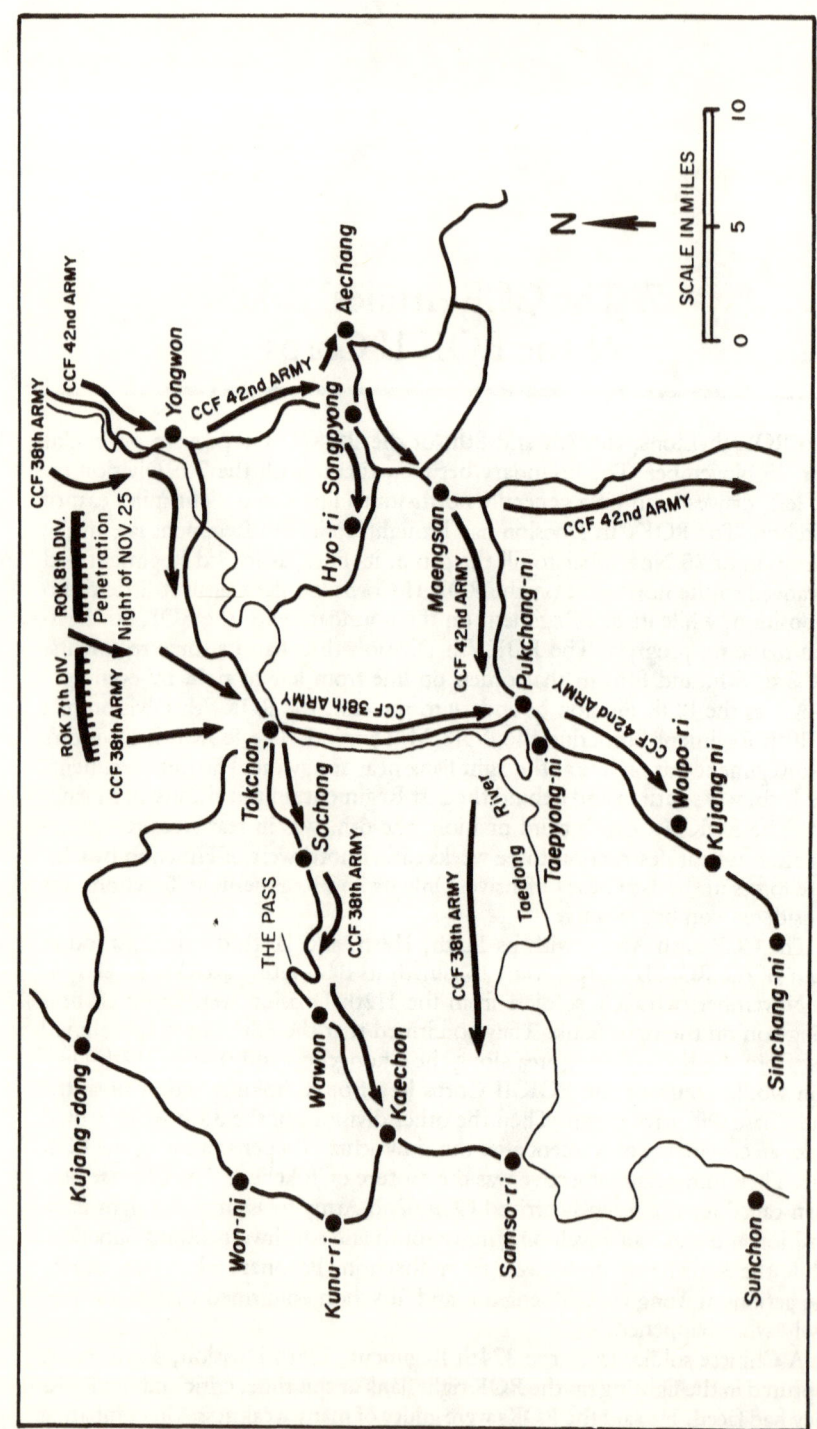

Map 4. The CCF 38th and 42nd armies' attacks on ROK II Corps, 25–30 November 1950.

the Chinese—he said they fired rifles and machine guns at random at night and built fires to keep warm, both actions revealing their positions. He advised the UN to enforce blackout and noise discipline at night and to use grenades in night fighting. He commented that machine-gun fire was ineffective at night.[2]

The Chinese 112th Division Splits the ROKs

It is a maxim in military theory that the best place to mass for an offensive strike is where enemy units have boundaries. It is here that weakness usually is found. The larger the unit boundary, the greater the weakness is apt to be, and the greater the chance for exploitation of a success. The Chinese throughout the Korean War demonstrated their ability by thorough night reconnaissance and patrolling to find unit boundaries, whether platoon, company, battalion, regiment, division, or corps. In this case, in planning their first major strike against the ROK II Corps, they chose to hit the center of the corps and to split it down the middle at the boundary of its two divisions. In so doing, they would also strike indirectly at the boundary of the ROK II Corps with Eighth Army to the west. If successful, their tactic would destroy the army's right-flank protection and set in motion a massive westward turning maneuver that might put them behind Eighth Army.

As daylight faded into near darkness, about 5 P.M. on 25 November, a Chinese assault force struck with precision and great energy on a narrow front at the boundary between the ROK 7th and 8th divisions in the center of the ROK II Corps line. The attack straddled the boundary between the two divisions. It overran the ROK infantry companies on either side of the boundary. Almost at once the Chinese had made a hole in the ROK line more than half a mile wide. Hundreds—possibly thousands—of Chinese, massed in echelon behind the assault force, at once poured through the gap and moved fast into the ROK rear areas. This penetration was about ten air miles northeast of Tokchon. After penetrating the ROK positions, the Chinese paid no further attention to the ROK front in that vicinity, and a perplexing quiet settled over the scene. But when the two ROK battalion commanders on either side of the division boundary tried to restore the line there by counterattacks, they found Chinese forces firmly established on both shoulders of the penetration and determined to hold open the gap through which the CCF 38th Army was sending large formations of its troops in the early hours of darkness on 25 November. All ROK counterattacks failed to close the gap.

The 8th Regiment of the ROK 7th Division and the 10th Regiment of the ROK 8th Division were not willing to bring their reserve battalions up by a three-mile approach march during the night through the jumbled terrain, with large but unknown numbers of Chinese soldiers now moving into their rear areas. Both ROK regimental commanders put their reserve battalions into defensive positions guarding the now exposed flanks south of the enemy penetration. The Chinese made no further effort during the night against the ROK 7th and 8th divisions. A patrol from the ROK 10th Regiment learned from a civilian that he had been forced to guide a Chinese force of at least 500 men to a mountain village three miles south of the battle line.

General Hue, the ROK II Corps commander at Pukchang-ni, 15 miles south of Tokchon, did not learn of the Chinese penetration of his lines until about midnight, four to five hours after it occurred. This delay was due in some degree to poor communications and partly to the fact that subordinate ROK officers were reluctant to report unfavorable developments to their superiors. Thus, 25 November ended ominously for the ROK II Corps.[3]

At daylight on 26 November, the 2nd Infantry Division, on the west or left flank of the ROK II Corps, did not know the full scope of developments in the ROK area on its right flank, nor did the rest of Eighth Army. But enough was known to give a picture that caused concern. The Eighth Army G-3 section report for 26 November said of the ROK II Corps front, "Practically nothing was known with respect to location of ROK units," except that elements of the ROK 3rd Regiment were in and behind the positions of the 38th Regiment, 2nd Infantry Division, that the 10th Regiment of the ROK 8th Division was east of Tokchon, and that Tokchon itself was in enemy possession.[4]

The IX Corps estimated that two enemy regiments had penetrated the right flank of the ROK 7th Division, and it was known that Chinese had established roadblocks in that division's rear along the MSR. A KMAG report to IX Corps at 9 P.M. stated that other ROK troops had reoccupied Tokchon and opened the MSR. This development, if true momentarily, did not last.

There were flurries of reports during 26 November from aerial observers over the Tokchon area (for that matter, over all the ROK II Corps zone of operations), trying to learn what had happened, and there were radio reports from various KMAG advisors with the ROK units giving bits of information known to them. These reports indicated a rapidly changing situation everywhere in the ROK corps area and real confusion as to the overall situation. A Mosquito plane over Tokchon reported at 9:30 A.M. that many refugees were moving south and southwest toward the town and that air strikes were taking place in the area. It requested that an escape route to the west and northwest from Tokchon be reconnoitered. It reported an enemy roadblock west of Tokchon. A patrol left Tokchon to disperse this roadblock, but about 500 enemy troops stopped the patrol and then moved on toward the southwest. Later in the afternoon a Tactical Air Control Party (TACP) asked for a helicopter to evacuate United States Army personnel from Tokchon. At 2 P.M., three L-5 planes landed at Tokchon and took off, carrying two enlisted men from the 38th Field Artillery Battalion and Major Keller, KMAG advisor to the ROK 3rd Regiment, 7th Division. When he landed at the Kunu-ri airstrip Major Keller said there were two enemy regiments in Tokchon. He had no information on the situation east of the ROK 8th Regiment.

Major Keller said that, after daylight that morning, a convoy from the 38th Regiment, comprising one ambulance with six wounded, a truck with 15 wounded, and three jeeps each with two or three wounded, had arrived at Tokchon. They reported they had run through an ambush behind the 3rd Battalion, 38th Regiment, on their way to Tokchon. This convoy ran into another enemy roadblock south of Tokchon, but some got back to Tokchon to report it. The 2nd Battalion, ROK 2nd Regiment, arrived at Tokchon at 10 A.M. from the east and was sent south to destroy this roadblock, but Keller had no information on what happened to it. An observation pilot reported during the day that Yongwon, at the northeastern corner of the ROK II Corps front, appeared deserted.

Another aerial report at 3:50 P.M. stated that Tokchon was under enemy mortar fire and that 15 to 20 ROK or American vehicles were burning there. This report said that between 600 and 700 ROK troops were retreating west from the town with 200 to 300 civilians mixed in with them.

Still another Mosquito pilot reported he took off from the Tokchon airstrip at 4:50 p.m. under fire from 20 to 30 enemy soldiers wearing white uniforms and armed with new equipment. He estimated 2,000 enemy were then in Tokchon and that 2,000 more, tactically deployed, were moving toward the town from the northeast and southeast.[5]

At 3:15 P.M., Eighth Army received a report that a control party of American advisors and ROKs were cut off northeast of Tokchon, and that 15 American personnel needed air evacuation from a small strip a mile east of Tokchon. This same report said air strikes were in progress against a CCF roadblock five miles south of Tokchon. About an hour and a half later, Colonel Burns informed Eighth Army that a Corporal MacMillan had been evacuated from the Tokchon airstrip at 3 P.M. Burns's call at 4:55 P.M. said none of the 15 KMAG advisor personnel waiting at the airstrip for air evacuation were wounded.

Brig. Gen. Francis W. Farrell, Eighth Army chief of KMAG, at this point ordered that no KMAG advisors attached to ROK ground forces be evacuated. He wanted to stay with the ROK troops to help keep them from disintegrating as combat units. Maj. Gen. Levan Allen, Eighth Army chief of staff, concurred in this order. At that time a regiment of the ROK 7th Division, it was thought, protected the airstrip.

In a matter of minutes, however, another report to Eighth Army said Chinese held the airstrip and Tokchon and that the ROK regiment had disappeared. Lieutenant Colonel Pearson, KMAG advisor to the ROK 6th Division, later said all the KMAG advisors attached to the ROK 7th Division were lost at Tokchon. At 5:40 P.M., apparently unaware of General Farrell's order that no American advisors to ROK ground troops be evacuated, a Lieutenant Richardson, a 25th Infantry Division liaison officer, flew to Tokchon to evacuate KMAG personnel. He reported that he was fired on when he tried to land, that seven to ten jeeps were burning on the airstrip, 15 vehicles north of Tokchon were being shelled and were burning, and that 200 enemy in blue uniforms were entering Tokchon. A column of vehicles reported earlier south of Tokchon had moved farther south. Lt. Col. Willard Pearson reported to IX Corps early in the afternoon that Korean civilians had reported large numbers of enemy moving around the flank of Yongwon and estimated that as many as two Chinese divisions were in the Songchon area. Aerial reports at the same time reported an enemy roadblock and ambush west of Tokchon on the road to Kunu-ri.[6]

When the ROK II Corps commander, General Hue, learned about midnight, 25 November, of the Chinese penetration northeast of Tokchon and the spreading chaos in his zone, he took immediate steps to counter the potential disaster. His only reserve close to the action was the ROK 2nd Regiment at Tokchon. He released it at once to the commander of the ROK 7th Division and ordered that it attack into and seal off the gap between the 7th and 8th divisions. He ordered the ROK division commander in the east to use part of his reserve regiment, the 16th, to patrol the area south of the Chinese penetration and to find and destroy any North Korean and Chinese soldiers found there. This was a desirable goal in theory but utterly impossible to execute in practice; the area was vast, and if the plan was feasible at all, its execution would take days and possibly weeks. None of his orders could be carried out as planned.

Three miles short of the Chinese penetration point, a strong enemy force met and blocked the ROK 2nd Regiment on the Tokchon-Yongwon road. And even before the ROK 16th Regiment was able to begin scouring the mountains back of the penetration, that order was superseded. When daylight came on 26 November, aerial observation, patrolling, and Korean civilian reports showed that strong Chinese forces of a regiment or more were enveloping the ROK 21st Regiment and Eighth Army's eastern flank along the Sangdong-Aechang road. This force included horse cavalry and undoubtedly were elements of the CCF 42nd Army. The ROK 16th Regiment now, instead of searching for enemy south of the penetration of the night before, was ordered to advance to meet this new force already south of and behind all front-line positions. The 16th Regiment made initial contact five miles north of the village of Toron. It was unable to stop or turn back the Chinese column. Instead it had to assume the defensive and try to delay the enemy advance, which, if continued, would reach the main roadnet behind the ROK positions. All day this fight continued, but the ROKs there were slowly forced back.[7]

After daylight of 26 November the ROK II Corps headquarters started moving south from Pukchang-ni. It encountered no enemy during its withdrawal. Colonel Gillette was the American KMAG advisor with the ROK II Corps, and he recounted what information the corps had at the end of the day. He reported at 9:45 P.M. that the enemy roadblock between Tokchon and Pukchang-ni had been eliminated, that four friendly battalions were in Tokchon—two from the ROK 2nd Regiment, one from the ROK 5th Regiment, and one from the ROK 8th Regiment. He reported four other ROK battalions were in covering positions north and east of Pukchang-ni but that three other ROK battalions were in a heavy fight in the vicinity of Maengsan.

But in view of other information that had been streaming into IX Corps and Eighth Army headquarters during the day by radio and aerial reports, this favorable summary of the situation at the end of daylight on 26 November seemed dubious at best. Instead of four friendly battalions holding Tokchon after dark that evening, the more reliable report was that 4,000 Chinese soldiers occupied the town. And there was a report that Lt. Col. Clark Campbell, senior KMAG advisor at Tokchon, had told all the KMAG officers and enlisted men gathered there earlier in the day that they were on their own, as all avenues of escape had been cut off. A Mosquito pilot reported just before dark that he saw six to eight American vehicles east of Tokchon, 100 abandoned vehicles on the road west of Tokchon, 100 more American vehicles abandoned in the vicinity of Yongwon. He said that enemy occupied the hills around Tokchon.[8]

The night of 26 November was cold and clear in the ROK II Corps zone, with a nearly full, brilliant moon spreading a silvery light over the landscape—a Chinese moon, in the parlance of Eighth Army. It provided optimum conditions for the Chinese to exploit their success thus far against the army right flank.

While the Eighth Army did not fully understand the situation on its right flank at the end of daylight on 26 November, it realized it was ripe for enemy exploitation. To protect itself, Eighth Army ordered the 1st Cavalry Division from army reserve to take positions in the area of Sunchon, Sinchang-ni, and Kachong-ni, behind the ROK II Corps area, and to be ready to stop an enemy turning movement against the Eighth Army from the east (right) flank. The IX Corps also ordered the Turkish Brigade during the day to move out east from Kunu-ri on the road to Tokchon to meet any Chinese threat from that direction. Eighth Army also changed the IX Corps boundary on 26 November, assigning the former ROK II Corps area west as far as Kujang-ni to it. Late in the afternoon of 26 November, groups of the ROK 3rd Regiment began appearing in the 38th Infantry sector. Colonel Peploe informed General Keiser, 2nd Division commander, who directed him to collect the ROKs coming into his zone.[9]

When the ROK 2nd Regiment failed to open the Tokchon-Yongwon road eastward to the area of the original Chinese penetration, it became vital to keep open the Yongwon-Maengsan road farther east. It was the only remaining supply and communications road that entered the ROK II Corps eastern positions. To accomplish this objective, the ROK 8th Division commander refused his right flank, turning his troops at right angle to face east instead of north. To make this front stronger, he had the 10th and 21st regiments send their reserve battalions to hills just west of the Yongwon-Maengsan road.

It seems incredible in this hour of crumbling defeat all across the ROK II Corps front that these units, upon arriving at their assigned defensive positions, seemed to be concerned only with their immediate physical comfort. The night was bitterly cold. The ROK battalions started fires on their hilltops to keep warm. These bonfires, twinkling over the mountain landscape, clearly marked for the Chinese the ROK positions. What happened that night can best be stated by an American officer, advisor to the ROK 10th Regiment of the 8th Division and present in the area. He wrote:

> The early part of the evening was quiet and peaceful. . . . At 2100 hours [9 P.M.], the entire corps front, covering a distance of 100 miles erupted with a violence that had not been witnessed previously in the Korean conflict. The Chinese launched simultaneous attacks in overwhelming numbers against the front, flank, and rear of the 8th, 10th, 21st, 16th, and 2nd Regiments. An effort was likewise made to eliminate the 3rd and 5th Regiments by multiple penetrations and pincers. The Maengsan-Yongsan road was cut at the important junction near the town of Songpyong. Other Chinese Communist Forces elements blocked the Maengsan-Tokchon road at Hyo-ri. The Chinese established defensive positions throughout the area, oriented to the north, along stream beds and ridge lines so as to complete the destruction of the ROK units after they had been split into small groups by the fury of the initial attack.[10]

The ROKs could not cope with this attack. After the first assault, they split into small groups, unit integrity was lost, and soon there was no communication with each other or higher headquarters. Each group under its own leader tried to fight its way to the rear, or it surrendered. By the morning of 27 November virtually all the ROK forces on the forward combat positions had been destroyed, except for the ROK 3rd Regiment on the left (west) flank adjacent to the US 2nd Division. This regiment drifted westward into the lines of the

38th Regiment of the 2nd Division, where Colonel Peploe, on 2nd Division order, tried to collect and reorganize them. The ROK 3rd Regiment was attached to the 2nd Division (it fought with the 38th Regiment) and was an effective combat unit in the following days, as the 2nd Division was forced to withdraw to Kunu-ri.

Many ROK leaders of groups numbering as many as 100 to 200 men fought their way back to friendly lines. To do this they had to work their way through mountainous terrain and fight CCF forces dug in across the most likely routes of escape southward. The ROK leaders had difficulty keeping their men moving, exhausted as they were after the climbing, marching, and fighting of the preceding days and nights. One ruse they employed was to have a small detail bring up the rear of their groups and fire close to the retreating men, thus creating the impression that Chinese pursuers were close on their heels. This stimulated them to further exertion toward escape.

On the morning of 27 November there could be no doubt that the CCF 112th Division and other enemy forces from the CCF 38th Army held Tokchon, although some remnants of the ROK 7th Division were in the vicinity, mostly south of the town in the direction of Pukchang-ni, the ROK II Corps headquarters. Maengsan was entirely surrounded by the CCF 42nd Army, if not actually in its hands. Large numbers of the 42nd Army had bypassed Maengsan and were south and west of it in the ROK II Corps rear. The road south from Tokchon to Pukchang-ni had been blocked repeatedly since the morning of 26 November, reopened several times briefly, and then blocked again. At noon on 27 November the CCF closed it for good. This caught the CP staff of the ROK 7th Division north of the block and closed this escape route. The ROK II Corps headquarters had to leave Pukchang-ni, and it took the road south. Some miles south of Pukchang-ni the ROK II Corps set up a defense position with elements of the ROK 6th Division and gathered up stragglers and groups from the ROK 7th and 8th divisions that had escaped the Chinese dragnet. The corps commander tried to reorganize these troops into usable units.

The ROK 5th Regiment had captured some prisoners in the vicinity of Tokchon. Korean interpreters interviewed them and learned that the CCF 112th Division had made the frontal assault on Tokchon, while the 113th and 114th divisions enveloped the town. By noon on 27 November, the ROK II Corps area of the Eighth Army front was almost entirely in enemy hands, and the corps routed.[11] The location of most units of the ROK II Corps was unknown.

From the ROK Corps left flank five companies of the ROK 3rd Regiment had escaped westward to the 38th Infantry positions, and they took up front-line duties with it. About 250 more ROK soldiers from the 2nd Regiment of the ROK 6th Division had come into the 38th Infantry lines as stragglers and were being reorganized there. Elsewhere, three companies of the ROK 7th and 19th regiments of the 6th Division had been left behind at Pukchang-ni, when the ROK II Corps evacuated the town, to delay enemy advance south of there. But theirs was only a temporary holding action at best. South of Pukchang-ni, units of the ROK 6th Division still intact took up a defensive position, behind which stragglers from the ROK 7th and 8th divisions assembled and regrouped, according to a message from a KMAG advisor with the ROK II Corps at 7:30 P.M. to IX Corps.[12]

Aerial reports during the day advised of numerous enemy formations converging on Tokchon and Yongwon from the north and the Huichon area, apparently to join and reinforce the drive southwest into the Eighth Army rear areas.

General Walker took several steps during the twenty-seventh to meet the growing crisis confronting Eighth Army. He ordered General Coulter, IX Corps commander, to assume control of the ROK II Corps sector. To help accommodate the larger IX Corps zone of responsibility, he changed the boundary between the US I Corps and the US IX Corps, moving it eastward, and as a part of this change the US 25th Infantry Division henceforth was in the I Corps zone. The boundary between the two US corps now ran south of the Chongchon River from Kunu-ri to Sunchon, with responsibility for the Kunu-ri–Sunchon road in IX Corps. Walker also released the 1st Cavalry Division from Eighth Army reserve and attached it to IX Corps, with orders that it should advance toward Pukchang-ni, the former ROK II Corps headquarters, secure it, and protect the Eighth Army east flank. The Turkish Brigade already had been attached to IX Corps and sent east from Kunu-ri toward Tokchon. As a further gathering of strength on the eastern flank, the British 27th Brigade had been ordered to an assembly area south of Kunu-ri.

During the day, the 7th and 8th regiments of the 1st Cavalry Division reached Sunchon, and the 5th Cavalry Regiment was on its way there. The 1st Cavalry Division was to advance on Pukchang-ni from Sunchon as early as possible on the morning of 28 November. The latest reliable information on the chaotic ROK II Corps situation on the southeast flank of Eighth Army came from Brigadier General Farrell, chief of KMAG, who was at the ROK II Corps headquarters in the afternoon. He reported there were about four battalions of ROK troops from mixed units assembled in the 11th Regiment, 6th Division, some artillery with them, and about 500 more ROKs from the 8th Division with some artillery pieces. They were in position about one mile south of Pukchang-ni. He said the road from Sunchon to Pukchang-ni was under fire at some points, indicating that some CCF units were already south of Pukchang-ni.[13]

Just after noon on 27 November, Eighth Army Deputy Chief of Staff Eugene M. Landrum telephoned Maj. Gen. Doyle Hickey, chief of staff, General Headquarters, Far East Command in Tokyo with a message from General Walker, which summarized the situation as he knew it. General Walker's message follows:

> Indications are that en is no longer on def but is taking off action in str. Main effort at the moment is against IX Corps (center) and II ROK Corps on our right. No important activity on our extreme west flank, but captured PWs indicate possibility of some str in that area. We are consolidating positions of I Corps until situation clarifies. IX Corps is resisting strong attacks but is under orders to resume the offensive. II ROK Corps on right has fallen back to general line east and west through TOKCHON. Situation in that corps still fluid. IX Corps is employing Turks to attack TOKCHON from the west to assist in stabilizing situation in II ROK Corps. 1st Cav Div being assembled east of Sunchon in rear of ROK as a precautionary measure.

To Walker's message, Landrum then added in conversation with Hickey, ". . . the general feeling up there is not pessimistic. But it's a tight situation brought about primarily by the lack of firmness on the part of our little friends."¹⁴ It is surprising to note in this message that Walker at midday, 27 November, apparently thought the IX Corps could still resume the Eighth Army offensive and that Landrum would say the American feeling at the front was not pessimistic.

CCF Exploit Breakthrough of ROK II Corps

During 28 November the Chinese were everywhere in motion during daylight, exploiting their breakthrough of the ROK II Corps. This daylight movement was in contrast to their usual practice of remaining quiet and hidden during daytime to minimize losses to air attack. Aerial observers at 8:55 A.M. reported two enemy regiments were approaching Pukchang-ni from the north. Another observer reported an enemy regiment moving west from Maengsan. A Joint Operations Center air report stated that a continuous stream of enemy soldiers was moving south from the Huichon area toward Tokchon, using all roads, trails, ridgelines, and gullies that afforded a route for foot movement. This activity continued all day. One report indicated that the troops were variously dressed, stating that an estimated 2,000 seen were dressed in white, another 400 to 500 in dark blue uniforms. Some of the troops had 40 to 50 pack animals with them. During the night or early morning of 28 November, the CCF occupied Pukchang-ni. Approximately four enemy regiments were there or in its vicinity after daylight of 28 November. Apparently the closest ROK defensive position was about three miles southwest of the town, where the ROK II Corps had organized parts of the ROK 7th and 19th regiments of the ROK 6th Division on high ground in an effort to stop further enemy penetration southward from Pukchang-ni.

At 9:30 A.M., an estimated regiment of Chinese with 20 mortars was reported to be in Pukchang-ni, another regiment a mile west of Taepyong-ni, two miles southwest of Pukchang-ni. The deepest penetration by enemy troops observed from the air was at Sochang-ni, where an estimated 2,000 enemy cavalry were seen. Sochang-ni was located on a trail or track about 12 air miles southeast of Pukchang-ni and almost directly east of Sunchon. At Sochang-ni, this force was many miles south of the ROK defensive position just established three miles below Pukchang-ni and moving around and behind it, apparently headed for Sinchang-ni and Sunchon.¹⁵ Another 2,000 men in civilian clothes were seen ten miles southeast of Wawon, moving west. The chief of staff of the ROK 7th Division arrived at the 1st Cavalry Division CP at noon on 28 November and reported his division had an estimated strength of 2,000 men. Eighth Army received a report during the day that the headquarters of the routed and fragmented ROK II Corps was at Sunchon.¹⁶

The Far East Command in its Daily Intelligence Summary for the 24-hour period beginning at 2:00 A.M. on 28 November admitted that the enemy in the last 48 hours had changed to "sharply aggressive counteroffensive with an apparent massing of his strength against 2nd ROK Corps which was swept aside to a depth of 5 to 25 miles. . . ." It then went on to say that the "probing attacks by the Eighth Army actually turned out to be a reconnaissance in force in which the enemy disclosed his real strength along the entire front." Here for the first time we see reference to the Eighth Army's attack that began on 24 November as "a reconnaissance in force," a term General MacArthur was later to use in describing what the Eighth Army had been doing, claiming that its action in disclosing the enemy's massed strength saved that army from annihilation.[17] This is not what the Far East Command had planned. It is a rationalization after the fact. Also, some misconceptions of the Far East Command intelligence section at this time are reflected in the previous day's intelligence summary, which implies that enemy action against the ROK II Corps came through the area of the gap between the Eighth Army and the X Corps. This, too, demonstrably, is not what happened.

At the end of 28 November, the leading CCF forces that had penetrated south and southwest of the ROK II Corps areas were swinging into the rear of the IX Corps front and threatening to move behind all of Eighth Army. General Walker counted on the 1st Cavalry Division to block that move. The collision of the 1st Cavalry Division with the CCF, primarily elements of the 125th and 126th divisions of the 42nd Army, will be described in a later section. First it will be necessary to go back a day or two and relate the story of the Turkish Brigade that had already met a strong force of the CCF 38th Army that drove west from Tokchon toward Kunu-ri, directly threatening to get in the rear of Eighth Army at the boundary of IX Corps and I Corps.

The Turks Meet Disaster

The Turkish Brigade was thrust into the battle for Tokchon on 26 November, their first appearance in combat in the Korean War. This United Nations contingent was the largest, except for the British, that participated in the Korean War alongside American and ROK troops.

Essentially, the Turkish Brigade, or Turkish Armed Forces Command, was a regimental combat team consisting of three infantry battalions and supporting engineers and artillery, with a brigade staff superimposed on it.

The advance party of the Turkish Brigade arrived at Pusan on 12 October 1950. The main body, numbering 5,190 troops, arrived there five days later, on 17 October. They unloaded the next day. The Turks were fully equipped, except for certain weapons. On 23 November, the Eighth Army G-4 Section carried the brigade as numbering 5,055 men for logistical support. Brig. Gen. Tahzin Yazici commanded the brigade. His principal staff officers were Col. Celal Dora as assistant commander, Maj. Faik Turun as G-3, and Maj. Recai Baturalp as G-4. The brigade went into bivouac just outside Taegu in South Korea for training exercises and to receive supplies and certain equipment. It was then attached to the 25th Infantry Division. One of the problems at first was to supply the brigade with enough bread to meet its requirements, as it was the major element of the Turks' diet. Bakers had to be trained to meet their needs, and US Army field ranges were provided for all Turkish kitchens. On 19 November the 25th Infantry Division left Kaesong at 6 A.M. and closed at Kunu-ri at 10 P.M. that night, after traveling 187 miles. The next day, 20 November, Eighth Army ordered the Turkish Brigade detached from the 25th Division and reassigned to IX Corps reserve. It stayed in that status five days.[18]

The Turks had the reputation of being rough, hard fighters. Most of those in the brigade were young and wore big, black mustaches that gave them a particularly fierce appearance. They wore a sidearm sword, as they called it, but to most Americans it looked like a long knife. No other troops in the UN forces were armed with a weapon of that kind. The Turks were proficient in its use for close combat.[19]

When the Turks arrived at Kunu-ri, "a little mud-and-stick village," as an English correspondent called it, they chanced to camp beside the Australian Battalion. A strange bond of affection and admiration between the two groups of young men sprang up, whose fathers had fought against each other at Gallipoli in World War I. This meeting between the two groups took place on a bitterly cold night, when they pulled up railroad ties, hacked down telegraph poles, and gathered rice sheaves to burn for warmth. This common tie seemed to cheer the Turks, who were indeed strangers in a strange land, with no understanding of either the English or the Korean languages, and whose customs were different from those all around them. The language barrier was to be a major difficulty in their military operations for some months. For one thing, the Turkish private would take orders from no one except his own officers.[20]

On 26 November the Chinese penetration of the ROK II Corps in the Tokchon area had assumed alarming proportions. General Coulter decided to send the Turkish Brigade from his corps reserve eastward on the road from Kunu-ri to Tokchon to defend that place. At 3:15 in the afternoon the corps attached a platoon of American tanks to the brigade and ordered the Turks to start moving toward Tokchon at once. The Turks' mission was to protect the right flank of the US 2nd Infantry Division, which, in effect, was at that time the Eighth Army's right flank. Trucks were to transport a battalion of Turks to Wawon, about 15 miles east of Kunu-ri, not quite halfway to Tokchon, unload them there, turn around, and return to transport another battalion to Wawon. The third Turkish battalion would for the present remain at Kunu-ri. From Wawon the Turks were to attack toward Tokchon on foot. The route from Kunu-ri that ran eastward behind the front lines was upstream along the Tongjukkyo River into the high mountain divide that separated the Chongchon from the Taedong drainage. Wawon was a small village on the road high in the mountains just west of the divide, where the headwaters of the Tongjukkyo River fanned out into numerous small streams that poured down from the divide to form the river.[21]

The first battalion of Turks to reach Wawon unloaded there in the afternoon of 26 November without tank support. It is not entirely clear just what happened at Wawon thereafter. The first word back to IX Corps at Unhang-ni, a few miles west of Kunu-ri, was that the Turks had met a force of Chinese, had won the ensuing fight in a wild knife and bayonet melee, and had captured some hundreds of Chinese. The IX Corps accepted this report as factual and, knowing now that the CCF held Tokchon, ordered the Turks to turn north from Wawon, advance into the mountains toward the right flank of the 2nd Infantry Division, and make contact with the 38th Regiment at Tomgi. The IX Corps headquarters immediately informed press representatives of the spectacular Turkish victory in their first encounter with the Chinese. Press releases recounting the story were sent at once to the United States and widely printed there and in Europe. But the story was entirely erroneous. It was never subsequently corrected in the press.

Word of the Turks' "victory" quickly reached the 2nd Division. It wanted to confirm it and to establish communications with the Turks, and at once sent a Nisei (Japanese-American) interpreter to Wawon. He reported back that the Turks actually had met about 200 ROK troops retreating from Tokchon, had thought they were Chinese, and had attacked them, killing many and capturing about 125. These ROKs were members of the ROK 6th and 7th divisions. There were no Chinese involved in this first fight the Turks had in Korea. This unfortunate incident was quickly covered over and not publicized – the public did not know what had really happened. The South Koreans bitterly resented being attacked and suffering many casualties by a force under Eighth Army command and in an area they thought was safe for their withdrawal from Tokchon.[22]

The Turks, however, can hardly be blamed for what happened. They had little reliable intelligence to guide them. They did not know a ROK force was retreating from Tokchon toward them. They did expect to meet Chinese somewhere on the road. They had none of their UN allies with them, who might have prevented the accident. They did not know either the Korean or the Chinese language. In their ignorance of the true situation and believing they were meeting enemies, their attack showed valor. The Turks stayed during the night at Wawon, astride the road they had traveled. They and the Chinese were almost certain to meet each other on the morrow.

Before the Turks could get started north for Tomgi after daylight on 27 November, they did indeed see Chinese soldiers. But the precise circumstances of the meeting are unclear. A message in the G-3 Journal, 2nd Infantry Division, says that the Turkish column was ambushed about three miles east of Wawon at 8 A.M. that morning. Eighth Army, aware on the morning of 27 November that Tokchon was in enemy hands, sent a message to halt the Turks at Sochang, for they reportedly had started toward Tokchon at 5 A.M. from Wawon and Wolbong-san. The latter is the high mountain at the divide east of Wawon. Just after noon on 27 November, at 1:10 P.M., IX Corps changed the Turks' mission to one of establishing a blocking position six miles east of Wawon, on Wolbong-san mountain pass. What happened to the earlier Eighth Army order is not known. From its blocking position ordered by IX Corps, the Turks were to patrol to the east, southeast, and north and to establish contact with the UN unit on their left. Presumably this would be the 38th Infantry Regiment of the 2nd Division, or possibly with ROKs of the 3rd Regiment who were still straggling into the 38th Infantry's zone. This message went to Lieutenant Colonel Weaver, who was the IX Corps liaison officer with the Turkish command.[23]

The flow of messages and changed orders to the Turks on the road to Tokchon on 27 November reflects the uncertainty and lack of precise information at IX Corps and Eighth Army of what was happening. It is certain, however, that during the day, and probably during the morning, Chinese ambushed the leading battalion of the Turks three to four miles east of Wawon and inflicted on it a decisive defeat. It appears that one battalion of the Turks lost most if not all of its vehicles in this fight, that their personnel losses were heavy, and that survivors took to the hills if they could not retreat back west on the road they were following. The records show only that the next morning, 28 November, many Turkish stragglers appeared in the zone of the 38th Infantry, north and northwest of the Wawon road, and that 2nd Division observers saw part of the Turkish command retreating west toward Kunu-ri.[24]

Information that filtered into IX Corps and Eighth Army headquarters a day or two later seems to indicate that the leading party of Turks from their 1st Battalion was ambushed in the pass a few miles east of Wawon. One message stated there were 100 men and six to eight vehicles in this party. After daylight the Turkish battalion commander sent a company forward, but it made no headway, and the entire battalion was then committed. The CCF probably could bring up a greater force than the Turks could muster, although there is no reliable information as to their strength. In any event, the Turkish battalion was surrounded, and there was close knife and bayonet fighting. One comment later was that about half the Turk battalion broke through the CCF force and withdrew west, reaching Taechon, a large village about seven miles southeast of Kunu-ri, where General Yazici had established his brigade headquarters CP. Two companies of Turks at that time were allegedly still fighting east of Wawon with about 400 wounded in their midst. It appears that these Turks held out at Wawon into the afternoon, and then those able to do so withdrew to another position two miles southwest of Wawon. Here they were soon outflanked by pursuing CCF and forced to withdraw farther on the road toward Kunu-ri. The CCF followed them closely.

In the meantime, General Yazici established a defense position half a mile east of Kaechon, where he attempted to reorganize his soldiers who escaped from the vicinity of Wawon. Some of the Turks fought delaying actions all the way from Wawon and slowed the CCF advance on Kunu-ri from Tokchon.[25] At 11 A.M. on 28 November, IX Corps attached the Turkish Brigade to the 2nd Infantry Division for operational control.

With information about the condition of the Turks so uncertain, General Keiser, 2nd Division commander, sent Col. John C. Coughlin, then attached to the 38th Regiment as an assistant to Colonel Peploe, to the Turkish Brigade CP at Kaechon to learn what he could of its condition. He found the Turks at the CP very excited. One battalion had been cut off at Wawon and vicinity, and they had no situation map posted and no communications with their forward units. He tried to get the Turks to send tanks up the road to the combat point, but the tanks kept coming back. He urged the Turkish command to stay where it was. The Turks there, however, seemed to expect the CCF to appear at any moment. That danger was certainly still many hours away.

Colonel Coughlin reported to Brig. Gen. Joseph S. Bradley, assistant 2nd Division commander, that he could not get the Turks on the line desired but that it would be farther to the rear, southeast of Kaechon and Kunu-ri. He also reported that he had found the Turkish command very indecisive. They would order the artillery forward and then order it back. In the meantime, the 38th Infantry Regiment, and indeed all of the 2nd Division, on the left of the Turks was withdrawing and trying to coordinate the Turkish moves on their right with their own.

Shortly after midnight, early in the morning of 28 November, the 2nd Division sent a message to General Yazici, through the American advisor attached to the Turkish Brigade, to move his troops on the right flank of the 38th Regiment, south of the Kaechon River and south of the town of Kaechon below Kunu-ri. The commanding officer refused to do so. Many American officers in touch with the situation felt that the Turkish command was weak but that the individual Turk was a good soldier and fighter. From this time on, the Turkish Brigade became fragmented. About 250 of them showed up at Anju in trucks, miles away from the front. Many others appeared at Sunchon far south of the battle front, and some even got as far away as Pyongyang. At 3:10 P.M. on 29 November, the G-3, IX Corps, received a message from Pyongyang stating that 125 to 150 Turks in about ten or more trucks, with an American KMAG advisor, had arrived there and asked, "What shall I do with them?"

The final collapse of the Turks in the battles of the Chongchon came about 4 P.M. on November 28 near Kaechon, when the 38th Infantry found they were withdrawing from their positions. Efforts to stop them and turn them around were unavailing. The CCF simply walked through them – those it found still in front of them. The CCF then got behind two battalions of the 38th Infantry because of the complete collapse of the Turks and attacked them from front and rear.[26]

The Eighth Army G-3 Operations Journal for 29 November reveals that the army command had little precise information on the situation surrounding the Turkish Brigade and was much concerned about it and that Gen. Laurence Keiser, commander of the 2nd Division, was on his way to the IX Corps CP to give as full a report as possible on the subject. Reports reaching Eighth Army at this time estimated about half the Turkish Brigade remained and that it was trying to hold just east of Kaechon but was short of ammunition, artillery, and tank support. Obviously, this report was incorrect, since the CCF broke through or walked past the Turks at Kaechon and vicinity and attacked the 38th Infantry from the rear. Another report stated that two companies of Turkish infantry had arrived at Sunchon bringing along about 400 casualties and that some other Turks were driving trucks and ambulances to Pyongyang.[27]

Until the late afternoon of 29 November, the Turks, in the face of crippling losses, had indeed held and delayed perhaps the major part of a CCF division that was advancing on Kunu-ri by road from Tokchon. But in the late afternoon of 29 November their opposition seems to have crumbled at last. At 4:40 P.M. that afternoon, Colonel Peploe reported to the 2nd Division that the Turks were not on position to his right and were unwilling to take a defensive position. Peploe urgently requested that everything be done to get them back in the defense line. Col. Gerald Epley, the 2nd Division chief of staff, telephoned Colonel Grunby, the principal American advisor with the Turks, asking him to get the Turks out of the village of Kaechon and into a defensive position. Grunby promised to try but said he did not think he would succeed. A few hours later the situation had deteriorated further. At 6:30 P.M., the division headquarters received a report that the Turks were milling around and appeared to be in such a chaotic and uncontrolled condition that they could not be used. At this very moment the CCF were pressing hard all around on the approaches to Kunu-ri. They especially threatened the survival of the US 2nd Infantry Division.[28]

Two weeks later, when all stragglers had been accounted for and the Turkish Brigade had assembled in a rear area for reorganization, it was found that, in their battles with the Chinese on the road from Tokchon to Kunu-ri and around Kaechon and Kunu-ri, the Turks had lost about 20 percent (roughly 1,000 men) in killed, wounded, and missing in action. They had lost approximately 90 percent of their communication equipment and vehicles. Only six artillery pieces remained to them.[29] Thus, in its destruction of the ROK II Corps, the CCF, it must be stated, also rendered combat ineffective the Turkish command of about 5,000 men.

On 13 December, General Walker presented Brig. Gen. Tahzin Yazici and 15 of his officers and men of his command with 15 Silver Star and Bronze Star medals for gallantry in action against the Chinese in late November. The Turkish Army gave no medals, so this presentation was an occasion the Turks remembered.[30]

The 1st Cavalry Division Checks Chinese Envelopment

The military situation had deteriorated on the army right flank in the ROK II Corps area so far by the evening of 27 November that the 1st Cavalry Division, in Eighth Army reserve, received a flash warning at 5:45 P.M., informing it that the division would be ordered to move to Pukchang-ni and to secure the town, protect the army right flank, and cover the ROK II Corps in its further withdrawals and reorganization. It was informed at the same time that about four battalions of mixed units were in the ROK 11th Regiment of the ROK 6th Division with some artillery and that about 500 more ROK soldiers from the ROK 8th Division with a few pieces of artillery had assembled about one mile south of Pukchang-ni. Also, the message said the road from Sunchon to Pukchang-ni was under fire at some points. Two hours later Eighth Army sent the 1st Cavalry Division orders to advance on Pukchang-ni as early as practicable the next morning, 28 November.[31] IX Corps assumed operational control of the 1st Cavalry Division at 1:40 A.M., 28 November.

Maj. Gen. Hobart R. Gay's 1st Cavalry Division headquarters on 27 November was near Pyongmyong-ni, about six miles southeast of Kunu-ri. The 5th Cavalry Regiment sent its Intelligence and Reconnaissance (I&R) Platoon from there at 8:40 A.M., 28 November, to make a reconnaissance of the road south to Sunchon. The 2nd Battalion, 5th Cavalry, left the Pyongmyong-ni area about an hour later, en route to Sunchon, following the I&R Platoon. The 2nd Battalion reported at 10:30 A.M. that a platoon sergeant and two enlisted men of the I&R Platoon had escaped back to it, reporting that Chinese had ambushed the I&R Platoon and taken all but themselves prisoners. They reported that the enemy were carrying small arms and automatic weapons.

The ambush site was about one and a half miles south of Chusong-dong and two and a half miles north of Samso-ri, where there was a ferry crossing of the Taedong River. The 2nd Battalion, 5th Cavalry, reached the ambush site just before noon. The troops dismounted from their vehicles and deployed for an attack, while their vehicles turned around to take a route farther west to Sunchon. F and G companies attacked the enemy positions and had hard going from the outset. By 4:30 in the afternoon the battalion had suffered 70 casualties. It requested a resupply of ammunition and evacuation facilities. The division immediately complied with both requests. The 2nd Battalion then renewed the fight.

The 2nd Battalion drove the Chinese south, and soon the fight centered on Hill 82, half a mile north of the river and east of Samso-ri and the road. Higher ground, Hill 167, west of the road and Samso-ri, gave dug-in enemy there a very strong position. The battle lasted until dark, with the 2nd Battalion unable to dislodge the Chinese. Later information indicated that the Chinese held these high ground positions in regimental strength. They apparently had the mission of preventing a UN crossing of the Taedong River at the Samso-ri ferry site. It became apparent that the enemy could not be dislodged without artillery support.

The 3rd Battalion, 5th Cavalry, already at Sunchon, sent K Company up to help the 2nd Battalion, but this reinforcement failed to alter the situation. K Company withdrew back to Sunchon, and the 2nd Battalion then quit the battle, reformed on the road north of the river, retraced its way to a bypass route it took around the Chinese roadblock, and went on to Sunchon. This action, in effect, left the Chinese in control of the main road south from Kunu-ri to Sunchon. The 2nd Battalion, 5th Cavalry, suffered heavily in this action, losing approximately 15 officers and 200 enlisted men killed, wounded, or missing. Because of this heavy loss, the 5th Cavalry assigned all its 105 replacements just received to the 2nd Battalion.[32]

Meanwhile, the 5th Cavalry Regimental headquarters and the 1st Battalion, aware of the strong enemy roadblock at Samso-ri, moved to Sunchon by an alternate road to the west. The Chinese force at Samso-ri may have continued on west and established the initial roadblock on the western alternate road to Sunchon from Kunu-ri that developed the next day and confronted the 2nd Infantry Division when it started to move south from Kunu-ri to Sunchon.

While these events were happening to the 5th Cavalry, the 7th Cavalry Regiment spent the day moving through Sunchon and on east and north toward Pukchang-ni. As a consequence of this maneuver, the IX Corps at 11 A.M. attached the ROK 6th Division to the 1st Cavalry Division for operational control.[33]

The enemy force that had seized control of Samso-ri and its ferry at a big bend of the Taedong River and turned back the 5th Cavalry from that road had a direct connection with the force the 7th Cavalry was advancing eastward to meet. The Chinese troops that had seized Samso-ri were in the vanguard of the Chinese 38th Army, which was moving westward after its capture of Tokchon. They had hurried south from Tokchon to Pukchang-ni and, after the capture of that place, had there turned due west, leaving the 42nd Army to continue on south and southwest from Pukchang-ni toward Sunchon. It was these troops from the Chinese 42nd Army that the 7th Cavalry would meet.[34]

When the vanguard of the 38th Army turned west from Pukchang-ni to get in the rear of the US 2nd Infantry Division, the leading elements of the 42nd Army had arrived there from Maengsan. The 125th Division led this army's enveloping movement. It left Pukchang-ni on the main road that ran southwest in a big loop through Wolpo-ri, Kujang-ni, and Sinchang-ni to Chasan, the last being six miles south of Sunchon. The 38th Army's mission was to cut off Eighth Army elements north of the Taedong River, while that of the 42nd Army was to engage in its broad, sweeping envelopment behind the whole of Eighth Army.[35]

The 7th Cavalry Regiment, now on a collision course with the advance elements of the CCF 125th Division, passed through Sinchang-ni and reached Kujang-ni, about 25 road miles northeast of Sunchon. It continued on a short distance and found the ROK 6th Division, with the ROK 7th Regiment in a defensive position astride the road just north of Wolpo-ri. A strong Chinese force was known to be not far north of this ROK position. Darkness soon settled over the scene on the evening of 28 November.[36]

The Kujang-ni Incident, 29 November At about 6:30 the next morning, 29 November, the 7th Cavalry Regiment perimeter came under Chinese attack, and the regiment that Lt. Col. George H. Custer commanded in the 1870s thus had its first battle contact with Chinese in the Korean War. The 1st and 2nd battalions of the regiment were on either side of the road, with the 3rd Battalion behind them, when the action began. The 2nd Battalion had a strong roadblock at Kujang-ni, facing north toward Wolpo-ri. Ahead of them at Wolpo-ri, they knew, was a ROK 6th Division mixed force, principally elements of the ROK 7th Regiment. Its strength on 29 November was given as about 1,200 men. No word had come back to the 7th Cavalry perimeter during the night of any enemy attack or activity at Wolpo-ri.

But suddenly before dawn, perimeter and roadblock guards heard the sound of firing to the north, and soon thereafter a long column of retreating ROK troops and equipment piled up at the 2nd Battalion roadblock, demanding to be let through. Maj. Gen. Hobart R. Gay, 1st Cavalry Division commander, had given Col. William A. Harris, commander of the 7th Cavalry Regiment, oral orders that he should not permit a retreating ROK unit, specifically the ROK 6th Division elements to the north of him, to retreat through his positions, in case of an enemy attack on the ROKs. There was always the danger that enemy dressed as civilians would infiltrate the retreating ROKs as refugees and either act as spies or suddenly open fire with concealed weapons and grenades to create confusion. General Gay had experienced several such incidents during the battles of the Pusan perimeter earlier in the year with the North Koreans. It was a well-known North Korean, and possibly Chinese, practice. It was also imperative to stop ROK withdrawals in the ROK II Corps area, to assemble and reorganize them, and to try to get them back in the fight.

When the retreating ROK column, with what appeared to be some civilian refugees mixed with them, came up to the 2nd Battalion roadblock near Kujang-ni, 1st Lt. John E. Sheehan, commanding officer of E Company, 2nd Battalion, went out into the road and began questioning some refugees in the halted column. During this discussion, a group of about ten enemy soldiers, posing as civilian refugees, suddenly opened fire with hidden small arms, killing Lieutenant Sheehan and another American soldier and wounding five others.[37] This incident caused further confusion, and no more refugees in the ROK columns were permitted entrance into the 7th Cavalry perimeter.

The Chinese attack on the ROK 6th Division elements at Wolpo-ri before dawn on 29 November caused a subsequent bitter dispute between KMAG officers with the ROK 7th Regiment and General Chang, commanding general of the ROK 6th Division, on one side, and the 7th Cavalry Regiment and the 1st Cavalry Division, on the other. Following the roadblock incident, the 7th Cavalry Regiment was immediately engaged with Chinese forces driving south from Wolpo-ri, an action that continued during the rest of the day and that night. The events at Wolpo-ri had some lasting repercussions and illustrated the nature of much of the fighting and military situation in Eighth Army at the time.

Maj. Thomas E. Bennett, the senior KMAG advisor to the ROK 7th Regiment, in a memorandum to General Gay a month and a half later, gives his version of the Chinese attack just north of Wolpo-ri and subsequent events. He was the closest responsible American officer to the scene. He wrote:

At 0602 hours 29 November 1950, I was awakened by a burst of machine gun fire from the high ground at the north side of Walpori. I sent my interpreter to the 7th Regimental CP to find out the situation; meanwhile I assembled my KMAG group.

At 0605 hours, our interpreters rushed into our billet calling, "Komunkwan! Danger! Go quickly!" Machine gun firing and small arms firing could be heard in the north side of Walpori.

At 0610 hours I put my KMAG Group on the road at the tail end of a long convoy of vehicles (exact numbers could not be determined because of darkness). Artillery howitzers and prime movers of the 27th Korean Field Artillery Battalion were in the column.

The vehicle column with my group just in front of the tail of the column began to move forward.

The column halted just after our three KMAG jeeps crossed a railroad south of Walpori. I sent my interpreter forward to find out what was delaying the column.

Machine gun firing and small arms firing at the tail of the column became more pronounced, still the vehicles were not moving.

Mortar shells (at least 81 mm) began to land off the road on the right and left of the column and abreast of my KMAG jeeps.

My interpreter returned and said that Americans would not let my Korean vehicles pass.

I made an estimate of the situation and decided that the steep drop-offs on either side of the road prohibited my taking my Group on the frozen rice paddies. When a mortar shell (at least 81 mm) hit the prime mover of a 105 mm howitzer just to the rear of Major Hewette's jeep, I told my KMAG Group to abandon jeep and we went off the road onto a frozen rice paddie at the left. Because of the darkness, the noise and the confusion, I told my group to keep contact by each officer calling the name of the other. We walked on the paddie about 25 yards before getting back on the road. A mortar shell (at least 81 mm) hit the road just in front of me. Two illuminating shells burst in the air off the right of the road. Fifty caliber tracers were passing over our heads. I could hear 50 caliber firing from our rear.

Suddenly the vehicles began to move. More mortar shells hit on the road around the vehicles. Because of the increase in firing from the rear, I told my group to catch rides on the vehicles going by. A vehicle, traveling fast, grazed my arm. . . .

Through my interpreter, Colonel Kim [ROK 7th Regimental commander] told me that a Chinese Communist Force of undetermined strength had attacked at 0430 hours 29 November 1950 along the road north of Walpori.

One platoon of the 1st Battalion was on the road; one company was on either side of the road. The colonel further stated that his men had fired until they ran out of ammunition. The Chinese had broken through.[38]

Lt. Col. Willard Pearson, as the senior KMAG advisor to General Chang, ROK 6th Division commander, wrote to General Gay on 16 January 1951, forwarding Bennett's statement and making charges on behalf of himself and other KMAG personnel with the ROK troops, alleging mistreatment by 1st Cavalry Division officers on 29 November at Kujang-ni. It must be remembered that the ROK 6th Division was attached to the 1st Cavalry Division at the time. Pearson alleged that General Gay had authorized General Chang "to drift" back on his MSR if the situation required it, yet his troops had been held outside friendly lines and there subjected to enemy small-arms and mortar fire. He acknowledged that the ROK 6th Division had subsequently been allowed to enter the 7th Cavalry perimeter and reorganize there, with less than one-third of its authorized strength. He alleged that the ROK 6th Division was required to protect the daylight withdrawal of the 7th Cavalry Regiment, and then the ROK troops had to withdraw on foot and establish its defense position that night on the MSR in the mountains after dark. Lieutenant Colonel Pearson wanted General Gay to consider the injustice done "to troops under your command." First Lt. Raymond Bishop, of the 27th Field Artillery Battalion, in support of the ROK 7th Regiment, added his complaints to those of Bennett and Pearson.

General Gay asked Col. William A. Harris, commanding the 7th Cavalry Regiment, for an explanation and reply to General Chang's, Lieutenant Colonel Pearson's, and the other KMAG advisors' charges. Colonel Harris replied to General Gay on 6 February 1951. According to Colonel Harris, the orders given to the ROK 6th Division, in his presence on 28 November, were that it was to hold for three days. Harris said he had not been informed of any authority granted by General Gay to General Chang to "drift back" along the MSR, that any ROK 6th Division plan of withdrawal had not been coordinated with him, and that his request for KMAG or ROK representatives to be stationed at his roadblock and at his headquarters had not met acceptance. He also said that no prior request to withdraw ROK artillery through the 7th Cavalry lines had been made, as stated by Lieutenant Bishop, and the offer of the 77th Field Artillery Battalion, supporting the 7th Cavalry Regiment, to shoot for the ROKs had never been acted on by the ROKs or their KMAG advisors. The ROK 6th Division fell back from Wolpo-ri to the 7th Cavalry lines at Kujang-ni, he said, without a single request for fire assistance and without notifying the 7th Cavalry of its actions. Colonel Harris added that, during 29 November and for several days thereafter, General Chang, Lieutenant Colonel Pearson, and other KMAG and ROK officers had contact with him and his staff officers and gave no indication of displeasure over the events that occurred on 29 November. His impression of their reaction, he said, was that they were happy to be out of a bad situation and to have the opportunity to reorganize behind the lines of the 7th Cavalry.[39] Resentment of imagined wrongs apparently built up in the ROK 6th Division commander and his KMAG advisors in the weeks following.

In the intervening two months between the actions themselves in late November 1950 and the charges submitted to General Gay in January 1951, one can be sure that this quarrel had echoed up and down the Eighth Army chain of command, involving General Farrell, KMAG chief, probably Generals Walker and Ridgway, the ROK army chief of staff, and President Syngman Rhee.

The facts of the attack by the Chinese 125th Division, 42nd Army, on the 7th and 19th ROK regiments, ROK 6th Division, north of Wolpo-ri, before dawn on 29 November seem to be that the Chinese made a frontal attack and at the same time outflanked both regiments, which then fled down the road. The KMAG advisors with them at the time seem to have been unavailable (we know from his own statement that Major Bennett and his group with the ROK 7th Regiment were in bed asleep at the time of the attack and made no effort to halt the retreating ROKs) at the front and exercised no influence on what quickly turned into a ROK precipitate withdrawal that was close to a rout. Both the ROK 7th and 19th regiments hurried south until they came up against the 2nd Battalion, 7th Cavalry, roadblock at Kujang-ni, where they were halted. The 27th Field Artillery Battalion lost all its guns, four 105-mm howitzers and eight 75-mm guns, their ammunition, and their trucks in front of the 7th Cavalry perimeter. Major Bennett alleged that, when the 2nd Battalion roadblock halted the retreating column, this resulted in considerable loss of life among the ROKs, who were then subject to enemy fire from the rear. He claimed he saw at least 12 ROK dead after daylight in front of the roadblock area. At this same time, the hotly pursuing Chinese came into contact with the perimeter defenses of both the 1st and 2nd battalions of the 7th Cavalry and a battle began that lasted most of the day and into the following night. Chinese prisoners identified themselves as members of the CCF 125th Division, 42nd Army.[40]

When KMAG personnel with the ROK troops were taken to Colonel Harris's CP and they explained the situation to him, he at once authorized the ROK column to enter the 7th Cavalry perimeter, which it did. It seems that Major Bennett, senior advisor to the ROK 7th Regiment, was taken to the CP of the 3rd Battalion, 7th Cavalry, which at the time of the incident was in regimental reserve inside the perimeter and behind the 1st and 2nd front line battalions.

Lt. Col. James H. Lynch, the 3rd Battalion commander, questioned Major Bennett about the whole affair, and it seems Major Bennett took exception to the line of questioning and what he considered rough treatment. It can be said of Lieutenant Colonel Lynch that he was a capable, tough, no-nonsense battalion commander, well tested in many battle situations. One may assume that Lynch had little patience with a KMAG officer who had been able to get out of bed and hit the road south away from the enemy in the short space of eight minutes. When the question of Lynch's treatment of Bennett came up later, other officers present said Lynch's questioning of Bennett was no different from his treatment and attitude toward his own officers.

The 7th Cavalry repulsed the Chinese attack against its perimeter by 8:20 A.M. Colonel Harris then ordered that the equipment abandoned by the ROKs during the early morning hours be recovered. Some 7th Cavalry patrols, or ROK detachments under protection of 7th Cavalry troops, went out in front of the perimeter toward Wolpo-ri and succeeded in recovering most of the equipment. Colonel Harris ordered that it be turned over to the ROK units. Meanwhile, the ROK units reorganized inside the 7th Cavalry perimeter.

Later in the morning of 29 November, General Gay ordered Colonel Harris to withdraw to the key road junction of Sinchang-ni, about seven road miles southwest of Kujang-ni on the MSR. The ROK 6th Division was to withdraw there first, and then the 7th Cavalry would follow. Snow showers that started in the morning continued until noon. Colonel Harris started his regiment toward Sinchang-ni at noon, and all its elements had closed there before dark. The 2nd Battalion acted as rear guard and covered the withdrawal. The Chinese followed closely.

Meanwhile, during the time the 7th Cavalry and elements of the ROK 6th Division were slowing down the enveloping movement of the Chinese 125th Division on the Wolpo-ri–Sunchon road, the 5th Cavalry Regiment had concentrated at Sunchon to cover the withdrawal south of the US 2nd Infantry Division. The 8th Cavalry Regiment, still taking in replacements and reorganizing after its ordeal a month earlier at Unsan, had been ordered to Songchon, 20 air miles southeast of Sunchon, on the main mountain road from Yongdok to the east. At Songchon the road forked, with one arm going northwest to Sunchon and the other southwest to Pyongyang, 30 air miles away. This route offered the CCF an opportunity to flank the Eighth Army and reach the North Korean capital. When the advance elements of the 8th Cavalry Regiment arrived at Songchon on 28 November they found it deserted. This was always a telltale sign that enemy troops were approaching. The civilian population always knew in advance of an enemy approach. The next day, 29 November, the 8th Cavalry Regiment reported that CCF forces had established three roadblocks around the town.

The Battle of Sinchang-ni At Sinchang-ni, the CCF closed up quickly and began a night attack against the 7th Cavalry Regiment. The latter's defense position was astride the road and adjacent high ground about two miles east of the town. By 10 P.M., the Chinese had engaged C Company in a heavy firefight and then overran the left-hand platoon. After a series of bugle-call signals, Chinese attacked the F Company CP. Still another enemy force overran the F Company roadblock and passed on down the road toward Sinchang-ni. By midnight, Chinese had reached the 1st Battalion CP and a close, hard fight developed there. The 1st Battalion Headquarters Company and C and D companies withdrew 1,000 yards to form a new line. The 3rd Battalion received news of the enemy penetrations and prepared a counterattack force composed of L Company with attached tanks and heavy machine guns. This force began its counterattack at 2 A.M. on 30 November. Five hours later, at 7 A.M., as daylight began to appear, the 7th Cavalry Regimental lines were reestablished. One of the twists of bad luck in this desperate night battle occurred just before midnight, when outposts thought a body of troops on the road were American, when in fact they were Chinese. Because of this error of perception, the Chinese drove a wedge between the 1st and 2nd battalions and were thus able to attack both battalions' CPs.[41]

In this night battle near Sinchang-ni, M. Sgt. Richard Beard, C Company, 70th Tank Battalion, was supporting a roadblock. His tank platoon was the object of a heavy enemy attack using mortars, automatic weapons, and small-arms fire. Sergeant Beard mounted the rear deck of his tank, fully exposed, directed the fire of his tank gun, and manned the tank deck machine gun. His fire caused heavy casualties in the attacking Chinese and forced their withdrawal. The enemy force reformed and came at his tanks again, but once more his machine-gun fire routed them. Beard later received orders to move his tank platoon to another location. When he was unable to reach one of his tank crews by radio, he dismounted and ran to the other tank through enemy fire. He delivered his instructions and ran back to his own tank. While directing his platoon's withdrawal to the new positions, enemy fire killed him.

During this night battle the Chinese overran the CP of the 77th Field Artillery Battalion. Capt. Gordon Sumner, Jr., of the artillery battalion was wounded in this action. He lay immobile in the overrun position, unnoticed by the enemy. Later, he reported that he saw two platoons of enemy horse cavalry in the initial attack, deployed perfectly. Just before midnight he watched about 300 CCF marching in platoon groups in a column of four pass near him. Subsequently, about 50 Chinese dug defensive positions in his vicinity. He said the Chinese had been very noisy in their attack, shouting and blowing whistles and bugles. While digging their defensive position, however, they were very quiet.

Despite the fact that the enemy overran two of its CPs, the 7th Cavalry did not withdraw during the night. But in the fighting on 29–30 November, the regiment had five of its tanks destroyed, 42 men killed, and 140 wounded. At Sinchang-ni alone, the 7th Cavalry Regiment had 38 of its men killed, 107 wounded, and 11 missing in action.[42]

During 30 November the 7th Cavalry withdrew to Sinchang-ni but did not remain in possession of the town very long. At 7 P.M. a KMAG officer with the ROK 6th Division reported to the 1st Cavalry Division that Chinese were in the town. During the day IX Corps ordered the 1st Cavalry Division to hold its positions at Sunchon and those near Sinchang-ni and at Songchon as long as possible to help the 2nd Division escape. That division was still many miles north of the enveloping forces of the Chinese 42nd Army and was then trying to withdraw south through Sunchon.

Early in the morning of 30 November, L Company in its counterattack against a Chinese penetration captured eight Chinese prisoners. They said the enemy attacking was the 374th Regiment of the 125th Division, 42nd Army. American intelligence had identified this unit as an elite Chinese assault force. One of the prisoners said their objective was to capture Sunchon and to let the main enemy body through in its sweep to the west behind Eighth Army. In its counterattacks and in restoring its lines at Sinchang-ni, the 7th Cavalry Regiment counted 350 enemy dead within its original perimeter and estimated that artillery had killed another 250 outside the perimeter.[43]

Chinese Analysis of Operations against ROK II Corps After the battles of the 2nd Phase Offensive in late November and early December 1950, the CCF 38th Army, comprising the 112th, 113th, and 114th divisions, published a bulletin reviewing its experiences in fighting ROK and American forces in that campaign. The CCF 38th Army had initially penetrated the ROK II Corps and rolled up the Eighth Army right flank. One or more of its divisions then swung west into the US IX Corps area and were influential in creating havoc in the US 2nd Infantry Division zone. While the 38th Army was doing this, the 42nd Army, and especially its 125th Division, was engaged in a deep enveloping move around the ROK II Corps and the US IX Corps east and south of the 38th Army.

UN forces captured an important document the 38th Army later issued. Its remarks about the 38th Army operations against the ROK II Corps are instructive. (The Chinese documents captured by UN forces during the Korean War tend to be objective and factual, reflecting the enemy's understanding of the events.) Eighth Army issued its own Combat Information Bulletin No. 13 on 13 March 1951, reproducing in it a major part of the document of the 38th Chinese People's Volunteer Army entitled "Experiences Gained in Three Battles since Entering Korea." The following excerpts relate to operations against the ROK mostly, but some refer also to other UN forces the 38th Army encountered:

> When counter-attacking, do not do so in full strength. In order to avoid confusion, light, aggressive assault teams should be organized, consisting of 10–15 men, each equipped with hand grenades, bayonets, and sub-machine guns. . . . These teams must stay under cover in suitable locations until they take up combat positions, which should not be more than 40–50 meters from the MLR [Main Line of Resistance]. . . .
>
> When the enemy advances, the artillery is not supported by infantry. We can turn this time to our advantage. On the defense, the enemy surrounds his artillery with mines, wire entanglements, and infantry support. This is hard to attack.
>
> Before entering into combat, we should try to locate enemy artillery according to our estimate of the situation and information from prisoners. Light special units should be organized. These special units break through the enemy lines until they reach the enemy artillery position by stealth. These units should be trained to act quickly, silently, bravely, and to fight fiercely. They should not reply to enemy fire, because at night both observation and communication are difficult and it is not easy to distinguish between friend and foe; the enemy fire is likely to be without effect. By advancing quickly without regard to casualties, the specialized team can accomplish its mission; to reach and destroy the enemy artillery. . . .
>
> Our experiences have taught us that daylight movement and combat are possible, provided our units are intermixed with the enemy in confusion (in the case of attack) and we have penetrated deeply inside the enemy territory. Examples: . . . In all three battles we moved in daylight without cover disguised as enemy troops and despite enemy air superiority, we suffered no losses from air attack.
>
> Prior to an attack, the assembly point must be located beyond range of the enemy's artillery in order to avoid heavy losses and, at the same time, to make air spotting of targets impossible.
>
> Surrounding ([translator's note]: double envelopment) tactics are a great threat to the enemy, and it is easy to succeed with such measures. The enemy has no great strength, their morale is low, and fighting ability is not good. Not only is their rear unguarded, a strict watch is not kept, but the enemy are careless of their guard to the front. Thus we can easily succeed in breaking through their lines and going around them. When we surrounded TOKCHON, the unit's objective was divided into two phases to cut through a gap between adjacent units, and to steal into the enemy's rear. During this movement, we frequently met enemy resistance at a unit boundary but the enemy did not dare to fight too long, and upon meeting our fierce attack, fell into disorder and re-

treated because they had not enough strength and did not fully understand our intentions. . . .

Consequently, in a meeting of engagement, our mission is to drive the enemy army away and open the route for our advance . . . however, the speed of advance should not be sacrificed for a small advantage. . . .

In our envelopment of TOKCHON, advance echelons of three units all demonstrated high morale and destroyed the enemy, opening the way for our advance. Our 338th Regiment [in 113th Division] used artillery to the best advantage in dislodging the enemy forces.

Our units can advance more quickly by attacking the enemy in rotation. When the enemy is not on the march, the advance guard squad of the advance guard platoon should attack the enemy and drive them away. After the way is cleared, another platoon of the advance guard company takes over the mission of advance guard and the unit continues to advance. If the enemy is encountered again, the process is repeated. Depending upon the situation, the attacking units retreat after the fire fight and fall in at the rear of their battalion or regiment.[44]

The ROK II Corps collapse on the right flank of Eighth Army was complete by 30 November. The ROK 7th and 8th divisions were out of the fight entirely and in rear areas of Eighth Army, trying to assemble stragglers and take in replacements to reconstitute their units. An exception was the ROK 3rd Regiment of the ROK 7th Division, which, on the extreme left flank of the corps, had moved into the zone of the US 2nd Division and had fought effectively alongside the US 38th Infantry Regiment. This ROK regiment was attached to the US 2nd Infantry Division and had fought with it during the Kunu-ri actions. The only division of the ROK II Corps still at the front and making a pretense of fighting the enemy on 30 November was the weak ROK 6th Division, which had been attached to the 1st Cavalry Division, and was now in the vicinity of Sinchang-ni. Its regiments, the 2nd, 7th, and 19th, were at very low strength, estimated by IX Corps on 29 November to number a total of no more than 3,700 men—1,200 men in the 7th Regiment, 1,500 in the 19th, and 1,000 stragglers in the 2nd. After the heavy fighting of the night of 29–30 November and during 30 November, the ROK 6th Division's strength was certainly even lower, although there is no reliable information as to the extent the ROK 6th Division engaged in the battles at Sinchang-ni.

To all intents and purposes, the ROK II Corps had ceased to exist as a combat-effective force. In five days and five nights of fighting, the CCF 38th and 42nd armies had penetrated 50 air miles south into the rear of the ROK II Corps area on the right flank of Eighth Army and 30 to 40 air miles west. At the end of the month the XIII Chinese Army Group held the imminent threat of a deep envelopment south and west around the right and center of Eighth Army, if not of the entire army.

It must be remembered that the CCF success at the army's right flank was not an isolated affair. At that same time, the CCF was attacking in great force clear across the rest of the Eighth Army front, except at its extreme western flank near the Yellow Sea.

8. Defeat of the US 25th Infantry Division

Just as the CCF 38th and 42nd armies were in position north and northeast of Tokchon on the Eighth Army right flank, waiting to strike the ROK II Corps, so was the CCF 39th Army waiting in front of the Eighth Army center. This part of the UN line was held by the US 25th Infantry Division in the Yongbyon and Ipsok area, on both sides of the south-flowing Kuryong River, which emptied into the Chongchon River about four miles northwest of Kunu-ri.

The 39th Army was no stranger to this part of Korea. Just a month earlier it had attacked and defeated the ROK 1st Division and two regiments of the US 1st Cavalry Division in the area around Unsan, on the west side of the Kuryong River, north of Kunu-ri. Subsequently it had driven down just short of the Chongchon River in the CCF 1st Phase Offensive. In the fighting around Unsan, the CCF all but destroyed the 8th Cavalry Regiment and turned back the 5th Cavalry when it tried to rescue the 8th Cavalry.

After the Unsan campaign, the CCF 66th Army, which at first stood in reserve behind the 39th Army, published a summary of battle conclusions reached as a result of their experiences in that campaign, the only one in the 1st Phase Offensive to engage large numbers of American troops. Now, as the CCF opened their 2nd Phase Offensive against the Eighth Army center, the ROK 1st Division, on line just to the left (west) of the US 25th Infantry Division, captured a copy of this document from the 66th Army on 26 November, the second day of the CCF 2nd Phase Offensive. A few of the conclusions stated in it may help explain their method of fighting and of using to advantage what they thought were fatal weaknesses of the American forces.

> Their infantry men are weak, afraid to die and haven't the courage to attack or defend. They depend on their planes, tanks, and artillery. At the same time, they are afraid of our fire power. . . .
> They must have proper terrain and good weather to transport their great amount of equipment. They can operate rapidly along good highways and flat country; not in hill country. . . .
> They specialize in day fighting. They are not familiar with night fighting or hand-to-hand combat. They are afraid of our big knives and grenades; also of our courageous attack, regular combat, and infiltration.
> If defeated, they have no orderly formation. Without the use of their mortars, they become completely lost and (as in the operation) [at Unsan, in October 1950] are killed off. They become dazed and completely demoralized.

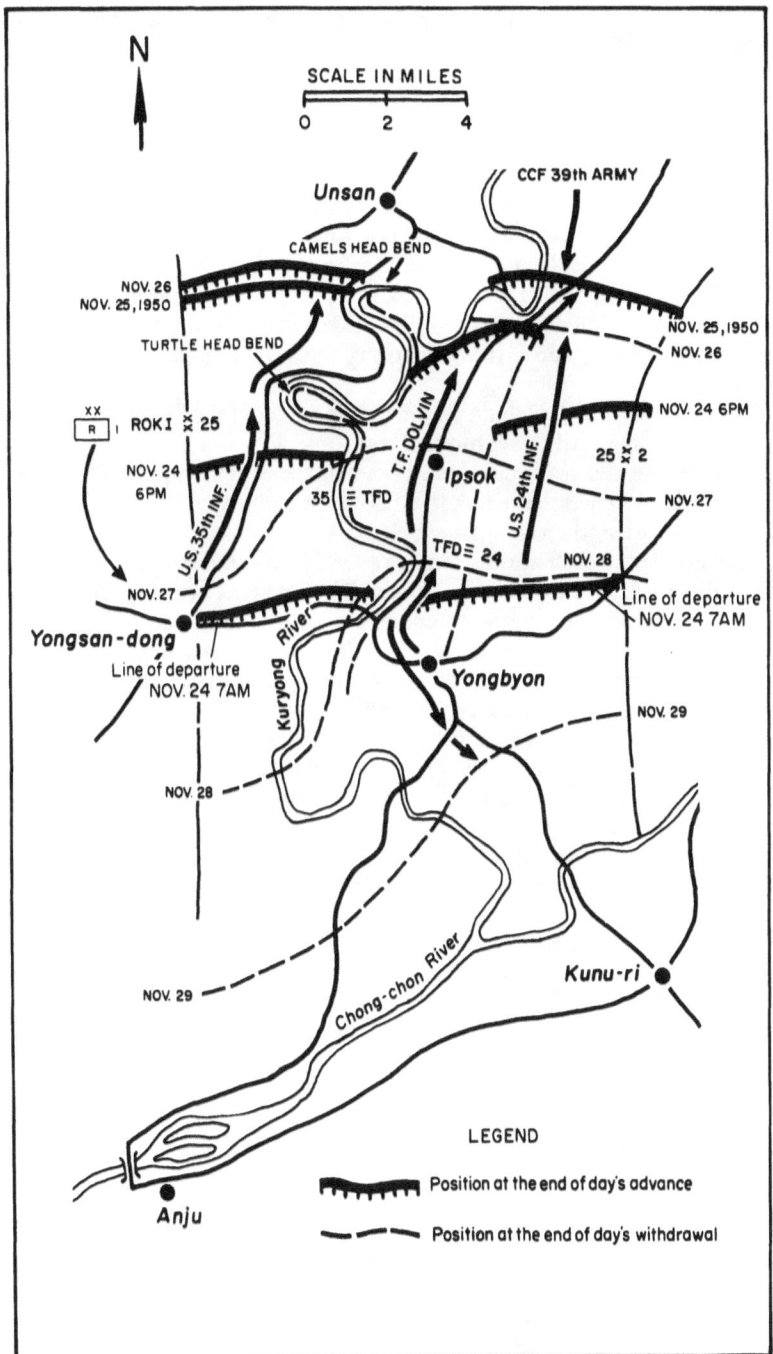

Map 5. The US 25th Infantry Division's attack and the CCF counterattack, 24–29 November 1950.

They are not good in a fight. At UNSAN, they were surrounded for several days yet they did nothing.
They are afraid when the rear is cut off. When transportation comes to a standstill, the infantry loses the will to fight. . . .
Those surrounded by us will think we are well organized and equipped with weapons. In this case, they will surrender rather than fight.[1]

An earlier chapter told of Task Force Dolvin's advance in the US 25th Division attack on 24–25 November. The task force was the specially created combat group to spearhead the division's attack north toward the Yalu. It was in the division center, with the 35th Infantry Regiment (–) on its left and the 24th Infantry Regiment on its right. Task Force Dolvin's composition has been given in an earlier chapter. It was a strong force of combined tank, infantry, and artillery.

Lt. Col. Welborn G. Dolvin, commanding officer of the 89th Medium Tank Battalion, commanded the combined task force. Dolvin's 89th Tank Battalion headquarters served as his task-force command staff. B Company, 35th Infantry, had been attached to the task force as its last component when the decision was made to strengthen its infantry element.

The task force led off north from Ipsok on 25 November in its continuation of the Eighth Army attack to the border. The Ranger Company and E Company, 27th Infantry, on the west side of the road, and B Company, 35th Infantry, on the east side advanced north under constant enemy observation and harassment. We have noted earlier that the Ranger Company had a very hard fight late in the afternoon taking Hill 205, a steep circular knob, immediately west of the road. This position was the northern-most held by Task Force Dolvin, although E Company, 27th Infantry, on Hill 207, a mile to the southwest, was almost as far. B Company, 35th Infantry, was on the opposite (east) side of the road on Hill 234, a mile and a half south of the Ranger Company. During the afternoon it had failed to advance abreast of the Ranger Company when a Chinese screening force on the ridge northward turned it back. E Company was on an elongated ridge a mile westward immediately above a big eastward bend of the Kuryong River and separated from the Ranger Company hill by a finger of land that was half a mile wide. Ascending ridges of high ground led into both hills from the north.

Task Force Dolvin had advanced on 24 and 25 November under Operation Order No. 6, dated 10:00 A.M., 23 November. An objectives overlay (1:50,000-scale map) accompanying this order located nine objectives, all high ground on both sides of the road north of Ipsok–only Objective 1 was south of Ipsok, about one and a half miles southwest of the town. Correlating the objectives overlay with a topographical map of the area gives the following hill locations and numbers for the objectives:

Objective 1–Hill 201, west of road, SW of Ipsok
Objective 2–Hill 205, west of road, NW of Ipsok
Objective 3–Hill 218, west of road
Objective 4–Hill 216, east of road, opposite Hill 218
Objective 5–Hill 200 (unnumbered on map), east of road
Objective 6–Hill 222, west of road

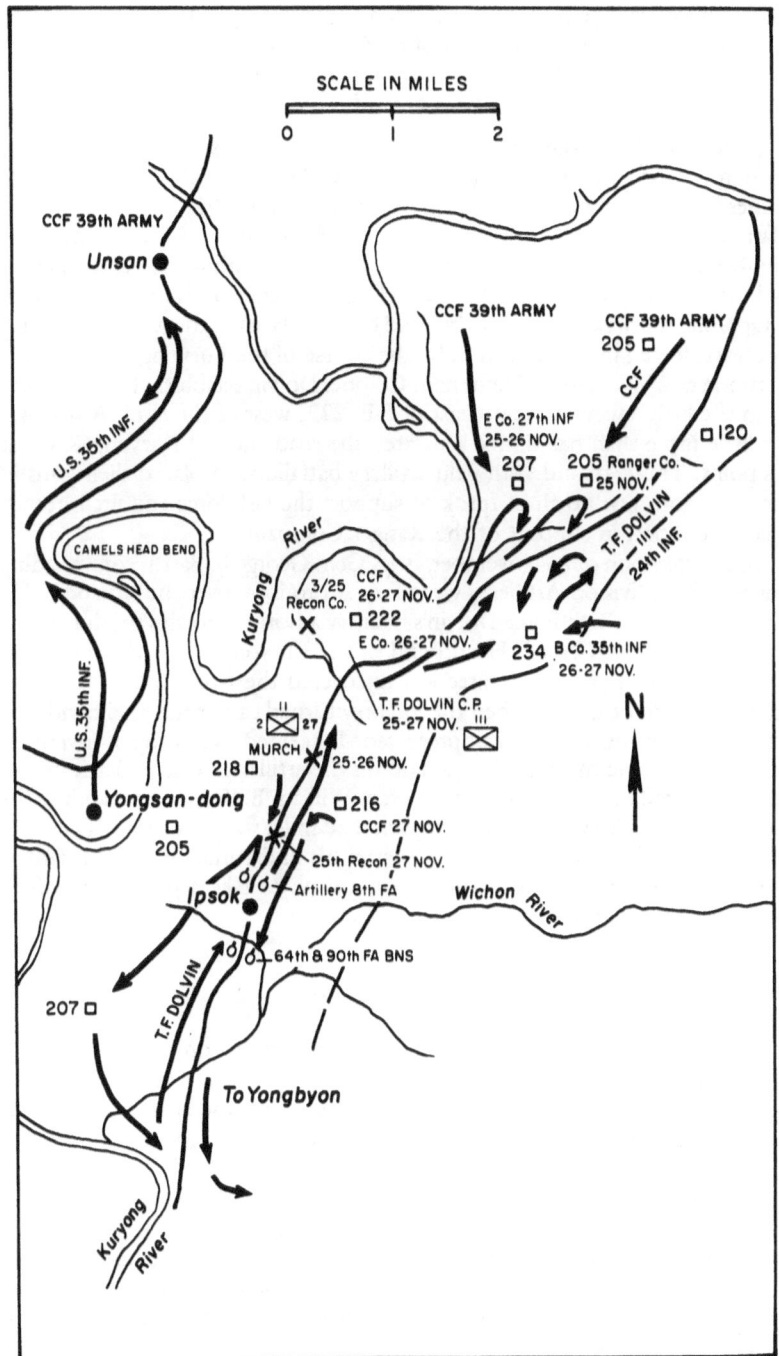

Map 6. Task Force Dolvin, 25th Infantry Division, 25–27 November 1950.

Objective 7–Hill 234, east of road
Objective 8–Hill 205, west of road
Objective 9–Hill 120–160 (unnumbered on map), astride road
Objective 10–Hill 207, west of road

At dark on 25 November Task Force Dolvin had passed over Objectives 1 through 6, occupying Objectives 7, 8, and 10. Only Objective 9 lay north of its lines. The Ranger Company was on Objective 8, Hill 205; E Company, 27th Infantry, was on Objective 10, Hill 207; and B Company, 35th Infantry, was on Objective 7, Hill 234. All these objectives were within the eight miles of road east of the Turtle's Head and Camel's Head bends of the Kuryong River.

Opposite the neck of the Camel's Head bend of the river, the road bent sharply northeast, forced in that direction by the course of the Kuryong River. In the afternoon of 25 November Lieutenant Colonel Dolvin established his task force CP in the little valley just southeast of Hill 222, west of the road. A distance of a little more than half a mile separated the road and the Kuryong River at this point. The 77th and 90th field artillery battalions emplaced their guns in firing positions just north of Ipsok to support the task force and fired heavily in late afternoon in support of the Ranger Company.

In the afternoon of 25 November, Brig. Gen. George B. Barth, commanding general, 25th Division Artillery, went forward to look over the situation. He noted that, where Task Force Dolvin's infantry advanced northward during the day and passed the Camel's Head bend of the Kuryong River, the road bent sharply east. This change of direction uncovered the two artillery battalions emplaced north of Ipsok. When the infantry turned east at the road bend, the artillery was left exposed and unprotected. It seemed like an open invitation for enemy to come through the gap and hit the artillery. General Barth immediately reported this weakness to Maj. Gen. William B. Kean, commanding the 25th Division, at his CP in Yongbyon, ten road miles south of Ipsok. The latter ordered Lt. Col. Gordon E. Murch to start his 2nd Battalion, 27th Infantry, immediately toward the scene and, upon arrival, to take a position north of the artillery for its protection.[2]

CCF Destroy Ranger Company

First Lt. Ralph Puckett commanded the 8213th Ranger Company–the Eighth Army Ranger Company, as it was then commonly called. The Ranger Company was the first of a new kind of special force unit the army was then experimenting with. Basically, it was an infantry-trained unit, with some special skills needed for special missions.

The Ranger Company went into the fight on Hill 205 in the afternoon of 25 November with two platoons, numbering in all only 85 men. Casualties in taking the hill late in the afternoon reduced the number of able-bodied Rangers left to defend the position during what threatened to be an unpredictable night. A platoon of B Company tanks, 89th Medium Tank Battalion, supported the Rangers.

Enemy probing teams arrived at the Ranger position about 10 P.M. It did not take them long to locate the defense line, and soon the hilltop was under heavy assault. The platoon of tanks and the 77th Field Artillery Battalion near Ipsok fired in support of the Rangers. The battle raged on the hill at close quarters for more than three hours. At 2:55 A.M. on 26 November, the 89th Tank Battalion headquarters section, serving as the task force's CP, received a radio message from tanks with the Ranger Company that they and the Ranger survivors had been forced off Objective 8, Hill 205. Lieutenant Puckett, the Ranger commander, was reported wounded; one of his platoon leaders, Lt. Charlie Bunn, had been killed, and the other platoon leader wounded. The Ranger survivors reverted to 25th Division reserve status at 10:30 A.M. that morning. Only 21 men came out of the Hill 205 fight.[3]

In contrast to the Ranger Company, E Company, 27th Infantry, had incredibly good luck on the night of 25–26 November, all things considered. Capt. Reginald B. Desiderio commanded E Company. He had been its commander for some time and already had left his mark on the company. His men considered him brave and a skillful and inspiring commander. He led them by example. Desiderio had quit school when 15 years old to enlist in the army. When his enlistment term ended, he finished high school. He was in the California National Guard when it was called into federal service in 1941. Desiderio became a second lieutenant in 1942. He earned his paratroop wings and served in the 70th Infantry Division in Europe in World War II, where he earned a Silver Star and two Bronze Stars. Now in Korea in 1950, he was about 30 years old, an experienced combat soldier and officer.

In moving toward Objective 10, Hill 207, a northeast-southwest ridge hard by the Kuryong River on its west side, on the afternoon of 25 November, E Company had had no trouble. As it neared its objective, some scattered long-range small-arms fire came to it from the right, probably from Hill 205, a mile away. Lt. William Otomo led a 12-man patrol ahead of E Company to Hill 207 and found it unoccupied. The main body of the company followed and occupied its objective without opposition. It seems strange that the Chinese had such a strong screening force on Hill 205, but none on Hill 207. Perhaps it was because Hill 205 was directly west of and overlooked the road leading north into their assembly areas, and they expected the Americans to be roadbound here.

Lieutenant Colonel Dolvin had ordered Captain Desiderio to post his company so that it covered all the little valley leading back to the task force CP. This may have been partly responsible for an unwise disposition of his troops at Hill 207. He placed only one of his rifle platoons, the 2nd, on top the hill. He sent Lt. J. C. Burch with his 3rd Platoon north of Hill 207 to outpost three knobs of high ground overlooking the valley northward. These knobs were about one-third of a mile beyond the main company position.

Burch put a squad on each knob. He stayed with the squad on the middle knob, on the top of which was a Korean graveyard, with stone burial slabs and burial mounds protruding upright at many places. He kept one of his machine guns with this squad; the other he sent with the squad to the knob on his right. The right-hand outpost-squad position was farther than the others from E Company's main position. By 5:30 P.M., at dark, Burch's squad was dug in on the middle outpost. Burch was unable to link his three squads by telephone, as his length of wire was too short.

Only two days past full moon and the sky clear, the landscape was flooded with a silvery half light and many shadows. This half darkness had scarcely settled when there was a sudden burst of machine-gun fire and a few rifle shots at the right-hand squad position. Then silence.

Burch and his squad soon saw two men, dragging two wounded buddies, struggling up the slope to their middle knob. The two told their story when they reached the top. They said a CCF fire-team had snuffed out the right-hand squad outpost in an instant. One of the squad members had left his foxhole to relieve himself. He was not seen again. Seconds later a group of Chinese soldiers swarmed over the crest and were man-handling the machine-gun crew before they were able to open fire. The machine-gun burst that Burch and his men heard occurred when the gunner opened fire aimlessly before he was struck down. The CCF apparently cut down most of the squad with rifle or submachine-gun fire. Private First Class Melzer, in spilling out the story to Burch, said he saw Private First Class Mays, firing his BAR, walk straight into the Chinese.

The main E Company position and the left-hand and middle outpost positions had remained quiet during this brief outburst at the right-flank outpost. But Melzer had hardly finished his story when Burch and others on the middle outpost began to hear a singsong jabbering on the slope below them. They could see nothing. Burch tried to get through on his SCR-300 radio to call for mortar and artillery fire on his forward slope, but the overcrowded channel was already full of other talk, and he could not get a connection. After about 20 minutes of this frustrating situation, the singsong jabbering in front of him stopped. The hill was quiet for a few moments. Then a shower of grenades exploded in the squad position among the gravestones. Chinese grenadiers had crawled undiscovered to within a few yards of the position.

Burch was still in the shadow of a gravestone trying to get through on his radio, but other voices cut in when he thought he was about to succeed. When the grenades came in, he looked up quickly and saw two of his attached ROK soldiers standing clear in the moonlight. They had given away his position. In the next instant a grenade exploded where they stood. Almost simultaneously a dozen Chinese came over the crest. Private First Class Navarro, the machine gunner, got off only one short burst. The enemy assault force went straight for the gun. A Chinese tommy gunner, standing directly over them, shot and killed Navarro and his assistant gunner, Private First Class Beverly. A grenade hit Sergeant Hawkins, who was lying next to Burch, shattering his leg and lifting him up. He fell back down on Burch. One of the men who had escaped from the right-hand outpost was hit again. Someone yelled, "The BAR's jammed!" All these things happened almost simultaneously.

Burch got loose from Hawkins, and now on his feet, he could see nearly 100 Chinese soldiers advancing in a semicircle formation so close he could have hit them with a rock. He knew his position was untenable and shouted the order, "Fall back on the company!" His outpost survivors took off at a run. Burch stood and covered their getaway with carbine fire. His carbine fired automatic with no malfunction, and at 15 feet he killed two Chinese who tried to rush him. Other enemy close to them hesitated when they fell. Burch turned and ran hard down the path. Not a shot followed him. The Chinese now seemed content to walk around among the gravestones on the captured outpost, yelling to the fleeing Americans, "Come on back, GI. Afraid, GI."

The 3rd Squad outpost on Burch's left had its contact with Chinese just after Burch and his survivors left the middle outpost. In the 3rd Squad outpost, Private First Class Fletcher, in his foxhole, was suddenly startled to see a man standing only 30 feet downslope in front of him. He said to Fletcher in perfect English, "I'm an FO [forward artillery observer]." Fletcher asked, "From where?" The man ignored the question and asked "How many men you got up there?" Fletcher fired but missed. The man ran into the underbrush. The Chinese then began their attack with tommy-gun and rifle fire. The crest was bare for perhaps 50 to 60 feet downslope, and visibility was good for the defenders. This made it hard for the Chinese to crawl to within good grenade range for a steep uphill throw. (The Chinese were reputed to have weak throwing arms.)

Burch, now back in the E Company position, called down fire from a 155-mm howitzer battery in front of the 3rd Squad outpost position. This fire and the determined defense by the outpost squad was so discouraging to the Chinese that they did not rush the position. When his squad ran out of ammunition, Sgt. Henry Pertree withdrew it about 2 A.M., 26 November, without losing a man. They rejoined E Company. There Captain Desiderio distributed the survivors from Burch's 3rd Platoon among the 2nd Platoon on Hill 207.[4]

Through the Valley of the Shadow of Death

While the 2nd Platoon of E Company dug in on the crest of Hill 207 and the 3rd Platoon took squad outpost positions on three different knobs of ground in front of Hill 207, the 1st Platoon rested on the rear (south) slope of the hill, interspersed among the tanks of the Assault Gun Platoon, 89th Tank Battalion, that were attached to E Company. Quiet still reigned. Captain Desiderio decided that the situation would be improved if he sent the 1st Platoon over to the Ranger hill to tie in there with the Rangers, who had both flanks open, and then to extend westward to tie in with the 3rd Platoon's right-hand squad outpost. M. Sgt. William D. Cox received Desiderio's brief instruction and led the 1st Platoon off in the shadowy darkness.

The Ranger hill, Hill 206, was about one mile almost due east of Hill 207 but northeast of its southern slope, the point from which Cox started with the 1st Platoon. A wide, open rice-paddy valley separated the two hills. At the southern end of this little valley, it was about half a mile across; farther north it narrowed to no more than a quarter of a mile. There is some indication that Desiderio did not give Cox full and explicit instructions about the distance to the Ranger hill and that the sergeant himself did not have the information. In any event, it seems that Sergeant Cox led his platoon *up* the rice-paddy valley west of Hill 205, instead of diagonally *across* it, passed on the west side of Hill 205, then crossed about half a mile of higher ground covered with scrub growth, and descended to another area of flat paddy ground, now a mile inside enemy territory and north of the Ranger hill. He was lost. Cox had led his platoon unknowingly into the enemy's midst. All this happened about the time Chinese overran the right-hand outpost of the 3rd Platoon in front of Hill 207.

The moon had been temporarily hidden by a cloud, but now as Cox led his platoon single file along a dike, its beams again illuminated the scene. The paddy system here was wider and more complex than it had been to the south. On the dike, Cox and his men heard firing in the distance, to his right rear (on the Ranger hill). Just in time, the leading scouts at the point detected a movement at the far end of the dike. They quickly dropped down along the shadow side of the high dike, and all others behind them slid down quickly. There now emerged from a darkened stretch of terrain two columns of Chinese soldiers, one on either side of the paddy ground. They were talking excitedly and dog-trotting south. The 1st Platoon literally held its breath. The Chinese hurrying south, not expecting any hostile troops in this area, passed the dike without noticing the American platoon hugging the darkened side of it.

Cox knew he faced the imminent appearance of more Chinese and that he must get out of the open paddy land. The nearest high ground was to the north—toward the enemy assembly areas. But Sfc. Maynard K. Bryers thought they should head quickly for it and get to the shadow at its base. Cox agreed. They had barely reached the base of the hill when another Chinese column rounded the hill and hurried southward.

Cox decided he had to get in touch with Desiderio by radio if possible and get instructions from him. When his radio call was answered, Cox described the situation, the type of ground he had traveled, and the nature of the topography around him. On consulting his map, Desiderio correctly estimated where Cox was and told him that he should go straight south 2,000 yards and he would come to a big ridge—the Ranger hill—and that he should join the Rangers.

Cox followed instructions but proceeded cautiously. He finally came to the end of the valley they had entered earlier and started uphill. This, they thought, must be the Ranger hill. They could hear sounds of gunfire and explosions toward the top. Then, several rounds of 155-mm artillery shells landed near them. No one was hurt, but they at once recognized this fire as coming from their own batteries near Ipsok and fired on the reverse slope of the hill to help the Ranger Company by interdicting enemy reinforcements. Cox and his men knew they could not take the risk of climbing the hill through this fire, and they decided to wait at the bottom until it stopped. They sat down and waited.

Before the fire stopped, Lieutenant Puckett and three other Rangers with him came off the hill and by chance encountered the 1st Platoon where it waited. Puckett was bleeding from two wounds, one in the arm and the other in the chest. Puckett thought he and his three companions were the only survivors. But others escaped individually or in groups of twos and threes in the same manner he had and eventually gained Task Force Dolvin's lines during the morning. In all, out of the 83 who had entered the fight for the hill the previous afternoon, only 21 or 22 survivors, many of them wounded, arrived at Dolvin's positions.

Now, with the situation changed and there no longer being a Ranger Company for him to join, Sergeant Cox once more got Captain Desiderio on the radio, explained the situation to him, and asked for instructions. Desiderio told Cox to rejoin E Company. This might be hard to do with CCF all around. In addition to capturing the Ranger hill, other CCF had overrun two of E Company's outposts and had the other one under attack. Cox realized the hazards facing him. He and Sergeant Bryers went from man to man, whispering instructions to each about what they were going to do and ordering each not to talk and not to fire a weapon under any circumstance unless ordered to do so. They would march single file, closed up, and holding hands in the line if necessary when they came to dark spots; they would try to avoid open and moonlit areas and would skulk from one bush to another. If they saw or encountered Chinese, they would freeze in their tracks and do nothing unless ordered. It was a throwback to early American frontier Indian warfare.

They started. Discipline was so good that they passed Chinese parties but were not themselves discovered. Cox finally led his men into E Company lines at 4:30 A.M., 26 November. In their entire adventure not a man had been lost. That their leadership and their own understanding and discipline had been good has to be assumed. In the entire adventure, not a shot was fired at them, nor did they fire at an enemy.[5]

There was no further action against E Company during the remainder of the night. Before dawn the Chinese soldiers withdrew from Hill 207 and from in front of E Company. Across the valley that separated them from the Chinese-held Ranger Hill 205, E Company could see artillery fire and white phosphorus shells bursting on Hill 205. While darkness lasted, the hill seemed to glow. Knowing that the Rangers no longer were on the hill, Lieutenant Colonel Dolvin had ordered the artillery to saturate it with shellfire so that no Chinese could stay alive on it. After daylight, aircraft came over in several waves, dropping bombs and napalm canisters, firing rockets, and strafing the hill. The Chinese who survived this ordeal fled northward to the next ridgeline. Ranger Hill 205 was a shell-pocked no-man's-land.

Elsewhere, B Company, 35th Infantry, reached Objective 7, Hill 234, on the east side of the road, a little more than a mile south of the Ranger Company. A platoon of tanks from B Company, 89th Tank Battalion, supported it. B Company continued on north and tried to take the next ridgeline, also numbered 234 on the map and almost directly opposite the Ranger hill. At 10:15 A.M., however, it reported to Lieutenant Colonel Dolvin that it was unable to take the position. He authorized it to withdraw to Objective 7. It established a defensive line there for the night.

Everything was quiet at B Company's position on Hill 234 until a figure approached the forward platoon and asked in fluent English how many men occupied the position. The men in the outpost gave the number. The figure disappeared. The man was a Chinese soldier. Soon after this incident a Chinese assault force attacked and overran the platoon. The remnants of the platoon escaped to another position. The B Company commander now committed his reserve platoon, which joined the others engaged with the enemy on the perimeter. The fight continued there until 3:30 A.M. on 26 November. Then the Chinese withdrew briefly. Twenty minutes later, whistles and calls in front of B Company preceded a renewal of the attack. Some Chinese got close enough to tanks with B Company to throw grenades at them. Toward dawn the Chinese withdrew.[6]

It seemed that Chinese groups had infiltrated all the way to Ipsok in the rear of all infantry elements. The 77th Field Artillery Battalion, firing from its emplacements just north of Ipsok, came under attack. Chinese overran one battery of guns and captured one of them. Several times CCF assault teams charged down the road toward two tanks guarding the artillery, throwing grenades at them, but the coaxial machine guns mounted on the tank decks cut them down. This CCF attack also ceased at dawn.

That night is remembered by those who lived through it as being exceedingly cold. One officer in Task Force Dolvin said, "It hurt to breathe." Second Lt. Robert K. Sawyer, commander of the 3rd Platoon, 25th Reconnaissance Company, was covering a ford over the Kuryong River behind E Company and guarding a section of the MSR in that vicinity. He said years later:

> My outstanding memory of this night is of the intense cold and how it affected us, men and machines alike. We humans huddled in our overcoats and fur-lined caps, reluctant to do anything except try to keep warm. The frigid air burned as we drew it into our lungs. I recall vividly my indecision about getting into my sleeping bag. I was tired and cold, and wanted to sleep, but I also thought about stories I had heard of G.I.'s being bayoneted in their sleeping bags. Sleep finally won out, however, and I curled up at last alongside one of my tanks. As for the vehicles, the guards were instructed to turn them over periodically during the night, and did so; but we had a real job getting everything moving the next morning.[7]

Lieutenant Colonel Murch Brings the 2nd Battalion, 27th Infantry, to Ipsok

After his visit to Task Force Dolvin on the afternoon of 25 November, Brig. Gen. George Barth reported to Major General Kean, commander of the 25th Division, that the two battalions of supporting artillery, emplaced just north of Ipsok, were without adequate protection and vulnerable to enemy attack. This information set in motion consideration of the need to reinforce the task force. When General Kean received reports of the hard fight the Ranger Company had in taking Hill 205 and afternoon aerial reports of large enemy troop movements north of the task force, he decided to send a battalion of infantry to the area without further delay.

At 7 P.M., the 25th Division sent an alert to Lt. Col. Gordon E. Murch, commander of the 2nd Battalion, 27th Infantry, which already was in an assembly area, having prepared to move on order to join Task Force Dolvin. Two and a half hours later his battalion, minus E Company (already with the task force), loaded on trucks and was ready to move. Ipsok was 11 road miles north of his assembly area. Murch's orders were to move the 2nd Battalion to Ipsok by truck, detruck there, and move the battalion on foot north of Ipsok. The main mission of Murch's battalion was to protect the artillery, trains, and supply and ammunition dumps that had been established at Ipsok during the day and to be a combat reserve for Task Force Dolvin.

Murch reached Ipsok without incident, detrucked his two rifle companies, F and G, and marched about two miles north along the MSR to an assembly area. The 2nd Battalion stopped there, more than a mile north of the 77th and 90th field artillery battalions and two miles north of the trains and ammunition supply near Ipsok, and about a mile south of Task Force Dolvin's CP. Murch was about four miles south of and behind the front-line positions of the Ranger Company and E Company, 27th Infantry.

Murch's battalion closed into its assembly area an hour before midnight, 25 November. It spent several hours digging in on a perimeter covering both sides of the road, with the bulk of its strength west of it. Murch believed the main enemy threat might come from the northwest, from the Kuryong River valley, which constituted an open avenue of approach. He outposted the perimeter with troops from his headquarters. On Lieutenant Colonel Dolvin's request, he sent a platoon from F Company to tie in on the northwest with Dolvin's headquarters perimeter. A platoon of tanks from C Company, 89th Tank Battalion, joined Murch's battalion. Murch sent two tanks to both the western and eastern ends of his perimeter to strengthen them. The night passed peacefully. His men heard no sounds of the heavy battle to the north of them at the Ranger and E Company hills.[8]

The daylight hours of 26 November did not project the prospect of moonlight for that night on the Chongchon. One who was there wrote of that day, "Skies which had been brilliant with moon and stars by night and sun by day, became leaden gray above the everlasting dust. There was a great white halo enclosing the fiery orange ball of the sun, and the heavy sky grew steadily more sullen all the 26th."[9]

As the skies darkened, so did the perception of Eighth Army as to just what was happening. The fog of war settled over the Chongchon River front on 26 November. There was much reason to wonder what was "on the other side of the hill." But Eighth Army still assessed the situation rather optimistically. Its appraisal was that, "except for vague situation on the east flank, the enemy reaction to EUSAK attack had been one of active defense with local counterattacks in strength. This last was believed the likely course of action."[10]

After daylight on 26 November, Lieutenant Colonel Dolvin learned that his task force was out ahead of adjacent friendly units–the 1st Battalion, 24th Infantry, on his right, and the 35th Infantry on his left across the Kuryong River. Where B Company of the 24th Infantry was supposed to be, Dolvin could see CCF troops occupying a hill to his right rear. What had happened to B Company, 24th Infantry, was a mystery to Dolvin and the 25th Division.

Nevertheless, Dolvin sent a message to the 25th Division G-3 at 7:45 A.M. that he wanted air strikes on Hill 205, the hill formerly held by the Ranger Company, and that then he would counterattack it. Presumably he intended to use B Company, 35th Infantry, from Hill 234, for this purpose. The G-3 told him not to attack the Ranger hill until General Kean approved it. But massive air, artillery, and tank fire was placed on the hill. An artillery forward observer reported large numbers of enemy were killed on the hill's rear slope as they tried to withdraw northward. After this saturation of the Ranger hill with shellfire, rockets, and napalm, Lieutenant Dickson, a liaison pilot, at 9 A.M. reported an estimated enemy battalion was digging in on Task Force Dolvin's Objective 9. Objective 9 was a ridgeline straddling the road a mile northeast of the Ranger hill. Artillery fire was now directed at it.

At 9:45 A.M., General Kean attached the 1st Battalion, 24th Infantry, to Task Force Dolvin and directed Dolvin to move B Company, 24th Infantry, up on line between A and C companies of the battalion and to secure a line from the 25th Reconnaissance Company at the Kuryong River to A Company's position on the right. The trouble with executing this order was that Task Force

Dolvin did not know where B Company, 24th Infantry, was. At the same time he gave this order, General Kean directed Lieutenant Colonel Dolvin not to resume an attack but to await further developments.[11]

In the meantime, the Ranger Company, all but destroyed, was withdrawn from attachment to Task Force Dolvin and at noon, 26 November, placed in 25th Division reserve. On the task force's extreme left, C Company, 65th Engineer Combat Battalion, relieved the 1st Platoon, 25th Reconnaissance Company, and the 3rd Platoon of the Reconnaissance Company shifted its position slightly to occupy a valley just east of the Kuryong River and south of Hill 222. Just west of this position the MSR turned due east and then bent northeast. Task Force Dolvin's CP was in this valley south of Hill 222 and adjacent to the road where it bent sharply eastward.[12]

During the morning of 26 November Lieutenant Colonel Dolvin received a message from the 25th Division G-3 that Brig. Gen. Vennard Wilson, assistant division commander, was on his way to assume command of the task force. General Wilson arrived at task-force headquarters at noon and assumed command 20 minutes later, at 12:20 P.M. The task force now officially became known as Task Force Wilson. General Wilson made Maj. Leon F. Morand, Jr., S-3 of the 89th Tank Battalion and of Task Force Dolvin, his own S-3, and Major Goolsby thereupon assumed the S-3 duties of the 89th Medium Tank Battalion.[13] In effect, Lieutenant Colonel Dolvin's staff automatically became the staff for General Wilson.

After his arrival and assumption of command, General Wilson ordered the task force to withdraw from Objectives 8 and 10 and to form a new defensive line based on Objectives 7 and 6, Hill 234 held by B Company, 35th Infantry, and an eastward knob of Hill 222. This knob was separated from Hill 222 proper by a shallow saddle. E Company, 27th Infantry, did not leave Hill 207 until just before dusk, and then it filtered back to position just behind Objective 6 and the task force CP. As it left Hill 207, it heard noises immediately in front of its old position – apparently CCF moving or deploying to the north of it.

Behind the task force CP, E Company was allowed to go into a rest bivouac for a good night's sleep, badly needed. It did not dig in there, as no one had any thought it would be engaged during the night. The men ate a hot meal, posted guards, and got into their bedrolls.[14]

At dark on 26 November, C Company of the 65th Engineer Combat Battalion was on the left of the task-force line at the Kuryong River, with the 3rd Platoon, 25th Reconnaissance Company, behind it. B Company, 35th Infantry, held the right end of the line on its Hill 234 east of the road. Murch's 2nd Battalion was behind this line, about half a mile from the task force CP and Captain Desiderio's E Company's bivouac. On General Wilson's order, Lieutenant Colonel Murch sent F Company, minus one platoon, to the left flank of the line to strengthen the security of the task force CP from that direction. Murch completed this move just before dark.

It should be mentioned that, during the afternoon, another change took place in the support forces accompanying Task Force Dolvin. General Kean, on Eighth Army order, withdrew the 77th and 82nd field artillery battalions from attachment to the 25th Division and sent them posthaste to rejoin the 1st Cavalry Division, which was about to be committed from Eighth Army reserve to the rear of the ROK II Corps front in an attempt to check the CCF breakthrough there. The 8th Field Artillery Battalion was hurried forward to Ipsok to replace the 77th Field Artillery Battalion. It arrived after dark on 26 November, and went into firing position at the northwest edge of Ipsok, behind Murch's 2nd Battalion.

The night of 26–27 November was a bad one for Task Force Wilson. The CCF were everywhere, all in motion, and everywhere, they launched crushing attacks. By dawn the task force had been decimated and was reeling. B Company was virtually destroyed; E Company barely escaped a similar fate; C Company, 65th Combat Engineers, was overrun; the task force's CP was attacked and had casualties; Murch's 2nd Battalion had been heavily engaged on the western part of its perimeter, and it had to send reinforcements to the task force CP to prevent the CCF from overrunning it; the Medical Company detachment and some of the trains of the 2nd Battalion were ambushed south of the battalion perimeter and destroyed; and the 8th Field Artillery Battalion on the northern and western edges of Ipsok came under persistent enemy close attack. Only the presence of Lieutenant Colonel Murch's 2nd Battalion, 27th Infantry, behind E Company and the task force CP and north of the 8th Field Artillery Battalion, saved Task Force Wilson from destruction during the night. General Kean never made a wiser decision than when he acted on General Barth's recommendation that he send a reinforcing infantry force to Dolvin on the evening of 25 November.

It seemed that the CCF came at all positions from all directions. At least once a column of Chinese marched right past part of F Company in its perimeter position without paying the slightest heed to it, apparently being on an assigned mission to go straight for Hill 216 on the east side of the road, get behind the task force there, and cut the road at that point.

In the midst of all this CCF movement and battle on all sides, 1st Lt. Robert K. Sawyer and his 3rd Platoon, 25th Reconnaissance Company, held a screening position on the east side of the Kuryong River south of Hill 222 and C Company, 65th Engineer Combat Battalion. Task Force Wilson's headquarters was located a mile eastward in the same small valley near the MSR. During the night, Sawyer lost radio contact with the reconnaissance company. He had put two machine guns on the point of a ridge north of the valley and some outposts where they should have been able to see and hear anything taking place near the 3rd Platoon's area. The platoon's tanks and vehicles were dispersed in the valley below the ridge and near the Kuryong River. The usual guards were posted. Sawyer sensed that everyone seemed on edge, as if they expected something to happen. Thus far, the platoon had not been engaged in any action with the Chinese. The outpost personnel were nervous and kept reporting strange noises. As night wore on, members could hear small arms firing, particularly to the south, and on occasion they saw brilliant tracers in the sky.

Sometime during the night Sawyer dozed off. He was shaken awake by someone who whispered, "Listen!" Sawyer struggled out of his sleeping bag and then heard distinctly the sound of troops moving from south to north across the valley floor behind his position. Later he said, "The padding of feet and soft clanking of equipment were unmistakeable. How I knew it was Chinese and not American feet, I cannot now say, but perhaps it was because of the rhythm.

Anyway, though I could see nothing in the darkness [it was an overcast night, with only an occasional opening of moonlight], I estimated that at least a company was passing behind us."[15] After a little while the sound died away. Sometime later, about daylight, Sawyer heard heavy small-arms fire and mortars behind his position toward the Ipsok road. He and his platoon luckily had occupied a small island of immunity in a hostile sea during the night.

General Wilson and Lieutenant Colonel Dolvin had been concerned for the past two days that the task force's right flank to the east was entirely open, because the 1st Battalion, 24th Infantry, had not come up there on the regimental boundary. It appeared to them that, unless the 1st Battalion, 24th Infantry, came abreast and formed a line with Task Force Wilson, the CCF could easily pass around its right flank and cut off its rear, as well as choose avenues of attack from that flank. Dolvin talked about this concern with Col. John Corley, the 24th Infantry Regiment commander.

Corley, one of the most decorated battalion commanders in World War II in the North African and European theaters, was not one to allow his regiment to loiter in its tasks if he could help it. Under his urging, the 1st Battalion did come abreast of Task Force Wilson the night of 26–27 November. But it did more—it passed Dolvin's line, apparently without knowing it and without establishing communications, and continued on north into Chinese territory. It was now out front and lost. With luck it might survive if the Chinese did not bump into it.

By this time, the Chinese assault forces in the area had located all the task force's positions and they concentrated their efforts on destroying Task Force Wilson. First, they attacked the front positions—B Company, 35th Infantry, on the right; C Company, 65th Combat Engineer Battalion, in the center; and part of the 25th Reconnaissance Company on the left. But soon they spread their attack to all parts of the task force, even to the artillery in its rear.

When Captain Desiderio and his E Company, 27th Infantry, were ordered to withdraw from Hill 207 in the afternoon of 26 November and to take a reserve position behind the headquarters of Task Force Dolvin, neither they nor the task force headquarters expected the company would have any action that night. It was supposed to be a period of rest and sleep for them. Half an hour after midnight, Lieutenant Colonel Dolvin telephoned Desiderio to have his E Company at the base of the hill just in front of headquarters in 15 minutes. Desiderio woke his men and hurriedly loaded them on five tanks of Headquarters Company, 89th Tank Battalion. They rolled into the CP on time. Dolvin told Desiderio to put his men on the small hill directly north of the CP. There was no enemy action there at the time, nor were enemy known to be on it or Hill 222 west of it near the Kuryong River. But there was the sound of battle to the front and rear.

The hill Desiderio had to climb merits a brief description, in view of what happened there that night. It was about 185 meters high, and on the east side a small stream separated its slopes from the MSR. A shallow saddle connected it on the west with Hill 222. In effect, the unnumbered hill was an eastern knob of Hill 222. The knob and the Hill 222 crest had been part of Objective 6 in the original Task Force Dolvin operation plan, and in the advance north past this objective on 25 November, these hills had been free of enemy. The entire

Hill 222 area extended more than a mile from the Kuryong River on the west to the MSR on the east, and it was generally more than half a mile wide in a north-south direction.

At the CP, Lieutenant Colonel Dolvin told Captain Desiderio to put his company on the knob about 500 feet to the north of where they stood. Desiderio walked with the company to the foot of the hill. The 1st Platoon, in the lead, had hardly taken five steps up the slope when enemy fire struck around the point. The men hit the ground. Enemy fire came from the west—from Hill 222. In a volley of fire and counterfire with the Chinese on Hill 222, Sergeant Cox got the 1st Platoon to the top of the hill, followed soon by Lieutenant Burch and his 3rd Platoon. Then Sergeant Lefler came up with the 2nd Platoon. Captain Desiderio directed them in digging in, facing generally west toward the known enemy position. Lt. Dell G. Evans brought up his mortars and the Weapons Company. After spotting the enemy position by their tracer bullets, he led his mortar men down the north slope of the hill into a depressed area and set up his mortars there. He then began lobbing mortar shells into the Hill 222 positions.

Meanwhile, both sides swept each other's positions with automatic-weapons fire. At their closest points, at the saddle, the Chinese and E Company were only about 200 yards apart. Desiderio quickly decided that he would need the help of tanks on top to hold the hill. The hill had an easy slope from the south, and the tanks should have no trouble in climbing up. Desiderio hurried down the hill to the task force CP and told Dolvin he needed the five tanks on top. Artillery support from the 8th Field Artillery Battalion was not available for E Company because the artillery themselves were under attack in the rear at the edge of Ipsok. Dolvin said to take the tanks.

Desiderio led the tanks up the hill. During Desiderio's absence, Evans's 60-mm and 81-mm mortars had been trying to saturate the Chinese position, the eastern slope of Hill 222 and the saddle, with mortar shells, including white phosphorus. The saddle was bare of tree growth but covered by dry grass. The white phosphorus shells had set this area on fire. The fire spread rapidly. Suddenly about 100 Chinese soldiers burst from their positions and ran rapidly toward the fire at the saddle. They stomped on the fire with their feet. But they paused only momentarily for this work before they divided into two parts. One group ran rapidly across the saddle toward E Company. This force, in full light of the burning grass fire, was cut down by 1st Platoon machine-gun and BAR fire. The other part ran into the valley north of the saddle and began to work its way around to the right flank of E Company.

At this juncture, the first two tanks reached the top of the knob and took under fire the Chinese in the flat ground below Burch's 3rd Platoon position. These tanks in the center of Burch's part of the line drew fire. Because of this, Burch soon had eight casualties, four of them ROK soldiers. Chinese bugles sounded at both ends of the line, and E Company men could see Chinese soldiers crawling toward them. They could also see many Chinese bodies in the saddle and in the valley to the right. The tanks spaced themselves about 25 yards apart, with riflemen between them. They fired their cannons at Hill 222, and their machine guns swept the intervening ground. The tank fire effectively silenced the enemy machine-gun and small-arms fire but did not find the Chinese mortars. These had found the range of E Company's position. They fired in salvos of four. Neither could Lieutenant Evans's mortars locate the enemy weapons. In this phase of the battle, E Company had about 14 casualties, most of them from enemy mortar fire. These same enemy mortars were firing salvos into Task Force Dolvin's CP. Also, enemy soldiers had infiltrated to within small-arms fire of it. In two hours of battle the Chinese on Hill 222 had not succeeded in reaching E Company's position, largely because of the great volume of tank fire against them—the tanks up to this time had fired 45 boxes of .50-caliber machine-gun ammunition.

Chinese bugles sounded recall. There followed a lull in the fighting, as the enemy regrouped and decided what to do next. Except where the burning grass fires had lighted up the landscape, the night was dark, with an overcast sky. During the lull, clerks and cooks from headquarters carried a resupply of ammunition to E Company, and the mortars received 400 rounds to replenish their exhausted supply.

The lull lasted an hour or more. Then before dawn, the Chinese were ready for another try. This time their tactic changed. At their main position on Hill 222, they had added two more machine guns to the four that had fired from there earlier. And under cover of darkness a line of grenadiers had crawled unseen to within 15 yards of E Company foxholes. Suddenly the six machine guns on Hill 222, perfectly trained on the E Company position, opened up with concentrated fire. At the same time, the grenadiers hurled their stick grenades into E Company and then jumped to their feet and rushed the foxholes. Some of these leading grenadiers fell from their own machine-gun fire from Hill 222, hit in the back as they ran toward the American holes.

Behind the grenadiers came another line of Chinese, armed with rifles and submachine guns. A bazooka team got into the perimeter and made for a tank. They hit the tread of one tank with their first round, disabling it. This team fell from BAR fire. Another bazooka team started for the tank. Rifle fire cut it down. But a number of grenades landed on the tanks' hulls, and their explosions caused many American casualties among soldiers grouped near the tanks. Enemy mortar fire also came in on the tanks. The Chinese obviously had decided that the tanks were the primary obstacle to their success. A mortar fragment wounded Captain Desiderio in the shoulder (he had taken his place near one of the tanks), and the same round wounded four other men in the vicinity, including Capt. J. C. Bayliss, E Company executive officer. One group of about a dozen Chinese got inside the perimeter; seven of them reached the tanks in a rush and clambered up the hulls. Sergeant Cox and his 1st Platoon were near this penetration. They left their positions on the line temporarily and ran for the tanks. At a range of only a few feet, they shot the seven Chinese soldiers off the tanks.

The battle was now at close quarters everywhere in the E Company perimeter, and many Americans fell dead or wounded. In the 1st Platoon position on the left, Sergeant Bryers with his machine gun and a squad of riflemen had stopped the enemy in the saddle. In the center of the line, the grenade battle continued in Burch's 3rd Platoon. Desiderio sensed that his men were nearing exhaustion. He went from one group to another, despite increasing weakness caused by his wound. Survivors say that he went around the hilltop yelling as loudly as he could, "Hold until daylight and you have it made."

Heavy mist had started to settle just before dawn. It was particularly bothersome at the far right of the line in the 2nd Platoon area, at the eastern tip of the hill, where thick brush covered the slope. An enemy force had found this weak point. A Chinese fire team had crawled close to the American machine gun, and suddenly they rushed the position. These Chinese were in the platoon position before Sergeant Lefler and his men knew what was happening. The Chinese grenaded the machine gun. Corporal Savage tried to fire his BAR into the Chinese. The gun quit. Savage fell dead a moment later, and an enemy burp gunner killed Sergeant Delotaba a few feet away. In a few moments 12 men of the 2nd Platoon were casualties. Lefler saw that his platoon in a matter of minutes would be completely wiped out. He yelled, "Follow me to the back slope!" Those still on their feet did so.

Meanwhile, the E Company mortar men had fired the last of their ammunition, and they now ran up the slope to the tanks. From there they could see and hear that the 2nd Platoon at the right had cracked and that part of the line was gone. Some of them started to yell, "The line's gone—get the hell out!" Two of the tank crews started their tanks off the hill. Desiderio and Lieutenant Otomo ran to the tanks, pounded on their hulls, and somehow got them stopped and back on the line.

The enemy were pressing in close, having seen momentary panic in the center among the tanks, and the right-flank position overrun. Desiderio realized the crisis was at hand. He told Otomo to take one side of the remaining portion of the line and he would take the other side. He had barely uttered these words when a Chinese burp gunner close to Desiderio ripped open his side up to the heart area. Desiderio pitched forward, dead within seconds. A short distance from Desiderio, Otomo was hit by a grenade at nearly the same time and badly wounded.

The Chinese were on the point of wiping out E Company. At this moment Sergeant Lefler and his remaining men of the 2nd Platoon reappeared on the hill. They had dropped only part way down the slope. Lefler reorganized the men with him, saw to it that each had grenades, and then told them they were going back up and retake their positions. They did just that. As he and his men neared the crest, they started throwing grenades. In one of the strange quirks of battle, the Chinese there broke and ran for the underbrush. It was nearly dawn, and the Chinese had apparently already decided they would call off the fight for the present. E Company survivors held the hill. But 60 of its men became casualties during the fight, eight killed. They had burned up all nine of their BARs, except one that had been knocked out by enemy bullets. The men of E Company mourned the loss of their dead commander. Desiderio received the Congressional Medal of Honor, Posthumously, for his staunch leadership that night.[16]

The Chinese force on Hill 222, at the same time it engaged E Company, also threatened to overrun the Task Force Wilson CP. It was only half a mile from the crest of Hill 222. Enemy snipers and infiltrators got into a ravine only 20 to 30 yards from the CP. One of their bullets killed Maj. Leon F. Morand,

Jr., the task force executive officer. The situation at the CP was so precarious by 1 A.M. 27 November that General Wilson telephoned Lieutenant Colonel Murch and asked him to send another platoon to restore the position. Murch sent a second platoon from his F Company to the CP, and after a fight with the Chinese there, the platoon drove them away.

Murch's battalion by this time was itself under fire. The enemy had launched a coordinated attack almost everywhere just after midnight against Task Force Wilson.

C Company, 65th Engineer Combat Battalion, on the defense line that night lost heavily. It was somewhere on Hill 222 or one of its finger ridges. It is possible that the unexpected midnight appearance of the strong Chinese force on Hill 222 that later engaged Desiderio's E Company, 27th Infantry, made a successful surprise attack that overran the Engineer Company and occupied its position. We do know that C Company, 65th Engineers, was overrun that night and that Capt. Anthony Pecoraro, its commander, and one of his platoon leaders were both missing in action, together with 34 enlisted men and 10 attached Korean soldiers. Only one of the missing later returned to the task force. But the ground where the Chinese overran the Engineers was never recovered, so it was not possible to know how many had been killed or severely wounded. An aerial report said that a body of men in the C Company Engineers area was surrounded by Chinese and that some of them were captured, but the observer could not identify the men as the Engineer Company. First Lt. Robert K. Sawyer, commanding the 3rd Platoon, 25th Reconnaissance Company, said that, when he arrived at Lieutenant Colonel Murch's perimeter on the morning of 27 November, he saw some C Company Engineers, without weapons, scrambling along ditches to the safety of the perimeter.[17]

On the evening of 26 November, B Company, 35th Infantry, held Hill 234 with 203 men in the infantry company, including attached ROKs; a section of mortars from the Weapons Company, 35th Infantry; and a platoon of tanks from the 89th Tank Battalion. Hill 234, Objective 7, was now the most advanced of the task-force positions. It was a large hill mass east of the MSR and nearly opposite Hill 222. There were good avenues of approach to its crest from nearly all sides, which constituted a weakness if exploited by the enemy. The Chinese did exploit this weakness and used all approaches to the top and B Company's positions during the night. Beginning about 15 minutes after midnight, the Chinese kept up an unrelenting assault on B Company, despite heavy casualties. By morning B Company had only 26 able-bodied men left out of more than 200, but its remnant still held the hill.

During the night, Chinese assault teams, including suicide groups, knocked out two of the defending tanks by bazooka and satchel charges. Young suicide attackers ran to the tanks and held satchel charges against them and were themselves blown to fragments in the explosions. Details of the B Company fight were not recorded in the official records or in personal recollections and interviews afterward, but its stand on the task-force right front after midnight of 26–27 November was a sacrificial one and helped save the entire force from being overwhelmed that night.[18]

Murch's 2nd Battalion, 27th Infantry—the Linchpin

Lt. Col. Gordon E. Murch's 2nd Battalion held the key to the survival of Task Force Wilson on the night of 26–27 November. Its G Company was on a hill south of the task force CP, facing west toward the Kuryong River; its F Company faced north toward the front line and the main battle position and was behind (south of) the task force CP. Already F Company had been weakened by sending a platoon to strengthen the task force CP toward the northwest—toward Hill 222. Another platoon after midnight would have to go to the rescue of the CP itself when Chinese almost overran it. Thus, F Company had only one rifle platoon on line during the critical hours after midnight, reinforced by nearly a platoon from G Company. In the afternoon Murch had sent a patrol forward of his position to Sangcha-dong on the Kuryong River to his left, just south of Hill 222. There was evidence that many enemy had been in that area.

G Company held a horseshoe-shaped hill south of F Company, the toe of the horseshoe pointing southwest. This put the open base of the horseshoe toward the northeast. The west side of the horseshoe faced the Kuryong River; the east side faced the MSR. Lieutenant Colonel Murch's CP was in a small valley north of the open base of the horseshoe. A saddle in the horseshoe-shaped hill mass made two low-lying hills for the F and G Company positions respectively. Two tanks and two machine guns were placed in low ground of the open end of the horseshoe, and they together with three 60-mm mortars guarded that approach at the northeast from the MSR.

Capt. Jack Michaely commanded G Company. He had 116 men, including 14 ROKs. The 1st Platoon of G Company was on the horseshoe prong on the northwest side of the company position. It had four machine guns sighted to fire north. Each platoon had a 57-mm recoilless rifle. Michaely's G Company had to send some of its squads to F Company to strengthen it when the latter sent two platoons to help save the task force CP.

The Chinese started their attack against Murch's 2nd Battalion about 1 A.M., the morning of 27 November. They first hit F Company. A group of Chinese succeeded in getting close enough, undiscovered, to grab a four-man fire team. Three of them wrenched free and ran toward G Company. The CCF held the fourth man and made him carry ammunition up the hills for them the rest of the night. He eventually escaped near daylight. After grabbing the F Company fire team, the Chinese set up a chant to F Company, "How many men you got up there?" The chant spread to the flank and rear of the company. This chant from three directions told everyone the company was nearly surrounded. A grass fire set by Chinese burned toward the F Company hilltop and reached the foxhole line. The men beat at the fire with anything they could find, but the 1st Platoon had to retreat to escape it. Captain Gough ordered his much reduced company to regroup into a tight perimeter on his left flank.

Then an unusual spectacle occurred. A force of about 70 enemy soldiers, apparently a Chinese company, marched straight up the hill in a column of fours and passed the left end of F Company where it had regrouped, at its boundary with G Company. At the crest they overran the recoilless-rifle emplacement, which happened to be in its path, killed its crew, and picked up the gun and threw it aside. They continued on, overrunning the F Company CP. They passed within a few feet of two jeeps and a pile of equipment but paid no attention to them. They looked straight ahead and never broke stride. Captain Gough from a distance of 50 feet watched them pass. He had a carbine but did not fire. The mortar section behind Gough's CP heard and saw the Chinese column coming. The mortarmen picked up their weapons and ran for a draw to the southeast. The Chinese could hardly have failed to see this movement, but they paid no attention to it. The enemy column could have turned slightly to its right after going through F Company and struck at G Company. It did not. It kept going straight ahead. This enemy force must have had the special mission of marching through the 2nd Battalion position and occupying Hill 216, on the east side of the MSR. The hill was straight ahead of them in their line of march. Later events showed that enemy did occupy Hill 216 about this time. After the main body of enemy had passed F Company, a few groups at the tail of the column peeled off to stop on the nose of the hill.

While all this was happening to F Company, G Company, only a mile away, remained quiet. Several times during the night, men in the company could hear Chinese talking on the lower slope of their hill, but nothing came of it.

The situation in front of and on the left side of Murch's 2nd Battalion was so bad that, at 2 A.M., 27 November, General Wilson and Lieutenant Colonel Murch decided they should send their numerous wounded in the Collection Station and the Medical Section personnel to the rear for their protection. An assistant S-3 officer was placed in command of this group and started toward Ipsok. Chinese ambushed the party about 600 yards south of the battalion's perimeter and killed, wounded, or captured all the men and destroyed the vehicles. Four wounded medical personnel escaped from their captors later in the night and reached Murch's CP to tell him what had happened. This calamity made it clear that enemy in force were behind Lieutenant Colonel Murch's 2nd Battalion and Task Force Wilson.

The next morning a tank officer who had come down the road from the task force (apparently a member of the 25th Reconnaissance Company) told a *New York Times* correspondent at Ipsok that, at the enemy roadblock where Chinese had ambushed the Medical Section and Collecting Station column the night before, human remains and mechanical wreckage lay scattered around for more than 100 yards. The tank officer was quoted as saying that he had been through two wars but had never seen anything quite so bad—"it was a terrible chewed up mess of dead men."[19]

At Ipsok during the night, the 8th Artillery Battalion had been under a very heavy Chinese attack, without infantry support, and had to fight off enemy within its own perimeter. Then sometime during the night a South Korean bearer and carrier party, moving from north to south in the Task Force Wilson area, came up against the Weapons Company roadblock at the southern end of Murch's 2nd Battalion perimeter. Mistaken by the roadblock force for Chinese, they were killed to a man.

On the edge of the high ground of G Company's position, Captain Eddington of the Weapons Company and Lieutenant Land of G Company thought they could hear enemy noises and digging across the MSR to the southeast of them. They notified Lieutenant Colonel Murch. He came up and joined them in the hour before dawn. Jointly they agreed it sounded like enemy digging in on the hill opposite them—Hill 216. When first light came, they could see a large enemy force still digging rifle pits along the Hill 216 ridgeline, which ran in an east-west direction. It dominated the MSR, which was only 300 to 400 yards from its lower finger ridges on the west side. Task Force Wilson was not only bruised and all but combat ineffective as a result of the night's numerous battles—it was now cut off from its only avenue of retreat as dawn came on 27 November.[20]

When Eighth Army ordered the recall of the 77th Field Artillery Battalion from Task Force Dolvin on 26 November, so that it could rejoin its parent unit, the 1st Cavalry Division, the 8th Field Artillery Battalion hurried north to Ipsok to replace it. Lt. Col. A. T. Terry commanded it. He put the battalion into firing position in the flat ground at the western and northern edges of Ipsok. A Battery was northwest of Ipsok, C Battery was just north of the village, and B Battery was southwest of Ipsok on the north bank of a small stream that flowed from west to east about 300 to 400 yards behind the two front batteries. The battalion headquarters and Headquarters Battery were at the east side of Ipsok. Observation posts were put out on high ground to the north, northwest, and northeast of the battery positions. A small valley ran north-northwest from Ipsok in front of the gun positions. Low ridge lines came down on both sides of this valley. To the east of the right-hand ridge, the MSR ran from Ipsok up to Task Force Wilson's positions. To the right (east) of the road, the 8th Field Artillery had a listening post and two machine-gun positions with a BAR team on a slightly elevated ridge, protecting the approach from that direction. The artillery battalion expected to be called on for its fires immediately. The 77th Field Artillery Battalion had lost two forward observers with Task Force Dolvin's infantry while it was at Ipsok.

Shortly before midnight, Capt. Lewis Millet, a forward observer, telephoned Maj. Joel M. Genung, operations officer, 8th Artillery, and told him that Task Force Wilson up ahead was being hit hard and that enemy forces were drifting to its rear. Headquarters Battery commander, Capt. Robert E. Dingeman, immediately aroused all members of the artillery battalion, distributed more machine-gun ammunition immediately, and sent three or four cases of grenades to each battery.

Earlier in the Korean War, the 8th Field Artillery Battalion had already been under close enemy attack and had learned how to serve as its own infantry to protect itself. About 1 A.M. on 27 November, C Battery reported to the Fire Direction Center that a column of men was marching down the road toward it. A few minutes later it reported another column of men coming toward it from the hill on the left. At 200 yards' distance, this force began blowing bugles. A Battery, to the west, now reported receiving small-arms fire and said that it too could see groups of men out front. The telephone line to Murch's position failed, and a wire team set out to find the trouble and repair it. This wire team ran right into the Chinese force on the road, which fired on it. The five men ran back. Sergeant Soloway helped one of them who was wounded.

The Chinese did not come right in; they seemed to be sending small groups forward to find specific locations of the battalion positions. But when C Battery opened up on a group of Chinese approaching from native huts on the right side of the road, blasting half a dozen or more of them into the air, the battle erupted all around it. One enemy group ran to one gun position and were quickly killed there. The artillery batteries raked the nearby hilltops and any other place CCF were seen. Machine-gun fire swept the open area down the road, and rockets blew apart houses near the perimeter. The battle lasted three hours, with the CCF using mortar and small-arms fire.

Beginning about 3 A.M., the 8th Field Artillery Battalion in the next two hours withdrew south 1,500 yards and joined the 64th and 90th field artillery battalions in their positions. It left one gun behind but recovered it the next day. The artillery battalion lost two men killed and about 10 to 12 wounded. After the fight, according to General Barth, Sgt. Manuel P. Viveiros, an old artilleryman, patted his carbine with satisfaction and said, "I always wanted to kill a bugler."[21]

A significant new development for Task Force Wilson took place early on 27 November. The CCF began a sharp attack on the 35th Infantry Regiment across the Kuryong River to the west, on the left flank of Task Force Wilson. Up to this time, the CCF had not carried their attack to the 35th Infantry and the left of Task Force Wilson, which they had so severely pressed since the night of 25–26 November. (The account of the 35th Infantry will be told in a subsequent section, but it is noted here to say that simultaneous increased pressure now fell on Task Force Wilson.)

Soon after daylight on 27 November, E Company, 27th Infantry, and B Company, 35th Infantry, received orders to withdraw from the hills they had barely held during the night. E Company had no more than a platoon of able-bodied men left, and in B Company only 26 men survived unhurt.

Everywhere in front of Murch's 2nd Battalion perimeter, troop units received orders to pull back after daybreak on the morning of 27 November. Already coming back in small groups, where they could escape, were E and B companies and C Company, 65th Engineer Combat Battalion. Among others, 1st Lt. Robert K. Sawyer's 3rd Platoon, 25th Reconnaissance Company, on the banks of the Kuryong River south of Hill 222, received orders to return to the road and to Murch's 2nd Battalion perimeter.

Sawyer told his platoon, untouched during the night of battle all around it, to start the tank motors and to get the other vehicles ready to move. Two outpost machine-gun crews stationed on a nose of ground above the little valley came down and loaded on a truck. Before starting, Sawyer checked to see that all personnel and equipment were accounted for. One of his sergeants told him a machine-gun outpost crew had left its machine gun behind. He made the men go back up the hill for it. They lost no time in getting back with the gun. On the way down the narrow, hill-rimmed valley, there was heavy machine-gun and small-arms fire falling on all the adjacent hills, and some mortar fire. What Sawyer thought was a rocket landed close to one of his tanks. It was not long, however, before the 3rd Platoon reached the road and entered Murch's perimeter. There Sawyer took position on the east side of the road. Some American vehicles were burning. In a ditch on the left of the road he saw men from C Company, 65th Engineer Combat Battalion, running toward his platoon. He said, "These men were crawling and scrambling, obviously frightened, and not one had a weapon that I could see."[22] From within the perimeter, American fire was being placed on the hills to the west. An officer within the perimeter told Sawyer the headquarters group had given up his 3rd Platoon as lost to the enemy during the night.

Safe inside Murch's perimeter for the moment, Sawyer made radio communication with his commanding officer, Capt. Robert H. Harrington, who was in Ipsok. Harrington told Sawyer to join the 25th Reconnaissance Company there.

During the night, the 25th Reconnaissance Company's 2nd Platoon had been driven from its position, and the company withdrew to Murch's perimeter after daylight. There, Harrington received orders to run an enemy roadblock known to be south of Murch's position, go to Ipsok, and help protect that place and the artillery, which by now had moved to the south of the village. Harrington made the run successfully with five tanks carrying riflemen on their decks.

Clanking down the road after receiving Harrington's instructions, Sawyer stood in the turret of the lead tank, "feeling very exposed." On the south slope of a low divide about a mile north of Ipsok, Sawyer's tank and vehicle column passed two tanks of the 25th Reconnaissance Company going north. When Sawyer arrived in Ipsok a few minutes later, Captain Harrington threw his arms around him and greeted him as one who had been given up for lost.

While they were talking, one of the men nearby ran across the road and excitedly told them the two tanks Sawyer had just passed were in trouble—one knocked out and the crews of both tanks pinned down by enemy fire—in the roadside ditches. Sawyer got back in his tank, and with Sfc. Floyd DeCorrevont, his 3rd Platoon sergeant, following in the No. 2 tank, they headed back up the road. Just beyond the point where they had passed the two tanks on their way south into Ipsok, Sawyer and DeCorrevont rounded a curve, and across a depression ahead saw a tank burning on the next curve. A second tank had stopped just behind it. Sawyer could also see a tank crew member lying in the road and two or three others huddled in the adjacent ditch. Sergeant DeCorrevont now came up, and the two dismounted from their tanks to discuss the situation. Heavy small-arms fire centered on the two tanks up ahead.

After a few exchanges, the sergeant said, "Lieutenant, those are our men." That ended the discussion. Sawyer and DeCorrevont started running down to the intervening valley and up toward the burning tank. They reached a point from where they could call to Staff Sgt. Raymond N. Reifers, who was one of the men in the ditch, to learn the condition of the tank crew. Reifers shouted back that a small Chinese boy had run to the lead tank and had thrown a satchel charge under its treads. He said he thought the man lying in the road had a broken back. Sawyer and DeCorrevont got to the man, who was conscious. Ammunition in the tank was exploding, and the tank itself was still burning. If the man was to be saved, he had to be dragged away at once. In response to a question, he nodded that he could endure the pain of being dragged away. Sawyer and DeCorrevont each grasped an arm and dragged the wounded man down into the valley, where they stopped a moment to rest. While Sawyer was shifting his slung M-1 rifle from his shoulder to his hand to carry it the rest of the way, he felt something like an electric shock hit him in the right ankle—a bullet that knocked him to his knees. Sergeant DeCorrevont helped him up the road to where they had left their tanks. Sawyer's crew lowered him down through the turret. Enemy fire hit all around while this was being done. The valiant platoon sergeant, DeCorrevont, was killed before the crews got the two tanks turned around.

Sgt. Raymond N. Reifers and William Anderson were last seen still in the ditch near the forward, knocked-out tank. They were listed as missing in action. During the day, Lieutenant Sawyer and 14 other wounded men of the 25th Reconnaissance Company were evacuated.[23]

There could be no doubt that enemy were on the road south of Murch and the task force all the way to Ipsok, and only a strong combat force had a chance to fight through. After daylight of 27 November it was indeed a question whether Task Force Dolvin-Wilson could be saved.

Decision to Withdraw Task Force Dolvin-Wilson

The CCF attack on the CP of Task Force Wilson stopped by 7:15 A.M., shortly after daybreak of 27 November, and the main enemy forces withdrew from the vicinity to avoid the punishing air strikes they knew would soon be delivered. When the last enemy attack of the night began at 5:30 A.M., the headquarters group had put every man on its defenses except one operator to receive and send messages. At daybreak only Lt. Col. Gordon Murch's 2nd Battalion was left as a combat-effective force, and even it had suffered many casualties by this time.

Brig. Gen. Vennard Wilson, the task-force commander, knew he had to try to get the remnants of the task force out of the area north of Ipsok during the day, or they would never get out. He established communication with General Kean, the division commander, and recommended that Task Force Wilson be dissolved, since it was no longer an effective fighting force. He explained the situation. General Wilson suggested that Lieutenant Colonel Murch be given command of an effort to extricate the task force with his 2nd Battalion, 27th Infantry. General Kean agreed to this proposal. About 9 A.M., General Wilson told Murch what was planned and asked, "Can you extricate this force?" Murch replied that he could. Both Wilson and Murch knew that the enemy were behind them all the way to Ipsok and that a strong enemy force held Hill 216, on the east side of the road, just a short distance south of Murch's perimeter. To get the task force started south, that hill had to be captured first. Murch immediately ordered preparations for F Company to attack it.

In preparing for the attack, Murch decided to leave G Company in its present position to support the attack on Hill 216 and to protect the various elements of the task force that were then within the 2nd Battalion perimeter. F Company had been engaged in a hard battle all night, but after daylight it was not under fire. It could maneuver from its position to the eastern side of the perimeter and from there prepare to launch an attack on Hill 216. Captain Gough of F Company had two platoons of his company that could still fight effectively, despite losses during the night. Murch reinforced Gough with a platoon from G Company, a tank section, two 75-mm recoilless rifles, a section of heavy machine guns from H Company, and all the battalion 4.2-inch and 81-mm mortars. Virtually all the battalion's heavy firepower was to be used in supporting the attack. Air strikes would help pave the way.

Captain Gough launched his attack at 11:30 A.M. with two platoons abreast, supported by tanks. An enemy rocket hit one of the tanks on the left flank of the line and killed the driver. Lieutenant Gallagher, 3rd Platoon leader, was wounded and out of action almost at once, and the other platoon leader, Lt. Clyde Force, was wounded by a mortar fragment and out of action at the beginning of the attack. These initial losses occurred almost at the line of departure when the assault platoons crossed the road, which the CCF swept with a curtain of fire from Hill 216. The two platoons raced for a rock ledge on the east side of the road and took shelter there. Lieutenant Mahoney, now commanding the 3rd Platoon, organized the men and arranged for a barrage of marching fire from that point on up the hill. When this fire was laid down, the men moved behind it. They overran a CCF .50-caliber machine-gun crew less than 200 feet up the slope. Captain Gough joined the assault line. He sent back for all the .50-caliber machine-gun ammunition that could be hurried up. Then he turned the captured gun around and gave Corporal Mosier the job of firing it on enemy farther up the hill. The large volume of mortar, machine-gun, recoilless-rifle, and small-arms fire delivered on the crest of the enemy-held hill caused the Chinese soldiers there to run off to the north into a ravine on that side to escape the hail of bullets and exploding shells.

Gough sent a tank along the road to a point where it had enfilading fire into this ravine, and Mosier and some men with him ran to the edge of the ravine, where they could see the bunched Chinese below. For them it was a shooting gallery. One Chinese ran from the group for the tank with a satchel charge, the fuse already burning. Mosier shot him just before he reached the tank. In another instant the charge exploded, and the Chinese soldier disappeared.

When the 2nd Platoon of G Company, in support of F Company, started across the road, an American jeep with two men in it sped right in front of the platoon. At that moment the jeep and the men in it went up in a big explosion, possibly from an enemy explosive charge buried in the road. Some parts of the bodies of the two men landed among the 28 men of the platoon, and the jeep's engine hit a ROK soldier and broke his leg. This incident only slightly delayed the platoon in joining Mosier at the ravine, where the men helped kill the last of the Chinese trying to climb out.

The G Company platoon then directed its fire at the crest while F Company climbed for the top. A small force, only six men, got there first. Others followed quickly. But at once, accurate, preregistered Chinese mortar fire hit the captured position. This mortar fire was devastating. The 2nd Platoon, F Company, lost 12 men there in a few minutes. Captain Gough guessed the enemy mortars were on the reverse slope of a ridge to the east of Hill 216, and he concentrated the fire of his 81-mm mortars there. This slackened the enemy mortar fire.[24]

Meanwhile, Task Force Wilson survivors within Murch's perimeter had loaded on trucks while F Company attacked Hill 216. They started down the road. Enemy snipers were close to the road on both sides, in brush and behind rocks. Their marksmanship was poor, and casualties from their fire were relatively light. Murch put these casualties on tanks and took them out ahead of the task-force command elements. F Company held Hill 216 while the vehicular column passed. Lieutenant Colonel Dolvin ordered the few men left in B Company, 35th Infantry, to occupy high ground at a former enemy roadblock site, and he ordered E Company, 27th Infantry, together with some tanks, to form a defensive line to cover the rear of the withdrawing task force. After the task force had cleared the perimeter, E Company was to load on tanks and follow. C Company, 65th Engineer Combat Battalion, escorted a convoy of wounded.

Air strikes now covered the withdrawal of F Company from Hill 216 with napalm drops, rockets, and .50-caliber strafing runs. F Company and its reinforcing units came down to the road. There the men went into a dogtrot alongside tanks that carried their wounded. After F Company had hurried off the crest of Hill 216, an air strike dropped napalm on it. This strike prevented Chinese from closing on the rear of the withdrawing task force, and it reached Ipsok. General Wilson had told Lieutenant Colonel Murch when the withdrawal started that he would collect the able-bodied men he could find at Ipsok and set up a delaying position south of the town. This was necessary to help the 35th Infantry west of the Kuryong River to withdraw eastward across a bridge farther downstream.

During the day 76 air sorties aided the 25th Division, more that day than for any other division sector. Air strikes destroyed one enemy roadblock near Ipsok. Fighter planes' strafing helped Task Force Wilson every mile of its withdrawal.

Task Force Dolvin-Wilson was now, on the afternoon of 27 November, only a remnant of the force that had started north four days earlier. B Company, 35th Infantry, had 18 men left; the Ranger Company had 22 men; the platoons of F Company of Murch's 2nd Battalion were now reduced to an average of 17 men; E Company, 27th Infantry, had about the same number; half the tanks of B Company, 89th Tank Battalion, had been knocked out; and many of the light tanks of the 25th Reconnaissance Company had been destroyed.

The large trains of the 25th Division that had followed Task Force Dolvin to the Ipsok area had already returned to Yongbyon, their starting point on 24 November. Enemy had infiltrated almost to the edge of that town. During 27 November a group of Chinese ambushed an ambulance just northwest of Yongbyon, killing the driver and his assistant.

Since the beginning of its attack north on 24 November, Task Force Dolvin-Wilson and other elements of the 25th Infantry Division had captured only nine Chinese soldiers—six from the 117th Division, two from the 115th Division, and one from the 116th Division, all from the CCF 39th Army. Intelligence from prisoners was so scanty that it is difficult to know just what Chinese units made specific attacks against any given American unit. Apparently the 117th Division carried most of the fight against Task Force Dolvin-Wilson.[25]

The Chinese followed hard on the heels of Task Force Wilson as it fought its way back to Ipsok. General Wilson collected all the useful combat elements of the task force at Ipsok, and when Murch arrived there about 4 P.M., his troops went into position on Hill 201, southwest of the town. This hill on the western side of the road, beginning at its eastern edge about half a mile southwest of Ipsok, extended about a mile west toward the Kuryong River and then turned abruptly south for another mile. It was a two-mile-long, dogleg-shaped ridge. F Company went into position on the west-running part of the ridge just below (south of) Ipsok; G Company took the southern leg of the ridge. In their greatly depleted strength these two rifle companies could not hope to cover the many-fingered approaches to their two-mile-long position. It was a precarious position.

Tanks of B Company, 89th Tank Battalion, held the road and some low ground east of the road just south of Ipsok. The 25th Reconnaissance Company guarded the crossing of an arm of the Wichon River just south of Ipsok, on the right flank of the F and G Company positions. The 8th Field Artillery Battalion remained to support Murch. The 64th and 90th field artillery battalions continued their withdrawal toward Yongbyon.

Murch and Task Force Wilson took this position just below Ipsok, instead of continuing a withdrawal south, to hold back the enemy on the east side of the Kuryong River in order to give the 35th Infantry Regiment, retreating on the west side of the Kuryong, a chance to reach and cross the bridge near Yongsan-dong and to escape through Yongbyon.

The pursuing Chinese soon arrived in Ipsok and began feeling out the new defense positions south of the town. The CCF attack against this new position began half an hour before midnight. Assault groups crawled close to the rifle line and hurled grenades in close attack. The thinly manned line was vulnerable, and it broke in places. At 1:30 A.M. on 28 November, General Kean asked for a report on the situation. He wanted to know if Murch could hold off the Chinese until Colonel Fisher's 35th Infantry had crossed the Kuryong River to its east side.

Murch said he would do his best. He ordered his rifle companies to hold where they were, and he then made an unusual request of General Kean to help them do it. He asked for a close-in air strike at night. Kean said he could get some B-26 planes over the area. They arrived about half an hour later. Murch marked the targets in front of him with white phosphorus mortar shells and communicated with the planes through his TACP leader. The planes came over the targets and strafed the northern slope and foot of the ridgeline, sometimes within 50 to 60 yards of the infantry foxholes. These B-26 bombers made a great effort that night. It succeeded. In the course of their attacks they also hit Ipsok and set many buildings in the town on fire. They burned brightly during the rest of the night. Murch's troops, with the critical help of the strafing in front of them, held long enough to permit the 35th Infantry to fight its way to the Kuryong River bridge and escape eastward on the Yongbyon road.[26]

As soon as the 35th Infantry had crossed the river, General Wilson at 2:30 A.M. ordered Murch to withdraw another mile and a half toward Yongbyon. G Company had to fight its way from its lines. Most of the remaining tanks of B Company, 89th Tank Battalion, went to F Company, on orders from Murch, and helped it break contact and start withdrawing. F Company had 23 able-bodied men left. This withdrawal ended with the task force taking a new position at Yongpo-dong above the Kuryong River bridge and a mile from Yongbyon.

Meanwhile, Captain Harrington and the 25th Reconnaissance Company remained in their positions guarding the crossing of the arm of the Wichon River immediately south of Ipsok. Its 1st Platoon was the last unit to leave as the leap-frogging platoons of the company started south, the rear guard of the taskforce withdrawal. Sergeant 1st Class Taylor of the 1st Platoon blew up an abandoned ammunition truck, and the exploding ammunition in it served as an effective roadblock for 45 minutes and helped his platoon disengage. It crossed the western fork of the Wichon River at 5 A.M., 28 November, and got away. The 25th Reconnaissance Company had 24 casualties in this night battle just south of Ipsok, lost one tank to a satchel-charge attack, and had three vehicles destroyed. The next morning, Sergeant 1st Class Taylor and Lieutenant Martin, with some riflemen aboard, got in a tank and recrossed to the north side of the Wichon River and picked up 18 stragglers of the task force, many of them wounded.[27]

Eighth Army Orders 25th Division to Withdraw to Chongchon River

At 5:45 A.M. on 28 November, Eighth Army ordered the 25th Infantry Division transferred to the operational control of I Corps. The division received this news from IX Corps 20 minutes later and sent a liaison officer to I Corps at once. This change was only one of several that Eighth Army took on 28 November as a result of defeats everywhere along its front and the need to make realignments to carry out preparations for a massive retreat, which the higher command now realized was necessary.

The date of 28 November can be remembered as the one on which Eighth Army withdrawal began as a planned operation everywhere on its front. On this day Task Force Dolvin and Murch's 2nd Battalion concentrated in the vicinity of Yongbyon, with the 89th Tank Battalion and the 25th Reconnaissance Company covering its rear. The 25th Division was ordered at noon to withdraw to the Chongchon River line. The divisional withdrawal began at 3 P.M. The 89th Tank Battalion, after covering the withdrawal of the main parts of the division south of Yongbyon to the Kunu-ri area, was to proceed southwest to Sudong on the north bank of the Chongchon, eight miles west of Kunu-ri, where there was a major ferry and tank ford of the river. It was to assemble there on an island in the river. The 25th Division had reached its Chongchon River line position north of Kunu-ri by 6 P.M., 28 November.

In the evening, Brig. Gen. Vennard Wilson sent a message to General Kean, recommending that the various elements of Task Force Dolvin-Wilson revert to their parent units. General Kean approved this recommendation, and the task force was dissolved effective 10 P.M. The 25th Division CP on the night of 28 November was a short distance southwest of Kunu-ri.

The companies of the 89th Tank Battalion remained with the 25th Division's regiments or battalions—B Company remained with Murch's 2nd Battalion, blocking on the Anju road westward; A Company was with the 35th Infantry on the Anju road; D Company was with elements of the 24th Regiment still north of the Chongchon, trying to escape pursuing Chinese. The tank companies of the 89th Tank Battalion had been widely separated from each other during the 25th Division attack and subsequent withdrawals. During this time the battalions and rifle companies of the 24th Regiment had become disorganized and were mostly ineffective.[28]

While the headquarters and CP of the 25th Division was south of the Chongchon River near Kunu-ri on the night of 28–29 November, all its combat infantry units were still north of the river on what was called the river line. This line in general varied from two miles north of the river on the right, or east, flank to five miles on the left, or west, flank. The major units on this line from left to right were the 35th Infantry Regiment, the 27th Infantry Regiment, and the 24th Infantry Regiment. During 29 November the division troops withdrew southward, always under pressure from Chinese, who followed them closely. Kunu-ri lay south of the 24th Regiment. The 25th Division line extended westward north of the river toward Anju. The bulk of the enemy action during the withdrawal on 29 November was against the 27th Regiment in the division center, south of Yongbyon. The 8th Field Artillery Battalion supported the 27th Regiment at this time, firing for all companies from its position near the Sudong Ferry at the Chongchon River, about eight miles west of Kunu-ri.

At 5 A.M. on 29 November, Chinese attacked both the 2nd and 3rd battalions of the 27th Regiment near Pong-dong, approximately three miles southeast of Yongbyon. The enemy overran K Company on the outpost line of resistance at 6:30 A.M. and then withdrew. Chinese then attacked L Company half an hour later. The enemy penetrated its right-hand platoon, continued on, and overran the company CP a little after 7 A.M. The company committed all its reserves. K Company regrouped and went back on the line between L and I companies. The Chinese closed to the foxholes of I Company. A hard fight followed, but by 9 A.M. the 3rd Battalion had regained its original positions. For a while around noon the 3rd Battalion lost contact with A Company, 24th Infantry, on its right flank, but contact was soon reestablished.

To the west of the 3rd Battalion, the 2nd Battalion, 27th Infantry, came under enemy fire at 5 A.M. Artillery fire helped greatly in repulsing the first attack. But soon an enemy group infiltrated past the 2nd Battalion boundary to engage L Company, 3rd Battalion, and cut the road behind both battalions. By noon, however, the two battalions had driven off the enemy in their front with the help of artillery fire and air strikes. At 4 P.M., all three battalions of the 27th Infantry withdrew under cover of air strikes. The 2nd Battalion marched 18 miles, closing on its bivouac area south of the Chongchon River at 11:30 that night. The troops waded the waters of several icy streams during the march. The 3rd Battalion had a similarly hard march, closing at Sangcham, on the south bank of the Chongchon, just east of its junction with the Kuryong River. The 1st Battalion, under only minor enemy pressure, withdrew six miles.

The right flank of the 25th Division in this withdrawal was held by the 25th Reconnaissance Company. It established a roadblock northeast of Kunu-ri and held a delaying position two miles north of the town. The CP of the 3rd Battalion, 24th Infantry, was in Kunu-ri, but its units were widely scattered. During the day the CP of the 25th Division moved southwest to a point five miles east of Sukchon on the Sunchon road, well below the Chongchon River.[29]

The 35th Infantry Fights Its Way Back from Unsan

It is necessary now to backtrack and follow the movements and actions of Colonel Fisher's 35th Regiment, 25th Division, which was separated by the Kuryong River from Task Force Dolvin-Wilson and the rest of the division. The 35th Infantry Regiment, minus B Company, which had been included in Task Force Dolvin, advanced from its point of departure on 24 November without enemy opposition. The most noteworthy event of its advance was coming upon the place south of Unsan where the CCF had surprised and overrun large numbers of the 3rd Battalion, 8th Cavalry, three weeks earlier, in the CCF 1st Phase Offensive. There, members of the 2nd Battalion, 35th Infantry, found a shambles of 31 dead men, most of them still in their sleeping bags, and about 30 vehicles burned.

In the afternoon of 25 November, Colonel Fisher from the eastern ridgeline of Hill 324, south of Unsan, could see into the town. He saw no sign of enemy activity. His advance troops were now a mile farther north than Task Force Dolvin that evening, which was eastward across the Kuryong River. The next morning, Fisher planned to send one battalion around Unsan to Hill 191, northwest of the town, and occupy it. Then he intended to advance into the town from the south along the road. By 10 A.M., his advance platoon that morning reached a bridge on a tributary of the Kuryong River, just south of Unsan. From there its members could look into the Unsan schoolyard, where they could see 10 to 12 vehicles of the 8th Cavalry Regiment still standing where they had been abandoned or destroyed nearly a month earlier. Neither this platoon nor any other part of the 35th Infantry advanced any farther, and no member of the regiment ever entered Unsan, now so plainly in view.

Before he left Yongbyon that morning, 26 November, to assume command of Task Force Dolvin, Assistant Division Commander Brigadier General Wilson had sent a radio message at 10 A.M. to Colonel Fisher not to advance farther but to hold in place and to be on guard for enemy action from his left flank. Enemy had hit the ROK 1st Division there hard during the night. This message did not mention the enemy's equally strong attack against Task Force Dolvin on his right flank. Thus far, the 35th Regiment had remained untouched between two seething cauldrons of battle. It bothered Fisher that he did not have contact with the ROK 1st Division on his left flank. He sent a patrol to Hill 598, a massive height southwest of Unsan, in an effort to reestablish contact. His patrol failed to find any ROK troops.

The first Chinese action against the 35th Infantry occurred at 3:45 A.M. on 26 November when a Chinese patrol of about 15 soldiers crept up on a mortar outpost of L Company, surprised it, and took five prisoners. They also killed one American and wounded two others in the course of his incident. Apparently this patrol had the specific mission of capturing prisoners for intelligence purposes. There was no enemy attack, however, immediately following this enemy patrol action.

Upon receiving General Wilson's order not to advance farther, Fisher ordered his 2nd Battalion, which had already started to move toward Hill 191, to turn around and dig in at its position of the night before. A platoon of A Company tanks, 89th Medium Tank Battalion, returned with the infantry. A platoon of

F Company remained at a roadblock it had established about five miles south of Unsan. From this vicinity, A Company tank fire killed some enemy seen trying to cross the Kuryong River, east to west, during the day. Chinese overran the F Company roadblock just after dark at 6:15 P.M., 26 November. Many of this Chinese force subsequently were killed.[30]

The immunity of the 35th Infantry on the night of 25-26 November and during the day of 26 November from Chinese attack, when it was general elsewhere across the Eighth Army front, seems to have been intentional. Later intelligence disclosed that the 39th and 40th CCF armies were massed in assembly areas near Unsan and that the 35th Infantry was advancing straight toward them. The CCF 66th Army was concentrated just a few miles farther west. The Chinese hit the ROK 1st Division, just to the left of the 35th Infantry, and Task Force Dolvin, just to the right of it, in strength on the first night of their 2nd Phase Offensive, 25-26 November. They could have done the same against the 35th Infantry, had they wanted. But with their attack forces advancing south of the 35th Infantry on both its left and right flanks and with the 35th Infantry having no physical contact with friendly forces on either flank, the enemy envisioned a perfect trap for the unit as it advanced into the heart of their assembly areas. The regiment then could have been cut off in the heart of enemy-held country and surrounded. Fortunately, the 25th Division CP realized the danger facing the regiment and stopped it on the morning of 26 November.

In its position on the night of 26 November south of Unsan, which was essentially the same as on the night of 25 November, 16 men from the F Company Platoon, which had been overrun at its roadblock, returned to the 2nd Battalion perimeter about an hour after midnight, and two hours later 13 more men made their way into its lines. Later, about 4 A.M., about 60 Chinese attacked F Company, but they were held off with artillery and mortar fire. Already the enemy had launched a very heavy attack against the 3rd Battalion.

Beginning about 3 P.M. on 27 November, Chinese assault groups drove in K and L Company outposts. The combat quickly became hand-to-hand in places, especially in K Company. Lieutenant Hinewood, a forward observer with K Company for the mortar company, had a fistfight with a Chinese soldier. Captain Hughes, K Company commander, stayed with his men two hours after being wounded. K Company held its lines against repeated enemy attacks and quickly sealed off one enemy penetration and subsequently restored its own position. An estimated two Chinese regiments assaulted the 2nd and 3rd battalions of the 35th Infantry during the night, withdrawing from the battle only with the coming of dawn. After daylight, a great many Chinese dead could be seen in front of the company perimeters. The dead were especially numerous in front of K Company. There were 374 counted enemy dead and an estimated 600 Chinese soldiers killed from the defensive fires and fighting of the 35th Infantry during the night. Six Chinese prisoners were captured, all from the 117th Division, 39th Army.

Brig. Gen. George B. Barth later stated that the stand of K Company in hurling back repeated Chinese attacks probably averted a major disaster. The Chinese attacks against it were particularly persistent because that is where the Chinese command intended to open a penetration. More than a division of enemy troops, about 10,000, according to prisoner information, stood ready behind the assault teams to pour through the penetration into the rear of the 35th Infantry lines if K Company had broken. This large enemy force subsequently shifted westward and exploited a penetration of the ROK 1st Division lines during the day. Despite the heavy fighting during the night, the casualties of L and K companies were not heavy—a tribute to good leadership, discipline, and professional use of weapons.[31]

On the morning of 27 November, the 25th Division headquarters informed Fisher that, during the night, the CCF had broken through the ROK 1st Division lines on his left and that he should withdraw. Fisher at 9 A.M. ordered his 2nd Battalion to prepare to screen the withdrawal of the regiment. By 10:30 A.M., the 1st Battalion had established a roadblock to cover the rest of the regiment. But enemy attacks against the 2nd and 3rd battalions developed. These had to be repulsed before any withdrawal could begin.

Enemy mortar and machine-gun fire still hit around the 2nd Battalion CP when the 2nd Battalion withdrawal started. At the same time, enemy forces struck at E and G companies. The tail end of the 2nd Battalion did not get away until midafternoon, and then it had to leave behind sleeping bags, six trucks, and five jeeps. The 3rd Battalion followed the 2nd Battalion, starting its movement about 3 P.M.

The regiment withdrew to the positions it had held north of Yongsan-dong when it began its advance northward on 24 November. During the withdrawal, Fisher had to turn rear units around to face enemy attacks on his rear. The 64th Field Artillery Battalion, as it too withdrew, continued to fire close support for the infantry when enemy forces threatened to close in. Fisher ordered that any vehicles at the tail of the column would be abandoned at once if they were trapped. Some were abandoned. But in this way he saved lives of men who might have tried to save the vehicles, and he also kept his column closed up and moving. That night, 27 November, Fisher established his CP at Yongsan-dong. His regiment went into position on the long east-west ridge of Hill 387, three miles north of the town.[32]

On the evening of 27 November, before dark, two groups of about 100 men each, dressed as Korean farmers, were seen assembling just north of Yongsan-dong behind the 35th Infantry lines. They were in fact CCF soldiers. In the hours of darkness they established a roadblock that cut the withdrawal road of the 35th Infantry, which passed through the crossroads town of Yongsan-dong. In the town, the 35th Infantry would have to take the road running due east to the bridge across the Kuryong River and, once across the river, continue on east to Yongbyon.

The road at the infantry defensive position three miles north of Yongsan-dong crossed a low saddle in the Hill 387 ridgeline and then ran south to Yongsan-dong. Control of this saddle was vital during the withdrawal, and the congested crossroads area in Yongsan-dong constituted a potential trap.

The Chinese began their attack on the 35th Regiment half an hour before midnight. It quickly spread across the regimental front. At the same time, unknown to the men on the forward line, a Chinese force had captured and occupied Yongsan-dong, three miles behind them. The 35th Infantry command-post personnel in Yongsan-dong barely escaped eastward.

The ROK 15th Regimental CP, ROK 1st Division, was also in Yongsan-dong that night. In fact, the division boundary between the 25th Infantry Division and the ROK 1st Division converged to pass through Yongsan-dong, a key crossroads point for both divisions. When the Chinese entered Yongsan-dong, they contrived to surround the ROK 15th Regimental CP, but the regimental commander and most of his staff escaped. The Chinese were now set to destroy the 35th Regiment, and they might have, had it been less disciplined and less ably led. The Chinese that night again had driven back the ROK 1st Division, which extended the army line westward from the 35th Infantry. Part of the enemy force cut the Yongsan-dong–Pakchon road south of Yongsan-dong and thus trapped large parts of the ROK 1st Division north of it. Both the 35th Infantry of the US 25th Division and the ROK 1st Division were now threatened with destruction.

The CCF coordinated attack had started first against the 2nd Battalion between 11 P.M. and midnight, striking all three infantry companies—E, F, and G. The fight lasted all night there, with hundreds of CCF killed. Colonel Fisher ordered a withdrawal, but it could not be undertaken at once. The battalion was not able to start its withdrawal until 6:15 A.M. on 28 November, shortly before daylight. The battalion lost many vehicles, but the main body of troops broke through the town of Yongsan-dong and headed east for the river.

Earlier, when the enemy roadblock north of Yongsan-dong became known, A Company, 89th Tank Battalion, with a company of infantry, went south from the defensive line to clear it. The CCF tried desperately to hold the block, and the fighting there went on for several hours. Eventually, the tank and infantry force partially cleared the block, losing two tanks in the effort.

In the general CCF attack that night, A Company, 1st Battalion, came under attack at 1 A.M. on the morning of 28 November. It held until after 4 A.M. It then began to withdraw but ran into the enemy roadblock north of Yongsan-dong. A and C companies found a little cut-off trail north of the town and turned east on it. The 1st Battalion was thus able to bypass the roadblock and the town. It continued on to high ground overlooking the Kuryong River. There it took up a defensive position to protect the Kuryong River bridge and to cover the withdrawal across it of the 2nd and 3rd battalions.

The 3rd Battalion S-3 Operations Journal gives a succinct summary of what happened to that battalion. At 1 A.M., 28 November, it was alerted for withdrawal when it received word that ROK forces on its left (west) had given way. Twenty minutes later CCF attacked L Company from all sides. An hour later all battalion vehicles were sent to the rear. Ten to 15 minutes later, artillery fire ceased because the 64th Artillery Battalion firing for it was under enemy attack. At 3 A.M., the plan for the withdrawal of the 2nd and 3rd battalions was put into effect. G Company of the 2nd Battalion and I Company of the 3rd Battalion would cover the withdrawal. I Company engaged enemy on the high ground west of the saddle at Hill 387. L Company joined it in the fight there and held the road open while the rest of the 3rd Battalion moved south and was then followed by the 2nd Battalion. A tank platoon of A Company, 89th Tank Battalion, covered the withdrawal of L and I companies when they started off the hill. In their withdrawal all had to fight their way through Yongsan-dong.[33]

Although it is apparent that the 35th Regiment had to fight its way south and through Yongsan-dong to the bridge crossing of the Kuryong River and just barely made it, a word must be added here about the part the ROK 1st Division played in making possible the withdrawal of the regiment. The ROK 1st Division, under Gen. Paik Sun Yup, had almost the entire CCF 66th Army to hold off in the battles around and south of Taechon from 25 November on. Shortly after midnight of 27 November, the Chinese broke through the ROK 12th Regiment, and at about the same time a massive enemy attack at close quarters broke the 15th Regiment's line two miles north of Yongsan-dong, adjacent to its boundary with the 35th Infantry. The Chinese then surrounded Yongsan-dong and quickly captured it. The ROK 15th Regimental headquarters there barely escaped. The Chinese in Yongsan-dong overran both the ROK 11th and 15th Regimental headquarters that night and both regimental commanders were killed or missing.

After daylight on 28 November General Paik left his headquarters near the Chongchon River and went north to the fragmented 11th and 15th regiments, gathered their scattered units, reorganized them, led them to positions where they again had the Chinese to their fronts, and ordered them to counterattack the Chinese. In this counterattack General Paik recaptured Yongsan-dong. Had it not been for his stalwart leadership and the response he was able to get from his troops, the safety of the 35th Infantry might have been in doubt during the morning of 28 November.

When his CP had been forced to flee from Yongsan-dong during the night of 27–28 November, Colonel Fisher crossed the Kuryong River to its east side. He then turned north to find Brigadier General Wilson and Colonel Dolvin with Murch's 2nd Battalion, 27th Infantry, at Yongpo-dong. He conferred there with General Wilson about the situation of the 35th Infantry. Apparently Colonel Fisher had ordered the withdrawal of the 35th Infantry on his own authority, but he knew that the regiment had to cross the Kuryong as soon as possible if it were to escape, because if the Chinese on the east side of the river broke through the ever-thinning blocking force of Murch's 2nd Battalion, his chance of getting the bulk of the 35th Infantry out of the closing jaws of the Chinese trap would be greatly diminished. Two batteries of the 64th Artillery Battalion and most of the tanks had crossed the river by dawn.

The 1st Battalion held its defensive positions on the west bank of the river, guarding the bridge and the Kuryong River crossing until 4:45 P.M., 28 November. At that time all other elements of the 35th Regiment had crossed the river. The 1st Battalion then left its covering positions and crossed the bridge. The 35th Regiment assembled at Yongbyon and saw the old walled city for the last time. The 2nd Battalion closed there at 2:45 P.M., and the 3rd Battalion at 5 P.M. After dark, at 6:30 P.M., the regiment started on south toward the Chongchon River, a march of ten miles.

Meanwhile, Lieutenant Colonel Murch's 2nd Battalion continued to hold its blocking position north of Yongpo-dong on the east side of the Kuryong River until all of the 35th Infantry had crossed the river and were on their way to Yongbyon. Then, at 5 P.M., 28 November, it followed the 35th Infantry. The service trains of the 25th Division departed Yongbyon on 28 November on short notice, headed for Kunu-ri, 22 miles away on the south bank of the Chongchon.[34]

It would appear that the CCF 117th Division of the 39th Army and elements of the CCF 66th Army, the latter in front of the ROK 1st Division west of the 35th Infantry, carried the fight against Fisher's 35th Infantry.[35]

All things considered, Task Force Dolvin-Wilson, the 35th Infantry, and Murch's 2nd Battalion, 27th Infantry, came off better against the surprise and massive Chinese attacks than might have been expected, and the Chinese must have been surprised at their escape. The Chinese attackers, using their well-tested tactics of frontal attack and double envelopment, failed to panic and destroy the two UN attack columns, even though they succeeded in surrounding both of them and in cutting off their withdrawal routes. Both forces fought their way through the Chinese behind them while holding against their continuing frontal pressure. It was a professional display of courage and soldierly competence by officers and enlisted men alike.

The "Deuce-Four" Regiment Loses Its Way in the Hills

It remains to follow the misfortunes of the 24th Infantry Regiment in its efforts as part of the US 25th Infantry Division's "attack to the border." The 24th Infantry was on the right (east) flank of the 25th Division, or east of Task Force Dolvin, which was the division center attack column. On the right flank of the 24th Infantry and the division was the 9th Infantry, the left flank of the US 2nd Infantry Division. There was no north-south road in the 24th Infantry's sector. The only decent road in its zone of operations was a southwest-northeast road that ran from Yongbyon, 25th Division headquarters site, northeast across the hills to strike the Chongchon River opposite Kujang-dong, a road distance of more than 15 miles. Most of the way, this road was from four to six air miles north of the river. The village of Unhung, or Muksi-dong on some maps, about ten road miles northeast of Yongbyon, was the only settlement larger than tiny villages on the road.

The valley of the Wichon River ascended eastward from Ipsok for a distance of eight miles to a point approximately two air miles north of Unhung, where its headwaters were trickles in the hills, topped by massive Hill 528. North of the Wichon valley there was a jumble of unbroken hills for many miles. Into this rough terrain, traversed only by poor trails, the 24th Infantry moved from the vicinity of Yongbyon on 24 November with its 1st Battalion on the left, the 3rd Battalion in the middle astride the Unhung road, and the 2nd Battalion on the right. The two flank battalions, the 1st and the 2nd, soon became lost.

The self-styled Deuce-Four, or 24th Infantry Regiment, the only black infantry regiment in Eighth Army, was commanded by Col. John T. Corley, a crew-cropped red-headed West Point graduate of the class of 1938, 35 years old. One of the most highly decorated battalion or regimental officers in the US Army, he had earned two Distinguished Service Crosses, eight Silver Stars, and a battlefield promotion to colonel. The Department of the Army and Eighth Army had a policy of trying to give the 24th Infantry the best possible leadership. The only other black infantry unit in Eighth Army was the 3rd Battalion, 9th Infantry Regiment.[36]

The 24th Regiment's battalion commanders were Lt. Col. Gerald G. Miller

(1st Battalion), Maj. George A. Clayton (2nd Battalion), and Lt. Col. Melvin R. Blair (3rd Battalion). The 159th Field Artillery Battalion supported the 24th Infantry, but for all practical purposes in the Chinese attacks of late November, it was of use only to the regimental headquarters and the 3rd Battalion on the Unhung road. It never advanced beyond positions just east of Unhung.

Strangely, the 24th Infantry met enemy resistance on 25 November that stopped two of its battalions. I and K companies of the 3rd Battalion attack came to a halt at midafternoon, largely because there were no adjacent units up on their flanks. The 2nd Battalion's F Company on its east flank advanced against no opposition, but E and G companies could not join F Company except by using roads that ran through the 2nd Infantry Division sector and then led westward into the hills from the Chongchon River valley at Kujang-dong. E and G companies were on their way through the 2nd Division zone to join F Company when the 2nd Division had to cancel its permission for the two companies to move through the 9th Infantry sector because it learned that CCF forces had established a protected roadblock on the road. The two rifle companies then decided to send their heavy equipment, tanks, artillery, heavy mortars, and vehicles back to the 2nd Battalion headquarters, while they tried to reach stranded F Company by climbing the mountain trails.[37]

The three battalions of the 24th Infantry became widely separated from each other on 26 November. The 2nd Battalion was in the hills north of the Chongchon River and west of Kujang-dong. The 3rd Battalion in the center reached Unhung during the day. The 1st Battalion on the west flank of the regiment slowly moved up on the flank of Task Force Dolvin but passed it during the night. Its companies became lost in enemy territory. Although attached to Task Force Wilson during the day, the 1st Battalion never joined the task force or operated with it as a combat force.

Colonel Corley lost communications during the day with many of his rifle companies—he did not know where some of them were, and this condition grew worse the next day. On the 26th, Corley visited Task Force Dolvin's CP, north of Ipsok, and conferred with Brigadier General Wilson. He learned there that his 1st Battalion had not come up on the task force's right flank. He promised to do what he could to get it up on line. As a result of this visit he knew that strong enemy forces had already attacked the task force and that the 1st Battalion would very likely meet the same opposition. Neither Task Force Dolvin-Wilson nor the 9th Infantry, 2nd Division, had contact with the 24th Infantry units that were supposed to be on their flanks, even though the 9th Infantry sent out a patrol to find them on the evening of 26 November.

On the 24th Regiment's right flank, E and G companies apparently reached Hill 273 and an adjoining ridge, with G Company on Hill 273 and E on the ridge, isolated far to the northeast of the 3rd Battalion near Unhung. CCF forces surrounded them there, deep in enemy territory. A liaison plane dropped a message to the companies to hold Hill 273 and await an airdrop of food. When the drop planes came over Hill 273, they found that Chinese then held the hill. E and G companies were nowhere in sight.

Before the drop planes arrived over Hill 273, the Chinese had attacked both companies, and in the ensuing fight both sides reported heavy losses. What happened is not clear. It seems that Capt. Leslie C. Terry, Jr., G Company commander, withdrew his company to the ridge where Capt. Frank O. Knoeller, E Company commander, had been able to hold his position. Maj. George A. Clayton, the 2nd Battalion commander, was also there.

After dark, Major Clayton employed a ruse to allow his men to escape. He built fires on one end of the ridge, and then withdrew his men to the other end. When the CCF attacked the area where the campfires burned, he and the two company commanders led the approximately 150 survivors southeast on a trail toward the 9th Infantry lines near the Chongchon River. They reached the 3rd Battalion, 9th Infantry. This 2nd Battalion, 24th Infantry, force remained with Colonel Sloane's 9th Infantry, 2nd Division, for the next several days and fought capably with it in the hard battles along the Chongchon. Colonel Sloane subsequently praised E and G companies for their efforts with his regiment.[38]

The records and other evidence are not clear as to what happened to the 1st Battalion, which was now ahead of Task Force Dolvin and in enemy territory. B Company led the 1st Battalion advance and was somewhere up in front of C Company. B Company led a charmed existence during the night of 26-27 November. It was supposed to come abreast of Task Force Dolvin, tie in with it, and hold there. Instead, it passed the task force in the dark and continued on into Chinese territory. In the hectic movements of Chinese forces throughout the night in their frontal attacks on Dolvin and flanking movements to cut the road behind it, they somehow missed encountering B Company. When daylight of 27 November came, Lieutenant Green, commanding B Company, chanced to see Chinese troops laying telephone wire some distance to his flank. He checked some small native villages near his position and found that enemy forces had occupied the villages until dawn. He realized he had spent the night in enemy territory.

Learning by radio of Green's predicament, Colonel Corley apparently ordered C Company to go to the help of B Company. At that time C Company must have been abreast on the east, or nearly so, of B Company, 35th Infantry (Task Force Dolvin), which was on Hill 234, approximately four air miles northeast of Ipsok. Capt. Milford W. Stanley, commanding C Company, 24th Infantry, started north with his company to find B Company. Subsequent events make it appear that he stumbled right into a strong Chinese assembly area. Colonel Corley claimed that evidence he obtained indicated that Captain Stanley surrendered the company without a fight and that, a few days later, Radio Peking broadcast the news that their troops in Korea had captured the company intact. The last word the 1st Battalion had from C Company on 26 November said it was withdrawing toward B Company, 35th Infantry, on its left flank. It was never heard from again, but one officer and six men from the company later came through friendly lines. The details of how this company happened to fall to the enemy almost intact are not known.[39] It is known, however, that the hills and ridges north of B Company, 35th Infantry, were in enemy hands from 25 November on, until Task Force Dolvin-Wilson made its fighting withdrawal from north of Ipsok.

The 3rd Battalion, in the 24th Infantry Regimental center, received an airdrop of supplies near Unhung at 4:15 P.M. on 26 November and maintained its positions there with the help of artillery and tank fire. Colonel Corley ordered the 3rd Battalion to withdraw more than a mile the next morning, as both its flanks were wide open.

The 25th Division headquarters early on the morning of 26 November realized that things were going poorly with the 24th Regiment. In the light of the heavy attacks against Task Force Dolvin and the 9th Infantry of the 2nd Division, on either side of the 24th Infantry, it appeared that a big gap in the Eighth Army line was developing on the 24th Infantry front. As early as 9 A.M. on 26 November, the 3rd Battalion, 27th Infantry Regiment, then in 25th Division reserve, received an alert for movement on one and a half hours' notice. The 3rd Platoon of C Company, 89th Medium Tank Battalion, was attached to the battalion. At 10 P.M. that night, the 3rd Battalion, 27th Infantry, received orders to move up behind the 24th Infantry. Twenty minutes before midnight it departed from its assembly area at Pong-dong, three miles southeast of Yongbyon, on the Kunu-ri road. At 2:12 A.M., 27 November, it closed in an assembly area at Unhung and established a perimeter defense there.[40]

On the morning of 27 November there was great confusion in the 24th Regimental headquarters and the 25th Division as to where various units of the regiment were located. Most attempts of communication with them had failed. The rough, hilly terrain made most of the company radios useless. In the early afternoon an air observer reported the 1st Battalion was located about three miles east of Ipsok and engaged with enemy.

On the right flank, F Company, which had survived by itself, started a motorized patrol of twelve men to go to the 3rd Battalion, 9th Infantry, to bring back E and G companies, but enemy small-arms and automatic fire turned it back with five men wounded and the loss of two jeeps. The 2nd Battalion headquarters and F Company, with the latter fighting a delaying and screening action, covered by fighter planes overhead, then started withdrawing toward Kunu-ri.[41]

At 9 P.M. on 26 November, Col. John H. Michaelis received orders from the 25th Division to move his 27th Regiment up behind the 24th Infantry. It closed at Unhung at 4:30 A.M. the next morning. The 3rd Battalion of the regiment was already there, as described earlier. The 24th Infantry line, now backed by the 27th Infantry, stretched eastward from Ipsok to the 9th Infantry and 2nd Division boundary near the Chongchon River. Most of C Company of the 89th Tank Battalion was with the 27th Infantry on 27 November when it went up to the line.

The 27th Infantry with the tanks went into position on the high ground north of Unhung, a long southwest-to-northeast ridge extending from Hill 208, a mile west of Unhung. It was an excellent defensive position covering the main road back to Yongbyon. This force held there for the next two days, covering the withdrawal of the 24th Infantry to the Kunu-ri area on the Chongchon River. It broke contact with the enemy on 29 November and then itself started withdrawal.

According to Colonel Corley, General Kean forced the hand of IX Corps in committing the 27th Infantry on the left of the 2nd Battalion, 24th Infantry, after the debacle of E and G companies on 26 November. The 1st Battalion, 24th Infantry, was attached to the 27th Infantry on 27 November.

On the morning of 27 November the 3rd Battalion, 24th Infantry, withdrew as ordered the previous evening. Chinese troops had established a roadblock about three miles east of Yongbyon on the road to Unhung, thereby cutting off the 27th Infantry and the 3rd Battalion, 24th Infantry. But Lieutenant Colonel Blair, 3rd Battalion commander, counterattacked this roadblock force with tanks and M Company, his Heavy Weapons Company, and destroyed it. Blair's rifle companies were farther forward than the battalion CP and M Company. On 27 November they came under heavy attack from an estimated regiment. The 1st Platoon of D Company, 89th Tank Battalion, with an infantry escort held a blocking position for them as they tried to extricate themselves. They thought their best chance to escape was to try to reach the 9th Infantry lines near the Chongchon River.[42]

Meanwhile, a patrol from K Company, 27th Infantry, with tanks left Unhung early in the morning of 27 November, and at 7 A.M. established contact with F Company, 24th Infantry, at a roadblock two miles southwest of Unhung. The 27th Infantry, with gaps on both flanks, kept patrols out to protect itself. The patrols were not allowed to go out of sight of the main assembly area.

All elements of the 24th Infantry withdrew toward the Chongchon River and the Kunu-ri area on 28 November. The regimental headquarters withdrew toward Yongbyon at 2 A.M. The 1st Battalion, under 27th Infantry control, withdrew southward after daylight to a point five miles southeast of Yongbyon and that night crossed the Chongchon River to a blocking position west of Kunu-ri on the road to Anju. Most of the infantry of the 2nd Battalion, E and G companies, were with the 9th Infantry Regiment of the 2nd Division and fought with that regiment in its withdrawal and blocking actions on the Chongchon River road south of Kujang-dong and toward Kunu-ri. The 2nd Battalion headquarters and F Company continued their withdrawal to Kunu-ri, and from there on south to Chosan.

The Weapons Company of the 3rd Battalion held its roadblock near Unhung during the night of 28 November. CCF attacked the roadblock at 2 A.M., 29 November. The roadblock force held its position until 4 A.M. and then withdrew southeast. D Company tanks of the 89th Tank Battalion helped cover the withdrawal of most of the 24th Infantry units, except for E and G companies with the 9th Infantry.

Behind the 1st Battalion, 24th Infantry, the 3rd Battalion, 27th Infantry, brought up the rear of the withdrawal from the left and center of the 24th Infantry zone, starting back from the Unhung area about 10 A.M. During the afternoon, it came upon equipment the 1st Battalion, 24th Infantry, had abandoned. A tank platoon accompanying the 3rd Battalion destroyed this abandoned equipment. Marching on foot, the 3rd Battalion, 27th Infantry, reached Pongdong, at 10 P.M., a town four road miles southeast of Yongbyon, on the main road from there to Kunu-ri. It established a defensive perimeter there for the night.[43]

By 29 November, Colonel Corley had only a fraction of the 24th Infantry under his control. The 1st Battalion was under control of the 27th Infantry, and most of the 2nd Battalion had joined the 9th Infantry temporarily to fight its way out with it, south along the Chongchon River road. Lt. Col. Melvin R. Blair's 3rd Battalion was the only battalion still under Colonel Corley's control. General Kean, according to Corley, was worried about the situation in the right, or eastern, part of the 24th Infantry Regimental zone, initially held by the 2nd

Battalion. That battalion's rapid disintegration there left a big gap next to the 9th Infantry, which had been hard hit by massive Chinese attacks beginning the night of 25 November.

To guard this area Corley shifted the 3rd Battalion eastward. It was the only sizable body of the 24th Infantry still north of the Chongchon River on 29 November. It essentially was along the east side of the regimental boundary, next to the 9th Infantry, just north or west of the Chongchon River, opposite Won-ni (or Pugwon, as some maps had it). The rifle companies of the 3rd Battalion were about five miles north of Kunu-ri on 29 November. The 24th Infantry and the 25th Division boundary here ran just east of Kunu-ri, almost straight north past the west side of Won-ni, and seven air miles to the north passed a short distance east of Unhung. This was also the boundary between I and IX corps.

Lieutenant Colonel Blair and his 3rd Battalion headquarters group were in Kunu-ri the night of 28–29 November. He had been in the rear of his rifle companies, and during his withdrawal, in an effort to contact them, he made a considerable detour on roads and trails, became lost when he turned northeast, got his jeep stuck, then turned his headlights on and turned back downstream toward Won-ni. The temperature was near zero. Blair took his party through water several times, and they got their feet wet before arriving at Kunu-ri. That meant danger of frostbite. When Colonel Corley saw Lieutenant Colonel Blair that night at Kunu-ri, he felt that Blair was suffering "combat fatigue."[44]

The story of the 24th Infantry in the Eighth Army attack of 24–28 November is largely one of disorder, ineptness, breakdown of communications, units getting lost in bad terrain, heavy personnel and equipment losses, and a cause of concern to friendly units on its flanks. It accomplished very little in action against the Chinese. Records and other information did not survive to allow a very detailed account of its many misfortunes, and regrettably many things about it are inadequately known.

9. Withdrawal of Eighth Army Left Flank to the Chongchon River

General Milburn's I Corps, which held Eighth Army's left flank, saw less action during the CCF 2nd Phase Offensive than did the army's other two corps. I Corps was composed of two infantry divisions on line. On its extreme left was the US 24th Division; on its right was the ROK 1st Division. This division, by general agreement, was the best in the ROK Army. Excepting its 5th RCT, the 24th Infantry Division had almost no combat in the 2nd Phase Offensive. After the ROK 1st Division came under heavy Chinese attack, the US 24th Division sent its 5th RCT to the division's eastern boundary, adjacent to the ROK 1st Division.

Leading the 24th Division advance in the Eighth Army attack on 24 November was Col. Richard W. Stephens's 21st Regiment, along the western coastal road. Trailing it was Col. Ned D. Moore's 19th Infantry Regiment. Back of both and echeloned to the east of them was Lt. Col. John L. Throckmorton's 5th RCT. Maj. Gen. John H. Church commanded the 24th Division. All these commanders were veterans of the Naktong perimeter battles.

Brig. Gen. Paik Sun Yup commanded the ROK 1st Division. He had led it since the beginning of the war, when the North Koreans crossed the 38th Parallel on 25 June 1950. General Paik had been a young lieutenant platoon leader with the Japanese army in China. His personal leadership and previous combat experience, together with his division's performance in the opening days of the war, quickly brought him to the fore among the ROK division commanders. The American commanders found that he and his division could pull their weight against the North Koreans and later against the Chinese. The ROK 1st Division was considered a reliable combat force.

It will be recalled that the 24th Division advanced from the vicinity of Pakchon along the west coastal road on 24–25 November as far as Chongju—approximately 20 miles. The 21st Infantry Regiment entered Chongju on 25 November and secured the town in the early afternoon. There had been no enemy resistance, although 60 North Korean soldiers surrendered to it. After the regiment occupied Chongju, K Company, 21st Infantry, sent a patrol to Hill 192 and lost one man killed there in an encounter with an enemy force. The next day, 26 November, Eighth Army ordered the 21st Infantry to remain at Chongju. It spent the day patrolling the vicinity. The division had one encounter with enemy forces during the day.

The 19th Infantry, behind the 21st Infantry, held the area in the vicinity of Naechong-jong (Napchong-dong on later maps). The 19th Infantry had received many civilian reports of strong Chinese forces around the town of O'hang, about five miles northwest of Naechong-jong and six miles northeast of Chongju. I Company of the 19th Infantry had occupied Hill 227. Just before 1 P.M. on 26 November, a Chinese battalion of horse cavalry, probably a reconnaissance and screening force, attacked I Company on the hill. The 13th Field Artillery Battalion fired in support of the company, and air strikes were quickly called in on the enemy force. The fight lasted about half an hour before the Chinese withdrew. Air strikes punished the cavalry unit considerably as it tried to get away. Ground and aerial estimates placed the number of enemy dead at approximately 250. At midafternoon the 19th Infantry Regiment ordered I Company to withdraw from the hill to the vicinity of Naechong-jong.[1]

Meanwhile, all day of 26 November, Chinese forces of the 66th Army had attacked the ROK 1st Division and had forced one of its regiments out of line. This threatening development on the division's right flank caused Lieutenant Colonel Throckmorton to move his 5th RCT forward and to take position on the right of the 21st Infantry near the boundary with the ROK 1st Division.

Beginning on the night of 25 November, the CCF attacked across the breadth of Eighth Army eastward from the 24th Division, which alone was spared. As a result of the nightlong battle elsewhere, General Walker ordered the 24th Division to hold the 21st Infantry at Chongju. If it continued its unopposed advance it would soon be far out in front of the rest of the army, with the CCF making inroads everywhere to the east of it. In such a situation, the division would be in danger of being surrounded.[2]

Throughout the Chinese 2nd Phase Offensive, the US 24th Division on the army left flank reacted to events elsewhere. By morning of 27 November these successful CCF attacks included important inroads in the zone of the ROK 1st Division on the immediate right flank of the 24th Infantry Division. The CCF 66th Army, concentrated around Taechon, on the night of 26–27 November struck the ROK 11th Regiment northeast of Taechon, and during the day attacked and forced back the ROK 12th Regiment.

At 8 A.M. on 27 November I Corps ordered General Church to send the US 19th Infantry to Pakchon as I Corps reserve and to withdraw the 21st Infantry from Chongju to Naechong-jong. There it was to establish contact on the main road with the 5th RCT on its right. During the day only the 5th RCT had important enemy contact.

Pursuant to division orders, Colonel Stephens's 21st Infantry at Chongju canceled at 8 A.M. all patrol orders and prepared to relieve the 19th Infantry at Naechong-jong. The 3rd Battalion started back at noon, and the 1st Battalion followed it an hour later. By 4:30 P.M., all 21st Regimental units had closed on Naechong-jong. When the 21st Infantry started back at noon on 27 November, it was 50 miles south of the Yalu River and the North Korean border. On 1 November, it had been located at Chonggo-dong on the coastal road, only 18 air miles south of the Yalu, the farthest north of an American unit in the Eighth Army. The 21st Infantry had no enemy contact during this latest movement northward. The CCF 50th Army was in assembly areas north of

Chongju and deliberately withheld action against the 21st Infantry, awaiting results of CCF attacks against Eighth Army elsewhere to the east.

The critical area for the 24th Division was now along its right flank, next to the ROK 1st Division. The 24th Reconnaissance Company and the 5th RCT covered this area. A 24th Reconnaissance Company patrol, with two tanks, encountered an enemy force, which local villagers estimated to number about 500 Chinese. The patrol caught most of this enemy force while its men were eating and, before they fled west, inflicted approximately 60 casualties.

Earlier, about 2:45 A.M. on 27 November, a Chinese force using heavy machine-gun fire forced a platoon of G Company, 5th RCT, to withdraw from its position. The company counterattacked after daylight and regained the lost ground at 9:30 A.M.

During 27 November, I Corps and the 24th Division were making plans to withdraw the division back to the Chongchon River line. I Corps at 10 P.M. issued its Operational Directive No. 25. It required the 24th Infantry Division to start withdrawing at 7 A.M. the next morning. The 19th Infantry, positioned east of the Taeryong River, was to be prepared to counterattack at any time in the ROK 1st Division zone during the withdrawal, but only on corps orders. Meanwhile, division troops and the 21st Infantry and 5th RCT were scheduled to withdraw without delay to a new defense line, called the Chongchon River bridgehead line. This was the same line the Eighth Army had held when it started its attack on 24 November. Heavy equipment and service trains not needed to support the immediate action were to go on south across the Chongchon River.[3]

The CCF 66th Army, from the vicinity of Taechon, carried out unrelenting attacks against the ROK 1st Division from 25 November on and, after the twenty-sixth, against the 5th RCT of the 24th Division. Two enemy divisions, the 196th and the 197th, of the 66th Army operated against the ROK 1st Division, and the 198th Division against the 5th RCT. Thus, the CCF 66th Army, with its main force against the ROK 1st Division, straddled the boundary between the ROK 1st Division and the 24th Division, with at least elements of one division driving south along the right flank of the 24th Division zone. The 5th RCT guarded this flank for the 24th Infantry Division. The CCF 50th Army, to the north of the 24th Division in the coastal area, apparently never entered the battle, or at most made only a few reconnaissance contacts.

The CCF 66th Army was on line with the 198th Division on its right (west) flank and apparently west of the main road that ran south from Taechon through Unsok-tong to Kasan. The road from Taechon south was the general boundary between the 24th Infantry Division and the ROK 1st Division. This meant that the road also was the boundary between the 5th RCT and the ROK 1st Division. The latter held the zone east of it to the divide between the Taeryong and the Kuryong rivers. East of the Taechon road, the CCF 197th and 196th divisions, on line from west to east, drove against the ROK 1st Division, pushing it back toward Pakchon. In effect, the CCF 66th Army was carrying out the Chinese right (west) flank attack of the 2nd Phase Offensive against the 5th RCT of the US 24th Division and the ROK 1st Division, with the ROK 1st Division bearing the brunt of the attack.

About 3 A.M. on 28 November, an estimated two Chinese battalions attacked the 2nd and 3rd battalions of the 5th RCT along the ROK 1st Division boundary. The enemy assault teams split K Company at three places and L Company at two places. Both companies had to withdraw. They reassembled on I Company, which was then in 3rd Battalion reserve. By 3:30 A.M., the 5th RCT repulsed this Chinese attack. It then disengaged and, on orders, withdrew to an assembly area southeast of Pakchon, where it closed by 3 P.M. that afternoon. At 4:20 P.M., the 24th Reconnaissance Company and E Company, 5th RCT, received the mission of securing the peninsula of land southwest of Pakchon between the Taeryong and Chongchon rivers. The 5th RCT now went into I Corps reserve, with one battalion taking a blocking position at the Chongchon River crossing site east of Anju.[4]

Meanwhile, the 21st Infantry Regiment received orders at 3:45 A.M. on 28 November to fall back to the old Chongchon River bridgehead line, west of Pakchon. Most of it arrived at its new position before noon. The 3rd Battalion brought up the rear, closing there at 3:30 in the afternoon. The 21st Regiment had no enemy contact during the move. The 19th Infantry remained behind to defend Pakchon.[5]

At 10:55 A.M. on 28 November Eighth Army sent an order by radio to I Corps and IX Corps, and to all divisions in the two corps, to execute a withdrawal to the Chongchon River bridgehead line. This line began on the west at the north bank of the river near the village of Kwanhae-dong, approximately 15 miles southwest of Pakchon, extending from there to Pakchon, where it turned slightly north of east for a distance of nearly 20 miles to Won-ni on the Chongchon River. There the line turned sharply southeast to Pukchang-ni, a distance of 25 miles, and from there continued on the same axis about 28 miles to the village of Taeul-li on the boundary between X Corps and Eighth Army. This defense line crossed the Chongchon River from the north to the south side at Won-ni. Eighth Army units were to organize, occupy, and defend along this line, utilizing the most favorable terrain, and be "prepared for resumption of offensive at an early date."[6] The most interesting part of this order was that calling for readiness to resume the offensive at an early date. It seems incredible that on 28 November General Walker and his Eighth Army staff could have seriously contemplated a resumption of the offensive in the near future.

At noon on 28 November I Corps issued its own Operational Directive No. 26, ordering its units to carry out the Eighth Army order, and gave some specific missions to the 24th Infantry and ROK 1st Divisions. The 24th Infantry Division was to establish defensive positions in the ROK 1st Division sector of the bridgehead line and secure the left flank of the I Corps; the ROK 1st Division was to defend while the 24th Division did this, then it was to withdraw through the 24th Division positions, reorganize, and take over the lines established by the 24th Division. Once the ROK 1st Division had taken over this defensive line, the 24th Division was to move south in army reserve and assemble in the vicinity of Sunchon—except for one regiment, the 5th RCT, which would assemble in the vicinity of Anju to protect the Chongchon River crossings until all I Corps troops had crossed to the south side of the river. These movements were to be executed at once—at the earliest possible time. At 5 P.M.

that afternoon, I Corps ordered the 24th Division to Sunchon, except for the 5th RCT. Eighth Army by this order transferred the 24th Division from I Corps to the IX Corps, but at the same time the 25th Division from IX Corps was attached to I Corps.[7]

On 29 November the 24th Infantry Division continued its withdrawal of all units to a point below (or south of) the Chongchon River and was out of contact with the enemy. Its destination, as fast as it could reach it, was Sunchon, 20 air miles south of the Chongchon River and in the IX Corps zone of operation. The 555th Field Artillery remained behind in support of the 5th RCT at the river bridges.

Chinese units were now boldly concentrating and moving in daylight in pursuit of Eighth Army units, everywhere in retreat. This was an unusual practice for the Chinese because it exposed them to crippling air attack. But with the entire Eighth Army suffering defeat and in retreat, the Chinese command apparently thought the results of hot pursuit in daytime worth the risk. At the same time, their trucks and pack convoys moved south in daylight from the Manchurian border to bring supplies to the front, and at night their trucks hurried south with headlights on.

On 29 November the 21st Infantry CP closed north of the Chongchon River at 2 P.M. and opened south of the river at Anju three hours later. The 24th Division G-3 telephoned the regiment to move all units across the river and those with transportation to continue on south to Sunchon. The 1st and 3rd battalions remained near Anju for the night but proceeded to Sunchon the next morning.[8]

On the 29th, the 5th RCT received an alert to move to its blocking positions at the bridgehead on the Chongchon River to cover the withdrawal of corps troops to the south side. The bridgehead blocking position was approximately five miles northeast of Anju on the Chongchon River road and across the stream from the village of Yongchon-dong. The 5th RCT closed into its blocking position at 5:30 P.M. 29 November. The 1st Battalion took its position at the river near the crossing sites; the 3rd Battalion blocked on the river road on the south side against attack from the north; and the 2nd Battalion remained in regimental reserve.[9]

The ROK 1st Division, commanded by Brig. Gen. Paik Sun Yup, was on the right of the I Corps advance in the Eighth Army attack that began on 24 November. Its axis of advance was almost due north from Pakchon toward Taechon. It straddled the Taeryong River, which emptied into the Chongchon near its mouth.

The Taeryong between Taechon and Pakchon ran a meandering course through low hills, none more than 1,000 feet high. Just northeast of Taechon, however, a high rugged mountain mass between 2,000 and 2,500 feet high formed a barrier between the Taeryong River on the west and the Kuryong River on the east; the two rivers were separated on average by about 14 air miles. The two highest peaks of this high ground were named Hyangjok-san, 782 meters high, and Mulsil-san, three miles westward, 750 meters high. The highest point in the eastern extremity of this mountain mass, near the Kuryong River and the boundary between the ROK 1st Division and the 25th Division, was Obongsan, 598 meters high. The ROK 1st Division advance on 25 November ran straight into this mountain east of Taechon. There the Chinese awaited them.

One of the main north-south roads in western Korea ran along the Taeryong valley toward the border, and it was certain to be a center of enemy concentration. It was a foregone conclusion that the ROK 1st Infantry Division would have tough going if the Chinese intended to attack Eighth Army or to defend against it in strength.

In studying the Korean War it is generally very hard to find reliable, detailed information about the actions of the South Korean Army. This is true even of those divisions attached to an American army corps. At this time, General Paik's ROK 1st Division was the only ROK division attached to an American army corps (I Corps) in Eighth Army. The Americans considered it a good division; it was well led, had more artillery support attached to it than any other ROK division, and had given an excellent account of itself in the war thus far. It was thus not far below, if not equal to, the standard of American divisions in its infantry action. But the American military records relating to the Korean War do not contain any South Korean unit reports of battalions, regiments, divisions, and corps. There are no South Korean staff S or G-1, -2, -3, -4 journals. The attached Korean units were not subject to the US Army's reporting system, and they made few if any written reports to their own government during the first year of the war.

The information one does find in American records comes from American Military Advisor messages to the Chief of KMAG, a member of the Eighth Army Staff. American advisors were attached to South Korean units down to battalion level. American units fighting adjacent to ROK units usually reported some incidents or the condition of the ROK troops at various stages of combat, because the ROK units on their flanks often affected them. The Eighth Army combined G-2/G-3 situation maps accompanying the daily G-2 Intelligence Summary often gave location data on ROK units.

Only these sources, as well as aerial observer reports, had the information that is needed to piece together a general account of ROK military action. A similar dearth of information exists in the case of the ROK 1st Division in the CCF 2nd Phase Offensive; some reference to it is found in the Eighth Army KMAG reports, I Corps reports, and reports of the 5th RCT, which fought on its western flank, and from reports of the 35th Infantry, which fought on its eastern flank. Aerial reports occasionally refer to the ROK 1st Division situation. But there is not available the amount of specific detail that is sometimes found in American records for US units. Personal accounts of ROK participants are almost never encountered.

For these reasons the ROK story is of necessity more generalized than the American, and it may also be not as reliable. However, the ROK action must be described to the full extent that the available facts will allow. The ROK 1st Division played an important part in the war, as did other ROK units at different times and places. Considering what happened in other sectors of the Eighth Army front in the last week of November 1950, the hard fighting of the ROK 1st Division stands comparison with the American divisions.

For the drive north, General Paik had established his division headquarters at Maengjung-dong, about five miles north of Sinanju on the main road from there to Pakchon. It happened to be about midway between the Chongchon River and the Taeryong River, where the road came to the east bank of the latter, seven miles south of Pakchon. At Maengjung-dong, the west coast main Korean rail line turned west to cross the Taeryong River and follow the westward bulge of the Korean peninsula to the Manchurian border. The town was an important rail and road center for control of military actions between the Chongchon River and the western part of Korea northward.

General Paik had an unusually large concentration of artillery attached to his division for the attack toward Taechon, in addition to the 17th Field Artillery Battalion, which was the division's usual support. Col. W. H. Hennig's 10th AAA Group had overall command of the artillery supporting the ROK 1st Division in this attack. It included the 78th AAA Gun Battalion, commanded by Lt. Col. Thomas W. Ackert; the 9th Field Artillery Battalion (155-mm howitzers), commanded by Maj. Thomas A. Arnold; and a rocket battery. Maj. John B. Coontz was the 10th AAA group liaison officer with the ROK 1st Division. In the initial approach to Taechon, the 78th AAA Gun Battalion supported the ROK 12th Regiment. Before the ROK 1st Division withdrew to the Chongchon River on the night of 29–30 November and while it was defending an extensive perimeter at the vital road center of Pakchon, two more artillery battalions, the 555th (105-mm howitzer) Artillery Battalion and the 68th AAA Gun Battalion, were added to its support.[10]

General Paik deployed his 11th Regiment on the division right and the 12th Regiment on his left as he advanced on Taechon. The 15th Regiment was in reserve. On the night of 24–25 November the 12th Regiment just south of Taechon had a quiet night, but the 11th Regiment about two and a half to six miles northeast of Taechon received a strong CCF attack. The ROK 11th Regiment was the most advanced unit of the ROK division. A Chinese force estimated to be a battalion struck it shortly after 3 A.M. on 25 November. In a battle that lasted until after dawn, the CCF forced the 1st Battalion back one and a half miles. With the coming of daylight, the enemy force withdrew from contact. During 25 November, the 1st Battalion reoccupied its lost position along the Taeryong River. It reported finding about 700 Chinese dead in the ground it reoccupied.[11]

Chinese prisoners taken during the night battle indicated that the 196th, 197th, and 198th divisions of the 66th Army were on the high ground and north and northeast of Taechon. Two of these divisions, the 196th and 197th, were in front of the ROK 1st Division to the north and northeast of Taechon. The third division, the 198th, it was learned later, initially held the west side of the CCF 66th Army front and was engaged mostly with the US 5th RCT of the US 24th Division west of the ROK boundary, although that division also was involved in fighting with the ROK 1st Division at times.

The Eighth Army situation maps for 25 and 26 November show that the ROK 11th Regiment's most advanced units were attacking the high ground of Mulsil-san and Hyangjok-san (2,000–2,500 feet in elevation) when the CCF struck them. The ROKs did not capture any of this high ground and were pushed back from the outset of the Chinese attack. During 25 November, the ROKs held their positions after the attack of the night before but made virtually no gain.

The CCF attack against the 11th Regiment of the ROK 1st Division northeast of Taechon during the early hours of 25 November was the earliest frontal attack against the Eighth Army in the CCF 2nd Phase Offensive. The ROK 1st Division had reached CCF assembly areas, and the CCF could not allow it to proceed farther.

CCF forces kept the 11th Regiment under attack from midnight on through 26 November, from the west, north, and northeast. The 2nd Battalion of the 11th Regiment came under a series of attacks, beginning at midnight. One enemy battalion hit the ROK 2nd Battalion by moving along a network of mountain trails, and another enemy battalion struck it from a more easterly direction, both from Hills 782 and 750 in the Hyangjok-san mountain mass, five to six miles northeast of Taechon. The ROK 11th Regiment, now quite disorganized, withdrew. It became necessary for General Paik to commit his reserve, the ROK 15th Regiment. It moved up on the right (east) of the 11th Regiment. Its 3rd Battalion took a position about seven miles east of Taechon between Sonhwa-dong and Tonggol, on the lower hills of the Hyangjok-san mountain. The 2nd Battalion was behind it and a little nearer to Taechon, but southeast of the town.

Another enemy force on the night of 25–26 November crossed the Chonbang River two miles south of Taechon and struck the ROK 12th Regiment. The Chinese achieved a penetration there, but the 12th Regiment quickly counterattacked and regained its position.

It seems likely that elements of both the 196th and 197th divisions of the CCF 66th Army were trying to overrun the ROK 11th Regiment. Their attack did not stop with the coming of daylight. Air strikes hit the northern slope of Hill 659, where enemy horses and soldiers were good targets. With the help of artillery fire and many air strikes, the 2nd Battalion, 11th Regiment, beat off the attacks from the northwest by noon. The Chinese attacking from the north and northeast changed tactics at this time to move around the east flank along the ROK division boundary with the 25th Division. This move was halted by 1:35 P.M. But an hour and a half later, two enemy companies penetrated the ROK line to Hill 358. A ROK counterattack forced the Chinese to withdraw from there.[12]

In the fighting on this day, 26 November, near Taechon, ROK troops captured a copy of a pamphlet in Chinese, entitled "Primary Conclusions of Battle Experience at UNSAN," printed from handwritten notes by the Chinese People's Volunteer Army Headquarters, 66th Army, on 20 November 1950. This pamphlet analyzed the fighting weaknesses, as the Chinese saw them, of the American troops in the battles near Unsan in the 1st Phase Chinese Offensive at the end of October, nearly a month earlier. As previously mentioned, this pamphlet, or extracts from it, was translated into English and widely distributed among UN forces in Korea.

During the night of 26–27 November the CCF continued their assaults on the ROK 1st Division. A Chinese attack struck the 2nd and 3rd battalions, 11th Regiment, after midnight. By 4 A.M., the regiment was badly disorganized, and it withdrew through the ROK 15th Regiment. The CCF gained about six miles in this attack on the right of the ROK 1st Division. The 2nd and 3rd battalions of the ROK 15th Regiment at 5 A.M. now had the task of holding the Chinese assaults on the division right.

At the same time, other Chinese formations attacked the left side of the ROK 1st Division south of Taechon. There, enemy attacked the 2nd Battalion, 12th Regiment, at 2:30 A.M. on 27 November, forcing it to withdraw. The battalion reorganized and after daylight counterattacked just after noon and regained its earlier position.

During the night of 26–27 November the combat was intense all along the ROK 1st Division line. The Chinese now held Taechon and the high ground above the town and from these places mounted attack after attack. In an unusual effort, the 78th AAA Gun Battalion during the night conducted seven different missions of marking enemy targets with white phosphorus for the Air Force. Night-flying planes then bombed and strafed those enemy targets. According to ROK patrols that went into some of these target areas the next day, the 78th AAA Gun Battalion fire and the resulting aerial bombing during the night resulted in hundreds of enemy dead.[13]

At 11:15 A.M., an estimated regiment of Chinese infantry and a squadron of horse cavalry hit the right flank of the ROK 1st Division, mainly the ROK 15th Regiment. These daylight attacks on 27 November were as unrelenting as the Chinese night attacks usually were. Now there was no respite when daylight came, even with air strikes helping to stem the enemy advances.

The ROK 15th Regiment had to withdraw farther south from its defensive positions around Kandong, six miles southeast of Taechon on the road to Yongsan-dong. The ROK 11th Regiment was now in the vicinity of Yongsan-dong, another six miles southeast of Kandong. At Yongsan-dong the road forked into two main escape routes for wheeled and tracked vehicles. The road to the east crossed the Kuryong River and went on to Yongbyon in the 25th Infantry Division sector; the road southwest led to Pakchon, ten miles away. By dark on 27 November, the ROK 1st Division was being pushed back at a rapid rate, and its 11th Regiment was hardly combat effective.[14]

The worst was still ahead for the ROK 1st Division when darkness came on the evening of 27 November. The ROK 12th Regiment was on the west side of the division front, about five miles south of Taechon, next to the 5th RCT of the 24th Division. In the center, 10 to 12 air miles southeast of Taechon, the reorganized remnants of the ROK 11th Regiment were in position a few miles northwest of Yongsan-dong to cover the road from Taechon. The ROK 15th Regiment was centered at Yongsan-dong, with its headquarters in that town and adjoining the 35th Regiment of the 25th Division immediately on its right (east). The 35th Regiment had to pass through Yongsan-dong to reach safety eastward across the Kuryong River. The Chinese after midnight pressed everywhere between the Taeryong and Kuryong rivers – against the 5th RCT of the 24th Division, all of the ROK 1st Division, the 35th Infantry, and Task Force Dolvin of the 25th Infantry Division. At 1:45 A.M. on 28 November a Chinese attack penetrated the ROK 12th Regiment and, after two and a half hours of battle, forced the regiment to withdraw through the 11th Regiment to a defensive position on the Chongchon River bridgehead line, south of Pakchon.

Even earlier, the coordinated attack of the CCF 66th Army, using all three of its divisions, started against the ROK 1st Division just before 1 A.M. The attack initially struck the ROK 15th Regiment on the division right and broke through it after only 15 minutes of close combat. The regiment carried on a fighting withdrawal of two miles to Yongsan-dong. The Chinese force followed up fast and got behind all three battalions of the regiment. They surrounded Yongsan-dong. The ROK 15th Regimental CP in the town was overrun, but some of the staff escaped. Either a part of this Chinese assault force or another from the west cut the road to Pakchon, southwest of Yongsan-dong. In the hours before dawn of 28 November it appeared that the Chinese had just about encircled the ROK 11th and 15th regiments and were in a position to destroy the division as a fighting force. The ROK 15th Regiment's surviving units were trying to hold positions approximately two miles southeast of Yongsan-dong on the Pakchon road.

The CPs of both the ROK 11th and 15th regiments were overrun during the night, and both regimental commanders were lost or missing. The artillery supporting the two regiments had to make quick decisions and act rapidly to save themselves. The 78th AAA Battalion received orders to go to Pakchon from its exposed firing positions to the northwest, from which it had been supporting the ROK 12th Regiment. The 9th Field Artillery Battalion of 155-mm howitzers moved to positions just northeast of Pakchon, and the two northernmost ROK batteries of the 17th Field Artillery Battalion also moved quickly to the vicinity of Pakchon. Pakchon was the crossroads in this vital area just north of the Chongchon River crossing areas near its mouth and around which a defense line had to be maintained if I Corps troops were to escape southward across the river.

In the critical hours before daylight on 28 November, Gen. Paik Sun Yup "accomplished the impossible," as one participant wrote later. With the 11th and 15th regiments cut off and without their regimental commanders, their strength critically reduced by killed, wounded, and missing, Paik went forward, found most of the scattered units, reorganized them, and brought the two regiments into positions where they once again confronted the victorious Chinese. He ordered counterattacks, which reestablished part of the line around Yongsan-dong, and recaptured the town. It is said that the ROK infantry who recaptured Yongsan-dong on 28 November counted 400 dead Chinese in the town, most of them killed by 90-mm artillery fire.

Acting on an Eighth Army order an hour earlier, I Corps at noon on 28 November ordered its units to withdraw to the Chongchon River bridgehead line. The ROK 1st Division was charged with initially holding the critical road junctions and areas around Yongsan-dong and southward long enough to permit the 24th Infantry Division to get through below Pakchon and establish a defensive line north of the Chongchon River. The ROK 1st Division was then to pass through the 24th Division and take over its defensive positions. In accordance with this order, the ROK 15th Regiment withdrew southwestward from Yongsan-dong at 9 P.M. that night.[15]

On 29 November, the ROK 1st Division held its positions around Pakchon while the 24th Infantry Division withdrew through the town and turned south toward the Chongchon River. The ROK 1st Division then began its own withdrawal southward, with the CCF 39th and 66th armies pressing hard against it. The ROK 11th and 15th regiments withdrew through the ROK 12th Regiment to the Chongchon River crossing sites. The ROK 12th Regiment held rear-guard defensive positions. When the 11th and 15th regiments had cleared to the south side of the river, the 12th Regiment followed. All these withdrawals were greatly aided by air strikes on an estimated 5,000 Chinese pursuing the ROKs and trying to break through on them. Heavy artillery fire of the 10th AAA Group in front (north) of the withdrawing ROKs also played a role in keeping the Chinese from closing in and driving through to the Chongchon River. This artillery fire against the advancing enemy was continued during the night.

The 10th AAA Group had remained uncomfortably close to the massed enemy in laying down their heavy and steady interdiction fires. But after dark the artillery began its withdrawal to the river. The 78th Battalion was the first to move, followed by the 17th, the 9th, then the 10th Group Headquarters, the Rocket Battery, and finally the 68th Field Artillery Battalion. This latter battalion maintained its fires against a major enemy crossing site of the Taeryong River just north of Pakchon, where the Chinese repeatedly massed battalion-sized groups for a crossing. The artillery in each instance broke up these attempts, with heavy loss of life for the Chinese. The 68th Battalion fired on this crossing site until 4 A.M. on 30 November, when it left its firing positions to withdraw. At that time the 78th and 9th field artillery battalions took up the barrages against the Chinese from the south side of the Chongchon. Observers reported the Chinese were still on the other side of the river north of Pakchon when the 68th Battalion began its withdrawal.[16]

At the end of the day on 29 November, the ROK 1st Division was south of the Chongchon River and moving to assembly areas southwest of Sinanju. The 10th Group Artillery Headquarters left Maengjung-dong at 7 A.M. on 30 November, and two hours later it was south of the river and on its way to Sukchon. I Corps withdrawal south of the Chongchon River had been accomplished.

The heavy fighting in the I and IX corps areas beginning the night of 25 November caused an increasing number of casualties to be brought to the K-29 airfield near Sinanju for evacuation, mostly to hospitals in Japan. On 28 November, 1,283 casualties were air evacuated from K-29. The Medical Battalion reported that never before in Korea had wounded been admitted to the Clearing Stations in such large numbers so quickly. Ambulances evacuated the wounded from the Clearing Stations. They included men from the 2nd, 25th, and 24th divisions, the 1st Cavalry Division, and Turks and ROKs. Since there were not enough ambulances to transport all the wounded to the Sinanju airfield, 2½-ton trucks were used to supplement them. On 29 November, 1,200 additional casualties were evacuated from K-29 airfield.[17] These figures of nearly 2,500 casualties evacuated by air rivaled figures for the evacuations by air from Hagaru-ri in the Chosin Reservoir fighting in the X Corps area of northeast Korea at nearly the same time.[18]

10. The CCF 40th Army Attack on the US 2nd Infantry Division

The US 2nd Infantry Division held perhaps the most pivotal position in the Eighth Army line. It straddled the Chongchon River in its advance north from Kunu-ri into the heart of the enemy area along the main highway and rail line that led northeast to the border area of Kanggye and Manpojin. The Chinese were certain to concentrate here, if anywhere, against an attack to the border.

The 2nd Infantry Division had no opposition in its advance on 24 and 25 November except that, on the twenty-fifth, its B Company, 9th Infantry, ran into stubborn enemy resistance when it tried to occupy Hill 219, just north of Sinhung-dong, on the east side of the Chongchon River. The Chinese screening force there still held the hill at dark when B Company, badly used up, withdrew down the slope to positions near its base. This was an unexpected setback.

Col. Paul L. Freeman's 23rd Infantry was to move up that evening to pass through the 9th Infantry the next morning, to lead the advance on Huichon, the division's immediate objective. But 2nd Division troops never got beyond Hill 219 on the river road. Hill 219 marked the place where the CCF 2nd Phase Offensive began against the 2nd Infantry Division.

The 9th Infantry, which led the 2nd Division up the Chongchon River on the first day of the advance, was split by the Chongchon River. The Regimental Headquarters and the 1st Battalion were grouped on the east side of the river near Sinhung-dong. The 2nd and 3rd battalions were west of the river. The 3rd Battalion was the farthest west, with I Company adjacent to the 25th Infantry boundary, approximately four miles from the river. K and L companies were on hills east and northeast of it on opposite sides of the Dry Creek bed that led to the Chongchon River a mile below Sinhung-dong. There was no communication between the three companies or the 3rd Battalion CP on the evening of 25 November.

The 2nd Battalion Headquarters and its E Company were on the east side of the river at Sinhung-dong, along with the 1st Battalion headquarters. The rest of the 2nd Battalion was in position on Hill 180 across the river from Sinhung-dong, on its west side. Hill 180 was just north of Dry Creek at its juncture with the Chongchon. It would seem that K and L companies of the 3rd Battalion together with the bulk of the 2nd Battalion on Hill 180 would dominate and control any enemy approach along Dry Creek to the Chongchon.

As described earlier, the 38th Infantry Regiment had requested and had been granted permission to move ahead of the rest of the division to a jump-off line that it felt would improve its starting point. It was on the right, or east, of the 9th Infantry, holding a series of hill positions along the Paengnyong River, which flowed from the east and emptied into the Chongchon just south of Sinhungdong. The 38th Regiment's western boundary with the 9th Infantry was at Hill 291, one and a half air miles southeast of Sinhung-dong. The Paengnyong River, a key feature in the 38th Infantry's zone of action, rose eastward near Tokchon in the divide between the Chongchon and the Taedong rivers.

Several hours before B Company of the 9th Infantry found enemy holding Hill 219, north of Sinhung-dong, the 38th Infantry before dawn on 25 November had started a company-sized reconnaissance patrol from the valley of the Paengnyong toward massive Hill 1229, five air miles north of the valley. A Company of the 1st Battalion drew this assignment. Its mission was to investigate aerial and other intelligence reports that a large enemy force had concentrated there. The twisting and steep mountain trails that led toward the crest of Hill 1229 from the Paengnyong valley must have been about three times the aerial distance—perhaps 15 miles. This patrol was the first unit of the 38th Infantry to encounter enemy and engage in hostilities—in the hills bordering the Paengnyong east of Sinhung-ni. At dark on 25 November, the patrol had made only about one-third of the distance to Hill 1229, harassed most of the way by enemy screening forces. The probability that it would ever reach the crest of Hill 1229 looked slim.

Meanwhile, the bulk of the 38th Regiment and its attached units continued their deployment eastward on the road leading from Kujang-dong toward Tokchon. The 38th Field Artillery Battalion of 105-mm howitzers, commanded by Lt. Col. Robert J. O'Donnell, the regular support for the 38th Infantry Regiment, with A Battery of the 503rd Field Artillery Battalion (155-mm howitzers) attached, followed the infantry regiment eastward on the Kujang-dong–Somin-dong–Tokchon road and went into position south of Col. George B. Peploe's 38th Regimental CP at Somin-dong.[1]

About 6 P.M. on 25 November, Col. Paul L. Freeman, Jr., and his 23rd Regimental Headquarters Company, with Lt. Col. Claire E. Hutchins, Jr.'s 1st Battalion and the 503rd Field Artillery Battalion (minus A Battery), came up behind the 9th Infantry elements on the east side of the Chongchon River at Sinhung-dong and went into bivouac along the west side of Chinaman's Hat for the night. Freeman did not at that time have control of his 2nd and 3rd battalions, but it was expected they would be available to him that night or the next day.

The CCF 40th Army Strikes Swiftly

The 40th CCF Field Army, composed of the 118th, 119th, and 120th divisions, had remained hidden for more than a week in assembly areas near Unsan and Kan-dong about 10 to 12 air miles north and northwest of Sinhung-dong and Kujang-dong. The 40th Field Army's mission was to attack any force that advanced up the Chongchon River toward Huichon. This Chinese Army was considered to be perhaps the best on all-around offensive and defensive capabilities of any army in the CCF XIII Army Group that confronted Eighth Army.

Chinese prisoners captured during the night of 25 November and the next morning on the east side of the Chongchon River in the vicinity of Chinaman's Hat provided a good description of how the CCF 40th Army moved into action against the US 2nd Infantry Division. It first hit the 9th Infantry Regiment on the division left because that regiment was athwart its approach march to the Chongchon River. The fast-moving enemy columns of the 120th Division, the lead division of the Chinese 40th Army, accidentally ran right into the 3rd Battalion. The 3rd Battalion, 9th Infantry, was virtually destroyed that night, and the rest of the regiment was decimated in the following 24 hours.

The CCF 40th Army had crossed the Yalu River at Sinanju on 24–25 October and had attacked the ROK 6th Division in the 1st Phase Offensive, rendering it largely combat ineffective. It then moved south and engaged American forces in other battles near the Chongchon, the 8th Cavalry Regiment suffering heavy casualties in these actions. The CCF Army reassembled at Unsan after the 1st Phase Offensive ended. There We Yu Shu, the cultural officer of the Heavy Weapons Company, 2nd Battalion, 359th Regiment of the 120th Chinese Division, captured at Chinaman's Hat on 26 November, said the Chinese 40th Army spent the time from 5 to 25 November 1950 in regrouping and reequipping. The 120th Division led the advance of the 40th Army to the Chongchon River on 25 November. He said his regiment received orders at 3 P.M. 25 November to advance that night to the Chongchon River at Kujang-dong.

We Yu Shu said the 359th Regiment started its march at dark, using mountain trails across country. It was thoroughly trained in night movement and warfare. Its strategy in night battle was to use rifles as little as possible, since that gave away positions, and to rely on grenades in close approach to an enemy. On leaving Unsan, each man had five days' rations of corn and millet and 100 rounds of small-arms ammunition. Each soldier also carried four grenades. Shu said the regiment arrived at the Chongchon River at midnight and waded across it in waist-deep water. While Kujang-dong was given as the regiment's destination, we know that it actually reached and crossed the Chongchon in the vicinity of Chinaman's Hat and Sinhung-dong, because that is where Shu and many other members of the 359th Regiment were captured during the night of 25–26 November and the next morning.

Another Chinese prisoner captured that night was Capt. Chang Han-chung, commanding officer of the 6th Company, 2nd Battalion, 359th Regiment. He had been a Chinese Nationalist soldier until 1948, when he was captured and incorporated into the Chinese Communist Army. He described the Chinese system of communication in the 120th Division as using courier at all levels, radio at regimental and higher levels, telephone (when wire could be laid) and signal flares at battalion level, bugle at company level, and whistles at platoon level.[2]

No map locations for K and L companies, 9th Infantry, have been found in army records. Their locations on the night of 25 November are therefore hard to plot. From survivor evidence, however, it appears that K Company was on a hill on the north side of the 30-foot-wide, sand-bottomed creek bed known only as Dry Creek in the records and in the personal recollections of

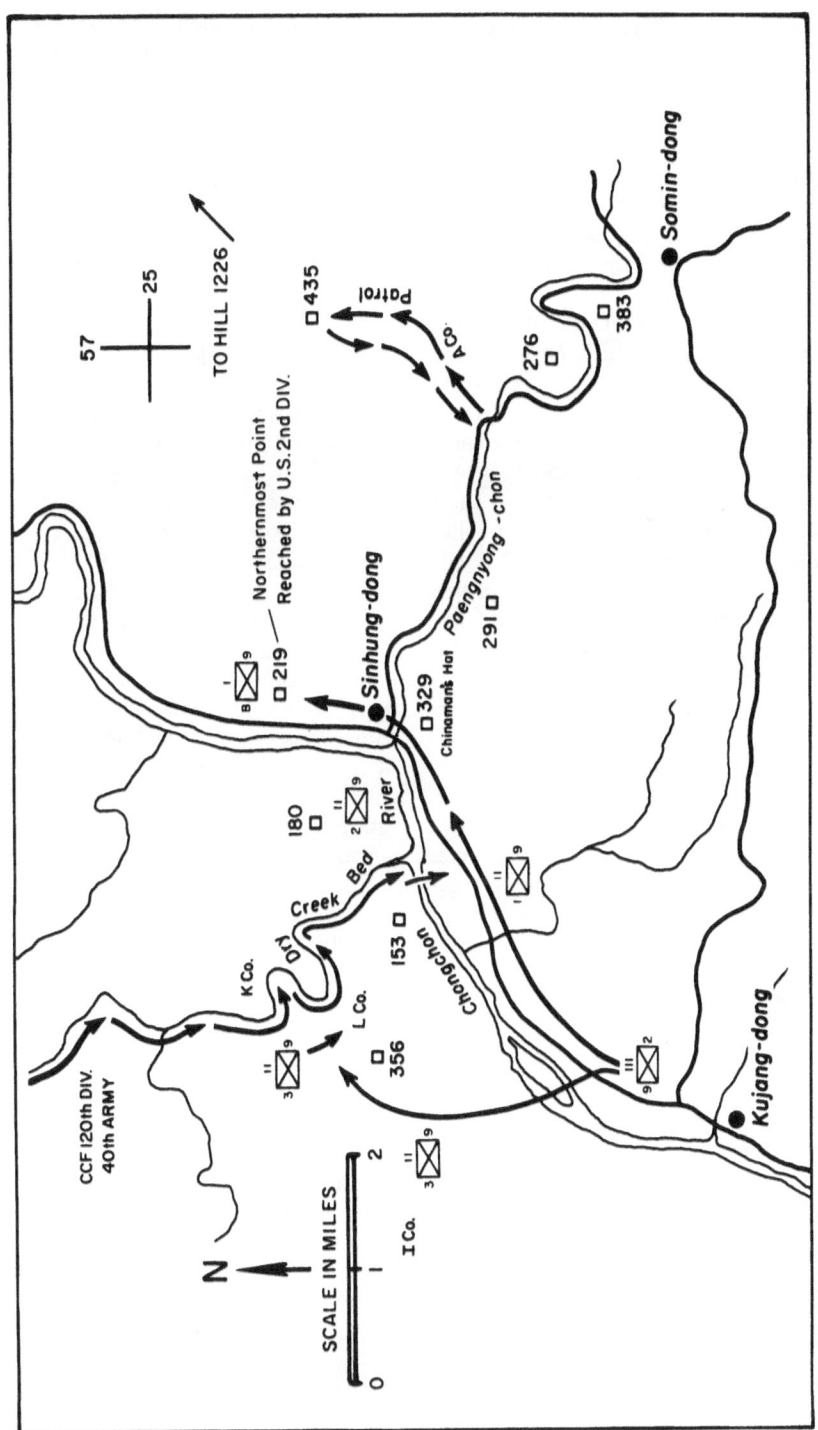

Map 7. The CCF attack on the 9th Infantry Regiment, 2nd Infantry Division, 25 November 1950.

participants. The company's position on meandering Dry Creek was about two air miles northwest of the creek's junction with the Chongchon River a mile west of Sinhung-dong, where the river in its own meandering course ran almost east to west. The distance to the river by the creek bed must have been about three miles. L Company was downstream, approximately one and a half miles from K Company, occupying a part of Hill 356 on the south side of Dry Creek. The third company of the battalion, I Company, was about a mile and a half west across the hills from L Company and Dry Creek. It was not in the path of the Chinese approach march and escaped enemy contact on the night of 25 November.

K Company, commanded by Capt. Benjamin J. Benton, was at very low strength, about one-third, having only 65 men in all, including attached ROK soldiers. It included only five BARs and two light machine guns. Some of its men had one or two grenades. Others had none. The company had marched all day in the hills, and when they reached their objective on Dry Creek, they were tired. They had not eaten since breakfast.

Captain Benton did not occupy the high ground of his position. He placed one platoon on a western knob of the hill ridge; the other two he placed at the bottom of the hill, facing them north and west toward the nearby Dry Creek. The west end of K Company's position was less than 100 feet from the bed of Dry Creek. The hill ridge itself was a weak position, as it had easy incline approaches to its crest from the creek bottom and from the north. Benton had communication with neither the 3rd Battalion nor L Company across Dry Creek southwest of him. He did not send out patrols to locate L Company. K Company was a weak force in a weak, isolated position on the night of 25 November.

Pfc. Louis Giudici was in an outpost position in what had been a cornfield along the creek bottom, at the west end of the K Company position, within 35 to 40 feet of Dry Creek. He manned a light machine gun. Two ROK riflemen guarded him. The moon was out and spread a bright silver sheen over the landscape. Giudici happened to glance at his watch and noted it was 7 P.M. At that moment he heard some small-arms fire to the south. A bugle sounded from the north and another from the west, and then other bugle sounds came from the south.

Within a few seconds Giudici heard the sound of tramping men. And then he saw them—coming down the creek bed toward him. Those in the lead were in small groups of about six men each, with small spaces between them. They seemed to carry no small arms. They came at double-time. Giudici saw them first at a distance of 250 to 300 feet. He waited to open fire when they came abreast of him, about 35 feet distant in the turn of the creek bed. But before that moment came, he saw a solid column of enemy infantry, four abreast, carrying rifles and submachine guns at port, moving at a rapid pace, following the advance groups. Giudici held his fire. For 17 minutes he watched the column go by, never pausing in its dogtrot pace. Horsemen, at intervals, rode alongside the men. He could hear them giving orders, apparently urging the men to maintain their speed.

The Chinese column, in regimental strength, did not discover Giudici and his two ROKs. Apparently they did not know that K Company was only yards away. K Company might have been spared, except that a rifleman with an M-1 had come down into the cornfield. As the last of the Chinese column started around the creek bend and would soon be lost to sight, the rifleman opened fire. Giudici thereupon cut loose with his machine gun, but after a few rounds it quit.

This one burst of automatic fire caused the tail end of the enemy column to hit the ground. When the automatic fire did not resume, Chinese rose and in a V formation walked straight toward Giudici's position. He, the two ROKs, and the rifleman ran up the hill. The K Company CP and its adjacent troops had not seen or heard the Chinese column pass.

The small-arms fire that Giudici had heard just before the Chinese infantry column came in sight had come from the 2nd Platoon at the other end of K Company's position in the valley below the hill. Apparently an advance scouting party had entered the creek valley there by chance. It may have had no direct connection with the enemy column that double-timed down the bed of Dry Creek toward the Chongchon. After its flurry of fire the 2nd Platoon had run for the hill. It did not see the enemy column pass.

With the presence of an American force now disclosed, about two companies of Chinese peeled off from the column, which never paused, and started to reconnoiter K Company's position north of the creek bed. Much of what happened thereafter is a matter of conjecture.

Pfc. Lawrence Brown in the 3rd Platoon manned the second light machine gun in the company. Two riflemen flanked him. Cpl. Eugene Mann was in a foxhole with a BAR a short distance behind Brown. None of these men had seen any targets or had fired their weapons. Without warning, a grenade dropped into the machine-gun position. Its explosion killed Brown and knocked over the machine gun. Mann saw the ROK soldier at Brown's side run for the hill. The American rifleman on the other side did not move—apparently killed by the grenade.

Mann cut loose with his BAR, although he saw no targets, and put about 50 rounds in front of the machine-gun position. Then he ran for the hill behind him. On the hill he met 2nd Lt. Al Raskin with about 15 men. There were no others in sight. Raskin told him they would have to get out. But there were two other groups of K Company men, one in the saddle between two knobs and another at the western base of the hill.

The group in the saddle was a small one of five men, consisting of Lt. George Williams and two American and two ROK soldiers. They saw a group of the Chinese soldiers that left the column at the creek bed. These enemy soldiers came toward them, firing as they came. Williams's group waited until the Chinese were within 100 feet, then fired their rifles and carbines at them. Some of the Chinese fell, but the others kept coming. The five men continued to pour small-arms fire into them. Thirty feet away, the survivors took cover. Behind them another enemy platoon was coming up the draw toward the saddle. At this point, the two ROKs ran for it. The front line of the approaching Chinese quit firing, apparently convinced that only a few men were in front of them. They apparently wanted prisoners. Suddenly, a small group of the Chinese in the first line that had taken cover rushed the three Americans, and a hand-to-hand fistfight took place. All three Americans, however, broke loose and escaped to the north side of the hill. There they barely escaped another enemy group and got away.

The other, larger group of Americans was at the west base of the ridge. It included what was left of the 3rd Platoon—about 15 men. In it were Captain Benton and Lieutenant Kreuger. The Chinese had not yet located them. According to one of the party, as he told it later, Captain Benton decided that, if any of them were to survive, they would have to abandon their position. The party moved north, the only direction that seemed to be free of enemy. But they ran into small Chinese groups even there and had frequent short firefights, losing some men. Those remaining turned east toward the Chongchon River, hoping to work their way back to friendly lines. But some of the men decided to hide out in rock ravines until daylight. Many of those who continued on were never seen again. Most of those who hid during the night eventually escaped.

Lieutenant Raskin and Corporal Mann's group fought their way out with the help of their perfectly functioning BARs. Not until survivors reached friendly lines on the Chongchon did any part of Eighth Army know what had happened to K Company that night.[3]

An incident that later became known about K Company should be told here. In the period after K Company survivors abandoned their position and individually and in small groups tried to escape, the CCF captured Captain Benton. They took him at once to a Korean house, where a Chinese officer interrogated him. The Chinese took his watch but did not mistreat him, except that they gave him no food. When Benton asked for food, a Chinese lieutenant told him he was sorry that he had none for him, since he had not anticipated his capture. The Chinese kept Benton separate from about 25 to 30 other American prisoners they had taken in the K Company fight. Two guards were assigned to him. This Chinese force of about five platoons soon moved on to another place, taking him with them. The Chinese marched in a column of platoons to the foot of a hill, where they deployed on a bugle signal. Benton later escaped and told American debriefing interrogators that the Chinese deployed without any confusion and that there was no noise or talking until they began their attack, which began about 20 minutes after deployment.[4]

L Company, 9th Infantry, was the closest American unit to K Company when the latter's position was given away to the Chinese column in its approach march to the Chongchon River. Capt. Maxwell M. Vail's L Company was stronger in manpower than K Company, numbering about 110 men. But it was short of ammunition and had neither bedrolls nor overcoats. It had stopped for the night on 25 November on the south side of Dry Creek on an elongated ridgeline that bent north in its center toward the creek. The ridge was noted as Hill 356. It was on the south side of Dry Creek, about one and a half miles southwest from K Company's position and therefore about a mile closer to the Chongchon River.

A supply party was supposed to bring food, ammunition, and bedrolls to L Company early in the evening. A carrying party of ten men had waited near the mouth of Dry Creek for the 2½-ton truck and a jeep carrying the supplies. But the drivers of the two vehicles got lost in the dark and ended up north of Dry Creek in the 2nd Battalion position. They then turned back to the rendezvous point.

Sgt. Charles Clark, leader of the carrying party, after waiting longer than he expected for the vehicles, decided they had become lost. He sent one of his men to look for them. This messenger found them a mile or more away and guided them south along the sandy bank of the Chongchon. They made slow progress but finally arrived at the rendezvous site, where Clark and his men started to unload the vehicles.

The carrying party had unloaded only a few items when sounds of a heavy firefight to the west, on the L Company position, reached them. At the same time, they saw masses of men running toward the Chongchon in the creek bed near its mouth, just north of them. They were the Chinese in the regimental column that had passed K and L companies. Clark hurried his men away from the vehicles to a small hill nearby. Although some of the carrying party had called out to the men in Dry Creek when they had first seen them, they received no answer. The CCF column never paused but continued on to the river. At this time a group of six men, escapees from K Company, joined Clark's group.

Back at the truck unloading spot, the drivers of the two vehicles had taken off in their trucks, for the river, and somehow got them across to the east side. Once there, they turned south toward the artillery positions at Kujang-dong. But they very soon ran into a Chinese roadblock. The truck driver was never seen again; Sgt. Joel Henry in the jeep was wounded twice in making his escape. These events explain why L Company did not get their expected bedrolls and an ammunition resupply that evening.

When the CCF regiment dogtrotted past K Company, it did not have far to go before it would come in sight of L Company's position. In less than a mile it would be abreast of its western edge. As it chanced, L Company had advance warning, but not by much, before Chinese appeared at its position. Two ROK soldiers who had escaped Chinese captors some days earlier were hiding out for the night in a schoolhouse on the northeast side of Dry Creek, about half a mile below K Company. It was only a matter of minutes after the point of the big Chinese column had passed K Company before it appeared in the creek bed in front of the schoolhouse, dogtrotting in the moonlight. The two ROKs watched in fascination and fear as the Chinese hurried past. They counted 25 horsemen interspersed in the column and estimated the enemy force as about 2,000 men, all carrying arms. As soon as the rear of the column passed, the two ROKs broke from the building and started on a run southward over the hills to a ridge where they had seen bonfires burning. They reasoned that these fires could only be on an American position. They were right. In a short time they came panting into the 3rd Platoon, L Company's position.

Squad bonfires stretched the full length of L Company's position, outlining perfectly the location and extent of the company. Captain Vail had authorized the bonfires when his men complained of the cold. One of the biggest fires was at his CP. Because the two ROKs had seen the bonfires from upstream, there could be no doubt the Chinese had seen them also, and as the creek bed curved north around the L Company hill position, they had good close-up views of the fires and the areas they lighted as they came abreast of it. As in the case of K Company, some companies of Chinese dropped out of the column and began enveloping the position. There was no firing or noise of any kind, even though one L Company outpost was within 200 yards of the creek. No one in L Company knew a Chinese column had just passed them. Their first knowledge came from the two ROK soldiers who burst suddenly into the western end of their position and said excitedly, "You are in great danger!"

A member of the platoon immediately took the two ROKs to the 2nd Platoon leader, Lt. Gene Takahashi. They told him what they had seen. Takahashi accepted their story. But he reasoned from it that the Chinese column had already passed the L Company position, since there had been no disturbance, and that the enemy column must have hurried on to the Chongchon River, only a short distance away. The ROKs repeated that they were all in great danger and should get out. Then they disappeared. They had no intention of staying there.

Takahashi walked down the back side of the hill to Captain Vail's CP and told him the story he had just heard. Vail agreed with Takahashi that the Chinese had probably already passed them, but he moved a part of the 3rd Platoon at the eastern end of the position to cover an approach route from the southwest–from the river side.

The squad warming fires still burned. L Company men stood around warming themselves. Their ridge positions looked like a lighted street. A forward observer from the 37th Field Artillery Battalion, Lt. Lynn R. Raybould, had been in his observation post in the 1st Platoon position in the middle of the line, where it approached closest to Dry Creek. But at the time the Chinese column went by, he had gone to Vail's CP on the reverse slope. He did not approve of the warming fires but apparently did not say anything about them when he saw that Vail himself had a large one. Takahashi was talking to Vail when Raybould arrived, but Raybould did not hear their conversation.

Sfc. Lionel King was in charge of the artillery observation post during Raybould's absence. He knew nothing of enemy in the vicinity and thought mistakenly that K Company was only a short distance north of him. Again, no patrols had established a connection between the two companies that evening. Some yards in front of the artillery observation post, two ROK soldiers occupied a foxhole. One of them reported to King that he could hear men digging in front of him. The other ROK said they were speaking Chinese. King went forward and listened. He could hear the digging but was uncertain about the source of it. He thought it might be caused by K Company men. Nevertheless, he moved seven men near him to firing positions facing the sound of digging. He then called out, "Are you guys from K Company?" The digging stopped and there was silence out front. He ordered his small group to fire. One of the men had a BAR. A loud scream came from the area in front of them. Then a machine gun fired on King's group from below them. Its fire was off target, however, and hit east of them among the 3rd Platoon.

This sudden outbreak of firing in front of the 1st Platoon left the 3rd Platoon uncertain and confused as to its source. They held their fire, while their platoon leader, 1st Lt. Clinton Jackson, ran toward the artillery observation post to find out what was happening. King told Jackson that Chinese had arrived in front of him. Jackson replied that he would go back to bring up a machine gun, place automatic fire from it on the enemy in front of King, and then King and his group were to withdraw from it to the company line in their rear. By now enemy fire from another direction, on the other side of the hill, fell in the L Company CP.

In this envelopment of L Company, there had been no blowing of whistles, bugles, or shepherd's horns and no firing of flares or similar communication signals and orders that often accompanied an impending Chinese attack at night. There was no need for them here. The squad fires had given the Chinese all the intelligence of the position they needed. The Chinese had by then just about surrounded it and were looking for the easiest gradient approach to the top. They found it—a long but gradual incline from the southwest.

Before any attack took place, Lieutenant Takahashi of the 2nd Platoon had returned to his platoon after talking with Vail. He started to extinguish the warming fires. He passed the word from platoon to platoon to do this at once. In carrying out this order, several times men moved directly into their glare. For the moment the Chinese held their fire at these individual targets. They had other plans. But one big fire could not be extinguished because of heavy enemy fire from Chinese when anyone was silhouetted by the firelight.

Takahashi's 2nd Platoon position at the southwest end of the company position was in the path of the easy gradient to the top. There the main enemy attack occurred. Takahashi went along the foxholes to examine them, and at the last, foremost one, he stood listening. He heard nothing. Suddenly, from only a few yards away a voice called out, "Hey there!" Takahashi answered, "Are you from K Company? If you don't answer, I will fire." An enemy burp gun from only a few yards away fired at him—and missed. Takahashi hit the ground. His men behind him opened fire. From a distance of about 200 yards, enemy rifle and automatic fire opened on the hill along a line of perhaps 400 yards long—the enemy had formed a curved line clear around the left flank of the hill and into the rear of the 2nd Platoon. The initial Chinese fire went high and did no damage. After a short time, Chinese soldiers in this line got to their feet and started toward the ridge, firing as they came. In the meantime, the group in the artillery observation outpost, covered by the machine gun that Lieutenant Jackson brought forward, successfully pulled back to the main defense line just as the Chinese started up the hill.

Takahashi, seeing the strong enemy force heading for his platoon, asked for reinforcement from the 1st Platoon. By now Vail's CP was receiving fire from below it on the reverse slope, and he moved some of the 1st Platoon to help defend it. Takahashi did not receive the reinforcements he had requested. The advancing Chinese skirmishers were now within 100 yards of Takahashi's line. At this point, Takahashi learned that his forward machine-gun crew was nearly wiped out and that the gun was nearly out of ammunition. He ordered Sergeant Cross, on the gun, and others in the front holes near it to fall back on him. This order started a withdrawal from the western knob of the ridge. The Chinese then quickened their advance on it, and Cross and others with him became intermingled with some of the leading Chinese riflemen. A melee occurred in which rifle butts and rocks were used against these Chinese. A few members of the 2nd Platoon grouped around Takahashi, and they momentarily succeeded in stopping the foremost Chinese skirmishers, now about 20 feet away, where they took cover among rocks.

Suddenly and for no apparent reason, the local enemy commander decided on different tactics. Two purple flares lit the sky, apparently a signal for the submachine gunners and riflemen to pull back and to let grenade throwers take the lead. A grenade attack now hit L Company. That company did not have a single grenade with which to counter this enemy attack, and it had to waste a diminishing supply of small-arms ammunition to reply at all. Several Chinese got to within ten feet of Takahashi's small party and lobbed grenades into it, wounding two men. Just moments after this grenade strike, everyone on the hill heard a shout from Vail's CP area, "The captain's hit!" Two bullets had struck him in the shoulder and arm. Lieutenant Jackson, with the 3rd Platoon on the east end of the line, had also been wounded.

Takahashi was now being pushed back on this platoon, where about 20 men remained. The Chinese had virtually overrun the hill, partly because American survivors on the east end had taken off with or without orders, singly or in groups of two or three.

The Chinese now let loose with a great blowing of whistles, and everywhere, it seemed, Chinese soldiers rose to their feet and walked toward the crest. The shouts of Vail, Jackson, and Takahashi did no good – the surviving men ran off seeking individual safety. Many of them were killed or captured as they tried to escape. L Company was finished as a fighting force. Some survivors escaped to friendly lines at the Chongchon River.[5]

Lieutenant Takahashi, the American Nisei who had led and directed most of the fighting in L Company, was captured on the hill. Eight Chinese soldiers seized him. His captors took him to a Chinese battalion CP. After some discussion there among the Chinese, Takahashi and another prisoner, First Sergeant Sims, were led off by two Chinese burp gunners who received instructions from a Chinese officer. Both men felt they were going to be shot. Some distance down the trail they were following, they made a break. Bullets from the guard behind him ripped Takahashi's sleeve as he went into a roll over the hillside. He escaped to tell his story.

I Company of the 3rd Battalion, 9th Infantry, was untouched during the night. It held a position just inside the western side of the 2nd Division boundary on the extreme left of the 9th Infantry sector, about one and a half air miles due west of L Company's position. Such was the topography of jumbled hills and ravines and its distance south of Dry Creek that it escaped all contact with Chinese that night.

Companies F, G, and H of the 2nd Battalion, 9th Infantry, were due west of Sinhung-dong, on the opposite (west) side of the Chongchon River during the night of 25 November. They had crossed to the west side of the river during the morning at a ford just north of Sinhung-dong. They went into positions on the south slope of big, round Hill 180, about a mile from the river and about the same distance north of the mouth of Dry Creek. A platoon of tanks and two quad-50s accompanied them. F Company was on the southeast base of Hill 180, nearest the river and their crossing point; G Company was on the southwest base of the hill; and H Company was south of the other two, centered between them. The tanks and the quad-50s were near the river east of H Company and could fire up and down both the river and the dry creek bed.

The big Chinese column that dogtrotted down the dry creek bed on the evening of 25 November did not know of their presence. Nor did the 2nd Battalion troops on and below Hill 180 know that this large Chinese force had passed just south of them.

During the day of 25 November, the 2nd Battalion on Hill 180 and at its base, west of the Chongchon, had been disturbed only by some enemy mortar fire from Hill 219 across the river and another enemy-occupied hill east of Hill 219. This fire fell on the Chongchon River ford leading to the 2nd Battalion position. To some degree it harassed, and in some instances stopped, supply vehicles from reaching the 2nd Battalion. Also, some of the mortar shells fell in F Company's position and killed two men during the day.

Maj. Cesibes V. Barberis, commander of the 2nd Battalion, did not accompany the bulk of his battalion to Hill 180 on the west side of the river on the morning of 25 November. He remained with his CP and E Company of his battalion on the east side of the Chongchon. His CP was just south of Hill 329, Chinaman's Hat. E Company stopped behind B Company of the 1st Battalion, 9th Infantry. When B Company attacked Hill 219 that morning, where it fought fruitlessly all day, E Company was on a hill southeast of it, less than a mile away. But during daylight of 25 November it was not engaged with the enemy.

Lieutenant Colonel Wolff, commander of the 1st Battalion, 9th Infantry, was not seriously concerned during 25 November when his B Company failed to secure Hill 219. But Col. Charles C. Sloane, the 9th Infantry Regimental commander, did not share his battalion commander's complacency. He insisted that the 1st Battalion's other companies, A, C, and D, be brought up behind B Company and faced to the northeast. Sloane thought this might be the place a heavy battle could begin. During the day, however, only B Company of his regiment was heavily engaged.

Prisoner information collected later indicates that all three regiments of the CCF 120th Division crossed the Chongchon River after dark of 25 November. At least one regiment crossed at or near the mouth of Dry Creek; another crossed below it and between Chinaman's Hat and Kujang-dong. Upon departing from its Unsan assembly areas, the entire division followed trails that led to Dry Creek some miles from the Chongchon and then followed the dry bed of that stream the rest of the way to the river, crossed it, and large parts of the division subsequently drove straight on to the southeast. At least one regiment fought a series of disjointed battles in the Hill 219, Sinhung-dong, and Chinaman's Hat areas during the night of 25-26 November. One of the enemy groups overran the 2nd Battalion's CP just south of Chinaman's Hat about midnight. Two or three hours later a strong Chinese attack struck south in the Hill 219 area, engaging the surviving parts of B Company and striking E Company, 2nd Battalion, on its hill position nearby on the north side of the Paengnyong-gang.

At dark on the evening of 25 November, remnants of B Company had consolidated for the night at the middle knob of Hill 219 and at the mortar position of the Weapons Company platoon near the southern end of the ridge. As the hours passed, everything there remained quiet. Fourteen men were in the mortar position. Some watched heavy tracer fire crossing the Chongchon River south of them. It grew in volume after midnight. This was all to their rear, and it worried them. They knew nothing, however, of the Chinese forces that had reached the river at the dry creek after destroying K and L companies of the 3rd Battalion.

Cpl. Walter K. Crawford, a 17-year-old squad leader of the mortar platoon, watched the tracer fire intently. He was fully alert. It was about 4 A.M. Pvt. John Howard was dozing in his foxhole a few feet away. Moonlight gave fair visibility. As if an apparition had suddenly intruded, Crawford saw a man standing by Howard's foxhole. Then he heard a low voice say, "Don't shoot. South Korean GI. Enemy come—many, many!" M. Sgt. Herbert Seegar saw the figure at the same time. He jumped to his feet, yelling, "He's Gook!" and fired his rifle in the man's face. The shot shattered it.

Everyone in the mortar position now was on his feet. Someone called out, "Bring your weapons; get back to the knoll." The men responded at once. They left the mortars and scrambled for the bit of high ground, carrying boxes of grenades and belts of ammunition. On the 16-foot-wide and 6-foot-high knoll, the 14 Americans made their stand. The knoll was dished on top and had a rock rim. This made it a small fortress and gave the group from the 4th Platoon, B Company, a chance. The battle was a close one—grenades and submachine-gun fire from the Chinese, who closed to within 25 feet; grenades, rifle fire, and sometimes rocks from the mortar men.

At the middle knob of Hill 219, survivors of the 1st and 2nd platoons on its northern slope became tense as a shepherd's horn repeated its two-note signal repeatedly from the bottom of the west side of the hill, toward the river. They could soon make out a skirmish line approaching the base of the slope from a cornfield below. Some of the Chinese in this line ran; others walked forward. The shepherd's horn continued its blasts. The Chinese now fired as they came forward—burp guns and rifles. As the men of Lt. Ellison C. Wynn's 1st and 2nd platoons hit the ground to escape this enemy fire, they caught faint sounds of the battle south of them in the 4th Platoon's position. The two actions were entirely separate. At this juncture, the 3rd Platoon on the south side of the big knoll of Hill 219 came under fire from machine guns below them. The entire company was now under attack in three separate places and surrounded in detail.

On the west slope, below the middle knob of Hill 219, the advance Chinese skirmishers were soon within 30 to 40 feet of the 1st and 2nd platoons. American fire stopped them at that point, and the Chinese survivors sought cover. The distance was just a little too far for the Chinese to reach with their grenades. But bullets began causing casualties in the 40-man force on top the middle knob. After an hour of this close fight, Chinese occupied the foxholes Americans had held when the fight began, and the American survivors were in a close-packed defense among the rocks on the ridge.

South of Wynn's group, the 14 men of the mortar platoon had a desperate time. Chinese got into foxholes at the mortar position, only 20 to 25 feet below them and within Chinese grenade range. The grenades that soon exploded in their position caused several casualties. But two men played Russian roulette with most of the grenades. Cpls. Walter K. Crawford and James C. Curcio, Jr., both still in their teens and very active, grabbed the grenades when they fell and threw them back. Others kicked hard at grenades that fell near their feet. In one hour the grenades came in at the rate of about one a minute. The men in the 16-foot saucer of ground estimated they threw back about 40 of the 60 grenades that landed among them.

The close-in Chinese had to be spurred to continue their attack. From time to time a whistle blast below the mortar position sounded, and each time a few Chinese would rise to their feet and try to rush the elevated depression. Grenades stopped them each time. When the clipped carbine ammunition was all used, four men who had been firing .45 Colts stopped that and concentrated on loading carbine magazines from a box of loose shells. But this supply finally was spent.

Seventeen-year-old Crawford now crawled from the position and got up the slope to where Wynn's group still held out—by this time from a better rampart than earlier. Chinese occupied all their earlier holes, but Chinese dead also lay in piles around them. When Crawford reached Wynn's group, he found it had three boxes of grenades left. Wynn gave Crawford one box, and Crawford with a few extra in his pockets crawled back to his own group. Grenades were passed to each man still able to pull a pin and throw.

Dawn was beginning to break. With it came another blast of enemy whistles and still another charge on the position. A shower of the recently acquired grenades dropped the Chinese. An enemy bugle sounded recall, repeated several times. The Chinese grenadiers started leaving their holes in the mortar position. Americans in the saucer position above jumped to their feet and fired carbines at the running Chinese. In their excitement they missed most of their shots. They hit only five Chinese.

On top the middle knoll, things were different with Wynn's group of men from the 1st and 2nd platoons. Their machine gun had stopped firing, BAR ammunition was gone, grenades were gone, and half or more of the men were casualties. They could no longer stop the Chinese who pressed in from the sides. Lieutenant Weathered from the mortar platoon shouted up to Wynn to bring his men down to his position—it was safer there. Wynn told his survivors to get ready to run and that he would cover them. Wynn had no weapon. He picked up rocks and several cans of C rations. Then as his men took off, he stood on the rim of their position and threw the rocks and cans at Chinese only ten yards away. Private First Class Frost stood beside him, ready to use his rifle as a club.

In the getaway, a Chinese with a tommy gun killed one man, already blinded, with a shot through the heart. An American named Smith carried a badly wounded man over his shoulder down the slope. All had left now except Wynn and Frost. As Wynn turned to go, a Chinese tried to rush him. Frost threw his empty rifle at the Chinese soldier. A grenade exploded and ripped the side of Wynn's face. He staggered down the slope bleeding badly, with Frost at his side.

Just as soon as the Chinese below the mortar position had withdrawn, some of the men rushed back to their mortars. Although the Chinese had possessed them for several hours, they had not tried to use them or to destroy them. There were ten rounds of high explosives and three of white phosphorus left. Since so few rounds remained, the group decided to use only one mortar and to fire it only for a specific purpose. This was to keep the Chinese from emplacing a machine gun on the middle knob above them just vacated by Wynn's group. If a machine gun could be emplaced and operated from there, it could kill or cripple every man below in the mortar position. The second round fired from the mortar landed squarely among a group of Chinese who milled around on the knob. Many of them fell; the others dropped down behind the crest. The mortar was now zeroed in on its target. Lieutenant Weathered posted seven riflemen to keep their eyes glued on the knob and shoot at any Chinese heads that showed. In this manner the B Company group kept the Chinese above them at bay. At 9:30 A.M. on 26 November an air strike came in on Hill 219 with napalm, rockets, and strafing. But the Chinese still tried to get a machine gun on the knob, and the fight went on. Wynn, although badly wounded by the grenade explosion, refused to leave his men, and he also refused bandaging and morphine, saying that others needed it more than he did.

Shortly after noon of 26 November, Wynn's group was all but out of ammunition. Corporal Crawford again volunteered for a necessary mission. He said he would try to get through to D Company's position south of Hill 219 and get ammunition and litters for wounded. Crawford took with him a wounded man who could walk but needed medical aid. They got through to D Company. There Captain Evers loaded several Korean bearers with ammunition and started them uphill to Wynn's position. In the meantime, Lieutenant Wynn had passed out from loss of blood and was carried down the hill to D Company.

After Captain Evers realized, from Crawford's account of the situation on Hill 219, that B Company survivors must be brought down, he succeeded in reaching the 9th Regimental CP by radio. He explained the situation and received instructions that B Company should withdraw to D Company and then that both of them should cross the Chongchon River and join the 2nd Battalion there. M. Sgt. Herbert Seegar with a squad covered the withdrawal of B Company survivors to D Company.

Out of 116 men who entered the battle with B Company the morning before, only 34 men, including several wounded, remained combat effective. In the first night and the following day's battles, the 9th Infantry Regiment had lost half its men. It had borne the brunt of the initial Chinese onslaught along the Chongchon.

By now, all of the 2nd Division was under attack. The CCF 120th Division that had dogtrotted down the dry creek the night before had crossed during the night and had infiltrated through and spread out almost everywhere behind the American front line.[6] The US 2nd Infantry Division never gained the initiative. And the Chinese never let up in their attacks on the division in the days that followed. The 2nd Division fought only defensive actions.

When B Company left the southern nose of Hill 219 on the afternoon of 26 November on 9th Infantry orders and, together with D Company, consolidated with the 2nd Battalion on the west side of the Chongchon River opposite Sinhung-dong, Eighth Army lost its foothold north of the Paengnyong-gang on the east side of the river. The 23rd Regiment of the division was now fighting desperately to maintain a foothold adjacent to Chinaman's Hat south of the Paengnyong-gang.

Chinese Wade the Chongchon River at Chinaman's Hat

The Chinese 359th Regiment of the 40th Army, although it dropped off enough troops to dispose of K and L companies of the 9th Infantry along Dry Creek on its way to the Chongchon, apparently had an assignment to destroy the American artillery near Kujang-dong, which they seem to have thought from their latest intelligence was unprotected by infantry. Both the Americans and the Chinese had surprises when the enemy force waded the Chongchon on the night of 25 November.

The 61st Field Artillery Battalion was the farthest north of any artillery unit with the 2nd Infantry Division on the Chongchon front. It was emplaced between Chinaman's Hat and the Chongchon River. This artillery battalion normally supported the 1st Cavalry Division. But because the 1st Cavalry Division was in Eighth Army reserve when the army drive to the border began on 24 November, two of its artillery battalions, the 61st and the 99th, were ordered to assist the 2nd Infantry Division in its attack up the Chongchon valley. The 61st Artillery of 105-mm howitzers arrived at Chinaman's Hat in the evening of 25 November after the 1st Battalion, 23rd Infantry, came up and went into bivouac there. As previously mentioned, the artillery battalion passed through the infantry and went into position more than half a mile in advance of them. This position may not have seemed so unusual, since the 1st Battalion, 9th Infantry, was in front of them.

The CCF 120th Division, 40th Army, led the Chinese Army's attack against the US 2nd Division. At least two of its regiments, the 358th and 359th, coming from Unsan, crossed the Chongchon River to the east side on the night of 25 November. Reports from prisoners captured that night and the next morning indicated the 359th Regiment led the division to the Chongchon, followed by the 358th Regiment. If that was the case, it appears that elements of the 359th Regiment overran K and L companies of the 3rd Battalion, 9th Infantry, on hills overlooking Dry Creek soon after dark on the evening of 25 November. It will be recalled that Private First Class Giudici's watch timed the arrival of the Chinese column at K Company's outpost position at 7 P.M. It would be four or five miles from there to the mouth of Dry Creek.

The first Chinese attack on the east side of the Chongchon in the Chinaman's Hat area came when Chinese from the 359th Regiment waded the river about 10 P.M. Captured prisoners said the next morning that they attacked across the Chongchon in seven columns, evenly spaced at intervals of about 100 yards, with about two companies totaling approximately 100 men to a column. They deployed undiscovered into these seven columns on the west side of the river. They began their crossings at about 10 P.M.[7]

It is not clear whether the first crossings were into the area of the 61st Field Artillery Battalion or into A Company, 23rd Infantry, half a mile farther south. The weight of evidence seems to indicate the crossings into the two American positions were made at about the same time.

Three of the seven columns of Chinese that crossed the Chongchon between 10 and 11 P.M. came directly into the bivouac area of the 61st Field Artillery Battalion. A Chinese prisoner later said that, at the river's edge, the Chinese soldiers undressed until they were completely naked and waded across the waist-

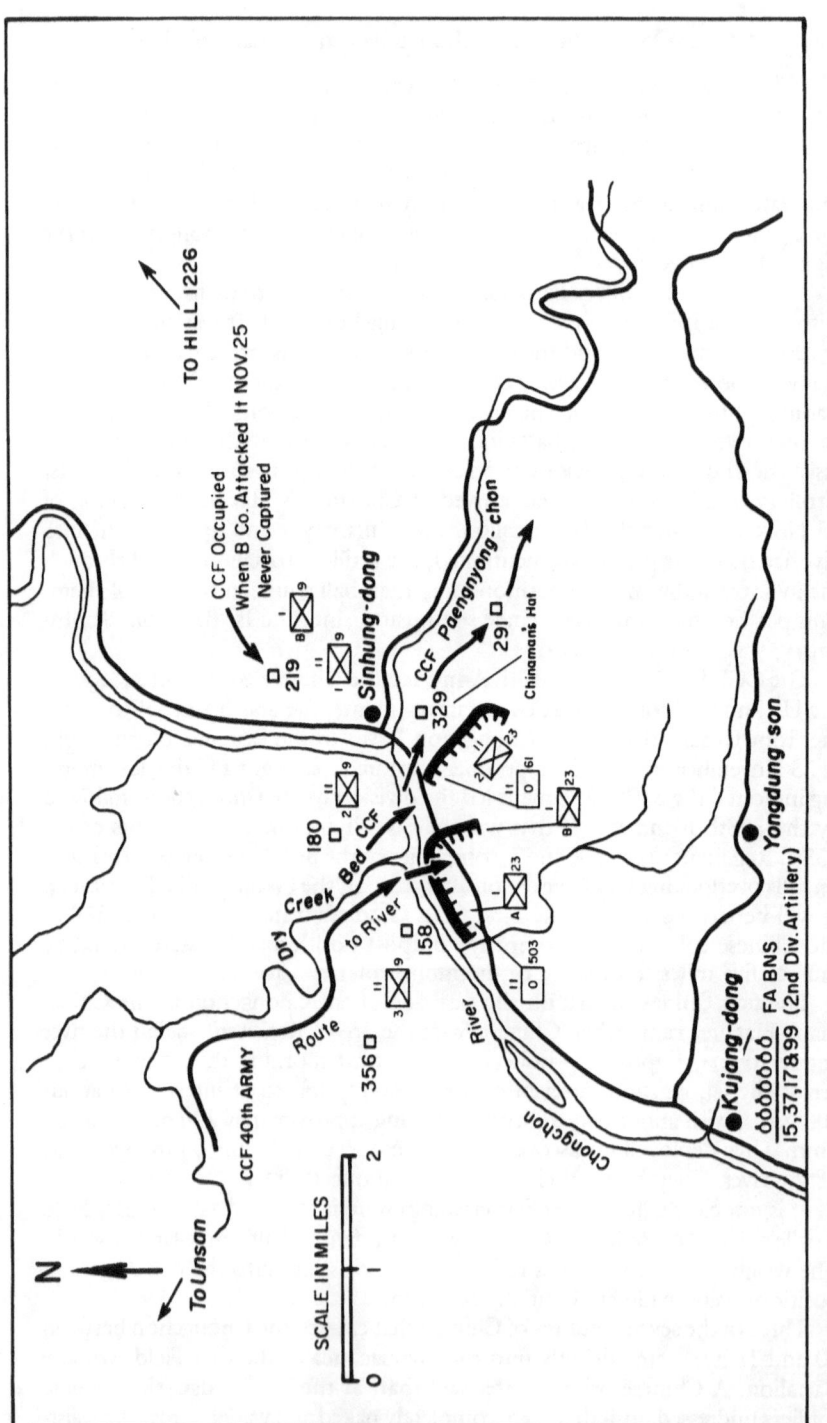

Map 8. The CCF 40th Army's attack on the 9th and 23rd infantry regiments, 2nd Infantry Division, and its crossing of the Chongchon River on the night of 25–26 November 1950.

deep river, holding their clothes and weapons above the water. Other evidence indicates that most of them removed only their shoes and trousers. Once on the east side, and virtually at the edge of the artillery position, some of the Chinese quickly put on their clothes, but others did not put on either shoes or pants but attacked immediately. The night was cold, and these men were wet. The Chinese assault caught the 61st Field Artillerymen completely by surprise. The Chinese overran the battalion quickly and occupied the gun pits. Most of the artillerymen fled south to friendly positions. Some ran through the camp of B Company, 23rd Infantry, going through the 3rd Platoon's line. Some continued their flight as far south as Kujang-dong, where they entered the 17th Field Artillery emplacements.

Capt. Melvin Stai, commander of A Company, 23rd Infantry, said that many of the 61st artillerymen came into his position, some in their underwear or barefooted, and that they barely had been able to get out of their sleeping bags before the Chinese soldiers were upon them. They left all their equipment and the howitzers behind. This sudden attack from across the Chongchon was also aided by other Chinese coming from the north, who had just overrun the CP of the 2nd Battalion, 9th Infantry. These enemy penetrated behind the artillery position about the same time as the 359th Regiment crossed the river from the west. About three companies hit the 61st Field Artillery Battalion area. The next day a count showed 61 members of the artillery battalion missing in action and Captain Gunnell, A Battery commander, and Lieutenant Peterson, also of A Battery, killed.[8]

Members of the 61st Field Artillery Battalion later charged that tanks of the 23rd Tank Company, in position south of them in support of A and B companies, 23rd Infantry, would not fire in their support although requested to do so. It is true that six or seven tanks were oriented to fire north, which would have been in the direction of the 61st Field Artillery Battalion. But at this time, A and B companies, 23rd Infantry, were under the same kind of surprise attack, and it would appear that the tanks could not fire in support of the artillerymen without running the risk of hitting them as well as Chinese who were already in their positions.

At the same time that three of seven Chinese columns waded the Chongchon River on the left flank of their deployment and completely routed the 61st Field Artillery Battalion, the other four columns, spaced about 200 to 250 feet apart, waded the river into the A Company, 23rd Infantry, position. There is a time discrepancy between official records and some interview material of participants as to when this happened. According to one source some members of A Company said the Chinese columns crossed into their front at dusk, about 6:30 P.M. The records put it some hours later, as does a credible interview report with responsible officers of A Company and the 1st Battalion.[9]

One recalls that Private First Class Giudici of K Company, 9th Infantry, timed the head of the enemy column by his watch at 7 P.M. when it reached his outpost position on Dry Creek. This same column waded the Chongchon opposite Chinaman's Hat to enter the 61st Field Artillery Battalion and A Company, 23rd Infantry, positions. It would have taken this enemy column at least an hour or longer to have reached the Chongchon River after passing Giudici's position, and additional time had to be spent in assembling and deploying the Chinese on the west bank of the river into the seven attack columns.

When Lt. Col. Claire E. Hutchins brought his 1st Battalion, 23rd Infantry, north to Chinaman's Hat on the evening of 25 November he expected to pass through the 9th Infantry the next morning and continue the attack upstream. No one had expected the 1st Battalion, 9th Infantry, to be held up at Hill 219. Accordingly, Hutchins put his battalion into a bivouac, but so disposed that it still resembled a perimeter defense, although it was not expected to be used as such. It occupied holes and trenches that had been dug by either American, ROK, or North Korean troops. Col. Paul L. Freeman, Jr., the 23rd Infantry Regimental commander, came up at the same time with his headquarters group to direct resumption of the attack the next morning.

The 1st Battalion, 23rd Infantry, was disposed around the 503rd Field Artillery (less A Battery), which had already arrived at Chinaman's Hat. A Company occupied a line of foxholes facing west toward the Chongchon River. Its 1st Platoon faced the river; the 2nd Platoon bent back from this line toward the road; and the 3rd Platoon was back of the 2nd Platoon in a reserve position near the company CP. Capt. Melvin Stai commanded A Company; 1st Lt. William J. Major was his executive officer. The mortars of D Company were south of the CP near tanks of the 23rd Tank Company. A Company had outposts on hills east of the road.

Pfc. Harvey M. Deshoen of A Company was on outpost duty near the river. Deshoen first alerted the A Company CP of enemy at hand. He was gazing straight to his front toward a growth of shrubs and small trees along the river bank when he noticed movement on the opposite bank. Watching closely, he could make out men removing their shoes and pants. He knew they could only be enemy. The river here was about 150 to 200 feet wide and three to four feet deep. It could be waded easily. Some small-arms fire could be heard dimly from the north. After Stai had alerted Lieutenant Colonel Hutchins that something was happening, but he knew not what, he ran toward his 1st Platoon near the river to see for himself.[10]

Sgts. Theodore A. Aspinwall and Robert Strahorn manned the 1st Platoon's machine gun on the platoon line. M. Sgt. Roger W. Remillard sat near them. The machine-gun position was in a large foxhole with an earth rampart around it. Remillard, gazing toward the river bank, which was lined with low shrubs, saw many Chinese soldiers, naked from the waist down, trying to get their trousers on, and some were pulling on shoes. He opened fire on them at once with a carbine. The nearby machine gun joined in the fire, as did the closest riflemen, and together they cut down the enemy in view. But others hidden by the bushes came on a run toward the 1st Platoon line. Some were naked from the waist down. Some of these had been able to get their shoes on, others had not, when the first American fire hit among them. Still trying to dress as they ran forward, this group of Chinese did not fire much as they came on.

Riflemen near the 1st Platoon's machine gun got up and ran toward it. As Captain Stai hurried toward the platoon, running riflemen passed him, going in the opposite direction. Then pursuing Chinese soldiers passed Stai, apparently without noticing him. Remillard had jumped into the machine-gun foxhole with Aspinwall and Strahorn. They stopped firing after they had cut down the first Chinese they had seen at the river bank. Now with the others charging toward them, they held their fire until these Chinese were quite close. They killed and wounded some, but onrushing Chinese passed them as if they were unnoticed. The three Americans then used only the one carbine and two .45-caliber Colt pistols to shoot at any Chinese who turned back toward the river. At different times three Chinese grenades landed in their hole, but none of them exploded. These three men held that forward part of the 1st Platoon line alone.

Stai, on meeting the running riflemen and pursuing Chinese, turned back and hurried to the 3rd Platoon bivouac. There he ordered 2nd Lt. John Gandy, the platoon leader, to form his platoon for an advance toward the 1st Platoon and to stop and incorporate into his 3rd Platoon any fleeing 1st Platoon soldiers he met. He also ordered Gandy to reestablish the forward line. Cooks and kitchen personnel had now grabbed their weapons and formed a makeshift position behind the front line. Gandy started his deployed platoon toward the river. By this time Chinese mortars, firing from the opposite side of the Chongchon, were dropping white phosphorus shells into the area back of the front line. On the American side of the river, the Chinese had also emplaced a machine gun near the southwest corner of A Company's position. Its fire swept across the flat ground that Gandy's men would have to cross. One of the American tanks had turned around to face this gun and fired on it with its own machine gun. This crossfire could have been deadly for Gandy's men and others still in the 1st Platoon position. Sfc. Tillman B. Leaphart ran to the tank and stopped its fire.

As Gandy's 3rd Platoon swept forward, Americans running hard suddenly appeared from the north and yelled "GI, GI!" as they hurtled through his skirmish line, never pausing. They were from the 61st Field Artillery Battalion half a mile north. Chinese had immediately occupied their positions. Many of these artillerymen ran through B Company's position where it extended A Company's line farther east to the road. Some B Company men jumped from their holes and joined the artillerymen in flight, illustrating the genesis of panic.

Gandy's platoon lost some men killed and wounded to the Chinese machine-gun fire, but the others bore straight ahead. Already most of the Chinese who had crossed the river in the first wave and had penetrated the front line had occupied American holes, sometimes as many as four or more in one hole. Most of them made no effort to fight as Gandy's men approached. The 3rd Platoon simply sprayed these holes with BAR, rifle, and carbine fire when they came up to them. Many carbines malfunctioned. Pfc. Robert L. Echard's BAR froze. He urinated on it, and the warm fluid unlocked the gun and again the BAR became a killer. Some men swung their inoperable carbines as clubs. Gandy completed his sweep when he reached the foxhole that the three men of the 1st Platoon still held with their machine gun.

Chinese who had taken over the 61st Field Artillery position were now firing south toward A Company with at least one machine gun. As Gandy came up to the 1st Platoon machine-gun position, a burst of enemy fire struck the staunch second lieutenant in the heart and killed him. Captain Stai was present when Gandy fell. To buttress the still-precarious 1st Platoon position, Stai moved some of the tanks that had been supporting the 2nd Platoon to join the 1st Platoon.[11]

While all this was happening, still more Chinese were crossing the river, for a second regiment of the CCF 120th Division had arrived. Captain Stai took command of the left side of A Company—the part that faced the river. First Lt. William J. Major, the company executive officer, took command of the right side, facing north. The tanks that had joined the 1st Platoon proved invaluable to its defense. Stai watched as 100 Chinese, holding shoes, pants, and weapons above the water, waded the river in the moonlight. Only when they had crossed to the east side and were putting on their shoes did he order all weapons to fire on them. This group was all but annihilated.

In front of the 2nd Platoon of A Company and in front of B Company, which faced north between the river and the road, heavy fire built up from Chinese who had occupied the position held earlier by 61st Field Artillery Battalion. The columns of Chinese that followed the first one down the dry creek bed could cross the river here unopposed to the east side. Some of them reinforced the first group that had stampeded the artillerymen; others continued on east and occupied all of Hill 329, Chinaman's Hat. This was a major enemy accomplishment. Still other Chinese forces of the CCF 120th Division pressed straight on east and southeast during the night to get behind the 38th Regiment.

Captain Stai was first aware of Chinese on top of Chinaman's Hat when, during the battle along the river, he noticed several flares fired from the top of the hill. The Chinese never gave up any ground they held on Chinaman's Hat. They were still there, looking down on all the American forces below them, when the latter withdrew down the river toward Kunu-ri.

When Chinese rifle fire from across the Chongchon River killed 1st Lt. Peter F. Charnetski of the 2nd Platoon, Captain Stai had lost all his original platoon leaders in little more than an hour. Before midnight, however, things were quiet in A Company. The enemy who initially had entered its perimeter were dead or had gone elsewhere. The battle had moved north and east into the areas of the 1st Battalion, 9th Infantry, where its remaining troops were fighting desperately but increasingly were becoming casualties. The enemy now reached the CP of the 23rd Infantry Regiment, east of the road.

By midnight of 25 November the Chinese 40th Army had crossed the river in force and was rapidly moving eastward. All front-line units of the 2nd Infantry Division were engaged. At the same time, it appears that part of the CCF 113th Division of the 38th Army, coming from the north, penetrated the left flank of the 38th Regiment, east of Sinhung-dong. In this first night of the Chinese 2nd Phase Offensive, the enemy hit the 2nd Infantry Division hard everywhere and made impressive gains. At the same time, the ROK II Corps was crumbling on its right.

One might wonder why the first regimental-sized Chinese crossing of the river did not accomplish more lasting results than overrunning the 61st Field Artillery Battalion, thereby securing an uncontested crossing place during the remainder of the night for other parts of the 40th Army. Very likely these troops were surprised to find strong infantry forces where they had expected to find only artillerymen. It has been noted that many of these first Chinese troops to arrive at the river did not carry personal arms but instead carried explosive charges, which apparently were intended to blow up artillery pieces. Some Chinese prisoners said this was the intent. The large number who dashed to the attack naked from the waist down must nearly have frozen in the cold night, even though some of them huddled four to five in a foxhole and gave little attention to carrying on a battle after the first rush. A dividend came to A Company at daybreak on 26 November when 74 Chinese soldiers crossed the river from the west side and surrendered.

After midnight of 25 November, the Chinese launched an attack against Colonel Freeman's CP and Headquarters Company. The CP and Headquarters Company were located on a small hill east of the road and at the southwest base of Chinaman's Hat. The Chinese came around the base of Chinaman's Hat and attacked the CP from the east. At this time they also attacked C Company, 23rd Infantry. The first enemy attack there was repulsed. But at 6 A.M., the Chinese drove C Company off the north end of its ridge. Parts of A Company were sent to help C Company hold the southern end of its position. Lieutenant Colonel Hutchins then moved his 1st Battalion CP 150 yards south of the railroad station.

A count of enemy dead after daylight put the number at approximately 400 in front of A Company. And there were 102 Chinese prisoners—an unusually high number under the circumstances. During the night the CCF had evacuated most of their wounded, the number unknown. The 2nd Division had about 200 casualties, killed and wounded, during the night.

An important reinforcement for the 23rd Infantry arrived at Chinaman's Hat. About 2 A.M. on 26 November Colonel Sloane, commander of the 9th Infantry, sent his tanks, B Company, 72nd Tank Battalion, to the area southwest of Chinaman's Hat. They went into the line at once with A Company, 23rd Infantry. Special Chinese assault teams tried to reach the tanks with explosive charges, but they failed, shot down by protecting infantrymen. When morning came, 17 dead Chinese, most of them carrying explosive charges, were found sprawled around one of the tanks. During the night-long battle, artillery concentrated at Kujang-dong (the 17th, 37th, and 15th field artillery battalions), four miles to the south, fired in support of the 23rd Infantry at Chinaman's Hat. They especially tried to knock out enemy mortars on the west side of the river and to interdict enemy approach routes. The 23rd Regimental Tank Company supported B Company in much the same manner that Sloane's tank company fought with and supported A Company.[12]

The elongated, curved high ridge known as Chinaman's Hat was the key position in this battle area. From the river bottom, where the American forces were concentrated, only the southern knob, in the shape of a conical Chinese hat, was visible. But to the northeast the ridge rose in two more knobs, the highest being 329 meters. The Chinese occupied all these knobs and the slopes around them. They were on the ridge in great force before daylight of 26 November. From their positions they could see everything below them and could direct machine-gun and mortar fire on the Americans. The hill had not been a crucial factor in the battles at its base during the night of 25–26 November. The enemy were then only in the process of occupying the hill with elements of the 120th Division, following the initial crossing of its 359th Regiment. From daylight of 26 November on, however, the hill was the dominant geographic factor in the situation.

After daylight of 26 November, the 2nd Division supporting artillery units at Kujang-dong collected members of the 61st Artillery who during the night had fled south to their emplacements. They then marched them back north to the Chinaman's Hat area. There at the 23rd Infantry line, they were ordered to go forward and reclaim their old gun pits. It was an easy task, for the Chinese who had remained there all night during the battle were now nearly all gone. All but two of the artillery pieces were operable or could be made so. After they captured them, the Chinese had failed to destroy or use them.

In the previous chapter the A Company, 38th Infantry, patrol was left on Hill 453, short of Hill 1229, its objective. Hill 1229 was an objective in the 38th Infantry phase line of advance. That morning, 25 November, after A Company was well on its way in the patrol, the 1st Battalion was relieved of its sector on the 38th Regimental left near Sinhung-dong, adjacent to the 9th Infantry right, but its A Company was not recalled from its mission. The 2nd Battalion, 38th Infantry, commanded by Lt. Col. James H. Skeldon, replaced the 1st Battalion. Thereupon, the 1st Battalion, minus A Company on its patrol, went into regimental reserve. The 3rd Battalion had extended the 38th Regimental position eastward into higher hills, where its boundary met that of the ROK 3rd Regiment and of the ROK II Corps some miles east of Somin-dong.

According to the records of the 38th Regiment, the A Company patrol reached the southern slope of Hill 625 by dusk of 25 November. This hill is about one and a quarter air miles directly north of Hill 453, but much farther by foot trail. At Hill 625, the trail turned northeast toward Hill 1229, still two and a half air miles distant and possibly two to three times that distance by foot trail. Enemy grenades and small-arms fire on the patrol at Hill 625 indicated that enemy troops occupied it. In radio discussion with the 1st Battalion CP, Capt. Leonard Lowery, 1st Battalion executive officer, who had accompanied Capt. Jack W. Rodarm and his A Company, talked with Capt. John L. Blackwell, the S-3 of the 1st Battalion on the situation. They agreed that A Company should pull back and set up a perimeter defense on top Hill 453 for the night. Accordingly, the company assembled there about dark and went into a defensive position.[13]

The crest of Hill 453 was in the form of a nearly level, rather narrow ridge, which sloped slightly down to the south. North of Hill 453 and across a shallow saddle was another ridge that ran toward Hill 453 at a slight angle from the northwest. This made Hill 453 vulnerable from that direction if enemy occupied the second and higher ridge. As far as the patrol knew, there were no enemy there at dark on 25 November. Captain Rodarm emplaced his A Company in a perimeter formation with his 3rd Platoon west of the crest and extending somewhat forward of it toward the saddle to the north. The 1st Platoon was in a similar position at the crest and eastward from it. At the southeastern part of the sloping ridge and directly behind the 1st Platoon and tying into it at its southwestern corner was the 2nd Platoon, which held that part of the perimeter. A party of about 20 Korean carriers formed a pocket within the 2nd Platoon position. West of the platoon and immediately south of the 3rd Platoon, the Weapons Platoon formed a circular position.

At 11:20 P.M. on 25 November, the 38th Regimental CP received information that F Company, on a hill just south of the Paengnyong River and several miles behind A Company, was under heavy machine-gun and mortar fire. Twenty-five minutes later it received radio information that a platoon of L Company on the right (east) of F Company was under attack. By midnight, enemy had penetrated between F and L companies far to the rear of A Company on Hill 453. A Company was unaware of this enemy action in its rear.

The enemy in front of A Company and in the Hill 1229 area were probably elements of the Chinese 113th Division of the 38th Army, which was on the left flank of the XIII Army Group with the mission of attacking the ROK II Corps. Major elements of both the CCF 113th and 120th divisions struck the 38th Regiment of the US 2nd Division on the night of 25–26 November. These two enemy divisions were on adjoining flanks of the boundary between two Chinese armies. The 38th Regiment happened to be in their paths, astride their boundary. The 113th Division attacked it from the north; the 120th attacked it from the west.[14]

In the A Company perimeter on Hill 453, the evening and night of 25 November passed quietly until just before midnight. A few minutes before midnight, M. Sgt. Thomas E. Weikel of the 1st Platoon bumped into a man he had not seen in the darkness just in front of his platoon position. When Weikel challenged him and raised his carbine, the man rolled away over the hillside. At the same time on the left front of the perimeter, in the 3rd Platoon area, Cpl. Renaldo Acosta was in front of the outpost when he saw a Chinese soldier standing ten yards from him. Before he could react, the Chinese vanished. There had been no noise of any kind, but an enemy force had moved in close to A Company. In a matter of minutes after these two Chinese had been encountered at the very edge of the forward American position, enemy machine-gun, submachine-gun, and rifle fire came in on A Company from the high ground just north across the shallow saddle. Rodarm could distinguish between the fire from two machine guns, some submachine guns, and many rifles. The enemy fire seemed to come from about 200 yards away.

The 1st and 3rd platoons returned the fire. During this exchange, tracer bullets from a 3rd Platoon machine gun started a grass fire in the saddle about 125 yards in front of it. Wind soon fanned the fire into a bright blaze. Chinese thereupon rushed out to stomp out the fire. They were good targets for the American machine guns, and most of them were casualties to the automatic fire. Others came out to take their places, making no effort to attack A Company—only to beat out the fire. Many of them, also, were killed or wounded, but still others came for the same task. It is not known how many scores or possibly hundreds of Chinese were killed in this one-sided action until the fire burned itself out. All this took place on the left front of A Company.

At the same time, enemy on the right front moved downhill a bit and started around the flank of the 1st Platoon. When they had moved south on the lower ground far enough to be on the flank of the 1st Platoon, these Chinese started up through scrub growth toward it. The 1st Platoon was unaware of this movement until a bugle downslope on its right flank warned it of what was happening. Then there were other bugle blasts and occasionally the sound of a shepherd's horn. The sound of men's voices in a chant came from downslope. This grew louder as the Chinese drew closer. But none was yet in sight in the direction of the noise. Nevertheless, the 1st Platoon fired down into the thicket that screened observation in that direction. The 1st Platoon fire apparently disorganized the enemy formation. But groups squirmed through the brush and up small gullies toward the platoon. Chinese stick grenades began falling into the platoon from less than 15 yards away, and it still had seen no Chinese. The squad nearest this enemy approach were all casualties within a few minutes.

Increased enemy fire had built up against the front of the 1st and 3rd platoons from the enemy hill to their front. Five instead of two enemy machine guns now were firing. After a while, three Chinese mortars joined the machine guns in firing steadily at A Company. The early mortar salvos struck behind the front platoons in the 2nd Platoon area and panicked most of the Korean carriers into running away. One mortar round critically wounded Lieutenant Claridge, forward observer for the 38th Field Artillery Battalion. Other mortar rounds hit in the Weapons Platoon, causing damage. Perhaps the single most destructive blow from the mortar fire came when a round landed in the 3rd Platoon's machine-gun position, destroying the gun and wounding some of the crew.

Captain Rodarm took stock of the situation and found he had five dead and 26 wounded, including five litter cases. At 1:30 A.M. on 26 November he told Captain Lowery he thought the company would have to withdraw. Lowery got Lieutenant Colonel Kelleher at 1st Battalion by radio and described the situation. Kelleher agreed the company should withdraw.

Rodarm ordered the 1st and 3rd platoons to withdraw through the 2nd Platoon, bringing all their wounded. There were no litter men with the company. Earlier they had taken wounded down to the valley. When they tried to rejoin the company, two had been killed on the way up. None arrived at the company perimeter. Riflemen or mortarmen, therefore, six to a blanket, had to be detailed to carry the blanket litters. There was no blood plasma, nor were any skilled medical personnel present.

In preparing for the withdrawal, the 2nd Platoon swung its machine guns to point north and placed its BAR men to face the same direction. All the withdrawing men left behind their sleeping bags, rations, excess equipment, and some ammunition. The withdrawal benefited when Chinese pursuers stopped at the 1st and 3rd Platoon positions to loot the abandoned food and equipment. The 2nd Platoon was able to take advantage of this to drop into line as tail in the company column without fighting as a rear guard. By 2:30 A.M., A Company had made it back to Hill 526, an E Company outpost, one air mile south of Hill 453. There the E Company platoon was about out of machine-gun and BAR ammunition but had a good supply of M-1 bandolier ammunition, which it divided with A Company.

From Hill 526, Cpl. Jack McKnight, now acting forward observer for the 38th Field Artillery Battalion, called in fire against Hill 453, which A Company had recently vacated. The responding barrages on the hill made at least two direct hits, one by high explosive and another by white phosphorus shells that set fire to the ration dump. From Hill 526, A Company men could see these hits and even silhouettes of Chinese moving about against the blaze.

It was not long, however, before Chinese pursuers caught up with A Company at Hill 526. About 3 A.M., four Chinese machine guns began firing on them. This fire killed two men in a short time. Captain Lowery decided it was time for a complete withdrawal back to the 1st Battalion; Rodarm agreed. Lowery was to take most of the company and try to keep it together in the withdrawal. Rodarm was to organize the evacuation of the wounded and, with the 2nd Platoon, which had seen the least action, fight a rear-guard protection of those who were ahead. Rodarm had the machine gun that the E Company platoon had left in position and about 20 small arms to keep up a constant fire on the Chinese while the others withdrew. Later, still firing their weapons, the 2nd Platoon withdrew. The Chinese pursued for about a third of a mile.

In the withdrawal, A Company splintered. Lowery and Rodarm retained control of the two largest groups, but others broke away and were on their own. Lowery with the walking wounded had the largest group from the lead platoons. Rodarm had the litter cases and part of the 3rd Platoon. The 2nd Platoon, or part of it, seems to have been between the other two main groups.

Captain Lowery with the leading group arrived near a footbridge they had crossed on the way up the morning before. At the edge of some shrubs and trees, they paused on the trail to look over the open ground ahead of them. They stood there immobile and silent for two or three minutes. Then they heard the soft thud of padded feet. A column of Chinese soldiers appeared in the half-moonlight, headed for the bridge. They came at the typical Chinese dog-trot when they were on the move, without any clanking of weapons or metal, in perfect discipline. The awed Americans heard only their heavy breathing and the soft padding of feet in rubber-soled shoes. Lowery estimated the force at about 500 men—a Chinese battalion. He waited 10 to 15 minutes after the Chinese had passed. Then he led his own party quickly across the footbridge and worked his way on down to the 1st Battalion CP.[15]

Captain Rodarm with his litter cases was the last of A Company to reach the low ground of the Paengnyong, where the regimental positions were having their own nightlong battles with Chinese. He followed the same trail as Lowery before him. The morning light, dimmed by fog, was at hand when he approached the footbridge. In time, he saw an enemy battalion camped adjacent to the bridge site. He swerved his party away from the area and skirted it undetected. Later in the morning Rodarm and his group entered American lines.

After daylight, liaison planes took to the air to try and locate A Company, since battalion and regiment had lost communication with it. One pilot reported he thought he had located it, that scattered groups were surrounded but were trying to fight their way back. By 8:14 A.M., 26 November, A Company stragglers were in F Company's hard-held hill perimeter near the Paengnyong River. By noon a total of four officers and 92 enlisted men from A Company and the E Company outpost from Hill 426 had entered friendly lines.[16]

One observation may be made about the A Company patrol. Although it was a costly and useless march into enemy territory and never came near to its objective (Hill 1229), it did make the farthest penetration of any American tactical unit of Eighth Army north into enemy territory when it reached the base of Hill 625 near dusk on the evening of 25 November. It was then north of Hill 219 along the east bank of the Chongchon River where Chinese stopped B Company, 9th Infantry—about four air miles east and one air mile north of B Company at its northernmost point at Hill 219. Perhaps theirs was an empty honor.

During the night, F Company had been surrounded on its Hill 383 position in a sharp bend on the south side of the Paengnyong, but it held there after prolonged and bitter fighting. Its fire killed or wounded many Chinese during the night as they crossed the Paengnyong River in front of it. F Company was reinforced during the night by the last of the 2nd Battalion reserve. Everywhere the front-line companies of the 38th Regiment had come under attack and were being forced back, except at the extreme right flank in the I and K Company positions, where there had been no action. An enemy attack had penetrated the 38th Regimental line at Somin-dong between the 2nd and 3rd battalions, and an unknown number of Chinese had passed through to the rear of the regiment.

Somin-dong was on the only escape route for the 38th Infantry back to the Chongchon River valley south of the Paengnyong. In this attack through Somin-dong, L Company was hurt most. I and K companies pulled back to block for it. A platoon of tanks from the blocking line went back into Somin-dong several times to pick up stragglers and to destroy American equipment that could not be salvaged.

After dawn an attack by elements of L and H companies and the Medical Company eastward reopened the MSR to Somin-dong, where the 38th Regimental CP was located. The 3rd Battalion on the right restored its original position. An air-liaison pilot reported, however, that heavy fighting was in progress in the I and K Company positions near the ROK boundary but that he could not locate G Company—that its foxholes were empty.[17] The story of G Company is told in the following section.

A Chinese Flute Serenade at Hill 291

The deployments taking place in the 38th Infantry on the afternoon of 25 November called for Lt. Col. James H. Skeldon's 2nd Battalion to relieve the 1st Battalion on the left side of the 38th Infantry's line east of Sinhung-dong. As part of this action, 1st Lt. Robert H. Rivet's G Company received orders to relieve C Company on Hill 291. This hill lay east of Sinhung-dong, about one and a half air miles southeast of Chinaman's Hat and three-quarters of an air mile south of the Paengnyong valley. A poor trail led to it from the valley of the Chongchon, perhaps three miles or more over broken ground, consisting of a series of ridges and knobs. C Company had had no enemy contact during the short time it had occupied the hill. Learning that G Company was going to relieve it on 25 November, it had dug no positions on the hill. Hill 291 was in the form of a large dogleg. The northern east-west part of the dogleg was about half a mile long with the crest on the east end. From there a mile-long ridge with several knobs ran on a slight slant a little east of south.

Rivet's company had a hot meal before noon and then started on its march to Hill 291. Counting attached ROK soldiers, the company numbered 164 men, larger than the average at that time. The men carried rifles, carbines, sleeping bags, an average of one grenade each, but no rations. Hot food was to be brought to them that evening. They had the usual company machine guns and light mortars. When G Company started, it did not appear to be a long or especially hard march. But it took the company nearly five hours to reach the hill. They took many rest breaks during the climb and were exhausted when they reached the top. G Company relieved C Company in place, platoon for platoon, making no changes in the initial position.

The C Company positions had been badly chosen. No one platoon position was in sight of another or of the company CP. Each of the four positions occupied what was essentially an isolated knob. The company CP was behind (south of) the nearest platoon position at the southern end of the long shank of the dogleg. The other platoon positions were farther north. It appears that the east-west ridge of the dogleg at the north end and the crest of Hill 291, which was closest there to the Paengnyong, were unoccupied. All the company positions were on the southern shank of the dogleg. Second Lt. Elster King's 3rd Platoon seems to have been north of and nearest to the company CP. Second Lieutenant Hollingsworth's 2nd Platoon was on a knob three-fourths of a mile from the CP, and M. Sgt. Felix Acosta's 1st Platoon was on a knob just below (south of) the crest of Hill 291 and about a mile north of the 2nd Platoon—a mile and a half or a little farther from Rivet's CP. Thus, by not independently considering the security of the defense position, Rivet inherited and accepted a poor position, with little opportunity for the several platoons and the company CP to be mutually supporting, or for the company commander to communicate with and control his several separated platoons.

Rivet's men made a desultory effort to dig in on their platoon positions but found shale and rock less than a foot below the surface. Fatigued from their climb, they quickly gave up, as there appeared to be no pressing need for holes. Some of the men piled slabs of slate and rocks around their individual positions. The company was isolated. There were no friendly forces on either side or in front or in its rear close enough to be of any help or even to know if it was under attack. Only Lieutenant King of the 3rd Platoon had contact, through an SCR-536 radio, with the company CP. Acosta's SCR-300 radio did not reach either the 2nd or the 3rd platoons. Lieutenant Hollingsworth's radio apparently could not make contact with either the CP or the 1st Platoon. Hollingsworth had to go personally to the company CP to confer with Rivet. There Rivet told him not to send out patrols until morning.

That night, moonlight illuminated the landscape. During the early part of the night, men in G Company could hear the distant sound of firing far to the west. Expecting the food promised for the evening meal, Rivet sent Cpl. Kenneth F. Johnson back on the trail to guide the carrying party with the hot food and ammunition to his position. Johnson ran into Chinese and barely escaped with his life. G Company had no hot food that night.

The night remained quiet around Hill 291 until sometime after midnight. Gradually, muffled noises reached Rivet from the trail to the left of his knob position. He could not tell just what it was. Rivet relayed an order through a ROK soldier to one of his most reliable KATUSA, An Jong Sup, to go down the hill in the direction of the noises to see what was happening. An Jong Sup worked his way quietly down the slope until he reached a large boulder about 100 feet from the bottom. From there he could see clearly the source of the strange noises heard on top. Several hundred Chinese soldiers were digging in on both sides of the trail and as far up the draw as he could see. While he watched this activity, a column of Chinese soldiers, in single file, appeared out of the draw, marching toward him. He watched them pass the digging Chinese, and just below him they turned south. He counted 150 of them. He still watched but did not report to Rivet what he had seen. After an interval another column came in view, following the first. They passed and also turned south. There were 113 in this group.

Inexplicably, An suddenly rose to his feet and emptied his carbine into the last of this group. He saw four or five of them fall. In a minute or two, a Chinese machine gun opened up on his position from the far side of the trail. An took to his heels and sprinted to the top of the knob. He had needlessly given away Rivet's position. When he reported to Rivet, the latter knew that he was in for it. The Chinese would certainly come for the hill.

Rivet at once radioed Skeldon and told him he was about to be attacked. Immediately afterward Rivet reached Lieutenant King and ordered him to move his two rifle squads of the 3rd Platoon toward the CP. King ran into Chinese in trying to reach Rivet and had a fight. He had only eight men, three of them ROKs, when he arrived at Rivet's position.

Rivet at this point seems to have decided suddenly that he should vacate his CP and move to higher ground northward, closer to the 2nd and 1st platoons. He did so, taking up a new position in rocks, trees, and shrubs, but only 150 yards away. He hoped the Chinese might miss him and ordered his men to remain quiet, not to fire even if Chinese were close to them, unless he ordered it. Rivet had 25 men with him. He faced them south in the direction from which he had just come.

As Rivet's men crouched among the boulders, they heard Chinese automatic fire sweeping the knob they had just vacated. About half an hour passed. Then three blasts from a whistle sounded—two short and one long. Following this signal, three Chinese appeared from the direction of their first position, walking calmly toward them. The three men were at intervals of about 100 feet. They appeared to be unarmed but each carried what looked like a short stick. They stopped short of the rise of ground from which Rivet's men watched. The moonlight gave good visibility. The three figures then raised what they carried to their lips and began playing a flute serenade of sweet music. They played unmolested for perhaps five minutes. Rivet's men were spellbound. After the initial serenade, many Chinese rose from among the rocks and bushes behind the flutists and danced and moved around them in three separate chains of men. One of Rivet's men could stand the strain no longer and fired his weapon. Then most of the others joined him firing at the Chinese. At the first shot the Chinese disappeared as if by magic. Then came four short Chinese bugle notes—the Chinese signal for reassembly.

In a matter of minutes, three enemy machine guns, several submachine guns, and perhaps 100 rifles were firing on Rivet's position. From the very first, this fire was accurate and took its toll. Lieutenant Rivet seems to have completely lost his judgment by this time. He told the 20 men who were left that he would lead them in a charge. But they went only a few steps before several dropped from enemy bullets. Those still on their feet quickly took cover. The Chinese made no effort to infiltrate or assault the hill. They probably believed that the men would never get away and that there was no need to attack. This strange fight and exchange of fire went on until just before dawn. Two Chinese mortars had by then been emplaced, and they began dropping their shells on the ridge. One of the mortar rounds killed Rivet. There were then two officers, five American enlisted men, and three ROKs alive on the knob, and only five of them were unwounded. Among them all there were only two clips of ammunition for two Colt .45 pistols and two clips for one carbine. The remnant agreed they had to try to escape.

Lieutenant King of the 3rd Platoon led the survivors down the slope to the east, then headed north in the direction of the 2nd and 1st platoons. But there were Chinese all around them, and in a series of encounters they found themselves in the midst of perhaps two companies of Chinese just as an American air strike came in on the enemy. An L-5 pilot had radioed the 38th Regiment that he had spotted about 300 Chinese in a valley behind G Company's position. In the confusion of the napalm and rocket strike, An Jong Sup raced up the slope through the Chinese in front of him. The rest were never heard of afterward.

An went north. Later he ran into two Chinese who let him come right up to them. They apparently thought he was friendly. At point-blank range he shot them both dead with his carbine. He then ran until he collapsed. Friendly troops later found him where he lay, still unconscious. They took him to Lieutenant Colonel Skeldon at the 2nd Battalion CP, where An told his story. Skeldon and the others who heard him believed his account. Except for An's account, no one would have known what happened to Rivet, his headquarters group, and the 3rd Platoon.[18]

Second Lieutenant Hollingsworth with his 2nd Platoon and Master Sergeant Acosta with the 1st Platoon, G Company, both only a short distance north on the Hill 291 dogleg from Rivet's position, escaped from the Chinese around them and rejoined Skeldon's 2nd Battalion to the north. But the fact that they did illustrates some features of the Chinese 2nd Phase Offensive. Hollingsworth's 2nd Platoon was approximately two-thirds of a mile north of Rivet's initial CP; Acosta's 1st Platoon was about a mile farther north. Both groups heard the distant sounds of battle. But neither had any idea that their company commander and his men and the 3rd Platoon were involved in a grim fight for life. They did not hear the sounds of that particular fight, and no message reached them of it.

About an hour after midnight, Hollingsworth decided he would go back to the company CP to find out why he had received no communications from it. Only a quarter of a mile from his own position, he made a turn in a small stream bed he was following to find directly in front of him about two companies of Chinese soldiers moving haphazardly around a small building. Perhaps an early breakfast break, he thought. He stopped and took cover and sent back his sole companion to bring up a machine gun. By the time the latter returned with it and an ammunition bearer, Hollingsworth had discovered another body of Chinese moving along a nearby ridge on a course that, if continued, would take them into his own 2nd Platoon position. He had already decided that it would not be wise to fire on the Chinese in front of him but that he should hurry back to his own men. Arriving there with his two companions and the machine gun, he swung the platoon around and reemplaced the automatic weapons to face south, where he expected the Chinese to appear. Hollingsworth forgot to send a runner to tell Acosta about the appearance of Chinese.

The Chinese column Hollingsworth expected to arrive in front of him got to within 100 yards of his easternmost squad before they were discovered, and that was only when the CCF opened up on the position with a sudden hail of submachine-gun fire—mostly from American Thompson submachine guns. In the firefight that now erupted, all the American BARs and the one machine gun jammed after firing briefly. With their automatic fire gone, the platoon lost morale.

Some of the attached South Korean soldiers jumped up and started running north toward the 1st Platoon. This caused some Americans to get to their feet as if to take off also. Hollingsworth decided at once that he had to get his men out of there and to gain time to restore their composure and try to clear the jammed weapons. He backed his platoon off the position in the direction of the 1st Platoon, learning in the process that nine of his platoon were casualties—killed, wounded, missing, or captured in the brief engagement. Halfway to the 1st Platoon, Hollingsworth stopped his platoon. He examined the machine gun and the BARs. He found that all the weapons except one of the BARs were hopelessly jammed. During this halt, Hollingsworth saw some Chinese leaving the position he had just vacated and moving in their direction. He now quickly led his men into the perimeter of the 1st Platoon.

For reasons not known, the Chinese did not attack the 1st Platoon position. There were hundreds, if not thousands, of Chinese troops now in the rear of the 38th Infantry front line. It is not clear where they all came from, but it is clear that enemy troops had penetrated the regiment's line at numerous places during the night of 25 November. It is known that large numbers crossed the Chongchon River from the west in the vicinity of Chinaman's Hat and that many others had come south from the Hill 1229 region and crossed the Paengnyong in the vicinity of Somin-dong. Both of these enemy forces, from different Chinese armies, had proceeded to send large forces swiftly behind the rear of the 38th Regiment and of the 2nd Infantry Division. The Chinese that surrounded G Company could have come from either one or both of these large penetrations. It is apparent that, by daylight of 26 November large numbers of CCF from the 40th Army, and probably also from the 38th Army, were behind Colonel Peploe's 38th Infantry east of the Chongchon River.

At the 1st Platoon position, now reinforced by survivors of Hollingsworth's 2nd Platoon, the excited Americans, however, remained undisturbed during the rest of the night and all morning of 26 November. Shortly after noon, Hollingsworth, now in command of both platoons, sent out two patrols to see whether a route of withdrawal was open. He and Sergeant Acosta decided they must get away from that location and try to fight their way out. The patrols reported back that enemy were on all sides of them. Yet Hollingsworth led the two platoons all the way back to Skeldon's battalion CP without firing a shot or being fired on. This could have happened only because the Chinese allowed it. Perhaps they were satisfied with having cut off the entire 38th Regiment during the night and now wanted to give all their effort to pressing farther into the

2nd Division rear. The escape of a platoon or two of isolated troops probably seemed unimportant to them in comparison to their larger mission.

Meanwhile, by the morning of 26 November, Lieutenant Colonel Skeldon had concluded that G Company must have been destroyed during the night. He reported this to Colonel Peploe, the 38th Regimental commander, and asked for a company to fill the gap that now existed between the 38th Regiment and the 9th Infantry west of it. Peploe released C Company to Skeldon, who put it into position on the west side of the regimental front. Only when Lieutenant Hollingsworth led his men into the 2nd Battalion CP about 5:30 P.M. that afternoon was it known that one officer and 60 men of G Company had survived out of the four officers, 115 American enlisted men, and 44 ROK soldiers the company had comprised the day before.[19]

The action at Hill 291 is an example of what can happen when there is poor leadership and no coordination, or poor coordination, at regimental boundaries. The right flank of the 9th Regiment and the left flank of the 38th Regiment had their boundaries at Hill 291. According to Colonel Peploe, the 9th Infantry made no attempt to establish contact with G Company on Hill 291. This resulted in a gap between the two regiments, which the Chinese were able to exploit for a successful penetration between them.[20] On the other hand, the Chinese who devastated G Company may have come from the north and east, and not through the gap between the regimental boundaries.

It is impossible to tell a coherent story of what happened to the 38th Regiment on the nights of 25 and 26 November. It is clear, however, that F Company, 2nd Battalion, on Hill 383, just south of and in a sharp bend of the Paengnyong River and about a mile northwest of Somin-dong, made a remarkable fight and killed hundreds of Chinese who crossed the river in front of it and tried to overrun its position during the night of 26–27 November. Capt. Nicholas Gombos commanded the company. He was in a strong position with a large supply of ammunition. The Chinese failed in their coordinated attack to take the hill and were deflected eastward from it. There they found Somin-dong straight ahead in their path. They made a major penetration at Somin-dong between the 2nd and 3rd battalions. Two Chinese prisoners said the force that hit F Company and subsequently penetrated the regimental line at Somin-dong came from the CCF 113th Division, 38th Army. This force, therefore, came from the north.

During the battle around Hill 383 and Somin-dong, F Company ran out of grenades. A platoon from E Company then reinforced it, and finally the last of the 2nd Battalion reserve had to join it on the hill. The outcome was in doubt for a while. For a time, Chinese held the crest of Hill 383. F Company at this point emplaced two 81-mm mortars to concentrate on the crest. The Chinese on top then emplaced three 60-mm mortars to fire on the 81-mm mortars below them. One Chinese salvo destroyed both the 81-mm mortars and wounded five men. From the top of Hill 383, these Chinese 60-mm mortars hit the 38th Regimental Collecting Station and the F Company CP at the southern base of the hill. They also placed interdicting fire on the F Company supply route. These enemy mortars remained active until daylight.

Gombos told his platoon leaders they must hold their ground and fight it out there, and they did exactly as ordered. The 1st Platoon had about 50 percent casualties. Before dawn, two red flares burst over the valley to the north. Afterward the enemy attack lessened, but the enemy on the crest of Hill 383 stayed there–until an air strike about 10 A.M. came in on them. An ad hoc platoon from remnants of E, B, and L companies then attacked the crest and drove off the remaining Chinese. This was one fight the Americans won. Dead Chinese were found on all approaches to the hill–from the north, east, and west sides and at the river crossings north of the hill.

Elsewhere in the 2nd Battalion front during the night, Chinese penetrated L Company, west of F Company. One of L Company's platoons withdrew into E Company. The 2nd Battalion CP in Somin-dong received heavy small-arms and mortar fire. Lieutenant Colonel Skeldon finally ordered the CP abandoned. An enemy mortar round made a direct hit on the only radio in the CP still working, and communication was then lost to all companies on 26 November. Many of the battalion vehicles were so cold they could not be started and had to be abandoned. H Company lost its mortars, and the regiment lost two tanks. Because the road west to Kujang-dong was closed to it at this time, the 38th Infantry had to evacuate 38 wounded eastward through Tokchon and Pukchang-ni.

The 38th Regiment by now had another problem on its right, or east, flank. ROK troops from the ROK 3rd Regiment in the ROK II Corps area were now streaming across the boundary into the regiment's sector. Colonel Peploe stopped them, attached them to his regiment, and put them into his defenses as best he could. The 38th Regiment's 3rd Battalion on that flank was itself pulling back. Colonel Peploe had started a movement by which he shifted his right flank and faced his regiment in a crescent-shaped perimeter to the north and east.[21] He was now being threatened not only from the west and north, but also from the east–and, one could easily have added, from the rear.

By the evening of 26 November, B Company, 9th Infantry, which the previous morning had attacked Hill 219 north of Sinhung-dong, was reduced to 34 men, some of them with light wounds, from the 129 men who had moved to it the previous day. E Company, 9th Infantry, had become involved in heavy fighting southeast of Hill 219 during the night of 25–26 November as the enemy pushed south around Hill 219 and its environs. It had lost 52 men killed and wounded during the night. When dawn of 26 November came, the 1st Battalion and parts of the 2nd Battalion east of the Chongchon River were virtually surrounded by Chinese and had to find some way to evacuate their wounded before they withdrew.

The 1st Battalion, 23rd Infantry, at Chinaman's Hat was in the same predicament. An enemy roadblock had been set up south of it on the road to Kujang-dong. This was the only route over which wounded could be evacuated.

The E Company commander, 1st Lt. Joseph Manto, selected Pfc. James L. Brown to take charge of getting casualties from the two battalions through the enemy roadblock south of Chinaman's Hat. The effective part of the roadblock was a group of 15 to 20 Chinese in a culvert under the railroad east of the road. Brown had the walking wounded lay down a covering fire on the culvert. At the same time he took two men with him and pushed a small handcar down the tracks, which gave them some protection. As Brown advanced toward the culvert, he eliminated small enemy fire groups along the way. In this way he approached close to the culvert, where he engaged the main enemy body with rifle fire and grenades. He successfully destroyed the roadblock, and the vehicles with the wounded then got through. His action also opened the way for many other troops to withdraw down the road, relatively free from hostile action.[22]

Brown earned the Distinguished Service Cross in the E Company fight that night, as did another man. Second Lt. Robert Gallardo remained with his platoon after being wounded, and after the company commander was wounded in a counterattack, Gallardo assumed command. He recovered an abandoned truck, supervised loading the wounded into it, and successfully evacuated them from the scene of action.[23]

Colonel Sloane ordered those still combat effective in E Company to wade the Chongchon River and join the 2nd Battalion, 9th Infantry, on the west side. At full daylight on 26 November, only three companies of the 9th Infantry —G, F, and H—were combat effective. Before dark that day, the regiment could account for only about half its men. In addition to battle casualties, the regiment had many men suffering from frozen feet and otherwise disabled by exposure.

During the night of 26-27 November, Chinese overran G Company, 9th Infantry, west of the Chongchon. In a devastating Chinese attack on the company that night, Pfc. Andrew J. Gasquet, Jr., a machine gunner with the 3rd Platoon, played a dominant role in enabling his platoon, and subsequently G Company, to escape destruction. Enemy mortar fire was heavy and enabled Chinese to penetrate the 3rd Platoon. First one squad withdrew—all except Gasquet, who voluntarily stayed with his machine gun. In a few minutes the entire 3rd Platoon followed the one squad that had fallen back and joined the 2nd Platoon on its left. Gasquet still stayed in his position, and by his automatic fire aided the 3rd Platoon in its successful withdrawal. Gasquet stayed with his gun until Chinese overran it. Within a few minutes all of G Company had left its position. Gasquet's fate is not known.[24]

Parts of F and G companies slipped back toward the tanks and the quad-50s. H Company suffered the least of the 2nd Battalion. The battalion's fight had been short and vicious. The attack had come just after Colonel Sloane had ordered Maj. Cesibes V. Barberis, the battalion commander, to load as many men as possible on tanks and other vehicles and cross to the east side of the Chongchon River into the perimeter of the 23rd Infantry. Sloane realized that his 2nd Battalion was being surrounded and probably could not hold during the night. The Chinese struck it from close-in on three sides just as the 2nd Battalion started to abandon its positions. Artillery of the 37th Field Artillery Battalion at Kujangdong fired heavily in support of the battalion on Hill 180 but had little effect on the close-in fight. From Hill 180, Barberis withdrew his battalion to Hill 153, south of the dry creek bed. There the Chinese soon attacked again.

Major Barberis later reported that the whole thing started about 11 P.M. on 26 November, when he sent out patrols to contact friendly units he thought were on his left (east) flank. The battalion had just moved to Hill 153, on the south bank of Dry Creek, close to the Chongchon River, preparatory to crossing to the east side of the river. The friendly troops Barberis thought were close were not there. Chinese were there instead. His patrols ran into large numbers of them, who were moving toward Hill 153. These Chinese enveloped the hill from three sides and attacked it. Barberis thought that only about three out of every ten Chinese in this force had rifles or submachine guns. The rest carried pouches of grenades tied to their waists.

On Hill 153, Barberis was opposite the positions of the 23rd Infantry at Chinaman's Hat on the other (east) side of the Chongchon River. From there Major Barberis was in the act of carrying out Colonel Sloane's order to cross the river into the perimeter of the 23rd Infantry. He put most of his men on tanks and quad-50s and started for the ford across the river.

A Chinese bazooka team ambushed the lead tank, and their rockets set it afire. The flames illuminated the column behind it, making it vulnerable to Chinese machine gunners. Many men on the vehicles were killed, and many wounded were left behind as the vehicles sprinted ahead and entered and crossed the river. Barberis's men tried unsuccessfully to save their 81-mm mortars, and others tried to carry out the machine guns, but most of those who made this effort were killed. By heroic effort the 2nd Battalion got about 150 wounded across the river. Those who could walk had to wade the icy Chongchon. After these wounded had gained the east bank of the river, Lt. Martin Kavanaugh and Lieutenant Haywood ventured back across the river and returned with their tank, loaded down with more wounded.

E Company, which had just joined the 2nd Battalion on the west side of the river, suffered very heavy losses. One of its platoon leaders, however, Lieutenant Manto, fought his way back to the east side with 40 wounded and then returned to the west side again to recover some abandoned equipment. When some of the Chinese tried to pursue him across the river, they were repulsed by the combined efforts of the 9th and 23rd infantrymen on the east side and the fire of eight tanks.[25]

While these heavy blows were falling on the 9th Infantry on 26 November and the night of 26–27, the 23rd Infantry on the east side of the river at Chinaman's Hat had a somewhat easier time until after dark. After daylight on the twenty-sixth, some of its infantry, supported by tanks, attacked north into the position the 61st Field Artillery had occupied the night before. They captured the position and 21 Chinese soldiers who were still there, including Culture Officer We Yu Shu. The 61st Field Artillery now recovered most of its lost guns and displaced them south.[26] Altogether, there were 102 Chinese prisoners taken during the night and in the clean-up the next morning at the 23rd Infantry lines adjacent to Chinaman's Hat, all of them from the CCF 359th Regiment, 120th Division.

The morning of 26 November at Chinaman's Hat was cold, with a freezing wind from the northwest, and the temperature only a few degrees above zero. Reinforcements arrived for the 23rd Infantry just after noon. At 1 P.M., Lt. Col. James W. Edwards brought his 2nd Battalion, 23rd Infantry, from Kujangdong into the 23rd perimeter. Edwards had little time to contemplate the situation. Colonel Freeman at once ordered him to attack Chinaman's Hat.

Lieutenant Colonel Edwards assigned Capt. John E. Emerson, Jr.'s G Company to attack the hill from the west and E Company to attack it from the southwest. G Company had to climb a 45-degree slope in its attack. By 8 P.M., it had reached a point 50 yards short of the crest. But E Company had not been able to move even from its line of departure.

At 8:30 P.M. the Chinese struck back with great force in full moonlight in a two-pronged attack. One part went right through E Company to the 23rd Regimental CP. The other came from the north around the west side of Chinaman's Hat to the 1st Battalion CP.

Earlier, in his attack toward the crest of Chinaman's Hat, Captain Emerson had led G Company in charge after charge—seven of them, according to one account. Now when the enemy gained G Company's rear, the battalion commander ordered Emerson to withdraw from Chinaman's Hat. To do so he had to lead a bayonet charge through a Chinese company that had cut him off. But he succeeded in getting his company back down to the flat ground and adjacent to B Company. Emerson then mounted a tank and fired its deck machine gun until he ran out of ammunition.[27] In two counterattacks during the night, the 23rd Infantry failed to regain its lost positions.

In these swirling battles around Chinaman's Hat, Sgt. John A. Pittman, C Company, 23rd Infantry, led a counterattack to regain lost ground, even though suffering from mortar fragment wounds. During this attack an enemy grenade landed amid his squad. He threw his body on the grenade. When a medical aid man reached him, Pittman's first words were to ask how many of his men had been injured. Pittman survived the war.[28]

The Chinese attack on the 23rd Infantry at Chinaman's Hat on the night of 26–27 November, following the failure of Edwards's 2nd Battalion to drive the Chinese from the hill, included an enemy force sweeping around the base of the hill and overrunning Colonel Freeman's CP. One Chinese tommy gunner ran through the CP tent, spraying bullets at random and wounding several men.[29]

After daylight on 27 November, the CCF who had captured the 23rd Regimental CP withdrew from it, and the regiment reoccupied it at 9 A.M. Most of its abandoned equipment was recovered at that time. The 23rd Regiment reorganized during the day and sent out patrols. These reported that Chinese were digging in east of the regiment. Stragglers from the 9th Infantry west of the river continued to come in to the 23rd Infantry perimeter, and others escaped downstream and crossed over to the artillery positions at Kujang-dong. Those suffering most from wounds and frostbite were taken to Kujang-dong to warming tents.

A harbinger of what was to come is found in the order received by the 17th Field Artillery Battalion (8-inch howitzers) at 10 P.M. on 26 November to move back from Kujang-dong 30 miles on the river road to Kunu-ri. This was the first official order that presaged the retreat of the entire 2nd Infantry Division. Already it was possible to read the cards. Although the 9th Infantry Regiment had greater losses than the other two regiments in the division, all had incurred heavy losses. The 2nd Battalion, 9th Infantry, for instance, on 25 November had approximately 28 officers and 750 men. Three days later it was down to 9 officers and 250 men. Although most of the 9th Infantry on the morning of 27 November were on the east side of the Chongchon with the 23rd Infantry at Chinaman's Hat, its strength was so low that the protection of the area of Kujang-dong northward depended largely on the 23rd Infantry. If the 23rd Infantry should come to disaster in the next day, the fate of the 38th Infantry might be in jeopardy. It could escape only if the Kujang-dong–Tokchon road junction with the Chongchon River road was held. That depended on the 23rd Infantry primarily.

Meanwhile, the 38th Infantry east of Kujang-dong was having its share of problems. On 26 November, after a night of battle almost everywhere on its line, the 38th Regiment was in a state of flux. One of the more serious factors was the movement of the ROK 3rd Regiment, westward into its lines east of Tongchang, which was the coordinating point between K Company on the 38th Regiment's right flank and the ROK 3rd Regiment on the ROK II Corps's left flank. This development left the eastern flank of the 38th Regiment, the 2nd Division, the IX Corps, and the whole Eighth Army completely exposed to Chinese encirclement and attack from the Tokchon area. It has already been noted that General Walker had directed the IX Corps to send the Turkish Brigade to Tokchon to halt the retreat of the ROK II Corps and to deal with the CCF threat from that quarter. But Chinese forces had met and defeated the Turks on the road to Tokchon.

Colonel Peploe reported to General Keiser the movement of the ROK 3rd Regiment into his sector. Keiser reported it to IX Corps, which confirmed him and Peploe in Peploe's having assumed control of the ROK regiment and any other ROKs that might enter the 2nd Division zone of operations. The ROK regimental commander accepted Peploe's control and cooperated fully with him. During 26 November Colonel Peploe sent two of the three ROK battalions to the left flank of his 1st Battalion to buttress his defense there.[30]

Evidence of intense enemy buildup of supplies and ammunition for use against an expected Eighth Army drive north toward the border, or for a general attack south of their own in this area, came to light in the 38th Regimental sector on 26 November. A patrol found a Chinese ammunition dump in an abandoned lead mine. It was only 300 yards south of the Ku-jang-dong–Somin-dong–Tokchon road. Two mine tunnels were used – in one tunnel, ammunition had been stored; in the other, billets had been built for troops. The stored ammunition included 500 cases of 60-mm mortar shells, 200 cases of 6.5 rifle ammunition, and 200 cases of 7.9 rifle ammunition – in all, about 18 tons of ammunition. Local civilians informed the patrol that about 100 Chinese soldiers came to the area on or about 9 November with a Korean interpreter and remained there for about ten days. During this period trucks and animal-drawn vehicles moved the ammunition into the mine tunnel. The Chinese worked only during the night. During daytime they remained hidden.[31]

Previously during 26 November Peploe had sent C Company to restore G Company's line on the east, but Chinese had encircled it. F and L companies were under fire. The 3rd Battalion was withdrawn under enemy fire to form a refused flank on the east of the 2nd Division line. In the middle, near Somin-dong, the 2nd Battalion lost two tanks before the battalion CP was abandoned. The battalion aid station also withdrew. In the fighting there, tank crew members said they encountered American-made rocket-launcher fire for the first time in Korea. The 2nd Battalion CP and parts of L Company withdrew one mile south of Somin-dong to Hill 404. I and K companies of the 3rd Battalion, two to three miles northeast of Somin-dong, meanwhile enjoyed relative calm.

By 6 P.M. on 26 November the 38th Regiment had established a new defensive line. The 3rd Battalion withdrew I and K companies from the original defense line a mile or more west of the Somin-dong–Tokchon road and turned them to form a line facing south in a refused eastern flank. The 2nd Battalion centered on Hill 404, a mile south of Somin-dong, and the 1st Battalion was southeast of Chinaman's Hat. Generally, the 38th Regimental line now protected both the 2nd Division and Eighth Army from sudden envelopment on their eastern, or right, flank. The regimental line resembled roughly a horseshoe, the toe pointed north. On its western flank, the regiment had assigned C Company, 2nd Engineers, to the 1st Battalion to replace A Company as riflemen, since A Company was now combat ineffective. A Company went into regimental reserve in rear of the regimental CP.

At the close of daylight on 26 November, the 2nd Division line consisted of remnants of the 9th Infantry along the Chongchon River on the west; two battalions, the 1st and 2nd, of the 23rd Infantry were east of the river at Chinaman's Hat; and the 38th Infantry on its horseshoe-shaped line ran generally east-west a few miles northeast of Kujang-dong. As stated earlier, some elements of the ROK 3rd Regiment were buttressing the 1st Battalion. The 38th Regiment was vulnerable in its position, as it had no north-south road in its sector. The only exit road was the lateral road running east-west from Tokchon to Kujang-dong, and Chinese had closed the Tokchon end. They had blocked the Kujang-dong end in the regiment's sector at different points for part of the time. In effect, the exit at Kujang-dong to the Chongchon River road from the regimental position was the only possible escape route open to the 38th Infantry. Friendly forces had to hold Kujang-dong to make the 38th Infantry withdrawal possible.

The 2nd Division's position grew worse as available transportation diminished. The division ordnance report for 26 November said that 20 vehicles a day were being lost, and the number increasing rapidly, because of a lack of spare parts. The division had abandoned 39 general-purpose vehicles and 47 track-laying vehicles for these reasons after stripping them of needed parts. But a favorable note concerned winter clothing. Three thousand parkas and 2,695 pile jackets arrived at Won-ni on 26 November, and they were issued to troops the next day.[32]

When Colonel Peploe had reached General Keiser on radio to tell him that the ROKs had collapsed on his right, that was Keiser's first information that his division's right flank was open and exposed. He instructed Peploe to use his own judgment as to how long he could hold his position. Keiser is reported to have said later that Peploe's prompt action in refusing his right flank saved the division at that time. He told Peploe to retire without further instructions whenever he felt it necessary to save the regiment. By this time the 38th Infantry had taken Chinese prisoners from three Chinese divisions, the CCF 113th and 114th from the CCF 38th Army, which hit him from the north, and from the 119th Division of the CCF 40th Army, which came from the west.[33]

On the night of 26–27 November, the Chinese renewed their assault against F Company on Hill 383. Again they captured some high ground there. Cpl. Robert K. Imrie and his platoon undertook to recapture the lost ground. They came under heavy machine-gun cross fire, which stopped them. Then Imrie alone charged the machine gun on the platoon's right flank under covering fire and, by automatic fire, succeeded in knocking out that position. But hardly had he accomplished this, than enemy machine-gun fire from the other flank hit and mortally wounded him. Imrie's platoon now attacked that machine-gun position and destroyed it.[34]

For a time during the morning of 27 November, the 38th Regimental CP had no contact with F, K, and I companies through their battalion CPs. Peploe, hard pressed everywhere, now used elements of the ROK 3rd Regiment to support his line at its most threatened points, always issuing his orders through the ROK regimental commander. Chinese were attacking Hill 404, south of Somin-dong, and drove I Company from it. At the same time, other Chinese attacked Somin-dong, just north of Hill 404, and drove K Company from it. This and other related action cut the MSR between the 38th Infantry and its 3rd Battalion to the east.

In hard fighting, I Company and a section of tanks counterattacked, broke out of the enemy encirclement, and fought their way through Somin-dong to a friendly roadblock half a mile west, held by the 2nd Battalion. K Company in counterattacks was still trying to hold parts of Hills 404 and 360 to the south.

Farther west toward Kujang-dong, a Chinese force penetrated between B Company and a ROK battalion of the 3rd Regiment on its left flank and reached high ground from which they could deliver fire on the 38th Regimental CP and the Collecting Station adjacent to it. An air strike on this enemy force greatly aided B Company in regaining its position. During the day of the twenty-seventh, there were 74 air sorties in the 2nd Division sector. One of the most spectaclar took place in the 38th Infantry's sector. This strike was directed against a mine shaft on Hill 943, where observers had reported a steady stream of enemy entering the mine. Air observers estimated this enemy force at 600, perhaps two battalions. The strike hit the mine entrance first with napalm and then with 500-pound bombs. The observers thought the strike closed the mine-shaft entrance and that possibly large numbers of Chinese may have perished inside.

Chinese even attacked the 38th Regimental CP on 27 November from its rear. Also included in this attack were the 38th Field Artillery Battalion, together with the attached A Battery of the 503rd Field Artillery Battalion. The headquarters personnel and the artillerymen beat off the attack, inflicting about 100 casualties on the Chinese.[35] ROK troops were south of the CP.

At dusk the 38th Regimental CP moved about one and a half miles west. Chinese followed, and at 2 A.M. they again attacked the CP. Peploe then moved his CP farther west to the vicinity of Lieutenant Colonel Skeldon's 2nd Battalion's CP.[36] This was the situation in the predawn hours of 28 November in the 38th Infantry. The regiment was now headed as rapidly as possible for Kujang-dong, but it had to fight almost every foot of the way.

11. The US 2nd Infantry Division Retreats to Kunu-ri

Full-scale retreat of the 2nd Infantry Division got under way during the night of 27–28 November. All day of the twenty-seventh, aerial observers had reported large numbers of enemy moving south from the direction of Huichon. Large numbers of Chinese perished from numerous air strikes, since many of these strikes caught groups and formations of Chinese in the open. While it will never be known how many Chinese lost their lives on 27 November in the 2nd Division sector from ground combat and from air strikes, the number must have been substantial by any standard. But the Chinese were willing to accept heavy losses to press their advantage.[1]

On 27 November Eighth Army was in the fourth day of its well-advertised "attack" to the North Korean border, but it was no longer an attack. It was now a retreat on all sectors of the front. The Chinese counterattack was rolling south and southwest against Eighth Army. With every passing hour it seemed to be assuming increased magnitude. To many, the picture was murky at best.

Meanwhile, on this day, 27 November, the X Corps on the other side of the peninsula in the Chosin Reservoir area was just beginning its offensive designed to drive west and cut off the Chinese who might be facing Eighth Army. While the X Corps offensive was doomed to failure and the corps's destruction itself was narrowly averted, it did not know on that day how critical the situation was in the Eighth Army front. And neither, apparently, did the Far East Command in Tokyo.

The night of 27–28 November was one of Chinese attacks almost everywhere against 2nd Infantry Division units. The 9th Infantry, still on the west end of the division line, and badly crippled, lost still more men. At this time, Lt. Col. Edgar V. H. Bell's 2nd Chemical Mortar Battalion (4.2-inch mortars) was attached to the regiment and served as light artillery for it. During the night, the mortar battalion lost almost all of its C Company. Of its vehicles, the company had only four jeeps left, and remaining personnel consisted of one officer and 24 enlisted men. Many of the missing, however, came in later to Clearing Stations or infiltrated back to friendly lines. After C Company of the mortar battalion was eliminated, Lieutenant Colonel Bell kept his A and B mortar companies in the fight. When the division withdrawal began, they were still with the 2nd Battalion, 9th Infantry, and among the last troops to cross from the west to the east side of the Chongchon River. The mortar battalion loaded the

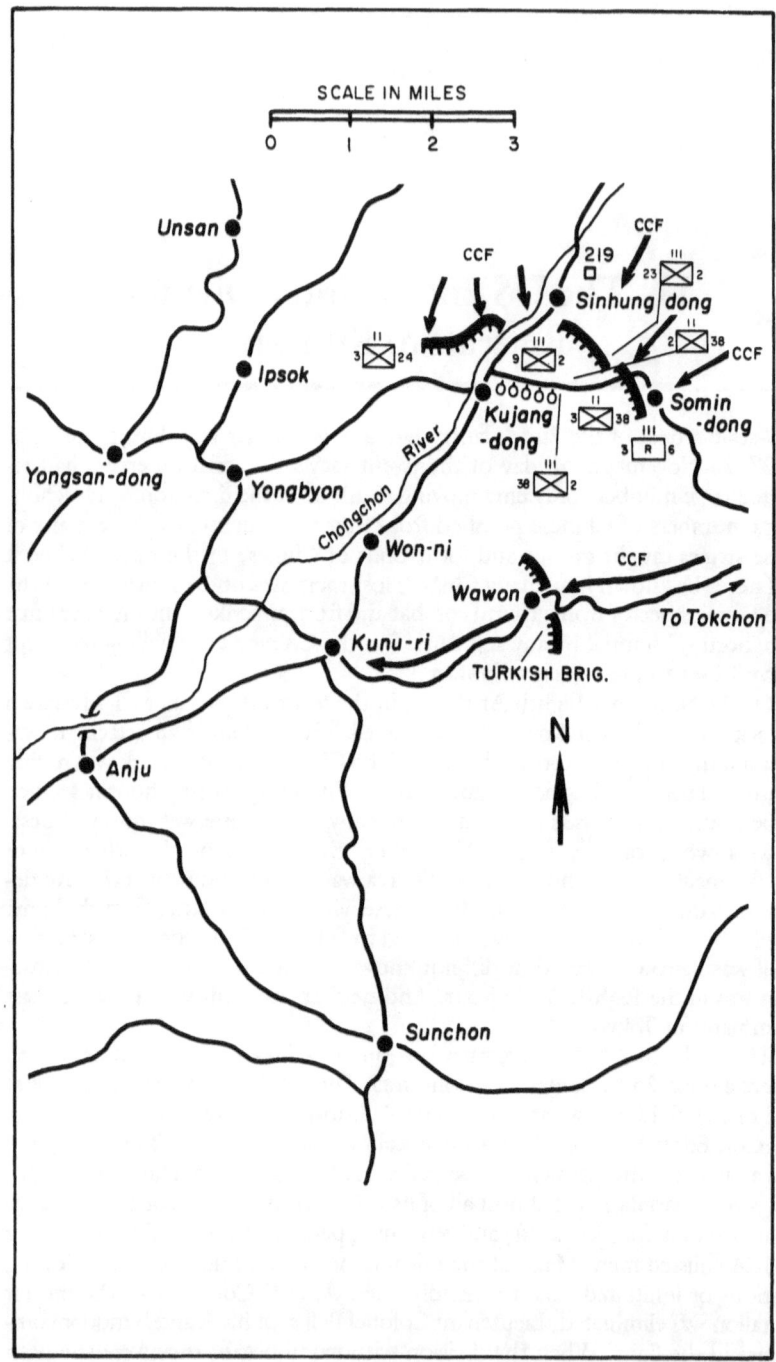

Map 9. The 2nd Infantry Division front line at 2 A.M., 28 November 1950.

The 8076th Mobile Army Surgical Hospital (MASH) at Kunu-ri, and its commanding officer, Lt. Col. Kryder E. Van Duskirk, on 27 November 1950. National Archives 111-SC 354715

274 officers and men left in the 2nd Battalion, 9th Infantry, on its vehicles and moved south to Won-ni, where the men set up a roadblock. It lasted only a short time. Bell said that at about 3:30 A.M. on 28 November, Major Barberis reported only 30 of his infantrymen left. The entire group then withdrew to Kunu-ri.[2]

At the same time, the 1st and 2nd battalions of the 9th Infantry were trying desperately to withdraw south. Chinese overran the CP of the 3rd Battalion during the night and its members joined the 2nd Battalion CP. It will be recalled that the 2nd Battalion, under heavy enemy attack, crossed to the east side of the Chongchon and entered the 23rd Infantry's perimeter before dawn of 28 November.[3]

During 28 November, the 2nd Infantry Division attached the 9th Infantry, minus the 2nd Battalion, to the 23rd Infantry. These troops blocked for the 23rd Infantry during its withdrawal at Won-ni. From the beginning of the Chinese attack against Eighth Army, from the evening of 25 November to 29 November, the three infantry battalions of the 9th Infantry had more than 50 percent casualties. The 2nd and 3rd battalions each had less than 400 men remaining as they moved southward toward Kunu-ri.⁴

On its extreme right flank, the IX Corps at 11 A.M. on 28 November attached the Turkish Brigade to the 2nd Infantry Division. The division in turn attached the Turks to Peploe's 38th Infantry Regiment, which held that flank. The 38th Regiment also had the ROK 3rd Regiment under its control. Thus, from 28 November on, Peploe's 38th Regiment had the difficult and critical task of defending the Eighth Army's right flank on the forward battle line as the entire army went into a rapid retreat. At the same time, Eighth Army moved the 1st Cavalry Division, with the ROK 6th Division attached to it, behind the collapsed ROK II Corps sector, in an effort to halt or slow the Chinese envelopment there from the southeast. The 2nd Infantry Division and the 1st Cavalry Division had no contact with each other. In between them, Chinese forces moved at will. The Eighth Army right flank was by this time in a most precarious position.⁵

On 28 November the 2nd Infantry Division issued an operations order establishing unit priority of movement with objectives the division staff hoped would result in an orderly withdrawal toward Kunu-ri. The 23rd Infantry, with the 2nd Battalion, 9th Infantry, and the 72nd Tank Battalion attached, was to cover the division withdrawal. The 9th Infantry was to move south first and attempt to secure Won-ni (Pugwon) and hold a defensive position there. The 38th Regiment, in the hills west of Kujang-dong and heavily engaged with the enemy, was to break contact and fight its way west to Kujang-dong and then continue south on the river road to Kunu-ri, where it was to take up defensive positions northeast of the town. The 23rd Infantry was to withdraw from Chinaman's Hat to Kujang-dong and there establish a defense position that would hold open the road junction with the river road of the Somin-dong–Tokchon road, by which the 38th Regiment was withdrawing. If the 38th Regiment was to escape with any of its equipment, transport, and artillery, this road junction had to be held until the regiment had passed it. The 38th Regiment was in great danger during the night of 27–28 November of being cut off and decimated before it could reach Kujang-dong. Once the 38th Regiment passed through Kujang-dong and started south on the river road, the rest of the division would follow it, while rear-guard elements tried to hold back pursuing Chinese.⁶

During the night of 27–28 November, the artillery at Kujang-dong massed its fires on all avenues of approach to the 23rd Infantry at Chinaman's Hat. The artillery commanders knew that Chinese were attacking that regiment in great numbers and that it needed all the help they could give it. All artillery units were ordered to strengthen their defenses, as it was considered possible that enemy forces might break through to them during the night. About midnight the division artillery at Kujang-dong received a radio message that one of their officers was to be present at division headquarters at 7 A.M. on 28 November to receive instructions. The division artillery S-3, Col. Walker R. Goodrich, was designated to attend the meeting.

At the conference next morning, Goodrich learned that a Chinese roadblock was in place between the 38th Infantry and Kujang-dong, that the 38th

Regiment was fighting its way toward Kujang-dong on the east-west road from that place to Tokchon, and that the regiment was expected to reach Kujang-dong in several hours. The artillery units were to hold their positions at Kujang-dong until the 38th Infantry reached that point, and then they would follow it and the 38th Artillery Battalion south in a withdrawal to positions south of Kunu-ri, on the road to Sunchon. When Goodrich returned to Kujang-dong, he relayed the 2nd Division's orders to all units, and a plan of withdrawal was prepared. The heavy artillery (17th Bn.) would go first, followed by the medium artillery (155th Bn.) and finally the light artillery (105 mm). All artillery battalions at Kujang-dong were ordered to send out reconnoitering parties to select firing positions south of Kunu-ri.[7]

About 10 A.M. on 28 November, an artillery air observer reported a column of approximately 200 to 250 soldiers dogtrotting along a ridge southeast of the Kujang-dong artillery positions. He maneuvered his plane above the column several times in an effort to determine whether they were ROK or Chinese, but without success. The artillery command informed the 2nd Division of the incident.[8]

All night of 27–28 November the 38th Infantry had fight after fight with the Chinese on the road west to Kujang-dong, with the Chinese trying to block its passage. The first task of the regiment was to break contact with the enemy and get on the road leading to Kujang-dong. It used vehicles and tanks for transportation when it could move; the ROK 3rd Regiment, having no vehicles, had to move on foot. The 2nd and 3rd battalions were to go out first, while the 1st Battalion held the road open for them.

Just after midnight, A and L companies, together with C Company of the 2nd Engineer Combat Battalion, began a four-hour fight for control of a hill overlooking the road. They lost the hill at one time, but in a counterattack, led by a tank platoon, they recaptured it. In the meantime, Chinese occupied the 38th Regiment's former CP and high ground on both sides of the road with about 300 men. In this action, they had cut off Lieutenant Colonel Kelleher's 1st Battalion, which was east of the former regimental CP. Colonel Peploe called Kelleher to come to him to receive his withdrawal orders. Kelleher had a dangerous and difficult assignment to carry out his instruction, which was to break contact with enemy forces east of the new big enemy roadblock and to fight his way at night westward through that roadblock to join the rest of the regiment.

In the effort, Kelleher had the help of a tank platoon and a company of the 3rd ROKs in attacking the roadblock. At dawn the ROKs, the tanks, and C Company of the Engineers engaged the Chinese at the roadblock in a savage fight. After 45 minutes they drove the Chinese off into the hills. In this fight, the Chinese knocked out two tanks with 2.36 rockets. L Company had joined the battle and, during the course of the fight, was reduced to one officer and 41 enlisted men. One platoon of C Company was cut off for a period. Tanks went back east on the road and delivered overhead fire while the ROK troops attacked up an almost vertical slope to reach the Chinese entrenchments. C Company escaped during this daring rescue effort. Then Henry Brown with some tanks ran back farther to rescue wounded. The tank drivers and assistant drivers ran the tanks with their hatches partly open so that they could see. One driver saw a face and a hand appear at the partly opened hatch. He snapped it shut, and four fingers fell off inside the tank. But in other instances, Chinese who climbed on the tanks pulled off American wounded who had been placed there. The Chinese infantry were very aggressive in attacking these tanks. Often they climbed on them to throw grenades inside the hatch. They also made every effort to blind the crews by heavy concentrations of small-arms fire and to knock out periscopes, radio antennas, and the deck machine gun.[9]

Leading elements of the 38th Infantry reached Kujang-dong and turned south from the 2nd Division Artillery CP about noon of 28 November. The regiment had cleared the Kujang-dong junction with the river road by 3 P.M. When the leading elements of the regiment first began arriving at Kujang-dong, the regiment received an order to take a defensive position east and south of the town, and the regimental staff made reconnaissance to do this. But before this first order could be carried out, another had the 38th Infantry continue its withdrawal on south toward Kunu-ri.[10]

When the 38th Regiment cleared Kujang-dong at midafternoon on 28 November, its companies were down to an average of two officers and 40 men. The regiment was ten miles south of Kujang-dong when it received division orders to take up a defensive position north and east of Kunu-ri. Facing north, the 23rd Infantry would be on its left (west), and the Turks would be on its right (east). During the day, the Fifth Air Force gave strong air support to the 2nd Infantry Division, but it could not dislodge the CCF. One air observer reported a column from the northeast that looked like ROK troops marching around Peploe's right flank. It was believed, however, that nearly all the ROKs had left this area. The strike planes flew low over the column, and pilots could see South Korean uniforms. The column paid no attention to the planes. A bit later this column vanished from view. It is likely that it was CCF dressed as South Koreans and moving straight into the 2nd Division rear areas.[11]

At 7 A.M. on 28 November, General Keiser ordered Colonel Freeman to move his 23rd Infantry to the vicinity of Won-ni. This regiment, still at Chinaman's Hat, was then the northernmost unit of the 2nd Division, although its 3rd Battalion was south of it, blocking the lateral road from Kujang-dong toward the 38th Infantry. Freeman's 1st Battalion and the regimental Headquarters Company were to go into a blocking formation just north of Kujang-dong, tying in there with the left flank of the 3rd Battalion. The 2nd Battalion was to remain in a blocking position 1,000 yards south of Chinaman's Hat until all of the 9th Infantry had passed through it.

When the 1st Battalion, 23rd Infantry, reached Kujang-dong, there was enemy fire on the area. The 2nd Battalion, 9th Infantry, meanwhile had been in a blocking position near Won-ni. After all elements of the 2nd Division had passed south through Kujang-dong, the 1st Battalion, 23rd Infantry, was to act as rear guard for the movement to Won-ni. To carry out this mission the 1st Battalion held a position just south of the Kujang-dong road junction. Once the 1st Battalion was in position there, the 3rd Battalion, 23rd Infantry, passed through it, then the 9th Infantry units, then the 2nd Battalion, 23rd Infantry, which had been fighting a delaying action south of Chinaman's Hat. By 5 P.M. on 28 November all elements of the 2nd Division had passed south of the 1st Battalion roadblock at Kujang-dong. The 1st Battalion started to follow, with its A Company, accompanied by tanks, the rear guard. Lt. Col. Claire E. Hutchins, the battalion commander, stayed with A Company in personal command.[12]

When the 38th Infantry passed through Kujang-dong at midafternoon, the artillery there followed south on the river road. The division Artillery Headquarters followed the 503rd Artillery Battalion. The movement was slow but orderly, with short halts from time to time. At dark the headquarters had reached the northern edge of Kunu-ri. There the artillery column met converging columns of the 25th Infantry Division, which was withdrawing from the northeast across the Chongchon River. In passing through Kunu-ri and for a few miles beyond, both divisions had to use the same road. Colonel Goodrich of the 2nd Division Artillery Headquarters and Colonel Dick, the 25th Division Artillery executive officer, joined at the Kunu-ri road junction to direct traffic of the merging columns. The last elements of the 25th Division cleared after 9 P.M., before those of the 2nd Division. After the 25th Division had cleared the road junction, Colonel Goodrich went on to the new 2nd Division Artillery CP. All artillery units completed their withdrawal that night without loss and were in firing positions south of Kunu-ri by midnight, 28 November.[13]

The 1st Battalion, 23rd Infantry, the last of the 2nd Division infantry battalions to move into the withdrawal march order, started its withdrawal from Kujang-dong at dusk, a little after 5 P.M. on 28 November. Infantrymen from its B and C companies loaded on the 15th Field Artillery Battalion vehicles. A Company, in the rear, rode on tanks, with their organic weapons in trucks. South of Kujang-dong the battalion came to a halt because of a jammed vehicular column ahead. The tanks and A Company infantry deployed in rice paddies on the west side of the road, and soon engaged in an exchange of machine-gun fire with Chinese pursuers. This stoppage lasted about half an hour. After the road ahead began to clear, A Company reloaded on tanks and proceeded another one and a half miles, when it again came up against a stalled column.

Here a sharp firefight with the Chinese developed. The CCF now had mortars in action as well as machine guns, and there was heavy small-arms fire from the railroad embankment west of the road. The moon was up and cast a bright light. Men in A Company could see Chinese troops moving around the column and could hear them talk. The last tank in line was protected by the shadows of a wooded knob near the road. The men with the tank saw a column of about 50 Chinese, four abreast, walking south on the road toward them. The Chinese did not see the tank. First Lt. William Majors and 1st Lt. Barrie E. Storrs, the tank platoon leader, happened to be with this last tank at the end of the A Company column. At a distance of 25 yards from the approaching Chinese, Storrs fired the 76-mm tank gun and Majors fired the tank .50-caliber machine gun. Sfc. Jack W. Warren on the ground by the tank fired his BAR. When this heavy burst of point-blank fire hit them, the Chinese screamed, and those still on their feet scattered. Warren walked up the road to see if all were dead. He disappeared from view and never came back.[14]

During this withdrawal on the night of 28 November, Lieutenant Colonel Hutchins was in radio communication with Colonel Freeman. Freeman kept Hutchins informed of the location of the tail of the main 2nd Division in front of the 23rd Infantry. During this fight at the last stop, Freeman told Hutchins the column was only a mile ahead of him. In these circumstances, Hutchins had A Company hold its position until it appeared that the Chinese were about to encircle them. Then Hutchins ordered A Company to mount the first seven of the ten tanks. Hutchins and Captain Stai were in the radio jeep at the head of A Company.

Between Kujang-dong and Won-ni, A Company, 23rd Infantry, stopped, deployed, and made five stands. In all but the last they had firefights with closely pursuing Chinese. According to the 23rd Infantry command report, A Company reached Won-ni at 10:30 P.M. There it passed through the 2nd Battalion, 9th Infantry, which was blocking just north of the village.

At midnight the 9th Infantry troops in their blocking position had a hard fight with Chinese. The 1st Battalion, 23rd Infantry, meanwhile, had gone through Won-ni but stopped one mile south of the village, where it went into a blocking position. The 2nd Battalion, 9th Infantry, then pulled back through it. The 2nd Division withdrawal from Kujang-dong down the main road for a distance of 15 miles had taken seven hours. In this withdrawal, involving four different firefights with Chinese, A Company, 23rd Infantry, had not lost a single vehicle and had suffered only a few casualties. It was a most skillfully executed piece of division withdrawal under fire and a model of combined tank-infantry rear-guard action in defense.[15]

When the 38th Infantry, leading the 2nd Division withdrawal to Kunu-ri, arrived at its assigned defense positions in an arc northeast of Kunu-ri the night of 28 November it found enemy already there. All day aerial observers had reported enemy forces moving south and east deep in the rear of the 38th Regiment. The 2nd Division CP itself had moved during the day from Unhung-ni, several miles west of Kunu-ri on the Chongchon River road, to a point six miles south of Kunu-ri on the road to Sunchon, and within the new IX Corps zone that Eighth Army had just established. When it arrived at the edge of Kunu-ri, the 38th Regiment had to fight to go into position. The Turkish Brigade was on its right (east) in a blocking position.

The 2nd and 3rd battalions of the 23rd Infantry stopped for the night about two miles north of Kunu-ri, on the left (west) of the 38th Infantry. Lieutenant Colonel Hutchins and his 1st Battalion stayed in a dug-in position a mile south of Won-ni for the rest of the night, 28–29 November. American stragglers came through its position all night and during the morning of the next day.[16]

On 28 November, war correspondent Homer Bigart filed a dispatch entitled "On Chongchon River Line" for the *New York Herald Tribune*. In it he charged that the "UN forces are now paying the initial price for the unsound decision to launch an offensive north of the peninsula's narrow neck. This move was unsound because it was undertaken with forces far too small to secure the long Korean frontier with China and Russia. Even without the open intervention of Red China, the UN Army was too weak to justify scattered garrisons along the Yalu River." Bigart wrote, "There are enough troops to hold the neck of Korea, provided the divisions now spread out on the northwest front can be brought back quickly. But the overall picture is grim." He saw the "United States faced with the ugly dilemma whether to accept a diplomatic defeat at the UN or launch a declared war and bomb Mukden."[17]

The British 27th Commonwealth Brigade

It is necessary to interrupt the story of the 2nd Infantry Division, which had now reached Kunu-ri, to describe how the British 27th Commonwealth Brigade was soon to find itself embroiled in the Kunu-ri battles. Eighth Army attached the British brigade to IX Corps at 3 P.M., 27 November. The 27th Brigade had ended very heavy fighting against the Chinese in the Pakchon-Kasan area in early November and were resting there in I Corps reserve when the Eighth Army attack to the border began on 24 November. They buried their dead (A Company of the Australian Battalion had 16 dead and 64 wounded) and also the numerous Chinese dead in their area. Then came their attachment to IX Corps and an order to move to Kunu-ri. The brigade at this time consisted of the Australian Battalion and the British Argyll and Middlesex battalions. Brig. Gen. Basil A. Coad commanded the brigade.

The British 27th Brigade began its movement to Kunu-ri on the afternoon of 27 November under a cloud-covered sky and a strong wind from the north. The Chongchon River was frozen over at their crossing point. The Australian Battalion closed into an assembly area south of Kunu-ri that evening, bivouacking in an extensive rice paddy. In the afternoon when a British correspondent with the battalion reached Kunu-ri, he learned that "something had happened." But no one seemed to know just what. He found much confusion in the IX Corps headquarters as to the situation.[18]

It chanced that, on this same day, the 3rd Battalion, 5th Cavalry, was relieved of responsibility for security of the Kunu-ri–Sunchon road.

When the Australian Battalion arrived at its assembly point south of Kunu-ri, it settled the question of how the men were to keep warm, by pulling down telegraph poles and digging out railroad ties from the nearby railbed. Smoke from innumerable fires blotted out the moon. American war correspondents at the IX Corps headquarters also found the situation at the CP confusing and unsatisfactory. Some of them charged there was indirect censorship, as IX Corps would not give information about what was happening at the front.

On the afternoon of the next day, 28 November, the 27th Brigade received orders to move south to Sunchon. The Argyll sergeant-major's verbal comments to the battalion were typical of the other battalion orders in the brigade. He said, "We are going to march south to Sunchon, where reports say the enemy has cut the road. You will carry full magazines for your rifles and Bren guns. If the road is clear you will march to Sunchon. If it is blocked you will fight your way to Sunchon. But you will go through to Sunchon."[19]

The Argylls led off to the skirl of the pipes. The Australian Battalion followed, and last came the Middlesex Battalion. The brigade marched single file in lines, one on each side of the road, leaving the middle for the passage of vehicles. Darkness had settled over the countryside before the last of the brigade got on the road. Before the column reached Sunchon, American trucks met them and carried them on into the town. The brigade arrived before dawn on 29 November. The 1st Cavalry Division had cleared the road ahead of them, and there was no trouble during their movement. The brigade, however, was moved quickly into outpost positions, as rumors were rife that thousands of Chinese troops were near and that an enemy attack was imminent.

On the twenth-ninth, the Argylls sent a patrol toward Pyongyang. At the same time, the Australians were hurriedly carried northeast to Yopa-ri on the Taedong River to keep open an escape route for the 7th US Cavalry Regiment, which was reported withdrawing in front of strong Chinese forces. Lieutenant Colonel Ferguson led the Australians to the river, where they dismounted and crossed the ice to a high mountain on the north side. A village at the river's edge burned from an American fighter-plane strike, and black smoke clouds rose against the background of white snow on the mountains. An Australian observer on the south side of the Taedong, watching the burning village, saw a number of Chinese mounted on Siberian horses ride around a house at a turn of the road. They halted and watched the Australians crossing for a few minutes, then wheeled their mounts and disappeared. The Australians stayed in their river position overnight. The next day, 30 November, word came that the 7th Cavalry Regiment had crossed the Taedong River farther downstream. The Australians then crossed back to the south side of the river.[20]

Meanwhile, the Middlesex Battalion was ordered north from Sunchon to the pass they had crossed the night before, which the 2nd Division also would have to cross in its planned retreat south from Kunu-ri. The battalion was to hold the pass open for them. As the Middlesex Battalion approached the south end of the pass (later known simply as the "Pass area"), it found that enemy held the high ground at the pass. In a firefight that developed, the Chinese drove back the battalion's advance troops. The battalion thereupon received orders to hold a defensive position eight miles south of the pass. The advanced company had hand-to-hand fighting with Chinese in making its withdrawal. The Middlesex Battalion now received reinforcements in the form of five American tanks, a platoon of C Company, 72nd Tank Battalion, and a battery of American 105-mm howitzers. The Middlesex Battalion made a second effort to reach the pass, and with the help of the American reinforcements, it arrived at a point three miles south of it. But it never controlled the pass or the high ground around it.[21]

Increasing Pressure from the CCF

Chinese columns of great size were in motion all day long on 29 November in the Eighth Army area. No longer did they hide by day and fight by night. They defied the UN air force to stop them. The Fifth Air Force put 148 close-support missions into the air on 29 November, 113 in the IX Corps sector, as against 25 in the adjacent I Corps sector. The Chinese realized by the end of 28 November that everywhere they had the Eighth Army in retreat. At many points they had large numbers of their troops behind the front lines of Eighth Army. This was particularly true on the American right (east) flank; and it was almost equally true in the army center. Most threatened was the US 2nd Infantry Division. It had a host of enemy troops bearing down on it day and night, from front, flank, and rear. The Chinese command must have felt that now they must not let up for a moment, even though their forces suffered heavily from daylight air attack.

Eighth Army took note of this feature. In its comments for 29 November, the army said in its war diary, "Unlike . . . N.K. units in early stages of the war, [instead] of losing contact for an extended period after withdrawals of Eighth Army units, the CCF Armies exerted almost continuous pressure in all sectors." It continued, "Bold daylight movements of regimental size units have been reported frequently in the past three days. These were partially shielded from air reconnaissance on the mountainous right flank by smoke caused by air strikes or fires set by the enemy." Eighth Army concluded on this day that the enemy was "capable of deep envelopment to strike at Pyongyang, or cut the roads to the city."[22]

On 29 November Eighth Army changed the boundaries of the IX and I corps to give the IX Corps full responsibility for the threatened area and the IX Corps main line of retreat from Kunu-ri south and southwest to Pyongyang. The IX Corps was responsible for the north-south road running from Kunu-ri through Sunchon to Pyongyang; I Corps was responsible for the area west of this road. Also, the army ordered Gen. John Coulter, IX Corps commander, to build a Class-50 floating bridge across the Taedong River without delay, east of the existing bridge, stipulating that the IX Corps and I Corps boundary should not coincide at that point.[23]

All during the night of 28–29 November and during the day of the twenty-ninth, the 2nd Division and attached troops moved south on vehicles on the Chongchon valley road through Won-ni toward Kunu-ri. The ROK 3rd Regiment marched in single file on either side of the road. While the 2nd Infantry Division was striving to reach the crossroads village of Kunu-ri, where it would turn south on the road to Sunchon, the Turkish Brigade on a road to the south of it was also converging on Kunu-ri from the east on the road from Tokchon. It was falling back in front of a Chinese force that was pressing it hard and had already inflicted heavy casualties. Kunu-ri was certain to become a bottleneck for all IX Corps troops seeking to escape from the encircling Chinese forces. Before the change in corps boundaries, most of the 25th Division had retreated to Kunu-ri, adding to the confusion there.

Meanwhile the IX Corps CP made ready to move south from Happacham (sometimes referred to as the Unhung-ni area), four miles west of Kunu-ri. The corps CP closed there at 1:30 P.M. on 29 November, and moved to Chasan, six miles south of Sunchon on the main north-south Kunu-ri–Sunchon–Pyongyang road. The CP was thus well south of the main battlefield of the next two days and in a position to move rapidly to Pyongyang in case of an emergency. About the same time, the 2nd Infantry Division CP moved from near Kunu-ri to a shallow, cove-like valley between hills in the Yonghyon area, six miles south of Kunu-ri, on the Sunchon road. The division chief of staff and his own staff arrived there at 8:30 A.M., 28 November. The rest of the division staff and Maj. Gen. Laurence Keiser arrived before dawn of 29 November.[24] The permanent defense force for the division headquarters included M16s (quad-50s) and M19s (dual-40s) from the 82nd AAA Battalion and three tanks from the 2nd Reconnaissance Company.

On 29 November, General Walker sent a message to all corps and division commanders indicating the course he had decided upon for the army in the immediate future. This order closed most of the Eighth Army installations at Pyongyang and relocated them farther south, most of them going all the way

Men of the 11th Engineer Battalion, I Corps, Eighth Army, construct an M4A2 floating treadway bridge over the Tong Dong River near Pyongyang, 2 December 1950. National Archives 111-SC 356051

to Seoul. These included the Medical Depot, the 34th Ordnance Depot Company, the 44th Ordnance Maintenance Company Depot, the 171st Evacuation Hospital, and the Prisoner of War Enclosure. Also closed were the Ammunition Supply Points (ASP) No. 17 at Sinanju and No. 21 at Kunu-ri. The Quartermaster Supply Points at Sukchon and Sunchon were closed. This order would indicate that, as early as 29 November, General Walker had decided not to defend Pyongyang but to pull the Eighth Army back to the vicinity of the Imjin River and Seoul.[25]

As explained in Chapter 3 above, Kunu-ri was a village on the northern edge of Kaechon, absorbed by the latter after 1950. In size, Kunu-ri was about one mile north-south and generally half a mile east-west. It lay at the southern edge of the Chongchon River floodplain, where hill country began, and was about three to four miles south of the Chongchon River itself, which swept past it in a north-bending arc. The Kaechon-gang and the Chotong-gang, both tributaries of the Chongtong River from the south, flowed northwest past the western side of Kunu-ri, the Kaechon-gang being the closer of the two to Kunu-ri.

The Chongchon valley road ran southwest from Won-ni (Pugwon) about five miles to the northern edge of Kunu-ri. Entering the town, it turned south for about a mile through the town and then turned west in the valley toward Anju and Sinanju. Near the point where the valley road turned west at the southern edge of Kunu-ri, another road ran south and then east toward Pongmyong-ni, Wawon, and Tokchon on the northeast side of the Kaechon River. This is the road used by the Turkish Brigade on its advance from, and then retreat to, Kunu-ri.

At Pongmyong-ni, a road turns south from the Tokchon road and winds generally almost due south to the Taedong River, where a ferry crossed at Samso-ri, and then continued on south to Sunchon. This was the best road in 1950 from Kunu-ri to Sunchon. But the Chinese cut the road at Samso-ri on 29 November and defeated efforts of the 5th Cavalry Regiment to drive them from the road. This made the road unusable to the 2nd Infantry Division in its withdrawal the next day.

The 2nd Division had to take another road south from Kunu-ri that branched off the valley road about a mile and a half west of the southern edge of the town and followed the valley of the Chotong-gang on a winding course southward through the hills toward the Taedong River and Sunchon. About eight air miles, and perhaps 15 road miles, south of Kunu-ri, the Chotong-gang has its source in the divide between the Chongchon and Taedong drainages. Here was the so-called Pass area that soon became so well known to all 2nd Division troops who traveled the road. There is little doubt that elements of the same Chinese formation that seized the main Sunchon road at Samso-ri on 29 November also established the first roadblocks on the alternate road from Kunu-ri only three miles west of Samso-ri.

A rail line ran south from the Chongchon valley at Kunu-ri, following generally the line of the Chotong-gang southward, but turning west to a better grade before reaching the Pass area. On the south side of the divide, the rail and road routes came together again and continued on, never far from each other, south to Sunchon.[26] In describing the situation around Kunu-ri, it is also to be noted that the three air miles of flat land between Kunu-ri and the Chongchon River was of a delta nature, bisected by numerous streams, large and small, with rice-paddy land in between. It had numerous trails crossing it, but no roads.

During the morning of 29 November dark, heavy clouds covered the sky, and there were snow showers until noon. Air support and aerial observation were largely missing for the continued withdrawal of the 2nd Infantry Division. At 6 A.M., the temperature stood at 21 degrees, but by midafternoon it had risen to above freezing–35 degrees. Everywhere on the 2nd Division front the Chinese closed up fast on the withdrawing troops.

The 3rd Battalion, 9th Infantry, with E and G companies of the 24th Infantry, 25th Division, accompanying it, withdrew under heavy enemy pressure south of Won-ni through the defensive position of the 1st Battalion, 23rd Infantry. It then started for Kunu-ri. On the west side of the Chongchon River below Won-ni, part of the 1st Battalion, 9th Infantry, held blocking positions to allow a part of the 24th Infantry of the 25th Division to withdraw to the south side of the river. These 9th Infantry troops then joined the 27th Regiment of the 25th Division in crossing the Chongchon. During the day, armor covering the 9th Infantry withdrawal lost six tanks to enemy action.[27] Colonel Sloane and his remnants of the 2nd and 3rd battalions, 9th Infantry, assembled near the 2nd Division CP six miles south of Kunu-ri.

At 11:15 A.M., aerial observers reported an estimated three enemy regiments —equivalent to a division of Chinese troops—crossing the Chongchon River to its south side below Won-ni. They moved in two formations. One entered Won-ni; the other, larger, body moved south along the valley a short distance and then climbed to the high ground southeast of the river to Hills 622 and 534, peaks in a large mountain mass four to five miles from the river. From there, only four air miles from Kunu-ri, they had it all downhill and could see in a broad arc to the west and southwest and to the road connecting Kunu-ri with Pongmyong-ni, where the Turkish Brigade was fighting a delaying battle. This new and very large enemy force was in a position during the day to threaten the entire 2nd Infantry Division, now in the Kunu-ri area, as well as the surviving elements of the Turkish Brigade. It could either move directly against them during the afternoon and night or head southwest into their rear.[28]

At 6 P.M. on 29 November, the Service Company and the 9th Regimental trains left Kunu-ri for Sunchon by way of the road west to Anju. News had come to the 2nd Division during the day that its MSR south to Sunchon had been cut by the enemy. An hour and a half later, at 8 P.M., Colonel Sloane received verbal orders from General Keiser that he was to attack the roadblock the next morning. For this task, Colonel Sloane organized the approximately 400 survivors of his 2nd and 3rd battalions fit for duty into a reinforced company.[29]

Meanwhile, the 38th Infantry, on the morning of the twenty-ninth, moved out to take its assigned defensive position, the hills northeast of Kunu-ri. Colonel Peploe still had the ROK 3rd Regiment on his left, facing north and adjacent to the 23rd Infantry, which was still north of Kunu-ri on the valley road hills. The Turkish Brigade was on his right facing north, in the vicinity of Pongmyong-ni and Sinnim-ni, about two miles farther east, on the Wawon-Tokchon road. It was all-important to the 38th Regiment that the Turks hold their defensive position as the regiment moved into its new assigned positions. Otherwise, that east flank of the regiment would be completely exposed and open to encirclement, and it could be cut off from the 2nd Division escape road leading south to Sunchon.

When the 2nd Battalion, 38th Infantry, reached its assigned position, it found Chinese there ahead of it. The Chinese fired on the battalion. Word came to the 38th Infantry at this time that the Turks farthest east, at Sinnim-ni, were surrounded, and they were to make a three-mile withdrawal. That would put all the Turks still combat effective on line in the vicinity of Pyongmyong-ni, near Kunu-ri. The Turkish CP was reported still to be in Pyongmyong-ni (Kaechon in the records), only five to six miles southeast of Kunu-ri.

In this situation, the 2nd and 3rd battalions of the 38th Infantry took up a defensive position during the morning of 29 November more than a mile farther back than those the 2nd Division had assigned them. At noon, Colonel Peploe received an order from the 2nd Division to send a rifle company to the division for use to help clear an enemy roadblock below it on the Sunchon road. Peploe sent C Company. Just before noon, a Chinese force drove the Turks out of Sinnim-ni. They began falling back on Pongmyong-ni and Kunu-ri in utter disorder.[30]

At 2 P.M., Chinese forces attacked the 3rd Battalion, 38th Infantry, from the north, east, and south. They overran the battalion right flank. The rest of the battalion held. At the same time, the Chinese struck the Turks at Pongmyong-ni and drove them back on Kunu-ri. Then the Chinese hit the 2nd Battalion, 38th Infantry, and drove hard against it. By now, with the rout of the Turks, the 38th Infantry's right flank (southeast) was completely uncovered. The 2nd and 3rd battalions were cut off from friendly forces. The Turks continued to fall back under a screen of smoke from burning buildings. Peploe's men could not distinguish friend from foe. Peploe ordered his 1st Battalion to reinforce his right flank. On its way to carry out this mission, the battalion encountered great numbers of Turkish soldiers and their vehicles on the road in complete rout. The 1st Battalion, caught up in this chaos, was unable to accomplish its purpose. It then received orders to take a position astride the Wawon road 2,000 yards east of Kunu-ri. The 2nd and 3rd battalions were ordered back to the regimental perimeter; they would have to fight their way out to get there.[31]

At 3:30 P.M., Peploe had radioed to the 2nd Division CP, asking if he could get through on the Sunchon road, as he had a lot of wounded. The division told him he could not, that he would have to evacuate wounded west through Anju. Accordingly, Peploe, now encircled and threatened with destruction southeast of Kunu-ri, that evening sent his wounded, Service Company, and trains west on the Anju road. When these vehicles arrived at Anju that evening, there were about 250 Turks on them. Just where and when they got on the trucks is a mystery.

According to a IX Corps G-2 report, there were some Turks still fighting in the area east of Kunu-ri on the right flank of the 38th Regiment as late as 5:15 P.M. About that time, or soon thereafter, these troops withdrew, leaving the 38th Infantry, the IX Corps, and the Eighth Army east flank open and exposed. At 6:10 P.M., a Turkish colonel and two Turkish soldiers arrived at Eighth Army headquarters in Pyongyang and reported that, at 9 A.M. that morning, an enemy division had surrounded the Turkish Brigade east of Kunu-ri but that from 500 to 1,000 Turks had broken through the enemy force and were at an unknown location. The Turkish colonel said he thought the Turkish commander, Brig. Gen. Yazici, was with them.

At 4:40 in the afternoon, Colonel Peploe reported to the division that his right flank battalion (the 3rd) was under enemy attack and that he could not get the Turks on its right to move into a supporting position. Col. Gerald G. Epley, the 2nd Division chief of staff, called Colonel Grunby, American advisor with the Turkish Brigade, asking him to get the Turks out of the village (apparently Pongmyong-ni, just east of Kunu-ri) and into the action. Colonel Grunby replied that he did not expect to succeed in the effort. He did not.[32]

At 4:30 P.M., General Keiser radioed to the IX Corps, telling General Coulter that the Chinese roadblock on the 2nd Division MSR south of the division CP was still holding. Keiser asked Coulter for urgent help from south of the roadblock, saying it was needed if the 2nd Division was to break it. Coulter responded by instructing the British 27th Brigade to send a relief force to help the 2nd Division. The brigade dispatched the Middlesex Battalion from Sunchon to move against the enemy roadblock below the 2nd Division. We have already noted that this battalion was repulsed by the Chinese as it approached the Pass from the south, and it gained only the low ground south of the Pass that evening.

General Keiser reported to General Coulter that night at 10:20 P.M. by voice radio on the situation at the 2nd Division. He told Coulter that his CP was then under enemy small-arms fire, that the remnants of the 9th Infantry (2nd and 3rd battalions) had reached his vicinity, that part of the 23rd Infantry Regiment was in the Kunu-ri area, that none of the 38th Infantry had reached his vicinity, and that Colonel Peploe had sent a radio message that two of his battalion headquarters had been destroyed.[33]

For General Keiser the most obscure situation that evening involved what was happening to the 38th Infantry. At 5 P.M., Peploe had a report that all roads into Kunu-ri were blocked, but he set about trying to save his regiment. Half an hour later, an ammunition truck, the lead vehicle in the 3rd Battalion's withdrawing column was disabled in a narrow pass on the road between Hills 182 and 107, about four miles southeast of Kunu-ri. It seemed impossible to move the vehicle. The 2nd and 3rd battalions formed a perimeter around the disabled vehicle and for several hours fought off Chinese attacks. The enemy onslaught began in earnest about 8 P.M. when an estimated two Chinese regiments attacked the right flank of the 38th Regiment through the vacated former Turk position. Smoke from burning buildings obscured the scene.

In this furious and chaotic battle, Capt. Nicholas Gombos, commander of F Company, who had been a conspicuous leader in previous days, was lost to the 2nd Battalion. Enemy machine-gun fire hit him in both legs. Some of his men put him in a jeep, but he was hit again in the area, where the disabled ammunition truck disrupted the withdrawal movement.[34]

While this critical fight was in progress, reconnaissance disclosed an alternate route of escape. The two battalions succeeded in getting some tanks and vehicles around the disabled truck. Colonel Peploe at his CP at this time had voice radio contact with the two battalion commanders, Lt. Cols. James H. Skeldon and Harold V. Maixner, who covered themselves with blankets so the Chinese could not hear them talking, so close were they. With tanks in the lead and the infantry on foot, part of the two battalions fought through to the 38th Regimental CP. But most of the infantry, guided by their officers, had to infiltrate through the enemy at different places to reach the 38th Infantry CP.[35]

West of the 2nd and 3rd battalions, the 1st Battalion, 38th Infantry, held Hills 133 and 110, about two miles southeast of Kunu-ri, blocking the road there into the town. The ROK 3rd Regiment survivors were on its left (west). When the 1st Battalion prepared to withdraw, Peploe informed the ROK colonel, through the 1st Battalion commander, that he could withdraw his men at the same time. The ROK 3rd Regimental commander replied, "No, my soldiers will remain on line until all American soldiers are out, and then I will come out." There was much praise from 38th Regimental officers and men for the ROK 3rd Regiment, which had fought with them from 26 to 30 November.[36]

An hour after midnight on the morning of 30 November, Kunu-ri was reported to be partly in Chinese possession. Still, the 2nd Division had a line holding on the northeast and south sides of the town, with the 23rd Infantry on the north and northeast and the 38th Infantry on the south.[37] By this time the 2nd Division G-3 had requested authority to move the division out on the road west to Anju. The IX Corps replied that it would have to clear the request with I Corps because this road was within I Corps's zone of responsibility.

During this furious fighting around the east and south sides of Kunu-ri, and in some cases within it, on the afternoon and night of 29 November, quad-50s and dual-40s of the Antiaircraft Artillery played important roles in helping the infantry units. They were special targets of Chinese attack. It would be impossible to say how many Chinese these lethal weapons killed or wounded in close-in fighting. But a few examples will indicate the nature of their effectiveness. One eyewitness told of finding one M16 (quad-50) with its entire crew dead beside it but about 500 enemy dead in heaps along the approaches to it (the number of enemy dead would appear to be an exaggerated estimate). In this case, the company clerk seems to have been the last man to fire the weapon after its crew had all been killed. In another instance, a Chinese soldier succeeded in carrying a bangalore torpedo to the platform of an M19 (dual-40) before he was killed. In this fight, Sergeant Denham directed the dual 40-mm guns on a nearby house and killed approximately 40 enemy who had been inside it. A few escaped. Later this gun battery's personnel went forward to pick up American wounded in the battle area. They found an American lieutenant alive but almost in shock behind a hump of earth near 40 dead Chinese.[38]

The 2nd Division had ordered the 38th Infantry in its withdrawal to clear the Kaechon River bridge southwest of Kunu-ri by 1 A.M. But the 38th Regimental Headquarters had to wait until 4 A.M. of 30 November for its 2nd and 3rd battalions to join it, the delay caused by the heavy night battles the two battalions had to fight in their withdrawal, before Peploe could move his regiment across the bridge to the south side of the Kaechon River and go into an assembly area. Peploe had some trouble reorganizing his regiment in the assembly area. The weather during the night had been biting cold, casualties in the 2nd and 3rd battalions had been heavy, units were mixed, and there were many stragglers.

In the withdrawal movement, which was to include the ROK 3rd Regiment, Peploe had ordered the latter, after it had crossed the bridge, to take a position southwest of the Kaechon River to tie in with the flank of the 23rd Infantry Regiment on its left and to extend from there eastward toward the river. This would put the ROK regiment north of the 38th Infantry assembly area, and provide protection for it and the nearby division artillery emplacements, as well as protect the right flank of the 23rd Infantry. For reasons unknown, the ROK commander, who had previously faithfully followed all instructions from the 38th Infantry to the best of his ability, failed to comply with this order. This failure left the 38th Regiment's assembly area uncovered and the right flank of the 23rd Infantry open to enemy infiltration. This situation was not discovered, however, until after daylight of 30 November. Peploe was preparing to send troops to close the gap for his and the division artillery's protection when he received division orders to withdraw to its CP two miles south. Peploe told the nearby artillery commander that his regiment was leaving and that there would be no protection for it from the north, after he left his position. The artillery commander said he would stay.[39]

The 23rd Infantry,
Rear Guard for the 2nd Infantry Division at Kunu-ri

During the morning of 29 November, the 1st Battalion, 23rd Infantry, stayed in its blocking position a mile south of Won-ni. All morning American stragglers passed through the battalion and were collected by it. There was no Chinese attack on the battalion in the morning. Although Chinese forces in great number were in the vicinity of Won-ni and on the hills to the east, they seemed intent on moving south and southeast around the 1st Battalion. At noon the 1st Battalion moved south, halting short of the regiment's 2nd and 3rd battalions. They were in blocking positions astride the road about two miles north of Kunu-ri on Hill 73, west of the road, and on a ridge of about the same height east of the road. At dark, the 1st Battalion moved through their blocking position, continued on to and through Kunu-ri, turned west at its southern edge, and at midnight crossed the bridge over the Kaechon River.

Lieutenant Colonel Hutchins put his 1st Battalion on two hills, one on either side of the road. This was the road that led west from Kunu-ri to Anju. At Hutchins's position, therefore, the road passed between these two hills in what might be called a saddle or a small pass. The 1st Battalion in its new position seemingly would control this road west of the Kaechon River and Kunu-ri. Hill 201, on the south side of the saddle, was the higher of the two hills.

Less than a mile west of the 1st Battalion's position at the saddle, the road coming north from Sunchon met the Kunu-ri–Anju road. This was a crucial road junction in the military situation that was developing. This road running south from the river road at that junction was the MSR for the 2nd Division in its projected withdrawal to Sunchon, and it was also the road on which the division CP and the division artillery emplacements were located. The 2nd Division CP was located four miles south of this road junction. The division artillery units were located in general about two miles north of the division CP and therefore that much closer to the road junction.

From midnight on, all kinds of American and UN troops passed Hutchins's 1st Battalion position, heading either west past the junction toward Anju and Sinanju or south from the junction toward Sunchon. There were men from the 25th Division, Turks, South Koreans, and the 2nd Infantry Division in this constant stream of units or stragglers seeking an escape route from the Chinese behind them. At one time during the night, a column of 24th Infantry, 25th Division, withdrawing from the northwest and another of the 23rd Infantry, from the northeast, met at an intersection in Kunu-ri. The commander of the 23rd Infantry unit argued with the military police at the intersection that he should let his unit through first. The MP stood his ground and ruled against the officer. Everyone was in a hurry that night to get through Kunu-ri.[40]

Meanwhile, the 2nd and 3rd battalions, 23rd Infantry, in their blocking positions two miles north of Kunu-ri on the valley road, did not have serious trouble until late in the afternoon. They had spent the day digging in on their position and keeping a close observation on all sides. By 5 P.M., the 2nd Battalion moved out under orders to follow the 1st Battalion to a position southwest of Kunu-ri. The 3rd Battalion remained in position as rear guard.

The 2nd Battalion had hardly disappeared southward on the road to Kunu-ri, with dusk at hand, when Chinese attacked the 3rd Battalion. A dogtrotting column of the enemy hit I Company. The company did not fire on the Chinese until they were within 15 yards. It was now dark. This point-blank fire killed or scattered these Chinese soldiers. At 10 P.M., the 3rd Battalion still held its position, but word had now come that the 38th Infantry on its right (south) had been forced to withdraw along the Wawon road west of Pongmyong-ni. Colonel Freeman now ordered the 3rd Battalion to begin its withdrawal to Kunu-ri. L Company and the 72nd Tank Battalion platoon remained behind as a roadblock to cover the withdrawal of the rest of the battalion and to protect the left flank of the 38th Regiment, which was in a desperate situation southeast of Kunu-ri. This blocking force was to remain in its position north of Kunu-ri until ordered to retire. Meanwhile, the 2nd Battalion of the 23rd Infantry passed through Kunu-ri, crossed the Kaechon River, and went into position on the right flank (south) of the 1st Battalion at its position astride the Anju road at Hill 201.

Colonel Freeman, commander of the 23rd Infantry, arrived at Colonel Peploe's 38th Infantry CP in Kunu-ri during the evening and there received orders from General Keiser to withdraw his regiment to the southwest of Kunu-ri but to cover the movement of the 38th Infantry across the bridge to high ground south of the town, where it would tie in with the 23rd Infantry. L Company carried out this mission in its rear-guard position two miles north of Kunu-ri. At midnight an estimated Chinese battalion made four strong attacks against L Company and its platoon of tanks but was repulsed. About 4 A.M. on 30 November, L Company received information that the 38th Infantry had completed its withdrawal and that it was returned to 3rd Battalion control and should join the battalion southwest of Kunu-ri. L Company and its tanks constituted the last American tactical unit through Kunu-ri. In moving through the town, it came under enemy small-arms fire but suffered no casualties. Chinese had begun to enter parts of Kunu-ri by midnight or soon thereafter. Lieutenant Colonel Maixner's 3rd Battalion, 23rd Infantry, closed in its position southwest of Kunu-ri, on the left flank of Lieutenant Colonel Hutchins's 1st Battalion. There the 3rd Battalion faced the rice-paddy land of the Chongchon valley to its northwest.

These movements during the night of 29–30 November placed the 23rd Regiment on line to protect both the Anju and the Sunchon junction roads from the north and northeast and replaced elements of the 25th Division on the Anju road. The 23rd Infantry line had its 3rd Battalion on the left, the 1st Battalion in the center, and the 2nd Battalion on the right. Because it commanded the Kunu-ri–Anju road and its junction with the Sunchon road, the 1st Battalion position was the most critical. It placed its B Company on the highest ground south of the road on Hill 201; its C Company was opposite it at the road pass or saddle and northwest of it. A Company was in reserve south of the road, behind B Company. The rest of the 2nd Infantry Division was by this time south or southeast of the 23rd Regiment. The left flank of the 38th Regiment was on the 23rd Infantry's right flank.

Thus, at dawn on 30 November two regiments held a defensive position in an arc west and south of Kunu-ri, covering the important roadnet that led west and south from it. The 2nd Division CP was about four miles south of them on the division's MSR to Sunchon.[41]

12. MacArthur Calls a Commanders' Conference

By the afternoon of 28 November, General MacArthur in Tokyo had decided that a crisis existed in Korea. Four days earlier he had confidently launched his attack to the border, which he had thought would result in the unification of all Korea. His Far East Command Headquarters, far from the Chongchon River battlefront, had been slow to realize that the Eighth Army there was being defeated in the series of battles that began on the night of 25 November in the center and eastern end of the army line.

A long message that General MacArthur sent to the Joint Chiefs of Staff in Washington on the afternoon of 28 November, and a communiqué he issued late that afternoon in Tokyo both indicated that he had reached a personal decision as to the critical nature of the crisis caused by the stunning success of the Chinese 2nd Phase Offensive against the Eighth Army in the west. Also, the Chinese IX Army Group in northeast Korea, in its surprise attack against the US X Corps on the night of 27 November (described in my *East of Chosin*) had achieved chilling successes at the very outset. Taken together, these events brought a sense of reality to General MacArthur.

The Chinese in their 2nd Phase Offensive had used no air power in their attacks. But the fear that it might suddenly descend on the UN troops, now not far from the border, had been growing in the minds of commanders. The Soviet MiG-15 fighter had first appeared near the Yalu River on 1 November, four weeks earlier, and rendered obsolete at once every US plane then in the Far East. The MiG easily outclassed the American Mustang and Corsair. It could fly at 660 miles an hour, 110 miles faster in level flight than the F-80C, and climb right away from the old Shooting Stars.

On 18 November, the US Navy's new F9F Pantherjets got into a dogfight with MiGs over Sinuiju on the Yalu. The MiGs were faster, they outclimbed and outdived the F9Fs, and they could turn inside the Panthers. But the Panthers shot down one MiG. The MiGs were based at Antung, on the north side of the Yalu, opposite Sinuiju. There, two gravel 6,000-foot runways had been converted to concrete, and taxiways were being hard-surfaced. Radar there gave them a 150-mile-radius early-warning system for spotting approaching American planes. The MiGs hugged the Yalu border and seldom made more than two passes before breaking off combat. The American planes were not permitted to follow them across the river. As a token of what might happen in the days ahead, on 28 November a light enemy liaison plane came over the Pyongyang airfield and dropped a fragmentation bomb, killing an American Air Force sergeant and damaging 11 Mustang fighters, three of them so badly they had to be junked.[1] These facts did not bolster American confidence at a time when their ground forces were everywhere in retreat.

On 29 November the *New York Times* printed a report from one of its war correspondents, datelined Washington, DC., 28 November, stating that there was surprise at the turn of military events. The account stated, however, that high-level defense officials had confidence that UN forces could hold a line against the Chinese. The article reported that some thought was being given to the possibility of a withdrawal from the present battlefront and that a defense line might be established at the narrow waist of Korea. It purported to reflect the feeling of responsible Defense Department officials on 28 November that events were taking an adverse turn at the Chongchon River front but that there was no real crisis.[2]

Unknown to the press at the time the above dispatch was printed, a long radio message arrived at the Pentagon from General MacArthur that was utterly pessimistic and jarred the Defense Department. MacArthur's message to the Joint Chiefs of Staff on 28 November was important because it showed a marked change in his view on the course of the war in Korea. It posed new problems for the Joint Chiefs and the president. Parts of MacArthur's message follow:

> The developments resulting from our assault movements have now assumed a clear definition. All hope of localization of the Korean conflict to enemy forces composed of NK troops with alien token elements can now be completely abandoned. The Chinese military forces are committed in NK in great and ever-increasing strength. No pretext of minor support under the guise of volunteerism or other subterfuge now has the slightest validity. We face an entirely new war. Interrogation of prisoners of war and other intelligence information establish the following enemy order of battle . . . comprising an aggregate strength approaching 200,000. The NK fragments, approximately 50,000 troops, are to be added to this strength. . . .
>
> It is quite evident that our present strength of force is not sufficient to meet this undeclared war by the Chinese with the inherent advantages which accrue thereby to them. The resulting situation presents an entirely new picture which broadens the potentialities to world embracing considerations beyond the sphere of decision by the theater commander. This command has done everything humanly possible within its capabilities but is now faced with conditions beyond its control and its strength.
>
> As directed by your JCS 92801, as amplified by your JCS 93709, my strategic plan for the immediate future is to pass from the offensive to the defensive with such local adjustments as may be required by a constantly fluid situation.[3]

General MacArthur's radio message, apparently sent about 3 P.M. on 28 November, Tokyo time (15 hours' difference between Tokyo and Washington time), was received at the Pentagon about 4 A.M. Washington time, 28 November. Col. John R. Beishline, on duty at the Pentagon, telephoned Lt. Gen. Matthew B. Ridgway, deputy chief of staff for operations, at his quarters at 4:15 A.M. to tell him he had just received a TS flash from the commander in chief, Far

East Command. General Ridgway asked that the message be brought to his quarters, and he read it there at 4:45 A.M. Ridgway immediately telephoned Gen. Joseph L. Collins, Army chief of staff and executive agent for the Joint Chiefs on Korean matters. He told him about the message and that Beishline was bringing it to him at once. An hour later, Ridgway telephoned Collins again and said he thought the Joint Chiefs would want President Truman to have the message soon after he had risen that morning. General Collins agreed and said he would telephone Gen. Omar N. Bradley, chairman of the Joint Chiefs of Staff.

Later in the morning, General Ridgway told Lt. Gen. Wade H. Haislip, Army vice-chief of staff, his immediate superior, that he thought it would be necessary to start planning for the possible evacuation of Korea at once but that such action should be confined to a small group. Ridgway suggested that Haislip discuss with General Collins the question of responsibility if disaster overtook Eighth Army and X Corps in Korea. Ridgway argued that the Joint Chiefs of Staff had a responsibility to the American people and to history in the matter and should issue instructions to General MacArthur.[4]

After sending his radio message to the Joint Chiefs of Staff, General MacArthur issued his Communiqué No. 14 at 5:25 P.M. in Tokyo. This communiqué was issued for worldwide consumption as his explanation of what was happening in Korea. Concerning enemy action of the past four days, it said that a major segment of the Chinese continental armed forces in army, corps, and division strength of more than 200,000 men were now committed against the United Nations in Korea. His communiqué continued in part:

> Consequently we face an entirely new war. This has shattered the high hope we entertained that the intervention of the Chinese was only of a token nature on a volunteer and individual basis as publicly announced. . . .
> It now appears to have been the enemy's intent in breaking off contact with our forces some two weeks ago, to secure the time necessary surreptitiously to build up for a later surprise assault upon our lines in overwhelming force, taking advantage of the freezing of all rivers and roadbeds which would have materially reduced the effectiveness of our air interdiction and permitted a greatly accelerated forward movement of enemy reinforcements and supplies. This plan has been disrupted by our own offensive action which forced upon the enemy a premature engagement.

An hour after the release of the communiqué, an additional paragraph was added to it.

> This situation, repugnant as it may be, poses issues beyond the authority of the United Nations military council—issues which must find their solution within the councils of the United Nations and chancelleries of the world.[5]

At the same time on the afternoon of 28 November, General MacArthur decided on a third step—to call Generals Walker and Almond, his field commanders in Korea, to Tokyo for a conference on the future course of the war. His summons to them went out that afternoon.

On the morning of 28 November, Maj. Gen. Edward M. Almond, X Corps commander in northeast Korea, flew from his Hamhung CP to Hagaru-ri, at the foot of the Chosin Reservoir, and went from there by jeep to the Advance

CP of the 1st Marine Division, where he conferred with Maj. Gen. Oliver P. Smith, the marine division commander. About noon he departed from that conference and flew by helicopter to the CP of the 1st Battalion, 32nd Infantry, on the east side of the reservoir. There he conferred with Col. Allan D. MacLean, 31st Infantry Regimental commander, and Lt. Col. Don C. Faith, Jr., the 1st Battalion commander. MacLean was then in the process of establishing his regimental Advance CP near the 1st Battalion, 32nd Infantry. Almond downplayed the seriousness of the heavy attacks of Chinese troops on the 1st Battalion the previous night.

General Almond returned to Hagaru-ri in the early afternoon. About midafternoon he flew from Hagaru-ri to his CP in Hamhung. Upon arriving there, he learned that a message had arrived from General MacArthur directing that he come at once to Tokyo for a conference.

General Almond had a hurried meeting with Maj. Gen. David G. Barr, commander of the 7th Infantry Division at 3:30, and then he spoke briefly with General Robertson, representative for British Commonwealth troops in Korea. At 5 P.M., he departed Yongpo airfield in Korea for Tokyo. Accompanying Almond were Lt. Col. William J. McCaffrey, X Corps deputy chief of staff; Lieutenant Colonel Glass, X Corps staff; Major Ladd, his senior aide; and one or two others. When Almond's plane arrived at Haneda airport, Tokyo, about 9 P.M., Colonel Clarke from General Headquarters, Far East Command, was waiting for the party. He said that General MacArthur was waiting with General Walker and desired him to proceed at once to the American Embassy, General MacArthur's residence.[6]

There is no comparable source detailing Lt. Gen. Walton H. Walker's movements as Eighth Army commander in Korea. In fact, the records of Eighth Army in the National Archives are so devoid of mention of General Walker that one has difficulty in knowing where the general was and what he was doing most of the time. One may presume that Walker received his summons from General MacArthur at a small advance CP he had established adjacent to the 24th Division CP at Anju in North Korea about the same time X Corps received its message for General Almond. In any event, we know that General Walker arrived in Tokyo ahead of General Almond and was waiting with General MacArthur and others when Almond arrived. From his radio message to the Joint Chiefs of Staff and his Communiqué No. 14, it is evident that General MacArthur had already made his decision to put his forces in Korea on the defense and abandon his offensive to the border, before the commanders' conference began.

The conference got under way about 9:30 P.M. It lasted until 1:30 A.M. the next morning, 29 November. In addition to the Far East commander and his two field commanders from Korea, only a few key members of MacArthur's staff and the top commanders of the Army, Navy, and Air Force were present. Except for a few staff officers, no one knew about Walker's and Almond's flights to Tokyo. Those present at the conference were the following:

Gen. Douglas MacArthur
Lt. Gen. Walton H. Walker, commander, Eighth Army in Korea
Maj. Gen. Edward M. Almond, commander, X Corps in Korea

Vice Adm. Charles Turner Joy, commander, Naval Forces Far East
Lt. Gen. George E. Stratemeyer, commander, Far East Air Force
Maj. Gen. Doyle O. Hickey, Far East Command chief of staff
Maj. Gen. Charles A. Willoughby, Far East Command G-2
Maj. Gen. Courtney Whitney, advisor on MacArthur's staff
Brig. Gen. Edwin K. Wright, Far East Command G-3[7]

General MacArthur and the eight other officers in the conference talked for nearly four hours, covering the situation in Korea as each understood it. General MacArthur asked many questions, most of them directed to Generals Walker and Almond. Occasionally, someone else would offer a remark or a suggestion or ask a question. Brigadier General Wright seems to have been the most active participant in the conference other than Generals MacArthur, Walker, and Almond. Apparently no official memorandum for record of this conference was made, and details of the discussions are not known. The principal points of view presented by the main participants are known, however, from statements made later by Major General Whitney, some radio messages from the Far East Command to General Almond at X Corps in Korea, and from interviews and conversations with General Almond.

The most surprising thing about the conference was the optimism of both Generals Walker and Almond about their military situations in Korea. Keeping in mind the worsening situation on the Eighth Army front in the west, where heavy fighting had been in progress for a period of three days and nights, it was to be expected that discussion centered on Walker's Eighth Army. When General MacArthur asked General Walker what he thought of the situation on his front and where the Eighth Army could make a successful stand, Walker replied that he expected to hold Pyongyang and to establish a defense line north and east of the city. When General MacArthur asked General Almond a similar question relating to X Corps, Almond euphorically answered that he expected the 1st Marine Division and his 7th Infantry Division to continue their attack west and northwest from the Chosin Reservoir and cut the enemy's line of communications in their rear, below Kanggye and the Yalu River.[8] That had been the X Corps's main mission in the attack to the border that began on its front on 27 November, the day before the conference was called.

General Walker's optimism is not surprising, given his stubborn and aggressive nature and the fact that not all was disaster when he left the Chongchon River front on the afternoon of 28 November. But it was not a cautious evaluation of the situation on his front, given the course of events and the amount of enemy combat intelligence that had been accumulated from Chinese prisoner-of-war interrogations that was in his possession at the time. In any event, five days later, on 3 December, his view had drastically changed, and he then informed General MacArthur that he could not hold Pyongyang and would have to withdraw, probably to the Inchon and Seoul river defense line far to the south.

General Almond's unrealistic view that he could continue his attack and reach the Mupyong-ni area is hard to explain. Just the day before, he had visited the 1st Marine Division front at Yudam-ni, and just that afternoon he had visited the 7th Infantry Division forward battalion position on the east side of the Chosin Reservoir, where he had talked with Colonel MacLean, the commander of the 31st RCT, and with Lt. Col. Don C. Faith, Jr., commander of the 1st Battalion, 32nd Infantry. At neither place was there any reason for optimism. Almond had badly misjudged the situation.

General MacArthur seems to have hoped that Walker could hold Pyongyang. But he apparently did not agree with Almond's view that he could continue his attack successfully to Mupyong-ni, although there is no evidence that he said so during the conference. His view was stated in his orders to Almond the next morning, and it also was in his radio message of the preceding afternoon to the Joint Chiefs of Staff.

During the conference, there was emphasis on what could be done that would most help Eighth Army. General Walker admitted he needed reinforcements desperately. In Korea, they could come only from the X Corps on the other side of the peninsula. But General Walker said he did not want the X Corps to give up its attack against the Chinese on his distant right flank and on the enemy's rear communications. General Wright suggested that General Almond might use Maj. Gen. Robert H. Soule's 3rd Infantry Division, then in the Wonsan area, to cross the Taebaek Range on a lateral, cross-peninsula road to Pyongyang and attack the Chinese XIII Army forces that were threatening to envelope Eighth Army's right flank.

General Almond strongly objected to this proposal, saying that the road to be used was on the map but did not in fact exist. This was a bit of an exaggeration – the road did exist, but it was a poor mountainous one, in places hardly better than a trail, and would be difficult for winter use by an American infantry division with its equipment and transport. Almond also stressed that there might be strong enemy guerrilla forces along this route and an attempt to move a division across it would be a hazard in which the 3rd Infantry Division might be lost. But he dropped opposition to the idea if the Eighth Army would assume responsibility for supplying the division once it had crossed to the west side of the Taebaek Range. General Walker did not promise he would do this. General MacArthur made no decision in the conference on this proposal. Later, on 30 November he ordered the 3rd Infantry Division or a task force from it to make the effort to join Eighth Army but canceled it before the venture could be started.[9] One may infer that only General Wright, the Far East Command operations officer, had any enthusiasm for the idea.

General MacArthur made no decisions and issued no orders to Generals Walker or Almond during or at the end of the conference. Before the two commanders left from Tokyo that day, however, to return to their commands in Korea, MacArthur did give them his instructions. He asked General Walker to hold the Pyongyang area if he could but to withdraw as needed to prevent the Chinese forces from getting around his right flank and into his rear. He ordered General Almond to end his offensive action and to withdraw and concentrate the X Corps in the Hamhung-Hungnam area on the coast. This order, no doubt, reflected his intention to evacuate X Corps from northeast Korea and to move it by sea to join Eighth Army in South Korea, or as far north as Eighth Army might be in Korea at the time. But he did not include that in his instructions to Almond on 29 November.

General Almond left Tokyo at noon on the twenty-ninth. Lieutenant Colonels McCaffrey and Glass and Major Ladd of his staff were on the plane with him. During the trip from Haneda to Yonpo airfield in Korea, the group discussed the situation. General Almond, acting on General MacArthur's directive to him, told McCaffrey and Glass to start preparing a draft of a X Corps order to concentrate the corps's forces at Hamhung, "and action against enemy wherever possible within good judgment."

Almond's plane arrived at Yonpo airfield at 5:10 in the afternoon. Almond, accompanied by Lieutenant Colonel McCaffrey, immediately flew to the X Corps CP. An hour later he began a conference there with his chief of staff, Maj. Gen. Clark L. Ruffner; his deputy chiefs of staff; and his general staff officers. An hour and a half later, at 9 P.M., the X Corps section chiefs presented a plan for Operation Order No. 8. The order, when issued, called for a discontinuance of the X Corps attack to the northwest and initiation of a withdrawal of X Corps forces. This order carried out General MacArthur's instructions to General Almond.[10]

Detailed information about Lieutenant General Walker's return to Korea and his actions is not recorded in the official Eighth Army War Diary for the day. But it may be assumed that he left Tokyo for Korea about the same time as did General Almond. Maj. Gen. Leven C. Allen, Eighth Army chief of staff in Korea, reported that General Walker, after returning to his CP at 5 P.M. on 29 November, ordered his forces to begin a withdrawal from the Chongchon River front.[11] In a sense, the order was redundant because the Chinese were already mandating it themselves.

Among the orders General Walker issued after his return to Korea was one instructing the 187th Airborne RCT to guard all bridges over the Taedong River. This protection was essential to ensure the ready crossing of the river when the withdrawing troops reached it. To the commanding general of the 187th RCT, Brig. Gen. Frank S. Bowen, Jr., General Walker said that it was "imperative to prevent movement of refugees over bridges Taedong River YD39122, YD405253, YD440320, and insure uninterrupted movement of military traffic through Pyongyang and across bridges. Responsibility yours until combat units I and IX Corps arrive bridge sites. . . . CG I and IX Corps assume responsibility to relieve 187th Abn. when arrive at bridges."[12] This order might indicate that General Walker was not planning on 29 November to have the entire army halt north of Pyongyang if the Chinese offensive continued.

It should be noted here that the Joint Chiefs of Staff on 29 November approved General MacArthur's plan to pass from the offensive to the defensive in Korea as stated in his radio message on 28 November. Their approval said that "strategic and tactical considerations are now paramount." But they also asked, "What are your plans re the coordination of operations of the 8th Army and X Corps and the positioning of X Corps, the units of which appear to us to be exposed?"[13]

In another development on 29 November, General MacArthur revived the proposal to use Nationalist Chinese troops in Korea against the Chinese Communists. General MacArthur's radio message to the Joint Chiefs proposed:

> The Chinese armies on Formosa represent the only source of potential trained reinforcements available for early commitment. Troops drawn from this source could be landed in Korea in approximately 14 days and a much larger force

than that originally offered would undoubtedly be made available if desired.

I strongly recommend accordingly that the theater commander be authorized to negotiate direct with the Chinese Government authorities on Formosa for the movement north and incorporation in the UNC of such Chinese units as may be available and desirable for reinforcing our position in Korea.[14]

That same day, the Joint Chiefs of Staff replied to General MacArthur, denying his request. Their radio said:

> Your proposal (C 50021) is being considered. It involves world-wide consequences. We shall have to consider the possibility that it would disrupt the united position of the nations associated with us in the UN and leave us isolated. It may be wholly unacceptable to the commonwealth countries to have their forces employed with Nationalist Chinese. It might extend hostilities to Formosa and other areas. Incidentally, our position of leadership in the Far East is being most seriously compromised in the UN. The utmost care will be necessary to avoid the disruption of the essential Allied line-up in that organization.[15]

Late on the night of 29 November, General Walker issued a memorandum for the press, stating that his attack to the border, which began on 24 November, had revealed the Chinese troop situation and had saved his army by discovering their deployment and intent in time. A British war correspondent then at the front wrote, "At first no one would believe that this was not a hoax, but when they knew it was meant to be serious, it spread consternation, anger and dismay among all ranks with whom I came into contact in the next few days."[16]

The *New York Herald Tribune* on 30 November printed an AP dispatch, datelined US Eighth Army Headquarters, 29 November 1950, which quoted General Walker. The statement apparently was intended to be a public-relations document to explain the Eighth Army action of the past week and to justify it, even though the army was in the midst of defeat and retreat at the time. It also buttressed General MacArthur's radio dispatches and communiqués he issued at Tokyo the day before. Because of the furor at the time and the continuing controversy it caused, Walker's press release is given in full:

> The assault launched by the 8th Army five days ago probably saved our forces from a trap which might well have destroyed them. Had we waited passively in place, the 200,000 Chinese troops thrown against my lines would have increased within a short time to double that strength. From beyond the Yalu they undoubtedly would have brought the 200,000 additional Chinese troops known to be assembled there. We naturally had hoped to find at least some semblance of truth in the public assurance of the Chinese Communist authorities that no formal military intervention had been perpetrated. However, only by assault tactics could the actualities have been fully developed. In my opinion this saved the army from possible destruction. The timing of our attack to develop the situation was, indeed, most fortunate.[17]

Thus began the frequently discussed theory that General MacArthur's brilliance in ordering the 24 November attack saved Eighth Army from destruction at a later date. This line of public-relations propaganda and excuse conveniently overlooked the fact that, at the time General MacArthur ordered the attack, he stated that it was to go to the Korean border, end the war, and unify Korea.

13. Withdrawal of Eighth Army South of the Chongchon River

By daylight of 30 November all major units of Eighth Army had received orders to withdraw south of the Chongchon River. By nightfall most of them had crossed and were headed in the direction of Pyongyang. A few units of the ROK 1st Division and of the 25th Infantry Division were still north of the river but rapidly approaching it. They would cross within an hour or two. The 5th RCT of the US 24th Division held the planned major crossing site east of Anju. The rest of the 24th Division had already crossed the river at Sinanju. The I Corps of the army, on the westernmost part of the line, was almost entirely south of the river before dark on 30 November. The last units of IX Corps to cross, the 3rd Battalion, 24th Infantry, of the 25th Division, escaped in fragments to the south side of the river just before dark, near Kunu-ri, with the help of strong, close air support and the tank and artillery fire of the 23rd Infantry Regiment, which still held its rear-guard defensive position southwest of Kunu-ri.

At this time, on the army's east flank, large formations of Chinese troops were executing flanking and encircling movements through the rear areas of the ROK II Corps and attempting to entrap the US 2nd Infantry Division before it could escape southward. Eighth Army had thrown in its reserve, principally the US 1st Cavalry Division and the British 27th Brigade, to check the enemy on the east in its enveloping move. Of all major units of the army, the 2nd Infantry Division was in the most danger on 30 November. It had in a real sense acted as the army's rear guard. Now it faced the continuing main frontal push of the Chinese XIII Army Group, while at the same time it was being encircled on its right flank and from the rear.

The US 24th Infantry Division, on the army's left (west) flank, was the first division to withdraw all its units south of the Chongchon River. Eighth Army had ordered the division, after it had crossed, to assemble its forces about 18 miles east of Pyongyang in the vicinity of Kang-dong. At the time of this order, the 21st Regiment was already assembled in the vicinity of Sunchon. Kang-dong was 20 air miles southeast of Sunchon and astride the important lateral road across the waist of Korea, which ran from Wonsan, on the east coast, to Pyongyang, the North Korean capital. At Kang-dong, the 24th Division was expected to protect Pyongyang from encircling Chinese forces, which were driving southwest around Sunchon, and it was also calculated to hold open the roadnet from the north by which Eighth Army would retreat south from the

Withdrawal South of the Chongchon River

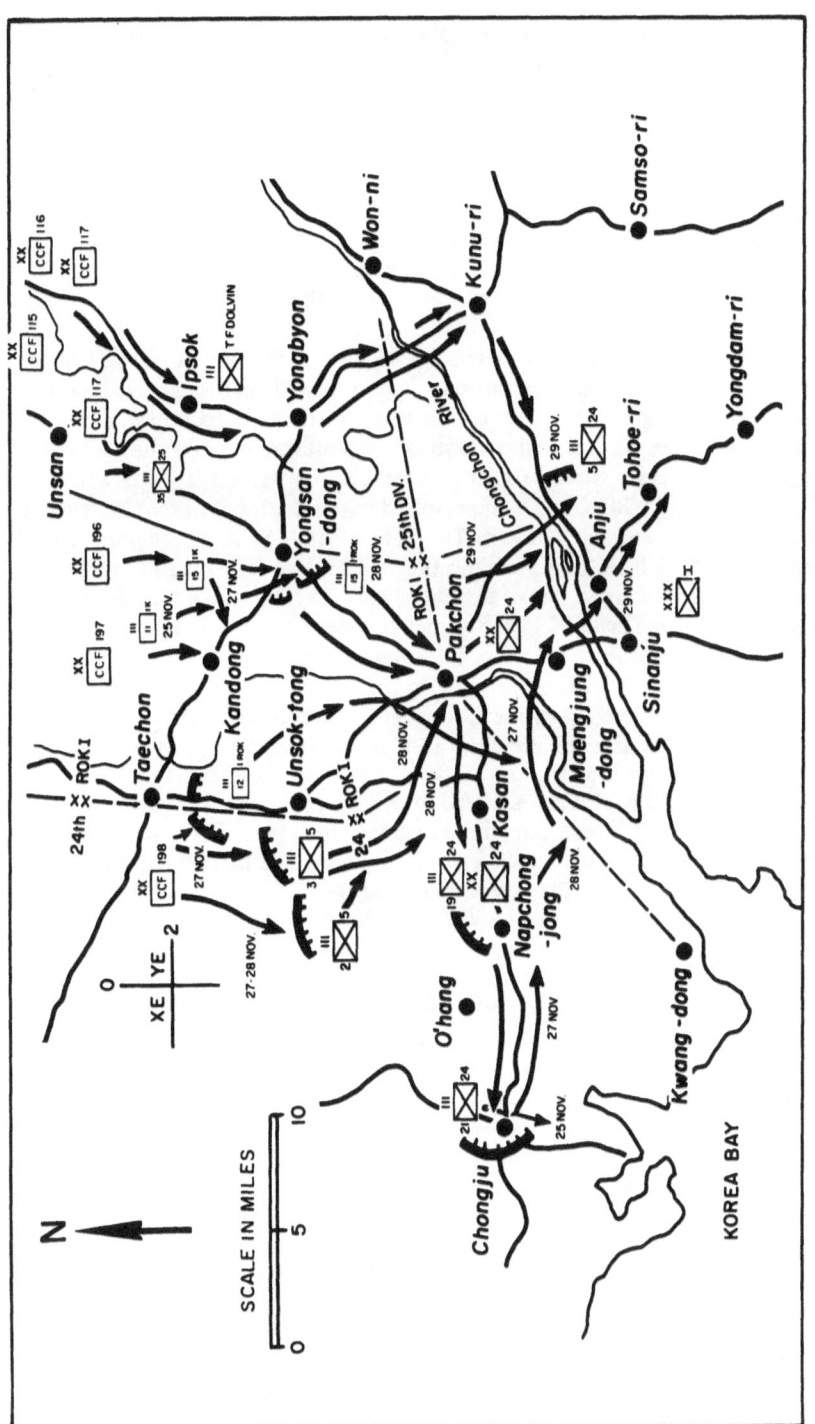

Map 10. The withdrawal of US I Corps, 25–29 November 1950.

Chongchon River front. Upon arrival at Kang-dong, the 24th Infantry Division reverted to Eighth Army control. In its movement to Kang-dong, Eighth Army ordered the division to destroy all supplies and equipment it could not evacuate and to carry out demolition that would slow down or obstruct enemy advance.[1]

I Corps closed its CP at Sinanju and moved south on the coastal road, opening its new CP at Yongju, at 8:20 P.M. on 30 November. Yongju was about midway between Sinanju and Pyongyang. At 2:15 P.M., I Corps had reported all its troops south of the river. That part of the 5th RCT still on the north side of the river at the bridge sites withdrew to the south side. At 4:15 P.M., the 5th RCT, on I Corps orders, destroyed the east bridge across the Chongchon, and one and a half hours later, at 5:45 P.M., it destroyed the west bridge. The next chapter will tell the story of why it waited that long–to allow the 23rd Infantry Regiment to escape westward on the Anju road from Kunu-ri. The 5th RCT, its mission well performed, then moved out west through Anju to Sinanju, where it turned south to assemble at Yongju in I Corps reserve.[2]

Meanwhile, the ROK 1st Division crossed to the south side of the Chongchon at Anju, or just east of the town. The 555th Field Artillery Battalion, which supported the 5th RCT in guarding the two bridges at Anju and in holding a block on the river road east of the town, gave covering fires for the ROK division as it crossed. The ROK 15th Regiment crossed first after daylight. The ROK 11th and 12th regiments followed, beginning their crossings about 10:30 A.M.

All had not gone well, however, with the supporting units of the ROK 1st Division in their crossing of the Chongchon. Some hours before daylight on 30 November, the last artillery unit of I Corps met enemy opposition as it approached the Anju bridges. Capt. Darrell Putnam, commanding a battery of 90-mm guns of the 68th AAA Battalion, which had been supporting the ROK 1st Division, said his men came under enemy small-arms fire at 4 A.M., when they were still more than a mile from the bridges. The battery had to destroy and abandon two guns they were unable to move.[3]

Lt. Col. Clarence E. Stuart's 555th Field Artillery Battalion covered all these crossings at the Anju bridges by delivering interdicting fire on enemy forces following the UN units to the bridges. His battalion remained in its emplacements covering the bridges and river roadblock until dark on 30 November, until after the 23rd Infantry Regiment from Kunu-ri had safely passed on the Anju road about dark. Stuart's battalion then withdrew down the Anju road without the loss of a vehicle or of a gun. But he barely got away unscathed. As he was leaving, he saw Chinese vehicles drive down to the river's edge opposite him on the north side with their lights on.[4]

The 25th Infantry Division had been the left-hand component of IX Corps during the heavy Chinese attacks and was on the right of the ROK 1st Division. It, too, had now escaped south of the Chongchon. Its F Company of the 27th Regiment was the last tactical unit of the division (except the lost fragments of the 3rd Battalion, 24th Infantry) to cross to the south side of the river during the night of 29–30 November. There it received orders to join the 89th Tank Battalion and the 25th Reconnaissance Company as a special task force to cover the Anju road west of Kunu-ri. F Company joined this force before dawn of 30 November. When the 23rd Regiment of the 2nd Division withdrew to its covering position southwest of Kunu-ri that night, it relieved the 25th Division of blocking on the Anju road just west of Kunu-ri. F Company then joined its battalion, and the 2nd Battalion followed the 1st Battalion through Anju. At Anju the regiment obtained much-needed food, and at 4:15 in the afternoon it resumed its march south. Trucks later met most of the 27th Infantry's troops and carried them to assembly areas. F Company and its 2nd Battalion rode the last 20 miles to their assembly area at Wolbong-ni, on the lateral road between Sukchon and Sunchon, arriving there at midnight. The 35th Regiment had closed at dusk that afternoon at Sunchon, the 25th Division's new area of responsibility.[5]

The last elements of the 25th Division to cross to the south side of the Chongchon were remnants of the 3rd Battalion, 24th Regiment. They escaped by the skin of their teeth. They reached the Chongchon about midafternoon of 30 November at a point opposite Kunu-ri, hotly pursued by Chinese. It chanced that the 23rd Infantry of the 2nd Division still held its defense arc northwest of Kunu-ri on the south side of the river when the 3rd Battalion remnants appeared on the north side opposite them. The 23rd Infantry thus could give vital fire support to the exhausted men of the 3rd Battalion and save some of them. Only an hour or two later the 23rd Infantry hurriedly left its positions and escaped west on the Anju road. Had it not been for the presence of the 23rd Infantry when the shattered 3rd Battalion, 24th Infantry, reached the Chongchon, it almost certainly would have been destroyed or captured by the Chinese that afternoon.

The story of the 3rd Battalion, 24th Infantry, 25th Division, is one of considerable confusion throughout the last days of November. More often than not, the regimental commander, Col. John T. Corley, had no communication with its commander, Lt. Col. Melvin R. Blair. It has already been told how Lieutenant Colonel Blair, with his headquarters, arrived at Kunu-ri on the night of 29 November, but he had no idea where his companies were. Blair himself seemed to be a case of battle fatigue. Colonel Corley finally located the troops north of Won-ni. At this point, however, there was no way to send a rescue party to meet them. Thus I, K, and L companies of the 3rd Battalion were largely on their own to fight their way through to Kunu-ri.

Even while Colonel Corley and Lieutenant Colonel Blair during the night of 29–30 November were holding a radio conversation, with Blair in his CP in Kunu-ri, Chinese attacked the CP. In this attack, the battalion sergeant major was killed, and the battalion executive officer, the battalion surgeon, and the artillery liaison officer were wounded, but they escaped. Lieutenant Colonel Blair also escaped. Most of the battalion command group infiltrated individually and in small groups out of Kunu-ri, and eventually, about 4:45 A.M. of 30 November they were able to join Corley's tactical CP southwest of Kunu-ri. This group stayed with Corley until about 7 A.M., when he sent them west on the Anju road.[6] All this left the infantry companies of the 3rd Battalion in limbo, their fate unknown.

Shortly after noon of 30 November word reached the 23rd Infantry Regiment in its rear-guard blocking position southwest of Kunu-ri that the missing 24th Infantry rifle companies were on the north bank of the Chongchon, trying to cross but hard pressed by pursuing Chinese. Colonel Freeman notified

Colonel Corley of this information after a captain and three enlisted men from the 3rd Battalion had crossed the Chongchon and reached his lines. The 3rd Battalion rifle companies were on foot, pursued by about two battalions of Chinese. Freeman moved two platoons of tanks to his left, in front of the 3rd Battalion soldiers trying to escape. The heavy fire of these tanks on the Chinese, together with massive air strikes by 20 fighter planes and three bombers on the pursuing Chinese, now in the open of the Chongchon valley rice paddies near the river, enabled most of I, K, and L companies, 24th Infantry, to reach the south side of the river and then to make their way across the two to three miles of flat delta land of the Chongchon valley at this point. Members of the 23rd Infantry saw several Chinese soldiers run up behind fleeing 3rd Battalion soldiers and capture them. This dramatic scene unfolded about 2 P.M. on 30 November.

In directing air strikes and artillery fire on the Chinese, an American Mosquito plane crashed three miles west of the Anju–Kunu-ri–Sunchon road junction. A tank went out into the no-man's-land and rescued the pilot and observer.

Meanwhile, the members of the 3rd Battalion who had escaped to the south side of the river and across the flat marshland there assembled on the Anju road within the 23rd Infantry lines. About 4 P.M. they loaded on 15th Field Artillery trucks and rode out to Anju. By 6 P.M., the last of them had cleared the initial point of traffic control in Anju, where Brig. Gen. Vennard Wilson, assistant division commander of the 25th Division, acted as traffic controller.[7] There were more Korean refugees fleeing south on the coastal roads, the 25th Division reported, than at any time since it had crossed the 38th Parallel.

At 2 P.M. on 30 November, the IX Corps closed its CP at Chasan, six miles south of Sunchon, and opened its new CP at Pyongyang at the same time. It is not known just when General Coulter arrived at the new CP in Pyongyang. It is known, however, that General Walker conferred with General Coulter, the IX Corps commander, and with General Church, commander of the 24th Division, at 4:40 P.M. at the IX Corps headquarters. We do not know the subject of that conference, but one might assume that it included the situation in the 2nd Infantry Division below Kunu-ri and the continuing Chinese envelopment of the army and the IX Corps right flank (or of the left flank, if one thinks of the army now being headed south).[8]

On that day, 30 November, the Eighth Army G-2 Section began moving from Pyongyang to Seoul. Some personnel files that day were taken in convoy to the South Korean capital. The Eighth Army G-2 staff report for the day said the evacuation of Pyongyang was a probability.[9]

Early that morning, at 2:05, Eighth Army sent an order to I Corps to destroy all supplies and equipment that could not be evacuated and to set demolitions and obstructions that would impede enemy advance. This was in fact the general policy pursued by all withdrawing units. As an example of what was done under this army policy in the withdrawal, the 24th Division destroyed by an air strike 62 vehicles at Anju, including 31 2¼-ton trucks that could not be repaired or towed. I Corps destroyed approximately 1,600 tons of ammunition on the ground.

The hasty abandonment or destruction of supplies had started the day before.

The IX Corps transportation officer on 29 November had left 2,000 tons of ammunition at the Kunu-ri ASP when the corps headquarters moved from near Kunu-ri to Chasan. In this case, however, Major Cleveland of I Corps, on learning of the incident, took a train to Kunu-ri and pulled out 1,500 tons of the ammunition and issued the remainder to troops in the Kunu-ri area. I Corps headquarters was still at Sinanju at the time.[10]

There can be no doubt that large quantities of military supplies of many kinds were left behind or destroyed as all Eighth Army and corps headquarters in the Chongchon valley hurriedly closed down their CPs there and hurriedly started south. The Ordnance Collecting Point at Sinanju in I Corps destroyed two M-46 tanks, three 90-mm guns, four M4 trailers, and 1,600 tons of ammunition because the vehicles could not move on their own power and there were no railcars available to move the ammunition. At Kunu-ri 500 tons of ammunition remained at the ASP there when enemy troops entered the town. At 4 A.M. on 30 November, the I Corps ordnance officer called for a napalm air strike at daylight to destroy this ammunition. When the strike planes arrived, they found Kunu-ri already in flames. At Sunchon, the 702nd Ordnance Company, and part of the 2nd Quartermaster Company that had arrived there ahead of the roadblock on the 2nd Division withdrawal route, left behind 39 vehicles "due to the emergency" when they continued on to Pyongyang.

At the same time, the rail transportation officer asked Eighth Army to order a temporary embargo on all rail movement of supplies north of Seoul. The rail station on the south side of the Han River opposite Seoul was full, and it looked as if anything moved north would be unneeded and possibly lost, since all movement was now south instead of north. This request was approved. But medical supplies and blankets to keep wounded warm until they could be evacuated continued to move north toward the battle front by airlift. On 30 November an emergency airlift delivered 2,000 blankets to K-23 airfield at Pyongyang.[11]

During all the hectic activity on 30 November with Eighth Army troops in movement everywhere headed south, it was mandatory that the Air Force extend its attacks on enemy formations to the maximum. The day dawned with broken clouds and an overcast—not the best harbinger for American air support during the day. But during the day 115 air sorties were flown, and aerial reports claimed heavy enemy casualties. In the vicinity of Tokchon and south of there, Air Force claimed it had destroyed 13 vehicles, 235 horses, an ammunition dump, a supply dump, 4 villages, a bridge, and 690 enemy soldiers and had strafed numerous troop concentrations, for which it gave no estimate of casualties inflicted. Aerial observers reported hundreds of enemy troops moving west in the hills. They also reported Chinese in possession of Kunu-ri at 9 P.M. About 8 P.M., an aerial observer reported there was a 20-mile long convoy of enemy vehicles moving south of the Yalu River between Sinuiju and Sonchon. Aerial strikes strafed and bombed this convoy. Since it was dark, no estimate was made of damage inflicted. There were other air reports of still more damage in the Tokchon area, including the destruction of more than 1,000 enemy troops. Another air report made the claim that air cover over the Kunu-ri area all day long had destroyed 2,500 enemy troops. There can be little doubt that aerial close support and deep interdiction in support of Eighth Army did result in the killing and wounding of an unknown, but very large, number of Chinese troops on 30 November.[12]

In another, far different aspect of aerial activity on 30 November, 740 army patients were flown out of Pyongyang, but 300 more were still there waiting to be removed to rear areas and to hospitals in Japan. There were also 130 more at the 8063rd Mobile Army Surgical Hospital and 300 at the 25th Medical Clearing Company for evacuation.[13]

On 30 November the one major unit that still was in contact with the Chinese in the Chongchon valley area, and indeed cut off on its assigned withdrawal route, was the 2nd Infantry Division. Its plan for 30 November was to break contact with the enemy and withdraw south. Gen. Laurence Keiser and his division staff had spent much of the night of 29–30 November preparing plans for the division's withdrawal from the vicinity of Kunu-ri to Sunchon, about 20 air miles due south. If it succeeded, then all of Eighth Army stood a good chance of escaping from the Chinese envelopment that was growing tighter by the hour, especially around the 2nd Infantry Division.

14. Withdrawal of the 2nd Infantry Division from Kunu-ri

When Eighth Army ordered its corps and divisions to withdraw from the Chongchon River front, General Keiser prepared to move the 2nd Division CP southward. For his new CP he selected a point on the Kunu-ri–Sunchon road about four miles south of the junction of that road with the Kunu-ri–Anju road. The 2nd Division's zone of responsibility, and also IX Corps's, on the west included the road south from the junction to Sunchon and the flanking-ridges west of it. The new division CP opened in a small schoolhouse about 5 A.M. on 29 November. It was still dark at the time.

The division headquarters staff had just arrived there, said Lt. Col. Maurice Holden, the division operations officer (G-3), "when some members of the Turkish Brigade arrived at the command post breathlessly and informed us that there was a road block several miles south of our CP on the Sunchon road." That was the first information the 2nd Division staff had that an enemy roadblock existed on the planned withdrawal route. The division staff was inclined not to credit the report fully, as they had received unreliable reports from the Turkish Brigade in the past several days during its first combat in Korea and considered the brigade somewhat excitable. Nevertheless, the staff took steps to learn what the situation to the south really was.

The division provost marshal, Lt. Col. Henry C. Becker, sent a military-police patrol at daybreak to investigate the report. Sometime between eight and nine o'clock, Lieutenant Colonel Becker reported to the division that the patrol had been "knocked out" and several of its members killed. This incident was said to have taken place three to four miles south of the division CP. Thus, the division CP knew definitely by 9 A.M. on 29 November that an enemy roadblock existed south of it on the Sunchon road.[1]

Upon receiving the report from Lieutenant Colonel Becker, the division decided to send Captain Kydland and his 2nd Reconnaissance Company south to open the road. Kydland had a reputation in the division as a battle-experienced officer, capable and dependable. The enemy were reported to be in a fireblock position; that is, the CCF were in firing positions with small arms and automatic weapons on both sides of the road. There was no physical roadblock on the road itself. Lieutenant Colonel Becker's MP patrol had determined this point. When the Reconnaissance Company reached the fireblock area, enemy fire almost immediately wounded Captain Kydland. A flash message to the division

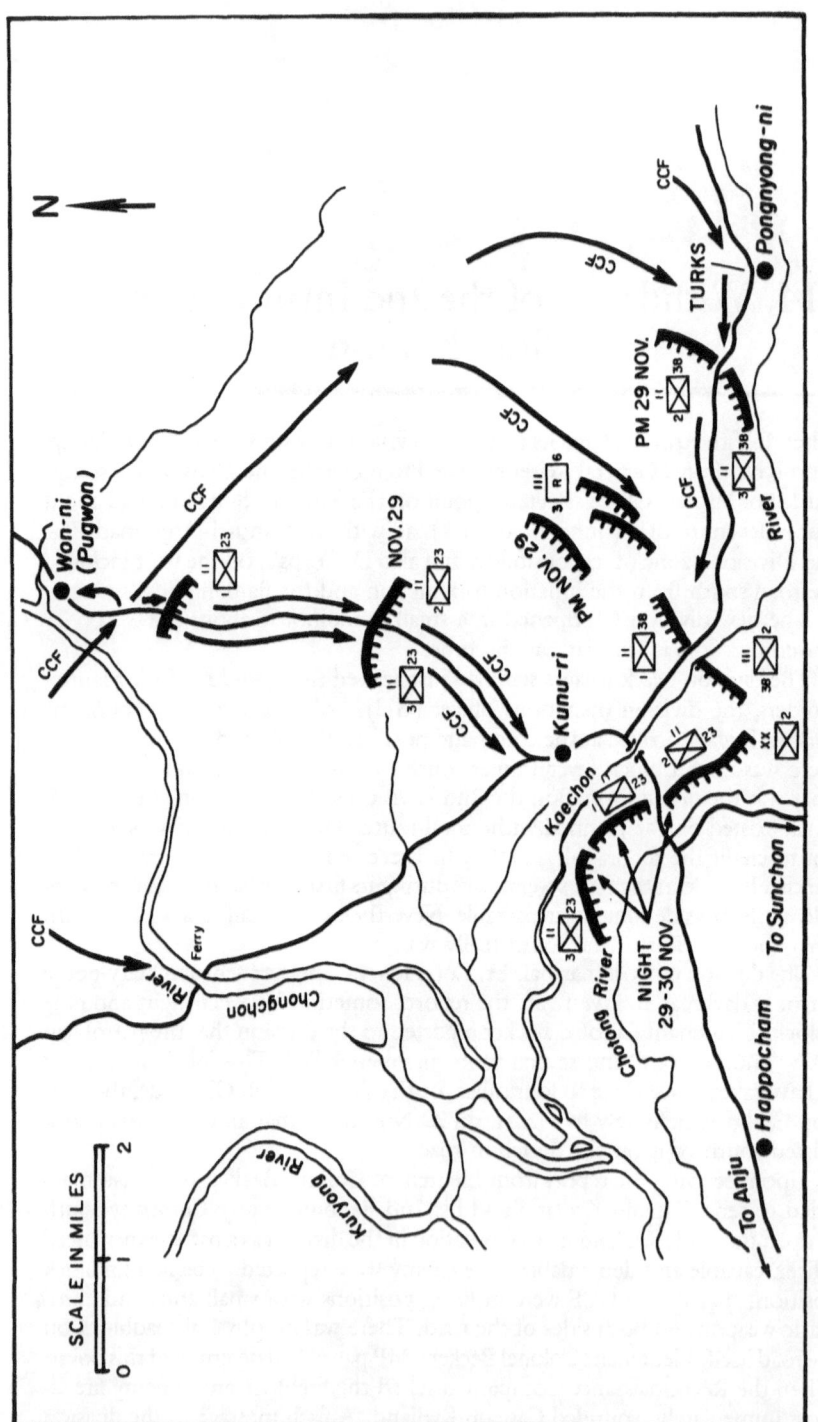

Map 11. 2nd Infantry Division positions in Kunu-ri and vicinity, 29-30 November 1950.

CP informed it that Kydland would have to be evacuated. By noon the division received further word that the Reconnaissance Company had failed to remove the enemy fireblock and that more strength was needed. General Keiser then ordered Colonel Peploe to send a rifle company from the 38th Infantry to reinforce the Reconnaissance Company. As stated earlier, Peploe sent C Company. It arrived at the division CP about 2 P.M. The company, seriously reduced by previous casualties, numbered only 60 to 75 men, less than half strength. The Division G-3 Section briefed the company commander, and Brigadier General Bradley talked with him, emphasizing the importance of opening the roadblock at once. The C Company commander asked, "What if I can't open this roadblock?" Bradley replied that his job was to attack and open it. Lieutenant Colonel Holden has stated that he believed at the time that the Reconnaissance Company and C Company would be able to clear the fireblock and that the division would be able to withdraw the next day.[2]

During the morning of 29 November, after the initial disaster to the 20-man MP patrol at the enemy fireblock, a platoon of tanks from C Company, 72nd Tank Battalion, left the 2nd Division CP to run down the road toward Sunchon to contact the British Middlesex Battalion, which was expected to attack north along the road. At 12:45, Lieutenant Harper, commanding the tank platoon, informed IX Corps Headquarters at Chasan, below Sunchon, that he had come through the fireblock, that one did exist about three miles below the 2nd Division Headquarters, and that he saw at least seven overturned 2½-ton trucks, some with trailers. He saw four wounded men at the overturned trucks. He said enemy mortar fire was falling on the road at that point and that the fireblock was held by an estimated battalion of enemy troops. The overturned trucks and wounded he saw were presumably the second ambush of the Turkish convoy.[3]

Lieutenant Harper's message said he had given the British Middlesex Battalion this information. Presumably it was also given to the 2nd Infantry Division, but there is no official record that it came through in that form. There is evidence that Harper or someone in his tank platoon radioed the 2nd Division that he had reached the Middlesex Battalion and found the road open – apparently he had meant there was no physical roadblock on it. As far as can be determined, Harper did not mention in his messages to IX Corps and the 2nd Division that he noticed the site of the first CCF ambush of the Turkish convoy about two miles south of the one he did report. After receiving the radio report from Harper's tank platoon, General Keiser had sent the 2nd Reconnaissance Company to the scene of the second and later Turkish convoy ambush.

When C Company, 38th Infantry, left the 2nd Division CP for the fireblock area, a platoon of tanks from the 72nd Tank Battalion accompanied it. This force, combined with the 2nd Reconnaissance Company, renewed the attack against the CCF who held high ground on both sides of the road from which they swept the road area with machine-gun fire. By dark of 29 November they had failed to clear the enemy from their dug-in ridge positions at the fireblock. The division then ordered the troops to break contact with the Chinese.[4]

Confusing the situation was another development. The Turkish survivors of the fireblock ambush early in the morning of 29 November, due either to their second ambush experience or to the language barrier, failed to tell the 2nd

Division staff that they had been ambushed twice on the way from Sunchon. The Turkish convoy had left Sunchon before dawn to carry supplies to the Turkish Brigade, which was fighting a strong enemy force east of Kunu-ri on the road to Wawon and Tokchon. The Turkish convoy had first run into a CCF fireblock two miles south of where they reported the ambush to the 2nd Division. This first fireblock, marked by destroyed Turkish trucks and dead Turkish soldiers, was not known to the 2nd Division until the next day, when its units passed the site and saw the evidence. Had the division known of the first ambush, it would have realized that the enemy fireblock was at least two miles in depth and not confined to the one fireblock site, where the Turkish survivors estimated there was about a company of enemy.

The initial report early in the morning placed the site of the Turkish ambush about three to four miles south of the 2nd Division CP. But by evening the Chinese seem to have expanded their fireblock north to a point only two miles below the Division CP, near the little village of Yangwon-ni. During the day, Korean civilian reports brought to the division headquarters other alarming news. These reports said that 30,000 Chinese troops had moved through Tokchon by 28 November and that three large columns of them were on their way west to Kunu-ri.[5]

An alarming and foreboding fact stood out at dark on 29 November for the 2nd Infantry Division. It had failed to clear the Chinese fireblock below it on the Sunchon road during all of 29 November, and it had even failed to learn its strength and extent. The division from the start had held a more optimistic view of the fireblock than the facts warranted. The division had failed during the day to acquire enough combat intelligence to understand the true situation. And IX Corps and Eighth Army had not helped it any in gaining this important intelligence.

It will be recalled that, before the 2nd Infantry Division moved its CP to the Sunchon road about daybreak of 29 November, the division artillery had already completed its withdrawal of firing positions southwest of Kunu-ri. These positions were north of the new division CP. There had been some discussion among the artillery officers that Kunu-ri was not a good place to halt the withdrawal because the division was open on its east flank to enemy envelopment and accordingly to enemy fireblocks and roadblocks on the roads leading south. They would have preferred that the withdrawal continue on south at least beyond the Pass on the Sunchon road, which separated the drainages of the Chongchon on the north and of the Taedong on the south, to the vicinity of Sunchon.[6]

But while tactically desirable from the viewpoint of the 2nd Infantry Division and its artillery concentration, it was hardly feasible because, from the IX Corps and the Eighth Army viewpoint, many troops of the 24th and 25th divisions were still north of the Chongchon River, and the army had to hold Kunu-ri for another day or two to give these units time to escape to the south side of the river. Many of them would have to use the road network centering on Kunu-ri for the river crossings. Thus, for compelling reasons, the 2nd Division had to be stopped in a vulnerable position at Kunu-ri for the benefit of the rest of the army. The successful withdrawal of Eighth Army to the south side of the Chongchon River in front of and west of Kunu-ri depended on the strength of the 2nd Division shield and the skill with which it was used to ward off repeated enemy blows on the army's right flank. From the night of 28 November on, this shield was at Kunu-ri and held facing north and east.

Chinese Fireblocks on the Anju-Sunchon Road West of Kunu-ri

It was not only the enemy fireblocks south of the 2nd Division on the Sunchon road that occupied attention on 29 November. There were also enemy fireblocks for a short time on the next road west, the road that ran on a diagonal from Anju to Sunchon. These enemy fireblocks on 29 November were the farthest west that Chinese troops reached in their encircling movement behind the rear of the Eighth Army front at the Chongchon.

On 29 November, the Chinese established two fireblocks on the Anju-Sunchon road, five and seven air miles southeast of Anju. They indicated that perhaps the CCF were trying to reach the Sinanju coastal road, Eighth Army's main withdrawal road. They are mentioned here because they were beyond (west of) the 2nd Division planned withdrawal road. They were on the road of withdrawal of the 24th Division from Anju to Sunchon, where Eighth Army wanted the 24th Division to concentrate to help stop the Chinese deep envelopment of the army's rear.

The 24th Infantry Division spent most of 29 November in moving from the Anju area southeast to Sunchon. Part of the division moved by the diagonal road from Anju. The first knowledge of enemy penetration to this road came at 10 A.M. on 29 November, when enemy ambushed a mail carrier for the 25th Division. He escaped and reported the incident. An army major reported that he had come under enemy fire at 12:30 while going north on the road from Sunchon. The Korean police chief of Yongbong-ni, about eight miles northwest of Sunchon, reported late in the morning that Chinese troops had appeared five miles north of his village. At 12:45, Lt. William Carr, commanding an ordnance detachment of the 25th Division located on the road and learning of the reported presence of Chinese nearby, evacuated all the vehicles he had that were operable and towed some others. At 1:30 P.M., Capt. Ivar Peterson prepared to destroy all the remaining 41 vehicles with gasoline. He destroyed them at 2:10 when small-arms fire erupted in his vicinity, and a large number of Korean civilians drew near. Twenty minutes later Lt. Jack Wadley of the 25th Ordnance Company destroyed at Yongbong-ni 15 truckloads of ordnance material, including 245 automatic pistols, 217 M-1 rifles, 119 carbines, 14 BARs, 40 .30-caliber machine guns, 54 .50-caliber machine guns, and 32 .45-caliber submachine guns. Military police of the 24th Division reported at 1:30 that there was an enemy roadblock five miles southeast of Anju on the Sunchon road. A medical detachment on the road turned back when it ran into a roadblock eight miles south of Anju. Korean civilians told the medical detachment that they estimated there were from 300 to 500 enemy in the area. At 3 P.M., the 519th Military Police Battalion of the 1st Cavalry Division at Sunchon reported an enemy roadblock on the Anju-Sunchon road, strength unknown, and that an engineer unit southeast of Anju was burning equipment and supplies.[7]

During the afternoon of 29 November the 19th Infantry Regiment, 24th Division, was moving from Anju to Sunchon by the diagonal road. A column of the regiment halted south of Anju when it received word of the enemy roadblocks farther down the road, and they rerouted back through Anju to Sinanju and Sukchon. At this time, about 2 P.M., the leading elements of the 1st Battalion, 19th Infantry, attacked the northernmost fireblock a little more than a mile below Tohoe-ri, where the enemy held Hill 273 on the west side of the road near Yongjon-ni (or Yongdam-ni on some maps). The 1st Battalion dispersed this enemy force, estimated at 150 CCF armed with mortars and machine guns, by 3 P.M., killing an estimated 15 and capturing three American-made 60-mm mortars.

The second enemy roadblock was about five miles farther south, near the village of Yongbong-ni, where an estimated 150 enemy were observed going into position on the high ground west of the village and road. An attack force composed of the 19th Regimental I&R Platoon and C Company, supported by B Company, 6th Tank Battalion, moved south to clear this enemy force from the road. Tanks and machine guns directed their fire on the hill, and an air strike hit the enemy position. But there were also Chinese close in—15 of them were killed within 150 feet of the road. The enemy in this second fireblock were driven off by 5 P.M. The road was cleared about dusk. The 19th Infantry closed on Sunchon at 11 P.M. that night.[8] This is the only instance known of Chinese troops getting in the rear of I Corps and Eighth Army in the Chongchon area west of the 2nd Infantry Division massive fireblock and roadblock.

An interesting fact emerges when one considers that, on 29 November, the Chinese established fireblocks on three different north-south roads behind Eighth Army about eight or nine miles below the Chongchon River, all on nearly an east-west line. These were (1) on the east at Samso-ri on the Taedong River at a highway-crossing site of the then main Kunu-ri–Sunchon road, where the Chinese turned back the 5th Cavalry Regiment, which tried to break the fireblock; (2) the CCF fireblocks on the secondary road five air miles westward of the Samso-ri road, which the 2nd Infantry Division had to use in its withdrawal attempt; and (3) and the weaker fireblocks on the diagonal Anju-Sunchon road just described, which the 19th Infantry did eliminate, about six air miles west of the 2nd Division withdrawal route. These enemy fireblocks covered all the usable roads over an air-mile distance of 12 miles behind the 2nd Infantry Division and parts of I Corps. Only the most western of the series of fireblocks, on the Anju-Sunchon road, was reopened after the fireblocks were put in place. It appears likely that the enemy who were driven from the Anju-Sunchon road fireblocks retreated eastward to join the forces at the 2nd Division fireblocks.

A captured enemy sketch map later showed that two regiments of the CCF 113th Division, 38th Army, made the cross-country movement from Tokchon to establish these fireblocks. One must say that the Chinese maneuver behind the 2nd Infantry Division was brilliantly conceived and well executed to force the withdrawal of Eighth Army from the Chongchon River front or to entrap large parts of its forces.

There is nothing in the Eighth Army and subordinate unit records, however, to indicate that the army so understood it at the time. As stated earlier, it appears that the 2nd Division did not know of the Chinese fireblocks on the Anju-

Sunchon road on 29–30 November, and nothing has yet been found to indicate that IX Corps or Eighth Army placed a correct interpretation on it. They did not understand the precarious position of the 2nd Division at dark on 29 November, or take necessary measures to help extricate it the next day. With sufficient units in reserve, the IX Corps and Eighth Army could have seized the Pass area on the Kunu-ri–Sunchon road and could have threatened the southern flanks of the Chinese on the east and west ridges along that road where the Chinese had positioned their fireblock forces. IX Corps and Eighth Army combat intelligence, or its interpretation, as well as that of the 2nd Infantry Division, in the Kunu-ri–Sunchon area was faulty at this critical moment.

During the day of 29 November the 2nd Division Headquarters staff and General Keiser were preoccupied with getting their 9th, 38th, and 23rd regiments settled in positions south and southwest of Kunu-ri to defend the division CP and to concentrate them for a general movement to Sunchon. Also, the 23rd RCT, with division artillery support, was to prevent any CCF from moving west from Kunu-ri toward Anju and Sinanju. The regimental actions of 29 November have been described. For the most part they were intense and dangerous for the 38th Infantry, and almost equally so for the 23rd Infantry. In the midst of this preoccupation, the 2nd Division may have given about all the attention it could to the CCF roadblock below it. The CCF formations were putting utmost pressure on the 2nd Division combat units blocking their way along the Chongchon River road and on the Tokchon road southeast of Kunu-ri. The division at this time had only two fragmented battalions of the 9th Infantry Regiment near its CP that could be used against the enemy fireblock.

On 29 November, the 2nd Division Headquarters could not locate the CP of the Turkish Brigade, which was supposed to be northeast of it. And later in the day it could not locate the headquarters of the ROK 3rd Regiment's troops. Neither did IX Corps Headquarters know their location. The 2nd Division wanted to move the Turkish troops that were still combat effective to the hills east and south of its CP to block there against the advancing Chinese. The division tried to get orders to the Turks through the 38th Infantry Regiment. Peploe confirms that the American advisor to the Turkish Brigade was at his headquarters at Kunu-ri at the time, along with a Turkish liaison officer. He thinks that, if an order came through for the Turkish Brigade, it would have been delivered to these officers. It would have been their duty to transmit it to the Turkish Brigade. But he does not know what happened to such an order.[9]

During the twenty-ninth, many 2nd Division supply vehicles were parked near the division CP. They had been directed to move to Sunchon, but the enemy fireblock to the south prevented their going farther south on the division road. Also, other vehicles began to pile up in the vicinity of the division CP. By 5 P.M., it became evident that the road to Sunchon would not be opened that day. Lieutenant Colonel Holden, the operations officer, went to see Lt. Col. Henry Becker, the provost marshal, who was in charge of all the vehicles assembled in the division area. Holden told Becker that, with so many vehicles in the area, their movement south on the Sunchon road would impede movement of tactical units. Holden proposed to Becker that they turn the column around and send it out west by the Anju road. Becker agreed. They sent vehicles north to the road junction and then west to Anju. When these vehicles started moving north, Lt. Col. Howard N. Tanner, Jr., the Division G-1, who was in charge of the division advance party, after a discussion with Holden, moved the advance party out the same way. Tanner left with his party about dusk. Both these division columns reached Anju without incident.[10]

During the afternoon, the G-3 Section of IX Corps informed the 2nd Division that it would move on the Kunu-ri–Sunchon road and that a battalion of British troops would attack north to help open the fireblock. The corps informed the 2nd Division that I Corps to the west of it had the 25th Division and many other units moving south on the Anju-Sinanju roads and that they were clogged with troops and vehicles withdrawing south. Lieutenant Colonel Holden remembers that, at some point in the afternoon or evening of 29 November, Lieutenant General Milburn, the I Corps commander, called General Keiser on the telephone and asked him about his situation and that General Keiser told him that General Milburn offered the use of the Anju road for the 2nd Division if it became necessary. Milburn and Keiser were close friends. In that conversation, Keiser asked Milburn if it would be all right to send his division advance party out that road. Milburn replied, "Yes."

As night came on, General Keiser became increasingly concerned about the CCF roadblock below the division. He decided that the 9th Infantry Regiment should attack the roadblock at daylight, and he set the hour for 7:30 A.M. Colonel Sloane and his S-3, Major Woodward, came to the Division Headquarters for a briefing on the situation they would face the next morning. Lieutenant Colonel Holden and Colonel Epley briefed them on their knowledge of the fireblock situation. Holden told Sloane the 2nd Division troops at the fireblock had broken contact with the CCF there at dark. Epley said the enemy fireblock forces amounted to about two companies. Colonel Sloane told Epley and Holden that all his riflemen would not total more than 400 to 500 men. It was a regiment in name only—actually little more than two rifle companies. After listening to Holden and Epley's briefing, Sloane appeared to think that his composite battalion, with supporting artillery and tank fire plus air strikes, could break the enemy fireblock. Sloane returned to his 2nd and 3rd battalions and spent the next several hours organizing them for their mission. He found that his effectives numbered little more than 400 men. The commander of C Company, 72nd Tank Battalion, was to join him the next morning with a platoon of tanks when he reached the 2nd Division CP.[11]

About 1 A.M. on 30 November, General Keiser called the assistant division commander, Brigadier General Bradley; Colonel Epley, chief of staff; and Lieutenant Colonel Holden, G-3; to his dugout. Keiser told them he had just talked with General Coulter, the IX Corps commander, who had ordered him to attack south with the 2nd Division at daylight and to withdraw the combat units along the Kunu-ri–Sunchon road. General Keiser further told the group that General Coulter said that he had flown over the road that afternoon (the twenty-ninth) in a liaison plane when he moved his headquarters from west of Kunu-ri to Chasan, south of Sunchon, and that he did not think the roadblock was very strong and that the division should be able to break through it. Coulter's remarks on the telephone to Keiser gave no hint that a large Chinese force might be in the area south toward Sunchon. Coulter confirmed to Keiser in this conversation that a British unit would start attacking north at daybreak to assist the 2nd Division. General Keiser, after discussing this telephone call with his principal staff officers, ordered Lieutenant Colonel Holden to prepare a plan for the division withdrawal, starting at daylight, and to use increased strength against the enemy fireblock. Holden started at once on the plan and worked most of the night on it. At times, Holden conferred with General Bradley for his opinions and help.

One problem that caused trouble was the need to work out an artillery fire plan with the G-3 of IX Corps that would prevent the 2nd Division from firing into the British troops that were to attack north. After a no-fire line was decided on and other matters such as a march order had been determined, the plan was sent to General Keiser, who approved it. Keiser at this time felt he had no choice but to go down the Kunu-ri–Sunchon road, since that is what the IX Corps commander had ordered.[12]

The 2nd Division Headquarters' fears that it was open to attack were realized during the night. About 10:30 P.M., enemy mortar, automatic weapons, and small-arms fire hit the CP area. Three tanks from the 2nd Reconnaissance Company and three dual-40s and quad-50s from the 82nd AAA Battalion, together with the Defense Platoon, returned the enemy fire. After about an hour the enemy fire ceased, and the rest of the night was quiet. The enemy fire killed a few men and wounded several in the miscellaneous units near the CP but otherwise did little damage.[13]

The 2nd Infantry Division Withdrawal Order

The 2nd Division withdrawal order, prepared and approved as related on the night of 29–30 November, listed the following units in march order, with the 9th Infantry leading after it had cleared the fireblock:

9th Infantry
ROK 3rd Regiment
2nd Battalion, 38th Infantry
2nd Reconnaissance Company
2nd Division Headquarters
Division Artillery
38th Infantry, minus 2nd Battalion (in march order earlier)
2nd Engineer Combat Battalion
23rd Infantry Regiment
15th Field Artillery Battalion, 72nd Tank Battalion (minus C Co.), B Battery, 82nd AAA Battalion (these units supported the 23rd Infantry and were part of the RCT)
(other miscellaneous units such as the Military Police and the Signal Company were placed generally in the march order after the Division Headquarters)

The next day there were several variations in this march order caused by delays of some of the major organizations in taking their places.[14]

When the withdrawal order was delivered to the Division Artillery commander, Brig. Gen. Loyal M. Haynes, he inquired as to the priority of the artillery battalions within the Division Artillery. General Bradley felt that the 17th Field Artillery Battalion of 8-inch howitzers, the only one in Korea at the time and thus considered the most valuable and hardest to replace, should lead the artillery units, followed by the 155-mm howitzer battalion, and then two of the three 105-mm howitzer battalions. Colonel Goodrich, the Division Artillery S-3, said the withdrawal order was received by telephone about daylight of 30 November.[15]

According to Colonel Epley, "The order of movement was designed for a fighting withdrawal if need be. Combat units were disposed front and rear. The Artillery and spare parts units were in the center."[16]

The withdrawal order as actually carried out in the afternoon and night of 30 November, in contrast to the march order given in the division order, was as follows for the major units:

2nd Battalion, 38th Infantry, with 2nd Battalion, 9th Infantry, riding on the 38th Infantry vehicles
2nd Division Headquarters
3rd Battalion, 38th Infantry
ROK 3rd Regiment, but parts mixed with other units
17th Field Artillery Battalion, 8-inch howitzers, and Division Artillery Headquarters
1st Battalion, 38th Infantry
2nd Military Police Company
37th Field Artillery Battalion, 105-mm howitzers
503rd Field Artillery Battalion, 155-mm howitzers
38th Field Artillery Battalion, 105-mm howitzers
82nd AAA AW Battalion (M19s and M16s), interspersed with artillery units
9th Infantry Headquarters Company
2nd Engineer Combat Battalion

The 23rd Infantry Regiment, together with the personnel of the 15th Field Artillery Battalion (the howitzers were left behind) and a company of 72nd Tank Battalion, went out west on the Anju road from its Kunu-ri defense position. This change of route was not contemplated in the withdrawal order.[17]

The command structure of the division artillery follows:

2nd Division Artillery—Brig. Gen. Loyal M. Haynes, commanding general; Col. Joseph H. Buys, exec. off.; Col. Walker R. Goodrich, S-3
17th Field Artillery Battalion (8-inch howitzers)—Lt. Col. Elmer H. Harrelson
503rd Artillery Battalion (155-mm howitzers)—Maj. Geoffrey Lavell
37th Artillery Battalion (105-mm howitzers), regular support for 9th Infantry—Lt. Col. John R. Hector
38th Artillery Battalion (105-mm howitzers), regular support for 38th Infantry—Lt. Col. Robert J. O'Donnell
15th Artillery Battalion (105-mm howitzers), regular support for 23rd Infantry—Lt. Col. John W. Keith
82nd AAA AW Battalion (M19s and M16s), organic to 2nd Infantry Division—Lt. Col. Walter Killilae

Brig. Gen. Loyal M. Haynes, commander of the 2nd Division Artillery, was one of the most senior brigadier generals in the US Army. Even so, he had had no combat experience prior to coming to Korea with the division in the summer of 1950. Some years before he had been in an airplane accident in Austria and had broken an ankle, which did not heal properly and left him with a gimpy walk. As a result, in Korea he seldom left his CP. When the division withdrawal started on 30 November, General Haynes got into his jeep and left with the command group. Colonel Goodrich, the S-3 operations officer, remained behind in the Division Artillery Fire Control Center.[18]

In the 2nd Infantry Division's withdrawal south from Kunu-ri to Sunchon, a distance of approximately 21 miles, it is important to know the disposition of the division artillery below Kunu-ri at the beginning. No arm of the 2nd Division suffered as heavy casualties as did the artillery. The artillery was in the rear part of the division position. In the withdrawal plan it was protected, however, by the infantry rear guard, the 23rd RCT. But when that unit, late in the afternoon of 30 November, suddenly left its place in the withdrawal column and instead went west on the Anju road, the artillery and the 2nd Engineer Combat Battalion were left without protection against the onslaught of a force of enemy infantry that continued to gain strength as night fell. The 2nd Infantry Division had had the largest concentration of artillery supporting it of any division in Eighth Army at this time.

The artillery units on the night of 29-30 November and on the thirtieth were concentrated in firing positions north of the 2nd Division CP and between it and the Kunu-ri–Anju and the Kunu-ri–Sunchon road junction, which the 23rd RCT defended. The 17th Artillery Battalion was farthest north of the artillery units, and east of the Sunchon road; the 15th Artillery Battalion was south of the 17th and also east of the road. The other three artillery battalions–the 503rd, the 37th, and the 38th–were west of the road and south of the two on the east side of the road. These three battalions on the west side of the road were just south of the 2nd Division Artillery CP but northwest of the 2nd Infantry Division CP.[19]

Lt. Col. Walter Killilae, commander of the 82nd AAA AW Battalion, had his antiaircraft weapons vehicles scattered among the 2nd Division units on 30 November. He broke down the 2nd Division Withdrawal Order into eight serials, which is helpful in understanding the sequence of unit withdrawals during the day and night.

- 1st Serial: Attack Force–two battalions of infantry from the 9th Infantry and two tank companies of the 72nd Tank Battalion
- 2nd Serial: One regiment of infantry–the 38th Infantry
- 3rd Serial: Division Command Group, Artillery Headquarters, Military Police Company, Reconnaissance Company, and part of Signal Company
- 4th Serial: 17th Artillery Battalion (8-inch howitzers)
- 5th Serial: Remaining parts of Infantry Attack Force (9th Inf.); one 105-mm howitzer battalion (37th); and Headquarters Battery, AAA AW Battalion
- 6th Serial: 503rd Artillery Battalion (155-mm howitzers), and 38th Artillery Battalion (105-mm howitzers)

7th Serial: 2nd Engineer Battalion (less heavy equipment, which had already left area)

8th Serial: Rear Guard—23rd RCT with all normal attachments

Killilae said the combat elements of the 82nd AAA AW Battalion were integrated into the column. The 2nd and 8th serials each had the AAA Battery normally attached to the 38th and 23rd regiments; the 3rd serial had a platoon normally attached to the Division Headquarters; and the 5th serial had the remaining three AAA platoons. Serials 1, 4, 6, and 7 did not have any AAA AW vehicles, because they were considered to have adequate ground-support weapons of their own.[20]

Only serials 1, 2, and 3 got through the enemy roadblock on the Sunchon road before dark. Serial 4 was going through the roadblock and fireblock at dusk and as darkness fell. Serial 8 never entered the fireblock—it traveled west on the Anju road. The roadblock and fireblock area was about six miles in depth—three miles longer if one includes the ford area at the blown bridge after dark. It helps to put the entire withdrawal in perspective to remember these facts.

The Situation on the Morning of 30 November

Sometime during the night of 29–30 November, Lt. Col. Henry Becker, the division provost marshal, informed Lieutenant Colonel Holden that he had received information from the 25th Division Military Police that enemy had established a roadblock on the Anju road about four miles west of Kunu-ri. This information proved to be untrue. But at the time, the 2nd Division accepted it. Col. Ed Messinger, executive officer of the 9th Infantry, telephoned Holden to ask why they did not go out the Anju road. Holden told him he had just heard that enemy had cut the road and that in any event they could not use that road except with permission from higher than division authority. Messinger said he thought there were some back roads paralleling the Anju road that they could use. He volunteered to send a reconnaissance patrol to see if 2½-ton trucks could get over them. Neither the 9th Infantry Regiment nor the 2nd Division Headquarters received further information that night on the results of the reconnaissance, which Messinger did make. Also, Col. John Hayden, executive officer, 1st Cavalry Division, told Colonel Buys of the 2nd Division Artillery later that the 1st Cavalry Division had improved this secondary road earlier on its way north. On the night of 29–30 November, General Haynes sent two reconnoitering parties in jeeps to check this road. Both parties had no difficulty in getting through on it, but they were unable to maintain radio contact with Haynes. Neither of the two parties returned to report their findings. This negligence may have contributed to the decision to send the bulk of the division artillery down the Sunchon road after dark, when it was under direct attack from the Chinese.[21]

As matters stood at daylight, the 2nd Infantry Division Headquarters was prepared to go south to Sunchon as soon as the enemy fireblock was cleared. Soon after daylight, however, the Division Headquarters received information that the enemy fireblock had been greatly strengthened during the night.

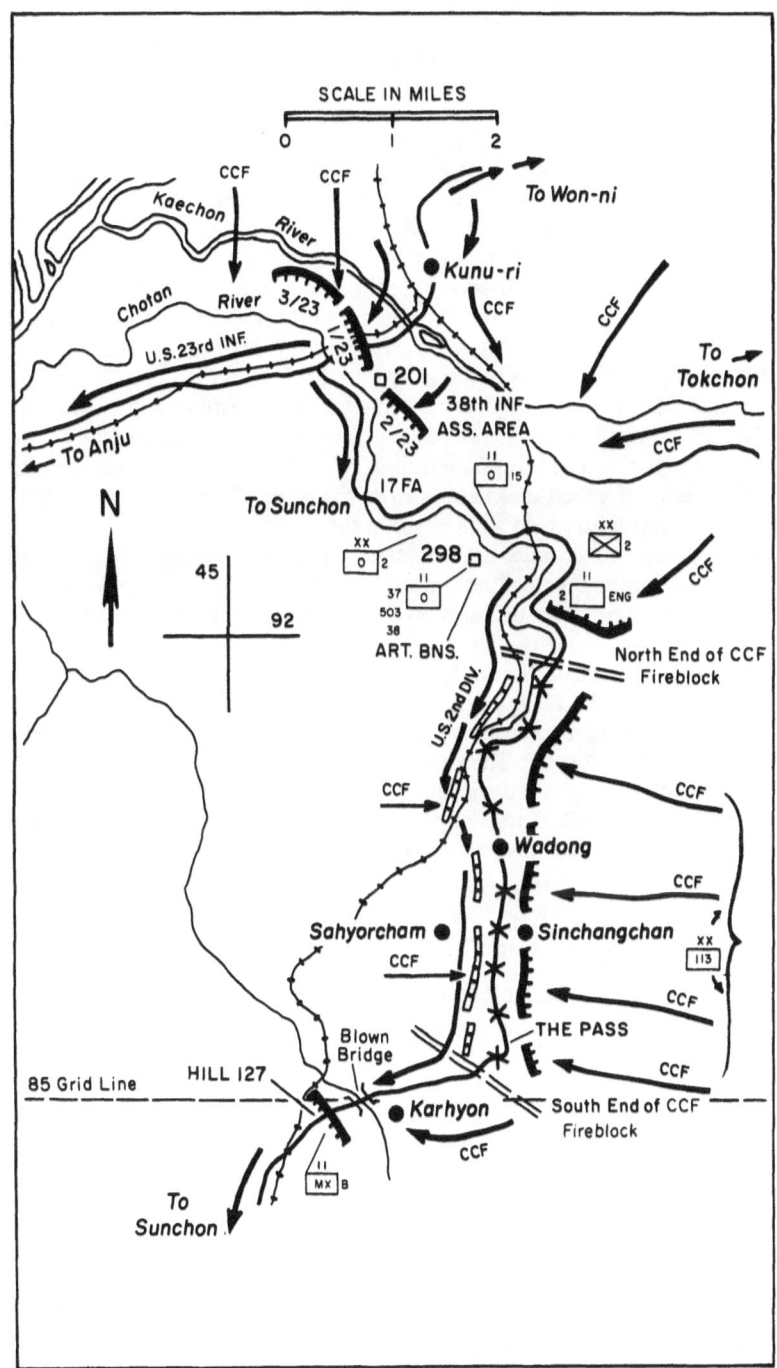

Map 12. The 2nd Infantry Division situation at Kunu-ri, 30 November 1950.

Moreover, this report said the Chinese were trying to extend their position northward to capture and occupy the dominant terrain just south of the division CP. The division CP was on the east side of the road in a small oval valley, opposite Hill 298 on the west side of the road. An east-west ridge of high ground was immediately south of the CP. The enemy were heading for this ridge.

This east-west ridge had one knob immediately adjacent to the road and another half a mile to the east at the village of Haryong-hyon. This half-mile-long ridge dominated the 2nd Division Headquarters, which was immediately north of it at its base. On receiving the news that the enemy was extending the fireblock toward this ridge, the division sent the 2nd Engineer Combat Battalion, which had bivouacked near the CP, to occupy the ridge and to hold it until all elements of the 2nd Division had cleared past it on the road, except for the 23rd Infantry, which was to be the rear guard.[22]

The 2nd Infantry Division on the morning of 30 November was surrounded by CCF on the north and west. The 23rd Infantry Regiment astride the Kunuri–Anju road, just west of Kunu-ri and short of the Sunchon-road junction with the Anju road, protected the division from the north. East of the 23rd Regiment, the 38th Infantry held a hill position two air miles south of Kunu-ri and about two and a half air miles north of the 2nd Division CP, affording temporary protection from the north and northeast. But both these regiments were under crushing enemy pressure, and no one could be sure how long they could hold.

As Colonel Sloane and his modest 9th Infantry force found out when they advanced in the predawn hours that morning to attack the CCF fireblock on the Sunchon road, Chinese were already moving north from it and were only a mile from the division CP. The Chinese had reached a point only half a mile from the east-west ridge south of the CP, which the division now hastily sent the 2nd Engineer Battalion to occupy. The 2nd Division had no time to waste on 30 November. It had to get away quickly.

Chinese Attack 1st Battalion, 23rd Infantry

It will be recalled that the 1st Battalion, 23rd Infantry, occupied both sides of the Kunu-ri–Anju road at the passage through the ridge west of Kunu-ri. Its key position was at Hill 201, which dominated the road from its south side about two miles southwest of Kunu-ri. The 2nd Battalion was south of the 1st Battalion on the continuing ridgeline. The 3rd Battalion, which arrived there about two hours before dawn of 30 November, took its position on the regimental left, north of the 1st Battalion and curving to the west so that it faced the rice paddies of the Chongchon deltalike area. The ROK 3rd Regiment was supposed to fill in the line east of the 2nd Battalion from Hill 201 to the Kaechon River, but it never arrived. It is possible that it did not receive the order to take this position in the line—that point is not clear. But if the ROK commander had not received his orders for that night, he should, as a responsible commander, have contacted Colonel Peploe. Whatever the facts were, he vanished from the defensive line during the darkness after midnight. As it chanced, the Chinese halted their attack during the night and did not cross the Kaechon River. In this instance, luck was with both the 23rd and 38th infantry regiments.[23]

But luck ran out for the 23rd Infantry before dawn. A force of about 100 Chinese, perhaps two companies, attacked B Company on Hill 201 about 4 A.M. on 30 November. Approximately 20 Chinese soldiers got to a point near the top before they were discovered in the darkness. Another 25 enemy reached the northwest lower end of the hill near the road, where they set up machine guns and fired into the battalion's tank-assembly area. The tanks fired back. But the tank fire carried high over the Chinese and into the lines of B Company on the hill, with deadly results there. Lieutenant Colonel Hutchins ran to the tanks to stop their fire. The Chinese near the top of the hill charged into B Company at this time and killed three men and wounded nine others before they were driven off.

During the American tank fire, which hit on the crest of Hill 201, 19 men slid off the southern end of the hill to escape the fire. They were all later missing in action. The 23rd Infantry Command Report for the period states that this friendly tank fire killed about 20 and wounded 70 men in B Company, one of the worst instances of casualties to friendly fire in the Korean War. In effect, B Company was driven from its key hill by its own supporting fires.

Captain Stai with A Company, in reserve behind B Company, counterattacked the Chinese on Hill 201 after Hutchins had stopped the tank fire, killing about 25 Chinese in this counterattack. He regained the lost position after an hour of fighting. Dawn came about 6:30, foggy, gray, and cold.

Lieutenant Colonel Hutchins called for an air strike as the Chinese fell back toward the Kaechon River bank. The air strike came in at 8:30, just as visibility was beginning to clear. The strike dropped napalm on the Chinese and then rocketed and strafed them. The Chinese ran in panic over comrades, some with clothing on fire. Survivors tried to escape to the paddy land. When good visibility developed about 9 A.M., Chinese soldiers were seen almost everywhere to the north, east, and west of the 23rd Infantry in the Chongchon River valley flat land. As the morning passed, other Chinese formations marched into view.[24]

Had the Chinese successfully penetrated the 1st Battalion line in their predawn attack at Hill 201 and exploited it by sending large forces through to the Sunchon-Anju road junction, they could have cut off the 23rd Infantry and directed a frontal attack against the 2nd Division artillery and the division CP area two and four miles respectively farther south. The Chinese were in Kunu-ri and vicinity in large numbers by this time, and more of their troops were arriving from the north and east with every passing hour.

Colonel Sloane's 9th Infantry Attack the Fireblock

When Colonel Sloane returned to his CP after his meeting with General Keiser on the night of 29 November, he called a meeting of his unit commanders. Sloane told the assembled officers that General Keiser had given the 9th Infantry the mission of attacking the enemy fireblock below the division CP at dawn and destroying it. He ordered the 2nd and 3rd battalions to prepare to march from their assembly areas to a point two miles beyond the 2nd Division Headquarters, where they would expect to find the enemy fireblock. There they would deploy and attack the ridges on either side of the road.

At 3:30 A.M. on 30 November, the 2nd Battalion moved out from its assembly area, followed by the 3rd Battalion, each with about 200 men. The 2nd Battalion was to attack west of the road; the 3rd Battalion would attack east of it. Sloane expected to be in contact with the enemy by 7 A.M.

The column stopped about one mile south of the 2nd Division Headquarters. There, Maj. Cesibes V. Barberis, 2nd Battalion commander, intended to send flanking patrols to the nearby ridgelines. Colonel Sloane started toward the head of the column, but before he got there enemy fire hit the leading 2nd Battalion. This was a surprise—the enemy were only a mile from the Division Headquarters, farther north than had been expected! By 7 A.M., Lt. Col. D. M. McMain's 3rd Battalion, deploying east of the road, came under enemy fire. The tank platoon of C Company, 72nd Tank Battalion, stayed on the road. It appears that, both on the west and on the east, Sloane's infantry took the ridge closest to the road, only to find that enemy fire from secondary ridges behind the first one then stopped them. In this initial attack, the Regimental Headquarters Company served as an improvised rifle company in reserve. One platoon of the 3rd Battalion's Weapons Company (M Co.) fired the 81-mm mortars and a heavy machine gun in support of the attack. But it stalled. Colonel Sloane called for an air strike on the ridge to the southwest, while men waited on the first ridge east of the road that they had taken. Despite a ground haze that hampered air support, the strike came in quickly. The planes dropped napalm and fired rockets on the enemy position. This sharply reduced the Chinese fire on the 3rd Battalion troops.

After the air strike, four tanks moved through Sloane's position and headed south on the road to meet the Middlesex Battalion, which was supposed to be attacking north from its overnight position north of Sunchon, but south of the Pass. The tanks passed down the road relatively unmolested. They did not meet the Middlesex Battalion, however, but arrived at its defensive position where it had remained overnight. From there they radioed their progress to the 2nd Division. The division understood the message to say that the road was clear—but it apparently was intended to mean that the road was free of physical roadblocks and the enemy fire they received was minor. The Chinese along the road apparently did not choose to make a fight of it with the tanks but waited for more vulnerable prey.

It was about eight o'clock when Colonel Sloane received word from the tanks of their progress. He then ordered his infantry to push south on the ridges, and he put an infantry platoon on tanks and started them south on the road. Enemy mortar and machine-gun fire immediately struck these units, quickly halting their advance.

Shortly after 9 A.M., the 2nd Division Headquarters sent the ROK 3rd Regiment, which had fought with Peploe's 38th Infantry since 27 November, to help Colonel Sloane. These troops had appeared at the Division Headquarters during the night and early morning, after being unaccounted for during most of the night. Colonel Chang, the ROK commander, assembled his men on the west side of the road and told Sloane he was anxious to join the fight. Sloane gave him the mission of passing through the 2nd Battalion and clearing the ridges on the west side. Major Barberis would then bring his 2nd Battalion to the east side of the road to help the stalled 3rd Battalion there. Chang said he would be ready to attack at 10:30.

Chang's ROK soldiers began their climb to the ridges on the right (west) of the road sometime before 11 A.M. An air strike hit the ridge ahead of them with napalm and rockets. The ROKs reached the crest of the first ridge and swept it clear of about 20 Chinese. They then advanced on the second ridge. American officers watching from the road could hear grenades explode as the ROKs closed with the Chinese. Then they saw the ROK line break and run down the slope, with about 50 Chinese in pursuit. The ROKs reformed at the base of the ridge and made a second assault, but not as energetically as the first time.

American tanks had played a role in the ROK failure. Despite the fact that the ROKs were carrying a cherry-red panel in their forward rank, two tanks of C Company, 72nd Tank Battalion, opened fire from the road area to help them reach the top of the second ridge, but their fire fell short and hit among the ROKs. Tank bullets knocked down the two leading ROKs. Two other ROK soldiers just behind them waved the panels at once to let the tank gunners know what they were doing. Then Chinese came out of their holes throwing grenades. Lt. Charles S. Heath, a 38th Infantry officer, saw all this happen and ran to the tanks to stop their fire.

The ROKs dropped their panel just short of the crest and ran down the hill. A ROK officer stopped the men at the base of the ridge and reformed them once again for another attack. The ROK line again approached the top. They were within a few yards of the dropped red panel when, for some inexplicable reason, the same two tanks started to fire and again their automatic fire hit the leading file of ROKs. This time the ROKs simply turned around and walked down the hill, some of them throwing away their weapons.[25]

The IX Corps Plan for the Middlesex Battalion

Before proceeding with the story of the US 2nd Infantry Division entering the enemy fireblock on the afternoon of 30 November, it is necessary to pause and see what was happening to the British battalion that General Coulter had ordered to assist the 2nd Division in clearing the Chinese fireblock by attacking north along the Sunchon–Kunu-ri road. Both Generals Coulter and Keiser expected the 2nd Division to meet the British force in the enemy fireblock area and that, by attacking it from both the south and the north at the same time, the two forces could eliminate it. At the time the plan was made on 29 November, there seemed a reasonable chance it could succeed. But it could be a reasonable assumption only if it was based on adequate American intelligence of the situation.

At the beginning of Eighth Army's attack on 24 November, the 27th Commonwealth Brigade was in reserve at Pakchon, in the I Corps zone. On 27 November General Walker ordered it to move to Kunu-ri, and it arrived there that night. The next day it was ordered to Sunchon, and most of the men marched a large part of the 22 miles, closing there at 2 A.M. on 29 November. There the brigade was attached to the IX Corps and placed in corps reserve. Eighth Army at this time was concentrating just about all its tactical units in the Sunchon area that were not committed at the front, because the CCF flanking movement around the east side of the army, in a southwesterly direction, would pass through the Sunchon roadnet. The Sunchon area, therefore, was a vital point in any attempt to check the CCF offensive flanking movement and to give Eighth Army time to withdraw its troops from the Chongchon River front. Among the reserves Eighth Army sent there as the battle developed were the 1st Cavalry Division and the 27th British Commonwealth Brigade. When the 27th Brigade was relieved at Pakchon it was supposed to leave Korea and sail for Hong Kong. The British 29th Brigade had already arrived in Korea as its replacement. That brigade's advance party, consisting of 94 officers and 1,877 men, had arrived at Pusan on 3 November. The brigade force totaled 540 officers and 8,771 men, and its equipment included 72 Centurion 50-ton tanks, the largest used in the Korean War. The 29th Brigade assembled at Suwon as rapidly as possible and then moved up to Kaesong, where it closed on 24 November. The battle crisis in late November prevented the British 27th Brigade from leaving Korea as planned, since the 29th Brigade had not arrived at the front to take its place.[26]

On 29 November, IX Corps started the Middlesex Battalion of the British 27th Brigade from the Sunchon area toward Samso-ri, where a strong CCF force held the crossing of the Taedong River against the 5th Cavalry Regiment, behind the Eighth Army front. During its movement toward Samso-ri, General Coulter sent a message to it at 8 A.M. about the enemy fireblock below the 2nd Infantry Division and changed the Middlesex Battalion's destination and mission. Its new mission was to move against the enemy fireblock below the 2nd Division, attack it immediately, and clear it. The Middlesex Battalion at 9 A.M. informed IX Corps that it was out of gasoline and had only seven trucks, not enough to move the battalion quickly. Half an hour later IX Corps sent it 13 more trucks.

It has already been described how, on 29 November, the Middlesex Battalion approached the Pass area on the Kunu-ri road, was stopped by Chinese fire, and then turned back on the afternoon of 29 November. British sources say the Middlesex Battalion found every ridge and peak under enemy control as it moved toward the Pass, and it was ordered to withdraw to hold a defensive position eight miles south of the Pass. There it was reinforced by a platoon of five American tanks and an American artillery battery of 105-mm howitzers. The Middlesex Battalion then moved up to attack again but had to turn back. In the words of the British source, "the Middlesex returned to the south end of the pass with orders to hold it for the 2nd Division if they could do so without getting cut off." One cannot know just what specific place was meant by "the south end of the pass," but the Middlesex Battalion in fact was some three miles southwest of the Pass, at Hill 127, on 30 November as the 2nd Division soldiers learned later. In its attempt to get control of the Pass area on the afternoon of 29 November the Middlesex Battalion took about 30 casualties in some hard fighting, including 2nd Lt. J. M. Lock of its A Company, killed by a grenade.[27] When the IX Corps asked the 27th Brigade at 6:40 P.M. on 29 November for the location of the Middlesex Battalion, the brigade replied that it did not know, because of communication problems.

The 16th Reconnaissance Company of the 1st Cavalry Division reported on 29 November that it had stopped single vehicles moving up toward the 2nd Division fireblock, holding them until a group had assembled for better protection, and then letting them through. It reported that the last five vehicles it had let through had turned around and come back and that five IX Corps vehicles had also turned back.

On this same day, Eighth Army ordered the British 29th Brigade to move to Anju, less one battalion, which was needed in the 2nd Division zone. The 29th Brigade, however, got no farther north than Pyongyang.

On the morning of 30 November the order for the Middlesex Battalion to attack north toward the 2nd Division was still in effect. General Coulter had reiterated this to General Keiser in his telephone call during the night of 29 November. It appears that, during the latter part of the night of 29–30 November, the IX Corps knew the location of the Middlesex Battalion because that information would be needed in settling on a demarcation line limiting 2nd Division artillery fire on the south so as not to strike the British Battalion position.

The 2nd Division seems to have thought on 30 November that the Middlesex Battalion would be just around the next bend of the road and would have cleared it southward. Communication between the 2nd Division and the Middlesex Battalion, as it turned out, was nonexistent that day, and the division did not know where it was until some of the division infantry reached its lines in the late afternoon. The IX Corps seems not to have maintained oversight of the Middlesex Battalion's actions on 30 November to assure its attack north went forward to help the 2nd Division. American and British communications at the battle scene that day were hardly better than that of the Chinese, if as good, despite their electronic equipment. In the hilly and mountainous country of northern Korea, there was constant trouble with infantry radios. Communication had to be by tank and artillery radio, when they were available.

An agreement for cooperation between the 2nd Infantry Division and the Middlesex Battalion in breaking the enemy roadblock on 30 November was reached during the night of 29–30 November between Lieutenant Colonel Holden, 2nd Division G-3, and the IX Corps G-3 staff. It called for the 2nd Division to attack south at first light. If its attack failed, it was to request the Middlesex Battalion to attack north toward it. Communication was to be by tank radio. The British Battalion was stated to be just south of the 85 grid line. The 2nd Division was not to deliver fire south of that line. The British Battalion, on its part, was not to deliver fire north of a line to be set by tank radio. The Middlesex Battalion was to be ready to attack not later than 8 A.M. on 30 November. In case tank radio did not establish communication, an alternate method was for 2nd Division liaison planes to drop messages to American tanks attached to the Middlesex Battalion. A IX Corps order, encompassing these terms, was issued at 3 A.M. on 30 November to both the 2nd Infantry Division and to the Middlesex Battalion. At 8:50 A.M., when the 9th Infantry troops under Colonel Sloane had failed to break the enemy fireblock below the 2nd Division Headquarters, the 2nd Division requested the Middlesex Battalion to attack north toward it.[28]

The 85 grid line mentioned in the IX Corps order was on the south side of the Pass area on the Kunu-ri–Sunchon road and ran past the northern edge of the village of Karhyon. In the 2nd Division withdrawal no units ever met any British troops of the Middlesex Battalion until they were south of Karhyon. As far as can be determined, the Middlesex Battalion did not attack toward the 2nd Division on 30 November, and it never reached the top of the Pass, which it was supposed to hold open for the 2nd Division. This failure is not explained in any official records, nor in other sources, including British writings on the subject. British writers say only that, on the afternoon and evening of 29 November, the Middlesex Battalion was stopped short of the Pass by Chinese. They do not explain its failure the next day to carry out the IX Corps order and its failure to respond to the 2nd Infantry Division request for it to attack north to help reduce the Chinese fireblock.

Herein lies one of the military failures of the day. If the Middlesex Battalion made an effort but was stopped short of its goal, it should have notified the IX Corps so that the latter could have assembled and sent into action reserve troops it had available in the vicinity of Sunchon, including part of the 1st Cavalry Division as well as units of the 24th Division. We know from testimony of the first groups of Americans to go through the Chinese fireblock and to reach the Middlesex lines that Chinese did not then hold the Pass area two road miles northeast of Karhyon in any strength. Capt. William E. Manning, who was among the early groups to reach the Middlesex Battalion position, recalled that the Middlesex were on Hill 127. This hill is just south of the 85 grid line but three miles southeast of the Pass.

The failure of the Middlesex Battalion (or of other IX Corps troops that could have been assigned to the attack north) to gain control of the Pass and to move on toward the 2nd Infantry Division was a critical case of IX Corps and Eighth Army mismanagement on the battlefield. The Pass area late in the afternoon and after dark on 30 November became the scene of some of the worst carnage in the six-mile-long Chinese fireblock. After the Chinese did extend their control to the Pass area, they emplaced mortars and machine guns on the high ground above the road cut at the Pass and exacted a heavy toll in terms of lives lost and vehicles destroyed.

The 2nd Infantry Division Starts into the Fireblock

The staff of the 2nd Infantry Division CP decided at about 10 A.M. that the 9th Infantry and other troops at the northern end of the enemy fireblock were too weak to break it. But the division could wait no longer to start its withdrawal. The division ordered the 38th Infantry Regiment to concentrate at the division CP. It was to lead the breakout attempt that General Keiser had now decided was the only option left to him. He ordered the Division Headquarters to get all the vehicles ready to go at any moment and instructed everyone to prepare to fight through the fireblock.

About the time General Keiser made this decision, he received an alarming report from Major Mezar, executive officer of the 23rd Infantry. Mezar reported by radio to Lieutenant Colonel Holden that Lt. Col. James Edwards, commanding officer of the 2nd Battalion, had told him of enemy pressure steadily building up on his front, with Chinese beginning to cross the Chongchon River to his front. Edwards's 2nd Battalion was then on high ground just southwest of Kunu-ri. The 23rd Infantry's position, only a few miles north of the 2nd Division CP and the artillery, might soon become precarious.[29]

General Keiser's order to the 38th Infantry to lead the division in its breakout effort did not find the regiment in the best of condition for such a mission, but there were no infantry troops available to Keiser that were better able to make the opening thrust. The 38th Regiment was pretty well worn out by its recent difficult actions with the Chinese on the approaches of Kunu-ri. During the previous night Colonel Peploe's 38th Infantry had spent until well after midnight fighting its way out of a Chinese encirclement south and southeast of Kunu-ri and did not reach its assigned defense position east of the 23rd Infantry Regiment until the early hours of 30 November. The regiment had lost all battalion aid stations during the night. It evacuated 90 wounded by sending them west that night on the Anju road. It still had 61 wounded it expected to carry out with it. The regiment, in its assembly area west of the Kaechon River, did not unload its trucks during the night. They remained ready to move at any time.

Colonel Peploe was so exhausted when the regimental headquarters stopped in the assembly area that night that he lay on a cot with his big overshoes on and his feet within six inches of a stove. He fell into a deep sleep. Others in the tent saw his overshoes start to smoke. They could not wake up the regimental commander, so they picked up the cot and moved it bodily away from the stove. Just about all the men in the regiment were as exhausted as Peploe, a strong, enduring man.

When Peploe received his orders on 30 November to move his regiment to the division CP, he started it south at once.[30] Lieutenant Colonel Skeldon's 2nd Battalion was the first unit of the 38th Regiment to reach the division headquarters, arriving there about 9 A.M. Skeldon reported to Lieutenant Colonel Holden, the Division G-3, who handed him a note for Colonel Sloane, confirming an oral message that Skeldon's 2nd Battalion was attached to his force to help clear the fireblock. There were now only about 220 men in Skeldon's battalion. Skeldon loaded his men, 20 to a tank, on the regimental tank company and went down the road to join Sloane's 9th Infantry. Skeldon joined Sloane about 11 A.M. at the head of the fireblock. There he watched the 9th Infantry and the ROK 3rd Regiment attack on the Chinese ridge positions and the accompanying air strikes on the enemy. He noted that I Company, 9th Infantry, was stalled on the ridge to the east.

Meanwhile, the rest of Peploe's 38th Regiment had reached the division CP and halted in an assembly area just south of it. There, Captain Manning saw a quartermaster crew burning supplies and ROK and Turkish soldiers helping themselves to shoes, socks, fatigue jackets, overcoats, and other items of clothing from a 25th Division dump. Tags attached to some of the clothing flapped in the wind. When Peploe arrived at the division headquarters, General Keiser told him to get the 38th Infantry moving, since the fireblock had been overcome, and reported that Sloane had cornered a small Chinese force that was still threatening the road. In fact, the road was never free of the fireblock at any time on 30 November.[31]

Colonel Peploe, upon receiving Keiser's oral order to lead the breakout, established his regimental march order, with the 2nd Battalion leading. The Regimental Headquarters, Special Units, the 3rd Battalion, and the 1st Battalion were to follow the 2nd Battalion in that order.

By noon all units of the division were assembled in the area of the Division Headquarters except the 23rd RCT and the artillery battalions. These formations were still in their positions, varying from two to four miles southwest of Kunu-ri, guarding the junction of the Anju–Sunchon–Kunu-ri roads and the 2nd Division south of it. It was vital that they hold their positions if the 2nd Infantry Division was to start its withdrawal in an orderly fashion.[32]

General Keiser accompanied Colonel Peploe and his men when they moved out to reach the beginning of the enemy fireblock. Soon after they arrived at Sloane's position, two companies of Turks appeared there. General Keiser ordered them to attack on the east side of the road, where increased enemy fire had developed, and where the attack by I Company, 9th Infantry, had stalled.

The 38th Infantry Enters the Fireblock

Lieutenant Colonel Skeldon's 2nd Battalion, 38th Infantry, was ready when General Keiser gave Colonel Peploe the signal to start his men down the enemy-dominated road. Keiser expected the regiment would meet the Middlesex Battalion within a short distance, although he had had no communication from it during the morning.

The 2nd Battalion of Sloane's 9th Infantry came off the hills as the lead tanks were preparing to start ahead of Skeldon's 2nd Battalion. Many of them, having no transportation to ride through the fireblock because the 9th Infantry trains had gone out the Anju road the previous night, got on Skeldon's tanks and any other vehicles they could reach. The lead tank, for instance, carried three officers and 18 men from the 9th Infantry.

Captain Hinton, commanding the 38th Tank Company, relayed the order from Colonel Peploe to Lt. James Mace, Tank Platoon leader in the lead tank, to go. In this way the division breakthrough started about 1:30 P.M. Lieutenant Mace fired his tank .50-caliber machine gun, sweeping every curve of the road when the tank approached it. The infantry troops riding the tank deck covered the sides of the road with rifle fire. This lead tank encountered five enemy machine guns in the first mile and a half but got past them without casualties. Then suddenly, Lieutenant Mace yelled to the tank driver to stop. Mace saw a physical roadblock just ahead. It comprised an American M-4 tank, an M39 ammunition carrier, and a 2½-ton truck. A wounded Turk was at the side of the road. The vehicles apparently were part of the Turk convoy that had been ambushed earlier. As the tank stopped, the infantry on its deck slid off and formed firing lines in the roadside ditches. Mace's tank pushed the immobile tank and truck off the road. The ammunition carrier, its brakes locked, could not be moved. When this was discovered, Lieutenant Heath, from the 38th Infantry and one of those riding on the tank deck, climbed aboard the carrier and tried all levers and gears he could find and finally stumbled onto the lateral levers and released them. Mace was then able to push the vehicle off the road. Heavy enemy fire fell on this spot as the men worked to clear the road. Lieutenant Mace held his tank until Lieutenants Knight and Heath got their men from the ditches and back aboard it. Then it took off down the road. This was a rare occurrence among the tanks that followed. When most of them stopped for any reason, they took off again as soon as they could and left their infantry riders stranded in the ditches.

As Mace's lead tank resumed its run, an F-51 came in strafing and firing rockets. One of the rockets hit close to the tank, and Lieutenant Heath was blinded temporarily in one eye. As Mace sped down the road, his tank passed other destroyed Turk convoy vehicles. The second tank in line had no infantrymen riding its deck. The third tank had 22 infantrymen on its deck and sides. Only ten of them survived the ride. One noncommissioned officer on this tank, Cpl. Jacob Schnabel, held two wounded men, one on either side of him, until enemy fire hit both men a second time and they slipped from his grasp.

Mace's tank, still in the lead, reached the half-mile-long Pass, a cut with steep 50-foot high slopes, approximately six miles from the starting point. Surprised Chinese in the cut ran off to the left and got away. At the south end of the Pass, six Chinese soldiers squatted eating a noonday meal. They too escaped. More wrecked Turkish vehicles were in the Pass. Heading downhill on the south side from the cut, Mace's tank ran into a barricade of three vehicles blocking the road. Chinese soldiers had piled all kinds of material on them. The tank rammed the barricade at full speed and ran over it. Later, Mace's tank met another coming toward it from a Middlesex Battalion outpost. American artillery at the Middlesex position apparently had been firing at Chinese on the hills to their north most of the morning, and enemy had kept up a harassing fire at times on them. But there is no indication that the Middlesex Battalion ever moved out and mounted an attack against the Chinese during the morning. Mace's tank radio, from the south side of the Pass, could not establish contact with the 2nd Division to give a report of what he had experienced.[33]

It appears that the 2nd Battalion, 9th Infantry, broke up as a unit when it came off the ridges and down to the road at the head of the fireblock. In groups or individually, the men boarded any 38th Infantry transportation they could find, either tank or truck, as Lieutenant Knight's group had done, and fought with them through the roadblock. Some of the 2nd Battalion, 9th Infantry, were in Sunchon by 4 P.M., among the first of the 2nd Division to get through the fireblock. The 3rd Battalion, 9th Infantry, on the other hand, now about half a mile into the fireblock, went into a perimeter defense on the road and held there while the 2nd Division units went through it and continued south into the fireblock. The 3rd Battalion, 9th Infantry, therefore was among the last of the division units to run the roadblock late in the afternoon. The 9th Infantry Headquarters, still back near the 2nd Division CP, did not start through the fireblock until late in the afternoon.[34]

When Colonel Peploe started his regiment through the fireblock, he had his infantry mount tank decks and get into artillery vehicles. All vehicles were ordered to keep moving. But the miscellaneous vehicles in the column did not keep pace with Lieutenant Mace's lead tanks. Most of the 2nd Battalion got only 500 yards down the road when the column stopped. Colonel Peploe, in one of the vehicles, described what happened:

I started through the block with my assigned driver at the steering wheel of my jeep. After we had gone a short distance the road turned abruptly to the right. There blocking the road were some empty vehicles with crews hugging the ditches on both sides of the road. Small arms fire was hitting the position from the nearby ridge on the right (west) side. We tumbled out of the jeep into the ditch on the left (east) side. Mortar fire from the east fell a short distance to our left. It was necessary to get the vehicles moving. So we scrambled into the jeep with Manning taking the wheel. It was overloaded with men. With my wounded Korean orderly on my lap we took off with the other vehicles following.[35]

Capt. William E. Manning of the 3rd Battalion had not originally been in Colonel Peploe's jeep. He had started with Special Units farther back in the column. When the column halted, Manning walked up the road to see what had caused the halt, was not fired on, and soon came upon Colonel Peploe trying to get the column moving. When Peploe and his men started for their jeep, Manning ran along with them and got behind the steering wheel. Manning drove the jeep around the stopped vehicles to take the lead, and then those behind started after them as soldiers from the ditches hurriedly reloaded into the vehicles.

After a short distance, Manning came upon a sergeant in the road. He stopped them and said there was an enemy sniper just ahead and that he had located him and would dispose of him shortly. Again the column halted briefly while the sergeant got rid of the sniper. Peploe's Korean orderly had been shot in the neck and was bleeding profusely, rapidly turning Peploe's new parka a new color. When the sergeant signaled that the sniper was no more, Manning started up again, this time going around a tank standing in the road. The tank followed him, and the other vehicles followed the tank. Manning drove the jeep rapidly down the road, the rest careening after him. Nothing happened until Manning came to a small hill pass near the village of Wadong (at map coordinate 4989), about two and a half miles from the beginning of the roadblock. Then, suddenly, automatic-weapons fire struck near the head of the column, and the enemy gunner sprayed fire down the column. The gunner apparently had meant to hit the lead vehicle, but he had not given his burst of fire enough lead at the moving column, and his first bullets hit behind it. The first few vehicles escaped unharmed, but the enemy machine-gun fire hit and knocked out six vehicles behind them. Again the column halted. The men scrambled from the vehicles into the roadside ditches and returned the enemy fire. In the resulting firefight, the enemy fire was mostly silenced. Again, the 2nd Battalion men got into and onto the operational vehicles and drove fast toward the Pass.

At the beginning of the Pass, mortar fire registered on the road and began to hit among the vehicles. Lieutenant Colonel Skeldon, the battalion commander, loaded his jeep with wounded men and sent it on. He walked through the Pass. While descending the south side, he got a ride on another vehicle. After getting to the south side of the Pass, the 2nd Battalion, without further trouble, drove on to Sunchon, and from there it went to Pyongyang.

Manning with Peploe and his overloaded jeep had now fallen behind the 3rd Battalion, 38th Infantry, which they were following when they reached the Pass. Enemy fire was coming mostly from the east side of the road. Manning, therefore, drove the jeep so that it hugged the three- to seven-foot bank on that side for defilade protection. The Pass area was beginning to get littered, and driving through it with any speed was difficult. But Manning maintained his speed. He said that Colonel Peploe "chewed him out" for his reckless driving, saying he would overturn the jeep. Years later, Peploe said he did not remember "chewing out Manning," commenting, "actually he did a marvelous job of driving."

Going into the top of the Pass, Manning went around an overturned Turkish truck and encountered a lot of debris on the road. Manning had kept the jeep in four-wheel drive all the way, and he now hurtled over the debris. Other vehicles behind him did likewise. One of them, right behind Peploe's jeep, was hit by enemy fire. Peploe had Manning stop, and they went back to push the knocked-out vehicle off the road. When they started up again they made the turn in the Pass and started downhill (map coordinate 494857). Peploe's jeep was hit several times on the left side by enemy fire coming from the east in its run through the enemy fireblock. Three miles farther after turning downhill at the Pass, Manning and Peploe came to the Middlesex Battalion on Hill 127 (map coordinate 464848). At last they knew where this battalion was. Hill 127 was on the northwest side of the road, and just east of the railroad track and stream the road crossed a short distance farther southwest.

Their first sight of the battalion was a red flag on a British Centurion tank, with a British officer sitting on the tank holding a swagger stick in his hand. The British battalion was not under enemy fire. Manning and Peploe asked why they had not attacked north up the road. They received no reply.[36]

Captain Manning's information as to the location of the Middlesex Battalion when the 2nd Infantry Division was trying to withdraw through the Chinese fireblock on 30 November 1950 is the most precise that came to light in this research. It corresponds, further, with all other general information that can be credited to a source, including the IX Corps G-3 information given to Lieutenant Colonel Holden on the night of 29–30 November that the Middlesex Battalion was then just south of the 85 grid line.

How long the Middlesex Battalion stayed in this position is a mystery. Had it been active after dark with the attached American tanks and artillery, it should have been able to suppress some of the enemy mortar and small-arms fire that was so damaging to the 2nd Division column at the blown bridge bypass at the south end of the Pass. The Middlesex Battalion seems to have withdrawn from its position sometime near or shortly after dark and was of no help during the night. Col. Walker R. Goodrich, S-3 of the 2nd Division Artillery, with others of the Division Fire Direction Center, went through the bypass shortly after dark and passed the place where the Middlesex Battalion had been during the afternoon. He states, "It would appear that the British withdrew shortly after 1700 [5 P.M.]. Although dark when I passed I saw no British there or S[outh] of there."[37]

Colonel Peploe and Captain Manning arrived at the Middlesex Battalion position about 5 P.M. Peploe spent some time at the First Aid Station talking to wounded of his regiment who had arrived there ahead of him. He and Manning thought the Middlesex Battalion was doing a good job in caring for the wounded. They took two of the badly wounded to an American Aid Station farther down the road. There Peploe left his wounded Korean orderly and never saw him again.

One factor that prevented more of the men exposed on the tank decks and in the trucks from being killed or wounded in running the enemy fireblock was the heavy cloud of dust the tanks stirred up on the road. The Chinese machine gunners on the hillsides were firing blind most of the time as the column passed them.

Colonel Peploe tells tersely of his arrival at Sunchon after getting through the fireblock:

> I stayed at Sunchon that night. A schoolhouse was selected as a temporary CP for the regiment. My baggage was placed inside. I walked a short distance to the division CP to confer [with Maj. Gen. Keiser] about future plans. When I returned the schoolhouse was in flames, but some thoughtful soul had rescued my baggage and placed it in my jeep. The next morning I went on to Pyongyang and conferred with Skeldon, the 2nd Battalion commander.[38]

The 2nd and part of the 3rd battalions, 38th Infantry, and the 38th Regimental command group had relatively easy going compared with those that followed. Because they and the 2nd Battalion, 9th Infantry, troops who rode out on the 2nd Battalion tanks and vehicles were the first in the division column, they met few knocked-out or damaged vehicles blocking the road and few wounded on the road requiring help. These factors built up hour after hour during the afternoon and into the night as the breakout progressed, and they worked against a rapid run through the fireblock and roadblocks. This increasingly adverse situation resulted in an ever-growing physical roadblock from destroyed vehicles and debris accumulating on the road. The subsequent serials of the division had greater difficulties.

The most vulnerable of the 2nd Division, 38th Infantry, were the infantry who rode on the open decks of tanks. They suffered heavy casualties to enemy fire. Some tank decks were covered with blood. The enemy machine guns were very effective where their range was no more than 200 to 300 yards. Those placed as far away as 500 yards did little damage. Just about all the enemy automatic fire came broadside into the road; strangely, there was almost no enfilading fire. During daytime few Chinese with small-arms fire were near the road. But once darkness fell they moved there in great numbers.

E Company of the 2nd Battalion was unlucky in the run through the fireblock. Forty-two men were riding tanks that drove off and left them stranded after the first stop. It appears that only two infantrymen were able to reload on the lead tank and none on the second, when the tanks started up after the first stop. Some of the stranded men started walking down the road, others waited in the ditch hoping to catch a ride. Of the 42 men in the company that started through the fireblock on the tanks, only 17 got to Sunchon.[39]

Capt. Reginald J. Hinton, commander of the 38th Tank Company, went out with F Company of the 2nd Battalion. When the company reached the defile just short of the Pass, Hinton saw an estimated 200 Chinese leave their hillside positions and charge toward the road and the vehicles. Lieutenant Colonel Skeldon was afoot in the Pass at the time, and 40 to 50 Chinese soldiers got near him. Skeldon shot a CCF rifleman at a range of about 30 yards. Three other Chinese jumped on a tank. American riflemen on the road shot two of them off. The third reached for the hatch with one hand; in the other he held a grenade that he intended to drop inside the tank. But at the moment the Chinese soldier reached for the hatch, a tanker inside pulled the hatch lid shut and clipped off the fingers of that hand. At the same moment someone outside the tank shot this Chinese soldier through the head. The situation was saved by air strikes that hit the Chinese on the road. And some of the tanks maneuvered so that they could bring their fire to bear on the Chinese who made this assault. It was a most unusual type of enemy attack in daylight during the afternoon. Very few of these Chinese escaped the combined fire of air, tanks, and the infantry.[40]

When a part of Lt. Col. Harold V. Maixner's 3rd Battalion, 38th Infantry, numbering 63 men, some riding on jeep hoods, reached the Pass, enemy fire had built up. Only about 45 of the men got through.

By the time the 38th Infantry had fought its way through the Pass area, the Chinese apparently recognized that this spot was one of their best fireblock positions, as well as being an effective physical roadblock of knocked-out and damaged vehicles. They now began to reinforce it with troops and weapons. The CCF buildup began about midafternoon and continued until dark. The Pass eventually became the worst fireblock and roadblock of the six-mile-long gauntlet.

Short of the Pass, Lt. Tom Turner, of the 38th Tank Company, had been knocked unconscious by an aerial rocket that hit close. When he regained consciousness he walked up the road alongside the column of stalled vehicles. He found a handhold on a truck when the column started, but enemy fire hit the bar he was holding and knocked him off. He tumbled into the ditch, again unconscious, and now with a sprained ankle. Again regaining his senses, he staggered up to the road and slumped down. He felt a prodding in his back. On turning, he saw a Chinese soldier holding a rifle, who motioned him to get to his feet. Other Chinese were only a few yards away clustered around another wounded American. These Chinese moved about in the ditch giving first aid to wounded Americans there. The Chinese leader spoke in perfect English to Turner, asking him if his sprained ankle would let him walk down the road. When Turner replied that it would, the Chinese told him to collect all the walking wounded he could assemble and make it on into his own lines. Turner collected three wounded who said they could walk. When he turned to look back, the Chinese had vanished.[41] This was a humanitarian vignette, unexpected, in a day and night of death and destruction. One may conjecture that this group of Chinese soldiers was from one of Chiang Kai-shek's Nationalist divisions now fighting with the Communist Chinese. Turner, with the help of a group of ROK soldiers who followed him after Americans refused to, subsequently rushed and knocked out an enemy machine gun close to the road that was causing many casualties.

Approximately 400 effective soldiers of the 38th Infantry reached the Middlesex Battalion in the afternoon. Throughout the night, stragglers made their way to Sunchon. Before midnight about 500 men of the regiment had passed through Sunchon and were assembling with the Service Company at the edge of Pyongyang. Later, between 500 and 600 men of the regiment were counted there.

The experiences of the 2nd Division units that followed the 38th Regiment showed that enemy driven from their positions by that regiment and air strikes during the first part of the afternoon were back at the same positions a short time later, often reinforced by new Chinese arrivals. The buildup of Chinese forces at the fireblock and the number of automatic weapons and mortars there grew larger as the afternoon wore on.[42]

During 1 December, Captain Manning returned from Pyongyang to Sunchon to learn how many of the last serials of the 38th Regiment had come in during the night. He found stragglers from the regiment still arriving at Sunchon. Lt. Col. William Kelleher's 1st Battalion was the last of the regiment to get out. It followed the 1st serial of the Division Artillery. Some of the battalion walked out, arriving at Sunchon during all hours of the night and on into daylight of 1 December.[43]

In an interview at the IX Corps CP on 21 August 1951 in Korea, then Brig. Gen. Peploe, IX Corps chief of staff, told the author that, in hindsight, he thought the 2nd Infantry Division should have established a regimental boundary between the 9th and 38th regiments, with each regiment responsible for the ridges on one side of the road, with at least one battalion sweeping the ridges and another in reserve—that the movement through the fireblock should have been a division attack. But Peploe thought the combat intelligence available at the time was misleading. He said that, when he entered the fireblock, Chinese on the west side were firing at close range into the road. Later the heaviest fire came from the east side. He said he and the division expected his regiment would meet the Middlesex Battalion about a mile down the road. General Peploe blamed very poor intelligence from higher authority in causing the 2nd Division to take the course it did to get through the fireblock. Both he and General Keiser, he said, thought the road was open at the time the 38th Infantry started down the road for Sunchon. The IX Corps had given them that impression. Otherwise, he said, the 38th Regiment would have taken a tactical formation, with tanks interspersed in the column. Peploe felt that the Chinese could have caused more damage than they did if they had developed their fireblock farther south on the road and enveloped more completely the 9th and 38th regiments. He said that the air strikes on 30 November were of the greatest help to the 2nd Divison, that they were effective.[44]

Somewhere behind the 38th Infantry, Colonel Chang led his ROK 3rd Regiment's survivors down the road at a dogtrot, according to observers, and if any of them fell to the ground, the others stepped over them and kept going. Other ROKs, many wounded, and most of the Turkish stragglers, wounded or stranded on the road, clambered on board any vehicle or tank where they could get a handhold. One Turkish soldier jumped right into a bunch of wounded in a truck. They clobbered him and threw him back on the road.[45]

The 2nd Division Headquarters Runs the Fireblock

For men in the 2nd Division Headquarters Company at the 2nd Division CP, the morning of 30 November was one of constant rumors about the enemy fireblock down the road, of American planes flying overhead and attacking adjacent hills and the ridges to the south, and of uncertainty as to just what they were to do. At 9:30 A.M., the men were told to load on vehicles and to move out. But they were then ordered to get off the vehicles and to go back to their perimeter defense positions. Finally, at 11:30 they were ordered back on the vehicles.

A little after noon, the Division Headquarters group pulled out of the compound, with General Keiser wrapped up in a parka, suffering from a bad cold. Brigadier General Bradley led the way. Some members of the G-2 and G-3 staff, with the command radio vehicle, were in the group. The command group went forward with Colonel Peploe of the 38th Infantry to meet Colonel Sloane and coordinate the reduction of the roadblock, if it was still in place. Colonel Epley, the chief of staff, remained behind and has written, "I did not see the CG or the G-2 and G-3 again until I reached Sunchon hours later. The remainder of the Division staff was in the CP area until about 3:00 P.M. I had available to me the Signal Company radio vehicle for communication."[46]

There was a shortage of vehicles, and the men of the Headquarters area who rode out with the command group jumped on any vehicle where they could find a seat or hold on for a ride. One of them, Pfc. Arthur J. Cohen, rode on the back of a G-4 trailer that was hitched to a G-4 jeep.

At the time the 2nd Division Headquarters left its CP and started for the fireblock, about two companies of Turkish soldiers with some of their officers had gathered at the CP. They followed the command group to the edge of the fireblock. There General Keiser ordered the Turks to try to clear the enemy from the ridges east of the road. They did go, and they cleared the enemy from the first ridge, but on attacking the second ridge, the Chinese there in unexpected force drove the Turks back. They drifted back to the road. There, they either trudged south on foot or tried to get a ride on any vehicle that came along. In this manner they became badly mixed up in the various division units trying to break out along the road. This body of Turks was only a fraction of the brigade that had by now fragmented. This group seems to have been the last Turks left in the Kunu-ri area. Private First Class Cohen said that, as the Division Headquarters group moved out of its CP, a Turkish officer came alongside the column and motioned to the men riding on the vehicles to come along with him, pointing to the hills. They waved him off and said, "Good-bye."[47]

A Military Police jeep led the Headquarters column, with five or six jeeps behind it; then came a tank, after it General Keiser in a jeep, General Bradley, some members of the G-2 and G-3 staffs, and more vehicles. Generals Keiser and Bradley and Colonel Epley had relinquished their vans so that they could be used to haul wounded. Epley arranged for personnel to accompany them and get the wounded into the vehicles. They were the most commodious and comfortable vehicles in the 2nd Division column. Planes were overhead pounding enemy positions. About a mile down the road the Division Headquarters column was slowed by the sound of firing ahead, and soon they came in range of enemy bullets hitting on and around the road. Cohen, who kept a diary of the last days of November, said of this serial's passage through the fireblock:

> The planes were continually flying over and dropping their napalm, rockets, and machine gun fire at the enemy at a dangerously low position. It appeared as though we could touch the wings of the planes because of the low range at which they were flying. Along the road was scattered just about every piece

of equipment that the army had in Korea. Anything from a .45 bullet to an 8″ shell could be found, every small arms weapon and some artillery pieces, vehicles of every nature, but worst of all, men. We made an attempt to get all the wounded out we could and even the dead but we didn't even have space to put in our own men and it hurt just about everyone of us to know that we had to leave even our own dead back there. Near the end of the pass, a mortar was shelling the road. At one time I counted 7 spotter planes out looking for it. They finally found it and an F-80 destroyed it with napalm.[48]

Most of the way through the fireblock, the 2nd Division Headquarters staff and personnel moved by spurts – their vehicles running pell-mell down the road until enemy fire stopped them. Then the men jumped into the ditches to return the fire and waited until air strikes or a lull gave them a chance to go on for another short distance – then back to the ditches. This they repeated until they reached the Pass, losing some killed and wounded on the way. At the Pass the mortar fire held them up until the F-80 had destroyed the enemy weapon. Then about 5 P.M., nearly dark, the column moved on without further trouble, passed through Sunchon, and stopped ten miles south of that place. Nearly everyone lost all his possessions except the clothes he wore and his personal weapon. They could not sleep in the cold that night, so they built a bonfire and grouped around it, including even General Bradley. The next day, 1 December, the Headquarters group loaded up at 2 P.M. and started for Pyongyang. They passed through Pyongyang about 6 P.M. after several hours of slow going in the heavy traffic, which traveled both directions on the road. The Headquarters group stopped for the night about 14 miles south of the North Korean capital.[49]

In the run through the enemy fireblock on the afternoon of 30 November, and during that night, nearly all the dead were left on the sides of the road. Many wounded were also left there and in the roadside ditches. When the column was held up at the Pass for about an hour because of the enemy mortar and small-arms fire there, General Keiser came to Lieutenant Colonel Holden, took him to the side of the road away from others, and asked if he thought he should order the men to abandon vehicles and continue on foot. Holden said he did not think that time had come. Keiser agreed, saying that he just wanted his opinion. At this point a shout from up ahead said the Pass was clear. The column moved on, and there was no more stopping until they reached Sunchon.

Innumerable gripping stories of personal drama and tragedy occurred every mile of the way to the Pass. At one time, Holden and Maj. Bill Harrington, assistant G-2, were kneeling behind a jeep firing at an enemy position. A burst of enemy small-arms fire knocked Holden's M-1 rifle out of his hands, and Major Harrington fell over on him dead – shot through the heart. At another place, Jack Thorpe, General Keiser's bodyguard, was killed while manning the machine gun on the general's jeep. The three vans of Generals Keiser and Bradley and Colonel Epley, carrying wounded, all had several bullet holes in them – Bradley's about 18, the driver said. Keiser's jeep had seven bullet holes. Much of the time during the numerous stops, Keiser was out on the road firing his favorite rifle (a Springfield) at the enemy and shouting encouragement to his men. Sgt. John H. Cook, the general's driver, said, "Believe me, the old man can get in and out of a jeep pretty fast. He'd holler, 'Dismount,' and we'd hit the ditch and fire away at the Reds. Then he'd yell 'Mount up,' and off we'd go." Sometimes Cook would fire the jeep machine gun, and then the general would bellow, "You're a simple minded S.O.B., but give them hell!" One bullet smashed through Keiser's windshield and hit the steering gear.[50]

Colonel Stebbins, Eighth Army G-4 and a close friend of General Walker, told the author that the pilot of a liaison plane that flew General Walker over the 2nd Division withdrawal road on the afternoon of 30 November told him that General Walker was furious at the chaotic scene he saw below him and yelled, "Get back there and fight, you yellow S.O.B.s," referring to the 2nd Division.[51] This comment, if actually made, was unfair. Many in the 2nd Division fought their battle without getting the help they expected and needed from higher authority. His reaction to what was happening as he saw it from the liaison plane does not answer the question, Where were the IX Corps and Eighth Army reserves on this day when they were needed to help the 2nd Division below Kunu-ri? And where was the Middlesex Battalion?

Although Colonel Epley had the Signal Company radio vehicle with him at the division CP after the command group left, he found that, once the command group began running the roadblock, he could not maintain communication with it. He wrote later:

> It was difficult to 1) locate the commander you wished to talk to, and 2), to get him to the radio so that you could communicate. When the units were in movement, we lost contact. This was especially true of the forward units. I tried without success to contact Gen. Keiser & the G-3 several times.
>
> I was in contact with Gen. Haynes, the Div Arty Commander twice. He was trying to get in touch with Gen. Keiser. He had been informed that the 23rd Inf. were preparing to use the Anju road and wanted to know if there had been a change in the Division order. I replied in the negative. The second time was somewhat later and he informed me that the 23rd was pulling out and again asked if there had been a change in the order. Upon being told No, he informed me that he was complying with the div plan and that the Div Arty, less those attached to the 23rd Inf would follow the Div special units.
>
> Gen. Bradley came back to the CP area once to my knowledge and used the Signal Company radio. I don't remember much of our conversation. He informed me that the situation up front was confused and he was vague about the whereabouts of Gen. Keiser. I believe he urged me to authorize the 23rd Inf to use the Anju Road, which I would not do in the absence of Gen. Keiser's blessing.[52]

In the meantime, Colonel Freeman began to feel that his 23rd RCT was becoming increasingly vulnerable to mounting Chinese attack in his positions north of the division, defending the road junction to Anju and Sunchon, southwest of Kunu-ri. He thought that his regiment should withdraw west on the Anju road, which was open, rather than act as division rear guard and follow the other units down the Sunchon road. It appears that he asked Chief of Staff Epley about noon, after the division command groups had started south, for authority to go west to Anju if he should think that was necessary to save his regiment. Epley told Freeman he could not give that authority. Freeman wanted to speak with General Keiser on the subject, but Epley could not establish radio communication with Keiser, who was then in the fireblock. About 2:30 P.M., Freeman was able to talk with General Bradley via Colonel Sloane's radio at the north end of the enemy fireblock. Bradley on that occasion did not give Freeman the authority to go west on the Anju road but said he would think about it. Colonel Freeman left his own CP and started south on the road to find someone who would authorize the move.

On his way south Freeman stopped at the Division Artillery CP, where he found Colonel Goodrich, the Artillery S-3 at the Fire Direction Center. Freeman arrived there about 3 P.M. Lieutenant Colonel Keith, commander of the 15th Artillery Battalion, accompanied Freeman. Freeman told Goodrich that he wanted him to place all the artillerymen still in position under Freeman's command to serve as infantry. Goodrich reports this incident:

> About 1500–1530 Col. Freeman and Lt Col Keith came to the FDC [Fire Direction Center]. Col. Freeman stated that he would be unable to hold his position unless all artillerymen were placed under his command and employed as infantrymen. Another unsuccessful radio attempt was made to reach the Div Arty Commander [Haynes] for his decision. I (S-3) did not have this decision authority.
>
> Freeman was told that I would drive S to contact the CG for a decision but until informed otherwise the Arty units would follow the Div order.
>
> The Opns Sgt was told to close the FDC and to move forward on the road to the rear of the column. When driving south the Bns Cos were told of Freeman's assessment and request, and my response.
>
> About a mile S of the artillery area I started to become aware of the seriousness of the situation. Troops prone in ditches on both sides of the road, dead and wounded both military and civilian. It was clear that they were or had been under fire although I was not conscious of any as I drove around vehicles for 3–4 days (estimate) until meeting the Div Arty CG in the road about 1 mile from the start up the Pass. His radio had gone dead.
>
> He stated that he would not agree to Freeman's request, and to my query whether I should return to the Bn COS with his decision he replied to the negative; that there was no need to confirm their orders. (My recollection is that this conversation took place about 1600.)
>
> As to the situation at the Pass he [Haynes] stated another tank-infantry attack up the Pass was being organized and when underway the column was to "smash" its way through . . .[53]

A little earlier in the afternoon, and preceding Goodrich's trip south on the Sunchon road, Colonel Epley left the old division CP to go south to Sloane's position to see what the situation was there. Epley found Sloane and his men spent and exhausted and some enemy fire falling on the road. He spent a short period placing some mortars and infantrymen on a ridge just north of a draw where the enemy fire came from and then, with his driver, continued on south down the road. About halfway to the Pass he came upon part of the division command group, including the Military Police Company, held up by fire from two enemy machine guns. There he met Lieutenant Colonel Becker, the division provost marshal, and 1st Lt. Leon D. Secton, assistant provost marshal. They walked ahead to determine the location of the two enemy guns and succeeded in spotting them. Lieutenant Secton went back to bring up an M19, dual-40 gun carriage, to fire on the enemy guns. Epley and his driver at this point started on up the road on foot, taking a defilade position in going around the enemy fireblock. They reached the top of the Pass without trouble.⁵⁴ Epley commented on his walk up to the Pass and back down:

> My purpose was to determine what obstacles, if any, lay ahead especially in the pass area. I expected to see elements of the 9th and 38th Regts and to touch base with the forward CP if I could find it. There were no friendly troops anywhere to be seen and none were defending the shoulders of the pass. We also encountered no enemy fire and no enemy. There were several ROK and Turk wounded along the road and I made signs that they would be picked up. I observed also some friendly and enemy dead. The pass area itself was clear of enemy and as far as I could tell so was the road and the downhill slopes beyond. No friendly troops were in sight. On the way back to the fireblock area several salvos of 155's from our artillery came in on the shoulders of the pass. One shell landed so close that the concussion picked me up and sat me down on the ground. My driver and I were unhurt as we were defiladed by the cut in the hillside.
>
> I returned to the area where our column had halted on the other side of the fireblock and passed the word that the pass was clear of enemy and that we should get going at once. At this time we were receiving no more enemy fire from the roadblock. Becker and I got the column moving again and after observing it for a time I remounted and rejoined the column. We continued through the pass, down into the valley and across the stream into Sunchon without further delays. We did receive some sporadic small arms fire on the way but as far as I could tell it was ineffective.⁵⁵

While Epley and his driver walked up to the top of the Pass and back down, Lieutenant Secton had brought up an M19, dual-40 gun carriage. He put it into position to fire on the two enemy machine guns. At the same time, fighter planes overhead were watching the impact area of the dual-40's fire. They delivered strikes on the same area. Between them and the dual-40, they silenced the two enemy guns. When Epley and his driver returned to the fireblock scene, Lieutenant Colonel Becker had already had the Military Police Company and other vehicles present organized to continue south. Capt. Richard S. Johnston's report for the Military Police Company confirmed Epley's statement that the company and the convoy of trucks behind it moved on south without further trouble and reached Sunchon.⁵⁶

As this episode shows, Epley was able to drive around the feeble fireblock at the north end of the enemy fireblock, where Sloane and some of his 9th Infantry were still in place, while the road ditches were filled with exhausted soldiers seeking cover. The determined action of Becker and Lieutenant Secton resulted in the quick removal of the two enemy machine guns that had held up the last part of the 3rd serial in the division withdrawal. If there had been similar determined action in all units of the withdrawal and officers with antiaircraft vehicles stationed at the north end of the fireblock to go to the aid of stalled units, the division withdrawal as a whole might have progressed better. The M19s and M16s were the best weapons in the division to reduce enemy fire.

In response to questions, Colonel Epley commented on the enemy fireblock at the time he was involved with it:

I went through the fireblock twice. Once on foot on a reconnaissance to the top of the pass. . . . The second time through the fireblock I was in my jeep. We received no enemy fire that I can remember while I was observing the movement of the column prior to rejoining it. There were no single vehicles in my memory. There was a solid column of vehicles with men jammed in and on them wherever they could find a place. For example, there were five or more in and on my jeep. I do not know when the enemy again closed the road and the pass. It must have been quite a while later because Div Special troops & Div Arty got through [only some of it], with some casualties.[57]

Epley estimated that he was in the fireblock area altogether about two hours. His account of little or no enemy fire during that time and no visible presence of enemy during several miles of the road and at the Pass (except the two machine guns mentioned earlier) agrees with Goodrich's comments when he went forward to find General Haynes. Epley must have arrived at the Pass after Haynes's party had passed through it and on south. Captain Johnston's report for the 2nd Military Police Company is consistent with Epley's account. This then raised the question, Where were the enemy during this lengthy period of mid-afternoon? Possibly the enemy force in the fireblock had run out of ammunition and was waiting for a resupply. Possibly they were regrouping or moving to what they considered would be more effective positions. Whatever the reasons, valuable time was lost for some of the later serials–those following serial 3. Had senior officers of the division command staff remained at the north end of the fireblock to act as regulators or traffic directors, they might have been able to keep the serials moving through the fireblock more rapidly as opportunity offered. But there were none there to perform that vital function. They had all left the scene in the 3rd serial.

At 7:30 P.M. on 30 November, Lieutenant Colonel Holden sent a message to Colonel Kunzig, IX Corps G-3, saying that 2nd Division Headquarters had arrived at Sunchon. He said the 38th Infantry got through with 400 effectives, but that the 9th Infantry, also through the fireblock, was in worse shape. He reported that the 23rd Infantry was still in place southwest of Kunu-ri but said that he had had no information from them since afternoon. (From this message one may assume that the 2nd Division Headquarters at 7:30 P.M. did not know that the 23rd Infantry had left its defense positions more than two hours earlier and was then safely out to the west by the Anju road.) Holden reported that the Division Headquarters had come out of the fireblock at 4:45 P.M., that enemy small-arms fire had been heavy, and that there had been some mortar fire. He said there had been ample air support. Holden told the IX Corps they had got through by the heavy fire they delivered from the ditches, with everyone joining in–clerks, cooks, and men of all ranks–in the intervals when they had to stop, and then barreling down the road again. Very likely the M16s and the M19s of the 82nd AAA Battalion, interspersed in the column with certain units, were the division's most effective weapons.[58]

Holden's report was good news for IX Corps, because at 5 P.M. it had received a report from a pilot that he could not drop an operational order to the 2nd Division command section, that there was much confusion on the Kunu-ri–Sunchon road, that there were gaps in the road column, and that at places men alongside stopped vehicles were in firefights with the Chinese. Fifteen minutes later, just before dark, another pilot reported to IX Corps that the fireblock had not been cleared and that the column was not moving.[59]

The 17th Field Artillery Battalion and Other Units Enter the Fireblock

Brig. Gen. Loyal M. Haynes, the Division Artillery commander, and his headquarters personnel, together with Lt. Col. Elmer H. Harrelson's 17th Field Artillery Battalion of 8-inch howitzers, were the first artillery units to enter the fireblock. But no artillery had completed the passage by dark.

The 17th Artillery had been as far north as Kujang-dong, but since 28 November it had been in firing position about two miles north of the 2nd Division at the side of the Sunchon road. On 29 November Lieutenant Colonel Harrelson and his staff reconnoitered the road south and found that an enemy fireblock did exist. That night, enemy began closing on the artillery, and the 17th Battalion began firing interdiction at a range of 18,000 yards with charge 7. By morning, that had shortened to a range of 1,300 yards, and it could see some of its shells explode on targets. Its direction of fire had changed during the night from north to east, where increasing numbers of enemy were in evidence and pressing on the division. The Division Headquarters had come under small-arms fire from the east just before midnight.[60]

During the night of 29–30 November, Harrelson received orders from General Haynes that on the morrow the 17th Battalion would go south on the Sunchon road. Until then, Harrelson had hoped the artillery could go out on the Anju road. At 8 A.M. on 30 November, Harrelson called his battery commanders together and informed them they would have to go south on the Sunchon road. An hour and a half later he told them the 17th Battalion would go out as a fighting column. The march order would be B Battery, A Battery, Headquarters and Service Company, and C Battery last. The tractors and howitzers would go first; the vehicles would follow. He said all tops and windshields would be down, machine guns mounted on vehicles, and the men would fight as infantry, with their individual weapons if necessary.

In moving south, the 17th Field Artillery Battalion passed the other division artillery battalions in their firing positions, the howitzers firing in different directions almost around the compass. Farther south on the road, the battalion came to an abandoned 25th Infantry Division quartermaster dump, where about 100 soldiers from miscellaneous units, including ROKs and Turks, lay on the ground resting, a captain apparently in charge. Everyone helped himself to anything in the dump that he might need. Overcoats were in demand. The 17th Artillery arrived at the dump about noon and stayed there about two hours, waiting word the road was clear. At 2:15 P.M., the battalion started moving again. The soldiers who had been resting at the dump climbed on board A Battery's vehicles. They were bumper to bumper on the dirt road. This road to Sunchon had been improved by US Engineer troops earlier when Eighth Army was planning to drive to the border, so that it was two-way in most places. Low hills lined the half-mile-wide valley here on both sides.[61]

The artillery group advanced slowly, with stops when enemy fire caused any part of the column ahead of it to halt and the men there to seek shelter in the ditches. About 4 P.M., the 17th Artillery again halted. This time it stopped in the vicinity of the villages of Sinchangcham and Sahyoncham. Machine-gun fire from a ridge south of Sahyoncham, on the west side of the road, at a range of about 400 yards, hit the artillery battalion on the road. Dusk was at hand, and all who looked could see tracer fire from the enemy guns. Brigadier General Haynes ordered a dual-40 up to the front, and it promptly began shelling the enemy hill with its two rapid-fire 40-mm guns. Some 105-mm howitzers, apparently from the 37th Field Artillery Battalion, had deployed on the east side of the road, and they too shelled the western ridges.

A jeep with a lieutenant of Military Police and his driver came running south and tried to pass the stalled column. A CCF sniper killed the driver; the lieutenant found a place on one of A Battery's jeep trailers. During this long stop, many disorganized ROK soldiers and some Turks, some now without their weapons, came off the hills east of the road, where they had earlier been engaged with the enemy and climbed on vehicles wherever they could find space. This took place just south of the northern end of the fireblock, where Colonel Sloane was located.

The infantry nearest to the artillery, if the Chinese elected to rush it during the oncoming dusk, was Lieutenant Colonel Kelleher's decimated 1st Battalion, 38th Infantry, which was in column about half a mile back. General Haynes called Kelleher up to his position and, with some of his artillery officers, discussed with him and Lieutenant Colonel Norum, the 38th Regimental executive officer, the question of where the infantry might set up a screen to protect the artillery during the evening and night, if necessary. Lieutenant Colonel Kelleher said he thought he could do it on Hill 122 on the east side of the road just north of Sinchangcham and on the long north-south ridge opposite, on the west side of the road. General Haynes said he would wait 15 minutes to see if the road cleared enough to allow them to proceed before making his decision whether to put the guns in a circle and set up a perimeter defense for the night. The jam at the Pass, nearly two miles from the head of the artillery column, cleared enough that the vehicles began to move before the 15 minutes had elapsed, and the artillery followed. It was now dark, except where burning vehicles lighted an area. For some unknown reason, the enemy guns remained quiet when the artillery started up again.[62]

The 17th Field Artillery Battalion drove on south under blackout. Visibility was generally not good, as the night just then had no moonlight. At one point, a vehicle came to a stop suddenly because another vehicle, motionless on the road, loomed up ahead of it. The driver waited a few moments to see what would happen, and then realized that both men in the jeep ahead were dead. He drove around the jeep. The artillery battalion arrived at the Pass without much trouble, although there was intermittent machine-gun fire from an estimated 8 to 12 enemy guns, emplaced 150 to 300 yards from the road. Up until dark, friendly strafing planes often drove enemy gunners from their guns.

After dark, enemy fire hit the battalion personnel truck. Its occupants abandoned it on the road without destroying its records. There was a bad accident south of the Pass when one of the 8-inch howitzers rolled over the road edge into a ravine while going down toward the bridge bypass, killing eight ROK soldiers riding on it.

The front of the artillery battalion cleared the Pass a little after dark. Small-arms fire on it ceased, and it reached the blown bridge on the south side of the Pass about 15 minutes later. The bridge was a two-lane concrete structure. A bypass was in use on its west side, crossing a stream about three feet deep. The south side of the stream bypass was about ten feet high at the stream bank and then crossed terraced rice paddies. Sometime earlier, a bulldozer had bladed down the two banks to provide ingress and egress from the stream. The 17th Field Artillery Battalion found one 2½-ton and two ¾-ton trucks stuck and abandoned in the stream, blocking their way. The lead tractor was uncoupled to pull them to the side just as two friendly tanks approached from the south side with their lights on. The bright beams from these tank lights lit up the scene and brought several enemy machine guns into play on the men working at the bypass. One Chinese rifleman was within 30 feet of the lighted scene and was in the act of shooting the A Battery executive officer, Lt. Donald D. Judd, when an artilleryman killed him. The tanks quickly turned their lights off and began firing at the enemy positions. Back on the road the second howitzer missed the bypass turnoff and pulled right up to the edge of the blown-bridge abyss. There the driver jolted to a stop just in time to avoid plunging over. The column behind had trouble backing up enough to let him get out. For the 17th Field Artillery Battalion, the bypass ended the CCF roadblock. A Battery cleared it and drove on to Sunchon. It had eight men wounded in the fireblock, and lost 26 vehicles altogether, including an M-4 tractor. B Battery lost one howitzer. And then, there were the eight ROK soldiers killed in the howitzer accident.[63] Compared to the other artillery battalions that followed it, the 17th was barely touched. According to Col. Walker R. Goodrich, the Division Artillery Headquarters and Headquarters Battery followed the 17th over the bypass.

Earlier we have described Colonel Goodrich's trip south on the Sunchon road to find General Haynes and to relay to him Colonel Freeman's request that the artillerymen of the 503rd and 38th artillery battalions, still north of the old division CP, join the 23rd Infantry RCT and fight as infantrymen under his command. When General Haynes gave his resounding "No!" to that proposal, he told Goodrich there was no need for him to go back to the artillery battalions, as they already had their orders. Accordingly, Goodrich joined Haynes's Artillery Command at the north end of the Pass and waited for an impending attack to suppress enemy fire on the Pass so that the column could proceed. His comments on ensuing events follow:

> Darkness had set in when the Arty Hdqrs started up the Pass. I (S3) was in the rear. A quad 50 was immediately ahead. The column was moving at a steady rate—estimate about 10 mph. Only once was I aware of any enemy fire and that was machine gun fire coming down across the road from a draw to the West and just short of the crest. A burst struck the road in the interval between the Quad 50 and the S-3 jeep. The machine gun was well positioned to damage, halt, and thereby back up the column.
>
> Driving down the pass was more difficult than going up. The roadway was

completely littered. . . . I saw no wounded or walking soldiers. Nor was I conscious of any enemy fire.

Next came the dropped bridge. The by-pass was as you have described it. The banks had been "bladed." Failure to negotiate it slowly in 4-wheel drive was the danger—motor flooding and stalling. However, all vehicles ahead had cleared it; there was no enemy fire; nor were there any British.

The drive from the by-pass to our assembly area near Sunchon was without incident.

A few vehicles passed over a period of about 1 hour and then no more—an ominous sign of major problems. The night was bitterly cold.

At daylight to my happy surprise was the presence of the Opn Sgt and the FDC team. His vehicle moved to and thru the Pass with no particular problem. The problem came when he reached the By-Pass. The area was clogged with vehicles and was being subjected to machine gun and mortar fire. The Sgt stated his driver got thru by bull-dog determination—(threatening to shoot anyone who blocked his way and by driving skill in skirting vehicles clogging the by-Pass). Comment: This information I passed on to Division officers early—about 0800 that morning. (I do not recall stating that it was a stalled 155 mm howitzer and prime mover that caused the trouble.) The FDC vehicle was ahead of the 503rd [155-mm howitzers]. Whether the FDC was ahead of the 37th FA I do not know. The 37th Bn was ahead of the 503rd and only 1½ firing batteries came through the block.[64]

It would appear from Colonel Goodrich's statement that traffic past his assembly area continued for only about one hour and then ceased and that the blown bridge bypass had become so badly clogged that it became impassable to vehicles about an hour after the Division Artillery Command Group passed over it.

When the 17th Field Artillery started for the Pass after its long wait at the enemy machine-gun positions near the village of Sahyoncham, Lieutenant Colonel Kelleher's 1st Battalion, 38th Infantry, survivors followed behind it toward the Pass. They had little trouble in getting there. Kelleher noted 22 burning vehicles and about another 100 wrecked or abandoned on the road or in the ditches. All sorts of equipment and litter lay about on the road and at its sides—tents, bedrolls, mattresses, packs, barracks bags. The road shoulders were littered with bodies. Wounded who could crawl from the ditch to the road often were seen among the dead, hoping for someone to rescue them and put them on a vehicle. Sometimes this happened. For many it never did. In the dark, the vehicles often bumped over rather soft objects on the road; they might have been American dead or badly wounded. In many places along the road, officers would stop their vehicles and search the road for American dead and wounded before they continued. In the chaotic scramble to get through the fireblock, however, there was no uniform practice in this matter. Kelleher had his 1st Battalion examine the road going into the Pass to see that they did not run over their own dead or wounded. His jeeps and vehicles, therefore, climbed to the top at a slow pace. At the top of the Pass, Kelleher found that the road was blocked again by a smashed jeep and trailer. A group of his men pushed the wreckage off to the side. Lieutenant Colonel Kelleher has told what he saw on the south side of the Pass:

> For the next 500 yards the road was temporarily impassable because of the numerous burning vehicles and the pile-up of dead men, coupled with the rush

of the wounded from the ditches, struggling to get aboard anything that rolled. When we checked to make a turnout, away from a blazing wreck, either there would be bodies in our way, or we would be almost borne down by wounded men who literally threw themselves upon us.

At one point, I got out of the quarter-ton to remove a body from the road. Then I saw that the man was still living. He was a wounded ROK soldier. I squeezed him into our trailer. But as I put him aboard, other wounded men piled on the trailer in such numbers that the jeep couldn't pull ahead. It was necessary to beat them off.

We got underway. Then I heard a scream behind me and stopped. The press of bodies had pushed a wounded Turk between the jeep and the trailer and we were about to tear him apart. Again I had to get out and wrestle off a dozen wounded who were trying to board us. There wasn't space for even one of them and I couldn't give my place because I had to keep my battalion moving.[65]

Kelleher's men received no enemy fire in descending the south side of the Pass. They went through the blown bridge bypass at the stream below, and then on south down the road. They were out of it.

While some military police patrolled the road alongside the 2nd Division, the bulk of the 2nd Military Police Company and the provost marshal's staff were in line behind Kelleher's 1st Battalion, 38th Infantry. They had more trouble than the 17th Field Artillery Battalion, and in some places more than Kelleher's men. Each succeeding unit in the march order faced increased danger and higher losses after dark as the night wore on. For one thing, enemy riflemen and submachine gunners moved closer to the road once darkness had fallen.

Lt. Col. Henry C. Becker had started out with his staff and the 2nd Military Police Company on 34 vehicles. Before they stopped behind the 1st Battalion, 38th Infantry, on the road near Singchanchong, they had not lost a vehicle. But as soon as they stopped, an enemy machine gun on the west side of the road began to riddle the line of vehicles. In the midst of this destruction came six explosions. Some of the men yelled from the ditches that it was mortar fire. But Becker could tell from the sound that it was not mortar fire but artillery. Furthermore, he recognized it as American artillery. Apparently, 155-mm shells from the 503rd Artillery Battalion, firing from the north and behind him on one of the enemy-held ridges, were "overs." This one salvo wounded 21 men, started one vehicle burning, and demolished five others. A jeep's horn began blaring from a wiring short and added to the tumult. About a third of the company was soon afoot because of vehicle destruction. Becker moved his group a little farther down the road, but again enemy machine-gun fire stopped them. Then a line of riflemen left the road and stalled vehicles ahead of him and started west toward the high ground beyond Sahyoncham, where the enemy machine guns were emplaced. Becker called out, asking who they were. They said they were Engineers and were going over to clear out that flank.

Becker ran back down the line of vehicles a short distance to two tanks. He ordered them up to the front of his column, telling the commander of one tank to start pushing the knocked-out and stalled vehicles off the road so mobile ones could pass. He told the other tank crew to put supporting tank fire on the ridge beyond the nearby village on the west to help the Engineers. When Becker turned away to attend to other matters, both tanks took off for the Pass. Lieutenant Secton, Becker's assistant, soon brought up a quad-50 from back in the column and placed it to deliver supporting fire for the Engineers. Under the effects of this combined attack, the enemy machine guns on the west ridge quieted down. Becker and Epley now got the column moving south again.[66]

The tanks in the division column did not cover themselves with glory. They showed a marked tendency to run off after a stop and leave the infantry who had been riding on their decks stranded in the ditches, and some of them deliberately left their assigned mission during the breakout to seek their own safety.

23rd Infantry Regiment Leaves Rear-Guard Position

It is necessary to interrupt the story of the 2nd Infantry Division withdrawal on the Sunchon road to tell of the unexpected development southwest of Kunu-ri that affected ruinously the sixth and seventh serials in the withdrawal column. As darkness descended, about half the division remained in, or had not yet entered, the enemy fireblock and roadblock area. The unexpected event disastrously changed the plan of withdrawal for them.[67]

The eighth and last serial in the withdrawal plan, the 23rd RCT rear guard for the division, the strongest infantry and combined arms regimental force now left in the division, left its rear-guard covering position southwest of Kunu-ri. This movement, unexpected by the rest of the division, began to unfold about 4 P.M., perhaps an hour before dark, and within another hour the entire 23rd RCT was hurrying west toward Anju, having broken completely with enemy forces. This ominous action was taken while the 17th Artillery Battalion and the 2nd Division Artillery command group were still trying to get through the Pass at the southern end of the enemy fireblock.

We must now turn to the 23rd RCT and its story during the afternoon to keep events in their proper sequence and perspective. On the morning of 30 November, the 23rd RCT held its rear-guard blocking position two miles southwest of Kunu-ri and about two miles north of the Division Artillery. The 2nd Division CP was about two miles farther south from the artillery, making it four miles south of the 23rd RCT. The 23rd RCT was under direct orders from General Keiser to act as the division rear guard and to follow the rest of the division south on the Sunchon road, continuing its mission of division rear guard. The division order, as stated earlier, derived from Major General Coulter's IX Corps order to General Keiser and applied to the entire division.

Colonel Freeman kept in touch with General Keiser by radio during the morning until about 10 A.M., informing him of the developing situation at Kunu-ri and along the Chongchon River, where Chinese had begun to cross to the south side directly in front of him. Colonel Buys states that the Division Artillery Headquarters had constant communication with Lieutenant Colonel Keith and his 15th Field Artillery Battalion, which gave direct support to the 23rd Infantry. After 10 A.M., Freeman had personal and radio contact with only Major General Bradley, the assistant division commander, and with Colonel Sloane and Col. Gerald Epley. This contact with Bradley and Sloane was over Colonel Sloane's 9th Infantry jeep voice radio. Epley, the division chief of staff, has said there was good communication with 2nd Division units until the Division Headquarters left its CP to enter the enemy fireblock about noon.[68]

Quite early in the morning of 30 November, about 6 A.M., the 23rd Infantry CP, as well as its front-line troops, received some enemy mortar fire. At that time the 23rd Regiment CP and the Service trains withdrew about 1,000 yards west on the road toward Anju and Sinanju. It appears that the regimental CP remained there until the regiment's withdrawal late in the afternoon. As the day wore on, it seemed to Colonel Freeman that enemy in his front were moving increasingly to the east of him. He thought they were going south to reinforce the enemy fireblock below the 2nd Division. He felt that the 23rd Regiment was being surrounded. He reconnoitered the road west toward Anju and found it free of enemy and roadblocks. It is apparent that Colonel Freeman began thinking that he should not take his regiment south on the Sunchon road as the division rear guard but that its survival depended on going west toward Anju. In the afternoon he made repeated efforts to get authority for this move.[69]

A previous chapter told how the 23rd Infantry helped to save parts of two companies, K and L, of the 3rd Battalion, 24th Infantry, of the 25th Division in getting across the Chongchon River and escaping to its lines, afterward reaching Anju and safety on the afternoon of 30 November. It was about noon when the 23rd Infantry made arrangements to try to help the two companies of the 3rd Battalion, 24th Infantry, escape from the large numbers of pursuing Chinese that had them pinned against the Chongchon and in the paddy lands just south of it. The 23rd Infantry arranged for a heavy artillery barrage to hit the Chinese and had a liaison plane drop a note to L Company that they should then make a run for it toward their lines. When the artillery barrage commenced, the soldiers started back, with the Chinese running after them. Observers in the 23rd Regiment saw Chinese soldiers run right up to many of them and push them to the ground and motion for them to stay there. About one-half of K and L companies, perhaps 175 to 200 men, made it to the Anju road and the protection of the 23rd Infantry. This episode gave Colonel Freeman the impression that the area in front of him and to the north was swarming with Chinese.

As this drama was unfolding in his front, an estimated regiment of Chinese soldiers, in three echelons, appeared in the flat plain of the Chongchon valley. Air strikes hit them with napalm and rockets and strafed them. Observers in the 23rd Infantry were astonished that the Chinese appeared to pay no attention to these punishing attacks and did not even break ranks. When they reached the impact area of the artillery, however, they executed a column left, still in formation, and moved north out of the artillery impact area.[70] There can be little doubt that the 23rd Infantry, and the 15th, 37th, and 38th field artillery battalions, which delivered this mass fire, saved those men of K and L companies who escaped. Some tanks and antiaircraft vehicles that were sent out behind some dikes to add their fire also contributed.

Colonel Freeman was by now obsessed with getting permission to take his 23rd Regiment out of his increasingly difficult position. It would have to be west on the Anju road, he thought. Before noon he reached Colonel Epley, the division chief of staff, by radio and asked for the authority. Colonel Epley refused it, as he felt it would violate a division and a IX Corps order. In the afternoon, Colonel Freeman reached Colonel Sloane of the 9th Infantry on the latter's jeep command radio at the north end of the enemy fireblock and asked him to have General Bradley get in touch with him by radio on the subject. At 2:30 in the afternoon, Colonel Freeman reached General Bradley via Sloane's radio and later reported his conversation with him:

> Not only was it appearing highly improbable that the tail of the 2nd Division including my force could withdraw via the main road before dark but [also] that the situation in the rear began to show signs of deterioration. The enemy was pushing hard on the rear guard position. I proposed to General Bradley that when the situation, in my judgment became critical and at least two hours before darkness that I be authorized to attempt to withdraw my force and any other force not clearing on the road. General Bradley replied that he would consider my plan and let me know.[71]

An hour later, at 3:30, Colonel Freeman again reached Colonel Sloane and asked that the 2nd Division give him a decision on his request, as a rapid deterioration was occurring in his situation. Half an hour later, General Bradley reached Colonel Freeman by Sloane's radio, and it was then, Freeman said, that Bradley gave him the authority to withdraw on the Anju road.[72]

It has already been related that, during the afternoon, Colonel Freeman had come to Colonel Goodrich at the 2nd Division Artillery Fire Direction Center and urged him to place all artillerymen under Freeman's command, to fight as infantrymen, and that Goodrich refused to do so. When Goodrich later found Brigadier General Haynes of the Division Artillery in the fireblock and repeated Freeman's request to him, Haynes exploded with an emphatic "No!"[73]

In considering Freeman's attempt to obtain authority to move the 23rd RCT west on the Anju road, rather than follow the division order to move on the Sunchon road as rear guard and the 8th serial in the withdrawal, one must keep in mind what such a move would mean to the 2nd Division units still in place, waiting their turn to enter the fireblock in the withdrawal, expecting the 23rd RCT would be their rear guard. This meant that two battalions of the Division Artillery, the 38th and 105th, and the 2nd Engineer Battalion, the latter still on the hills where they had guarded the division CP all day, would suddenly be exposed. They would have no protection from Chinese that were now massing in front of and to the east of the 23rd RCT position and crossing the Chongchon River to its south side by the hundreds with every passing hour. These enemy troops had only to move south, after the 23rd RCT had gone out on the Anju road, and in two or three miles they would be upon all the above-named major units of the rear serials of the 2nd Division. This would happen when darkness was approaching or had already fallen.

There was the almost certain prospect that, in these conditions, the 38th Artillery Battalion would lose all its 105-mm howitzers and vehicles, that the 503rd Artillery Battalion would lose its 155-mm howitzers and vehicles, and that few of the 2nd Engineer Battalion would escape. The personnel losses in these organizations would most likely be heavy. Those who escaped would have to walk out over the hills. Furthermore, there would be no possibility of mounting a division attack or defense on the withdrawal route because the one infantry force strong enough for such an attempt would not be present.

It can hardly be surprising that there existed in the 2nd Division and in Eighth

Army for a long time the feeling that Freeman's 23rd RCT should not have been allowed to depart from its planned role as division rear guard. Many participants believed that General Keiser was to blame for the change, because S. L. A. Marshall in his book *The River and the Gauntlet*, published in 1953, said that General Keiser had given Freeman authority to leave by the Anju route.[74] Marshall's book was widely read after it appeared, both by participants and survivors of the Korean War and by the general public. Placing the blame on General Keiser for Freeman's departure from the division withdrawal plan and order bestowed on Keiser an untrue and unjustified reputation. After reviewing the manuscript for *Disaster in Korea*, one major participant in the catastrophe said that he had thought for the past thirty years that Keiser had authorized Freeman's departure from the division withdrawal order.

Colonel Freeman's withdrawal of his regiment by the Anju road and then south from Sinanju over the I Corps main supply and withdrawal route later caused a welter of charge and countercharge about his failure to withdraw on the Sunchon road as General Keiser had ordered. In the research for this book, an effort was made to uncover the facts of the matter because the 2nd Division, IX Corps, I Corps, and Eighth Army official records contained no data on the issuing of an order authorizing Colonel Freeman to withdraw his 23rd RCT on the Anju road. A letter from then Maj. Gen. Joseph S. Bradley made clear at least one thing—that it was indeed he who authorized Colonel Freeman to take his regiment out on the Anju road. General Bradley wrote in part, "I accept full responsibility for Col. Freeman's actions. It was not what was desired but as presented to me by feeble and interrupted radio and Colonel Freeman's strong recommendation. I authorized him to use his best judgment in extricating himself from what he implied was immediate 'suicide' to comply with orders. As Colonel Freeman could not reach General Kaiser [Keiser] by radio I felt as his deputy, I had authority to act."[75]

Colonel Freeman, then, finally had authority at approximately four o'clock in the afternoon to withdraw his regiment and any other troops in the vicinity west to Anju instead of south on the Kunu-ri–Sunchon road. Freeman said he informed the units near him of his plan and asked them if they wished to accompany him. Lt. Col. Robert J. O'Donnell, commanding the 38th Field Artillery Battalion, declined and started south on the Sunchon road. Major Hinkley, commanding the remnants of the 1st Battalion, 9th Infantry, rear echelon, told Freeman he had already formed a rear guard to protect the tail of his column, as ordered by Colonel Sloane, and would go south on the Sunchon road. In addition to the 23rd Infantry Regiment, the other units in the vicinity were the 15th Field Artillery Battalion; B Battery, 82nd AAA Battalion; and elements of the 72nd Tank Battalion. Colonel Freeman ordered the 15th Field Artillery Battalion and B Battery, 82nd AAA Battalion, as parts of the 23rd RCT under his command, to accompany him. Tanks of the 72nd Tank Battalion supporting Freeman's regiment decided to accompany him.[76]

Freeman throughout the day had conferred closely with Lt. Col. John W. Keith, Jr., commanding officer of the 15th Field Artillery Battalion. Freeman asked Keith how long it would take him to get his artillery battalion ready to move out in a withdrawal column. Keith answered that it would take from one and a half to two hours. Both Freeman and Keith agreed, once Freeman had authority from General Bradley to move out toward Anju, that they did not have much time—not the two hours Keith had stated. Both agreed that the artillery would be a hindrance to a fast getaway and might make the column vulnerable to successful enemy attack on the road. They decided the best thing was to fire all the artillery ammunition at Chinese targets, destroy the 105-mm howitzers, position the artillery vehicles for a fast loading of infantry from the front-line positions, and make a rapid departure. All the operable vehicles were to be stationed in the vicinity of Singham-ni near the junction of the Kunu-ri–Anju road with the Sunchon road. Freeman then gave the order to Lieutenant Colonel Keith to carry out this plan for the artillery.

It happened that the forward observers for the 15th Field Artillery Battalion were then adjusting fire on three enemy objectives. Two of them were two large columns of Chinese troops approaching the north bank of the Chongchon River opposite the 23rd Regiment's perimeter. An estimated 400 Chinese were in the closest column at a range of just under two miles from the artillery; the second column of about 500 Chinese soldiers was a bit farther away, about two and a third miles distant. The third target was the river crossing at the trail and road junction village of Won-ni (Pugwon) about six and a half miles northeast, a center of enemy traffic for troops bearing down against the 2nd Division. C Battery adjusted on Won-ni at extreme range; A and B batteries adjusted on the two columns of troops approaching the river in front of the 23rd Infantry. For 22 minutes these three artillery batteries fired as fast as they could load. They delivered approximately 3,200 rounds of 105-mm howitzer shells on the enemy, about eight rounds a minute for each gun firing, according to one calculation. The artillery fired all its ammunition and just about burnt out its gun barrels. At the same time, Colonel Freeman sent tanks out onto the flat land up to some dikes, and they also delivered fire on the Chinese approaching the river. The artillery forward observers said the Chinese columns stopped and started digging in frantically as this extreme volume of fire started falling on them. Chinese fire on the 23rd Infantry now fell off.[77]

Colonel Freeman ordered his three infantry battalions to leave their positions in the order of the 2nd Battalion, the 1st Battalion, and the 3rd Battalion. This meant withdrawing the line from right to left. The troops were to hurry to the waiting vehicles on the road and load quickly. The troops did not load strictly by unit, but took any vehicles they could reach. By the time the 3rd Battalion began its withdrawal, enemy troops could already be seen in the 1st and 2nd Battalion positions. The 3rd Battalion was hard pressed in its withdrawal and loaded on 72nd Tank Battalion vehicles. The artillerymen and infantry were all loaded and ready to leave at 4:30 P.M. Everyone was hurrying to get the long column away before dark.

Air cover was still overhead when the column began to move out. A Mosquito plane relaying target messages from the ground to fighter and bomber planes was shot down at this time, three miles west of the Kunu-ri–Anju–Sunchon road junction, in the flat paddy ground north of the withdrawal road. A tank went out and picked up the pilot and observer.

As the men of the 15th Field Artillery were preparing to evacuate their guns and make a run for the waiting trucks, Colonel Freeman sent Second Lieutenant Smith with a platoon of about 34 men from L Company, which had been on the extreme left of the regimental line, accompanied by two tanks, to guard the withdrawal of the artillerymen. The L Company platoon went south on the Sunchon road toward the 15th Field Artillery position. This platoon never got out; the men were either killed or captured. The last any of the artillerymen saw of them, they were north of the road junction and firing at enemy. Some artillerymen saw Chinese enter the first of their abandoned gun positions as they were making their getaway.[78]

Sometime between 4:30 and 5:00 P.M., the 23rd RCT column started west toward Anju. Darkness was falling. Freeman ordered drivers to turn on vehicular lights and to keep the column closed up, and shouted, "Get the hell out of here, and don't stop!" A section of tanks, 72nd Tank Battalion, led the way, followed by officers in a jeep. The rest of the column of jeeps, trucks, and tanks followed. There was some scattered small-arms and machine-gun fire against the tail of the column at dark as it pulled out, but no serious damage resulted from this last enemy fire in the Kunu-ri area. Tanks brought up the tail of the column.[79]

The withdrawing 23rd Infantry had no trouble on the Anju road. After about eight miles, the head of the column came to the 5th RCT, 24th Division, blocking positions at the Chongchon River bridge crossings, five miles east of Anju. On the way, it ran into stragglers from many UN units—Turks and American soldiers. The 5th Infantry held its positions until the last of the 23rd Infantry column had passed westward. The IX Corps Headquarters picked up a radio intercept from the 23rd Infantry at 7:25 P.M. saying, "We are 30 minutes out of Sinanju." The regimental column by this time was strung out over several miles. At Sinanju the 23rd Infantry turned south on the coastal road. It began arriving at Sukchon about 11 P.M., but the last of the column did not arrive until about 3 A.M. on 1 December. There it stopped at fires for warming, hot food, and a little rest. Later in the day it continued on to Pyongyang.[80] Freeman had saved his 23rd RCT, but the cost to the rear serials of the 2nd Infantry Division in the withdrawal from Kunu-ri to Sunchon is incalculable.

In the controversy that followed Colonel Freeman's action, he apparently never wavered in his opinion that he did the right thing. He stated his view on 9 December 1950 for the record when he wrote: "I . . . realized . . . that I could not have followed the main body down the 2nd Division withdrawal route. I can also state with every degree of certainty that my force could not have held its rear guard position an hour longer than it did. There is no doubt in my mind that the correct decision was made. I feel that the 23rd RCT made its maximum contribution to the withdrawal of the 2nd Division and could have done no more without annihilation."[81] Condemnation of Colonel Freeman for not following the 2nd Division down the Sunchon road as its rear guard, according to General Keiser's orders, was very strong and quite widespread in the 2nd Infantry Division and in Eighth Army in general.[82]

The 503rd and 38th Battalions of Division Artillery Destroyed in Fireblock

When the 23rd RCT left its rear-guard position, the last major elements of the Division Artillery, the 503rd and 38th artillery battalions, became the rear elements of the 2nd Infantry Division on the Sunchon road. They were now open to attack from the gathering Chinese forces to the north and to the east of them. Two miles south of them the 2nd Engineer Combat Battalion was still on the hill ridges overlooking the division CP area. The survival of all these units now depended on their getting on the road and moving swiftly toward Sunchon.

The 37th 105-mm howitzer battalion had already moved out in the withdrawal, following the 17th 8-inch howitzer battalion. Next scheduled in the march order to withdraw was the 503rd Artillery Battalion of 155-mm howitzers. It was second only to the 17th Battalion as the most important artillery battalion in the withdrawal. The 38th Artillery Battalion was to follow the 503rd. It was the last artillery battalion in the withdrawal movement on the Sunchon road.

Some elements of K and L companies, 3rd Battalion, 38th Infantry, had been ordered in the morning to stay with the 503rd Artillery Battalion and to ride out on its vehicles in its withdrawal. There were not enough vehicles to carry all the 3rd Battalion troops when it left earlier in the division column. Lt. Douglas D. Grinnell, of I Company, 38th Infantry, was in charge of these men who had remained behind with the 503rd Artillery. Maj. John C. Fralish, S-3 of the 503rd Artillery, rode out with 155-mm howitzers.

After its entrance into the enemy roadblock area, the 503rd Artillery proceeded south on the road about one mile before Chinese machine guns opened fire on it. Accompanying this enemy barrage of automatic fire, bugles blew and a large force of Chinese soldiers rushed to the road. In the ensuing melee they completely overran B Battery of the 503rd. The enemy soldiers looted the battery, and what they did not want to carry away, they threw on the road. It was stated later that only two officers and 20 enlisted men from B Battery survived passage through the fireblock. After looting the battery, the Chinese vanished back into the brush and hills near the road. They left behind an ammunition truck burning on the road. Several Korean huts alongside the road here were also burning. These large fires illuminated the area around the ammunition truck.

While the attack on B Battery was under way, Major Fralish and Lieutenant Grinnell came forward to the scene. They discussed the grim spectacle. Grinnell knew some quad-50s were in the rear. He wondered if they could be brought forward and blast a way through for the artillery. Fralish hunted up Major Geoffrey Lavell, Lieutenant Colonel O'Donnell, and Major Carl Kopischkie. He put to them the question – should the artillery and vehicles be put to the torch and destroyed with explosives and the artillerymen fight out on foot, or should the column go into a perimeter defense for the night? No one of the senior artillery officers present made a decision – indecision ruled. Some of the artillery began firing from the road to the eastern ridge. Four or five enemy machine guns returned the fire, but it was wild and went overhead.

Major Fralish then got Major Lavell and Lieutenant Colonel O'Donnell to go with him to the head of the column to the wreckage of B Battery. An enemy machine gun opened up on them from only 40 yards away, dead ahead. O'Donnell went down with five bullets in him. Lavell and Fralish hit the dirt unharmed, except for a bullet that creased Fralish across his upper lip. Lavell crawled to O'Donnell and came back to tell Fralish that he was dead. Lavell still could not give Fralish an answer as to what he wanted to do. Soon afterward Lavell disappeared, and his men never saw him again. A story circulated in the division later that someone had seen him with a leg wound. There were now four enemy mortars and five machine guns firing at the immobilized artillery column on the road. But the Chinese here did not rush to the road as had the Chinese unit farther down when it overran B Battery. Much later it was learned that Major Lavell died in a prisoner-of-war camp in Korea, 8 February 1951. It appears that he was wounded and captured the night of 30 November.[83]

Lieutenant Grinnell told Fralish he thought the best way to counter the enemy fire was to go back down the line and pull out all the AAA vehicles he could find—he knew there were several back there—and bring them up to a firing position. He found three quad-50s (M16) and two dual-40s (M19). These five AAA gun carriages together had terrific firepower. He put one of the dual-40s at the front, and Major Fralish pointed out its target. It let loose with both automatic guns, and in a few moments it had silenced the closest of the machine guns and killed its crew of six Chinese soldiers. Fralish and Grinnell then put the five AAA vehicles at the front of the column with instructions to keep moving ahead, firing constantly when they met enemy fire—some to the front, others to either flank.

Before they started, however, Fralish thought about Lieutenant Colonel O'Donnell. He went back to where his body lay to make sure he was dead. He was conscious! But he was badly wounded from the five machine-gun bullets in his body. Lieutenant Warneke wrapped O'Donnell in a blanket and carried him to the lead dual-40 and lashed him to it with ropes. In this way O'Donnell rode through the fireblock and survived to tell his story. The AAA gun carriages led the artillery forward to the Pass. Their concentrated fire silenced the enemy as they entered the Pass. These quad-50s and dual-40s, and some of the trucks and jeeps behind them, must have been the last vehicles to get through the Pass and the bypass ford across the stream south of it. None of the 155-mm howitzers got through the ford. By the time they arrived there, it was clogged to their passage and the Chinese had the ford again under heavy mortar and machine-gun fire.

After going over the Pass and turning downhill, the trucks in the column carrying wounded came in view of the village of Karhyon, two or three miles to the southwest at the bottom of the hill. The small village of about 20 huts was burning fiercely and lighted up much of the surrounding area. Many Chinese could be seen within the glare. In a quick conference at the spot officers decided to send the AAA gun carriages and the trucks with the wounded on a run past the burning village, with the AAA vehicles in front, and each to fire all weapons at Karhyon as it passed. A driver and two guards would ride each truck with the wounded. The remainder of the now bunched-up men, about 100, would strike off into the hills and attempt to walk out. Capt. Simon J. Stevens, commanding officer of A Battery, 82nd AAA Battalion, led the quad-50s and dual-40s. He lost two of his five-gun carriages in running down the hill and past Karhyon. One quad-50 was knocked out by enemy fire. The other missed the turnout for the bypass and ford at the blown bridge and dropped into the hole at the bridge site.[84]

Meanwhile, Fralish and Grinnell and their approximately 100 men started up the hill to circle around and pass east of burning Karhyon, Grinnell in the lead. They circled the burning town and then turned south toward Sunchon. There was some straying from the column for one reason or another, and soon individuals or groups of two or three were on their own. The main party stopped at 5 A.M. to rest. Two hours later, at daybreak, they reached a high point of ground. From there they could look back and see Karhyon. Through field glasses the ruined village looked as if it were in the center of a large enemy encampment. Mongolian pony picket lines were visible. In another direction, Grinnell's party saw in the distance a party of walking men and subsequently joined them. Together they waded across the Taedong River. At this point a small American plane landed on a sandbar in the river and delivered water, rations, first-aid packets, and maps to them, with information as to how best to reach Sunchon.[85]

Writing many years later about the ordeals of the Division Artillery in the fireblock below Kunu-ri, Col. Walker R. Goodrich of the artillery wrote, "Too much credit and recognition cannot be given to Major Fralish, S-3, 503rd for his actions as you have described them. Of all artillerymen his courage, coolheadedness, stamina and leadership was the most outstanding."[86]

We return briefly to the 503rd and 38th artillery battalions in their attempted passage of the fireblock and their ultimate fate. In connection with the 38th Field Artillery Battalion, its commander, Lt. Col. Robert J. O'Donnell, whom Major Lavell had thought dead, survived the war, and in a letter to the editors of *Combat Forces Journal* in 1953, he told what happened to him and his battalion as he remembered it:

> When the head of the 38th FA Bn column was stopped by the tail of the 503rd FA Bn column, I walked forward to determine the cause of the holdup. Before I reached the head of my battalion column, enemy fire from small arms and mortars hit one of the firing batteries. The battery returned the fire and temporarily silenced the enemy. From my existing knowledge of the situation I realized that I was faced with the decision of destroying our howitzers and fighting out on foot, or attempting to continue farther south on the road. The essential element of information lacking was "How effectively was the road ahead blocked?" In such a crucial decision I felt that first-hand knowledge was essential.
>
> Accordingly, I instructed Major Kopischkie, as executive officer, to assemble the battalion in a defensive area, and to be prepared for either decision. I then walked forward and found Major Lavell and Major Fralish at the tail of the 503rd column. I asked them to report on the extent of the physical block on the road ahead, and was informed that the 503rd column had been hard hit but that they did not know whether it was possible to get our trucks and howitzers past the damaged vehicles. Without delay I continued to walk forward with the intention of personally determining the effectiveness of the block. As related by Major Fralish I was then fired upon and seriously wounded. Believing me dead, Fralish and Lavell returned to the rear of the 503rd column and informed the 38th officers of my death. From accounts I have since received, Major Kopischkie then decided to destroy the materiel and to fight out on foot.[87]

It would seem from the above that the 38th Field Artillery Battalion destroyed its pieces on the road, and the personnel then tried to make it out on foot. But what happened to the 503rd Field Artillery Battalion of 155-mm howitzers just ahead of it? Some of the howitzers and personnel were lost to enemy fire on the road, but most of the howitzers made it over the Pass and to the bypass at the blown bridge. Lieutenant Colonel Holden gives one version of what happened there to the 503rd:

> About three miles south of the road block area, there is a little mining town [Karhyon]. It is the first town north of Sunchon as I recall. On the south [west] side of this town, there had been a two-lane concrete bridge. Someone had blown the bridge several days before we got there. There we were forced to bypass it and to ford the river. The Division headquarters crossed this river at approximately 1730 hours. The water was quite deep and so it was difficult for jeeps to make it, but with the help of some manpower, we made it without any trouble. At the time we made this crossing, we received some very long range machine gun fire, possibly .50 caliber from about 500–700 yards due west. I remember the Division Air Controller was with us and he immediately put an air strike against this enemy position and the firing stopped.
>
> Now, here is apparently what happened. The 8-inch Howitzer battalion, which was pulled by tractors crossed the ford without any trouble, but the first 155 Howitzer, pulled by its M-6 tractor, stalled in the middle of the ford. The men tried to get the howitzer and the tractor out of the way but were unable to do so. This ford constituted a serious threat and stopped all traffic to the rear. I feel that if this unfortunate incident had not happened, we would have gotten all the artillery pieces out intact . . . all the vehicles to the rear were trapped. Personnel had to abandon their vehicles and escape on foot.[88]

Despite Lieutenant Colonel Holden's statement, made in February 1952, about one 155-mm howitzer and its tractor blocking the ford, which in the first instance was based on hearsay evidence, the bypass may have been blocked by other factors and before the first howitzer of the 503rd Artillery Battalion reached the ford. Holden gave Colonel Goodrich as his authority for the statement to him that the first 155-mm howitzer to enter the ford got stuck and closed it to subsequent traffic. Goodrich wrote many years later in a personal letter that he did not recall having made such a statement and that the Artillery Fire Direction Center operations sergeant, who was ahead of the 503rd Artillery Battalion, found the ford virtually closed when his driver barely got across it.[89] The sergeant's description of his crossing of the ford has already been given. It is possible that, after 30 years, Lieutenant Colonel Holden confused Goodrich in his memory with someone else. We also know that, whatever closed the ford (if indeed it was totally closed), the 38th Field Artillery Battalion, following behind the 503rd, could not have crossed in any event because it was destroyed by its own men several miles back in the fireblock, as stated by Colonel O'Donnell. The facts concerning the final end of the 503rd Artillery Battalion are uncertain. We do know, however, that it did not get across the bridge bypass at the river opposite Karhyon, south of the Pass.

With regard to C Battery of the 82nd AAA AW going through the bypass ford earlier in the day with the 2nd serial, Lieutenant Colonel Killilae, commander of the 82nd AAA Battalion, wrote subsequently that elements of the 38th Infantry and two sections of C Battery "were pulled out of the column and placed in an emergency assembly area with some tanks. These vehicles were given the mission of assisting others in getting out. Twice the M-19s reentered the roadblock area to silence enemy fire and tow other vehicles through the ford."[90] We know from this account that vehicles were getting stuck in the ford by midafternoon and that some had to be pulled through by full-tracked vehicles. We do not know how long the M19s remained at the south end of the bypass to help in this work, but those of C Battery had left before the congestion reported by the operations sergeant of the Artillery Fire Direction Center an hour or two after dark. It is certain that after dark it became increasingly difficult for vehicles of any kind to cross the ford. This problem was compounded after enemy began arriving at Karhyon in considerable force and placed the bypass area under mortar and automatic-weapons fire. Just when this began to take place is not certain, but it was well before midnight. The first 155-mm howitzer and its tractor may well have become stuck in the bypass, known to have been already badly clogged, and completed its closure. It may be stated with some certainty that the 155-mm howitzers of the 503rd Artillery Battalion and the 105-mm howitzers of the 15th and 38th artillery battalions were all left behind or destroyed north of the bypass.

Casualties in the 38th and 503rd battalions were heavy during the night of 30 November, but many men of both artillery battalions walked out with other men caught in the last units of the division withdrawal column.

Among the last troops to start south from the vicinity of the now-abandoned 2nd Division CP was the 9th Infantry Regimental Headquarters Company, stragglers of the regiment who had arrived at the CP during the day, and some stragglers from the 2nd Engineers.

The 9th Infantry Headquarters Company moved out at 4 P.M. but progressed very slowly, coming to a stop about 7 P.M. It had reached the beginning of the fireblock, only a mile or less from where it started. There it sat for two hours, with no chance to move farther–the road was blocked ahead of it. Some of the Headquarters Company officers walked up and down the sides of the stopped vehicles telling the men they were at the fireblock and would run for it when they could move. There was no enemy fire on the vehicles at this time. The officers suggested that the men fortify the sides of the trucks. This was done by piling sleeping rolls, bags, and any equipment at hand along the sides.

After a long wait, enemy small-arms fire began to come in from the east side of the road. The troops ignored it for a time and stayed in the trucks. Shortly, however, the fire became intense. The men in the vehicles piled out onto the road and milled about. Soon an excited sergeant came along and asked, "Doesn't anyone here know what to do?" "Not me" or "I've always been a medical soldier" came the answers. The sergeant turned to Sgt. Richard H. Shriver and put the question to him directly. At that, Shriver walked down the line of vehicles and told the men to get into the ditches, to scatter along it, and he told them where the enemy fire was coming from. They all seemed to welcome being told what to do, and they acted on Shriver's suggestions at once.

In a few minutes Lt. Jim Wise, the Headquarters Company's executive officer, came along and ordered everyone to move up to the head of the column. Some of the men were hit by enemy fire while doing so. The rest gathered near the head of the column of vehicles, which stretched two abreast for about a quarter of a mile on the road. Most of the men, apparently, expected to go back to the trucks, because they took no personal possessions with them when they got out. But they never returned to the trucks.

Shortly after they had assembled, about 9:30 P.M., Capt. Lincoln Wray and 1st Sgt. Larry Craften formed the approximately 300 men into two single-file columns. Captain Wray ordered the men to follow, as he and Sergeant Craften led them west from the road into the hills. On top the first crest they stopped to get their bearings and study the situation below on the road. During this stop, the sound of much shouting, blasts from bugles, and small-arms fire came to them from the road below. They moved deeper into the hills. The moon was out at this time, the temperature near zero. As the party went farther south into the hills, they continued to hear bugle calls and sounds of firefights in their rear. Sometimes the column broke into a dogtrot; no one wanted to be left behind, and all tried to keep up.[91]

An hour before midnight, the men stopped on a high rise of ground to rest. While there, another group of American soldiers joined them after a flurry of fire between the two groups. The newcomers proved to be mostly men from the 2nd Engineers. The combined group then continued, often skirting groups of Chinese soldiers. Some of the Chinese sat around fires they had made. About 4:30 in the morning of 1 December, the men came to a road that they believed would lead into the 2nd Division MSR–the road to Sunchon. Much relieved, they stopped for a drink, only to find their canteens had frozen solid. They started on down the road. Within a short distance they were challenged in English. Captain Wray answered, "GIs." They were told to come through single file, five yards apart.

The foremost started, when the voice said again, "Are you all Americans?" The American soldiers never used the word "American" in referring to themselves. At this last, suspicious challenge, all the men scurried back for cover. The outpost they had run into opened up with small-arms fire. No one was hit, and the group got back on high ground. Captain Wray later told Shriver he had seen two tanks. This must have meant that Wray and his men had encountered a Middlesex Battalion outpost somewhere southwest of the Pass. The party, however, skirted the place. The time was 6 A.M. They knew it would be daylight about seven o'clock. At 6:30, Captain Wray, looking from a hilltop, said he thought the Sunchon road was just beyond. He was right. At daybreak they came to the Sunchon road. The group now numbered about 200, as individuals and small parties had dropped off during the night or had become lost.

Soon after daylight it developed that there was an unidentified lieutenant colonel with them who had kept quiet all night. Now he began to act like an assistant commander. He deployed the little force into the paddies on either side of the road, with a point out ahead, as they followed down the road. A Korean interpreter with them said they were about 12 miles from Sunchon.

During the morning a jet plane came over from the south. One of the men grabbed a panel from a nearby knocked-out truck and waved it, and the newly found lieutenant colonel told all to stand up and wave so the pilot would know they were friendly. The plane dove down at the group as if it was going to strafe, but it did not. It circled them a few times, then continued on north. Soon a propeller plane came over, presumably as a result of a radio report from the jet, and dipped its wings. Then another plane arrived and at 11 A.M. dropped a message that read, "You are on the right road, keep following it as you are and Sunchon is about 10 miles farther on. There will be trucks waiting for you."[92] The happy group now limped on down the road. Nearly all had blistered and bloodied feet. Some men, however, just dropped by the side of the road and lay there. Some of these men were never heard of again.

The trudging, bedraggled men who could stay on their feet reached Sunchon about 2:30 P.M. on 1 December. Someone in the 9th Infantry Headquarters Company estimated that the mixed body of men had traveled about 40 miles across mountainous terrain in the 17 hours that had elapsed since the main party had left the road near the north end of the enemy fireblock.[93] An estimate of 30 miles would seem a more reasonable figure.

Since the 9th Infantry Company Report for 30 November–1 December 1950 does not mention members of the 503rd and 38th field artillery battalions with Major Fralish and Lieutenant Grinnell being with this group, it must be assumed that they came in separately about the same time.

After arriving at Sunchon, a few of the group climbed on some tanks there and went another seven miles south. Most, however, waited for trucks, thawed out water at fires, and found some food. Shriver wrote of Sunchon at that time, the afternoon of 1 December: "All that was left in the town were a few MPs and a scattering of others who had waited for us when the planes had informed them we were up the road. A few jeeps traveled up the road we had come as far as they dared to pick up stragglers and wounded." The trucks came during the afternoon, but so few that the men had to pack into them, 40 to a truck. They were in the trucks about eight hours, and at 3 A.M., 2 December, they finally were delivered to an assembly area at Chunghwa, 15 miles south of Pyongyang. That morning, the exhausted, sleeping men were roused to fall in line to form platoons. In the platoons, where there had been 50 men five days before, there were now from 18 to 30.[94]

The 2nd Engineer Battalion's Fate as Rear Guard

When the 2nd Engineers went to the two hills just south and southwest of the 2nd Division CP about midmorning of 30 November, they went in a defensive role to prevent CCF from reaching the CP from the south and southeast while the 9th Infantry and other units were trying to clear the northern end of the enemy fireblock. As it turned out, they were the rear guard of the 2nd Division in the evening when it was in the fireblock below Kunu-ri. Just what happened to the 2nd Engineers at the end is not known precisely. It is known, however, that it suffered one of the highest rates of battle casualties in all of Eighth Army in the CCF 2nd Phase Offensive. Its authorized strength was 977 men. It numbered only 266 men when a count was made after the 2nd Division withdrawal through the Chinese fireblock on 30 November and 1 December.[95]

The 2nd Engineers stretched in an arc from northwest to northeast in their position near the old 2nd Division CP. When the 23rd Infantry Regiment pulled out posthaste on the Anju road about four miles northwest of them, the 2nd Engineers were the northernmost 2nd Division foot troops still in position. They were also now wide open to attack from all the CCF pouring south across the

Chongchon River and from those enemy who had been attacking the 23rd Regiment from the east, as well as the Chinese that had gathered at the north end of the fireblock, south of them. The story of the 2nd Engineers, as far as it is known, is sketchy. At dark the 2nd Engineers stood alone – no match for the thousands of enemy that now surrounded them on all sides.

Apparently the last contact the 2nd Engineer Battalion commander had with anyone in the 2nd Infantry Division with authority to give any instructions or orders was Division Chief of Staff Gerald G. Epley, about 3 P.M. This was shortly before Epley left the old division CP in the afternoon to go south in a reconnaissance of the Sunchon road condition, from which he did not return to the CP. Epley wrote:

> I was in contact with the commander of the Combat Engineer Bn, whose troops were deployed on the hills surrounding the CP area. They were under continuing enemy pressure. I saw him personally just before the CP rear echelon departed and authorized him to assemble his unit and follow the artillery [this was no change from the earlier division withdrawal order]. Unfortunately, the Engineers never were able to complete their assembly. Darkness and the enemy closed in and many including their commander were captured.[96]

We know from Shriver's account of the withdrawal of Headquarters Company, 9th Infantry, late in the afternoon that some men from the 2nd Engineers were among them, and others joined it later in the hills. Maj. Lawrence B. Farnum, of the Division Artillery, has stated that, when the 503rd and 38th field artillery battalions were halted in the massive road jam and fireblock on the night of 30 November, "a portion of the engineer battalion was in column behind the artillery pieces at the time the column was completely blocked." He gives them credit for being the last troops in the column and for being the division rear guard. These Engineer troops must have been on the southernmost of the two defensive hills the battalion had occupied, and it was from this hill that some escaped. The 2nd Infantry Division War Diary for November 1950 says, "The 2nd Engineer (C) Battalion continued to hold the two critical hills southwest of the old 2nd Division Command Post until well after darkness. Not a man escaped from the northernmost of the two hills." The G-4 Section of the War Diary says further, "The Engineer Bn. was almost completely wiped out as an effective unit and lost over 95% of their T/O&E equipment." Col. Pascal N. Strong, Eighth Army Engineer, writing in the *Military Engineer* two years later said, "In an effort to hold the road open to permit the divisional artillery to get out, the 2nd Engineers were committed as a rear guard. They were hit on all sides. When they finally extricated themselves, half of the officers were killed, or missing, among them the battalion commander, half of the men were casualties, and all of the equipment was gone."[97]

It is interesting that Major Farnum and Lt. Col. Robert J. O'Donnell, commanding officer of the 38th Field Artillery, both wrote letters to the editors of *Combat Forces Journal* to comment on and to correct statements of S. L. A. Marshall in his article "They Fought to Save Their Guns," in the May 1953 issue, which was a part of Marshall's book *The River and the Gauntlet*. In that book Marshall gave the impression that the Division Artillery units were the rear guard of the 2nd Division on the Sunchon road. Major Farnum took the trouble to say specifically that they were not the rear guard but that the 2nd Engineers were behind them.

At least part of the 2nd Engineers, in column behind the 503rd and 38th artillery battalions, must have been the group that joined the 9th Infantry Headquarters Company in the hills southwest of the Pass and walked out with them to Sunchon on 1 December. It is a matter of regret that some of the Engineer survivors did not leave a record or that a report was not assembled soon after the event and made a part of the official records of the 2nd Division. Such a record would have revealed details of this unit's valor below Kunu-ri in the afternoon and evening of 30 November 1950.

Location and Extent of the CCF Fireblock

Perhaps it is desirable to summarize and define rather precisely the location, extent, and nature of the Chinese fireblock southwest of Kunu-ri on 29 November to 1 December 1950 that enmeshed and decimated the 2nd Infantry Division, even though much has been said already in preceding pages about it. Map 12 attempts to illustrate the situation.

When the roadblock and fireblock were first reported to the 2nd Division CP by elements of a Turkish convoy about dawn on 29 November, and when a subsequent MP patrol confirmed its presence, it seemed to be at only one place, about three miles south of the CP. Subsequently, it was learned that the same convoy had first encountered an enemy ambush in the Pass area about four miles farther south. Thus, there were at least two places where enemy had established fireblocks on the Sunchon–Kunu-ri road by dawn of 29 November. There may have been other places and more extensive fireblocks at that time not known or suspected. But on the basis of the Turkish report early on the morning of 29 November, and by subsequent reconnaissance, the 2nd Division estimated that not more than an enemy battalion was involved.

We know from a captured enemy sketch map that two regiments of the CCF 113th Division of the 38th Army were dispatched from Tokchon to establish a fireblock on the Sunchon–Kunu-ri road. But we do not know when they arrived there in full force. It may be that not more than a battalion of enemy were established at the known fireblocks early on 29 November. But it is evident from succeeding events during that day and the next that the enemy constantly reinforced the fireblock, and it is reasonable to assume that, by afternoon of 30 November, two entire regiments of the 113th Division or more had arrived at the scene.

By the time the 2nd Division CP and Headquarters started through the fireblock about midafternoon on 30 November (they reached the beginning of the fireblock before that time but waited as the 38th Infantry attacked through it), there were enemy machine gunners and mortar crews, as well as infantry, dispersed along a six-to-seven-mile stretch of the road running south toward Sunchon from the northern end of the fireblock, which by then had reached to within one mile south of the Division CP. The enemy fireblock for most units during the day and into the early hours of the night ended at the top of the Pass. The Pass marked the divide between the drainage north to the Chongchon River and the drainage south to the Taedong River. The Pass was about 12 road miles south of Kunu-ri and 16 road miles north of Sunchon. At the top of the Pass, the secondary dirt and gravel road, made two-way for most of its distance by earlier work of US Engineer battalions, turned sharply from a southerly direction to the southwest for a distance of a little more than three miles, where it turned south again toward Sunchon.

The village of Karhyon lay on the south side of the road about a mile and a half west of the Pass. About 400 yards west of Karhyon, the road crossed over a stream by a two-way concrete bridge. This bridge had been blown by the time the 2nd Division arrived there in its withdrawal, and the 30-foot wide, 3-foot deep stream had to be crossed in a bypass. The bypass had the banks cut down for vehicular use, apparently the work earlier of a US Army Engineer bulldozer. The bypass bent sharply down to the stream on the north side just short of the blown bridge. On the south side the bypass climbed a sharp ten-foot bank to a series of terraced rice paddies. This south side of the stream, an uphill, rough climb for vehicles, was the worst part of the bypass. Many vehicles could not climb up this incline out of the stream on their own power.

After dark, perhaps by 9 P.M., enemy fire from Karhyon hit on the road near and on the bypass, where many vehicles floundered in the stream as men tried to free them. This enemy mortar and automatic fire became severe as the night passed and as more Chinese arrived. If the enemy in Karhyon are considered part of the fireblock in its later stages, then the fireblock and roadblock after dark would be longer in extent than the six or seven miles usually given for it. In its later stages the enemy fireblock would have to be described as being from nine to ten miles long.

In attempting to gain perspective about the CCF fireblock established on the Kunu-ri–Sunchon road during the night of 28–29 November, it seems clear from an examination of enemy sources that enemy moving westward across country from Tokchon first established the fireblocks. In the late afternoon of 30 November, about an hour or two before dark, the nature of the enemy fireblock seemed to show a marked increase in firepower, especially in mortars and machine guns. Then near dark, and about the same time the 23rd RCT left its rear-guard position and went west on the Anju road, Chinese forces seemed to build up in great numbers as new enemy formations arrived at the fireblock.

In considering the nature of the enemy fireblock below Kunu-ri, it must be recognized that, by 29 November the 2nd Infantry Division had two Chinese armies converging on it, one coming down the valley of the Chongchon and another driving the 25th Infantry Division south before it in an approach to the Chongchon River crossings in the vicinity of Won-ni and Kunu-ri. The 112th and 113th divisions of the Chinese 38th Army were bearing down against its front and left flank, and the 118th and 120th divisions of the Chinese 40th Army were approaching it from the north and northeast. From the Tokchon area and east of Sunchon, another Chinese army was moving against the rear of the 2nd Infantry Division.

Enemy troops that crossed the Chongchon at Won-ni and Kunu-ri in the afternoon and evening of 30 November in large numbers certainly account for the rapid enemy buildup at the northern end of the fireblock after dark set in.

At the same time, large numbers of troops began to show up at the southern end of the fireblock south of the Pass and near Karhyon. By midnight, and after, Chinese were in ever-increasing numbers below Kunu-ri, moving toward Sunchon.[98]

A special word should be said about aerial support for the ground troops at Kunu-ri. As the Chinese 2nd Phase Offensive began rolling back the Eighth Army on the Chongchon River front in late November, the Joint Operations Center of the Fifth Air Force gave more and more of its close ground support missions and some bombing missions to the 2nd Infantry Division, which was fighting a critical, delaying rear-guard action for the entire army. The division held the vital pivotal position where the enemy had to be slowed to prevent a massive flanking movement around the army's eastern, or right, flank after the Chinese routed the ROK II Corps on that flank in the first night and day of their offensive. The 38th Infantry on the extreme right of the division, for instance, received aerial strikes one day that sealed a mine shaft in its rear, where an estimated 600 Chinese soldiers were seen to enter and where it was believed many perished. Another typical strike caught about 50 Chinese soldiers in the open and dropped napalm on them, burning just about all of them to death. The most air strength, however, was assembled and put over the 2nd Division on 30 November when it was trying to break through the Chinese fireblock south of Kunu-ri. General Keiser on 30 November sent an urgent call to the Fifth Air Force for maximum close support for his troops. It was given until darkness came. There appears to have been little air presence, however, for a period in midafternoon.

East of the Kunu-ri–Sunchon road, Fast Carrier Task Force 77 flew in two propeller-plane strikes involving 14 Corsairs and five ADs. They dropped 14 tons of napalm on enemy troop concentrations in the 2nd Division area. To help the Fifth Air Force on 30 November protect the division, Carrier Task Force 77 divided its sorties between X Corps and Eighth Army. It sent armed reconnaissance flights through the big bend of the Taedong River northeast of Sunchon and along the route of the retreating 2nd Division, ready to unload their munitions on any target selected for them by any controller they could reach. Unfortunately, they found the controller situation chaotic in this area, and their potential effectiveness was not used to its maximum. Of four jet flights over the 2nd Division, only one made contact with a controller.

A weak air-controller situation over the 2nd Division on 30 November was due, in part at least, to the fact that enemy advances had forced the Fifth Air Force from its forward staging field at Sinanju, that many of the TACPs with the ground troops had been lost by then to enemy action, that irreplaceable radio-control equipment had been lost, and finally that the Mosquito control planes based at Pyongyang were being evacuated from there. But despite some failures, there was strong air support along the fireblock during daylight hours. Later, General Keiser praised without reservation the aid given by the close support and said that those of his division who escaped might never have made it through the Chinese fireblock without that aerial aid.[99]

There was not universal praise, however, for the air support over the Kunu-ri–Sunchon road on 30 November. Chief of Staff Epley said that, in the two hours or more that he was in the enemy fireblock area in midafternoon to late afternoon, he did not see a single aircraft. Some of the Division Artillery officers had similar observations.[100] It seems to have been a mixed picture in that the air support was excellent when planes were over the fireblock area, but there were some gaps in their presence there.

Many survivors who rode, walked, or scrambled through the Pass at the end of the fireblock have left comments about the ferocity of air attacks in the late afternoon on the Chinese soldiers who occupied the heights above the Pass, a defile about 450 yards long at its highest part where embankments of rocks and dirt rose 50 feet high on either side of a cut. This part of the fireblock was initially free of enemy machine-gun emplacements, but by the latter part of the afternoon enemy observers saw the importance of this strategic spot and rushed enemy gunners and mortar crews to it, emplacing machine guns on either side. It then became a scene of carnage, and the road was repeatedly blocked by knocked-out vehicles and debris. Fighter-bombers hit the Pass repeatedly during this period with napalm, which spilled down the embankment sides to the road; .50-caliber bullets from strafing planes chipped a cascade of rocks and dirt from the sides; and rockets hit with concussion blasts.

Some of those who benefited from the air strikes thought they destroyed more enemy soldiers and gun and mortar positions than the ground troops themselves in trying to force a passage. This may not, however, represent a balanced judgment. Overall, the air cover would certainly have been more effective if there had been adequate Mosquito planes and ground forward controllers with more of the various division serials who could have conveyed target information to the strike planes.

Air strikes on masses of enemy in the flatlands of the Chongchon River valley in the vicinity of Won-ni and Kunu-ri to the northeast of the fireblock area, however, seem to have been devastating to the Chinese caught in the open there, but they came on in spite of it. Air cover here was most telling in delaying enemy forces from engulfing the 2nd Infantry Division sooner than they did.

IX and I Corps Actions on Keiser's Option to Use Anju Road

It may be useful in reflecting on the fate of the 2nd Infantry Division at Kunu-ri to review briefly actions taken by the IX and I corps in connection with proposals made on 29 and 30 November that the 2nd Division might or should use the Anju road through the I Corps sector, not the Kunu-ri–Sunchon road in the IX Corps sector, in withdrawing from the Chongchon River front and Kunu-ri after the CCF fireblock was established on the Sunchon road below the division.

Many of the communications during this period between the two corps and the 2nd Division were verbal over voice radio or telephone and were not made a part of the G-3 Journal entries and therefore were never officially recorded. Also, it must be remembered that, while the I and IX corps records for this period survived, those for the 2nd Infantry Division did not. Records for the division that survived predated the evening of 29 November, when the Service trains were sent out on the Anju road. For the critical day of 30 November, no division records got out. In fact, few were ever entered on paper that day. The records for the 2nd Infantry Division, such as they are, were compiled later from the memory of a few participants. But even so, certain facts can be established with reasonable certainty concerning the roles played by Maj. Gen. John Coulter, IX Corps commander; Maj. Gen. Frank W. Milburn, I Corps commander; and Maj. Gen. Laurence Keiser, 2nd Infantry Division commander. So far as has been determined in this research, Lt. Gen. Walton Walker, Eighth Army commander, played no direct role in the matter of the withdrawal route of the 2nd Infantry Division. Perhaps he should have.

An examination of the I Corps G-3 Journal entries shows that there is only one message recorded on the subject. On 29 November at 7:15 P.M., the IX Corps transmitted a message to I Corps stating that "2nd Division requests use of road from Kunu-ri to Anju." There is no record of a message of approval from I Corps.[101] The IX Corps G-3 Journal contains no entry on the subject, although two officers who were on duty at the time in the IX Corps G-3 Section stated a year later that a 2nd Division request was received and cleared with I Corps and transmitted to the division.[102] We know, however, that I Corps did receive such a message at 7:15 on 29 November.

We have indicated earlier that General Milburn gave General Keiser his approval by telephone to use the Anju-Sinanju road on the evening of 29 November for the movement of the 2nd Division Service trains and such noncombat units as the G-1 Section. C Battery of the 1st Observation Battalion also went out on the Anju road. According to Lt. Col. Maurice C. Holden, 2nd Division G-3, Generals Milburn and Keiser were close personal friends. It appears from all the evidence available that General Milburn was willing to let General Keiser use the Anju-Sinanju-Sukchon road in his I Corps sector, but he was not, of course, in command of the 2nd Division—Maj. Gen. John Coulter was. About noon of 30 November, General Milburn telephoned General Keiser and offered use of the Anju road if he thought it necessary to get his division out. Colonel Epley, the division chief of staff, said General Keiser told him of this conversation immediately after it had taken place. And General Milburn said in early 1952 that he had telephoned General Keiser and offered use of the Anju road to him and that he would hold the 5th RCT roadblocks in place east of Anju until his columns had passed.[103]

In response to the question, "Did the 2nd Infantry Division ever receive clearance from I Corps *through IX Corps* for using the Kunu-ri–Anju road?" Lieutenant Colonel Holden said "The answer is emphatically *No.*" We know, as stated earlier in this chapter, that, about 1 A.M. on 30 November, General Keiser called his principal staff officers together in conference and told them he had just finished a telephone conference with General Coulter of IX Corps and that the latter had ordered him to take the 2nd Division out south on the Kunu-ri–Sunchon road within the zone of IX Corps. General Coulter never countermanded it. In these circumstances, General Keiser believed he was not free to accept General Milburn's offer to use the Anju road.[104]

In summary on this point, one may say that General Keiser never received from his superior commanders, either from General Coulter or from General Walker, authority to use his judgment as to whether he should withdraw his division on the Anju road, nor did he receive an order to do so. Rather, he had a definite order from General Coulter to take the division down the Sunchon road within the IX Corps zone of operations.

General Keiser faced a most difficult task to get his division out on the Sunchon road, given the nature and strength of the CCF fireblock there, without incurring very heavy losses in men and equipment. If the IX Corps commander or the Eighth Army commander had kept fully abreast of developments on 30 November, and had strongly reinforced the Middlesex Battalion and mounted an attack from the south end of the Pass against the CCF fireblock, coincident with a 2nd Division attack from the north, the 2nd Division might have escaped with only a fraction of the loss in men and equipment it sustained. The IX Corps and the Eighth Army had the troops at hand in the vicinity of Sunchon to accomplish this. Available were the British 27th Commonwealth Brigade and about four battalions of the 1st Cavalry Division. Also, the 19th and 21st regiments of the 24th Division were west of the Taedong River near Sunchon on the morning of 30 November and could have been used. None were. Had the Pass been held by friendly troops, one of the most difficult obstacles to the passage of vehicles would have been eliminated.

The IX Corps and the Eighth Army command must be charged with underestimating the critical nature of the situation on the 2nd Division front, of wrongly interpreting its intelligence of the enemy drive against the 2nd Division, and of not using its reserves to help the 2nd Infantry Division. One cannot fairly accuse General Keiser of being responsible for the disaster that overwhelmed the division on 30 November 1950. It was a higher-command failure as well.

2nd Infantry Division Casualties at Kunu-ri

In the chaotic conditions prevailing on 30 November and the loss of all 2nd Infantry Division records for the day, it is impossible to be exact in stating division personnel casualties in the enemy fireblock. Some generalizations are possible. It is known that the casualties were very great—crippling, in fact, for some units—and that the division was declared combat ineffective, having only about half its authorized strength at the beginning of December. For some units, it was possible later to be rather precise in giving casualties for 30 November–1 December.

The 82nd AAA AW Battalion, organic to the 2nd Division, lost 12 officers and 263 men, mostly from its Headquarters Battery, in the action south of Kunu-ri in the enemy fireblock. This battery was caught on the road when CCF fire blew up two ammunition trucks and halted all movement behind them. In the ensuing action the enemy came off nearby ridges and swarmed over the road in one of the few instances this occurred during the period they enforced the fireblock.

Some figures come from units (the 5th Cavalry Regiment and the 1st Cavalry Division) stationed at Sunchon while the 2nd Division was trying to reach that place. General Walker had made the 1st Cavalry Division responsible for covering the withdrawal of the 2nd Division south of Sunchon. A 5th Cavalry Regiment report stated that, on 30 November more than 700 wounded men from the 2nd Division and the Turkish Expeditionary Force passed through its aid stations and evacuation facilities. The 1st Cavalry Division War Diary states that more than 500 casualties passed through its medical and evacuation facilities on 30 November. They did not have enough ambulances to transport these wounded farther to the rear and had to use 2½-ton trucks. In this way, the 1st Cavalry Division moved more than 500 wounded through its Clearing Station in less than 24 hours. It also arranged with Eighth Army to send a train with four coaches from Pyongyang to Sunchon with medical supplies and to assist in evacuation of wounded.[105]

The 2nd Infantry Division G-1 report for November 1950 states that, during the month, the division had 4,935 battle casualties, most of them near Kunu-ri and in the CCF fireblock. This figure includes 1–2 December, as it is impossible to separate those two days from 29–30 November in connection with casualties incurred below Kunu-ri. The division lost 237 officers in this period. The G-1 (Personnel Section) estimated that the division lost one-third of its strength in the period 27 November–2 December. The 2nd Engineer Battalion lost all its field-grade officers and many company-grade officers. The 2nd Division Medical Company lost all but one of its officers. Lt. Col. James Tanner, the 2nd Division G-1 Personnel Officer, gave the figures in tables 4 and 5 for the 2nd Division at the end of November.[106]

The tabulations show that, of the three infantry regiments in the 2nd Division, the 9th Regiment suffered the greatest number of battle casualties in the battles along the Chongchon in late November. The Division Artillery suffered more casualties than any of the infantry regiments. This was caused in large part because of the extremely high casualties in the 6th serial of the withdrawal from Kunu-ri. After the 23rd RCT abandoned its rear-guard role, the remaining two battalions of artillery were badly hurt.

In comparing the two tables, one learns that the 2nd Engineer Battalion suffered far more casualties in relation to its actual strength at the end of November than any other unit of the 2nd Division. The 23rd Infantry Regiment had less than half the casualties of the 38th Infantry, and only a little more than a third those of the 9th Infantry. The 2nd Division was a little more than half strength at the close of the Chongchon River and Kunu-ri battles at the end of November.

One regiment of the division, the 9th Infantry, made a tabulation of its casualties in November, most of them occurring 27–30 November. This count reveals its losses by battalions: 1st Battalion, 428; 2nd Battalion, 331; and 3rd Battalion, 397. These figures do not include the casualties of its special units

Table 4. Casualties for US 2nd Division, as of 30 November 1950

Unit	Battle Casualties	Nonbattle Casualties	Total
9th Inf. Regt.	1,267	207	1,474
23rd Inf. Regt.	485	60	545
38th Inf. Regt.	1,075	103	1,178
Div. Arty.	1,461	68	1,529
2nd Engineer Bn.	561	8	569

or of attached ROKs. It lost 6 battalion staff officers, 11 company commanders, and 5 medical officers.[107] The three rifle battalions of the 9th Infantry had only 35 officers and 751 enlisted men, for a total of 786 men.

Some indication of the number of wounded and severe frostbite cases that had accumulated at Pyongyang, behind the lines, by 30 November is indicated in the fact that, on that day, 740 patients were flown out of Pyongyang for treatment in hospitals farther to the rear or in Japan, that 300 still awaited evacuation, 130 more were at the 8063rd Mobile Army Surgical Hospital, and 300 were at the 25th Medical Clearing Company for evacuation.[108] Not all of these were from the 2nd Division.

The US 25th Infantry Division was adjacent to the 2nd Infantry Division on the west and had heavy fighting and resultant heavy casualties during the Chinese 2nd Phase Offensive. It reported 1,313 battle casualties for November, second highest for the American divisions, but this was only one-fourth those of the 2nd Division.[109] This is a measure of the 2nd Division battle casualties as compared with other American divisions in this ill-fated "drive to the border."

Generally in a military disaster, the losses at first seem larger than a later count reveals. As the days pass following any defeat and loss of a battlefield, stragglers and sometimes groups of men who have had to take to the hills on foot begin to come in and increase the number of survivors. So it was about 30 November at Kunu-ri. During the first week of December, a total of 724 men returned to their units and were removed from the missing-in-action status. After the first week of December, however, there were few further arrivals of stragglers. Just about all who were ever to regain friendly lines from the Kunu-ri action had done so, and it was possible then to make a reasonably accurate count of the losses.[110]

As elements of the 2nd Infantry Division arrived at Sunchon in the late afternoon and night of 30 November they were instructed to go to an assembly area seven miles south of the town. Some personnel did not stop when they got there but continued on to Pyongyang. The bulk of the division, however, stopped at the designated assembly area, where the division had established its CP. There the division received Eighth Army orders for it to go into army reserve and move to the vicinity of Chunghwa. There it would try to regroup if the current front line could be held and stabilized.[111]

Table 5. **Strength of US 2nd Division Units, 30 November 1950**

Unit	Authorized Strength	Actual Strength
9th Inf. Regt.	3,793	1,406
23rd Inf. Regt.	3,793	2,244
38th Inf. Regt.	3,793	1,762
Div. Arty.	3,695	1,970
2nd Engineer Bn.	977	266
Div. Headquarters Co.	190	166
Other, smaller units	2,690	2,455
Total	18,931	10,269

Perhaps the most reliable assessment of the damage suffered by the 2nd Infantry Division at Kunu-ri is set forth in Lt. Col. A. E. Lancaster's report to Colonel Dabney, Eighth Army G-3, on 5 December 1950. Lancaster was a staff officer in the G-3 Section. He was sent to the 2nd Infantry Division on 5 December when it was in the Munsan-ni area, for the purpose of obtaining its latest count on personnel and equipment losses at Kunu-ri. It was thought at that date the count would be reasonably accurate. Lancaster's report on the 2nd Division status showed the following major facts:

> The 2nd Engineer Battalion came out with six vehicles and about 300 men. All field-grade officers were lost.
> The Division Artillery lost all 155-mm howitzers and all but eight 105-mm howitzers. The 38th Field Artillery Battalion had only 65 enlisted men left.
> The 9th Regiment had 1,400 officers and men, a capability of one battalion, plus.
> The 23rd Regiment had 2,200 officers and men, a capability of a regiment, minus.
> The 38th Regiment had 1,600 officers and men, with a recount in the regiment increasing the number to 1,801 men and 51 ROKs, a capability of 1 battalion, plus.
> The 72nd Tank Battalion was in fairly good shape, with 33 tanks.
> The 2nd Battalion, 38th Infantry, had lost all company commanders.
> The 3rd Battalion, 38th Infantry, had lost its entire battalion staff and the battalion commander was seriously wounded and evacuated.
> The Turkish Brigade had a strength of 4,118 officers and men. It reported a loss of 68 men killed, 238 wounded, and 630 missing in action.[112]

2nd Infantry Division Equipment Losses at Kunu-ri

The loss of the 2nd Division in artillery pieces at Kunu-ri was easily the heaviest of any action in the Korean War. Three artillery battalions—the 503rd, the 38th, and the 15th—lost all their pieces. The 15th Artillery Battalion, attached to the 23rd Infantry Regiment, left its artillery in position but destroyed vital parts of the firing mechanism when the 23rd Regiment hastily broke contact with the enemy and withdrew its personnel about 4:30 or 5:00 P.M. west on the Anju road from the hills southwest of Kunu-ri. In the enemy fireblock on the Kunu-ri–Sunchon road, the 38th Field Artillery Battalion abandoned its howitzers. The 503rd Artillery Battalion, likewise, abandoned or lost all its howitzers on the withdrawal road when the bypass ford at the blown bridge near Karhyon became impassable near midnight, 30 November. The 37th Field Artillery Battalion got out with eight howitzers. Of the five artillery battalions with the 2nd Infantry Division, only the 17th with its 8-inch howitzers, and the first of the artillery battalions in the march order through the enemy fireblock, got out with nearly all its guns. Table 6 gives the artillery strengths and losses of guns at Kunu-ri, 30 November, as best as can be determined.

The 82nd AAA AW Battalion's M19s and M16s were interspersed, as described earlier, in the march order of the division column. They were without any doubt the most effective defense weapon in the division column in going through the enemy fireblock. It seems appropriate to list the commanding officers of the several batteries:

> 82nd AAA AW Bn.–Lt. Col. Walter Killilae, CO
> A Battery–Capt. Edgar L. Casey, CO; Sgt. Lewis E. Chaney
> B Battery–1st Lt. C. T. Hathaway, CO; Sgt. Bobby F. Dill
> C Battery–Capt. Robert Adams, CO
> D Battery–Capt. Simon Stevens, CO

One eyewitness of the scene told of finding the entire crew of an M16 dead beside their vehicle on the road and more than "500 dead CCF on approaches" to it. While this is certainly an exaggerated count or estimate of enemy dead, the impression that the M16 killed a lot of the CCF before its crew were overrun and killed may be considered valid. One M19 with its two Bofors automatic 40-mm guns with the 38th Infantry was credited with knocking out three enemy machine guns in the fireblock.[113]

Other heavy weapons and equipment losses at Kunu-ri included 40 to 50 percent of all signal equipment, 45 percent of crew-served weapons (the Engineer Battalion lost 90 percent of its crew-served weapons), and 30 percent of all vehicles. The Turkish Brigade lost 50 percent of its artillery, 90 percent of its signal equipment, and 90 percent of its vehicles.[114] The 2nd Infantry Division and Eighth Army finally settled on the number of men lost in the division at Kunu-ri –killed, wounded, and missing–as 4,037. The 2nd Division at the end of the Kunu-ri action was given an overall capability of one regimental combat team.[115]

Maj. Gen. Laurence B. Keiser–Scapegoat?

Maj. Gen. Laurence B. Keiser was 55 years old when he rode and walked through the CCF fireblock on 30 November, fighting his way more like an infantry pri-

Table 6. US 2nd Division Artillery Losses at Kunu-ri

Unit	Weapon	Strength	Pieces Lost
15th FA Bn.	105-mm howitzer	18 guns, in 3 firing batteries	18
37th FA Bn.	105-mm howitzer	18 guns, in 3 firing batteries	10
38th FA Bn.	105-mm howitzer	18 guns, in 3 firing batteries	18
503rd FA Bn.	155-mm howitzer	18 guns, in 3 firing batteries	18
17th FA Bn.	8-inch howitzer	12 guns, in 3 firing batteries	1
82nd AAA AW Bn.	M19 (dual-40s)	–	23
	M16 (quad-50s)	–	26
Total lost			114

Source: The number of weapons in the artillery battalion is based on Goodrich, letter to author, 16 Mar. 1982, giving strength as of 24 Nov. 1950. The losses are based on Lancaster, Report, and the known loss of one 8-inch howitzer that turned over in a ravine nearing the blown bridge, killing ROK troops riding on it. The count does not include artillery lost by the Turkish Brigade.

vate than the commanding general of a division. After the 2nd Infantry Division command staff left its CP six miles south of Kunu-ri and started through the CCF fireblock toward Sunchon in the afternoon of 30 November it lost communication with just about all its subordinate units, and there was no command control of the division column. It was largely a case of every unit, and often every individual, for itself or himself. In this chaotic afternoon, General Keiser showed personal courage equal to that of anyone in the division, over which he no longer had any control. Was he to blame for the sorry situation of and the thousands of casualties in this exhausted combat division that had covered Eighth Army in its exposed extremity for the past five days and nights? This question is interesting, if unanswerable.[116]

On 30 November General Keiser was not in the best of condition. He suffered that day and later from a bad cold. On 28 November, according to Capt. William E. Manning, General Keiser seemed to be in excellent health. Two days later, when the division was preparing to fight its way through the enemy fireblock, Manning said Keiser had a bad cold and was bundled up in a heavy parka. Others who saw him at different times in the fireblock said he appeared to have a heavy cold and was using a bandanna handkerchief frequently. He loaded his jeep to the limit of its capacity with wounded as he went through the fireblock. His jeep acquired seven small-arms and machine-gun bullet holes, but remained operational, in getting through the fireblock. Many persons saw General Keiser using his old Springfield 1903 bolt-action rifle in returning enemy fire at the frequent stops he made in the fireblock.

At the pass, General Keiser was on foot most of the time, trying to find soldiers he could organize into some kind of effective resistance. He walked down the south side and then turned back toward the top. By now he was very tired. One story has it that he failed to lift his booted foot high enough to clear the body of what appeared to be a dead soldier in the road and accidentally stubbed his toe against it. The supposed corpse jerked upright and cursed the man who had stumbled against him. General Keiser, astonished, said, "My friend, I'm sorry," and continued on up the road to the point where he had left his jeep.

Colonel Epley saw General Keiser at Sunchon when he arrived there and reported to the 2nd Division CP on the evening of 30 November. Epley wrote of that meeting, "One of the first questions I asked General Keiser when I reported to him at Sunchon after reaching the Division assembly area was—Did you authorize the 23rd RCT to withdraw via the Anju route? His answer was an emphatic 'No!'"[117]

The next day, 1 December, Capt. Perry Davis, the division information officer, saw General Keiser. At that time Davis said Keiser had a bad cold. In the following days, Captain Manning said Keiser had a bad cough, was quite hoarse, and was often blowing his nose. Colonel Carle, the division surgeon, recommended that General Keiser go to a hospital. According to the Chief of Staff's Journal in the 2nd Division Command Report for December 1950, an entry at 6:30 P.M. on 5 December said that General Keiser was taken to a field hospital because of a "serious illness." Brig. Gen. Loyal M. Haynes assumed acting command of the division. He held this post until 1:45 P.M. on 7 December, when Maj. Gen. Robert B. McClure arrived to take command of the division.[118]

The Eighth Army Command Report on 5 December, in its G-3 Section, carried its first official record that General Keiser was being evacuated from Korea to Japan for treatment of a cold influenza and "pneumonia" and was being replaced by Maj. Gen. Robert B. McClure as commanding general of the 2nd Infantry Division.[119] General Keiser did not consider himself that ill and always thought the charge to evacuate him for medical reasons to Japan for treatment of pneumonia was nothing more than an excuse to relieve him of command of the 2nd Division because of what happened to it south of Kunu-ri.

When the 2nd Division had withdrawn south as far as the Han River in early December, it set up its CP at Yongdong-po on the south bank, opposite Seoul. There, on 6 December General Keiser received what was said to be an army order to go to Japan for medical and hospital treatment. He left the next day for Japan. The official word passed out was that he had pneumonia. He never returned to the division. There is no official record that he was relieved of command of the 2nd Division, and there appears to be no adverse reprimand or other comment from the Eighth Army commander about him in the records.

The fact is, however, that Maj. Gen. Leven Allen, Eighth Army chief of staff, on General Walker's orders, went to Yongdong-po and verbally relieved Keiser of command of the 2nd Division. Lt. Gen. Walton Walker, therefore, relieved General Keiser of command of the 2nd Division, apparently believing him responsible for the disaster that overtook the division below Kunu-ri on 30 November 1950.[120]

Some years later, after General Keiser's death in 1969, S. L. A. Marshall, an analyst for a private firm that contracts with the military to make operations studies for it, published a newspaper article dealing with General Keiser's relief from command of the 2nd Division. Marshall was at Yongdong-po at the time of Keiser's relief from command in December 1950, and was acquainted with Keiser. His article purports to be a summary of what General Keiser told him immediately after Keiser visited Eighth Army Headquarters in Seoul after he had learned that he must report to a hospital in Japan for treatment. Keiser was angry at the time, Marshall said, and felt that he was being made a scapegoat. He walked into Army Chief of Staff Maj. Gen. Leven Allen's office and said to Allen, "You can see that I do not have pneumonia." Allen replied by asking, "You are going to comply with an order, aren't you?" Keiser answered, "Yes, I'll go along with it because it is an order; but I want to make it plain that my health is not the reason." Allen then said, "Gen. Walker will take care of you with a job around this headquarters." Keiser allegedly shouted his reply that he would have nothing to do with such a job, in a voice loud enough to make sure that Walker, in the next room, would hear it. Marshall concludes his article speculating that perhaps not Walker but someone else in a higher headquarters wanted Keiser removed from command of the division.[121] No evidence has surfaced to support Marshall's speculation.

After General Keiser had been in Japan for a week and had recovered somewhat, he visited Mrs. Margaret Almond, wife of Gen. Edward M. Almond, the X Corps commander. The Keisers and Almonds had been longtime friends. General Keiser told Mrs. Almond about being relieved of his command in Korea and commented about the terrible ordeal of his division. At one point he wept openly. He said one of the worst things for him personally was when he had to take the dead body of one of his aides (probably his bodyguard, who had been killed) from his jeep in the fireblock and lay it at the side of the road south of Kunu-ri to make room for a badly wounded sergeant, whom he carried through to safety.[122]

When General Keiser was ordered to Japan for hospital treatment, the question arose as to who would be in temporary command of the 2nd Division. Maj. Gen. Joseph S. Bradley, the assistant division commander, telephoned higher authority for information, probably IX Corps, where General Coulter presumably referred the matter to Eighth Army, and received back the answer that the senior officer in the division should assume command. Brig. Gen. Loyal M. Haynes, commander of the 2nd Division Artillery, was the senior officer, and he assumed command of the division temporarily.[123]

It is clear that General Keiser never recovered from being relieved of command of the 2nd Infantry Division for what he believed was a false and unwarranted cause that tarnished his reputation thereafter. Perhaps Keiser's feelings about Kunu-ri are best reflected in what he said to Colonel Epley. The latter wrote, "In the days and years following Kunu-ri I saw and conversed with Gen. Keiser on several occasions. His attitude concerning Kunu-ri became and remained, 'It is over—it is done, Let it lie.'"[124]

As stated earlier, Maj. Gen. John B. Coulter of IX Corps and Lt. Gen. Walton H. Walker of Eighth Army must share a large burden of responsibility for what happened to the 2nd Infantry Division at Kunu-ri. They did not send an adequate force of the available troops from the Sunchon area to attack the Chinese fireblock area from the south on 30 November and to help the exhausted 2nd Division. While the Middlesex Battalion of the 27th British Commonwealth Brigade was under orders to attack north on 30 November for this purpose, it never did so. It had demonstrated on the previous day that it could not even reach the southern end of the Pass. Higher command at that point should have reassessed the situation. It had added reinforcements at hand on the morning of the thirtieth to join in the attack north to meet the 2nd Infantry Division.

Pondering the question of why Kunu-ri happened and where and how errors of command judgment were made, one keeps coming back to a precept that General Ridgway stated several times, that in battle, "the place for a commander, certainly from Regiment up through Army, is where the crisis is, anticipating it if possible, but if not, then getting there as quickly as possible after it has developed."[125] He also believed there was seldom more than one real crisis at a given time. The crisis for Eighth Army, and for its subordinate 2nd Infantry Division in covering the final stages of the army withdrawal from contact with the Chinese forces along the Chongchon River on 30 November 1950, was along the 2nd Infantry Division withdrawal route from Kunu-ri to Sunchon. There was no other crisis at that time for Eighth Army—all the other subordinate units of the army had broken contact with the enemy and executed successful withdrawals or were in the final stages of doing so. Only the 2nd Infantry Division, after covering the right flank of the army and the successful withdrawal of the army units in the center and on the left, was in danger in its own efforts to break contact with the Chinese and then to withdraw successfully. There was the crisis for the 2nd Division, the IX Corps, and the Eighth Army on 30 November. Applying Ridgway's dictum for battle leadership, one may ask where

General Coulter of IX Corps and General Walker of Eighth Army were on that day of crisis, 30 November 1950, and what they did to help the 2nd Division, the major army unit enmeshed in the crisis.

General Coulter closed his CP at Happacham (Unhung-ni), four miles west of Kunu-ri on the Anju road, at 1:30 P.M. on 29 November, and opened his new CP at Chasan, six miles south of Sunchon at the same time. His CP remained at Chasan until 2 P.M. the next day, 30 November, when he closed it and opened his new CP at the same time at Pyongyang. There in Pyongyang, he conferred with Generals Walker and Church at 4:30 P.M. Just when on the thirtieth Coulter went to Pyongyang is not known, but presumably it must have been, at the latest, in the early afternoon of that day, because he opened his CP there at 1:30 P.M. In the afternoon of the thirtieth and that night, he was nowhere near the place of crisis and battle—the enemy fireblock and roadblock on the road from Kunu-ri to Sunchon. He was in Pyongyang.

General Walker's movements during the last days of November 1950 are hard to trace. He kept a sort of Advance CP near that of I Corps and the 24th Division in the Anju-Sinanju area. He probably left that CP when I Corps departed from its CP in Sinanju at 8:20 A.M. on 30 November. General Walker apparently left in a liaison plane and flew over the 2nd Division withdrawal route from Kunu-ri to Sunchon on the thirtieth, since his pilot told Colonel Stebbins, Eighth Army G-4, about it later. Walker's reaction to the 2nd Division on that occasion has already been stated. Walker apparently went on to Pyongyang to the Eighth Army main CP there. Just when he arrived is not known, but he certainly was there by 4:30 P.M., when he conferred with Generals Coulter and Church. Walker apparently did nothing on the thirtieth to help the 2nd Division, even though from the air he had seen that it was in trouble.

Neither General Coulter nor General Walker, the superior commanders responsible for taking action to assist one of their subordinate units in its crisis, did anything on 30 November or that night, nor is there evidence that they gave any special thought to it. Where did the greater failure lay? With General Keiser in whatever mistakes he may have made in trying to carry out General Coulter's orders, or in the indifference or carelessness of superior command in failing to keep on top the developing situation with regard to the 2nd Infantry Division and to intercede with whatever force was necessary to save it from disaster? In judging General Keiser one must not forget also that he never knew until after the event that his rear-guard RCT did not carry out its planned mission in his division movement.

15. Back to Pyongyang

When the stragglers from the 2nd Infantry Division arrived at Sunchon on 1 December and were carried on to Pyongyang and points south during the next few days, all other units of Eighth Army were already on their way to Pyongyang, the North Korean capital, except for some 1st Cavalry Division and 27th British Brigade units covering the army east flank at Taedong River crossings south of Sunchon. Although General Walker had told General MacArthur in Tokyo on the night of 28–29 November that he expected the army to hold a line north and east of Pyongyang and to retain control of the North Korean capital, he made no effort to do so when the moment for decision arrived. General Walker did not officially order the evacuation of Pyongyang until 3 December. But from 30 November on, he and his senior staff officers knew that no battle would be fought north of the city or in its vicinity and that the city would not be held.

The continuous movement of troops through and south of Pyongyang during and after 30 November, and the destruction and abandonment of supplies there and elsewhere built up day after day into a hectic rush to get south. There was no indication of an intent to stop, face about, and confront the enemy. And there was none until Eighth Army reached the line of the Han and Imjin rivers, 20 air miles north of Seoul and 100 miles south of Pyongyang. This was in fact the old defense line between the two Koreas, virtually on the 38th Parallel. In effect, the movement south from the Chongchon River front that was in full swing on 30 November carried Eighth Army south without pause until it had abandoned practically all of North Korea.

Tokyo-Washington Jitters at the End of November 1950

A short digression from events at the battlefront in Korea is necessary to put in perspective the state of mind in the military and political high commands in Tokyo and Washington, caused by the alarming course of events in Korea. Even at Pusan, several hundred miles to the south of the battlefront, the course of events on the Chongchon was reflected by 30 November. There all ships loading received orders to stop. LSTs and other resupply vessels that were discharging cargo were ordered to hasten their unloading and to stand by for further

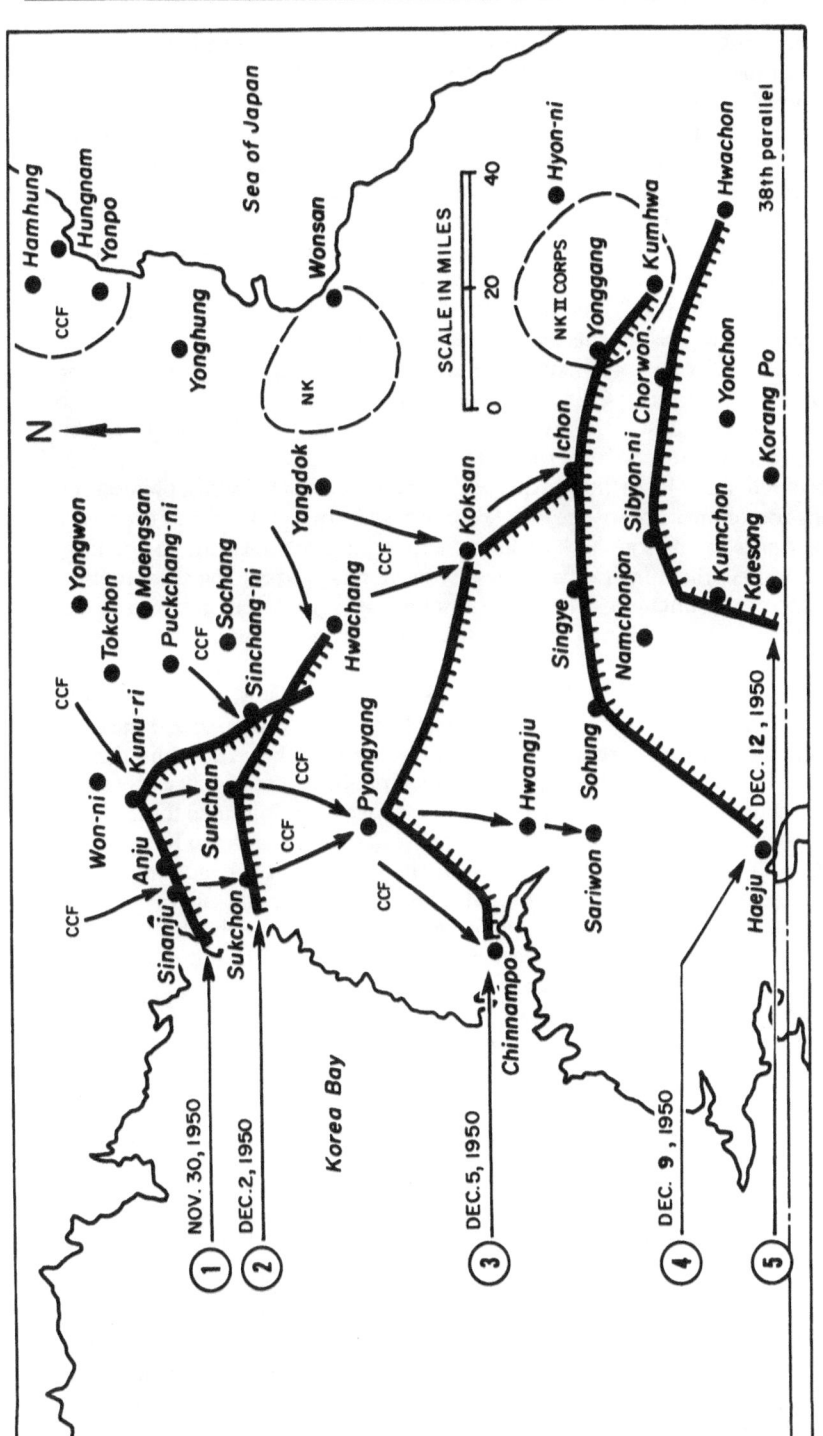

Map 13. Eighth Army withdrawal positions, 30 November–12 December 1950.

instructions. Evacuation of Eighth Army obviously was already in the minds of Eighth Army transportation officials and higher authorities.[1]

A series of messages on 30 November between General MacArthur and the Joint Chiefs of Staff reflected some of these thoughts. General MacArthur sent two messages that day to the Joint Chiefs in which he said that Chinese reinforcements from the Manchurian border could reach the battlefront in Korea in two night marches and result in a heavy and continuous buildup of their forces numbering several hundred thousands of additional troops. He added that "it is quite evident that the 8th Army will successively have to continue to replace to the rear." This message indicates that MacArthur as early as 30 November contemplated the evacuation of Pyongyang.

In an earlier message that day he said that the X Corps in Northeast Korea had tied up six to eight Chinese divisions that otherwise would have been available for the attack against Eighth Army and that the Chinese could not safely penetrate southward in the west until the threat of the X Corps to their eastern flank had been nullified. MacArthur further said that any concept "of actual physical combination of the forces of the 8th Army and X Corps in a practically continuous line across the narrow neck of Korea is quite impracticable due to the length of that line, the numerical weakness of our forces, and the logistical problems due to the mountainous divide which splits such a front from north to south."[2] Yet such a line was formed later and at a wider part of the peninsula on a weaker defense line.

The Joint Chiefs of Staff replied the same day to MacArthur that his plans "are causing increasing concern here." The Joint Chiefs expressed fear the enemy could move strong forces between the X Corps and Eighth Army, and therefore the X Corps and Eighth Army should be brought together sufficiently so that their actions could be coordinated. Their message then continued to clarify what they considered the mission given to the Far East Commander in Korea, saying, "Regarding the mission assigned you by the UN the entire region northeast of the waist of Korea should be ignored except for strategic and tactical considerations relating to the security of your command."[3] (A later chapter will discuss what might have been accomplished if the UN command had seized and established a defense line at the waist of Korea.)

The next day, 1 December, General MacArthur said his lack of authority to act against the Chinese north of the border in Manchuria was "an enormous handicap without precedent in military operations." When asked about the use of atomic bombs, MacArthur replied it would be "inappropriate at this time" for him to comment on their use in Korea.[4]

Clement Atlee and Truman Meet on the Atomic Bomb Issue

The jitters now building in Washington as a result of the disastrous news from Korea is shown best by a remark of President Truman to reporters at a press conference on 30 November. He said the use of the atomic bomb was under consideration. This comment produced a shock, and nowhere more than in England. Many observers and listeners erroneously jumped to the conclusion that President Truman meant to leave the decision to General MacArthur as to how and when to use the bomb. That same day, 30 November, Clement Atlee, the British prime minister, asked to be received for a visit to Washington to discuss with Truman the meaning of events in Korea and the potentials in the future course of the war. The conference was arranged promptly. It was to begin on 4 December. On the third, South Korean Defense Minister Shin Sung Mo added his voice to the call for use of the atomic bomb. He said its use immediately was necessary to prevent his country from being conquered. He went as far as to avow that the people of South Korea would rather perish in an atomic holocaust than become slaves of the Chinese Communists.

Before he left England, Atlee conferred with leaders of the Commonwealth nations and with the French premier and foreign minister. In the United States the secretary of defense, the secretary of state, the Joint Chiefs of Staff, and presidential advisor Averell Harriman met to discuss their position and advise the president on his forthcoming talks with the British prime minister. The British were known to oppose General MacArthur's Korean proposals, which they feared might widen the war. If the British withdrew support for the Korean War at the UN, no one could foretell the consequences.

At the time, General Collins, Army chief of staff and agent for the Joint Chiefs of Staff for the Korean War, was in Korea assessing the situation. The consulting group decided on 3 December that it would not submit recommendations to President Truman until General Collins returned from his trip. It was known to the group and to President Truman that Prime Minister Atlee was strongly opposed to use of the atom bomb before consulting with him and believed that it should not be used in China. On 4 December, the day President Truman and Prime Minister Atlee began their talks, the State Department and the Joint Chiefs of Staff sent to the secretary of defense their view that the president should not make a commitment to Mr. Atlee restricting American freedom of action in using the atomic bomb.

Serious differences developed between the State Department and the Defense Department on a proposal to Prime Minister Atlee as to the course of action in Korea. The Defense Department considered the State Department proposals too rigid and binding on freedom of action of the military for protection of its forces in Korea, and too specific in proposed lines for withdrawal, including the possibility of withdrawing from Korea to Japan. The Defense Department insisted that the Chinese must not be offered too much for too little and that the UN commander (General MacArthur) must not be restricted operationally. The Joint Chiefs of Staff found the State Department proposals unacceptable. They revised the State Department proposals to embody their own. President Truman agreed with the view of the Joint Chiefs of Staff.

President Truman, Secretary of Defense George C. Marshall, Secretary of State Dean G. Acheson, Prime Minister Clement Atlee, and the British ambassador to the United States met at the White House on 4 December and daily thereafter through 9 December, six days in all. Truman told Atlee that, if the enemy proposed a cease-fire, the United States would accept it but would pay nothing for it. If a cease-fire was not proposed and the Chinese continued their offensive, the United States would fight as hard as it could. After the meeting on 7 December, President Truman and Prime Minister Atlee agreed there would be no voluntary evacuation of Korea in the current conditions.

On his return from Korea, General Collins reviewed with the two heads of government on 9 December the military situation in Korea as he judged it to be, saying he thought the UN forces there could take care of themselves without further heavy losses. In the end, the complex negotiations between Truman and Atlee ended with agreement that, if solutions could not be found for a peaceful settlement of the Korean, Formosa, and Indochina problems in Asia, the American and British troops would fight in Korea until they were forced out. Prime Minister Atlee went home with the understanding that the atomic bomb would not be used unless an unforeseen and wholly disastrous situation should develop.[5] General MacArthur received résumés of these discussions as they occurred, but it is doubtful whether many on his Far East Command Staff knew of them in any detail, and probably only some press accounts reached a few persons in Korea.

MacArthur Faces a Lack of Reinforcements

By 1 December the stated objective of Eighth Army was to disengage from enemy on all its fronts and to move rapidly south out of contact. By the end of the day it had done this, except for a few patrols and one or two larger-unit contacts on its eastern, or right, flank. On 28 November General MacArthur had queried the Joint Chiefs about picking up Generalissimo Chiang Kai-shek's offer in June 1950 to send Chinese Nationalist troops from Formosa to help repel the North Korean invasion. General MacArthur now wanted to raise the size of the Nationalist Chinese contingent to 50,000 or more, rather than the 33,000 Chiang Kai-shek had originally offered. The Joint Chiefs of Staff rejected this proposal, feeling that it would create more problems in the UN, and particularly with British allies, than it would be worth. The only other source of reinforcements for the UN forces in Korea in this crisis, other than relatively small UN contingents that had been pledged, would have to come from the United States. In view of the need for immediate and rather sizable reinforcements in infantry and supporting arms in Korea to confront the victorious Chinese and a rapidly growing reorganization of the North Korean Army that was expected to join the Chinese at the front in the near future, the status of United States Army reserves at this time came under review at the Pentagon.

On 1 December, Gen. Charles L. Bolte, acting chief of staff, G-3, Department of the Army, had sent to Gen. Matthew B. Ridgway, acting chief of staff for administration, a memorandum outlining the US Army's capabilities. It listed approximately 220,000 current forces available in Korea to the commander in chief, Far East, of which 153,000 men were in Army forces, with an augmentation of 23,000 ROK troops; the 1st Marine Division, numbering 25,000 men; and about 20,000 in other UN allies contingents. The United States Army units in Korea, with 153,000 men, were 65,000 under strength. The 220,000 current forces, however, did not include the 121,000 men in the ROK Army. These were available to General MacArthur as UN commander. The total, therefore, available to him would be 342,000 rather than 220,000.

General Bolte listed the reinforcement capabilities as follows:

January 1951–82nd Airborne Division
June 1951–Two National Guard Divisions (43rd and 28th)
July 1951–Two National Guard Divisions (45th and 40th)
August 1951–4th Infantry Division
September 1951–2nd Armored Division; one RCT of the 11th Airborne Division

To get these forces equipped and combat ready would deplete the reserve and take equipment items from reserve components. There would be no further divisions available until August 1952. Thereafter, beginning in November 1952, the Department of the Army could have two additional divisions ready monthly.[6]

From this inventory of US force availability, only one division could be sent to reinforce the UN forces in Korea within a month, and then it would be mid-1951 before any other Army reinforcements could be sent to Korea–not a happy prospect for the commander, Far East, or the commanding general in Korea, to contemplate in the crisis of early December 1950. In effect, it meant that, whatever happened in the immediate future, the American forces in Korea–an understrength and battle-weary force–could not be reinforced and that they would have to get along with what they had.

Eighth Army Falls Back on Pyongyang, 1–3 December

The major objective of the initial phase of Eighth Army's and the UN retreat from the Chongchon River front and of breaking contact with the enemy on 1 December and the week that followed was to protect the Pyongyang-Seoul highway, its MSR from South Korea. While the army was engaged in its initial movements to accomplish this purpose, the 187th Airborne RCT guarded the approaches to Pyongyang and the ROK 2nd and 5th divisions were placed in positions flanking the Pyongyang-Seoul corridor on the east.[7] The two ROK divisions were sent to the so-called Iron Triangle area east of the MSR to deal primarily with enemy guerrilla forces that infested that area northeast of Seoul, far behind Eighth Army's front line, and that threatened to cut or harass the army's main withdrawal route. In a subsequent chapter more will be said about the increasing guerrilla threat behind Eighth Army.

On 1 December, the combat-effective units of Eighth Army were the 24th and 25th Infantry and 1st Cavalry divisions, the ROK 1st Division, the 27th and 29th British Commonwealth brigades, and the 187th Airborne RCT. The 2nd Infantry Division and the Turkish Brigade, as well as the ROK II Corps, were considered combat ineffective. In the ROK II Corps, the 7th Division on 1 December reportedly had 6,793 men, and the 8th Division only 5,761 men.

The Eighth Army line on 1 December started at Sukchon on the west, about 50 miles north of Pyongyang, and ran generally east through Sunchon to a point about five miles east of the town to control the crossings of the Taedong River in that vicinity. On this line from west to east were the 12th and 15th regiments of the ROK 1st Division, with the 11th Regiment in reserve; the 27th, 24th, and 35th regiments of the 25th Division; the 1st Cavalry's 8th Regiment, in the vicinity of Songchon; the 5th Cavalry Regiment, northwest of Sunchon; and the 7th Cavalry Regiment, east of Sunchon in the vicinity of Unsan-ni. Remaining elements of the ROK 6th Division were on the left of the 7th Cavalry Regiment and attached to it. The British 27th Commonwealth Brigade was on the right (east) of the 7th Cavalry Regiment on the extreme right flank of the Eighth Army line. The 24th Infantry Division was in Eighth Army reserve. Also under Eighth Army control were the 187th Airborne RCT, the Netherlands Battalion, the French Battalion, and the Thailand 10th Expeditionary Force—all of the UN contingents had recently landed at Pusan and were on their way north to join Eighth Army.

In the next two weeks Eighth Army withdrew south 120 miles to the Imjin River line, north of Seoul. During that time there was no contact with the Chinese after 3 December, and American intelligence concerning the CCF was spotty and incomplete. It depended entirely on aerial observation and on Korean civilian reports.

Army engineers had by now reconnoitered the routes south that Eighth Army could take in its withdrawal from North Korea. Their report, studied and confirmed by the G-3 section of the army, reached the conclusion that only two routes were feasible. One would proceed from Pyongyang through Chunghwa, Sariwon, Namchonjom to Kaesong, and hence to Seoul; the other would go south to the port of Haeju and then east to Kaesong. Any other route, it was decided, would be too far to the east and would have to pass through North Korean guerrilla country, and hence was not safe. As it developed, almost the entire army took the main road south through Sariwon and Namchonjom to Kaesong.[8]

The elements of the 2nd Infantry Division that came through the CCF fireblock north of Sunchon during the night of 30 November were still coming into Sunchon after daylight of 1 December, and were the northernmost combat troops of Eighth Army still moving south, except for the 1st Cavalry Division, which was holding a defensive position around Sunchon, and the Middlesex Battalion north of Sunchon. The movement of the 38th Infantry Regiment, 2nd Division, survivors may be taken as typical of the rest of the division in leaving the battle area. At 8 A.M. on 1 December the 38th Infantry received orders to move from Sunchon to Chunghwa, 18 miles south of Pyongyang. The next day orders came to continue 125 road miles farther south to Munsan-ni, on the south bank of the Imjin River. The 2nd Division and the Turkish Brigade hastened south to the Seoul area in a practically nonstop motorized movement, where they were to reorganize (and the 2nd Division take in replacements) and to reequip to become combat effective again as quickly as possible. The 38th Infantry, leading the way, closed at Munsan-ni on 4 December.[9]

The British 27th Brigade and the 1st Cavalry Division were the last of Eighth Army, on its right flank, to have combat contact with the Chinese. After the trickle of soldiers from the 2nd Division coming through Sunchon had ended in the afternoon of 1 December, the Middlesex Battalion moved south to Chasan, six miles south of Sunchon, where it joined the Australian Battalion. That afternoon Eighth Army, acting through the IX Corps, attached the British 27th Brigade to the 1st Cavalry Division for operations. The next day the Australian Battalion moved ten miles southeast from Chasan to defend a bridge that was

Eighth Army troops pass Korean refugees as they withdraw from Sunchon to regroup at Pyongyang, 1 December 1950. National Archives 111-SC 355303

being built across the upper Taedong River at Apa-ri, as it is shown on some maps. This bridge and the road over it were expected to serve as the escape route of parts of the 1st Cavalry Division and the British 27th Brigade. CCF forces were already on the hills north of the river when the Australians arrived there. In an attack on the enemy, the Australians dislodged the CCF, but an enemy buildup took place during the night. Other CCF had moved around and behind nearby 1st Cavalry Division troops and forced them to withdraw westward. A heavy snow fell during the night of 2–3 December. Between 3 and 4 A.M. on 3 December the Australians withdrew south across the river at Apa-ri. When the Australians left Apa-ri and the Taedong River, they moved south 94 miles in 12 hours to Hayu-ri. Reportedly they did not like this "bugging out," as they called it.[10]

The Argyll Battalion of the British 27th Brigade, meanwhile, attached to the 7th Cavalry Regiment, was on a flank-guard mission east of Unsan-ni. There they marched and countermarched through the hills, encountering no enemy, for a period of 36 hours. They lost some tanks and troop carriers with thrown

Troops of the British Eighth Kings Royal Irish Hussars on top of a Centurion tank cover the withdrawal of UN troops from the Pyongyang area, 3 December 1950. National Archives 111-SC 354735

tracks, and one tank was destroyed when it became wedged in a narrow place in the road. The Argylls derisively called this period "the Cavalry Canter." The British 27th Brigade, under orders, withdrew after these misadventures to Pyongyang. On the evening of 3 December it crossed the Taedong River near Pyongyang, and on 4 December passed through the newly arrived British 29th Brigade, which was holding the Taedong bridgehead for troop withdrawals from the north. From Pyongyang the 27th Brigade continued on south 112 air miles to Uijongbu, which it reached on 11 December.[11]

The 1st Cavalry Division Breaks Enemy Contact on Right Flank

On 1 December the only Eighth Army contact with the CCF was on its right flank, where the 1st Cavalry Division and the attached Argyll Battalion were deployed to guard against a threatened strong enemy push around that flank. The enemy had at least one roadblock south of Songchon and above Kangdong, about 30 road miles northeast of Pyongyang. There were continuing reports of enemy movements on the lateral (east-west) road from Yangdok to Songchon in the central part of the peninsula, indicating probable enemy use of the road from Wonsan on the east coast west toward Pyongyang. This was in the area often referred to as the waist of Korea. There was no evidence on 1 December that the CCF were trying to close rapidly on the Eighth Army rear, as they had done in the previous several days when they had shown a strong desire to close in combat, even in daytime, on the army front along the Chongchon. In its right flank-guard deployment, the 1st Cavalry Division had all three of its regiments in defensive positions east and south of Sunchon, together with the attached 27th British Brigade and its three infantry battalions, the Australians, the Middlesex, and the Argylls. Also, the remnants of the ROK 6th Division were in positions to help hold this flank while the rest of Eighth Army moved south out of the battle zone. On 1 December, one battalion of the 8th Cavalry was still near Sunchon, and two battalions of the 8th Cavalry Regiment had firefights with CCF in the vicinity of Sunchon.

During the night of 30 November–1 December, CCF drove Korean refugees into the 8th Cavalry lines at Songchon and then followed them with some of their own troops. This CCF force of approximately 50 men captured the 8th Cavalry roadblock at Songchon, but an American platoon attack recaptured it at 5:30 A.M. on 1 December. Enemy soldiers during the night occupied high ground around the town, and the 8th Cavalry defenders, low on ammunition, decided during the day to abandon it. The two battalions retreated to Kangdong to the southwest. This withdrawal from Songchon was unauthorized by higher authority. At 3 P.M. in the afternoon, when Eighth Army learned of the withdrawal, it directed the 1st Cavalry Division to order the two battalions of the 8th Cavalry to return to Songchon, retake the town, and hold it. Soon after daylight on 2 December the two battalions regained Songchon. The commanding officer of the 8th Cavalry Regiment sent a message to the G-3 of the 1st Cavalry Division that it was impracticable to hold the town against a night attack, but he was ordered nevertheless to stay there.[12]

Air observers in the afternoon of 2 December, however, reported so many enemy troops moving in the vicinity of Songchon that to them "the ground seemed to be moving." A Mosquito plane directed fighter planes on enemy in the vicinity of Songchon that were estimated to number perhaps as many as 8,000 men. The fighter-bomber planes made strikes on this enemy concentration all afternoon. They were not dug in but on the move and apparently prepared to attack. The 7th and 8th regiments had to withdraw in the face of this approaching force. The 7th Cavalry Regiment and the 3rd Battalion, 8th Cavalry, followed the road leading to the crossing of the Taedong River at Apa-ri, west of Songchon. There they encountered a CCF roadblock and enemy in position on Hill 335. They turned back and eventually, together with the British 27th Brigade, successfully withdrew by a more westerly route through Chasan and Sainjang, south of Sunchon.[13]

In its actions on the army right flank along the Taedong River, the 1st Cavalry Division had many cases of frostbite and other foot ailments. At this time one observer saw a bit of grim humor at the division CP. On its bulletin board was a newspaper clipping carrying huge headlines saying "Americans Due to

Leave Korea by Christmas." Pinned to it was the joker from a deck of cards.[14]

There were a few other instances of enemy contact on the army right flank east and south of Sunchon on 2 December. The most important of these was on the Taedong River, east of Sainjang, where B Company, 8th Engineer Combat Battalion, had been building a dam across the river. The 16th Reconnaissance Company protected the engineers at the site. A liaison plane dropped a message to the Reconnaissance Company to send a patrol five miles north to rescue wounded who had been seen there. It did so, and rescued ten men. At 9:40 A.M., an estimated enemy battalion attacked the engineer troops. A firefight between the engineers, the 16th Reconnaissance Company, and apparently some British Argyll troops that arrived at the scene and the Chinese continued until the early afternoon. Air strikes were called in. These caught the enemy in the open and decimated them. In this fight, the American ground forces claimed 200 Chinese killed. The air strikes killed an estimated 500 more Chinese. If these claims were near the facts, a Chinese battalion was destroyed. The Middlesex Battalion then reinforced the ground troops in the vicinity of the bridge site.[15] On 3 December the 7th and 8th cavalry regiments continued their withdrawal on the right flank of Eighth Army and reported some minor contact and exchange of fire with Chinese forces.[16]

As might be expected, the Fifth Air Force kept the Chinese on the Chongchon River front under constant surveillance and continuing attack in the first days of December, while Eighth Army was withdrawing south. Quite noticeable was the continuing heavy CCF crossing of the Chongchon River, both infantry columns on foot and vehicular columns south of Kunu-ri. All available aircraft, including naval air, was sent there, and between 40 and 50 aircraft kept the river crossings in the vicinity of Kunu-ri under constant attack during 1 December. During the day there were 183 sorties in the IX Corps area alone. These sorties reported 13 different enemy troop concentrations attacked with an estimated 825 men destroyed. On the ridges southwest of Kunu-ri, pilots said they attacked an estimated 10,000 enemy and estimated 300 of them killed. Just southwest of Kunu-ri, air strikes caught an estimated 1,500 Chinese halfway across the Chongchon River, and pilots estimated 400 of them were killed. South of Kunu-ri, aircraft pilots reported seeing many enemy wearing captured American clothing.[17]

Another air observer reported seeing about 1,000 enemy troops change from their uniforms to white civilian clothes four miles southeast of Kunu-ri. All day there were enemy targets moving in the open, either crossing the Chongchon River from Won-ni on the north to west of Kunu-ri or moving south after crossing the river. Some of these enemy groups and columns were estimated to number in the thousands. The full force of UN air strength was directed against them. That hundreds and probably thousands of CCF were killed or wounded in the air attacks on 1 December cannot be doubted, but the exact number can be only speculated.[18]

The Army Destroys Supplies in Its Rush South

When Colonel Freeman's 23rd RCT hastily mounted trucks and tanks for a quick departure on the road west to Anju, they joined the tide of soldiers and transports that had preceded them on the coastal road west and then south. Only the 5th RCT, still manning the roadblock five miles east of Anju, remained to follow them. The next morning before daylight a small, lone enemy plane strafed Sukchon. Maj. Sam Radow of the 23rd Infantry said later that, at Sukchon, everyone seemed to be blowing up ammunition and running wildly about making preparations to move farther south. Rumors were rife, he said, that the army was going to evacuate Korea and that orders were to get on the road and move south—and to keep going.[19] This view was generally prevalent among Eighth Army personnel as the big retreat began. As it progressed, the idea of getting out of Korea seemed to become a settled conviction for most.

With it came massive traffic jams on the main coastal road running south, where very quickly most of Eighth Army funneled itself, as intelligence and rumors mounted that enemy were encircling the army's right flank, and there was increasing danger that they would cut the main road south to Seoul. With this haste to get away came a quick destruction or abandonment of equipment and supplies that would be encumbering.

The 25th Infantry Division on 30 November found the road south to Sunan so congested that northbound travel was virtually impossible. An official report said there were "numerous accidents and mechanical failures. Disabled equipment that could not be evacuated on the spot was pushed off the highway to permit continuous flow of traffic." The 40-mile road trip from Yongyu to Pyongyang took six and a half hours for one group, an average of six miles per hour. At Sinanju, I Corps reported there were five M-46 tanks needing repair. Three of them were repaired so they could be driven south. The other two were destroyed. Many ordnance items were destroyed at Sinanju and vicinity because of lack of transportation to move them south quickly. Included among these items were three 90-mm antiaircraft guns and four M-4 tractors. On the road south from Sinanju to Pyongyang, two officers of I Corps said they saw a tank retriever, a tractor and its 8-inch howitzer, and ten high-speed tractors pulled off the road and burned. The air officer for I Corps said later of the first days of the Eighth Army retreat:

> I think probably the most harrowing experience was the withdrawal from Sinanju when we had to fall back from the Chinese Communists in November of last year. There was a lot of equipment abandoned and a great deal of confusion resulting from the lack of communications and people trying to get through the roads. Vehicles jammed bumper to bumper and the aspect of what might happen was worse than what actually happened. . . . Everyone was anxious to get back and set up where they could protect themselves. There were no known front lines and everyone was trying to get back and get organized.[20]

When Eighth Army's massive retreat began from the Chongchon River front, there were few railroad locomotives and only a small number of cars of any kind that far north to evacuate matériel and supplies from Sinanju and other points north of Pyongyang. Most of the rail equipment was between Pusan, the southern port, and Seoul, bringing supplies northbound. Every effort had been made prior to 24 November to build up a stock of supplies at the Eighth Army front sufficient to support an advance. Ironically, this readiness had just been achieved when everything was put in reverse. Now everything that was to be saved had to be put on the single-track railroad at Sinanju and Sukchon and on the two-lane highway, running south. ASP 17 at Sinanju had just been built up to 3,000 tons daily when the order came to evacuate it. Only 15 railcars were available to do it—not enough. I Corps had to destroy 1,600 tons of ammunition there because there was no transport available to move it.[21]

The port of Chinnampo, 35 miles southwest of Pyongyang, the seaport for the North Korean capital, was just reaching its unloading capacity when Eighth Army turned back south. The US Navy had just completed what it said was the greatest mine-sweeping task in its history, clearing a 65-mile-long channel to the port so that supplies could be brought in for the army. From Chinnampo an improved highway and a rail line ran to Pyongyang, and from there to the front. This new avenue of military supplies was abandoned just after it reached operational state. The 24th Division, which expected to receive most of its supplies through Chinnampo in the drive north, reflects the story rather well in the movement of its Quartermaster Company in six hectic days. On 25 November the company moved north to Pakchon to support the advance. On 28 November it withdrew suddenly to Sinanju; the next day it went back farther to Sukchon, and on 30 November it fell back to Pyongyang. From there it went all the way back to the outskirts of Seoul. In the general movement south, Chinnampo was again destroyed. Some supplies accumulated there were evacuated, some destroyed, and some fell to the Chinese.[22]

In the rapid withdrawal of Eighth Army from north of Pyongyang, the necessity for most of the units to go through the city caused some slowdowns. Physical and geographic features that characterized and surrounded the city caused the problems. The Taedong River split the city in two parts on a line running from northeast to the southwest. This mandated two supply points for Eighth Army, one on the south side of the river for cargo and supplies arriving by rail and air from the south, and a second one on the north side of the river for supplies arriving from Chinnampo and those trucked across the river from the south. In the withdrawal movement, a large amount of supplies being evacuated from points north of Pyongyang could have been hauled by truck to rail stations south of the city and the Taedong River for further evacuation if more trucks had been available. Since adequate transport was not present, large amounts of supplies were lost north of the river.[23]

The nearly nightly raids of a lone enemy light plane on Pyongyang and other supply centers on the MSR had certain disruptive effects. On a few occasions this nighttime harassing caused damage. As early as 19 November an enemy single-engine plane bombed Sunchon and strafed US troop positions along the Chongchon. The worst of these hit-and-run nighttime attacks occured at 3 A.M. on 28 November, when a single enemy light plane, a night heckler that American troops called Bed Check Charlie, dropped a string of fragmentation bombs across the 8th Fighter Bomber Group parking ramp at the Pyongyang airfield, killing an Air Force sergeant and damaging 11 Mustangs, three of them so badly they were left there when the field was abandoned a few days later in the evacuation of the city.[24]

The 24th Division effort to move its large supply dumps from Sukchon to East Pyongyang illustrates some aspects of the problems that faced the entire army in its withdrawal. A little after noon on 30 November, verbal orders passed down from the 24th Division G-4 through Lieutenant Colonel Cocheu, the division quartermaster, to Maj. James W. Spellman, his executive officer, to evacuate the Sukchon Quartermaster Supply Point to East Pyongyang. About 2 P.M., the larger part of the 24th Quartermaster Company left Sukchon for Pyongyang. There were no trucks left for evacuation of supplies.

But 14 trucks belonging to the company were then on their way to Sukchon from the K-29 airstrip, 17 miles to the north at the edge of Sinanju. They were hauling gasoline, because the previous evening the officer in charge at K-29 had told Captain Overmeyer of the 24th Quartermaster Company that he intended to burn all the gasoline still left at the airstrip on the morning of 30 November. When these trucks arrived at Sukchon they could be used to load railcars with priority supplies for evacuation. But these trucks encountered great delay in arriving at Sukchon because of slow-moving, southbound military traffic from Sinanju. Lieutenants Zabilski and Osterhout, in charge of the trucks, finally walked several miles into Sukchon to report truck movement was at a crawl. It was 4:30 P.M. before the first trucks of the 24th Quartermaster Company were loaded at the Sukchon Supply Point. In their shuttle movement to and from the railhead, they had to move a short distance on the main highway, and this they found almost impossible to do. Southbound traffic was using both lanes. Northbound vehicles found it impossible to break into this bumper-to-bumper mass of traffic. Just to get rations to the supply point, Major Spellman had to send a detachment of 25 Philippine scouts on foot to the rail head to carry back boxes of rations.[25]

In the meantime, reports came from Sinanju that ammunition and supplies not already evacuated had been destroyed at 5 P.M. on 30 November. A captain of the 724th Ordnance Company reported to Major Spellman that he had abandoned about 60 unserviceable vehicles near Anju and was moving south. At Sukchon, Major Spellman continued to shuttle trucks from the supply point to the railhead, loaded with priority supplies, including winter clothing, as fast as he could get them through the traffic on the main road south. He had only six trucks for this purpose because eight of the 14 returning from the K-29 airstrip with gasoline had been ordered to continue on to the 24th Division rear with fuel to support its move to Pyongyang.

At 1 A.M. on 1 December, three trucks fully loaded returned from the railhead to the supply point. Lieutenant Zabilski, accompanying the trucks, reported that a lieutenant colonel in command at the 3rd Transportation Military Railway Service at the railhead told him no more cargo was to be loaded on the eight railcars standing there. Six of the cars were fully loaded, but the last two were only partially loaded. The commander at the railhead said the only available engine was going to depart immediately with the train. It was charged later that this officer had closed the rail service at Sukchon 24 hours early; otherwise, all supplies could have been evacuated from there.

When Major Spellman received the report from Lieutenant Zabilski that the Sukchon railhead was being closed, he put all possible supplies on the six trucks he had and ordered the rest of the supplies to be burned. This was done at 2:15 A.M. on 1 December. At this time a loud explosion indicated that nearby ammunition had been destroyed. Half an hour earlier the enemy's Bed Check Charlie had flown over Sukchon, strafing various targets. By the time Major

Spellman had loaded his six trucks and burned warehouses and the supplies that remained, traffic from the north had practically ceased. One may say, therefore, that virtually all of Eighth Army using the coastal road had cleared Sukchon by 2:15 A.M. on 1 December. Spellman, his 24th Quartermaster detachment, his Philippine scouts, and six trucks reached Pyongyang by 7:30 A.M.[26] The 24th Division's records of supplies lost in the withdrawal disappeared when the truck carrying them broke down on the road and was abandoned.

The suddenness of orders to various Army and Air Force units to evacuate their positions near the Chongchon River front and move south in withdrawal can be illustrated by an Air Force unit at Sinanju. The commanding officer of the 606th Squadron of B-26s received an order in the afternoon of 29 November to evacuate the field within three hours. He had no chance to destroy radar and camp equipment. He could only get the men out. Col. Gilbert Myers, deputy for operations, Fifth Air Force, said, "A million and a half dollars worth of equipment . . . was lost for the lack of a few trucks."[27]

When the 35th Regiment of the 25th Division was withdrawing south from the front, Col. Henry Fisher, its commander, said, "I saw a warehouse burning. It had trench coats in it—enough for a division of 15,000 men, I was told." The building and its contents were being burned to prevent capture by the enemy.[28] The US I Corps had ordered such destruction on Eighth Army orders, that all stocks of food and supplies in warehouses, military or civilian, should be destroyed if they could not be evacuated. As a result of these orders much winter clothing for American troops, not yet issued, was burned in division dumps. In some cases the winter clothing reportedly was not issued earlier because of fear that the troops would throw it away before cold weather. Most of the winter clothing, however, was late in getting to the front because the quartermaster organization in the United States had not foreseen or been informed that it would have to provide Eighth Army for a winter campaign in North Korea. The winter clothing, in general, was being issued to the troops as rapidly as it arrived and arrangements could be made. With nearly all units moving daily in the course of constant battle, there sometimes was no opportunity to issue the winter clothing on the hour or day of its arrival in the division dumps.[29]

Lt. Col. Clarence E. Stuart, commanding officer of the 555th Field Artillery Battalion, attached to the 5th RCT, 24th Division, spoke of passing an ordnance dump south of Anju during the army withdrawal and observing guns and prime movers being left there. He reported the matter and was instrumental in having men and equipment sent back to get this expensive heavy equipment out. His battalion passed an Air Force dump during their withdrawal south, and his men were able to help themselves to what they called "fancy clothing," probably meaning excellent cold-weather leather jackets.

Concerning the attitude of the men in his artillery battalion in the withdrawal, Lieutenant Colonel Stuart said, "The attitude of the men astounded me. They were proud of having done a good job and they had not been hurt much. Many of them thought the army would fight north of Seoul." Stuart felt that the 24th and 25th divisions were not defeatist at this time and, with the exception of the 24th Regiment of the 25th Division, were ready to engage the enemy again whenever ordered to do so. He said the rapid, nonstop withdrawal confused the infantry and the artillerymen in these divisions.[30]

The effect of the long retreat on soldier morale is seen in the remarks of a few weary soldiers who led the advance of the retreat into Seoul. Army PXs there had been rationing cigarettes but now suddenly were selling them in larger quantities. GIs were queued up at one of the PXs when the tired arrivals from the front passed by and shouted to them, "Wait a few days, Joes, and they'll be passing out that stuff free so the Commies don't get it."[31]

It must be recorded that some units did not carelessly throw things away or think only of getting south as fast as possible. The Ordnance Company of the US 25th Division provides an example. During the first days of December, the 25th Division was one of the first to move south of the Chongchon on orders and to keep on moving south after it reached Pyongyang. The division's order of march is an example of good road organization for protection of all parts of the division in a withdrawal; first, the division trains, followed by service companies, two infantry regiments, ordnance armored maintenance platoon, tank battalion, the last infantry regiment, and lastly, demolition teams. The ordnance armored maintenance platoon was to repair or evacuate equipment that failed on the march and, on call, to return past the last infantry regiment and the tanks and repair or evacuate equipment. When the 25th Division reached Chunghwa, about 18 miles south of Pyongyang, it had about 20 trucks that could go no farther. They were grouped near a crossroads, and all units following were invited to cannibalize them. Eight tanks could go no farther without new engines. It was important not to leave them. In temperatures of ten degrees below zero that night, the Ordnance Company erected tents and built bonfires in an area adjacent to an intersection in Chunghwa and then started pulling out the worn-out engines and installing new ones. The work began about 6 P.M. By 6 A.M. the next morning, all eight tanks had new engines and lived to fight another day.[32]

On 2 December it was apparent that Eighth Army was speeding up plans to evacuate Pyongyang and to hurry south. In that connection, Eighth Army adopted a "scorched-earth" policy in its withdrawal, ordering all its subordinate units to destroy everything that could not be evacuated. This included food such as rice, wheat, barley, and millet that was staple food items for the Chinese and North Koreans.[33]

The 2nd Division was ordered to continue on to Munsan-ni, and the 24th Division received orders to continue guarding the army's east flank south of Kangdong. The division's 19th Infantry still held its blocking position northeast of that town. At midafternoon, the 2nd Division returned to army control. Another combat-ineffective force, the Turkish Brigade, by Eighth Army order, issued through the IX Corps, was to assemble in the vicinity of Kaesong, where it would become attached to the 2nd Infantry Division. The Turkish Brigade at the time of this order had about 3,000 men assembled at Pyongyang, another 300 were at Kaesong, and some others were as far south as Seoul. A flurry of excitement came to Pyongyang at 2 A.M. on 2 December when a light enemy plane dropped from six to nine bombs on the Pyongyang airstrip.[34]

The American Air Force continued air strikes in enemy-held territory south of the Chongchon River. The G-3 Air Report for the day stated that 91 sorties were flown in the IX Corps area on the army's east flank. In these strikes aircraft hit two villages ten miles west of Songchon, where enemy had sought shelter, and destroyed an estimated 950 CCF soldiers. Air strikes hit three other enemy troop concentrations, with unknown results. And at Yangdok, air strikes hit two concentrations of 1,000 enemy each, but again with unknown results.[35]

The Far East Command intelligence summary for the day concluded that the CCF, with the NK guerrillas operating behind the Eighth Army lines, had the capability of seizing Kaesong, preventing the Eighth Army from retiring toward Seoul, and completing the destruction of US field forces in Korea.[36] This was indeed an alarming intelligence estimate and reflects the agitated state of mind that existed in at least some quarters of the Far East Command in Tokyo.

General Walker Orders Evacuation of Pyongyang on 3 December

A significant troop movement on 3 December for the protection of the Eighth Army retreat involved the 5th RCT of the 24th Division, which had reverted to 24th Division control on 2 December. The 5th RCT was ordered to Yul-li, where it closed during the day. Yul-li lay 25 road miles south of Kangdong on the main road south from that place to Suan, Singye, and Sibyon-ni. At Yul-li the 5th RCT controlled a main road that ran from there, northwest to Pyongyang. The 5th RCT remained at Yul-li, blocking there for the army until 8 December.[37]

The most exposed American division on 3 December was the 1st Cavalry Division, which had been disposed on the east and south of Sunchon, covering the army's right flank there and collecting stragglers from the US 2nd Infantry Division. On 3 December it received orders to withdraw to Singye, 75 miles southeast of Pyongyang. Before it could break contact with the enemy, its 8th Cavalry Regiment moved into an enemy ambush just before daylight on the third. Some of the Chinese involved in the ambush tied themselves to trees and stumps and, in the dark, looked as if they were dead. After the 8th Cavalry unit had passed them, most of these supposed corpses came to life and shot many Americans in the back. In this encounter, northeast of Pyongyang, the 8th Cavalry had 24 casualties. They seem to have been the last American and UN casualties to enemy fire in breaking contact with the Chinese south of the Chongchon River. The CCF 42nd Army constituted the enemy force engaged in the deepest movement around the right flank of Eighth Army, and some of its troops probably were involved in this incident. The 1st Cavalry Division now, on 4 December, began moving to its assigned assembly area three miles south of Singye, arriving there the next day. The ROK 6th Division remnants were detached from the division's control at this time.[38]

On 3 December, also, the 24th Division, attached to IX Corps, received orders to place one battalion on the north bank of the Taedong River to cover the withdrawal of the 1st Cavalry Division over the river bridges at Pyongyang. The 1st Battalion, 19th Infantry, took up the defense position. After the last of the 1st Cavalry Division had crossed the river, the 19th Infantry blew up the bridges at 6:45 A.M. on 5 December. The 1st Battalion, 19th Infantry, was certainly one of the last American infantry units at the Taedong River.[39]

In the withdrawal from Pyongyang, the ROK 6th Division, on being detached from the 1st Cavalry Division, was reassigned to control of the 24th Division, which made it responsible for the western half of its division sector. On 3 December, Eighth Army considered its defensive line to be south of the Taedong River. Korean civilians reported in the evening that CCF soldiers at 5 P.M. were in Sukchon, 25 miles north of Pyongyang.

The North Korean refugee problem was a huge one at Pyongyang for the withdrawing army, thousands of Korean civilians were fleeing in advance of the approaching Chinese. It was a human wave that threw itself onto the bridges across the Taedong from the north part of the city and the country to the north. They crowded the roads leading south, already jammed with army vehicles and personnel. Often enemy agents infiltrated the refugees, dressing like them and then gathering intelligence or creating chaos whenever an opportunity arose. In Pyongyang, refugees accumulated in ever-increasing numbers, despite efforts to keep them back.

On 3 December, when the army had broken contact with the Chinese, the executive officer of the 3rd Battalion, 35th Infantry Regiment, 25th Division, wrote in his official journal a truth that characterized one of the American forces' weaknesses during all of 1950 in Korea, to be corrected only after General Ridgway assumed command of the army, and then only gradually as he insisted on the change. The officer wrote, "One error that stands out during and prior to the [Chinese] attack and was a proximate cause of the surprise effected upon us was the lack of ground reconnaissance to the front."[40] After 3 December this condition became pronounced. There was virtually no American or UN patrol or other reconnaissance to the north of UN forces to learn the location and movements of the enemy. The Eighth Army was virtually blind for the next two weeks as to where the Chinese were and what they were doing. But in practical terms perhaps it made no difference—the UN forces moved south so rapidly the Chinese could not keep up with them, and they did not try to do so.

As the Eighth Army retreat got under way and the troops approached Pyongyang, the Joint Chiefs of Staff queried General MacArthur whether he could establish and hold a defensive line across the waist of Korea, using both the X Corps and Eighth Army. General MacArthur replied on 3 December to this suggestion that it was not practicable to attempt to join the two forces and would not add to UN strength. He was already below the waist of Korea.

On the third, the 9th Infantry Regiment of the 2nd Division started on a long motorized movement to Munsan-ni, below the 38th Parallel. The men loaded on all vehicles available, including tanks, where they covered the decks. Jeeps often carried six men and three or four more on the trailers they pulled. The regiment closed at Munsan-ni at 3 A.M. the next day, covering the 121 road miles in 21 hours, an average of six miles an hour.[41] Col. Charles C. Sloane, Jr., the regimental commander, was evacuated for medical reasons on 6 December, and Col. Edwin J. Messinger succeeded to command of the 9th Infantry. The regiment moved on to Ascom City, between Seoul and Inchon on 7 December, closing there at 10:20 P.M.

Another major unit, the Turkish Brigade, left Pyongyang the same day for an assembly area far in the rear where it could reequip. It entrained on the south side of the Taedong River, at Pyongyang, and started for Kaesong.

At this time a report was finally available as to the strength of the ROK II Corps, which had been routed and disorganized, with an untold number killed, wounded, and missing the first night and day of the CCF 2nd Phase Offensive on 25–26 November. Stragglers from the corps had been assembled in the rear until now it seemed that all who would ever be recovered were on hand. In the ROK rout on the extreme east flank, 300 troops of the ROK 8th Division, after having been cut off, had made their way on east through the mountains into the US X Corps zone in northeastern Korea. They had crossed the famous gap. These ROKs were being returned to their division by water transport down the east coast of Korea to the Eighth Army area. The tabulation of the ROK II Corps strength on 3 December appears in table 7.[42]

General Walker issued the order on 3 December that Eighth Army would withdraw from Pyongyang, beginning at 8 A.M. the next morning. The Army Service Trains had already started for Seoul. Consistent with this order, the Eighth Army Advance CP at Pyongyang closed at noon, 3 December, and opened at the same time at Seoul. Army Operational Order 107 that day indicated an initial defense line would be established in an arc passing through Chunghwa, about 18 miles south of Pyongyang, with a secondary defense line extending from Haeju eastward through Sinmak and Singye to Ichon, 40 air miles south and southeast of Pyongyang. It was well understood in most Eighth Army commands that these two lines were merely phase lines in a general withdrawal to the Imjin River and the defenses of Seoul. The Fifth Air Force had anticipated this withdrawal on 27 November, a week earlier, when General Partridge informed General Stratemeyer that he was making plans for the possible evacuation of the airfields at Sinanju and Pyongyang and all air facilities there because of the course of ground action.[43]

Table 7. **ROK II Corps Strength, 3 December 1950**

Unit	Officers	Enlisted Men
ROK 7th Division		
Division Headquarters[a]	166	1,882
3rd Regiment	139	2,395
5th Regiment	78	1,493
8th Regiment	48	592
Subtotal	431	6,362
ROK 8th Division		
Division Headquarters[a]	213	2,543
10th Regiment	42	798
16th Regiment	104	1,250
21st Regiment	46	765
Subtotal	405	5,356
Total	836	11,718

Source: Eighth Army, Command Report, G-3 Sec., G-3 Journal File, 3 December 1950, Box 1136.
[a]Division Headquarters includes Artillery and special troops.

16. Evacuation of Pyongyang

We have noted that General Walker, on 3 December, ordered the evacuation of Pyongyang. The formal evacuation of the city was to begin the next morning, 4 December. But in fact, Eighth Army's withdrawal through the city and continuation of the movement south had been in progress from 1 December. The troops had not paused in Pyongyang but had continued on south in most cases. General Walker personally made the decision to abandon Pyongyang. Just when he reached this decision is not known, but the pattern of Eighth Army troop movements from 1 December on affords circumstantial evidence that he decided on or about 1 December. Only two days earlier he had assured General MacArthur that he could hold somewhere above Pyongyang.

The inference that General Walker had decided by 1 December that he could not hold Pyongyang and must have informed General MacArthur that day or the next of his decision, probably in a radio telephone conversation, is given some support by the trip to Korea that Maj. Gen. Doyle Hickey, Far East Command acting chief of staff, and Brig. Gen. Edwin K. Wright, Far East Command G-3, made on 2 December. Apparently MacArthur sent these two staff officers and advisors to Korea to check the situation with General Walker and to judge whether there was any chance of holding the city. According to Maj. Gen. Leven Allen, Eighth Army chief of staff, they concurred in General Walker's decision to abandon Pyongyang.[1]

According to Colonel Stebbins, General Walker made the decision because he thought it was necessary in order to save Eighth Army. Walker had witnessed the failure of the ROK 2nd and 5th divisions to drive out the strong North Korean reconstituted army units and guerrillas in Eighth Army's rear to the southeast in the Iron Triangle area. Also, he had realized the continuing menace of Chinese formations south and southeast of Sunchon and to the east of Pyongyang that were engaged in a sweep around the army's right flank and threatening to cut off Eighth Army in the Pyongyang area unless he withdrew the army rapidly. It would appear that General Walker also had some fear that further defeat would cause the ROK forces to crumble everywhere and to desert. He apparently did not have confidence that Eighth Army could confront the enemy and win a general battle against the CCF in the vicinity of Pyongyang. He was unwilling to accept a situation where some CCF units and the North Korean and guerrilla forces would be in the rear of Eighth Army during such a battle.

General Walker must have known that the great bulk of the CCF in his front, now engaged in the pursuit phase of their victory along the Chongchon, were virtually without ammunition and food and that they were in no condition to meet the Eighth Army, which could select a perimeter defense or a series of such defense positions and which had an adequate supply (and resupply capability) of ammunition and food. With armor and air support, the Eighth Army should have been able to hold those positions and then destroy the CCF in detail, unless they were heavily reinforced quickly from Manchuria. Some commanders might have thought the chances good to win such a battle at Pyongyang. General Walker apparently did not. The examples of German success against vastly superior Soviet forces in World War II were either unknown to General Walker, or he chose not to equate them with his own situation.

The failure of the UN forces to make a defensive stand at Pyongyang was probably one of the important tactical mistakes of the war. With its air power almost uncontested, with strong armor forces at hand against none for the CCF, with far superior artillery and mortar fire, with the nearby port of Chinnampo now open and the logistic support of Eighth Army, including a repaired railroad line reaching the Taedong River at Pyongyang, the best it had been thus far in the war, well-selected hedgehog-type defense perimeters should have given Eighth Army a good chance of turning back an attack by the CCF, whose logistic and resupply situation at this point must have been inadequate for a sustained assault.

As Eighth Army G-4, Colonel Stebbins had the staff responsibility to evacuate war material, food, and supplies of all kind from the depots around Pyongyang and north of the city, ahead of the troop withdrawal itself. He said he started clearing supply points on his own initiative when he sensed that Eighth Army was not going to stand at Pyongyang. He could not get information in advance of the dates the city would be given up, and as a result he estimated he lost two days' worth of army supplies at Pyongyang. Stebbins said he also did not get word later of the intent to evacuate Inchon.[2]

After trying to evacuate supply points at Pyongyang for some days, Stebbins finally received word from Maj. Gen. Leven Allen, Eighth Army chief of staff at Seoul, to proceed with the evacuation of supplies of all kinds. After this, Colonel Stebbins said he endeavored to get the supply situation in hand so that, if Korea were to be evacuated, he would be able to get most of Eighth Army's supplies and equipment out of the country. General Walker wanted to destroy everything that might help the Chinese and the North Koreans supply themselves. Colonel Stebbins said that General Walker intended to do just what General Ridgway did later: withdraw Eighth Army south of the Han River to a defensive position based on what might be called the Pyongtaek-Ansong-Chungju line, 50 air miles south of Seoul. There, he said, General Walker intended to stand, or farther south, depending on how rapidly the CCF and North Koreans could pursue south of the Han River, and just when the X Corps could become an effective part of Eighth Army in an integrated battle position across the breadth of Korea.[3]

The Stebbins view as stated above of General Walker's intentions is supported by verbal statements of Lieutenant Colonel Bullock of the Eighth Army G-3 Section, but it is not buttressed by documentary evidence. Some verbal testimony, such as that of Col. Richard W. Stephens, commanding officer of the 21st Infantry Regiment, 24th Division, goes to the contrary. He said General Walker came around to division and regimental commanders during the withdrawal and told them, "Don't worry, I am going to get Eighth Army out. Not going to lose more good men in this country." Stephens understood the Army would leave Korea.[4]

The British 29th Brigade Covers the Evacuation of Pyongyang

General Walker assigned the newly arrived British 29th Brigade to cover the evacuation of Pyongyang. The brigade took positions on the northern outskirts of the city on 3 December, with the mission of preventing enemy units from entering the city from the north and northeast until the city had been evacuated. It was then to withdraw south across the Taedong River bridges. The composition of this new and important reinforcement was as follows:

HQ, 29th Independent Brigade Group–CO, Brigadier Thomas Brodie
1st Battalion, Royal Northumberland Fusiliers–CO, Lt. Col. K. O. N. Foster
1st Battalion, Royal Ulster Rifles–CO, Lt. Col. R. J. H. Carson
1st Battalion, Gloucestershire Regt.–CO, Lt. Col. J. P. Carne
8th Royal Irish Hussars (two squadrons of Centurion tanks and C Squadron of the 7th Tank Regt.)–CO, Lt. Col. J. W. Phillips
45th Field Regt., Royal Artillery–CO, Lt. Col. M. F. Young
55th Field Squadron, Royal Engineers–CO, Maj. A. E. Younger[5]

Brigadier Brodie was a veteran of the Burma Campaign in World War II. He had the reputation of being a tough Scottish soldier.

As the 29th Brigade arrived at Pyongyang, its sister brigade, the 27th, was passing south through the city in its withdrawal from covering the Taedong River crossings northeast of the city. There was camaraderie between the two British formations as they met, and the 29th Brigade had a chance to hear some of the 27th Brigade's comments about the Chinese enemy. On the very day the British 29th Brigade went into position north of Pyongyang, 3 December, a small detached group of soldiers from the 27th Brigade was trying to get a stalled weapons carrier started in their withdrawal column from one of their positions northeast of Pyongyang. Absorbed in this effort, they did not notice a group of Chinese infantry approach them. They came up to the working Englishmen unseen. One of them said in good English that they did not intend to hurt the British but wished they would leave Korea. The Chinese soldiers then pushed the weapons carrier free and helped to get it under way.[6] Such was one of the many quixotic and generous actions they were capable of during the war.

In its mission as rear guard on the north edge of Pyongyang during 3–5 December, the British 29th Brigade had no combat or contact with the Chinese, as the enemy had not yet pressed that far south, although aerial reconnaissance reported them 20 miles north of the city on 4 December, and in both Yongju and Sunchon.

The bridges across the Taedong River at Pyongyang were obviously bottlenecks to the movement of troops and transport going south. All of them were temporary ones built by Army Engineers on the way north in the past six weeks. Prior to Eighth Army's capture of Pyongyang on 20 October, the Fifth Air Force had destroyed all the bridges across the river. In passing through the city, the Taedong River, generally flowing from northeast to southwest, changes course and runs almost due south, splitting the city into eastern and western parts. While one generally refers to the north and south banks of the Taedong River, to be exact within the city limits of Pyongyang, one would have to speak of the east and west banks. The main part of Pyongyang, with the important public buildings and the North Korean capitol building, where Eighth Army had its headquarters, lay on the north or west side of the river. A large, relatively new industrial suburb sprawled opposite on the south side.

Two railroad bridges of the Pusan-Seoul-Mukden Railroad had crossed the Taedong, but they were in ruins now from American bombing earlier in the year. Immediately on the north side of the river the railroad bridges led into an extensive rail yard, with the main station adjacent. Upstream from the railroad bridges approximately one and a half miles was the main highway bridge. It, too, had been destroyed, but Army Engineers had constructed a timber bridge at the site, and it now served as the main north-south vehicular bridge across the Taedong. The I Corps had built other temporary bridges farther upstream (northeast) to help carry the heavy military traffic. The Taedong River averages about a quarter of a mile wide at Pyongyang and has a swift current.

The two largest airfields in the Pyongyang vicinity were named on the Japanese maps then in use the Airport and the Military Air Base. They were adjacent to each other, the Airport being just east of the river at the northeastern edge of the city; the Military Air Base was immediately east of the Airport. The Military Air Base became what the US Air Force called K-23. A rail spur ran to the Military Air Base, as did a good highway spur from a major road about half a mile south of it. On the south side of the Taedong in the new industrial section of the city, there were rail assembly yards and extensive warehouses and a good roadnet.[7]

As soon as all of Eighth Army had cleared to the south side of the Taedong River, the British 29th Brigade was to give the signal for I Corps Engineer troops to destroy the three bridges within the city. At 2 A.M. on 5 December the Class-15 bridge was destroyed. The north span of I Corps's 50-ton bridge was destroyed at 6:55 A.M., and about 25 minutes later the south span over the Taedong was blown. With its job completed, the leading elements of the British 29th Brigade left Pyongyang at 7:32 A.M., and the remainder of the brigade followed. East of the city, the 1st Battalion, 19th Infantry, destroyed a bridge at 6:45 A.M. after the 1st Cavalry Division had crossed it. One of the last units to leave Pyongyang was D Battery, 865th AAA AW Battalion, which had been emplaced at the Military Air Base (K-23) and had provided antiaircraft defense for the field.[8]

After the British 29th Brigade crossed the Taedong, the demolition work within Pyongyang was actually carried out by I Corps Engineer units. The Engineer Section of I Corps reported to the I Corps commander on 5 December that all planned demolitions in Pyongyang had been completed by 8 A.M. that morning. These demolitions had been in progress since the morning of

4 December at least and covered scores of individual structures and military facilities. Some of these demolitions were in the southern part of the city.

The Eighth Army demolition policy General Walker ordered was to destroy everything that could be of military use to the enemy. As to bridges, the criterion was that demolition should be extensive enough that building a new bridge would be easier for the enemy than repairing the old one. Usually this meant the complete destruction of all spans, piers, and abutments, rather than dropping only one or two spans, which would have been adequate to accomplish a tactical delay in enemy movements.

Initially, Eighth Army held to itself final authority on the execution of demolition targets except river crossings and railroads. On 3 December, however, the day General Walker ordered the evacuation of Pyongyang, the final authority was given to the commander of I Corps, who in turn delegated it to the I Corps Engineer, Col. Emerson C. Itschner. He in turn sent written instructions to all I Corps Engineer units.[9]

The Engineer demolition work took cognizance generally of the following principles:

1. Keep at least one good route of withdrawal open for each corps (for practical purposes this meant the US I and IX corps).
2. Execute any demolition that would delay the enemy.
3. Destroy all military equipment and supplies that might fall into enemy hands.

It is worth noting that one long railroad bridge nearing completion under UN forced labor one afternoon was destroyed the next afternoon (4 December).

At the same time that demolition to delay the enemy was in full swing, construction was in progress farther south to allow the withdrawing army to cross the seven rivers that traversed its planned route of withdrawal. It was a rule that each river must have two bridges in a corps sector capable of carrying the heaviest military loads. One bridge would probably carry all the traffic, but a second bridge would provide assurance that a withdrawal would not be interrupted. At the beginning of the withdrawal, most of the rivers had only one bridge—either a floating bridge of the modified treadway (or an M-4) type or a combination causeway-timber trestle bridge. Eighth Army Engineer units in rear areas, however, planked over two railroad bridges and built one trestle bridge to provide the second bridge for three rivers. Corps and division Engineers put bridges across two other rivers. At the time, there was only one heavy-capacity bridge across the Taedong River at Pyongyang. A pontoon bridge was built a few miles east of this bridge to give the necessary back-up facility. In blowing bridges behind a retreating army, it was essential that the timing be carefully controlled. If a bridge was blown too soon, it would isolate friendly troops on the far shore and cut off their retreat; if it was delayed too long, it might allow the enemy to come up and seize it. A classic example of the latter was the Remagen Bridge across the Rhine River that the Allies seized in World War II.

The greatest concentration of demolition targets was in Pyongyang. Just about every bridge along the withdrawal route was destroyed. In Pyongyang the most important demolition targets were the Taedong River bridges. The rear-guard commander authorized the time of their destruction. The Rail Transportation

Officer (RTO) north of the Taedong was also authorized to order execution of the demolitions. There were several large buildings in the heart of Pyongyang that were marked for demolition.

Colonel Itschner called a meeting on 2 December of all engineer officers who would be responsible for executing demolitions. Each officer was required to give a verbal description of his targets and his plans for their demolitions. Some of these major demolitions will be described subsequently. The work went pretty well on schedule, and at 6 P.M. on 4 December information indicated that all troops would have passed through the bridgehead perimeter by 3 A.M. the next morning, 5 December. Meanwhile, heavy equipment and troops not needed to carry out the demolitions had already moved south. During the night, word came that the last troops from the north would pass through the perimeter approximately two hours earlier than estimated. This allowed a speeding up of demolition work. While the Engineers' work was confined largely to bridges, Service troops of organizations in and around Pyongyang tried to destroy all supplies that could not be evacuated. The last planned demolition in Pyongyang was the destruction with napalm of a large supply of bombs at the airfield. Black clouds from the napalm and the thunderous explosions of the aerial bombs could be seen and heard as the last Engineers cleared the southern edge of Pyongyang.[10]

Exodus from Pyongyang on 3–5 December

When the CCF began closing in on Pyongyang, it was clear that the army units left on the west end of the line in I Corps were under the least enemy pressure. The MSR from Sinanju leading south to Pyongyang, in fact, was free of enemy interference. The CCF pressure was farther east, in the IX Corps sector, concentrated against the US 2nd Infantry Division at Kunu-ri, and also into the void left by the defeated ROK II Corps farther east and southeast. As late as 2 December a ROK 1st Division patrol returned to Sinanju airport and salvaged several tons of rice. The coastal road was still free of Chinese troops.

On 3 December Korean civilians began leaving Pyongyang in droves. Barges and small boats ferried civilians across the Taedong River, until the boats were destroyed to prevent such movement south, which clogged the roads the army would need for its withdrawal. No Korean civilians were allowed to cross the army bridges. But they could not be prevented from crossing the ruins of the great steel bridge that had been the main crossing point before American bombers destroyed and dropped the south span into the river. On 3–4 December Korean civilians by the thousands crossed the river on this bridge, climbing to the top of the steel girders and crossing on them, many with great bundles and packages on their backs. It seemed a feat possible only for a tightrope walker. It was an act of desperation. It is not known how many fell to their death in the river below. An Associated Press photographer caught a dramatic and fearsome view of this Korean mass of humanity crossing on the arched beams of this destroyed bridge, every top girder on the sides a solid line of people climbing up or sliding down the steeply pitched steel pathway. Back at the central

North Koreans fleeing from their homes in Pyongyang and crossing the Taedong River to the south side, 3 December 1950, as Eighth Army evacuates the North Korean capital. National Archives 111-SC 355229

part of the bridge, which still stood, a solid mass of people waited their chance to take the same desperate risk.[11] It was estimated that 300,000 civilians were trying to leave the city. On 4 December it was apparent that only the most heartless suppression by force could have prevented these Korean civilians from crossing to the south side of the river, and attempts to stop them largely ceased. Great numbers then waded the river at its shallower spots.

On 3 December, some 1,500 Korean city officials and others who had aided the UN forces while the latter occupied Pyongyang were allowed to cross the river and escape south. At the same time, the thousands that applied at the city hall for permits to flee the city were told there was no transportation available to help them. There was great fear that an enemy fifth column would start to operate in the city. There was a rumor that enemy airborne troops would drop on Pyongyang. And on the third, the body of a civilian who had been bound and shot was found near the airfield.[12]

Railroads and the Evacuation

In the withdrawal from Pyongyang the movement of both personnel and supplies depended to a large degree on the Korean National Railroads. All locomotives were steam operated and required large amounts of water. As the Eighth Army moved north into recaptured and later captured territory, after the Inchon landing and the army breakout from the Naktong perimeter in the late summer and early fall, the Corps of Engineers had to install 480-gallon pumps and 100-kilowatt generators for the rail shops, roundhouses, and pumping stations. Along the rail lines nearly all the communication lines had been destroyed—from Seoul to Kaesong, destruction had been 100 percent. Until December, only Korean communication repairmen could be used. There was no copper wire for the rail communication lines. Field wire would function for only a day or two. SCR-399 radios were tried at each main station, but they too were unsatisfactory. By early December a good line had been established between Kaesong and Pyongyang, but it was mid-December before the line between Seoul and Kaesong functioned properly. Beyond Pyongyang north to Sinanju at the Chongchon River, the rail communication line never operated.

The most important help to rail communications came from the Mukden cable, which was buried under the main highway north through Pyongyang to Sinanju and on north to the border, where it crossed at Sinuiju to continue on to Mukden, Manchuria. In late November and early December, Eighth Army had the cable operating from Pyongyang southward, with circuits to Pusan, Taegu, Taejon, and Chonan. Rail communication at Pyongyang was assigned directly to the 3rd Transportation Military Railway Service. During the Eighth Army withdrawals from late November into January, there was no difficulty with rail communications. It had been restored just in time for the withdrawal.

Prior to the army withdrawal from the North Korean front, US Army Engineers had built what was called a "Shoo-Fly" expedient rail bridge across the Han River to Seoul, another over the Imjin River, and a high-level bridge across the Yesong River at Hanpo-ri. Except for these, South Korean bridge and track gangs of the Korean National Railroads repaired the rail lines as Eighth Army advanced from September to December. They worked rapidly and could outperform the US Engineers in the type of work they did. They repaired rail lines mostly by using sand bags, timber trestling, and rail stringers.

By late November, completion of the high-level bridge at Hanpo-ri over the Yesong River, about 25 miles north of Kaesong, made possible continuous rail operations north as far as the Taedong Station, opposite Pyongyang on the south side of the Taedong River. By 1 December rail service operated to Sinanju, but since there was no rail bridge across the Taedong River at Pyongyang, this rail service had to begin at the north bank of the river in that city. This made it necessary, in transporting supplies or personnel from north to south or in the opposite direction, to unload at the station nearest the river bank on both the north and south sides, reload on trucks that crossed the river on a pontoon bridge, then reload onto railcars on the opposite bank. The importance of the rail system in Eighth Army operations can be seen in the 4,000 tons daily that were coming into Pyongyang when the CCF 2nd Phase Offensive began in late November. One estimate states that the Korean National Railroads moved about

95 percent of military tonnage to the front. When Pyongyang was evacuated, all the railroad locomotives and rolling stock north of the Taedong River necessarily were lost and were destroyed. Rail yards were stripped of supplies, inoperative locomotives were destroyed, bridges, switches, control towers, and other equipment were blown up. This process continued south of the Taedong after Eighth Army had evacuated Pyongyang and hurried south toward Seoul.[13]

In the Eighth Army withdrawal, the Signal Service was destroyed as completely as were the transportation facilities. Col. Thomas A. Pitcher, of the Signal Section, Eighth Army, wrote the following: "The destruction of signal equipment was systematic during the withdrawal during the winter of 1950–1951. We didn't know whether we were leaving Korea, but we took no chance of leaving anything behind which could aid the enemy. We did a thorough job of destroying the repeater stations, cable, and open-wire lines."[14]

Troop movements through Pyongyang continued apace on 4 December, all of it southward. The 35th Infantry Regiment, 25th Division, moved from Pyongyang ten miles south. It was not a long distance in miles, but converging roads entering Pyongyang from the north and northeast poured a constant stream of military traffic into it and held the 35th Infantry column north of the city for several hours. The ROK 1st Division cleared Pyongyang and crossed the Taedong River bridge to the south side just before midnight. The 24th Infantry Regiment, 25th Division, now south of the city, on orders tried to return to Pyongyang during the fourth to bring out supplies left there by various army units but found it impossible to reenter the city. It was on fire, and explosions there could be heard from a considerable distance. The returning troops considered it unsafe to cross into the city and abandoned their mission.[15]

During the day, I Corps reported that withdrawal of the 5th, 7th, and 8th cavalry regiments, the 27th British Brigade, and the ROK 6th Division proceeded on schedule. When the 7th Cavalry moved south out of Kangdong that morning, a report from the TACP with it relayed a pilot report that CCF with self-propelled artillery was behind it. A Mosquito plane was shot down just after noon. It crashed nine miles south of Sunchon. An aerial investigation at the crash site showed no sign of the pilot, but four enemy soldiers were standing around the plane. During the day all elements of the 1st Cavalry Division and the British 27th Brigade crossed to the south or east side of the Taedong River. There was no enemy contact during the day except by patrols, although ROK stragglers reported that a company of ROKs was surrounded in or near Sunchon and had engaged in a firefight with Chinese during the early hours of 4 December. The enemy did not seem to be pressing a pursuit.[16]

The destruction of all military facilities in Pyongyang began on 4 December and continued during the day and that night, on into early the next morning. The British 29th Brigade began the systematic destruction as soon as the ROK 1st Division had cleared through the city.

In its retreat from Sunan, eight miles north of Pyongyang, the 1st Battalion, 24th Infantry, reported at 5:30 P.M. on 4 December that all ammunition railcars there had not been completely destroyed but were left burning. There were 11 boxcars and a gondola. The 1st Battalion notified the 25th Division and requested an air strike on the cars to complete their destruction. When the Indian Field Ambulance Unit joined the British 27th Brigade at Pyongyang, it

The ROK 2nd Division withdraws ten miles south of Pyongyang, 5 December 1950. National Archives 111-SC 353863

received orders to burn all its stores, a six-months' supply. The commanding officer of the unit was horrified. Rather than comply, he found a locomotive, filled the boiler with water from jerricans passed along a human chain. His men then cut wood, fired the engines, found two men who said they could run the locomotive, and then got their supplies over the river bridge to the train at 4 A.M. on 5 December, just an hour before it was blown.[17]

The entrainment of the 2nd Infantry Division Rear personnel at Pyongyang for movement to Seoul affords an example of the difficulties, delays, and growing chaos in the North Korean capital as Eighth Army hurried to evacuate the city. About 8 P.M. on 2 December, the train began loading. Personnel loaded into coaches; division records and personal equipment and belongings were placed in open gondola cars. Enemy air activity over the city, with at least one plane dropping bombs, caused intermittent blackout conditions. Probably it was only the nightly visit of Bed Check Charlie. The train remained in a substation until 4 P.M. the next day, when it moved to the main Pyongyang rail station. In making this short move, the train passed thousands of ROK soldiers, many wounded and most without their individual weapons. In the station, the train's locomotive was uncoupled and put on a hospital train that had higher priority in movement. The 2nd Division train had no choice but to wait for another locomotive. Guards were placed on each boxcar and gondola.

At daylight on 4 December the 2nd Division train still sat in the Pyongyang rail station. The commanding officer of the 3rd serial of the train at 8 A.M. called the personnel of the various sections together and told them that there was a good possibility the train would have to be abandoned and that the Division Headquarters section would have to decide whether to destroy the equipment that could not be carried and have the men walk south or to wait on the train and hope that a locomotive would be available for it. The decision was to wait. As many as 125 men crowded into a coach. At 11:30 A.M., the postal officer began to burn money-order files, letters, and money on instructions of the train commanding officer. An hour later, soldiers and civilians in Pyongyang began to loot boxcars on the tracks in the Pyongyang rail yard, anticipating that they could not be moved south. Leather jackets were a popular choice. At 1 P.M., a locomotive was hitched to the train, but the RTO at Pyongyang said it could be used only for the movement of personnel. All records and equipment in the open gondolas were left behind when those cars were detached from the train. The 38th Regiment lost all its personnel records, the adjutant general of the division lost most of his files, and the Division Rear personnel lost nearly all their personal belongings. The train pulled out of the station at 5:20 P.M. on 4 December. A few miles south of Pyongyang it hit the back of another train, killing several refugees hitching a ride on the rear car.

The train reached Sariwon early on 5 December, only about 40 miles south of Pyongyang. The next day the train crossed the 38th Parallel at 9:45 A.M. At the last rail station north of the 38th Parallel, refugees crowded everywhere. They had been stopped there and forbidden to cross the parallel. Most of them were in tears. Snow now covered the ground. The train continued slowly, passing through Kaesong at 4:10 on the sixth. On 7 December the 2nd Division Rear train arrived at the outskirts of Seoul early in the morning, and about 5 P.M. in the afternoon had crossed the Han River to the new 2nd Division Headquarters in Yongdong-po on the south side of the river.[18]

A Special Problem with the Turkish Brigade

After the Turks' fighting retreat from Wawon on the road from Tokchon to Kunu-ri, where the Turks and the Chinese first met in battle, and their subsequent battles around Kunu-ri, Turkish soldiers were found in widely scattered places west and south of the fighting front, some as far west as Anju and Sinanju, and others as far south as Pyongyang, while the bulk of the brigade was still engaged at the southeast edge of Kunu-ri. In the big enemy fireblock south of Kunu-ri, most of the surviving Turks intermingled with 2nd Division troops and attempted to pass through the enemy fireblock, with varying luck. Most of them turned up in Pyongyang on 1 and 2 December. It was apparent even then that the Turks were in a foul mood at what had happened. In Pyongyang on 1 December, Capt. Ismail Catalogy, aide to Brig. Gen. Tahsin Yazici, the Turkish Brigade commander, said of the Turks, "Many men are bitter–bitter because of requested air strikes which did not come, a lack of transportation to get us out of our rough spot, a shortage of food and ammunition, and the fact that we were not advised on occasions of withdrawal plans. Some think they were let down by the Americans, but we are explaining that everyone had a bad time up there."[19] Captain Catalogy estimated that at least 500 Turks had been killed or wounded.

As quickly as possible Eighth Army had to move the Turks out of Pyongyang and get them far behind the front lines for rehabilitation and reorganization. They were sent south to assemble at Kaesong, on the MSR and the railroad that ran north from Seoul to Pyongyang. Upon arrival at Kaesong, the Turkish Brigade was to be attached to the 2nd Infantry Division, which was also moving to the rear for reorganization. Just before midnight or 3 December about 1,100 Turkish soldiers arrived at Kaesong by truck. The next day two train elements were expected to arrive there with another 2,000 Turks.[20]

The Eighth Army G-4 records indicate that, by the afternoon of 4 December a crisis was reported developing at Kaesong, where the Turks alleged there was no food for them. Immediate action was taken. Nine trucks were sent to Ascom City, a general supply depot between Seoul and Inchon, and two railcars of rations were loaded and arrived at Kaesong at 4 P.M. the next afternoon. At the same time, steps were taken to airlift 8,000 blankets and 4,000 sleeping bags to Kaesong for the Turks. They arrived there on 5 December. The Turks were short on everything, but food, blankets, and sleeping bags were considered of immediate importance.

The situation was considered so serious in the Turkish Brigade that Eighth Army sent a liaison officer to Kaesong to make a report on the situation. His report was included in the Eighth Army G-3 Journal for 5 December. The report said there were 2,500 Turks at the Kaesong assembly area and that 1,000 more were expected there by train. The personnel losses in the brigade were reported as 20 percent. Equipment losses were reported as 90 percent of communications equipment and vehicles. The latter included jeeps (112 lost out of 125), 1½-ton trucks (56 lost out of 77), and 2½-ton trucks (87 lost out of 139).

As a result of the Turkish Brigade's heavy losses around Kunu-ri in late November, Brigadier General Yazici complained that his forces were employed without regard to their relative immobility compared to that of American infantry forces–they had 60 percent fewer vehicles than a comparable-sized American force. The matter of the Turkish Brigade's alleged improper employment in the November actions was being discussed in Turkish by General Yazici and members of the Turkish-Korean delegation. Although the Eighth Army liaison officer attended this conference, he did not understand the language and could not report on it. He did report, however, that Kaesong was the wrong place for the brigade to be assembled, that it was blocking and interfering with military traffic there, and that it was difficult to control the Turks because of the language barrier. He estimated it would require 15 days to reorganize and re-equip the brigade. He emphasized the brigade would have to be moved to another location. He also stressed that a senior staff officer of Eighth Army should be sent to talk with General Yazici and his staff to avoid embarrassing complications arising from any misunderstandings between Turkish and Eighth Army officers. The Eighth Army issued orders at once that the Turkish Brigade should move to a new assembly area, Sosa-ri, a few miles east of Inchon on the main road between that place and Seoul. The Turks were expected to close on Sosa-ri on 7 December, and at that time would revert to Eighth Army control.[21]

There is little doubt that the traffic jam at Kaesong at this time was unbearable for a large army that was trying to funnel through it southbound. One official Eighth Army journal at the time says that, on 6 December the "traffic situation at Kaesong is terrible. Turks, Indians, British, ROKs, Nubians [Ethiopians] are running in all directions." And there were no military police in town. The confusion that reigned at Kaesong is reflected in a delayed report on 7 December of ten trucks dispatched to Kaesong with supplies for the Turks that arrived at 4 P.M. in the afternoon of the fifth, but the noncommissioned officer in charge of them could not locate the British officer who was to be his contact or anyone else who could speak English. He finally was able, with considerable difficulty, to get Turkish soldiers to unload blankets from the trucks and turned them over to a Turkish captain at 7:30 P.M. Two trucks were loaded with rations for the Turks. He even had trouble in getting the Turks to unload the food intended for them. In the end, two trucks were not unloaded.[22]

Other Complications in the Evacuation

While it is impossible to give an account of unit after unit of service troops and depots of various stores and equipment that were evacuated from Pyongyang and other nearby storage centers, even if the information were available, some examples of what happened to several of them will illustrate the general situation during the evacuation of the city. The 15th Quartermaster Company supported the 1st Cavalry Division. On 29 November the Quartermaster Company opened a supply point at Sunchon, around which the 1st Cavalry Division was posted at various points to guard against CCF units outflanking the army from the east. But it never issued any supplies at Sunchon, withdrawing before it could do so. On 1 December its most advanced supply point was in Pyongyang. The next day it began clearing out its clothing and petroleum supplies for movement south. Lt. Col. Marcus E. Cooper, the quartermaster of the 1st Cavalry Division, requested of Eighth Army 10 to 11 boxcars to evacuate the supplies. The army was unable to supply them. Cooper already had two partly loaded boxcars, so he filled them quickly so they could be moved out that night. The next morning, 3 December, four empty boxcars and two gondolas of empty gasoline drums were found in the freight yard. The RTO agreed to allow the 1st Cavalry Division to use the cars. It unloaded the empty gasoline drums and loaded the cars with quartermaster supplies. About 8:45 P.M. that evening, before the cars could be moved, an ammunition dump several city blocks away caught fire. Shells began to explode, at which time all locomotives in the area departed. Two of the Quartermaster warehouses burned as well as the two gondolas. The four boxcars survived.

The next morning, 4 December, locomotives returned to pull out loaded cars. When the boxcars began to move, they derailed. It was then learned that the ties had burned under the cars and the track had collapsed. The Quartermaster unit unloaded supplies from the boxcars and put them on trucks. These trucks were taken to the road, where a Quartermaster soldier stood by and offered to all units that passed anything they wanted or could take with them. During the night of 3 December and on 4 December, the Quartermaster Company hauled food and gasoline from Pyongyang across the river, where its personnel stopped vehicles and offered to them what they might be able to use. At 6 P.M. that evening it destroyed the gasoline and rations it could not give away or evacuate. Between 15,000 and 30,000 gallons of gasoline, all of it in drums, was destroyed. By 8 December, this Quartermaster Company delivered the supplies it had been able to truck away from Pyongyang to Ascom City, near Inchon.[23]

All night of 4 December the streets of Pyongyang were warm from many fires. Roaring flames sent a rosy glow over the ice along the edges of the Taedong River and parts of the city.

In the evacuation of Pyongyang there were many mishaps for any number of reasons, and evacuations of many supplies and much equipment were not carried out before bridges were blown. Some of it was due to the lack of sufficient railcars to load the material on, and locomotives were frequently lacking to pull the loaded trains out of the rail yards. For reasons not clear (perhaps just because of plain oversight), 16 new M46 Patton tanks were still standing on flatcars in the railyard and not evacuated when the city was abandoned. An examination of them by a tank unit passing by showed that some parts were missing, such as carburetors, and they could not be driven away on their own power. On learning this condition, the passing tank unit stopped long enough to send maintenance men to salvage other parts it could use.[24]

When the 3rd Battalion, 8th Cavalry Regiment, crossed the Taedong River, it stated in a message that 20 new tanks and six cars of equipment were still standing on a railroad trestle east of Pyongyang. The evacuation of the city was not an example of superb planning and execution; it was done in great haste. In its last days in American control, the situation was chaotic and characterized by too much haste and fear in Eighth Army that the Chinese would appear, although intelligence was adequate to indicate there was still time to save and evacuate military supplies and equipment.[25]

In passing one of the airports on his way from the Chongchon front, 1st Lt. Francis Nordstrom said that he saw the Air Force burning a lot of parkas and that he would have liked to halt his D Company of tanks, 89th Tank Battalion, long enough to get one for himself—but he could not stop the tank column. At the airstrip at the north edge of Pyongyang, he said all kinds of supplies were burning as they passed it.[26]

One of the greatest losses for any unit at Pyongyang occurred in the 822nd Engineer Aviation Battalion. It had a good start in loading its equipment for evacuation and had most of it on flatcars. But before its trains could move, an explosion erupted in one of the ammunition cars in the main rail yards and stopped all further rail movement from there. About 185 carloads of engineering equipment and supplies, approximately 75 percent of the battalion's property, had to be abandoned for destruction.[27] Army Service units and supply installations were so sorely pressed for time in accordance with orders delivered to them for evacuation that 8,000 to 10,000 tons of supplies and equipment were unnecessarily lost. The regrettable aspect of these losses is that most of them could have been prevented if two or three days more had been given for evacuation.[28] It seems certain that this amount of time was indeed available if panic had not seized those in authority. The Chinese did not enter Pyongyang, or come close to it in any numbers, for at least that length of time after the final evacuation. The rear guard, the 29th British Brigade, was never engaged, and other troops could have been held close to the city for possible engagement of advanced elements of the CCF moving toward Pyongyang if they had threatened the city before it had been evacuated in an orderly way.

One of the larger ordnance units with a depot in Pyongyang when the withdrawal started was the 44th Ordnance Company. It was the first field ordnance depot to arrive in Korea, entering Pusan harbor on 8 July 1950. Its mission then was to supply ordance equipment to the US 24th Division, the first American infantry division to be committed in the Korean War. Later the ordnance company supplied I Corps with ordnance equipment. In execution of this mission it arrived at Pyongyang on 31 October, and established itself at the Military Academy of North Korea on the north side of the Taedong River, the personnel occupying some of the then-empty buildings. Its supplies and equipment were trucked to it from Pusan and Inchon, with some reaching it from Chinnampo in the last few days prior to withdrawal. A truck round trip to and from Pusan required ten days.

The Pusan railroad became operational to Taedong Station on the south side of the Taedong River at Pyongyang only about two weeks before all of Eighth Army was in full retreat from the city. At this time the 44th Ordnance Company Depot carried 550 tons of stock, three times its normal capacity and intended to supply 25,000 troops. Its 550 tons of stock was considered able to supply one army corps. In addition to the 550 tons of current serviceable supplies, it had 1,500 tons of captured enemy and unserviceable UN and American supplies. Capt. Wayne Kallimuki commanded the 44th Ordnance Company at the time; Capt. Robert M. Elser was executive officer.[29]

The drill field of the North Korean Military Academy was large, about 15 to 20 acres. From the beginning the 44th Ordnance Company used this big open space as a collecting point for disabled ordnance. In November it had collected here a vast amount of items held for repair. There were between 30 and 40 US tanks, none of them operational; 200 2½-ton trucks; 300 weapons carriers and jeeps; one 8-inch howitzer; three or four 105-mm howitzers; 10 to 15 high-speed tractors used as prime movers for artillery pieces; and about 2,000 boxes of truck engines, transmissions, differentials, and transfer cases. When the word for withdrawal came, the Ordnance Company closed the collecting point; no more damaged or inoperable ordnance was received, and every unit with such items had to try to get its equipment out to safety as best it could. The amount of transportation in Pyongyang when the Eighth Army began its withdrawal made it almost certain that very few inoperable items would ever get out. This prospect applies to the huge collection point of the 44th Ordnance Company. Because of this situation, the gates of the collecting point were opened on 2 December, and cannibalization of the equipment invited to all who could make use of parts to keep their own organic equipment operational for the withdrawal.[30]

The 44th Ordnance Company received an alert at 9 P.M. on 30 November to be ready to move from Pyongyang no later than 2 December. Captain Kallimuki started at once to load less critical items such as tank treads, engines, and other items that normally would not be needed for use at once. The more critical items such as tires, the GMC front springs, spark plugs, fan belts, small arms, and antifreezing compounds were issued to the division ordnance companies. The 15 105-mm howitzers it had were issued to the 24th Infantry and the 1st Cavalry Divisions. Other supples and equipment available were issued on request, regardless of whether such units would normally be authorized to draw them. On 1 December, 35 railcars were made available to the company at the rail station, which was nine miles from the ordnance depot. It required two hours for a truck from the depot to make a round-trip to the rail station in the snarl of traffic it had to pass through. The loading of the boxcars at the station continued throughout 1 December and after dark. The night was cold, and the ordnance personnel built a bonfire to keep themselves warm during the unloading and reloading. Moonlight during part of the night helped. By daylight of 2 December all boxcars had been loaded. The remaining supplies and equipment were loaded on 2½-ton trucks and 15-ton semitrailers at the ordnance depot. At 8 A.M. on 2 December 18 semitrailer vans and trucks started from the ordnance depot, crossed the Taedong River, and headed south on the MSR. The 44th Ordnance personnel rode on 15 trucks.

An Engineer detachment with some bulldozers arrived at the depot and pushed all equipment that could not be evacuated into a large pile, where it was burned. When the convoy left the depot, five semitrailers were left parked there because prime movers were not able to pull them.

The ordnance convoy found that, out on the road, traffic was bumper to bumper, with average speed for a while at one and a half miles an hour. March discipline seemed to be completely lacking on the road, with numerous accidents and blockages. Snow started falling on the night of the second, and by morning of 3 December there was six inches of it on the ground. The 44th Ordnance Company arrived at Yongdong-po at 8 P.M. on 3 December.

Captain Kallimuki detached five tractors from the semitrailers they had been pulling and, on 4 December sent them back to Pyongyang to bring out the five loaded semitrailers left parked in the 44th Ordnance Depot, north of the river. When they arrived at the Taedong River, they found the bridge had already been blown, and they could not cross to the north side. The guard that had been left with the five semitrailers had left on 4 December. Since the bridges were blown on the morning of 5 December, and the tractors arrived there that day, it can be seen that a short delay in destroying the Taedong bridges would have saved this ordnance matériel. It is not known what happened to these five loaded semitrailers. Each semitrailer was loaded with 15 tons, making a total of 75 tons of ordnance lost. The 44th Ordnance Company had successfully evacuated 18 vans loaded with 10 tons each for 180 tons, and 2½-ton trucks brought out another 20 tons, for a total of 200 tons saved. Captain Elser said he did not know what happened to the 35 railcars loaded with ordnance matériel they left ready to be pulled out in the Pyongyang rail yard. Since he and the 44th Ordnance Company never heard of them again, there is a presumption that they did not get out.[31] Sfc. John H. Wright of the Ordnance Company said that, at this time during the evacuation of Pyongyang, if anyone got cold he would burn his spare tire for warmth.

On 27 November, the 57th Ordnance Recovery Company, Capt. Willard Baker commanding, was at Anju and Kunu-ri. It was an I Corps unit, its mission to undertake battlefield recovery of disabled tanks and to assist in recovery of other disabled ordnance items. Two days later it was getting caught in the early withdrawal of heavy ordnance equipment. The 2nd Platoon arrived at Pyongyang and bivouacked at the large drill grounds of the North Korean Military Academy, where the 44th Ordnance Depot Company was established. At 4 P.M. the afternoon of 29 November, Captain Lawrence, the motor officer of the 6th Heavy Tank Battalion, arrived at the platoon's area tired and excited. He told Captain Baker that nine tanks of the 6th Tank Battalion were some miles north of Pyongyang, limping along, and needed help. Some of the tanks were on the main road toward Sukchon, others were on the road from Sunchon. These two roads converged about two miles north of Pyongyang, where the Sunchon road joined the main Sukchon-Anju-Sinanju road. Captain Baker asked his operations officer, Lt. Gentle S. Banks, if he could help. Banks replied he thought he could. Banks together with Lts. Robert L. Brown and LeRoy Ingram went to the motor pool to see what they could send out to help the tanks get in. They found they could send five tractors on the rescue mission. Lieutenant Brown took the Sukchon road, and Lieutenant Ingram took the Sunchon road. Southbound traffic was heavy on both roads.

A regimental officer of an infantry column moving south met Ingram's tractors and ordered Ingram to pull them off to the side of the road, because they were interfering with a tactical withdrawal. Ingram pulled his tractors off to the side for an hour while the infantry column passed. He then continued toward Sunchon, and nine miles from Pyongyang, at 11 P.M., he found some of the tanks. Their drivers had pulled the tanks off at the side of the road and had built a fire. They were cold and dispirited. Ingram attached his three tractors to three Patton tanks and pulled them into Pyongyang. On the Sukchon road, Lieutenant Brown met crippled tanks 13 miles north of Pyongyang at 9:30 P.M. and pulled two more Patton tanks into Pyongyang. Ingram and Brown pulled these tanks over the pontoon bridge to Taedong Station on the south side of the river. They arrived there about midnight.

The next morning, Lieutenants Banks and Ingram went to the Taedong Station to make arrangements with the RTO for use of flatcars to evacuate the tanks. They learned no cars were available at the station. Lieutenant Banks then decided to move the tanks over a dirt road to Sadon Station, a small rail-marshaling yard five miles east of Pyongyang. On the way the lead tank damaged a bridge, and there was a delay until Engineers made necessary repairs. The tanks arrived at Sadon Station just before noon. The tractors left the tanks there and returned to their own organization to pull their own trailers south across the Taedong River.

At Sadon Station, Lieutenant Banks had urged the RTO to load the tanks, saying that two of them had special, secret new equipment—torquematic transmissions and bore evacuators—that could not be allowed to fall into enemy hands. Lieutenant Flicker, the RTO, told Banks that Eighth Army had given the Air Force priority loading privileges at Sadon Station. The Air Force was loading an assortment of boxes, tables, chairs, and office equipment. Banks told Lieutenant Flicker that he would need the use of the ramp to load the tanks but that the Air Force could load its equipment without the use of the ramp. Flicker then pointed out that Banks had no cars at the station to load the tanks, even if he had use of the ramp. Banks said he would try to get some cars. Flicker said he would talk with the Air Force lieutenant colonel who was in charge of the Air Force loading operation, to see if he would agree to give up use of the ramp. Banks overheard the conversation that followed. The Air Force officer flatly refused, saying he had priority and he wanted to use the ramp and all the cars. The situation at Sadon Station remained unchanged throughout 30 November.

The next day a switch engine arrived at Sadon Station at 8 P.M. with six flatcars of replacement tanks for the 6th and 70th tank battalions. The Air Force crew left just about that time, and the ramp became available. In leaving, the Air Force abandoned much of its equipment at the rail yard. Banks told the North Korean locomotive operator to switch the cars and bring the flatcars to the ramp. The newly arrived replacement tanks were then unloaded. It was then found that two of them would not start. The 57th Ordnance Recovery Company had all the tanks unloaded before midnight, but only two disabled tanks were loaded during the rest of the night. The next morning, loading resumed and went faster. At 8 A.M. that morning, 2 December, Banks received orders that the 57th Ordnance Recovery Company had to leave Pyongyang by noon the next day, 3 December.

According to Lieutenant Banks, 17 disabled tanks had been loaded on the flatcars by 9:30 A.M. on 3 December—14 disabled M-46 Patton tanks, the two M-46 Patton replacement tanks that would not start, and one M-26 Pershing tank. Banks notified Flicker, the RTO at Sadon Station, that the tank loading was completed and the cars could be pulled out of the station. Lieutenant Flicker could not give assurance they would be moved—there was no locomotive there. Banks then telephoned Lt. Col. Herbert W. Wurtzler, I Corps ordnance officer. Wurtzler was not in his office to take the call, but it was relayed to him. He in turn notified Eighth Army that the tanks were loaded and ready for evacuation. A locomotive was needed. Eighth Army said it would be sent. A little later, the RTO at Sariwon notified Lieutenant Colonel Wurtzler that three locomotives had started for the Sadon Station. None ever arrived there. The last train that left Sadon Station carried the 14th Engineer Battalion, but no tanks.

On 4 December the Air Force reported a daylight attack of F-51s and F-80s that destroyed eight and damaged six friendly tanks in the vicinity of Pyongyang. Two days later, on 6 December, the US I Corps Ordnance Section received a report from the Air Force that it had destroyed 16 tanks at Pyongyang— 15 M-46 Patton tanks and one M-26 Pershing tank. These were the tanks that Lieutenant Banks and personnel of the 57th Ordnance Recovery Company had tried so hard to evacuate from Pyongyang. Thus, we see the devoted work, frustration, and final failure of a less than smoothly running Army machine in the course of a major defeat and its aftermath.[32]

The personnel of the 57th Ordnance Recovery Company were under firm orders to evacuate Pyongyang by noon, 3 December. On the way south, about 15 miles below Sariwon, military police would not allow the company to stop to retrieve one of its wrecker vehicles that had slid off the road. They insisted that to do so would interrupt traffic moving south. The Ordnance Company had another defeat in that it had to pour gasoline on the vehicle and burn it. In their withdrawal, company personnel saw many other vehicles burned along the side of the road.

In Pyongyang, where explosions and fires were becoming ever more common on 3 and 4 December as the evacuation continued, one stood out above all others. It started as an accident. A British truck loaded with ammunition accidentally caught fire at 11 P.M. on 3 December at the British ASP 16 near the Pyongyang K-23 airfield. The burning truck and exploding ammunition in it started a chain reaction of explosions in the Ammunition Supply Point that continued until 100 tons of British ammunition and 900 tons of American ammunition had been destroyed. Among the losses were 10,000 rounds of 105-mm howitzer shells and 1,000 rounds of 155-mm howitzer shells. The burning and exploding ammunition at ASP 16 continued through the early hours of 4 December. All traffic on the roads near it was stopped for a period of three hours. This big fire and the thunderous roar of exploding shells, heard throughout the city, caused chaos during the night. It also caused a delay in the departure of some military units in the withdrawal.[33]

In the developing crisis in Korea during the first days of December, the Joint Chiefs of Staff decided that their agent for Korean Affairs, Army Chief of Staff J. Lawton Collins, should visit Japan and Korea for the purpose of making a personal appraisal of the situation, talk with Generals MacArthur, Walker, and Almond, and then report back to them. Collins's arrival in Tokyo nearly coincided with the big explosions at ASP 16 in Pyongyang. Collins conferred hastily with MacArthur on the morning of 4 December, immediately after his arrival, and then left for Seoul, Korea. General Walker flew from Pyongyang to Seoul that day to meet Collins, who later in the day continued on to Sariwon, where he met General Milburn, commander of I Corps.

The next day, 5 December, Collins flew to Hamhung in northeast Korea, where he conferred with General Almond. That night he returned to Tokyo. The next day he conferred with General MacArthur, Admiral Joy, and General Stratemeyer, together with Generals Hickey, Wright, and Willoughby of MacArthur's staff. On 8 December General Collins was back in Washington, where he reported to the Joint Chiefs of Staff.

Collins had submitted an interim report to the Joint Chiefs on 4 December after his first meeting with MacArthur and before he left for Korea. In it he said that the X Corps had been ordered to assemble in the Hamhung area, that Eighth Army would hold the Pyongyang area as long as possible, but that the Far East Command felt it would "ultimately have to fall back to Seoul-Inchon area. No estimate now on this timing."[34] It is difficult to understand this last analysis of the Eighth Army situation because General Walker had already the day before informed General MacArthur that he could not hold Pyongyang, and on 3 December he had ordered its evacuation.

In his conference with General Collins at Seoul on 4 December, General Walker told Collins that he could continue the Eighth Army withdrawal without further serious losses unless he were ordered to defend the Seoul-Inchon area. In that event he felt the Chinese could encircle him. He felt that an evacuation of the army from Inchon would be costly and that, if an evacuation of the army from Korea became necessary, it should be made from Pusan and not from Inchon. Walker felt he could safely get the army into a defensive position at Pusan and hold there for an indefinite time if the X Corps joined him there. At Hamhung, Collins found that General Almond believed he could hold the Hamhung-Hungnam area for an indefinite period and could withdraw from it successfully when ordered. General Collins agreed with these assessments.

When General Collins returned to Tokyo on the evening of 5 December he knew the views of Generals Walker and Almond. He spent the next day going over the several options General MacArthur presented for action during the period ahead. General MacArthur told General Collins that, if the CCF continued their attack and he received no reinforcements from the United States or from the Nationalist Chinese, if he were not allowed to mount air attacks against China, and if there were no blockade against China, his forces would have to be withdrawn from Korea. Use of the atomic bomb in North Korea was discussed. General MacArthur agreed with General Walker that, if the UN troops were withdrawn from Korea, it should be done through the port of Pusan. General Collins agreed. The other options considered need not be discussed here, as the conditions that did prevail as policy decisions in Washington were those just mentioned. General MacArthur made it clear to General Collins that he felt impossible restrictions were being placed on him in conducting the war.[35]

The Last Troops out of Pyongyang

While the British 29th Brigade was the tactical infantry organization for the protection of Pyongyang from possible CCF attack during its evacuation, the I Corps Engineers carried out the destruction of the Taedong River bridges, the rail and warehouse facilities, and selected targets within the city. It is impossible to know precisely what unit was the last to leave Pyongyang. It is reasonably clear, however, that, when all tactical units had passed through their perimeter and crossed the Taedong River during the night of 4–5 December, the British 29th Brigade informed the Engineer demolition units to start their final work–the destruction of the bridges crossing the Taedong River. These were blown by 7:20 A.M. on 5 December. I Corps Engineers reported to the I Corps commander at 8 A.M. that morning that all planned demolitions had been completed.

Within the British 29th Brigade, the Royal Ulster Battalion is credited with being the last infantry unit to cross from the north to the south side of the river, at 6:30 A.M. on 5 December. Some Engineer units of I Corps crossed later after their last demolitions north of the river. Maj. Gen. William F. Marquat, of the Antiaircraft Artillery (AAA AW), says that D Battery, 865th AAA AW Battalion, engaged in airfield defense at Pyongyang, was the last American unit to leave the city. It is probable, however, that some unidentified Engineer demolition squad of the I Corps Engineers were the last troops to leave Pyongyang.

In any event, all UN troops were out of Pyongyang by 9 A.M. on 5 December, except possibly for a few inevitable stragglers.[36]

On 5 December, as Eighth Army completed the evacuation of Pyongyang, it requested that General MacArthur change the boundary between the X Corps and itself to give the army control of all the area eastward not occupied by X Corps and then for the boundary to follow the 39th Parallel eastward to the coast. It also requested that the Navy be required to watch the east coast south of Hamhung and to land ROK Navy patrols there to question civilians about potential and actual enemy activities. Eighth Army also asked for air surveillance of this area. These requests reflected Eighth Army's concern about CCF and North Korean troop movements in the central and eastern parts of the Korean peninsula and their potential of outflanking the army on the east and cutting it off from Pusan.[37]

Chinnampo Evacuated

The decision to evacuate Pyongyang carried with it necessarily the decision also to abandon its port, Chinnampo, situated 30 air miles southwest on an estuary of the Taedong River where it empties into the Yellow Sea. This event was particularly ironic in that, at tremendous effort, the US Navy, in its greatest minesweeping effort ever made, had just cleared the 84-mile-long channel leading to the port. Supplies for Eighth Army in support of its operations north of Pyongyang had just started arriving from Chinnampo. All that the Navy had accomplished at Chinnampo was speedily undone. It literally went up in smoke.[38]

It chanced that, on 1 December US Navy Transport Squadron 1, with APA (attack) transports *Bayfield, Bexar,* and *Okanogan,* and AKAs (cargo ships) *Algol* and *Montague,* with Capt. S. G. Kelly in the *Bayfield,* commanding, were en route from Japan to Inchon. While steaming north in the Yellow Sea on the afternoon of 3 December Captain Kelly intercepted an urgent message from Eighth Army to the commander, Navy Far East, to divert these ships to Chinnampo to help evacuate that port. Captain Kelly did not receive any immediate orders from the Navy Far East to change his destination, and for five hours he continued on course. Then, on his own initiative at 10 P.M., he changed course and headed for Chinnampo. The next morning at 3:30 on 4 December, Kelly intercepted a naval message that six destroyers were available to protect his transports and that the *Ceylon* was leaving Sasebo, Japan, to join them. Unknown to Kelly, Admiral Andrewes, in the aircraft carrier *Theseus,* and four destroyers were also preparing to sail for Chinnampo.

Meanwhile at Chinnampo, Lt. Comdr. Henry J. Erekson, with the destroyer escort *Foss,* was providing the town with electric power. Off the mouth of the Taedong River, a mine-sweeping group was still at work. There was a small South Korean naval base with three motor launches at Chinnampo. About 3 A.M. on 4 December, the South Korean naval-base commander reported to Erekson that Eighth Army had ordered him to leave at once, and that he had 100 sailboats available to remove some refugees. Of the 50,000 refugees on hand, he estimated he could take only 20,000 out by sea; the remaining 30,000 would have to go by land.

The American transports under Captain Kelly through the night continued on their way toward Chinnampo. At 9:30 A.M. on 4 December his group of five ships, with the exception of the *Bexar*, had reached the outer end of the 84-mile swept channel and started in. Believing that surrounded army units were awaiting rescue, Kelly gave orders to man all guns, lower all boats, commence loading at once, and keep steam up to the throttles. About this time he received a succession of radio messages that the destroyers were on their way to give protection and that the next day the *Theseus* would be there to give air cover. Captain Kelly was now in charge of the Chinnampo evacuation.

Kelly and his transport crews quickly learned that the only army troops at Chinnampo were 1,700 port logistics personnel and about 7,000 South Koreans, some of them wounded soldiers; others were government workers, military and political prisoners, and police. The *Bexar*, coming up the channel in the dark, had now arrived. With the loading rapidly nearing completion, the main problem ahead was to get safely back down the tortuous channel. It was considered best to leave Chinnampo as soon as possible because it was a poor place in which to be caught. Hills came down to the harbor's edge. From the reverse slope enemy mortars could hit the ship anchorage. Word came that Chinese were in Pyongyang, and that some of their forces were closing on Chinnampo—an erroneous report. At 9 P.M. on the night of 4 December the six destroyers had reached the mouth of the Taedong and started in to protect the transports at Chinnampo. Two of them never made it, one going aground and the other fouling a screw propeller in a buoy cable. The latter turned back. By 2:40 A.M. on 5 December the other four destroyers (*Cuyuga, Athabaskan, Bataan,* and *Forrest Royal*) anchored off Chinnampo and trained their guns on the waterfront.

Loading continued on the morning of the fifth, mostly refugees packing into sailboats, which then slipped downriver. In the afternoon, aircraft from the *Theseus* arrived over Chinnampo. Half an hour after noon, the American transports began leaving the Chinnampo anchorage individually, and by 2:30 P.M. the beach was nearly empty. But then, suddenly, 3,000 more Korean refugees arrived. The unexpected arrival of another ship, which had not received notice of diversion to another destination, solved that problem, and the refugees were taken from the dock to this ship. At 5:30 P.M. on 5 December, the *Bexar*, the last of the transports to leave, headed downstream together with the destroyer escort *Foss*. LSTs, having the port logistics personnel aboard, anchored in the harbor for the night. The destroyers then bombarded the oil storage tanks, harbor cranes, railway equipment, and everything else considered of military value to the enemy. After daylight on 6 December, the destroyers and the LSTs made an uneventful trip down the channel. The night before, the *Bexar* had grounded north of Sokto but got herself free without damage. A blinding snowstorm raged over the mouth of the Taedong and the Yellow Sea on the sixth. The passage through the open sea was not without danger, as floating mines were frequently encountered. About 2,000 tons of military supplies at Chinnampo were destroyed in the evacuation of the port.[39]

After the evacuation of Pyongyang, the rumor spread (and was repeated by some officers of the army) that a large amount of highly secret enemy materials, collected by a special American task force in the first hours after the capture of Pyongyang in October, had been lost in the hectic evacuation of the city on

4–5 December. Lt. Col. Ralph L. Foster, G-2 of the US 2nd Infantry Division, had led this task force, known as Task Force Indianhead, named from the shoulder patch of the 2nd Division. It had been attached to the 1st Cavalry Division for the entry into Pyongyang. Its mission was to enter the city with the leading 1st Cavalry troops and to secure and protect certain government buildings and foreign compounds until they could be searched for intelligence materials. Highly classified Soviet and North Korean materials were obtained in this way. The rumor that this material had been lost was untrue. The material, collected by Foster's group and Counter Intelligence Corps (CIC) agents, was turned over to a Far East Command General Headquarters Team from Tokyo, headed by Maj. Eugene Kryloff, and flown back to Japan to ATIS. The rumor regarding the loss of this material apparently derived from the fact that a copy of a summary report on it was lost with all 2nd Division G-2 records in the withdrawal from Pyongyang.[40]

The Last Hours of Eighth Army Headquarters in Pyongyang

If one counts 5 December as the last day any Eighth Army and UN troops were in Pyongyang, American troops had held this oldest of Korean cities for 47 days. First Lt. James H. Bell's F Company, 5th Cavalry Regiment, had reached outskirts of the city about noon on 19 October. The ROK 15th Regiment of the ROK 1st Division was the first unit to cross the Taedong River and reach the main part of Pyongyang later in the day. On 24 October, five days later, when Lt. Gen. Walton H. Walker arrived in Pyongyang to take personal command of the Eighth Army Advance CP, which Col. William A. Collier, deputy chief of staff, had established in the North Korean capitol building two days earlier, he took over Kim Il Sung's room as his office. No one ever disturbed Joseph Stalin's picture in its place on the wall of the room, and it was still there when Eighth Army abandoned the city.[41]

It seems appropriate to describe the last days of the Eighth Army occupancy of its Advance Headquarters in Pyongyang, especially since we have, in Cpl. Randle M. Hurst's manuscript, an eyewitness account. He appears to be the last American soldier to have left the building in the evacuation of Pyongyang. Hurst, a member of the 502nd Reconnaissance Platoon, General Walker's personal bodyguard, gives an intimate view of what the CP was like in the midst of the hectic withdrawal from North Korea.

Hurst was a native of Oklahoma City. He volunteered for the army at the age of 19, in 1948, and arrived at Yokohama, Japan, in October 1949. He was assigned to the 519th Military Police Battalion. In it he was a member of "the General's Platoon," C Company, and was present for duty on 19 October 1949. The platoon numbered about 25 soldiers, who guarded Lt. Gen. Walton H. Walker's residence and his Eighth Army Headquarters office in downtown Yokohama. In the spring of 1950, the General's Guard Platoon of C Company, Military Police, was changed to the 502nd Reconnaissance Platoon. It then had about 45 men.

On July 7, a short time after the North Korean Army invaded South Korea, 32 men of the 502nd Reconnaissance Platoon learned they were to go to Korea at once. Hurst was one of them. The next day he was one of an advance detail of ten men leaving by plane for Korea. On 9 July the advance group landed at Taejon. There the group reported to General Dean's 24th Division Headquarters. But they learned they were at the wrong place. They returned to the airfield and took off for Taegu, where Eighth Army's Headquarters opened that day. General Walker arrived at Taegu on 13 July, and Hurst says he was the first guard to go on duty at the general's door. From that time on he was one of those who guarded the general and stood guard post at his CP or at his residence. Hurst felt from what he saw and heard that two older officers on the general's staff, Cols. William A. Collier and Eugene M. Landrum, ran the headquarters. General Walker always called Landrum "General Landrum." Walker's and Landrum's offices and homes were always adjacent to each other, he said. Hurst considered General Walker a very moral and conventional person and strictly "business" with everyone.

General Walker used two special jeeps in dashing around to his troop positions in the battles of the Pusan perimeter. He followed much the same pattern in North Korea most of the time. Often Hurst's job was to handle the .50-caliber machine gun in the second jeep, which carried a guard detail to protect the general. These trips were always marked by fast driving to keep up with the general's jeep, which was driven by M. Sgt. George Belton, who was considered by the others to be an extremely fast and sometimes reckless driver.

Corporal Hurst reached Pyongyang on or about 12 November, and thereafter often stood guard at the post just outside the general's door if the general was in his office, or, if the general was absent, he stood guard inside the office. He often looked at the general's desk, formerly used by Kim Il Sung, and gazed at Joseph Stalin's portrait on the wall behind the desk.

Hurst said that security at the Eighth Army Headquarters in Pyongyang was tight. The 502nd Reconnaissance Platoon used two tanks in their perimeter guard posts, and at night the motor of one of them was always kept warmed up. Hurst said that Walker was not in his office much of the time in November – perhaps he would be there for a short time half of the days. And after 24 November, when Eighth Army's attack to the border started, he was seldom there. The impression in the guard platoon was that he was somewhere in the Anju area and that he traveled almost entirely by plane wherever he had to go.

Hurst describes the Pyongyang Army Headquarters building as having a large marble lobby just inside the entrance. At the back of the lobby a large staircase curved up from either side to the second floor. The offices of General Walker and his principal staff were on the second floor. From the staircase landing, Colonel Collier's office came first on the right along the hallway that ran the length of the second floor. General Walker's office was just beyond it at the end of the hallway. A guard, usually from the Military Police, stood at the bottom of the staircase on the first floor; another, from the 502nd Reconnaissance Platoon, stood either just outside Walker's door if he was inside or in the room if the general was absent.[42]

On 3 December, Lt. George Duckworth, commander of the 502nd Reconnaissance Platoon, came to Hurst, who was walking guard around General Walker's residence, and told him that he and another member of the platoon, Corporal Barns, would have to stay in Pyongyang another night. The two of them would have to provide security for a group of Eighth Army Headquarters

Company who had been left to ransack the building for any documents left behind when the headquarters departed. When this group finished its work and left, then Hurst and Barns could go.

Hurst and Barns had a jeep from their rifle section, with a .50-caliber machine-gun pedestal mounted on it. Barns had loaded the jeep with his and Hurst's gear, and he was waiting for him at the front steps of the capitol building. The Eighth Army Headquarters security officer, a captain, Duckworth said, would tell him when to cease guard duty at the residence. Then Lieutenant Duckworth said, "Goodbye, Randy; I'll see you in Seoul." Shortly after noon Hurst saw a captain walking toward him from the capitol building. He came directly to Hurst and said, "Corporal Hurst, you are relieved of duty at this guard post." Hurst saluted and headed for Barns.[43]

It was noon or a little after on 3 December, when Hurst walked over to Barns's jeep in front of the North Korean capitol building. Hurst's words pick up his story:

The 502 Rec had departed at least by 1000, and many units of 8th Army Headquarters had departed the day before. Barns and I ended up sitting on our jeep right in front of the front steps of the NK Capitol building watching the last of 8th Army Headquarters leave. We made C-ration coffee on our little coleman stove on the hood of our jeep and watched Col. Collier and several of the G-staff officers climb into a jeep and roll away. Col. Collier sat in the rear of the jeep and at least two generals were in the jeep with him. I do not recall who drove the jeep. After that we saw the last 519th MP jeep leave and I think Pvt Hollis was driving it. Pvt Hollis was formerly Sgt Hollis of Company C, 519th Battalion. I do not recall what he got busted for. Pvt Hollis did not know Barns, but knew me and shouted, "See you in Seoul, Randy," and away he went.

Barns and I chaffed [chafed] as we sat in front of the NK Cap building. We wanted to be on the road to Seoul like everyone else. As the afternoon wore on, on that bitter cold day, the area got strangely quiet. Pretty soon there was no one moving about anywhere. During the preceding 18 days, the traffic circle in front of the NK Cap building was quite busy and required traffic control by C Company MPs. British, Turks, South Korean officers, war correspondents, and people from I Corps and divisions forward were constantly coming and going in that traffic circle. Bed Check Charlie even visited us nearly every night, drawing fire from all the 40 mm in town. But now the place was deathly quiet. No civilians in sight anywhere. All buildings were deserted in the area except the NK Cap building. Very late in the afternoon, a fat master sergeant leaned over the 2nd floor balcony railing . . . and said to us, "What's the matter with you guys?" Barns replied, "We want to get going to Seoul." The fat m/sgt replied, "You guys come on up and have a beer." So Barns and I went up on the 2nd floor and drank beer and sat on desk tops while the pencil pushers were bundling up papers and junk to take with them to Seoul. Nothing, not even toilet paper, was being left in that building. Finally, when it was dark, the fat m/sgt said that the task was completed and every one could head for Seoul. There were no commissioned officers present at all. I mean none anywhere. The pencil pushers had a lot of beer. We all ended up on the ground floor in the left wing. . . . Barns and I decided to drive down to the bridge across the Taedong River and see if we could get across. That bridge was the standard Army plank bridge. One of our exercises in drafting training at Ft.

Belvoir, Va., was to draw the profile plan of that bridge. When we got to the highway that crossed that bridge, we found it jammed with traffic bumper to bumper . . . just an incredible procession of vehicles crossing that bridge and going south. The I Corps MPs guarding the bridge were surly and would not let us break into the traffic crossing the bridge. They had never heard of our outfit and thought all of 8th Army Headquarters had gone south days ago. Finally, Barns and I drove back to the NK Cap building to spend the night. We fell in with some other I Corps MPs who were wandering around. We all parked our jeeps in front of the NK Cap building and ate C-rations in the offices and in the lobby of the building.

As it grew dark, that night of 3 December 1950, I wondered if we should not check out the upper floors of the building. There were no commissioned officers anywhere. There were about 20 pencil pushers and maybe 5 or 6 I Corps MPs, all enlisted men, some drunk, and none too much worried about security until it got dark. Barns and I talked it over with the MPs and we agreed that Barns and I would guard until midnight, then the MPs would guard until daylight, then we would all leave. At this point I decided to check out the upper floors of the building. I took my M-3 submachine gun with two mags (60 rounds), my .45 caliber pistol, and two frag grenades with me, and before I ascended the stairs, I warned everybody not to come up because I planned to work from the top down and I would riddle anything moving on any upper floor. All agreed to remain on ground floor. So then I went to the very top floor of the building . . . and checked out every office and every corridor in that whole building. I did not go up on the roof because I could not find the way up there. It was as cold inside the building as it was outside. I had cover open and bolt back on that submachine gun so I could shoot with one trigger pull, and I poked my nose and my submachine gun into every room in that whole building, including the General's office. . . . I found no one. The place was just a huge haunted house. It was an eerie experience and well after dark by the time I descended to the first floor for the last time. I told the group gathered around the hibachi that the NKs had not moved in above us yet.

Several times that evening I strolled along the front of the building, looking around. There was no one anywhere. Traffic was moving on the road south, but that road was not near enough to the NK Cap building for us to hear or see the traffic, as I recall. I do not recall hearing or seeing it. Barns set up our cots in an office on the right of the front entrance. . . . I continued to circulate around the ground floor of the building until midnight. Several pencil pushers and MPs were worried. The fat m/sgt was sound asleep in a hammock he had improvised. At midnight the MPs supposedly took over the guard, and Barns and I sacked out in our sleeping bags in that office.

Barns and I awoke when a terrific blast shook the building. I jumped out of the sack in my long handles and stocking feet, grabbed my M-3 submachine gun, and ran out into the lobby. The pencil pushers and MPs had left. There was no one in that whole building but Barns and me. Our jeep was still in front. We had removed the bug so it was inoperable. We pulled on our clothes and boots, rolled up sleeping bags, folded up our cots, gathered all our stuff, and piled it all on the jeep. We saw no one. Several more heavy explosions occured as Barns and I were frantically getting ready to roll. It must have been about 0600 4 December, and it was bitter, bitter cold. The explosions were across town. Each one lit up the sky briefly. Barns and I were scared. There was just no one in sight. . . . I loaded the gun [.50 caliber machine gun on pedestal mount]. . . .

... When Barns and I arrived at the bridge, we stopped to talk to the MPs. They had a bonfire going. I unloaded our 50 cal as I did not want an accident. Then some jeeps approached from the north and we started across the bridge behind them. Here is what happened. The jeep in front of us suddenly spun around on the icy bridge and the left front wheel jumped over the bridge rail, which was a low rail made out of timber. The whole bridge was a timber bridge. . . . Barns and I stopped to help the driver of the jeep that spun around. But when I looked under the canvas top of that jeep, there was no one behind the wheel. Another jeep stopped behind ours and we were all mystified. Then a man came walking toward us from the south end of the bridge and he was moaning. (It was dark and cold, mind you.) One of the men from the jeep that had stopped behind us shouted, "What the hell you doing?" The man who was moaning and walking toward us said, "I was thrown clear out of the jeep and landed on the ice down there." We looked over the edge of the bridge and there was ice on the river about 15 feet below. When the jeep spun around, the driver, alone in the jeep, was pitched out and over the rail onto the ice below. He fell about 15 feet. He was not hurt, apparently, but badly shaken. We lifted his wheel off the rail of the bridge, turned his jeep around, and he drove off. Barns and I climbed back into our jeep and headed south. . . .

. . . We soon overtook vehicles as the road south of us was jammed. Barns and I were a couple of pirates. We passed everyone. Officers yelled at us. The MPs stopped us several times and chewed us out for doubling the convoy, etc. We just kept going. We had great difficulty passing M-26 tanks. All of them are nearly 10 feet wide and they used both sides of the road. They all had infantry on their fenders, and they were bedraggled looking infantry too. Barns and I did not try to read any bumper numbers or tank numbers. We didn't care whom we were passing. We just passed at every opportunity. Several times we saw overturned vehicles along the sides of the road. Also, pitifully, we saw refugees trudging along the road carrying all their possessions on their backs. I felt sorry for those wretched people. We offered no rides to anyone. We just kept going.

All traffic was going south until we got down below Kaesong, and then we encountered long truck convoys carrying infantry north. Again I did not read any bumper numbers. I have no idea who they were except that they were American troops, all infantry, going north somewhere south of Kaesong. The highway was now quite congested. Traffic going north and traffic going south at the same time.

I forgot to mention one fatality we saw on the road near Sariwon, I believe. This incident occurred about noon or shortly after. (It took all day to drive the 140 miles to Seoul.) We caught up with 2 DUKWs [amphibious trucks] laboring along the highway. They stopped in front of us and we saw a man lying in the road behind one of the DUKWs. He turned out to be a South Korean soldier who was one of a group who had thumbed a ride on the DUKWs. He fell off the rear deck onto the road and his friends shouted at the DUKW drivers so loudly that both vehicles stopped. Barns and I stopped also. No one attempted to help the man in the road. Everyone just stood around looking at him. He was lying on his back and not moving. So, I took his pulse, or tried to take it, and found none. The fellow was a young South Korean soldier, tall and slender in build. He sure seemed dead to me. Barns and I got back into our jeep, passed the DUKWs, and caught up with a Lt. Col. whose jeep was stopped way up ahead, and he was looking back at the DUKWs. We told him what had happened and then went on. . . .

Barnes and I found the 502 Recon back in the Women's Med College where we had been before. . . . The 502 Recon had resumed pulling guard at the office, the General's van (where he was staying each night), at the residence provided by the Repub of Korea . . . and around our own area. Everyone was gloomy.[44]

Chinese Enter Pyongyang on 6 December

Air observers covered the city of Pyongyang and the areas north and east of it all day of 5 December to report on enemy movements. There are many reports of enemy troop movements on the right (east) flank of Eighth Army, and several observers reported enemy troops crossing the Taedong River to the south side during the day. By noon, these reports said, Chinese troops had occupied two abandoned airfields east of Pyongyang. One observer reported 500 enemy troops with five camels in view below him farther east. As early as 10:10 A.M. on the fifth, an aerial observer reported enemy troops were moving onto the main Pyongyang airfield. An hour later he reported large numbers of others crossing the Taedong River, headed for the airfield. About 12:25 P.M., other reports said that UN air attacks killed an estimated 200 to 250 enemy troops at the river-crossing sites four miles east of the airfield. Two hours later another aerial report stated that strafing attacks killed an estimated 300 more enemy at the same river crossings. Still other aerial reports said five boatloads of enemy troops were destroyed at 5 P.M. at river crossing attempts 11 miles east of Pyongyang.[45]

It seems clear from aerial observer intelligence that large numbers of Chinese troops were crossing the Taedong River east of Pyongyang and that they had occupied the airfields on that side of the city during the afternoon and evening of 5 December. There is no proof, however, that they entered Pyongyang itself during the day. Korean civilian agents left behind in the city reported the Chinese did not enter the city until 6 December.[46]

On 5 December the Operations Section of Eighth Army gave its interpretation of the situation at that time as follows: "Major concern at the present time is the intentions of the enemy. Very little contact has been made with the enemy and his capabilities include envelopment around the east flank and complete occupation of Southern Korea. All plans and orders are designed to discover the enemy's movements and to delay him without becoming inextricably involved with his numerically superior forces."[47] This can be interpreted to mean that Eighth Army had no intention of fighting a major engagement with the CCF in the foreseeable future or of trying to halt its advance southward.

17. The Waist of Korea

In military action the narrow part of a peninsula always has tactical significance, especially for defensive action. From the narrow section of Korea's "waist" there is an ever-widening bulge northward, where it expands toward the east and the west until it joins the vast expanse of Asia, at Korea's 700-mile border. There is also a widening bulge south of the waist that becomes a thick finger with its tip at the port of Pusan, where the Korean Strait separates the peninsula from Japan. The waist of Korea did not play the important military role in the Korean War that it might have because General MacArthur wanted to unify all of Korea, and that plan meant carrying the sword all the way to the northern border.

Had the UN and the American forces stopped at the waist of Korea, they would have had the best defensive line north of the 38th Parallel to defend what had been gained. The American Joint Chiefs of Staff in the fall of 1950 thought the waist of Korea should have been the limit of UN advance. Great Britain thought the same thing. One question is paramount—could General Walker have made a stand there and have fought a successful battle to hold the waist of Korea at the beginning of December 1950, instead of retreating all the way to Seoul and giving up all of North Korea to the Communists, with the result that the UN might have to withdraw entirely from Korea?

General Walker adopted the military precept that, if he had to withdraw to save Eighth Army, he had to break contact with the enemy sharply and then withdraw as rapidly as possible over the full extent of the line and outrun pursuit to a considerable distance, where he might have time to reorganize his troops and to establish a defense line. That is what he did.

A good general description of the topography in the waist of Korea is found in an early American government report. It suggests why lateral travel across the peninsula was difficult almost everywhere, especially in the northern half of the country, where the Northern Taebaek Range of mountains, a southern extension of the Northern Korean Highlands, which extend across the Yalu into Manchuria, is the dominant geographic feature of the land.

> Here ridges trend mostly north-south but valleys extend in all directions. The region is rugged, partly forested, and well-drained but unfavorable for cross-country movement. Hills and ridges are generally 1,500 to 5,000 feet high and are steep. Valleys are narrow, gorge-like, and extremely winding. In their upper reaches the larger westward flowing rivers, such as the Chongchon, the

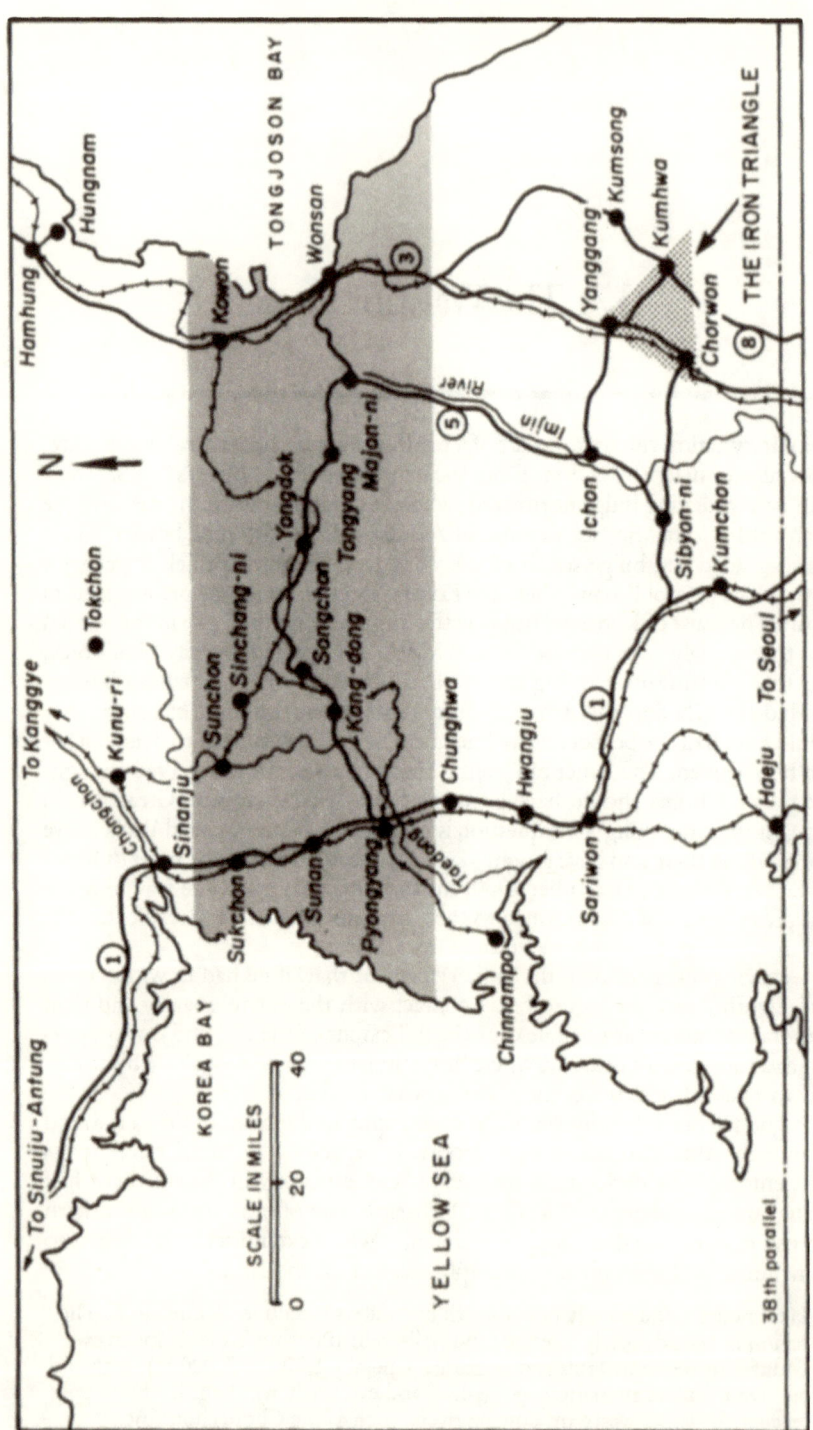

Map 14. The waist of Korea. Circled numerals indicate highway numbers.

Taedong, the Yesong, and the Imjin, flow in narrow, steep-sided valleys or gorges which provide no room for extensive movement or deployment. No routes suitable for rapid, large scale movement cross the region in any direction. Existing roads are narrow and winding and cross steep passes 2,000 to 3,600 feet high.[1]

The 39th Parallel may be identified closely with the waist of Korea. The parallel runs through Pyongyang on the west side of the waist and emerges into the Sea of Japan only 12 miles south of Wonsan on the east side.

The waist of Korea runs laterally from west to east from the North Korean capital of Pyongyang on the west side of the peninsula to Wonsan, a major port on its east side, an air-mile distance of about 100 miles. A vehicular road and a railroad connect the two places, winding through the Northern Taebaek Mountains most of the way. The vehicular road is approximately 150 miles long. This road in December 1950 was a poor one, dirt all the way, and in some places only one track wide.

If one extends the southwestern terminus of the waist of Korea corridor to the Korea Bay and includes the port of Chinnampo, 30 miles southwest of Pyongyang, then the waist of Korea would be about 125 air miles from sea to sea, from the Yellow Sea on the west to the Sea of Japan on the east. The vehicular road would be about 180 miles long. It would be logical to include the Chinnampo area within any defense line across the waist of Korea, since Chinnampo, the port for Pyongyang, would be of great logistic importance in defense warfare at the waist of Korea. There is no vehicular road or railroad crossing the peninsula north of the waist of Korea, although there are several of both crossing Korea laterally south of the waist. This fact obviously was of great importance to adversaries located on either side of the waist.

North of the waist of Korea there was a meager population living in small villages for the most part, with only the most primitive communications and transport system in a mountainous area. South of it there was an increasing density of population and a far better developed transportation and communication system. All the large cities in Korea were in, or south of, the waist of Korea except for the port of Hungnam and the nearby city of Hamhung on the east coast, north of Wonsan. These factors would strongly favor any military force occupying the waist of Korea and the land south of it. Those defending at the waist of Korea against a hostile force from the north would be in a favorable position.

The highway across the waist of Korea, starting at Wonsan on the east, passes through the principal towns and villages of Majon-ni, Tongyang, Yongdok, Songchon, and Kangdong. At Kangdong it meets the Taedong River and from there follows its course generally west to Pyongyang, twenty-odd miles away.

The lateral railroad at its eastern end does not follow the vehicular road from Wonsan but starts west across the waist from the town of Kowon, about 25 miles northwest of Wonsan, where it meets the main east-coast railroad, which continues on to Soviet Siberia. From Kowon the railroad goes nearly due west for approximately 25 air miles and then bends sharply south to Yongdok, where it meets the vehicular road from Wonsan. Thereafter, it generally follows the course of the road until it reaches Kangdong, where it crosses the road and continues south for about 15 miles and then turns directly west toward Pyongyang.

Of the towns mentioned on the vehicular road, the railroad after leaving Kowon goes through only Yongdok and Kangdong, but it passes close to Songchon.

For the most effective use of the logistic values of the railroad, the waist of Korea defense line would have to include the area as far north as Kowon on the east side. The defense line would have to encompass both the railroad and the vehicular road and be located to protect them from the north. Such a line would have to be located by engineers and tactical officers after a careful reconnaissance of the area to include the best topographical features. Such a study was never made.

The drainage pattern in the vicinity of Majon-ni, including the headwaters of the Imjin River and the lower course of the Taedong River, would probably have influenced the location of such a defense line. For the rest there would have had to have been selection of commanding ground and communication intersections on the north side of the lateral rail and vehicular road which required protection. Strong defenses would have had to be established at both Wonsan and Pyongyang. Naval forces could have been used to good advantage offshore at Wonsan and to a lesser extent at the mouth of the Taedong River estuary at and below Chinnampo.[2]

Aside from air reconnaissance, UN forces had very little firsthand knowledge of the condition of the lateral road from Pyongyang to Wonsan. Research revealed only one party of American soldiers who passed over it from end to end. According to Lt. Gen. William J. McCaffrey, USA, Ret. (a lieutenant colonel in charge of X Corps Advance CP at Wonsan in October 1950), Lt. Col. Olinto Barsanti with a small party in three jeeps drove from Wonsan to the Sukchon-Pyongyang area in late October 1950 to establish contact with the 187th Airborne RCT.[3] McCaffrey, who flew in a light plane from Wonsan over the eastern part of the road, said it was deserted at the time. He saw no enemy but noticed empty foxholes on ridges along both sides of the road at some places. The road itself looked to be hardly passable at many points.

The importance of the waist of Korea lay in the short distance across the peninsula from sea to sea on both flanks and in its communications and logistic facilities to the party that held it. This value is attested in a study published by the Far East Command in 1953, in which it stated that "the majority of [enemy] supply installations . . . are located contiguous to the major traffic arteries and the bulk of the enemy's major supply installations are encountered in the area adjacent to, and just below, the 39th parallel."[4]

This study stated that the road from Chongjin to Wonsan (No. 5), the coastal road from the Soviet border along the east coast to Wonsan, carried a surprisingly large amount of traffic and was maintained by a tremendous amount of repair work in the face of concerted UN efforts to disrupt its traffic. This road connected at Wonsan with the lateral route across the waist of Korea (No. 6). It said that, other than routes of entry into Korea from the Soviet Union and Manchuria, this lateral road was among the most important to the enemy in all Korea. The study stated further:

> Among the most important [roads] is undoubtedly Route No. 6 (Pyongyang to Wonsan) which runs generally along the 39th Parallel and through the major enemy supply complexes in NK. This route is the only major East-West route available to the enemy in Korea and consequently considerable stress has

been placed on its maintenance and repair. This route is a one and a half to two lanes gravel surfaced road with paved stretches as wide as thirty feet in urban areas, but has steep grades, sharp curves, and frequent defiles, particularly in the mountain areas. Due to constant enemy maintenance efforts along this route, it appears capable today of sustaining more traffic in relation to its originally assessed peace-time capacity than any other road in NK.[5]

The rail line from Kowon on the east coast to Pyongyang and to Sinanju via Sinchang-ni and Sunchon is listed as being 143 miles to Sinanju. About two-thirds of the way across the waist, a branch of the main rail line slants northwest to Sinanju via Kunu-ri, to make connection with the main west-coast rail line from Antung in Manchuria. Thus, there was rail connection from both main coastal rail lines into the heart of the waist of Korea. The Far East Command study, previously cited, stated that the enemy had made "special effort to keep this east-west link of the rail line open and operable. The main supply complexes of the enemy armies in N Korea are located contiguous to this line."

These observations, made two years after Barsanti and McCaffrey noted the primitive nature of the roads at the end of 1950, show how important the communications across the waist of Korea became to the Chinese and North Koreans following the UN retreat south of this strategic area in Korea in December 1950. They would have been equally important to the UN forces had they held this area, which they might well have done.

Some of the better informed and more perceptive war correspondents in Korea were aware that for the UN army to go north of the waist of Korea was a risky and dangerous adventure. One of them, Homer Bigart of the *New York Herald Tribune*, in a dispatch from the Chongchon River front on 28 November charged that the UN was beginning to pay the "initial price for the unsound decision to launch an offensive north of the peninsula's narrow neck." At that time he thought there were enough troops in Korea, if the X Corps in northeast Korea could be united to Eighth Army quickly, to hold "the neck of Korea." A week later he dispatched another report to the *Herald Tribune* from Seoul in which he alluded to the decision of the UN command to go beyond the waist of Korea. Events had proceeded faster and with more devastating results than even he had conceived possible just a week earlier. Now he wrote:

> Already some thoughtful officers are beginning to question the sanity of recent military decisions which may not have caused, but which certainly accelerated, this crisis. The most questionable decision of the last few weeks was MacArthur's abortive offensive. Before the offensive was launched, it was noted by some observers that any attempt to push beyond the neck of the peninsula would be unsound—even if the Communists withdrew. To fan out on a 700 mile frontier made no sense. It was an invitation to disaster.
>
> Adequate vigilance of the frontier would have required a force many times that of the UN . . . certainty of border incidents would compel UN troops to remain in Korea indefinitely.[6]

In Washington, there had been for a long time much worry over General MacArthur's tendency to ignore, or to talk his way around, instructions from the Joint Chiefs of Staff about how far north he should go in Korea. It was the settled opinion of the Joint Chiefs, the secretary of state, and the president, as well as the British prime minister, that the UN forces, except possibly the ROK troops, should not go beyond the waist of Korea and that they should stop there and establish a well-fortified defense line. The trouble was that the Joint Chiefs did not make MacArthur toe the line laid down. He was always able to protest their decisions and in the end obtain a modification or some vagueness that allowed him to scramble through to suit his own ends. On 29 September in Washington, President Truman, Secretary of State Acheson, and Secretary of Defense Marshall, with military situation maps of Korea in front of them, unanimously decided that MacArthur should "occupy, fortify and hold the line Pyongyang-Wonsan"–the waist of Korea. North of that line they thought South Korean troops might operate.[7]

Directives were sent to MacArthur on 30 September that reflected this viewpoint. On 25 October the Joint Chiefs of Staff protested MacArthur's attack order of the day before as a violation of his orders of 30 September.[8] Acheson says that "the Joint Chiefs and Marshall fumed, saw the danger involved, but . . . were not willing to order MacArthur back to the September 30 line."

On 30 November 1950, General MacArthur sent a message to the Pentagon saying that the idea of joining the Eighth Army and the X Corps across the narrow neck of Korea was quite impracticable because of logistic problems posed by the mountainous divide. The Joint Chiefs responded the same day, saying, "regarding the mission assigned you by the UN the entire region northeast of the waist of Korea should be ignored except for strategic and tactical considerations relating to the security of your command."[9]

When the evacuation of Pyongyang was imminent, the Joint Chiefs on 1 December asked MacArthur again if he could establish and hold a defensive line across the waist of Korea. He replied on the third that it was not practicable to do this. The irony of his reply is that it was true—most of Eighth Army was already south of the waist of Korea and could not possibly be used in an effort to hold it.[10]

It really made no difference now what the Joint Chiefs thought. It was too late to make any effort to hold the waist of Korea. It had been given to the enemy. Any commonsense appraisal of the dialogue between the Joint Chiefs of Staff and MacArthur on the conduct of the war in Korea has to end with the conclusion that the Joint Chiefs did not exercise their superior command function over General MacArthur to hold him to a course they thought best served the US national interest. They, too, failed in their duty.

North Korean Guerrilla Action behind Eighth Army

In October, after the Inchon landing and the capture of Seoul, when Eighth Army hurriedly drove north toward Pyongyang and subsequently on toward the Yalu border, it ignored the many fragments of North Korean Army units left behind, many of them in mountains along the Seoul-Wonsan corridor between the South and North Taebaek ranges. These defeated and disorganized groups of regular North Korean Army soldiers varied in size from squads and platoons to nearly regiments. Some of them continued north to a general rendezvous in the Kanggye area in the central mountains near the Yalu. There they reorganized, filled their ranks with conscripted Koreans, and reequipped and trained for recommitment to battle. Other depleted units crossed into Manchuria, where they reequipped, retrained, and reorganized. But large numbers of the defeated North Korean Army remained in mountainous parts of central North Korea, where they took up guerrilla operations against supply and transport routes and service units in the Eighth Army rear areas. These guerrilla operations southeast of the waist of Korea took their toll and spread increasing uneasiness in the UN command.

In the Eighth Army sector, the North Korean harassing operations in the army rear north of the 38th Parallel centered in a key strategic area that became known as the Iron Triangle, with corners at Pyonggang (not to be confused with Pyongyang) on the north, Kumhwa at the southeast, and Chorwon at the southwest. Chorwon lay only 45 air miles north of Seoul.

This hotbed of enemy guerrilla action lay 80 to 100 air miles southeast of Pyongyang, deep in the Eighth Army rear. There was always the threat that this enemy force, if it increased in size and organized under a unified command, could cut the MSR north from Seoul to the Eighth Army front. From ancient times, Chorwon had been on the main invasion route to Seoul, and indeed it had been the main route to Seoul in the North Korean invasion of South Korea only six months earlier.

It was noticeable that North Korean guerrilla operations in the Iron Triangle area increased markedly in late October and throughout November, reaching a new high when the CCF launched their 2nd Phase Offensive in the last week of November. The question arose, Was there coordination between the two?

As early as 9 November a force of North Koreans attacked Chorwon in the Iron Triangle, and scattered guerrilla actions there continued throughout the month. The Eighth Army command was particularly disturbed by increasing enemy action that far behind its front lines. The level of activity of these bypassed North Korean elements in that part of the army's rear reached such proportions that the ROK 2nd and 5th divisions, far understrength and untested, were assigned the task of driving guerrillas from the area and then of holding it. On 22 November, a force of approximately 1,500 North Koreans attacked the ROK 17th Regiment, 2nd Division, at Chorwon from east and southwest of the town. At the same time, the 31st and 32nd regiments of the ROK 2nd Division came under North Korean attack in the Kapyong area, about 35 air miles southeast of Chorwon and only ten miles west of Chunchon.

The next day, 23 November, a strong North Korean force ambushed the ROK 3rd Battalion, 17th Regiment, between Yonchon and Chorwon, in which the ROK battalion lost three truckloads of ammunition. That day the 1st Battalion withdrew from Chorwon. Fighting continued in the Kapyong area. The following day an airdrop near Chorwon resupplied the 1st and 3rd battalions, ROK 17th Regiment, and they then moved across country to join the rest of the regiment six miles south of Chorwon. Chorwon remained in North Korean possession. Eighth Army officials considered the situation critical at Chorwon.[11] In the meantime, the 1st Battalion, 31st Infantry, ROK 2nd Division, attacked from Hongchon toward Chunchon to clear that area of guerrilla forces. An enemy force estimated to number 2,000 met it four miles southeast of Chunchon, repulsed it, and forced its withdrawal ten miles southeast.

The night of 24–25 November, the night before the CCF 2nd Phase Offensive struck Eighth Army, North Korean army units hit in the ROK II Corps rear with especially devastating effects. A North Korean force descended on Yonchon, where the ROK II Corps had a rear-area supply point. The 60 South Korean police guarding a bridge five miles south of Yonchon were either killed or captured, and the bridge destroyed. ROK army supplies at Yonchon were either captured and taken away or destroyed. In the Kapyong area, ROK 5th Division forces failed to dislodge North Korean troops.[12]

Finally, at 6 A.M. on 26 November the ROK 2nd and 5th divisions undertook a coordinated counterattack to sweep the North Korean guerrillas from the Iron Triangle and adjacent areas centering on Chunchon, Hwachon, and Yonchon. Intelligence estimated at the time that there were two enemy regiments totaling about 7,000 soldiers at Chorwon and about 3,500 in the Kapyong-Chunchon areas. Chorwon was considered the strongest enemy point, with the reconstituted NK II Corps Headquarters there. At Chorwon, the North Koreans were astride the railroad running south from Wonsan.[13]

On 29 November, the Eighth Army G-3 staff indicated it had received reports that CCF troops on its right flank had linked up with guerrilla forces, elements of the NK 10th and 7th divisions, which had been fighting the ROK 2nd and 5th divisions in the Iron Triangle area and near Chunchon. Eighth Army intelligence reported that guerrilla activity in these areas was being coordinated from a higher enemy headquarters, with the intent to disrupt conditions in the American rear areas until CCF troops could arrive.[14]

The next day, the Northumberland Fusiliers, a unit of the British 29th Brigade, newly arrived in Korea and on its way north to the Pyongyang area, received an enemy attack between 3 A.M. and 7:30 A.M. by an estimated 1,200 enemy in the vicinity of Sibyong-ni, 40 miles west of Chorwon. These enemy troops had to be North Korean. In beating off this attack, the battalion committed two companies and fired 200 or more rounds of artillery. At the end of the month the US IX Corps G-2 Section estimated that North Korean units behind American lines included elements of the NK 10th and 15th divisions in the Koksan area; of the NK 2nd, 7th, and 43rd divisions in the Kangdong area; of the 8th, 33rd, and 34th regiments in the Ichon area; of the NK 4th Division in the Yonchon area; and of the 9th Division in the Kumhwa area. The intelligence report stated the first two groups were well organized and believed to be under the command of Gen. Kim Paek's newly organized NK II Corps, with his CP at Kumsong, just northeast of the Iron Triangle. The NK II Corps strength was estimated to be about 15,000 men. Gen. Kim Paek enjoyed the reputation of being an excellent guerrilla leader.[15]

In effect, North Korean remnants of many divisions of its original army had defeated the ROK 2nd and 5th divisions by the end of November and held control of the vital Iron Triangle in central Korea, north of Seoul. At exactly this same time, the CCF 2nd Phase Offensive had hurled the Eighth Army back from the Chongchon River front, far to the north, and the US 2nd Infantry Division was trying desperately to escape south through the CCF fireblock on the Kunu-ri–Sunchon road.

On 1 December Eighth Army estimated there were 2,000 North Korean guerrillas northeast of Pyongyang, 4,000 east of Sariwon and southeast of Pyongyang, and 5,500 in the Iron Triangle. Eighth Army believed that these enemy behind the lines intended to attack south. The IX Corps intelligence officer reached the conclusion that the North Korean guerrilla forces behind the UN line had the capability of cutting the Pyongyang-Seoul MSR on the Yangdok-Kumchon-Kaesong axis.[16]

ROK troops were never able to regain control of the Iron Triangle, although some ineffectual efforts were made again in the first part of December. On 10 December aerial intelligence showed much enemy activity in the Pyonggang area. At Yonchon there were new enemy installations visible, and nine roadblocks made of felled trees, rocks, and wood crates obstructed the north-south highway. A motorized patrol from the 1st Battalion, 5th RCT, US 24th Division, advanced toward Chorwon on 10 December to investigate the situation. At Taegwan-ni it encountered an estimated company of North Korean troops, armed with 82-mm mortars, automatic weapons, and small arms. In the ensuing firefight the patrol had two men seriously wounded.[17]

On 13 December the 5th RCT was again sent toward Chorwon to help elements of the 19th Regiment fight out of a guerrilla roadblock south of Yonchon. The infantry element was supported by C Battery, 555th FA Battalion, to which was attached A Battery, 26th Antiaircraft Battalion. That night about 10 P.M., an enemy force of 60 North Koreans infiltrated to within a few yards of an M16 (quad-50), on outpost duty at the perimeter. Sfc. Neal M. Morris commanded the quad-50 and had seven men including his weapons crew with him. The enemy infiltrators wounded the quad-50 driver, and the others escaped to a point about 75 yards from the quad-50. From there, Morris and his men crawled back to within 10 yards of the quad-50. Morris continued on to the M16 and got his wounded driver out. He then went back to try to start the motor that operated the four .50-caliber machine guns. An enemy grenade blew Morris, mortally wounded, from the quad-50. The remaining small group of seven then drove off the North Korean infiltrators. A little later about 200 North Koreans overran a part of K Company and the 3rd Battalion's trains. Survivors withdrew to C Battery. After midnight an L Company platoon and a tank helped recapture the overrun mortars. About daylight that morning, 14 December, an estimated 300 North Korean guerrillas struck the C Battery perimeter but were repulsed, with heavy loss. During the day the ROK 6th Division cleared Yonchon of enemy, and the 5th RCT began withdrawing its 3rd Battalion under cover of supporting artillery fire from south of the Imjin River.[18]

The ROK 10th Division was dispatched to occupy old concrete pillboxes built by the North Koreans before their invasion in June. These fortifications were in the Hwachon area, and the division's mission was to secure the Hwachon Dam. The ROKs did not hold these positions long. Nearby, the North Korean 9th Division was reported to be in Kumchon. Such was the unhappy situation just north of the 38th Parallel and in the Iron Triangle at mid-December as the Eighth Army was settling into its new defensive positions along the Imjin River line north of Seoul.[19]

Later in the Korean War, intelligence collected from prisoner-of-war interrogations and captured documents produced a clearer picture of events in the Iron Triangle in November and December 1950. It indicated that, at the end of October 1950, the North Korean 4th Division, composed of the 5th, 18th, and 29th regiments, was just north of the 38th Parallel in the Yonchon-Chorwon area. On or about 8 November, other parts of the division moved south to the Chorwon area. On 9 November the 18th Regiment attacked Chorwon, capturing hand grenades, antitank ammunition, and other military supplies held there. The 4th Division thereafter remained in Chorwon, behind UN lines, and operated as a guerrilla force. For its successes in these operations, the division received an honorary title and was known as the Kim Chaek Division. It took part in the Chinese 3rd Phase Offensive, the New Year's offensive that began after dark on 31 December 1950, and was in contact with UN forces near Seoul on 4 January. After this it apparently withdrew to Pyonggang in the Iron Triangle for reorganization.[20]

Aside from a short-lived and limited attempt by a part of the 5th RCT of the US 24th Division from 10 to 13 December to penetrate the North Korean stronghold in the Iron Triangle, the entire effort to hold that vital area for the UN command was made by poorly trained ROK troops. It failed.

The North Koreans certainly were wiser than the American command in late 1950 in recognizing the importance of controlling the Iron Triangle area, even though for a period it was like an island in a surrounding sea. The dividends would have been high for the UN forces if General MacArthur had used the X Corps to hold Wonsan on the east coast and the rail and road communications corridor south from it to the Iron Triangle and had established there a strong connection with the right flank of Eighth Army, rather than try to occupy all of northeast Korea to the border. But such a course would not have held forth the promise of ending the war with a unified Korea.

Could the UN Have Defended the Waist?

As one ponders the question whether General Walker could and should have tried to make a stand against the pursuing Chinese at Pyongyang in the first days of December 1950, the fact emerges that he and his staff had never developed a plan for such a contingency. Walker told General MacArthur in the conference at Tokyo during the night of 28–29 November that he hoped to hold Pyongyang, but there is no indication how he expected to do it. The 2nd Infantry Division had not yet been destroyed, and perhaps he felt that plain luck would ride with him and his army or that the Chinese push would run out of steam and come to a halt.

For an enemy halt to take place or to be enforced on it, a start toward that end would have had to take place along an east-west line from Sukchon to Sunchon to Sinchang-ni, with a refused right flank holding in the vicinity of Kangdong. But instead of Eighth Army slowing and assuming a position there to halt the Chinese, it rushed right on south, with Walker making no effort to slow its pace and instead apparently doing everything he could to accelerate it. When there was no effort to regroup the army for a stand north of the Taedong River at Pyongyang, the die was cast. It would now be a frantic and headlong retreat—where it would slow and stop, no one could at that moment tell. The waist of Korea was to be abandoned.

The troops had not been prepared for a long retrograde movement, and as the speedup of retreat became apparent, there were indications all around of a near hysteria, involving the abandonment and uncalled-for loss of military equipment. The Eighth Army command and the army as a whole seemed frantic. Not until the army had passed Sariwon did the panic start to abate. By that time morale had been shattered, and no one thought of stopping and of giving battle to the Chinese, although they were now far in the rear.[21] Some soldiers had a sardonic laugh upon reading this notice tacked up in a latrine: "At this moment you are the only one in the army who knows what he is doing."

Some months later, Eighth Army could tolerate with some humor the circulation of a joke that had started: "How many platoons in a horde?" The answer came, "Three swarms equal a horde, two hordes equal a human wave, two waves equal a human tide, and then followed the bottomless ocean of Chinese manpower." At the beginning of December, no one seemed to think that the Chinese soldier was human, that his legs would ever weaken under him, that he must now be exhausted, or that a week earlier he had started out with no more than ten days' supply of food. One captured Chinese officer said that his supply was six kilograms of hard wheat bread and six kilograms of millet, carried in a stockinglike roll on his back when he left Manchuria, and that he had not been resupplied since.[22]

More experience with Chinese preplanned major attacks against the UN forces showed that the Chinese soldiers began to weaken after about the third day of an offensive; by that time, their food and ammunition had been exhausted. The UN forces could then counterattack and win back what they may have lost, and the Chinese enemy were generally defeated. That probably would have happened in early December 1950 if the Eighth Army had made a stand near Pyongyang and the soldiers and their leaders had retained fighting morale. But cool common sense had fled, and the army never stopped to test its will and strength against an all-but-exhausted enemy.

Whatever Eighth Army might have tried to halt the Chinese short of Pyongyang and the waist of Korea in December 1950, it would have had to do alone. It was too late to expect any help from the X Corps. When Eighth Army faced its crisis in the first days of December, the bulk of the 1st Marine Division was still trying to fight its way from Yudam-ni to Hagaru-ri at the Chosin Reservoir. It did not accomplish that until 4 December. The 31st RCT of the 7th Division on the east side of the reservoir had been destroyed as a tactical unit by 2 December, as told in *East of Chosin* (1987). The 1st Marine Division and some hundreds of mixed army troops did not begin their retreat from Hagaru-ri to Hungnam until 6 December, and the leading formation in this retreat did not arrive there until 11 December. Not until 24 December were the last of X Corps troops taken on board ships at Hungnam and the port destroyed by explosives and naval gunfire.

This was another price paid for separating the two forces. In a crisis for either, the other could be of no help. The X Corps could have taken care of itself indefinitely in a tight perimeter defense at Hungnam with offshore naval support. But for the Eighth Army, only its own will and ability would decide the issue. It did not have the will; whether it had the ability will never be known.

In any attempt to estimate the Eighth Army's chance of containing the Chinese offensive short of Pyongyang and the waist of Korea in early December

1950, several variant factors applying to both sides must be noted. The enemy, the Chinese XIII Army Group of the Fourth Field Army of the People's Liberation Army (PLA), had been in the attack for five days and nights without resupply. They had moved through the region almost entirely on their legs. Their food supply of grain was exhausted, and thousands of them had become casualties. They had had no resupply of either food or ammunition, other than what they could salvage from the battlefield. They had poor footgear for winter (a type of tennis shoe), and frozen feet and frostbite had exacted a heavy toll. Their arms were those of light infantry—rifle, submachine gun, grenades, small mortars, a few 57-mm recoilless rifles—no artillery, no heavy mortars, no combat aircraft over the battlefield, no armor, few radios, few vehicles. The soldiery were a mixture of Communist regulars with a large contingent of former Nationalist soldiers of Chiang Kai-shek's army. One authority estimates the composition of the PLA in 1951 as follows: 15 percent were World War II Communist soldiers, 25 percent were veterans of the Chinese civil war, 30 percent were former Nationalist soldiers, and 30 percent were young Chinese inducted since 1948. Most of the soldiers were of peasant origin, with a high rate of illiteracy at the beginning. The XIII Army Group, however, was more cosmopolitan than most of the Chinese formations, including many urban workers from Mukden and other cities in Manchuria.

A weakness of the Chinese army in 1950 was the miscellaneous origin of its weapons. Its heavier weapons such as the 57-mm recoilless rifle, the small mountain gun, and the mortars were of mixed Chinese, Japanese, German, and Czech patterns and manufacture. Each had an uncertain ammunition resupply. Perhaps its most potent small arms were of American manufacture, such as the Thompson submachine gun, the Springfield rifle, and the 60-mm mortar, which had been captured in large numbers from the Nationalist Army during the civil war. The Chinese army at this time had no Soviet arms or equipment.[23] Its major assets were stamina, foot power, willingness to climb hills and to exist on poverty rations, and capability to achieve surprise.

In contrast to the characteristics of the Chinese enemy, the UN force, mostly American, had complete control of the air over the battlefield, with napalm, rocket, bomb, and strafing weaponry; it had light and medium artillery in quantity; it had armor, although Korea was a poor place to use it; it had large numbers of light, medium, and heavy mortars; it possessed a vast quantity of trucks and other transport vehicles; it had a normally good resupply system of both ammunition and food, and an array of radio and telephone equipment for communication; it had better clothing and footgear than the Chinese; and it had naval gunfire on both sides of the peninsula and uncontested control of the coastal waters. Its small arms were a good rifle (the .30-caliber M-1 Garand), the .30-caliber M-1 carbine, a .45-caliber pistol, and the .30-caliber BAR. In automatic weapons it possessed a liberal quantity of both light and heavy machine guns (.30 and .50 caliber). In its artillery were the 105-mm, 155-mm, and 8-inch howitzers, and some antiaircraft artillery—the M16 quad-50 half-track .50-caliber machine gun and the M19 dual-40 40-mm full-track. Both of these weapons carriers were capable of horrendous human destruction with their rapid rate of automatic fire.

One side was a modern force with the latest in weapons and a good communications, transport, and resupply system with naval and air supremacy; the other was a primitive force of light infantry with only light hand weapons for the most part, almost no resupply capability, and primitive communications and transport systems.

Given these contrasting characteristics, it would seem in any commonsense evaluation of their capabilities that the Eighth Army should have been able to set up a series of hedgehog-type strong points in front of and around Pyongyang and hold out against any attack the Chinese could have mounted in the first days of December 1950. The Germans found in their campaigns against the Russians on the eastern front in World War II that such defenses could hold off numerical forces in a ratio of 1 to 6 and at the same time could inflict devastating casualties by machine-gun fire. With adequate leadership and a decent morale in the soldiery, this could have been done in North Korea at Pyongyang. The Chinese "hordes" were an appearance and a perception in the minds of the American leadership and their soldiers for the most part and derived largely from the typical Chinese method of attacking in line formation – squad behind squad, platoon behind platoon, company behind company. The formation behind always stepped into the place of the one ahead of it if the former faltered or was destroyed, until, like the dropping of water in the same spot, its effect was to wear down the defenders at that narrow point where there seemed to be no end of enemy soldiery and the line gave way or was penetrated. Thus was born the "human wave" concept.

But at Pyongyang there was no intent, attempt, or effort of any kind to make a stand and fight the Chinese in a defensive battle, which the UN should have been able to win. The essentials to win such a battle – the will to fight, morale to contest the outcome, confidence of the professional leadership – were lacking in the top leadership and the officer corps, and in the rank-and-file as well. The rank-and-file might have responded had the leadership been up to it. But it was not. Eighth Army as a whole panicked and fled; it was a shameful performance. At Pyongyang there was nothing of Chipyong-ni, where in February 1951 French and American UN forces achieved a decisive victory.

18. Big Bugout or Skillful Retreat?

The story of the two weeks following the evacuation of Pyongyang is one of Eighth Army moving as rapidly as possible toward the 38th Parallel, 90 miles south, where it might take up a defensive position in the old defenses north of Seoul, anchored on the lower Han and Imjin rivers. There was no thought of stopping anywhere short of that line. In all that two weeks the Eighth Army had no contact with the Chinese army, nor did it try to establish contact. The Eighth Army was essentially blind as to the location of the Chinese forces, their centers of concentration, and their intentions for the immediate future. In this headlong race for the 38th Parallel, General Walker's UN forces violated one of the fundamental rules of war. It lost contact with the enemy. It did not leave behind any screening forces to report on enemy advances, their routes and speed of advance, and their directions of future concentrations—or whether there was any pursuit at all.

About 20 December Chinese advance reconnaissance and probing elements appeared in front of the UN forces where they were waiting in defensive positions south of the Imjin River. It was the Chinese and North Koreans who reestablished contact, not Eighth Army. It would appear that, when the Chinese reached Pyongyang, they were exhausted and desperately in need of food and resupply of ammunition, and in the days that followed they would have been vulnerable to counterattack. They halted at Pyongyang and vicinity until they had rested and achieved some degree of resupply before venturing farther south.

On 6 and 7 December, Chinese forces appeared in Pyongyang together with North Korean units and began the occupation of the city. A South Korean agent in Pyongyang reported that on 6 December between 3,000 and 5,000 Chinese soldiers entered the city, arriving from Sunchon and Kangdong to the northeast and east. ROK stragglers reported CCF soldiers guarding the Taedong River bridge sites in Pyongyang just before noon on 7 December. Still other agents reported during the period 6–8 December that Chinese were arriving in Pyongyang and moving to the south side of the city, but there was no general movement of enemy troops more than a few miles south of Pyongyang. One of the North Korean soldiers who entered the city at this time, later captured, said they were surprised to find still intact the large underground arsenal in one of the numerous coal mines at the edge of Pyongyang, with its store of ammunition and machinery, hastily abandoned when the North Korean Army and government officials fled north in October. This North Korean arsenal had about 1,000 pieces of machinery and manufactured small arms, Soviet-type machine guns, and grenades.[1]

About the same time enemy troops entered Pyongyang, other enemy units reached the port of Chinnampo, at the mouth of the Taedong River, and began crossing to the south side. Aerial observation confirmed that enemy troops were crossing the river by ferry near Chinnampo on 6 December but did not confirm that enemy troops were yet in the city. Large numbers of Korean refugees fled in front of the Chinese, about 10,000 of them being reported in the Chinnampo area. After 6 December, Eighth Army tried to keep Korean refugees off the main supply roads leading south and shunted them westward to the Haeju Peninsula below Chinnampo. Korean civilian reports said the enemy were screening large masses of refugees for conscription of young men to fill depleted North Korean units. Other agents reported a small group of Chinese soldiers in Sariwon on 13 December, but this was refuted by other reports that none arrived there until 17 December.[2]

In its retreat south from Pyongyang, Eighth Army prevented many refugees from using the main road south, but refugees crowded the railroad trains, hanging on to every place imaginable on the outside of the cars and the top of boxcars. All trains were stopped at Kumchon, a few miles north of the 38th Parallel, and there the refugees were forced off. Some estimates placed the number of Korean refugees in the Haeju Peninsula, between Chaeryong and Haeju, as 30,000 to 50,000 on 9 December.[3] The army did not want these masses of refugees in the area north of Seoul along the Imjin River, where it expected to form a defense line. Since they were North Koreans, it tried to prevent them from crossing the 38th Parallel into South Korea. Already military writers in the United States seemed to be preparing the American people for disaster in Korea. Hanson Baldwin of the *New York Times* wrote in the 6 December issue, "The dangerous alternatives of another Munich or Oriental Dunkerque loomed yesterday as the Korean crisis darkened."[4]

There were plenty of snafus in the army movement south. For example, Engineer troops destroyed a rail bridge north of Namchonjom prematurely on 9 December, as a 30-car train was bringing the ROK 1st Division from Sinmak to Namchonjom. With the bridge out, the troops had to transfer to trucks. But there was no enemy interference—they were far behind. From 9 to 19 December, I Corps reported it had no enemy contact. Disorganization was common at this time. Even with no enemy near, there were tragic accidents caused by extreme nervousness. At night on 13 December, an artillery forward observer with I Company, 35th Infantry, was killed when a guard shot him during a halt for identification.

The weather caused trouble for the retreating army. On 8 December large amounts of floating ice took out the pontoon bridge over the Imjin River at Munsan-ni, and troops going south there were rerouted over the decked railroad bridge. And while the roads south of Pyongyang were congested with Eighth Army movement south to the 38th Parallel, the docks at Pusan on 10 December were jammed with 60,000 tons of supplies. Four hundred railcars were needed to move this logjam to allow further unloading.[5]

Meanwhile, the major units of Eighth Army were approaching, or already were south of, the 38th Parallel and nearing their intermediate goal—the defense positions north of Seoul. The 2nd Infantry Division had moved all the way to Yongdong-po, south of the Han River, where it was to reequip and take in replacements. The Turkish Brigade was at Sosa-ri, between Yongdong-po and Inchon to reequip and reorganize. The 24th Division had closed on Uijongbu, about 12 miles north of Seoul, by 10 December. The next day the British 29th Brigade, released from 1st Cavalry Division control, was attached to the 24th Division but remained under IX Corps control.

On 13 December, IX Corps issued its Operational Plan No. 4, which called for the 24th Division to cover the corps withdrawal through Seoul if enemy pressure should force it. The 24th Division now took its place on the defense line south of the Imjin River, known as Line B. The 1st Cavalry Division moved to Sibyon-ni on 8–9 December, and on the eleventh it moved to a new assembly area only six miles north of Seoul in Eighth Army reserve. But four days later, Eighth Army ordered the 1st Cavalry Division to move to Kapyong, 35 miles northwest of Seoul, to an important point on the Chunchon road, south of the Iron Triangle, where resurgent North Koreans were threatening the UN right flank. Col. Harold Johnson replaced Colonel Palmer in command of the 8th Cavalry Regiment, and Col. Marcel G. Crombez assumed command of the 5th Cavalry Regiment on 14 December.[6] On 13 December 1st Cavalry Division motorized patrols had gone as far east as Chunchon, Hongchon, Wonju, and Chipo-ri without enemy contact.

In the midst of the withdrawal, Eighth Army on 9 December rescinded its earlier "scorched-earth" policy and its order that all villages be burnt.

The two weeks following Eighth Army's evacuation of Pyongyang saw a bewildering succession of army orders and operational plans. Some were drawn up and not issued; others lasted only a day or two. They apparently represented an effort by the army G-3 staff, and by General Walker, to give the withdrawal some logic and orderly behavior. But few, if any, of these operational plans meant anything in what happened. The army simply went on south as fast as it could, and hardly anyone expected an army order to be acted on, because it would be obsolete and overtaken by time and space before it could be implemented. For instance, Army Operational Plan No. 17 stated that the army final defense line would be from the mouth of the Yesong River on the west to Kumchon, Sibyon-ni, Chorwon, Chigyong-dong, and Hwachon. On 7 December it was modified to change corps boundaries. Then the next day, the army issued Operational Plan No. 18, which set up new delaying positions farther south, which would become effective on further army order. On 9 December, the army announced that plan 18 would become effective at 6 A.M. on 11 December. Then on that same date General Walker sent a letter to the commanding general of the 2nd Logistical Command at Pusan, directing him to construct a series of defense lines between the Naktong River and the port of Pusan.[7] It soon became clear that the avalanche of orders only gave an appearance of formality to what in effect was a rapid retreat to the Seoul and Han River area and seemed to project a continuation from there to the southern extremity of the peninsula, and a possible exit from the country through the port of Pusan.

On 11 December the I Corps Engineers blew up the bridge over the Yesong River, just west of Kaesong, and during the day destroyed all the bridges across

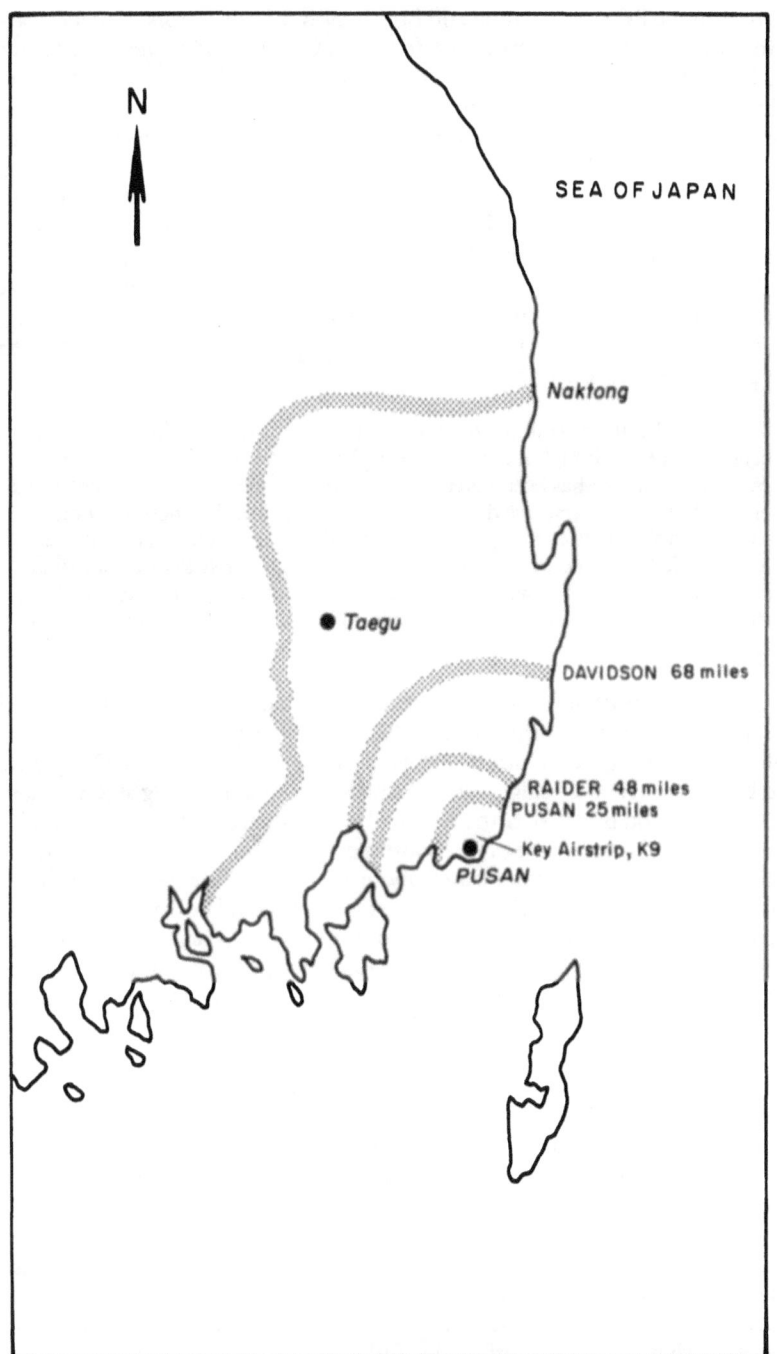

Map 15. The plan for withdrawal defense lines given in Operational Plan 12 in an Eighth Army order to the 2nd Logistical Command, 11 December 1950.

the river in the ROK 1st Division and British 29th Brigade sectors. General MacArthur on that day made a hasty trip to Korea. General Walker met MacArthur and his party at Kimpo airfield, and they drove back to Seoul for a conference. What was discussed at this meeting is not a matter of record, but it can be assumed that part of the discussion centered on General MacArthur's order to X Corps that it should outload at Hungnam and come by sea to the Pusan area and then join Eighth Army. The 1st Marine Division had just reached Hungnam after its long two-week fight to escape the Chinese forces at the Chosin Reservoir. It is also likely that General MacArthur wanted to appraise General Walker's state of mind, since it is known MacArthur was disappointed that Eighth Army did not establish and try to hold a defensive position above Pyongyang. General MacArthur made another of his public relations statements to the press after his visit to Seoul. He said:

> The United Nations command, in spite of its recent heavy fighting, is in excellent shape, with high morale and conspicuous self-confidence. . . . Every possible advantage has been taken of the premature disclosure of surreptitious enemy build-up operations designed to encompass our destruction by one massive stroke. This enemy plan has failed. All our units are intact and the losses inflicted on the enemy have been . . . as high as ten to one compared with our own. . . . Notwithstanding the enormous danger inherent in the drastic change I consider that the command for the time being is relatively secure.[8]

On 15 December air reconnaissance reported that the Chinese had repaired the highway bridge over the Taedong River at Pyongyang and that vehicular traffic had been sighted south of the city. I Corps reported that its Engineers had blown the railroad bridge over the Imjin River that morning at 2 A.M. and that the pontoon bridge over the river had been salvaged and evacuated. It also said that all UN troops were on the south side of the Imjin. The Eighth Army's G-3 Operations Section complained about meager intelligence, stating that it had no indication where the expected enemy attack would be made, if and when it came. Another Chinese envelopment of the army right flank on the east was generally feared. It was to strengthen the ROK troops there that the army's reserve force, the 1st Cavalry Division, had been sent to Kapyong to prevent an enemy approach from there toward Seoul.[9]

At this time a serious disturbance involved the Turkish Brigade. The Turkish Brigade had been attached to the 25th Infantry Division on the afternoon of 13 December. The division had responsibility for the western end of the army line and accordingly had its left boundary on the sea. South of Kaesong and northwest of Seoul, and on the south side of the Han River where it emptied into the sea, the large island of Kanghwa-do, cut off from the Korean peninsula by a narrow inlet between the Han River and the sea, formed the western extremity of the 25th Division's zone of responsibility. It assigned the Turkish Brigade the mission of patrolling the island and watching for attempted enemy crossings of the mouth of the Han. The Navy and the Air Force were to cooperate with it. On 15 December the Turkish Brigade established a number of outposts on the island. The next day the 25th Division operations officer informed Eighth Army that the Korean Civil Police protested that the Turkish

Brigade had fired on Korean refugees crossing the river at Monju and had killed many of them. The refugees had been trying to land from their boats when fired on. The Korean refugee traffic was very heavy through Kaesong, only five miles south of the 38th Parallel, and the incident had occurred where local authorities had been channeling fleeing refugees. US Navy vessels patrolled the area along with South Korean naval vessels.

A Navy message to Eighth Army confirmed that Turkish Brigade troops had killed some refugees. The Navy and ROK messages to Eighth Army requested that action be taken to prevent a recurrence of the incident. At the same time, word came that there was bad feeling and trouble between the South Korean island governor and the civil assistance staff with the Turkish troops on the island. Assistant 25th Division commander, Brig. Gen. Vennard Wilson, visited the Turkish Brigade on 19 December to straighten out the matter. On his return his plane crashed on takeoff. Wilson was injured in the crash and was evacuated to Japan.[10]

By the middle of December Eighth Army was moving into the Imjin River defense line. The 25th Division was south of the Imjin on the west flank by 14 December. There it had a special problem in controlling the movement of refugees, who were especially numerous in that part of the line. East of the 25th Division the ROK 1st Division was in place. The ROK 6th Division was on line east of the ROK 1st Division, and east of it the US 24th Division was moving into line. Eighth Army considered the area held by the ROK 6th Division a weak sector, and on 16 December it sent the 1st Cavalry Division to the Kapyong area to backstop the ROK division. The ROK 7th and 8th divisions of the ROK II Corps had taken positions in the Wonju area in the unprotected central corridor of the peninsula.

The 8213th Ranger Company, which had been decimated in its first battle north of Ipsok on the night of 25 November in the initial Chinese onslaught against Task Force Dolvin of the 25th Division, had been reorganized and replacements taken in, and the company had trained in the Pusan area. It was now ready for recommitment. On 17 December the 25th Division attached it to the Turkish Brigade, which also received the 79th Tank Battalion at this time.[11]

Signs that the enemy might be approaching the Imjin River began to appear. On 16 December an aerial report indicated that Chinese forces were in Sariwon. A ROK 1st Division patrol on 18 December reported contact with enemy north of the Imjin. The next day it reported its patrols had encountered enemy platoon- and company-sized groups north of the river.

On 20 December, F Company, 21st Infantry, 24th Division, sent out patrols to capture enemy prisoners. The army needed information as to the enemy strength and whether Chinese or North Korean formations were in that part of the enemy buildup. The patrol got into a firefight with an enemy force at Hill 216 but took no prisoners. The patrol had seven casualties in this fight and estimated it had killed about 30 enemy. The location indicated the enemy force was probably North Korean.

On that same day, the ROK 1st Division reported its patrols had contact with a small enemy group north of the Imjin that they believed to be Chinese. ROK patrols from this division crossed to the north side of the Imjin River nightly to scout the area to its front for intelligence. On 20 November the ROK I, II, and III corps in the eastern and central parts of the peninsula reported no enemy contact. The US I and IX corps reported only light patrol action. But by this time it was clearly evident that strong North Korean forces held the Iron Triangle and vicinity, and while Eighth Army had virtually no knowledge of the location and strength of the Chinese that might be in its immediate front because it had no contact and its patrol actions were weak, signs were beginning to appear that the Chinese, who had remained static for nearly two weeks after the capture of Pyongyang, were once again on the move. Again on 22 December the US I and IX corps reported no significant enemy activity to their fronts but offered the view that the central area was likely to be the scene of the next enemy attack. I Corps believed there was a CCF buildup of three divisions north of Munsan-ni.[12]

It is doubtful if General Walker was greatly cheered on 19 December when President Syngman Rhee decorated him with the Republic of Korea's Military Order of Merit with gold star for bravery and professional skill in his defense of the Pusan perimeter during the preceding summer.

During this period of UN withdrawal in the west, from the Chongchon River south to Seoul and the Imjin and Han rivers line, the US Navy played hardly any role after evacuating UN forces and supplies from Chinnampo. It was during this period that virtually all US naval forces in the Far East were concentrated on the east coast of Korea at Wonsan and Hungnam for the evacuation of the US X Corps from northeast Korea. That was a massive undertaking, the largest American sealift since the Okinawan campaign of World War II. The Navy completed the evacuation of X Corps at Hungnam on 24 December and carried out the final stages of transferring the corps to the Pusan area at the southern tip of the peninsula, where it was to prepare to move into the Eighth Army line, which at that time rested in the vicinity of the Han River and Seoul.

While the Navy had little part in the Eighth Army withdrawal in the first part of December to the Seoul area, it was faced with increasing demands to prepare for the possible evacuation of all UN forces from Korea. On 7 December Admiral Thackeray received orders to start removal of army supplies from Inchon, the west-coast port for Seoul. On 20 December, Eighth Army headquarters left Seoul for Taegu, although President Syngman Rhee refused to move the South Korean government. In anticipation of future enemy activity in the western part of Korea below the 38th Parallel, Eighth Army requested the Navy to plan for providing naval gunfire along the entire western coast of Korea.[13] One had only to lift a finger into the wind to know which way it was blowing.

Demolition Policies of the Eighth Army

It is necessary to comment on the Eighth Army demolition policy in its withdrawal from Pyongyang because it had tremendous importance in the future conduct of the war. According to Maj. Gen. Leven Allen, Eighth Army's chief of staff at the time, the Far East Command ordered General Walker to destroy everything that might be of use to the enemy, to adopt a "scorched-earth" policy.[14] After the bulk of Eighth Army had passed south of Sariwon and neared the 38th Parallel, the policy was modified to rescind destruction of villages and civilian property. But the policy still called for destruction of every bridge and transportation facility the army passed in its withdrawal. This order was still in effect when Eighth Army evacuated Seoul and crossed the Han River, withdrawing farther south, in January 1951. This continuing destruction was interpreted by many in the army to mean that it would never move north again and that the facilities destroyed would never again be needed in American military operations in Korea.

Later, when General Ridgway turned Eighth Army around and started back north, the army was constantly slowed because virtually all bridges and other transportation facilities had to be rebuilt, with great cost and enormous effort by engineering units and Korean labor.

Col. Pascal Strong, chief engineer of Eighth Army, opposed this demolition policy, recommending that only major bridges be partially destroyed. He pointed out that the Chinese and North Koreans had few vehicles and little heavy equipment and that destruction of all bridges would impede them very little. General Walker overruled him, in some instances directing that rails on the railroad system be lifted and destroyed. The destruction continued after Walker's death and into January 1951 because General Ridgway did not know at first the extent of the destruction. When Eighth Army in the late winter of 1950–51 started back north, Colonel Strong and the Engineers had to rebuild 23 bridges between Chonan and Seoul on the road back to the Han River in 1951. All of this reconstruction was in South Korea.

Colonel Strong so disapproved of the army demolition policy in the withdrawal from North Korea that he said the army would have been "better off if every block of TNT had been destroyed and dumped into the ocean." General Walker personally ordered the destruction of the port facilities of Inchon, over Colonel Strong's objections. Strong pointed out that, in any event, the CCF and North Koreans could not use the port of Inchon while the US naval forces controlled the sea and held blockade power over the area. Under General Walker's policy at this time, heavy bridging supplies, including some Bailey bridges already in Korea (but not bridging construction equipment), were sent back to Japan in December and January. After the ground forces had destroyed bridges and transportation facilities, the Air Force subsequently increased and widened the destruction by repeated bombing.[15]

At one time Colonel Strong said Army Engineers were using 1,000 tons of bridging materials a day in trying to restore the roads and railroads for army use in the drive to push the enemy forces north out of South Korea in 1951. By that time General Ridgway had changed the policy so that only key bridges or other structures were damaged when the CCF or North Koreans gained temporary success in their repeated major offensives in the first half of 1951. In contrast to the American policy, the enemy rarely destroyed transportation features when the fortunes of war went against them and they had to withdraw from a battle area.

Many of the unit commanders in the UN forces disagreed with the American demolition policy. For instance, Col. Harold K. Johnson, then commanding the 5th Cavalry Regiment and later US Army chief of staff, thought the policy went too far. The burning of haystacks and villages and dwellings alienated the native people, he thought, and the destruction of transport facilities was later a tremendous handicap to Eighth Army when it turned and started back north in 1951. Brig. Gen. James Brittingham, I Corps Artillery officer, held similar views. He said, "We blew everything–never expected to come back. Now, we never knock them out to that extent again. We are only now [July 1951] getting the high level bridges back again." Captain Bodkin, of the 2nd Engineer Combat Battalion, said he tried to receive authority in the withdrawal to leave bridges intact, but was overruled by superiors carrying out the army demolition policy.[16]

The US Air Force: Unhindered over Korea

While the Eighth Army was out of contact with the CCF on the ground for more than two weeks during its withdrawal south in December, the US Air Force, Far East, increased its sorties and attacks on enemy troops and targets in North Korea right up to the border. The Air Force carried on the war during this period and tried in every way possible to inflict enemy casualties and to impede, if not stop, southward advance of the CCF.

A new situation developed in the air over Korea in the border region when American Mustang pilots met their first MiG-15 fighter planes. These Soviet planes clearly outclassed the American fighter planes in Korea during the month of November. Among their armament the MiGs had 23-mm cannon. Operating from an all-weather field at Antung, just across the Yalu River from Sinuiju, the MiG-15s took a toll of American B-29 bombers and other aircraft during the month. The MiG-15 fighter plane was generally piloted by poor pilots, by American standards, and they did not do the damage they might have in the hands of expert fighter pilots. The developing situation in the air over North Korea, however, required immediate attention.

On 8 November, Gen. Hoyt Vandenberg, US Air Force chief of staff, offered to send an F-84E Thunderjet and an F-86A Sabre Wing to Korea, if usable fields for them could be prepared. The offer was accepted by Generals Partridge and Stratemeyer the same day, and Vandenberg ordered the 4th F-86A Sabre Fighter Interceptor Wing and the 27th F-84E Thunderjet Fighter Escort Wing to Korea. The F-86A Sabre was the best fighter plane the United States had. The two wings flew to San Diego, California, where they were deck-loaded on aircraft carriers and a fast tanker. They arrived in the Far East in early December. General Partridge had planned to put the 4th Sabre Fighter Wing at Pyongyang airfield and the Thunderjet Fighter Escort Wing at Kimpo airfield near Seoul, but by the time they arrived in Japan, the situation in Korea on the ground had changed drastically. Eighth Army was in precipitate retreat, and the Pyongyang airfield could not be used. General Partridge sent a part of the 4th Fighter Wing of Sabres to Kimpo in South Korea and the Thunderjet Fighter Escort Wing to Taegu.

The Thunderjets at Taegu flew their first mission on 6 December. On 15 December the Sabres flew an orientation mission from Kimpo over North Korea. General Partridge gave the Sabres a simple but hard assignment–to fly combat air patrols over northwest Korea, to meet and, if possible, to destroy the MiG-15s, and to establish air superiority. The Sabres were the only plane the United States had that could compare with the MiG-15, and since they had never met in combat, the outcome was uncertain, but the Sabre pilots felt confident they could win.

The first Sabre combat flight took off from Kimpo airfield on 17 December and headed for the Korean border. The Sabres carried six .50-caliber machine guns and gyroscope computing gunsight with an electric range-control system. It had a limitation in its flight range of only 490 nautical miles. Lt. Col. Bruce H. Hinton commanded the 336th Squadron and led the flight. When he arrived near the border at midafternoon, he sighted a flight of four MiGs below him. The MiGs were climbing up to meet Hinton's flight and apparently thought they were the old and slow F-80s that they had met before. The Sabres put on a burst of speed and dove toward the MiGs. The startled MiG pilots tried to dive away toward the Yalu. Hinton tailed the second MiG and gave it three long bursts from his machine guns. The MiG burst into flames and spun toward the ground. Hinton was the first Sabre pilot to destroy a MiG-15 in aerial combat.[17]

A little experience soon taught the Sabre pilots they should arrive over the Yalu at high speed and not try to save fuel. Otherwise, their slow speed on arrival would place them at a disadvantage in a sudden encounter with the MiGs. The new procedure would give them only ten minutes of time over target. On 22 December Lt. Col. John C. Meyer, commander of the 4th Group, led two Sabre flights that met more than 15 MiGs near the Yalu. The ensuing dogfight lasted 20 minutes and ranged from near ground level to 30,000 feet. Meyer's Sabres shot down six MiGs and lost one of its own planes. A MiG pilot caught Capt. L. V. Bach in a tight turn and shot him down. The fight for control of the air over the border escalated during December. On 30 December 36 MiGs rose to meet a flight of 16 Sabres, but they were very cautious by this time, and the Sabres were able to damage only two of the MiGs. The Sabres established superiority over the MiGs by the end of December, and the anxiety about enemy threat of air control over North Korea subsided.[18]

In the short period when the MiG-15 pretty well ruled the skies over the Yalu border, the question of "hot pursuit" became an urgent issue. The American pilots were prevented by the policy of the Joint Chiefs of Staff from crossing the Korean-Manchurian border at the Yalu in pursuit of enemy planes. They had to break off combat over the river while the enemy planes descended to their sanctuary at the Antung airfield. The American pilots chafed over this restriction, and their morale was lowered by what they considered a limitation that imperiled them and made it all but impossible for them to destroy the enemy air strength. The issue reached the Joint Chiefs in Washington, where on 7-8 December the Joint Chiefs proposed lifting the restriction and allowing what it called hot pursuit for a limited distance beyond the Yalu. Gen. George C. Marshall, secretary of defense, fully supported the proposal. His testimony on 7, 8, and 11 May 1951, before the Senate Armed Services and Military Affairs Committee and the Senate Foreign Affairs Committee tells what happened to that proposal. In response to a question from Senator Russell, chairman of the Senate Armed Services and Military Affairs Committee, on 7 May 1951, General Marshall said that hot pursuit "was considered, concurred in by me, as a matter of fact I had urgently recommended it, and was concurred in by the Secretary of State and approved by the President, and the Secretary of State was directed to take that up with the thirteen nations involved with us in fighting. . . . They voted solidly against it, so for the time being we had to drop that."[19]

Beginning about 1 December, after the CCF had driven Eighth Army south of the Chongchon River, the Chinese battle forces began moving in the open during the daytime, something previously not done. This willingness to move openly lasted for the first half of December. During this period the Fifth Air Force had its golden opportunity of the war. Daily it roamed the skies over the Chongchon and south of it, strafing and bombing enemy caught in the open. It especially sought targets of CCF transport such as trucks now moving on the roads leading south from the border. At the end of two weeks of this kind of aerial action, General Stratemeyer on 16 December estimated that the Fifth Air Force had killed or wounded 33,000 enemy soldiers. Also, by this time the supply trucks again disappeared from the roads during the daytime and moved only at night. A Chinese prisoner, an assistant platoon leader in the CCF 113th Division, told interrogators that his division moved during this period by day until aerial attacks had destroyed nearly all its trucks. The division then reverted to its customary practice of moving during darkness.[20]

At the same time, bombers struck the major towns of North Korea, its airfields, and its railroad marshaling yards. On 4 December Fifth Air Force B-29s bombed Tokchon, Anju, and Pukchang-ni. The next day the B-29s hit Sunchon, Songchon, and Sukchon. On 10 December they cratered two airfields at the northeast edge of Pyongyang. Four days later they hit the railroad marshaling yards in Pyongyang and the storage yards south of the river to destroy a large amount of military supplies the Eighth Army had left there in its withdrawal. On 21–22 December, as Eighth Army settled into its position on the Imjin River line, the US Bomber Command sent its entire force against North Korean bridges. On 23 December General MacArthur asked that two-thirds of the B-29s be used against towns and villages where enemy troops might be sheltered. But the Joint Chiefs of Staff refused MacArthur's request to bomb Racin on the northeast coast, about 35 miles south of the Soviet border. Racin was a railroad and highway center for supplies coming into Korea from the Soviet Union. The Joint Chiefs and Secretary of Defense Marshall felt that "it was a question of the risk involved in an operation so close to the Soviet frontier, and as to the question of ships in the harbor, and other mishaps that might occur."[21]

As Eighth Army continued its retreat toward Seoul, the Air Force began to question how long its planes could continue to operate out of airfields it then held. On 6 December, Maj. Gen. Edward J. Timberlake, deputy commander of the Fifth Air Force, presided at a conference in Seoul to consider the subject. He reported that Eighth Army had not yet decided whether to plan on holding a beachhead in the Seoul-Inchon area, or at Taegu-Pusan. He said if the beachhead was to be in the Seoul area, then the Air Force units at Taegu, Pusan, and Pohang-dong would have to be evacuated. If the beachhead was to be in the Pusan area, then the Air Force units at Seoul and Kimpo would have to move. Within the next day or two, the Fifth Air Force learned that Eighth Army would try to hold Seoul as long as possible and then withdraw toward Taegu and Pusan. The Air Force now began to prepare for the evacuation of its airfields at Seoul, Kimpo, and Suwon, the latter two on the south side of the Han River. On 10 December, the 8th Wing of Mustangs at Seoul began to move back to Itazuke, Japan. On the same day the 51st Fighter Interceptor Wing began moving its main organization to Itazuke, leaving behind a combat group at Kimpo, organized in a way similar to the recently arrived 4th Fighter Interceptor Wing. Five days later, the 18th Fighter Bomber Wing at Suwon departed for the airfield at Chinhae (K-10) on the southern coast of Korea, leaving behind only a servicing detachment. Then, on 20 December, Eighth Army moved its main CP from Seoul to Taegu, and both the Fifth Air Force and the Joint Operations Center followed it.[22]

While this movement of aircraft away from the Han River was in progress, the Far East Air Force on 15 December implemented its Interdiction Plan No. 4, which divided Korea above the 37th Parallel into 11 zones on the basis of the country's main transportation routes. It named 172 specific targets: 45 railroad bridges, 12 highway bridges, 13 railroad tunnels, 39 railroad marshaling yards, and 63 supply centers. The Naval Forces Far East assumed responsibility for destroying similar targets in the three interdiction zones on the eastern coast of North Korea from Wonsan north to the Siberian border. If the interdiction campaign was able to keep all the railroad bridges listed knocked out, there would be no stretch of rail line in North Korea above the 37th Parallel longer than 30 miles that would be serviceable.[23]

The North Korean Army Is Reborn

In December 1950 the recently shattered North Korean Army was reborn from the fragments that had survived and reached sanctuary in Manchuria or had found a haven just south of the border in the mountains of the Korean highlands near the Yalu. The new North Korean Army headquarters established itself in Pyongyang as soon as the city was reoccupied.

According to an interrogation report of a North Korean Army headquarters signal officer who surrendered to the 23rd Infantry on 27 May 1951, the North Korean Army headquarters crossed back to Korea at Sinuiju on 27 November, as the CCF 2nd Phase Offensive was making rapid progress. From Sinuiju, the North Korean general headquarters moved by convoy to Pyongyang, entering the city on 6 December. It made its headquarters at Moran-Bong, adjacent to the Pyongyang racetracks, and used the underground ammunition dumps that the UN had failed to destroy before evacuating Pyongyang. There were many large coal mines northeast of the city that the North Korean Army had used in the early part of the war, and after its return to Pyongyang, it again used them for various military purposes. There they were protected from aerial attack. This North Korean officer said he left Pyongyang Army headquarters on 27 April 1951, for temporary duty with the NK V Corps Headquarters, and after six days of jeep travel via the Pyongyang-Wonsan road, reached Kosong, where he joined the V Corps headquarters.[24]

Another document based on a number of enemy interrogations outlines what was a typical experience for recently defeated and decimated North Korean Army units after the fall of Seoul in late September 1950. Advance groups of the retreating NK 12th Division passed through Inje, situated virtually on the

38th Parallel, and there turned northwest to reach Pyongyang about the end of October. Aircraft attacked them constantly, and the journey was one for survival. Stragglers from many other North Korean units joined them en route. From Pyongyang the 12th Division group continued north to Sunchon, Anju, and from there turned northeast up the Chongchon River road toward Kanggye, which they reached about 10 November. The interrogations gave the information that Kanggye at that time was the reorganization and retraining center for the defeated NK Army. The remains of the original 12th Division were absorbed into the mass of North Koreans assembled there, and the original division ceased to exist. A new 12th Division was organized and activated in late November, having three rifle regiments, each numbering about 2,000 troops. About 40 percent of the new division were veterans of the original North Korean Army that fought the summer battles; the other 60 percent were freshly conscripted men. The combat veterans of the new 12th Division came mostly from the original 7th, 9th, and 12th North Korean divisions. The men were issued winter uniforms and armed with Soviet rifles and hand grenades. The new North Korean 12th Division was assigned to the NK V Corps. The 12th Division left Kanggye on 25 November, headed south toward the battlefront, and was to operate as an organized guerrilla force.[25]

During the second week of December, strong and active North Korean guerrilla groups were dominant in the Iron Triangle area, defeating the ROK 2nd and 5th divisions that had been sent there to secure the area for the UN. This vital area obviously was fast falling into the hands of North Korean Army forces. They began making probing attacks wherever they found UN forces. These North Korean forces belonged to the NK II Corps, which now held the Hwachon and Yonchon areas. The newly organized NK V Corps arrived during this period from Kanggye with its reorganized 6th, 12th, 31st, and 38th divisions. It went into positions in the mountains east of the NK II Corps, athwart the important central mountain corridor that led south. The NK V Corps reached as far east as Inje. The preliminary indications seemed to be in mid-December that the two recently formed North Korean II and V corps, holding the area from the Iron Triangle eastward to Inje, was forming an attack force along the central mountain corridor leading into South Korea at the same time the Chinese moved south to the west of them and formed a line from the coast to the Iron Triangle in the area north of Seoul.[26]

In an effort to meet the growing threat that the North Korean Army was making to establish control of the central part of Korea east of the Iron Triangle, Eighth Army on 10 December ordered the ROK III Corps to move to Yongpyong ten miles south of Yonchon, and to assume control of the ROK 2nd, 5th, and 7th divisions. At the same time it ordered the ROK II Corps to move to Wonju with the ROK 8th and 9th divisions. The ROK 1st, 2nd, and 3rd security battalions were reorganized and given the mission of extending the UN line, or the eastern ROK portion of it, eastward from the Wonju-Hoengsong area to the Sea of Japan on the east coast at a point three miles north of Yonpori. Here we see Eighth Army's first attempt to extend its line all the way across the Korean Peninsula and to counter the North Korean infiltration into the central corridor for a potential drive south. On this same day General Walker had a conference with President Syngman Rhee and his cabinet in Seoul.[27]

On 11 December the Far East intelligence report estimated that 40,000 North Korean guerrillas were in the Iron Triangle area, controlled by Gen. Kim Chaek and his staff by radio from Kisan-ni. There Kim Chaek and his staff lived in the village and nearby farmhouses and wore civilian clothing. It is noteworthy that Kim Chaek had formerly been vice-premier of North Korea.[28]

Eighth Army's uncertainty of what the enemy's next move might be seemed to be clarified in a broadcast picked up from Moscow on 12 December. The broadcast said Kim Il Sung of North Korea had ordered his forces and the Chinese fighting with them to push the American army into the sea.[29] With the hastily devised Eighth Army line in the center of the peninsula running through a concentration of North Korean forces, and many of them in the rear of the ROK troops just sent there, the Far East Command on 12 December evaluated the situation on the army's right flank as a threat to its entire defense position, and unless this threat could be eliminated, further withdrawals would be necessary.[30] To strengthen this part of its line, Eighth Army on 14 December ordered the ROK II Corps to assume command of the ROK 9th Division on the east coast, and the ROK 3rd Division was ordered to Wonju to strengthen the ROK II Corps.[31]

The US 2nd Infantry Division's first entry into potential future action on the central front came on 14 December when its 23rd Regiment, the only combat-ready part of the division, received orders to send a patrol to contact the ROK 5th Division and to report on the condition of roads and bridges in the sector. The motorized patrol reached Chunchon just after noon on 15 December. There it contacted KMAG representatives of both the ROK 5th and 8th divisions, who reported that both divisions had been under daylong attack by an estimated four North Korean divisions. These divisions were about half strength. The North Koreans had penetrated the left flank of the ROK 5th Division, but it had just been restored in counterattack.[32]

On 16 December, the 2nd Infantry Division G-2 Section reported that there were many indications of a rapid North Korean buildup. It thought the NK II Corps could mount a heavy attack on the Eighth Army right flank and that the NK V Corps could start a deep envelopment in conjunction with any CCF resumption of a frontal attack. It found from previous CCF prisoner interrogations that the Chinese preferred to fight American soldiers "because they abandoned so much usable equipment during retreats, including personal clothing, weapons, and many luxury items."[33]

On 17 December a new development occurred on the east coast of Korea. The South Korean Capital Division of the ROK I Corps, which earlier had almost reached the Soviet border in the X Corps zone in northeast Korea, came ashore from sea transport at Samchok below the 38th Parallel. There it was on a line almost due east of Seoul. In landing the division there, Eighth Army hoped to build up an eastern flank anchored on the sea to tie in with the ROK forces it had hurriedly moved to the central part of Korea. If this could be done, Eighth Army would then have a defense line across the width of Korea, roughly following the 38th Parallel. On this same day Eighth Army reported there was still no word of CCF contact on the Eighth Army front, nor had it been able to confirm that CCF forces in strength had moved south from the Pyongyang area. But it had by this time identified five reconstituted North Korean divisions on the central front. The next day, 18 December, Eighth Army abruptly changed its evaluation to say that intelligence reports indicated that CCF units were beginning to displace south and east from Pyongyang.[34]

It appeared by 20 December that North Korean forces on the central front were carrying out a systematic probing of the UN positions trying to locate its main line of resistance, particularly in the Ichon-Kumhwa-Hwachon area, and covering the three main routes leading south to Seoul. These routes followed the Yonchon-Uijongbu axis, the Kumwha-Uijongbu axis (these two coming together at Uijongbu), and the Hwachon-Chunchon axis, which struck the Pukhan River and could then follow it downstream southwest to Seoul. The latter axis could also continue south from Chunchon through Hoengsong, Wonju, Chechon, and Chungju, along the spine of the Lower Taebaek Range toward Pusan, bypassing Seoul entirely. It appeared that the NK V Corps was now moving into this front to reinforce the NK II Corps already there. Aerial observers saw many horses and some camels in the vicinity of Hwachon, south of the reservoir of the same name, and by 21 December all enemy roadblocks previously in place between Ichon and Hwachon had been removed.[35]

In a night attack on 21 December an enemy regiment hit the ROK 8th Division and by 7 A.M. the next morning had cut the lateral road between its 10th and 16th regiments, gaining a penetration about two miles deep. The ROK 8th Division sent its reserve 21st Regiment into the gap and stopped the advancing North Koreans. These enemy troops were wearing American overcoats and were armed with American M-1 rifles (apparently all captured recently either by CCF or themselves). Elements of the ROK 3rd Division helped stop this enemy penetration near Chunchon. The enemy troops were not identified, but they were undoubtedly North Korean. Also on 21 December, just before noon, aerial observers counted 20 camels, not loaded, and about 400 troops near Chorwon. The presence of so many camels led to the speculation that these troops were Chinese. Other reports, not confirmed, placed Chinese troops in Ichon and Yonchon on 19–20 December.[36]

It was clear by the end of the third week of December that reorganized North Korean divisions, most of them at about half strength, were taking over a section of the enemy line, generally south and east of where the CCF had operated in late November and in early December. Signs indicated that, in any renewed offensive, the CCF would move south to form the western end of the line north of Seoul, and the North Koreans would pick up the line somewhere in the vicinity of the Iron Triangle and carry it on eastward into the central mountains in a sector that might be called the central front.

ROK Army Reorganization in December 1950

In December 1950 the ROK Army needed reorganization and training almost as much as did the North Koreans after the fall of Inchon and Seoul and their defeat in South Korea. Of the ROK divisions, the 1st was generally considered the best, and indeed it had been so considered from the beginning of the war. Gen. Paik Sun Yup's division had been part of I Corps after American forces entered the war, and it had been placed between American divisions. It had held its own, had good discipline and high morale, but it had more firepower than the other ROK divisions. The two ROK divisions of I Corps on the east coast had performed well most of the time. These divisions, the Capital and the 3rd, moved from the X Corps area of northeast Korea to join Eighth Army in South Korea on its extreme eastern flank. The 7th and 8th divisions of the ROK II Corps had been virtually destroyed in the opening days of the CCF 2nd Phase Offensive in the vicinity of Tokchon in late November. Several other ROK divisions were then being organized but were untrained and had no combat experience. As the Eighth Army went into its Imjin River line at mid-December, the entire central and eastern parts of Korea were held, and only recently, by largely inexperienced ROK divisions, except for the two of the I Corps on the east coast. It made for an insecure situation in the central part of the new UN line.

Much has been said and written about the basic qualities of the Korean soldier. With proper training and good leadership, the South Korean was a good soldier, as was the North Korean soldier. But after the near destruction of the South Korean Army following the North Korean invasion across the 38th Parallel in June, just about all the experienced noncommissioned officers and junior officers of platoon and company level had been lost. There were no adequate replacements for them on short notice. The training of such leadership required establishment of the proper schools and several months of training by competent supervisors. The United States took a leading part in establishing such a system of schools and training schedules, but it was not until the summer of 1951 that young officers with such training were filling the ranks of the Korean divisions. During the first half of 1951, the early difficulties with ROK soldiers in large part continued. Maj. Eldon B. Anderson, who had been the Korean Military Advisor (KMAG) in artillery to the ROK 9th Division from November 1950 to December 1951 gave a debriefing report at Fort Sill, Oklahoma, in March 1952. In it he summarized rather well the qualities of the ROK soldier in the first year of the war and the limitations under which he fought. Major Anderson answered the question, Does the Korean soldier do as well as other nations' soldiers if given the fire support? In the course of his response he said:

> Given the fire support, the training, and the leadership, the Korean soldier can't be beat. . . . He is a wonderful soldier. He is obedient, intelligent . . . and they have a good fighting spirit. They lacked leadership and still do to quite an extent, and they lacked training. A year ago, the infantry soldier got only 7 to 10 days training before being assigned to an outfit. They lack fire support. Even in the infantry regiment they didn't have nearly as much fire support as we do. They have only three squads per platoon; they don't have the fourth squad that the American Army does which has the machine guns. Until recently they had no recoilless 57s or 75s; they don't have the 4.2″ mortar company in the regiment that we have; they don't have any tanks; they don't have any antiaircraft. As a consequence, the Korean division should be considered as no more than an American combat team [regiment reinforced]. That was a source of a great deal of trouble in Korea. The Americans could not understand, even on a higher level apparently, that the Korean division represented a unit only as large [not in numbers but in effective firepower and combat effectiveness] as one-third of an American division. Many times,

Korean divisions were given missions similar to those given American divisions and naturally they could not accomplish them.[37]

Another side of the coin is that ROK soldiers in the first part of the war did not have the technical knowledge to use much of the communication equipment, the artillery, the tanks, and other weapons the American divisions possessed. Nor did they have as much transport as the American division. Usually every ROK division had an American battalion of 105-mm howitzers attached to it for fire support, and some had tank battalions attached to them. As the war progressed and their competence to use and protect the more sophisticated and technical weapons improved, they got them. But this condition did not prevail at the end of 1950 and on into much of 1951. The United States Army tried to remedy the situation for the ROKs and to make them more combat effective in the winter of 1950–51 by placing an ROK division between two American divisions, so that each of the latter could deliver fire support for the ROKs from either side.

Of the new ROK divisions being put into the line by mid-December 1950, the 2nd and 5th lacked combat experience. The others were being filled with relatively untrained recruits. When General Collins returned from his trip to Korea in early December to assess the situation for the Joint Chiefs of Staff, he reported to them that, among the ROK divisions, the 5th was in fair shape, the 6th was being reassembled after the battles along the Chongchon, the 7th was being reassembled in the vicinity of Suan, and the other ROK forces in the Eighth Army sector could not be depended on except for outpost duty. This did not include the ROK Capital and 3rd divisions in the X Corps sector of northeast Korea, where they had given a good account of themselves. These two ROK divisions were subsequently put ashore, as already stated, at Samchok on the east coast to form the eastern anchor of the Eighth Army line at the end of December 1950.[38]

The ROK divisions that were being put into the line in central Korea were disappointingly slow in reaching and taking up their positions. Frequent enemy ambushes slowed their progress, but the main difficulty was the lack of adequate transportation.

The east coast of Korea was still undefended by any troops when Eighth Army went into its defense positions at the Imjin River on 14 December. The ROK 9th Division had been relieved of its security mission in South Korea and had been started for the coast, but the rough terrain and lack of transportation slowed its progress. On 18 December the situation changed for the better on the east coast when 12,000 troops of the ROK I Corps made an unopposed landing from the sea north of Samchok. The ROK I Corps headquarters and the Capital Division composed most of these troops; the ROK 3rd Division soon joined them. In the meantime, the ROK 9th Division arrived at the coast. The ROK I Corps deployed the Capital Division along the coast and placed the 3rd and 9th divisions on its left flank inland in high mountains. Maj. Gen. Kim Pac Il commanded the ROK I Corps at this time. Brig. Gen. Song Yo Chan commanded the Capital Division, and Brig. Gen. Rhee Chong Chan commanded the 3rd Division. On 19 December the ROK I Corps passed to the operational control of Eighth Army.[39]

Nearly every day in December the Fifth Air Force flew between 300 and 400 sorties, trying to observe enemy movements and, by its repeated strikes, to delay or prevent them from advancing south. On 16 December, however, it flew only 54 sorties, because of heavy snow.

UN Reinforcements in December 1950

The 11th Report of the United Nations Command Operations in Korea for the first half of December 1950 to the Security Council stated that ten nations were then represented by combat forces in Korea: Australia, France, Greece, the Republic of Korea, the Netherlands, the Philippines, Thailand, Turkey, the United Kingdom, and the United States. Combat forces of four nations arrived in Korea in the first half of December, at a time when Eighth Army sorely needed their additional strength. These were from France, the Netherlands, Greece, and Canada.

The French force was in battalion strength, including 39 officers, 172 noncommissioned officers, and more than 800 enlisted men—approximately 1,250 men altogether.[40] It departed Marseilles, France, on 25 September and arrived at Pusan, Korea, on 30 November. It was not entirely ashore until the first days of December. This battalion was to have an enviable combat record in Korea.

The advance party of the Dutch, or Netherlands, Battalion arrived in Korea on 24 October, but the full battalion did not arrive until early December. It consisted of two rifle companies and a heavy weapons company, for a total of about 600 men. It came from Indonesia, where it had been fighting, and its combat effectiveness was considered high. But it had come from a warm climate to a cold one in December 1950.

The Greek Battalion of 840 infantrymen arrived in Korea on 9 December. The officers of the battalion were specially chosen for their knowledge of English. The rest of the battalion was taken from one of the Greek Brigades. The Greeks also distinguished themselves in Korean combat.

The 2nd Battalion of the Princess Patricia's Canadian Light Infantry sailed from Seattle on 25 November, when the Korean War seemed to many to be about over. Its troopship entered Yokohama's harbor on 14 December, when the situation in Korea had changed drastically. The battalion consisted of 45 officers and 873 enlisted men. The Princess Pat Battalion began disembarking at Pusan on 18 December.[41]

On 10 December Eighth Army issued a letter that listed the permanent attachments of major UN units then in Korea or due to arrive soon, to become operational on Eighth Army order:

Parent Unit	*UN Unit to Be Attached*
1st Cavalry Division	Thailand, 21st Infantry Regiment
	Philippine 10th Battalion Combat Team
	Greek Expeditionary Force
2nd Infantry Division	Netherlands Infantry Battalion
	French Infantry Battalion
	Belgian Infantry Battalion

24th Infantry Division
25th Infantry Division
British Commonwealth
   29th Brigade

British Commonwealth 27th Brigade
Turkish Brigade
2nd Battalion, Princess Patricia Canadian
   Light Infantry

No time was wasted concerning the French and Netherlands battalions. On 12 December, Eighth Army attached them to the US 2nd Infantry Division, which in turn on 15 December attached the French Battalion to its 23rd Infantry Regiment, and the Netherlands Battalion on 13 December to its 38th Infantry Regiment.[42] These two battalions of infantry, comprising together more than 1,800 men, helped considerably in building up the strength of the division and in shortening the time before it could once again take its place in the battle line.

One of the most important tasks confronting Eighth Army after the battles along the Chongchon was the rehabilitation of the US 2nd Infantry Division to combat readiness. The division was transported as quickly as possible to the south side of the Han River opposite Seoul, where it went into assembly areas to take in replacements, receive new equipment, undergo retraining, and, it was hoped, be able to take its place in Eighth Army's combat-effective forces at an early date. By evening of 8 December all divisional units had completed their moves to the rear and were in their assembly areas. The 2nd Division established its CP at Yongdong-po on the south side of the Han River on 7 December. The next day its 23rd Regiment received a defense assignment in guarding the Han River bridge. At 1:45 P.M. on 7 December Maj. Gen. Robert B. McClure assumed command of the division.[43]

On 10 December, the 2nd Division received an Eighth Army order to reconnoiter the roadnet from Seoul to Chunchon and Chungju. The next day, Col. John G. Coughlin became the Division G-3, replacing Lt. Col. Holden. Throughout December the division had sent details to Pusan to drive back vehicles in reequipping its transportation. In early December the Far East Command had relayed to the Pentagon an urgent request to ship the weapons and equipment for a full division to replace losses in the X Corps and in Eighth Army.

The losses of the 2nd Infantry Division and in the Turkish Brigade were uppermost in mind. On 4 December General Larkin, Department of the Army G-4, ordered the immediate loading of needed equipment. On 5 December four ships were to dock at San Francisco and another four were to dock at Seattle to load the equipment, with departure dates for the Far East set for 9 December. Deadline for arrival of cargo at the two ports was 8 December. It developed that only three instead of four ships were needed at each port. All were loaded and sailed on the scheduled date, 9 December, except one ship. It remained an extra day to await arrival of an air shipment from the east coast. Some liaison planes, general purpose vehicles, some ammunition, and certain items that technical chiefs said were not needed for combat were stricken from the regular table of organization and equipment in the loading of the six ships. Some items included in the loading were:[44]

Medium tanks	140
Heavy machine guns	40
Light machine guns	160

.50-caliber machine guns	354
.50-caliber quadruple AAA machine guns (for quad-50s)	32
40-mm AAA guns (twin guns; for dual-40s)	32
Automatic rifles (BARs)	412
Garand M-1 rifles	6,913
.30-caliber carbines	7,474
3.5-inch rocket launchers	465
105-mm howitzers	54
155-mm howitzers	18

Meanwhile, General MacArthur ordered the immediate shipment to Korea from depot stocks in Japan of major equipment for two regimental combat teams.

Nearly all the replacement personnel arriving for Eighth Army from the United States in December went to the 2nd Infantry Division or the 25th Infantry Division. Most of the replacements went to the 2nd Division because it had the greatest need, having lost 4,163 men, according to Army figures, between 27 November and 2 December. Units of this division began taking in replacements as soon as they arrived. On 7 December, for instance, the 23rd Regiment took in personnel replacements as well as replacement equipment. The 9th Regiment took in more than 500 replacements at Ascom City between 8 and 14 December. On 11 December, Eighth Army G-3 Section stated it made liaison visits to the 2nd Division daily to check on the progress in replacing personnel and equipment. On that day it placed the strength of the three infantry regiments at 2,180 (9th Infantry), 2,450 (23rd Infantry), and 2,650 (38th Infantry). The division's total strength on that day was 12,813, and it had 90 of 134 tanks authorized. It was then considered to have a capability of two regimental combat teams, but one of them at 50 percent combat effectiveness.[45]

In addition to filling in its own organic regimental units, the 2nd Division also had attached to it the newly arrived French Battalion, the Netherlands Battalion, and the reorganized Ranger Company, which had previously been attached to the 25th Infantry Division. It was now renamed the 1st Ranger Company. Capt. J. P. Vaun was the new commander of the Ranger Company. He transferred from the G-4 Section of the 25th Infantry Division when he asked for a combat assignment. On 15 December, the 2nd Division G-4 said the division had been reequipped sufficiently to make it combat effective. It was nearing the point where it could once again assume a combat role in the rapidly expanding Eighth Army line across the width of Korea. This rapid reequipment of the 2nd Infantry Division had been made possible by emergency shipments from the United States and prompt shipments of some major equipment from depot stocks in Japan.

From 13 to 19 December there was a bewildering series of changes in plans for the 2nd Infantry Division. Most of the division was instructed to buttress the western defenses around the mouth of the Han River, Kimpo airfield, and the Seoul bridges. But the 38th Infantry Regiment received instructions to prepare to move to the central area around Wonju. The Division Operational Plan No. 1, 16 December, called for the division to move to the Wonju-Hoengsong-Chungju area in the central mountains and to establish blocking positions to deny enemy movement south along the Hoengsong-Chungju axis. The army made a final decision on the employment of the 2nd Infantry Division on 19 December when it issued a Top Secret Operational Directive ordering the 2nd Infantry Division to the Chungju area. The division began moving to the new area on 21 December over icy roads. The 38th Infantry Regiment on 22–23 December arrived at an assembly area six miles south of Chungju, and the 9th Infantry moved to Chungju during 23 and 24 December. It had only 50 percent of its organic transportation when it received the order to move. The 23rd Infantry moved to Chungju on the twenty-second, closing there on 23 December.

On 23 December, 2nd Division Operational Order No. 13 gave the division mission as securing the Eighth Army east flank. The 23rd Infantry was to block on the Wonju-Chungju and Chungju–Chipo-ri roads; the 38th Infantry was to occupy Wonju and defend the Wonju-Chechon-Andong road; the 9th Infantry was at Chungju in division reserve; the 72nd Tank Battalion was in the vicinity of Sangju, south of the main mountain barrier that was an obstacle to north-south movement; and the 1st Ranger Company, attached to the 38th Infantry, was to maintain contact with the ROK II and III corps. Thus the 2nd Infantry Division before the end of December was committed on the mountainous central front, surrounded by ROK units on either flank, and charged with the main responsibility of stopping an enemy thrust southward through the central mountains, which the Eighth Army now feared was about to take place.[46]

Chungju was 40 air miles south of Wonju. Supply of the division was difficult. It had to truck all its gasoline 90 miles from Kumchon to Chungju over a route that included a six-mile-long mountain pass. The division requested Eighth Army to establish a Class I, II, and V supply point and an ammunition supply point at Wonju. The closest Class V supply points were at Taejon and Taegu, prohibitive distances away.

While the 2nd Division had been taking in several thousand replacements and reequipping, it had also been engaged in an intensive training program for all its combat units, most of them now having a considerable proportion of replacements. This training tried to profit from the recent combat experiences with the Chinese. It emphasized night-combat problems such as fire discipline and premature exposure of defense positions, which had been costly to it in late November and early December. The training emphasized holding a position during the night at all costs rather than withdrawing in darkness, for daylight would bring help from air and armor. Sleeping bags were not to be used in front-line positions. Warming fires were prohibited there. A minimum of equipment was to be carried, but having a basic load of ammunition was high priority, and a good supply of hand grenades was emphasized. Care of feet to avoid frostbite was given special attention. Long marches had been frequent in order to inure the troops to fatigue.[47]

Eighth Army Defense Preparations

The American divisions of X Corps were taken by sea to the Pusan area and unloaded there near the end of December. It was evident that the X Corps could not get into the new Eighth Army line and be of practical help until January

1951, at the earliest. For this reason, Eighth Army sent the 2nd Infantry Division to the central mountains at the end of the third week of December to bolster the ROK troops there in the event of an enemy attack down the central corridor toward Pusan.

Definite planning to join X Corps with Eighth Army in South Korea took official form on 6 December, however, when Brig. Gen. Edwin K. Wright, Far East Command Army G-3 operations officer, recommended to General MacArthur that he move the X Corps to South Korea and place it under Eighth Army command. MacArthur approved the recommendation the next day, even though he had some reluctance in placing General Almond under General Walker's command. When General MacArthur discussed his intention to join X Corps with Eighth Army with General Almond, he gave Almond the choice of coming under Walker's command as a part of Eighth Army, or of rejoining the Far East Command as chief of staff, which Almond still was on paper. Almond unhesitatingly said he preferred to remain in command of X Corps under Walker's command.[48] General MacArthur notified both Walker and Almond on 7 December of his intention, but he did not then specify the effective date. The Joint Chiefs of Staff in Washington approved the proposal on 8 December.

On 16 December, Eighth Army sent the X Corps a letter outlining the mission it expected to assign it after the corps had assembled in the Pusan area and had reorganized and reequipped under the 2nd Logistical Command in Pusan. It would go into the army line east of IX Corps and assume an active combat role at the earliest possible date. Three days later, Eighth Army sent IX Corps its top secret plan to use the 2nd Infantry Division in the Wonju area. The next day the army ordered the 2nd Division to move there without delay.

The 1st Marine Division was the first of X Corps's combat divisions to arrive in South Korea. It opened its CP in an old assembly area near Masan on 16 December, and by 17 December, all units were at Masan. The 7th Infantry Division debarked at Pusan on 22 December and moved at once to Yongchon, north of Pusan and on the lateral road between Pohang-dong and Taegu. Its advance party had been there for more than a week, and the 31st Infantry Regiment was already there. The X Corps Headquarters and the 3rd Infantry Division arrived in the Ulsan area during the last week of December. In the meantime, Eighth Army ordered its I and IX corps on 20 December to select and organize a bridgehead line north of the Han River and the Seoul bridges. This line passed in the vicinity of Uijongbu and then turned south toward the Han River.[49]

At the same time Eighth Army was going into its defense positions along the Imjin River line north of Seoul and the Han River, it was also moving all supply points south of the river and clearing out the large accumulation of military supplies at Inchon and Ascom City, four miles east of the port. To naval authorities, Eighth Army indicated that Inchon might have to be evacuated before X Corps had cleared from Hungnam, where most of the available shipping had concentrated. Admiral Joy asked MacArthur to order shipping to be worked 24-hours a day. Inchon had a capacity of loading 3,000 tons daily. Ascom City, on the main road to Yongdong-po and Seoul, had become the main storage center of supplies brought in through Inchon. And at Yongdong-po, on the south side of the Han, railcars were held fully loaded so that they could be hurried south at a moment's notice. Evacuation of supplies from the Seoul-Inchon area went forward during December by both rail and sea. By 18 December all critical supply materials had been moved from Ascom City, and two days later the 3rd Logistical Command (Inchon) reported that only an Eighth Army Engineering staff remained there. All ammunition supply points had moved south of the Han River. On 12 December ASP 23 at Kaesong closed, and two days later ASP 26 at Munsan-ni, on the south side of the Imjin River, closed.[50]

As early as 13 December Eighth Army and IX Corps had plans in readiness to evacuate Seoul if enemy pressure should dictate a withdrawal south of the Han River. On that date, IX Corps Operational Plan No. 4 called for the 24th Infantry Division to cover the withdrawal through and from the Seoul area. On 20 December IX Corps Operational Plan No. 5 extended some features of Plan 4 and called for the removal or destruction of the Han River bridges in the Seoul area. The British 27th Brigade (minus one infantry battalion), the 6th Medium Tank Battalion, and the 19th Engineer Combat Battalion, under a unified task-force commander, would constitute the covering force for the withdrawal. The next day 24th Division Instruction No. 81 gave the details of the withdrawal and covering force plans and the details of the march order. The 24th Infantry Division was on line in the Uijongbu area almost directly north of Seoul. The withdrawal plan called for the movement to end in the Suwon area, about 25 miles south of Seoul. On 22 December, IX Corps made minor changes in its 20 December Operations Order No. 5.[51]

Plans for withdrawal south of the Han River to the Suwon area, however, did not stop there. Defense lines were laid out for the withdrawal of Eighth Army all the way to Pusan, at the southern tip of the peninsula, and the possible withdrawal of the army through that port from Korea to Japan. On 10 December Eighth Army commented on these plans in its command report: "Enemy slow in his follow-up, but even so, the enemy, with so overwhelming a force as he had at his disposal, could not be decisively stopped with the forces available to EUSAK on any defensive line it might establish . . . planning contemplated continued withdrawal to successive defensive lines until (if necessary) a final line was reached covering the army's withdrawal from Korea."[52]

The successive defensive lines Eighth Army referred to had already been located and defined. They were four in number, named from north to south.

> The Naktong line, similar to the defense line of that name, used in the summer (4 Aug.–16 Sept. 1950) to defend Pusan from the North Koreans
> The Davidson line – 68-mile perimeter
> The Raider line – 48-mile perimeter
> The Pusan line – 28-mile perimeter

The Davidson line, given priority in construction, had been partially completed in August 1950, in preparation for a possible forced withdrawal from the Naktong River line in defense of Pusan. This line was named for then Brig. Gen. Garrison H. Davidson, assistant division commander, 24th Infantry Division, and an Engineer officer, who was in charge of laying out the successive defense lines.

The 2nd Logistical Command, headquarters at Pusan, received orders from Eighth Army to complete these four lines. Part of the construction work on the Davidson line called for building a lateral road behind the line, from Miryang in the west to Ulsan on the east coast. The 44th Engineer Battalion, with X Corps, on its arrival in South Korea, was to supervise the construction of the road. The commanding general of the 2nd Logistical Command was ordered to utilize Korean labor in carrying the work forward. Instructions for the defense lines included the following:

1. Double fox-hole shelters for combat personnel and crew served weapons.
2. Clear necessary fields of fire in front of the lines.
3. Install tactical and protective wire.
4. Make plans for mine fields and stock mines where they could be obtained and laid quickly.[53]

On 16 December the 2nd Logistical Command issued Operational Plan "Stop Gap," which required the command to organize four provisional battalions from its service troops (two of them composed of American personnel and two of them from ROK personnel) that could be used in a defense mission, on Eighth Army order, to reinforce and plug gaps in the army's main line of resistance if enemy forces should penetrate them. The 2nd Logistical Command completed the organization of these four battalions during December.[54]

At the beginning of December, General Walker had a number of defense lines on paper to defend in North Korea and, if necessary, south of the Han River as long as possible, pursuant to General MacArthur's orders to him. These lines were labeled alphabetically from north to south:

Line Able—north of Pyongyang
Line Baker—along the lower Imjin River and then eastward along the 38th Parallel generally
Line Charlie—a crescent around Seoul and east of Hongchon and on to the east coast
Line Dog—below the Han River, from Pyongtaek to Wonju to Samchok on the east coast

If forced south of Line Dog by the middle of December, there were the four final defense lines already mentioned reaching down to Pusan.

As events developed, Eighth Army in December retreated all the way to Line Baker, the Imjin River line, before it stopped to take up a defensive position. This was a retreat of 120 miles before it stopped to see what the CCF would do. Eighth Army was in this line by the middle of December, with a scramble continuing to nearly the end of the month to move ROK divisions into the central and eastern parts of the line.

Line Baker tried to take advantage of the lower Imjin and Han River barriers in the west; in the central part it had the numerous south- and southwest-flowing tributaries of the Han River as enemy corridors of advance to deal with in uneven and difficult terrain. In the east it had the high divide of the Taebeck Range, only 30 miles on average from the east coast, and mountainous terrain from it sloping down eastward to the Sea of Japan. It was the first attempt of the UN forces to establish a defense line across the breadth of Korea above Seoul. It extended about 135 miles.

The western end of the line was in the low-lying ground of the west coastal and estuary regions of the lower Imjin and Han rivers. Water barriers there made defense fairly easy. Eastward, the south- and southwest-flowing tributaries of the Han River made it all downhill for the enemy in approaching Seoul from central Korea by several corridors leading into the Han valley. The main roads followed these tributary streams, and once in the Han valley, a main road followed it west to Seoul. The main enemy corridors of advance toward Eighth Army defense lines were, from west to east:

1. from Kaesong and Munsan-ni, southeast to Seoul
2. from Chorwon, almost due south through Uijongbu to Seoul
3. from Kumhwa, southwest to Uijongbu, where this corridor joined that from Chorwon
4. from Kumhwa and Hwachon southeast to Chunchon in the Pukhan River valley and then to the Han River valley and hence west to Seoul, or from Chunchon south through the central mountains to Hoengsong and Wonju; from there several possible routes lead to the rear of Eighth Army, allowing enemy to outflank it from the east or drive on south toward Pusan

East of Wonju there was no feasible north-south corridor other than the east coastal road. A study of the terrain indicated that securing Seoul from attack was feasible on the north and northeast only if the Han valley and its tributary corridors could be defended and blocked to enemy advance. Otherwise, enemy forces could outflank Seoul on the east.

On Line Baker's main line of resistance, Eighth Army had ten divisions; two American and eight ROK. A third American division, the 1st Cavalry, was in reserve near Kapyong in the Pukhan River valley, west of Chunchon. The divisions and attached units were on the main line of resistance from west to east in the following order:

> US 25th Infantry Division
> ROK 1st Division
> ROK 6th Division
> US 24th Infantry Division
> ROK 2nd Division
> ROK 5th Division
> ROK 8th Division
> ROK 3rd Division
> ROK 9th Division
> ROK Capital Division

In Eighth Army reserve there were the following major units:

> 1st Cavalry Division
> British 27th Brigade
> British 29th Brigade
> US 2nd Infantry Division
> ROK 7th Division

Actually, the US 2nd Infantry Division was moved just back of the main line of resistance on 22–23 December behind the ROK 5th Division in the Wonju area and could actually be considered as part of the main line of resistance. The Baker Line as taken up by the UN forces curved northeast from north of Inchon and the mouth of the Imjin River up the Imjin River to Munsan-ni, on to Yongpyong, and hence east to pass just north of Chunchon. It then continued on an irregular line northeast, passing just below Inje and hence northeast through the mountains to reach the east coast a few miles north of Yangyang–a total distance of 135 to 140 miles.[55]

The prepared defenses varied greatly over the extent of Line Baker. Most of the ROK divisions in the center and in the east had little more than their individual foxholes and some gun emplacements. In the western part of the line, above Seoul, and particularly in those sectors held by American divisions, the prepared defenses were formidable. These were the sectors held by the 24th and 25th infantry divisions. There the pontoon bridges over the Imjin River on the MSR in the 25th Division sector were removed on 14 December. The next day the infantry troops on the north bank that had protected the engineers in this work crossed to the south side of the river and took up their defense positions. I Corps reported that all M-4 floating bridges (pontoons) had been removed at 3 A.M. on 15 December, and that all UN troops were on the south side of the river. These bridges were salvaged, not destroyed.

Between 16 and 23 December the 25th Division in this vital area placed barbed wire, antipersonnel mines, and flares in front of their positions. Some rifle companies had as many as 14 machine guns emplaced. One battalion front used 800 rolls of barbed wire, 950 flares, and 400 antipersonnel mines on its part of the line.[56]

In the period between 17 and 22 December the Eighth Army G-2 concluded that, if the enemy crossed the 38th Parallel, they would make their main effort down the Uijongbu-Seoul axis; that a secondary advance would be made south on the Hongchon-Wonju axis; and that a deep envelopment of the army and Seoul might be attempted from the Inje area.[57]

The CCF Resume Contact with UN Forces

The CCF had by now moved up to contact with the Eighth Army and other UN forces in Line Baker. For more than two weeks after the Chinese and some North Koreans entered Pyongyang on 6 December there had been, in effect, a no-man's-land from Pyongyang to the Imjin River line, where Eighth Army stopped in its headlong retreat. This no-man's-land was vast, about 70 to 75 air miles. This situation did not, however, exist in central Korea, in the Iron Triangle area, where North Korean guerrillas held strategically important ground.

There is reason to think that the CCF were surprised when they found Eighth Army had not regrouped to fight a major battle against them north of Pyongyang in early December. It would appear that the CCF 2nd Phase Offensive in late November and early December 1950 had as its goal the capture of Pyongyang in the west and Wonsan in the east. At any rate, that is where the CCF advance stopped. For the next two weeks the CCF army in the west in the Eighth Army zone regrouped and resupplied, and its leaders considered what should be their next move when they found that the UN forces had disappeared to their front.

In the northeast, the CCF were so badly used up after the X Corps evacuated that part of Korea that the CCF IX Army could do no better than just rest and gradually bring in replacements to become combat effective again. This enemy force in the east caused no end of surmises among American and UN commanders as to what they were doing and planned to do. The fact is that these troops and units did not appear in the front lines that developed subsequently until four months later, in March 1951.

By 23 December various forms of intelligence disclosed that CCF troops were appearing in front of Eighth Army in the lower Imjin River area in the sectors held by the US I and IX corps. The CCF had moved south from Pyongyang by foot, oxcart, sledge, pack horse, and even the two-humped Bactrian camel. Some trucks moved at night.

Reliable sources reported on 13 December that there were no CCF in the Kaesong area. One agent reported he had traveled from Haeju, Yonan, and Kaesong and saw no enemy personnel on the fourteenth. Residents in those areas said they had seen no enemy in those areas south of the 38th Parallel. ROK police in Haeju, 75 air miles northwest of Seoul on the main west coastal road, refused on 13 December to evacuate the city because there had been no enemy activity there. The Far East Command intelligence summary for 14 December stated that the bulk of the Chinese forces was east-west along the Taedong River in the Pyongyang area. It surmised that the CCF were regrouping under a screen of North Korean troops farther south, which were probing to determine Eighth Army's positions. On 19 December, the same source stated: "Whereabouts of CCF and reasons these units out of contact for such a long period continue in the speculative realm . . . seems to indicate enemy may not yet be ready to resume the offensive."[58]

In Tokyo on 20 December, General Stratemeyer, commander of the US Air Force, Far East, frustrated that no one knew where the Chinese were, ordered General Partridge, commander of the Fifth Air Force, to use his entire reconnaissance force to locate them—in his words, "to find out where these communists are." During a period of ten days the Fifth Air Force reconnaissance squadrons photographed a 40-mile-deep zone north of Eighth Army's lines. At Taegu, photograph interpreters examined 27,643 aerial photographs made on these flights but found few enemy. They were unable to locate the Chinese armies.[59]

On 21 December the first concrete evidence surfaced that Chinese were closing on Eighth Army. Line crossers from the ROK 1st Division that day reported they had seen large numbers of CCF in front of the ROK 1st and US 25th divisions, on the western end of the UN line. That same day, elements of the ROK 1st Division captured two prisoners a mile north of Korangpo. They were identified two days later as being from the CCF 116th Division, 39th Army. These same enemy organizations had fought against the 25th Division north of the Chongchon in late November. On 19 December I Corps intelligence had reported enemy in platoon and company strength opposite the corps on the north side of the Imjin River but had not been able to identify them positively as CCF. The next day it concluded that Chinese were approaching the Imjin River.

After the ROK 1st Division had taken its two Chinese prisoners on 21 December, I Corps concluded that day that a Chinese regiment was in the Korangpo area.

On 23 December, an air report stated that an aerial attack at 10:20 A.M. had killed an unknown number of enemy and four or five camels on the road ten miles west of Chorwon. The next day, the Far East Command intelligence summary cited recent announcements from North Korean premier Kim Il Sung and from CCF leaders that they planned to drive the United Nations forces from Korea. It set the probable date for an offensive between 25 December and 10 January. It estimated the enemy had 650 planes in Manchuria that could be used to support such an offensive.[60]

A Chinese prisoner, taken in the vicinity of the Imjin River, said that his 117th Division of the CCF 39th Army passed through Pyongyang on 15 December and arrived at a point about 15 miles north of Kaesong on 23 December. About this time an American soldier who had been a prisoner returned to American lines. He reported that, while he had been a prisoner, an English-speaking North Korean officer had asked him, "When the CCF cross the 38th Parallel, what will the UN course be?" Then on 28 December, two South Korean agents escaped from their CCF captors north of the Imjin River, opposite the ROK 1st Division, and reported that a CCF division was near Korangpo and that members of it had said they would attack prior to 1 January.[61]

Intelligence available on 23 December and subsequently indicated that a strong concentration of the CCF 39th Army was opposite the ROK 1st Division in the Korangpo area. This town was a road center on the north bank of the Imjin River, approximately halfway between Munsan-ni and Yongpyong. At the latter place the Eighth Army line turned east from the north-bearing arch it had followed thus far from the west coast up the Imjin River. Opposite Korangpo, on the south side of the Imjin, a major roadnet led nearly directly south to Seoul. This axis was in the US I Corps sector.

Bugout or Skillful Retreat?

Was Eighth Army's precipitate retreat from the Chongchon River front 120 miles south to the Imjin River, just short of Seoul in early December 1950, a "bugout," as many termed it at the time and later? Or was it a skillful and timely retreat that saved Eighth Army, as General Walker claimed and as General MacArthur stated to the world?

British troops and their commanders fighting with Eighth Army could not understand the long and hasty retreat and were critical of it. Brig. Gen. Edwin K. Wright, the able G-3 operations officer of the Far East Command in Tokyo, said that neither he nor General MacArthur thought at the time that Walker's Eighth Army would be forced back of the Pyongyang line but believed that it would rally and hold the North Korean capital. It was initially, therefore, a severe shock to MacArthur when the army headed speedily south for the 38th Parallel. General Wright said that General MacArthur never laid down tactical rules for ground forces. There is some indication that Walker lost favor with MacArthur because of his handling of the battles with the Chinese in

November and early December and his precipitous retreat. It may be speculated that Walker would have been replaced as commander of Eighth Army, had not his sudden death on 23 December made such a question academic. But General Wright agreed with the view developed in this research that General MacArthur had an unrealistic faith in the ability of American air power to destroy the Chinese in North Korea and that this led in part to his stunned disbelief when the CCF first stopped Eighth Army and then forced it to turn about in massive retreat.[62]

If General Walker had lived, would he have taken Eighth Army out of Korea, or would he have turned it around at some point and confronted the CCF in a major battle? As previously stated, there is evidence on this question pointing in both directions.

What was the prevailing opinion and feeling of the Eighth Army officer corps in general and of the rank-and-file in early December as it undertook the long retreat? For a time, at least, the situation looked like a "bugout." There was a tremendous amount of talk in all ranks of Eighth Army in 1951 that the army was indeed headed for Pusan in December 1950 and in following weeks and that its leaders had no wish to stay longer in Korea. Even when General Ridgway, early in 1951, started to turn Eighth Army around, there was at first the term "wrong-way Ridgway" applied to the new Eighth Army commander. The comment was heard with astonishing frequency in 1951 from all ranks in Korea that the men in Eighth Army thought they were heading out of Korea for good at the end of 1950. That view was also reflected in some of the official reports of the army, but generally the subject was avoided there, for obvious reasons. The 25th Division G-4 Section report for December 1950 said, "The apparent careless abandon and indifference with which some troops were observed to burn and destroy equipment with the slightest excuse is almost criminal. . . . It is impossible to name them [acts of destruction] since they range from abandoning individual clothing and equipment to burning vehicles and trailers, but it was clearly indicated that positive command action is called for in this matter."[63]

Lt. Gen. W. B. Palmer, writing later, but with the Korean War in the period of late 1950 in mind, said of American supply discipline:

> It appalls me to think how many failures occur in this very last link of the logistical chain. Equipment is manufactured at great expense. It is shipped 5,000 miles by train, ship and truck. It is issued to the troops eventually, with great labor, carried to the top of a mountain in Korea. How many times, at that last point, has this whole enormous effort been thrown away, as carelessly as a burnt match, by the happy-go-lucky negligence of the very people whose lives depended on their keeping the stuff in shape?[64]

One of the most interesting, and perhaps indicative, actions reflecting prevailing opinion in the retreating UN forces in December was the destruction on 15 December of 1.9 billion Won (Bank of Chosen currency). This mass of South Korean currency was estimated to weigh 100 tons, and it required 50 hours to destroy it. Had it fallen into enemy hands, it was thought the money would have been used by them as valid currency in South Korea.[65]

In debriefing statements following the combat in November–December 1950, several American officers said that esprit de corps among American troops was poor, often below that of South Korean troops with whom they worked; that the American troops "had the retrograde movement fever, . . . the feeling among several of my NCOs was that it was foolish to stay and fight. They wanted to pull out."66

One officer told of hearing American soldiers cheer when they passed the 38th Parallel going south in December. Another officer said, "We were always glad to hear of withdrawal to the next phase line—we intended to leave Korea. When an announcement was made over the radio about the possibility of leaving or being forced out of Korea, we would say 'Good.'" Some of the officers, however, felt badly about the precipitous retreat southward and said neither they nor their men could understand why the whole army was going back.67

When Eighth Army was falling back on Pyongyang, war correspondents with the army, according to one dispatch on 2 December to the *New York Herald Tribune*, said, "Reporters have been wandering like lost souls for the last few days looking for front lines. CPs from which reporters depart in the morning are not there by nightfall. Fighting shifts rapidly often before newsmen at corps headquarters can get to the scene of action. Jeep-loads of reporters stop frequently along the way to ask about conditions ahead. The answer usually is 'I don't know any more than you do!' "68

Brig. Gen. Basil A. Coad, commander of the British 27th Commonwealth Brigade, writing later about the retreat, said, "A series of withdrawals now took place. One of these was in a 132-mile withdrawal from a position 35 miles north of Pyongyang, for, as far as we could see, no apparent reason other than some ominous red arrows marked on the operational maps, showing that the whole of the U.N. forces were about to be encircled."69

Another British writer commented, "It would be idle to pretend that the retreat had not had an effect on the Eighth Army. In the two British and Commonwealth brigades morale was high, but the men were puzzled by the poor military situation. They felt that western troops, with their wealth of military experience in World War II, and equipped with modern weapons, should have been able to stand their ground in face of the Chinese enemy, however great their numbers."70

A member of the Australian Battalion of the 27th British Commonwealth Brigade who was present during the withdrawal in the last days of November and the early days of December had written:

> The morale within the [8th] Army was very bad at the time of the withdrawal. We had participated in a number of rearguards and seemed to be continually on the move in conditions of bitter cold. The attitude of other units with which we came in contact was of despair. The transport units we used seemed very low in spirit and the talk of the drivers was of the masses of Chinese and that self-inflicted wounds seemed the only way out. . . . We seemed to receive conflicting orders throughout the withdrawal and to get little or no information about the enemy.71

The term "bugout" became a new word that the Korean War added to the English lexicon. It is of uncertain origin. Some soldiers say it was used in Japan before the war by members of the all-black 24th Infantry Regiment, 25th Division, in talking about someone who had gone AWOL. It suggested the way bugs and insects would scurry frantically, seeking new cover, when their shelter of a rock or log was turned over. It was used in Korea to mean that soldiers or a unit just simply ran away when confronted by an enemy force. The troops "bugged out" without fighting.

General Milburn said that he was first aware of the term during Eighth Army's breakout from the Naktong perimeter in mid-September 1950, and that it then referred to North Korean soldiers who changed from their uniforms into Korean white civilian clothing and fled north. Colonel Fisher, commanding officer of the 35th Infantry, 25th Division, said the first time he heard it was in August 1950, when Lieutenant Colonel Wilkins, one of his battalion commanders, called him on the radio and said, "OK, colonel, you can get in your jeep now. The Gooks have bugged out." General Kean, the 25th Division commander, has also said he heard the term in the summer of 1950 in the Naktong River area fighting, referring to fleeing or dispersed North Korean soldiers.[72]

Research for this book indicates the probability that this descriptive American phrase was probably coined by black soldiers of the 24th Infantry and may have first been used by them in Japan, but that it spread to armywide use in Korea in the summer and fall of 1950. Ironically, it found its widest use to describe Eighth Army's withdrawal from the Chongchon River front in North Korea in late November and in early December 1950. It became perhaps the most widely used American idiom of the Korean War.

Col. Emerson C. Itschner, US I Corps Engineer officer, summed up quite well the concept of "bugout" that prevailed in Eighth Army at the end of 1950 in Korea. He wrote: "You will not find 'Operation Bug-Out' mentioned in any official report. Nevertheless, officer and G.I. alike serving in Korea have the name for the retrograde movement which commenced with the withdrawal shortly after Thanksgiving Day, 1950, from positions considerably north of the Chungchon River, and ended six weeks later when a defensive line was drawn across Korea 300 road miles to the south."[73]

There is little doubt that there was a "bugout" mentality among many men in Eighth Army in December 1950. They wanted to get going south fast and keep going. The command echelon of Eighth Army also seems to have wanted to put a lot of distance between themselves and the Chinese in early December 1950—in order to save the army, they usually said.

Tokyo and Washington Policy Actions, 6–22 December 1950

From the evacuation of Pyongyang on 5 December to the death of General Walker on 23 December, policy actions taken in Washington anticipated the course of military action in Korea in the immediate future. When Army Chief of Staff Gen. J. Lawton Collins discussed the Korean situation with General MacArthur in Tokyo on 6 December, MacArthur told Collins that, unless he received substantial reinforcements in a reasonable time, he anticipated he would have to evacuate American forces from Korea. General Collins told MacArthur that he should not expect any reinforcements in the near future. In Washington the question was also under discussion. Maj. Gen. Charles L. Bolte, the acting chief of staff for operations, G-3, proposed on 3 December that the 82nd Airborne

Division, the only combat-ready division in the United States, be sent to Japan at once, where it could be available to protect the Japanese base or be sent to Korea if a decision should be made to use it there. General Bolte said the division could be in Japan within 34 days after being alerted.

The Army G-4, Maj. Gen. William O. Reeder, agreed the division could be sent but did not recommend it. Gen. Matthew B. Ridgway, deputy chief of staff for operations and administration, recommended to General Haislip, the acting chief of staff, that a decision on the matter be withheld until General Collins returned from Korea. General Ridgway later stated that he told General Haislip the 82nd Airborne Division should not be sent to Korea under any circumstances, "that it was our only Army reserve capable of immediate combat." When Collins returned to Washington on 8 December, he disapproved the proposal to send the 82nd Airborne Division to Japan or Korea.[74]

On 28 November General MacArthur had requested the Joint Chiefs of Staff to approve Chiang Kai-shek's offer during the summer to send 33,000 Nationalist troops from Formosa to Korea to help the UN, and also to request that he increase the number beyond the original amount. The Joint Chiefs of Staff did not approve the request but said it was under consideration, pointing out the difficulties in the proposal in such a way that it should have been clear it would not be approved. Then on 18 December, MacArthur asked the Joint Chiefs to call to duty four National Guard divisions and send them to Japan immediately. By 23 December the Joint Chiefs had told MacArthur that he could not expect any of those divisions in the foreseeable future.[75] Thus, by 23 December, MacArthur knew he would receive no reinforcements from the United States or from Formosa and that, except for possible small UN contingents from other countries, he would have to meet future war contingencies in Korea from the troops already there.

The Joint Chiefs of Staff in Washington at this time were:

> Gen. Omar Bradley, chairman
> Adm. Forrest Sherman (Navy)
> Gen. Hoyt Vandenberg (Air Force)
> Gen. J. Lawton Collins (Army)

The Joint Chiefs operated under the general jurisdiction of General George C. Marshall, secretary of defense, who reported directly to the president of the United States, Harry S Truman. On matters transcending the purely military and reaching into foreign policy, the president would normally consult the secretary of state, Dean G. Acheson. The above men were the top policymakers in the United States government at this time, reviewing and acting on General MacArthur's requests and recommendations in the crisis period in Korea in December 1950.[76]

On 6 December, the secretary of defense issued a directive to all military commanders, warning them to avoid statements of public policy concerning the conduct of foreign affairs that had not been cleared in Washington. This order was to have serious consequences in the future for MacArthur, but it did not mention him directly. Later, however, in response to a question from Senator Russell, chairman of the Senate Military Affairs Committee, General Marshall stated that General MacArthur's statements in early December, at the time of Eighth

Army's defeat along the Chongchon and the failure of his 24 November offensive, criticizing the restrictions placed on him and his command in responding to the Chinese offensive, were the reasons for issuing the directive. It was in fact directed at General MacArthur and was intended as a direct warning to cease making such comments. In response to another question by Senator Russell, General Marshall said that MacArthur, subsequent to 6 December, had violated this directive.[77]

On 7 December General MacArthur sent a radio message to General Walker in Korea stating that "current planning provides for a withdrawal in successive positions, if necessary, to the Pusan area. 8th Army will hold the Seoul area for maximum time possible short of entailing such envelopment as would prevent its withdrawal to the south." This same message informed General Walker that the X Corps was being evacuated from northeast Korea and would join Eighth Army as soon as practicable, and at that time would pass to control of Eighth Army.[78] All of General Walker's decisions concerning Eighth Army after 7 December must be considered in the light of this instruction from General MacArthur.

At this time, after the Joint Chiefs had refused to allow the Far East Command to bomb the Yalu River bridges and after his conversations with General Collins on 6 December, which made it certain he would receive no reinforcements from the United States, General MacArthur subsequently said he decided to resign from his post as commander, Far East. He wrote a dispatch on 7 or 8 December to the Joint Chiefs of Staff, tendering his resignation. According to his later statement, "I at once asked for immediate relief from assignment to duty in the Far East. In my bitterness I told my able Chief of Staff, General Doyle Hickey." MacArthur then continues, "By some means the enemy commanders must have known of this decision to protect his lines of communication into North Korea, or he never would have dared to cross those bridges in force." General Hickey protested to MacArthur that he should not take the action he proposed in the crisis then existing. General MacArthur added, "I tore up my dispatch."[79]

Soviet Penetration of American War Policy

While this work is a combat history of the Korean War and not a political history of the UN alliance that fought it, it seems essential to mention briefly a charge that General MacArthur made in late 1950 and early 1951 (and repeated later) that the Soviet Union and the Chinese government were well informed of American and UN policy concerning limits imposed on him for the conduct of the war. If true, this charge meant that the Chinese knew in advance of the UN forces' actions at the end of 1950 that there would be no reprisal against them on the mainland of Asia and that they had a sanctuary across the Yalu River in Manchuria. Therefore, there would be little risk to them in sending their troops across the border into Korea to fight UN forces in November and December. The Soviets and the Chinese could know all this only if their agents, working in either the United States or England, had penetrated the highest levels of policy-making offices of the two governments. If the Soviets and the Chinese did in fact know in advance that UN and United States policy would be to engage in no military action against China beyond the confines of Korea, this knowledge would obviously affect the course of their actions and of the war.

General MacArthur believed that the Chinese Communists and the Soviets did know these policies in advance. And he believed this information had reached the Soviets and the Chinese through espionage agents operating within the British Embassy in Washington and within the British government in London, and indirectly through the United States Department of State.

It is a matter of record, in public documents and in UN actions, that the British government was hostile to General MacArthur's proposals in November and December 1950 to take military action against Chinese bases in Manchuria and against the Chinese mainland after the massive Chinese intervention in Korea. We have already mentioned the trip Prime Minister Clement Atlee of Great Britain made hurriedly to the United States on 4 December 1950 and his subsequent conversations with President Truman, Secretary of State Dean Acheson, and the Joint Chiefs of Staff. His trip was almost wholly to make sure the United States government would not accede to General MacArthur's recommendations and would not use the atomic bomb, which President Truman had suggested might be used against CCF forces in Korea. Atlee and his government feared that any of these actions, if taken, might involve Great Britain, as an ally of the United States, in a war with the Soviet Union.

General MacArthur raised the question, Were British subjects working within the British Embassy in Washington as Soviet agents at this time? And if they were, would they have access to State Department and American war-policy decisions on Korea? The answer on both counts has to be yes. Not only were British subjects working as Soviet agents in positions of high authority in the British Embassy in Washington, but their network encompassed the British Foreign Office and British Intelligence in London. Specifically, the agents Kim Philby, Donald MacLean, and Guy Burgess were traitors to their country, and their espionage actions directly affected the United States in the Korean War.

In the early summer of 1950, Philby was transferred from Istanbul to Washington as Secret Service liaison officer in the British Embassy to work with the American CIA and the FBI. Burgess was transferred from London to the British Embassy in Washington as second secretary in October 1950. He imposed himself on Philby, whom he could blackmail, and lived in his home for 18 months. At the same time, MacLean was back in London and assigned to the American desk in the Foreign Office. The three men could hardly have been placed in better positions to serve their Soviet masters. All three were bitterly hostile to General MacArthur for his efforts to expand the war so as to win it, as MacArthur thought. They were all afraid he might dominate American policy in Korea. MacLean in London "provided for the Moscow Centre microfilmed copies of every vital document that passed through his hands," according to a foremost student of the espionage ring.[80]

There is no certain knowledge, publicly known, as to just what the British espionage agents in 1950 and 1951 may have transmitted to the Soviet Union about UN and American war policy concerning China in the Korean War. And there is no certain knowledge, publicly known, as to how much of this information the Soviet Union may have passed on to China. If American intelligence has any knowledge on these points, it is still locked in secrecy. Possibly it is all still held in the secret files of the Soviet Union, and perhaps part of it in those of China.

All of this is not to imply that Soviet and Chinese intelligence gained by any source, including that which may have been transmitted by Philby, MacLean, and Burgess, about the limitations Great Britain, the United States, and the United Nations imposed on MacArthur, caused the loss of North Korea to Chinese intervention and nearly the entire war. It may very well have been one of several factors in the dismal outcome. But it was not the most important. It was open knowledge that Great Britain would exert itself to contain the war and hold a checkrein on General MacArthur's plans for extending the war beyond the Yalu. In a coalition war, such as was the Korean War, it is a commonplace of history that allies leak to, or are penetrated by, an active enemy intelligence apparatus to learn coalition secrets. So what is new in the case of Korea? When China intervened on a massive scale in late 1950, even though it had intelligence that it would have an inviolate sanctuary north of the Yalu, it nevertheless had to accept the risk that this might not be so. Any cautious commander must know that he cannot count with certainty on *anything* in war working out as he has planned it.

The mistakes that General MacArthur himself made after the Inchon landing and the capture of Seoul, and the subsequent linking up of Eighth Army from the south with the X Corps in the Seoul area, constituted the origins that led to disaster in Korea. MacArthur tied up the port of Inchon for weeks in outloading the X Corps for ferrying it to northeast Korea, preventing the bringing in of supplies for Eighth Army to continue the attack north. Instead of attaching the X Corps to Eighth Army for unified command to operate from the Seoul area and in western Korea, MacArthur kept it as a separate command under his own control. Rather than the long, inefficient movement of X Corps by water all the way around Korea to the Wonsan area of northeast Korea, he could have marched the corps overland from Seoul to Wonsan in a week, and while doing so have taken possession of the key Iron Triangle area and its communications. Subsequently, after Eighth Army captured Pyongyang, he could have used the X Corps from the Wonsan area in conjunction with Eighth Army in the Pyongyang area to establish control of the waist of Korea and established there a defense line with an ocean port at either end for ready supply and logistic support of the UN troops.

When General MacArthur decided to go to the Korean border, scatter his X Corps troops in far-flung positions that were not mutually supporting, and leave numerous North Korean guerrilla units behind his front, both in the east and in the west, he created a precarious military situation. A wise general would have established a secure line across the waist of Korea before he ventured farther. If the 38th Parallel was crossed because it did not offer a good defensive line (one of the reasons given for crossing it), then the advance should have stopped at the waist of Korea if such a line was being sought. Even if the Chinese had not intervened in Korea initially in late October and subsequently in far greater strength in November and December, it seems certain that the ROK Army and the Republic of Korea could not have established and maintained civil government throughout all of Korea up to the border. This would have been especially unlikely in northeast Korea along a 500-mile border from Manpojin to the Sea of Japan. General MacArthur can be accused of violating one of Clausewitz's dictums that military ventures should not be undertaken beyond what political policies and capabilities could support after military victory had been won.

General MacArthur's own decisions after Inchon and the capture of Seoul, rather than the effect of successful Soviet espionage in the United States and England, were the main causes of the Korean disaster. His decisions and policies were militarily unrealistic and unsound in the circumstances and conditions that prevailed in Korea and its border territories and in the light of the conventional military resources available to the United States and the UN.

As conditions worsened in Korea in the first half of December, ranking officers in the Department of the Army, including Generals Collins and Ridgway, urged that President Truman declare a state of national emergency. On the evening of 15 December the president in a radio address to the nation said that the United States was in "great danger" and that a state of national emergency existed. The next day he issued a formal proclamation to that effect.[81] That same day the People's Republic of China rejected the UN plan for a cease-fire in Korea.

19. The Death of General Walker

Two days before Christmas 1950, on a Saturday, Lt. Gen. Walton H. Walker, Eighth Army commander, left his headquarters in Seoul about 10:30 A.M. for Uijongbu, about 20 miles north on the MSR. He rode as usual in his special jeep, driven by his longtime driver, Master Sergeant Belton, and with his bodyguard. A second jeep with his armed escort followed close behind the first jeep. General Walker was scheduled to present the Republic of Korea Presidential Citation to the US 24th Infantry Division and to the British 27th Brigade for roles they played in the defense of the Naktong River line perimeter during the preceding summer. The ceremony was to be held at the IX Corps headquarters at Uijongbu.

Approximately two to three miles south of Uijongbu at a few minutes before 11 A.M., General Walker was killed in an accident involving the lead jeep in which he was riding. The ceremonial presentations were not held that day for the paraded British 27th Brigade, which waited in vain for the arrival of General Walker. Maj. Gen. Frank Milburn, US I Corps commander, did make the presentations the next day as acting commanding general of Eighth Army.

The official United States Army records present a mystifying silence on details of the accident that caused Walker's death. All one finds is the terse statement that he was killed about 11 o'clock in a traffic accident while on his way to present the citations at Uijongbu. The most commonly heard hearsay elaboration of this cryptic announcement was that a truck driven by a ROK soldier pulled out of the southbound traffic lane in front of Walker's jeep and collided with it.[1]

Gen. John Coulter described the setting for the accident. He was awaiting General Walker at his IX Corps CP, only two to three miles from the scene of the accident, when word came to him of Walker's death. He went at once to the scene. General Walker, he said, had been traveling north rather fast. In the southbound lane of the road a British 27th Brigade truck had stopped because of some mechanical trouble. A ROK 6th Division vehicle going south came up behind the stopped British vehicle and started to pull around it. At that moment General Walker's jeep came over a rise just ahead, running fast. The two vehicles narrowly missed averting a collision, but the left-hand three inches of the ROK vehicle bumper grazed Walker's jeep, causing it to swerve and skid over the side of the road and turn over down an embankment. The road at this point crossed a bund, or raised fill, over low paddy ground. General Walker was pinned under the jeep and had a broken neck, according to General Coulter.[2]

The men in the second jeep, following General Walker, had a close-up view of the accident. They lifted the jeep off the dead general and carried the other injured men to the roadside. They also witnessed the arrival of two generals and other men from IX Corps. A bit of background is necessary in understanding what had become a normal practice of travel in the general's jeep and was a factor in the accident.

Before the outbreak of the Korean War, General Walker in Japan had four special jeeps, two of them painted white, the other two Army olive drab (OD). All of them were modified in certain respects. When Walker came to Korea in mid-July 1950 to take command of the troops there, he brought the two OD-colored jeeps with him. Jeep No. 1 had a .30-caliber machine gun on a pedestal mount between and behind the driver and General Walker, who always rode in the front right-hand seat. Two escort guards, one of them behind the .30-caliber machine gun, rode in the backseat. Lt. Col. Joseph Tyner, the general's aide, usually rode in the lead jeep with the general. The jeeps were not armored, although it is believed the general's jeep had a piece of armor plate on the floor to protect him against a possible road-mine explosion. The jeeps had flashing red lights and sirens mounted on each front fender, and a steel handrail welded to either side crossed in front of the windshield. The general often stood up and held on to the bar. The jeeps also had rear overhang compartments welded to the frame and body. In Japan they had been used to carry luggage for the general and his staff. In Korea they were used to carry machine-gun ammunition. The ammunition weight in the rear tended to shift the jeep's center of gravity toward the rear wheels. At high speed the jeeps would ride front wheels high, making steering uncertain and treacherous. In Korea the dirt roads were often deep in dust, increasing the danger in driving these jeeps at high speed.

The second jeep, called by the escort guards the machine-gun jeep, had a .50-caliber machine gun on a pedestal mount but otherwise was similar to the first jeep. The driver of Walker's jeep was nearly always Master Sergeant Belton. The other members of his party, except his aide, Lieutenant Colonel Tyner, were all members of the 502nd Reconnaissance Platoon. Their sole duty was to protect the general and to do escort duty for him and guard duty at his CP and residence or van, in which he normally slept. The original Jeep No. 2 had been destroyed in an accident in August at the Naktong River front. At the time of the accident on 23 December it had been replaced by a normal jeep from the 502nd Reconnaissance Platoon Scout Section, mounting a .50-caliber machine gun. The accident in early August caused serious injury to Colonel Dabney, Eighth Army G-3, and Sergeant Davidson, who were riding in it. That jeep in trying to follow Belton was caught in a cloud of dust; the driver could not see the road and crashed head-on into a self-propelled gun.

Everyone in the 502nd Reconnaissance Platoon talked about Belton's fast driving, often at 50 to 60 miles an hour in traffic and dust on the bumpy dirt roads. A common jest in the platoon was "Shoot Belton and save the general." But Belton's driving must have satisfied Walker, because he would have no other. Walker was often impatient with slow travel caused by road traffic congestion, and those who rode escort with him said that sometimes he would pull out his .45 automatic pistol and fire it into the road to clear a path. His jeep usually traveled with sirens blaring and red lights flashing.³

On the morning of 23 December, Jeep No. 1 carried the following persons: driver Master Sergeant Belton, General Walker in the right front seat, Lieutenant Colonel Tyner in the back seat, and Cpl. Francis S. Reenan in the back seat. Jeep No. 2 carried driver Sgt. Eugene Donlin, Sgt. Emerson A. Sullivan, and Corporal Long. There may have been another person in the jeep, but this is not certain. Cpl. Randle Hurst was not in Jeep No. 2 on this trip. He had the eight to noon guard duty outside General Walker's office in Seoul that morning. Learning the details of the accident from his friends in the general's escort later in the day, Hurst later wrote that the two vehicles approached Uijongbu

> at a mad-man's speed when they met a ROK three-quarter ton weapons carrier headed south. Belton did not reduce speed. The jeep side-swiped the 3/4 ton, the jeep turned over clock-wise as seen by the men in the second jeep. They all saw it and it was Belton's fault. General Walker was under the jeep and the hand rail came down on his head. The entire jeep was upside down on the ground on the general. Sgt. Belton was also partly under the jeep and suffered a broken back. Major [Lt. Col.] Tyner also suffered a broken back. Both men (Belton and Tyner) were conveyed away from the scene in ambulances, neither walked around while awaiting the ambulances, and none of us in 502 Recon ever saw either of them again. . . .
>
> The ROK truck stopped and three South Korean soldiers on it helped our men in the second jeep lift the jeep off the general. Then the three South Korean soldiers got back on their weapons carrier and drove away. . . . The weapons carrier was not damaged, and all this information I got straight from Donald Waters, Donlin, Sullivan, and Long.
>
> Corporal Long gave us all the lurid details of the general's injuries. He "looked" dead when they got the jeep off him. Long said his head was visibly deformed and "his eye ball was in his mouth." Two generals came from Uijongbu along with other rescuers and one of the generals made Long hold the general's head in his lap as they drove to a field hospital. When Long and the rest of the party returned to Seoul later in the day, I saw the blood on Long's pants. I think the generals who came to the scene of the accident were from the corps headquarters. I do not now recall the names of the generals.⁴

To President Syngman Rhee and the ROK high command, it was a tremendous shock and disgrace when they learned that the commander of the UN forces in Korea had been killed in an accident involving some of their soldiers. They immediately ordered a thorough investigation of the accident. It was carried out under the supervision of Gen. Chang Chang Kuk, provost marshal of the ROK Army. His findings confirmed General Coulter's account.⁵ Thus ended the life of the defender of the Pusan perimeter, the famed commander of the "Ghost Corps" (the XX Corps) of General Patton's Third Army. This corps was the driving force that led the Allied armies from Normandy across France and Germany into Austria.

Cpl. Randle Hurst was one of the detail that guarded General Walker's body during the dead general's last night in Korea. General Walker's body was placed in a heavy casket and brought to the University of Seoul's auditorium. (The university served as Eighth Army's CP and headquarters.) The guard detail, drawn from the 502nd Reconnaissance Platoon, stood that night of 23–24 December in silent post beside their dead general. Hurst wrote a letter to his parents in Oklahoma City on 25 December, only one day after the general's body was flown to Japan on its way to the United States, describing those hours. It follows:

> We guarded our general all night long in the cold and drafty auditorium. Six candles illuminated the area immediately around the coffin. The flag was draped appropriately over the top. A guard stood at rigid parade rest at each corner of the coffin. Three guards stood at the door, parade rest also. No lights were shown except for the six candles in the entire building. We stood at our guard posts in immaculate uniforms. We pulled four hours on and four hours off all night long. We shivered in the cold, but we never moved or spoke a word throughout our tours of duty. Everyone was permitted to pay their respects. Division commanders and high ranking officers came and went all night long. It was so quiet you could hear a pin drop.
> At 0500 hours in the morning, the 24th, all our vehicles were rolled out, guns uncovered, and a convoy was formed. We moved the casket into a 2½ ton truck. Our convoy was reinforced by the 503rd Reconnaissance Platoon vehicles. Also, the vehicles containing the high ranking commanders of all the forces in Korea brought up the rear. Our platoon led the convoy. We drove slowly through the frigid early morning darkness toward Kimpo Air Field. When we arrived an Army band [ROK] played a mournful dirge while we loaded our general for his last homeward voyage. We stood at present arms until the great transport plane had roared away into the dawn of the east.[6]

The plane that carried General Walker's body to Japan was a Constellation, undoubtedly General MacArthur's Constellation No. 1. General Partridge, commander of the Fifth Air Force, was at the controls as it took off from Kimpo airfield. Mrs. Walker arranged for brief observances at Yokohama, the home base in Japan of Eighth Army. Then the body was flown to Washington, D.C. Funeral services for General Walker were held there on 2 January 1951, and he was buried the next day in Arlington National Cemetery.[7]

Maj. Gen. Frank W. Milburn, I Corps commander, had assumed temporary command of Eighth Army at 3 P.M., 23 December. At the same time, Maj. Gen. William B. Kean, commanding the 25th Infantry Division, temporarily took command of I Corps. Both Milburn and Kean returned to their regular posts on 26 December when General Ridgway assumed command of Eighth Army.

During General Milburn's three-day command of Eighth Army, the army became increasingly tense as the CCF built up strength in front of the western end of the army line. And in the central part of Korea, a large buildup of North Korea's revitalized divisions threatened the understrength and largely raw-recruit ROK divisions that had hastily taken positions there. It was evident that a new enemy offensive was being prepared, this time with the CCF concentrated on the western half of the line and with the North Koreans, for the first time in more than two months, taking an active and important role in the action, concentrating their strength in the central and eastern part of the peninsula along and just below the 38th Parallel. There is no evidence that the enemy knew immediately of General Walker's death and a change in Eighth Army command. This event had no part in the enemy's plan for a renewed offensive.

On the day that General Walker died, North Korean forces in the central area hit the ROK 8th Division again, forcing back the ROK 10th Regiment two miles, leaving gaps between its battalions. The ROK 3rd Division moved westward into the ROK III Corps area. The unstable ROK eastern part of the Eighth Army line now was organized so that the ROK III Corps was east of the US IX Corps, the ROK II Corps was east of the ROK III Corps, and the ROK I Corps was at the eastern end of the line in the mountains and along the coast near Yangyang. At the same time, elements of the ROK 1st Division in the US I Corps area along the Imjin River regained the important river-crossing village of Korangpo on the north bank of the river after Chinese forces had driven the ROK 1st Division Reconnaissance Company and the I&R Platoon out of the village the day before. In some places American units had an early Christmas Day dinner, including most units of the 25th Infantry Division, as they prepared for an enemy Christmas Day offensive, widely anticipated in Eighth Army.[8]

The ROK 1st Division did not hold Korangpo very long after retaking it on 23 December. During the twenty-fourth, elements of the ROK 11th Regiment captured ten Chinese near Korangpo. But that night two companies of CCF captured the town for good and drove remaining soldiers of the ROK 1st Division across the Imjin River to the south bank. This was the ROK division's main battle line.

The Chinese prisoners taken near Korangpo were from the CCF 116th Division, 39th Army. They said their mission was to determine the depth of the Imjin River, locate fords, learn the condition of any bridges, and find out the disposition of UN troops along the river. They said the CCF 39th Army's CP was at Uichon, six miles southwest of Sibyon-ni, that the CCF 50th Army was assembling near Kaesong, and that the NK V Corps was in position to the left (east) of the CCF 38th Army, which was to envelop Yonchon and Pakchon. This would put the CCF 50th Army on the American left flank in the west, the 39th Army next to it eastward, and the 38th Army east of the 39th in the area of the Iron Triangle, the Yonchon-Chorwon area, astride the main route south toward Seoul. The Chinese-North Korean boundary seemed to be at the eastern edge of the Iron Triangle, with the North Korean concentration in the vicinity of Chunchon. Elements of the ROK 6th Division captured two Chinese prisoners during the day from the 38th Army, southeast of Yonchon, seeming to confirm this report. Later events showed that the CCF 66th Army was east of the 39th Army, and the CCF 42nd Army was behind the westernmost North Korean divisions and northeast of the CCF 66th Division.[9]

Aerial observers reported during the day seeing about 500 haystacks with no snow on them between Kumhwa and Hwachon, and 50 haystacks close to the road at one place with vehicle tracks to them. Several hundred stacks of odd shape were observed near Ichon. The next day, a haystack exploded when it was strafed.

Just about all of Eighth Army expected an attack on Christmas Eve or Christmas Day. Army intelligence expected the main CCF attack to be down the Uijongbu-Seoul corridor from the Yonchon-Iron Triangle area held by the CCF 38th Army, with a secondary attack by North Korean divisions in the Chunchon area toward Wonju to outflank the UN forces north of Seoul. But Christmas Day came and went without an enemy general attack.[10]

On the east central front in the ROK Army positions, there was bad news. Strong North Korean forces there shifted their attack somewhat eastward from the ROK 8th Division to strike the ROK 9th Division in a very mountainous and almost roadless area. The ROK 9th Division was composed of inexperienced troops, and the North Koreans made a deep penetration in the ROK 9th Division. It was never closed off, and large numbers of North Koreans got not only into the rear of that division but also into the rear of the ROK 3rd, 8th, and 2nd divisions farther west.

On 25 December there was little activity anywhere at the front, except in the remote mountains of the ROK I Corps near the east coast. Communications with the ROKs there were poor, and the confusion that prevailed in the ROK 9th Division resulted in very little firm information. In the US IX Corps sector, B-29s bombed the important enemy buildup centers of Kumhwa, Sariwon, and Pyongyang. Far East Command intelligence issued a statement that 11 reconstituted North Korean divisions had appeared on the central and eastern Korean front in the past ten days and that it had reports that 130,000 North Korean troops were in training in Manchuria.[11]

Christmas Day in Korea saw the continuation of American troop movements toward the central front as a result of the US 2nd Division Operational Order of 23 December. On 25 December, the 2nd Reconnaissance Company established a patrol base at Hoengsong, 12 air miles north of Wonju, in rear of the crumbling ROK II and III Corps divisions. The 2nd Division units that had just moved from the Seoul area to Chungju in the central mountains reported an unceasing flow of South Korean civilians drafted for the South Korean Army, estimated at 75,000, going south to training camps. The 72nd Tank Battalion, part of the 2nd Infantry Division, was still near Sangju, south of the main mountain barrier that cuts across this part of east-central Korea. It was under orders to be prepared to move north or east against a possible enemy penetration of the ROK troops to the north of and in front of it. To help the US 2nd Division in moving into battle positions or critical areas, markers with the names of villages and towns in English were to be placed on their outskirts in this zone of action.[12]

In different areas of the Eighth Army front, Christmas dinner was served over a period of four days, from 23 to 26 December, as circumstances dictated. The twenty-sixth was much like the days that preceded it, except that Eighth Army's new commander, Lt. Gen. Matthew B. Ridgway, arrived from the United States and assumed command. In the eastern central front, North Korean attacks against the ROK 8th and 9th divisions continued with enemy success, and the situation there became worse by the hour. Patrols from both US I and IX corps on the western half of the front encountered enemy groups. At this time the IX Corps CP was three miles east of Seoul.

In its Daily Intelligence Summary for 26 December, the Far East Headquarters intelligence section wondered "Why CCF delay?" It surmised that the enemy had been surprised at their initial success in late November and that they were now acting cautiously. It also surmised that the CCF in the west were delaying further attack until CCF troops of the IX Army Group that had fought against the X Corps in northeast Korea could move into position in the Wonsan-Hungnam area to help the North Koreans there. Intelligence projections by

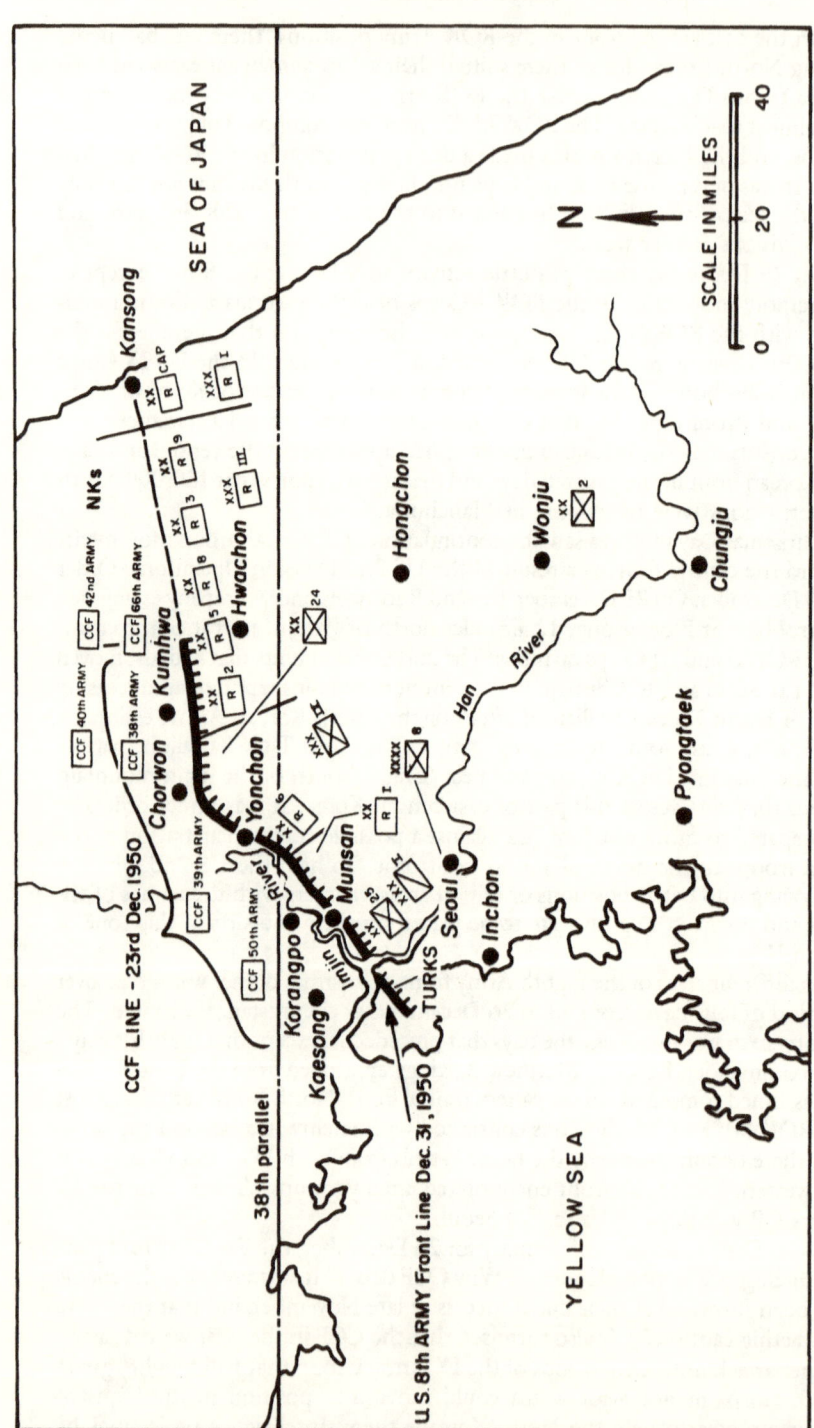

Map 16. The Eighth Army front line, 31 December 1950.

Eighth Army gave the same reason for the CCF delay in renewing attack.[13] Both were wrong. And they continued to be wrong in this matter for the next three months. This is an unusually good indication of the condition of UN intelligence of enemy troop disposition and potential in Korea at this time. The fact is, the CCF IX Army Group lay crippled in the Hungnam area and was incapable of taking combat position anywhere. Those CCF divisions had to rebuild with recruits and rearm and reprovision before they could reappear in the front lines. They first reappeared in the central front in March 1951.

In its intelligence summary covering 26 December, the Far East Command intelligence section thought the enemy attack was at hand. It noted that, during the previous 48 hours, enemy troops, supplies, and artillery had been arriving in forward areas on all roads and trails, coming south from Sibyon-ni, Chorwon, and Kumhwa. The largest buildup seemed to be on the Yonchon-Seoul axis and the Kumhwa-Uijongbu axis. Air reports said there was displacement of artillery and 5,000 troops to the vicinity of Yonchon. Enemy patrols tried to penetrate the 24th Infantry Division to determine its extent, and an enemy patrol was encountered seven miles southeast of Yonchon.[14]

The death of General Walker on 23 December when his Eighth Army was taking defensive positions just north of Seoul and new South Korean divisions were hurriedly being placed in defense positions in an extension of the army line to the central mountains and beyond to the eastern coast, to meet an imminent Chinese–North Korean offensive, marks the logical place to bring this volume to a close. A new phase of the Korean War was about to open with a new commander for the UN forces as the new year, 1951, awaited only a few dawns away.

Lt. Gen. Matthew B. Ridgway, the American leader of airborne troops in World War II in Europe, came to his Asian assignment on very short notice, direct from the Pentagon in Washington. He inherited a dispirited army. The disastrous chain of events that unfolded following General MacArthur's orders on 24 November 1950 to resume the attack to the northern border of Korea had ended in the loss to Chinese Communists of all North Korea. The question now was, Would South Korea—all of Korea—follow?

Notes

Abbreviations used in these notes include the following: Act. Rpt. = Action Report; Comd. Rpt. = Command Report (designation for monthly reports to Eighth Army after November 1950); DIS = Daily Intelligence Summary; GO = General Order; HQ = Headquarters; Jnl. file = Journal file (especially important for G-2 and G-3 sections); Msg. = Message; Narr. = Narrative; PIR (Periodic Intelligence Report) = G-2 Daily Intelligence Report; POR (Periodic Operations Report) = G-3 Daily Operations Report; PLR (Periodic Logistics Report) = G-4 Daily Logistics Report; (The PIR, POR, and PLR were daily reports from the major staff divisions of Eighth Army.); Sec. = Section; Summ. = Summary; WD = War Diary (designation for monthly reports by elements of Eighth Army up to November 1950).

Chapter 1

1. A detailed history of the Korean War from its onset in June 1950 to 24 Nov 50, including the Chinese 1st Phase Offensive, appears in Lt. Col. Roy E. Appleman, *South to the Naktong, North to the Yalu* (official US Army history of the Korean War, 25 June–24 Nov 1950; Washington, D.C.: GPO, 1961).

2. Ibid., pp. 758–60.

3. Edgar Snow, *Red China Today: The Other Side of the River* (1962; reprint, New York: Vintage Books, 1971), pp. 116–17.

4. Peng Dehuai, *Memoirs of a Chinese Marshal: A Cultural Revolution "Confession" by Marshal Peng Dehuai (1898–1974) Covering His Career from Service in China's Warlord Armies to Command of the Chinese People's Volunteers in Korea*, 1st English edition (Beijing: Foreign Languages Press, 1984), pp. 472–73.

5. Ibid., p. 477. The Party Central Comm. voted on 6 Oct to enter the war.

6. The information on Han Xianchu is based on the article "A Biography of Comrade Han Xianchu" (trans. Ellis L. Melvin), *People's Daily* (Beijing), 12 Oct 86, p. 4. I am indebted to Ellis L. Melvin of Tamaroa, Ill., for all the foregoing information about the establishment of the Chinese People's Liberation Army of Volunteers and its commander, Marshal Peng Dehuai. Melvin translated several chapters of Wei Wei's "Marshal Peng" from *Kunlun* magazine and supplied machine copies of relevant material from his copy of *Memoirs of a Chinese Marshal*. Melvin served as a senior translator in Asia and the United States until 1964, after having studied Chinese Mandarin in 1953–54. He served in Korea in 1954–55 and has been reading Chinese for more than 30 years. Mel-

vin, a retired member of the United States armed forces, has tried to keep abreast of publications in China relating to the Korean War.

7. This account is based on *Khrushchev Remembers,* with introduction, commentary, and notes by Edward Crankshaw, trans. and ed. Strobe Talbott (Boston: Little, Brown, 1970), pp. 367-73. It was reported during the war that Mao Tse-tung's son, a general, was killed in an American air raid on a Communist force CP in Korea.

8. Appleman, *South to the Naktong, North to the Yalu,* p. 766n.57.

9. Estimates of the number of boats of all kinds being assembled on the Chinese coast opposite Formosa reached 100,000 – an incredible number. Necessarily they included vessels that could carry only a few persons. Such craft could make a crossing of the 90-mile wide Taiwan (Formosa) Strait only if favored by good weather and if they encountered no significant air or naval opposition.

10. Appleman, *South to the Naktong, North to the Yalu,* p. 751.

11. This estimate of Chinese troop strength is based on experience and intelligence gained in the course of battle and from prisoner interrogation and captured enemy documents. While there was some variation in the strength of Chinese divisions, they averaged about 8,000 men. Full strength of a Chinese division was supposed to be 10,000 men, but this strength was rarely attained in the Korean War.

12. Appleman, *South to the Naktong, North to the Yalu,* p. 751.

13. Xenophon, *The Anabasis* (The march up-country), trans. W. H. D. Rouse (London: Thomas Nelson and Sons, 1947). There are several editions of Xenophon's famous work. For Roman Legion performances, see Flavius Vegetius Renatus (Vegetius), *The Military Institutions of the Romans,* ed. Brig. Gen. Thomas R. Phillips (Harrisburg, Pa.: Military Service Publishing, 1944); William Duncan, *Caesar* (London: Jones, n.d.), includes Caesar's *Commentaries* and *A Discourse Concerning the Roman Art of War.* Many editions of Caesar's *Commentaries* are available in English.

14. The movement and marches of the Chinese soldiers in the example given are fully documented in Appleman, *South to the Naktong, North to the Yalu,* p. 770n.65. The figure of 210,000 Chinese soldiers in position to confront the UN forces in Korea by mid-Nov 1950 is based on an average division strength of 8,000. Intelligence gained from prisoner interrogation and captured enemy documents subsequent to Nov 1950 justify this figure. This estimate of enemy strength omits some supporting groups of service and cavalry reconnaissance units and one Chinese army of four divisions that at first remained in reserve at Linchiang, Manchuria.

15. Gen. Matthew B. Ridgway, interview with author, 21 Oct 75.

16. The discussion of the CCF in 1950 and the leaders of the Chinese "Volunteer" forces that entered Korea is based on many sources, including the following: Department of the Army, *Pamphlet No. 30-51, Handbook on the Chinese Communist Army, September 1952* (Washington, D.C., 1952); Far East Command (FEC), "Chinese Communist Military Operations in Korea," *Intelligence Digest* 35 (1–15 Nov 52): 44–51, National Archives, Federal Records Center, Record Group 407, Box 766 (hereafter, similar citations give box number only); ibid., 6 (16–31 Aug 51), Box 513; Edgar Snow, *Red Star over China* (New York: Random House, 1938); idem, *Red China Today;* Stanley Karnow, *Mao and China: From Revolution to Revolution* (New York: Viking Press, 1972); Han Suyin, *The Morning Deluge: Mao Tse-tung and the Chinese Revolution, 1893–1954* (Boston: Little, Brown, 1972); Nikita Khrushchev, *Khrushchev Remembers: The Last Testament* (Boston: Little, Brown, 1974).

17. Department of the Army, *Pamphlet No. 30-51, Handbook on the Chinese Communist Army, September 1952,* pp. 28–29. This handbook was prepared from a vast array of intelligence information and material captured in the first six months of the Chinese intervention in Korea, including the interrogation of Chinese prisoners, and it is supported by hundreds of detailed combat reports of American and UN units.

18. Information regarding the movement of the XIII Army Group into Korea is based primarily on a captured enemy document that was reproduced in FEC Daily Intelligence Summary (DIS) No. 3207, 21 June 51, Box 473. The document carries the heading "Volunteer Headquarters." There are many intelligence summaries throughout Nov and Dec 1950 that give the same information as to the enemy order of battle for the Chinese units in front of Eighth Army, based largely on the testimony of Chinese prisoners captured in the fighting. They identified their units without hesitation. The only question concerns the 167th Division of the 50th Army. It may not have been with the 50th Army when it first crossed the Yalu but may have joined it at a later date.

19. Appleman, *South to the Naktong, North to the Yalu*, pp. 667–716, gives the story of the Chinese 1st Phase Offensive in detail. This summary is based on that account.

Chapter 2

1. Lt. Col. James F. Schnabel, Ret., *Policy and Direction the First Year: The United States Army in the Korean War* (Washington, D.C.: Office of Chief of Military History, US Army, 1972). Lt. Col. Schnabel's work is a study of the official records of the Far East Command in Tokyo and of the Joint Chiefs of Staff (JCS) in Washington, together with other related materials, bearing on the policies, command methods, and high-level political and military decisions of the United States in conducting the Korean War during its first year. It is documented in detail and relies heavily on the cable traffic between the two command centers. My treatment of this subject is based largely on Schnabel's work.

2. See ibid., pp. 182–83, for the 27 Sept 50 directive from the JCS to MacArthur.

3. Ibid., pp. 250–56, gives a detailed account of the exchange of messages between MacArthur and the JCS, of discussion in the National Security Council, and of exchanges between the JCS and the president on this issue.

4. Gen. Douglas A. MacArthur, *Reminiscences* (New York: McGraw-Hill, 1964), pp. 359–60; Almond testimony before the Judiciary Committee, 83rd Cong., 2nd sess., 23 Nov 54, pt. 25, pp. 2103–2104. MacArthur held that the "terrain was such that there was little prospect that any enemy might drive an effective wedge between the two forces and initiate flanking operations against either or both, and no such attempt was ever made."

5. Map of Korea, 1950 and later editions, 1:50,000 scale; JANIS, *Study of Korea*, Apr 1950, and map "Mountain Ranges of Korea."

6. The discussion of the so-called gap between Eighth Army and the X Corps is based in part on Appleman, *South to the Naktong, North to the Yalu*, pp. 745–48, which is documented in detail from official records of military units on the edges of the gap. Additional studies on the subject since that work was published have only confirmed my stated conclusions.

7. 2nd Inf. Div. Comd. Rpt., G-3 Act. Rpt., Nov 1950, Box 2435.

8. Some of the specific information on this ROK patrol will be found in Lt. Col. Robert C. Cameron, KMAG advisor to the ROK 10th Regt., in "The Lost Corps," *Military Review* 33, no. 2, (May 1953): 10–18.

9. This sketch of efforts by both Eighth Army and X Corps to establish contact in the gap between them is based on the following documentary evidence: 3rd Inf. Div. WD, G-3 Jnl., Msg. CG X Corps to Eighth Army, at 1500 [3:00 P.M.], and journal entries at 1020 [10:20 A.M.], 2220 [10:20 P.M.], 13 Nov 50; ibid., G-3 Jnl. entries at 1330 [1:30 P.M.], 14 Nov 50; X Corps PIR No. 49, 14 Nov 50; 65th Inf. Regt. Comd. Rpt., Nov 1950, p. 4; Eighth Army WD, G-3 Sec., 14 Nov 50; Eighth Army POR No. 379, 15 Nov 50; 2nd Inf. Div. WD, POR No. 315, 18 Nov 50; 38th Inf. WD, 16–18 Nov 50. (Subsequent references to the time of messages, journal entries, telephone conversations, etc., may appear only in the 24-hour system used by the military.)

10. James A. Field, Jr., *History of United States Naval Operations in Korea* (Washington, D.C.: GPO, 1962), pp. 237–42; 24th Inf. Div. WD, Narr., Nov 1950, Box 3512. Field's book is an excellent work, based on official primary US Navy sources.

11. Eighth Army WD, Summ., Sec. 1, 17–19 Nov 50, Box 1122.

Chapter 3

1. Brig. Gen. William A. Collier, review comments on "South to the Naktong, North to the Yalu" MS, Dec 1957, and letter to author, 10 Mar 58. During the time Gen. Walker was at the advance CP near Anju, Collier seems to have been in charge of the Pyongyang Army CP. Collier was well known in Eighth Army and highly respected for his efficient performance of duty. During the army attack toward the border, Milburn may have had his I Corps Headquarters (HQ) at Sinanju, or at its outskirts. This seems to be indicated in the I Corps records, but I am not clear on this point. In any event, Sinanju and Anju are only four or five miles apart, and some confusion as to exact location may have arisen from this fact.

2. Norman Bartlett, *With the Australians in Korea* (Canberra: Australian War Memorial, 1954), pp. 44–45; 3rd Bn., 27th Inf., 25th Inf. Div. WD, Box 3764.

3. Pfc. Arthur J. Cohen (HQ Co., 2nd Inf. Div.), "Diary of a Week," 23 Nov–1 Dec 50, Kunu-ri, Korea (copy in author's possession); Col. Robert K. Sawyer, letter to author, 14 June 74.

4. Col. Henry G. Fisher, commander of the 35th Inf. Regt., interview with author, 5 Jan 52. Also, Sawyer, letter to author, 14 June 74. In Nov 1950 Sawyer was a platoon leader of the 25th Recon. Co., 25th Inf. Div.

5. FEC DIS No. 2999, 25 Nov 50, Box 99.

6. Eighth Army WD, 24 Nov 50, G-2 PIR No. 135, and G-3 Sec.

7. 38th Inf. Comd. Rpt., Summ., Nov 1950, Box 2473; Eighth Army WD, Summ., Sec. 1, Nov 1950, pp. 16–23; 2nd Inf. Div. WD, Summ., Nov 1950, Box 2435; 35th Inf. WD, Nov 1950, Box 3764.

8. Eighth Army WD, G-3 Sec., 23–24 Nov 50; *Operations in Korea* (25 June 1950 to 1 April 1951) (West Point, N.Y.: US Military Academy, Dept. of Military Art and Engineering, 1951), Map 8; Bartlett, *With the Australians in Korea*.

9. Eighth Army WD, 22 Nov 50, G-4 Sec., Annex A to PLR No. 133, Arty. Rpt. No. 15. The relative firepower figure is determined by the formula: $RFP = D + W + R$, where D is the range, in thousands of yards; W is the weight of the projectile divided by 5; and R is the normal number of rounds per minute of the weapon fired.

10. Eighth Army WD, 23 Nov 50, G-4 Sec. See Sec. 3, par. 5, Operations, for organization of artillery with Eighth Army, pursuant to Operational Plan No. 15.

11. Eighth Army WD, G-3 Sec., 23 Nov 50; ibid., Opn. Plan No. 16, 23 Nov 50. The UN concern about the power plants was grossly exaggerated, as it turned out. Many that were captured were found to have had all the machinery removed, and some of the plants had never been completed.

12. See table 2. The most important document relating to the Chinese order of battle for the 2nd Phase Offensive against Eighth Army is translated and reproduced in FEC DIS No. 3207, 21 June 51. It was issued by the CCF Volunteers HQ, giving the composition of that headquarters and including the organization of the XIII Army Group. It is noteworthy that the document is headed "Volunteer Headquarters." The Chinese placed much importance on the fiction of their forces in Korea being "volunteers."

13. Schnabel, *Policy and Direction*, p. 273.

14. The exact number of troops in the Chinese order of battle cannot be determined. At full strength a Chinese infantry division was supposed to number 10,000 men. The

X Corps and the 1st Marine Div. in the Chosin Reservoir campaign reached the conclusion that the divisions of the IX Army Group there numbered, on average, about 7,500-8,000 men. It seems likely that the divisions of the XIII Army Group in the west were similar in strength. The POW interrogation intelligence on this subject is conflicting.

15. JANIS, *Mountain Ranges of Korea,* Map of Korea, 1:50,000 scale, April 1945. Certain place-name suffixes on maps of Korea indicate "river," "island," "village," or "mountain." River names usually carry the suffix *ch'on, gang,* or *kang* (Chong*chon* River, for example). Mountains have a suffix of *bong, pong,* or *san.* An island usually has a suffix of *do.* A settlement may be indicated by one of several suffixes, such as *dong, gol, kol, li, ni,* or *ri* (such as Kunu-*ri* or Hagaru-*ri*).

16. Appleman, *South to the Naktong, North to the Yalu,* pp. 670–72; Map of Korea, revised 1950 edition, scale 1:50,000 (1¼ inches to 1 mile) (Washington, D.C.: US Army Corps of Engineers, 1950), is used throughout this work in discussions of topography, except where otherwise noted. Numerous war diaries and other records of combat units of Eighth Army have also contributed much to this brief generalized analysis of the key terrain where Eighth Army and the CCF had their initial engagements and ensuing combat in the last week of November 1950. These will often be cited in discussing these particular events.

Chapter 4

1. Eighth Army WD, 24 Nov 50, G-2 PIR No. 135.
2. Eric Linklater, *Our Men in Korea* (London: HMSO, 1952), p. 28.
3. Col. Henry G. Fisher, interview with author, 5 Jan 52; Col. Albert K. Stebbins, Jr., interview with author, 4 Dec 53.
4. Appleman, *South to the Naktong, North to the Yalu,* pp. 773–74.
5. 24th Div. WD, 1–30 Nov 50; 21st Inf. WD, 24 Nov 50, Box 3538; Col. Gines Perez, CO, 21st Inf., interview with author, 6 Aug 51.
6. 5th RCT Unit Rpt., Nov 1950, Box 4691; IX Corps WD, Vol. 2, G-2 Spot Rpt., Boxes 1769 and 1767, G-2 Act. Rpt., 24 Nov 50 in I Corps WD; IX Corps WD, G-3 Spot Rpt., 24 Nov 50; FEC DIS No. 3000, 26 Nov 50, Box 99.
7. Col. John T. Corley, commander of the 24th Inf. Regt., interview with author, 4 Jan 52. Col. Corley had commanded the 24th Inf. since Sept 1950. He told the author that Gen. Kean, 25th Div. commander, usually placed the 24th Inf. in the least critical part of the division's zone of action. The regiment's record in the early part of the Korean War was not good, and it was considered unreliable. There was only one other all-black infantry unit in Eighth Army—the 3rd Bn., 9th Inf., 2nd Inf. Div. The personnel of both the 24th Regt. and the 3rd Bn., 9th Inf., were integrated into other units of Eighth Army in the fall of 1951.
8. 25th Div. Hist., Bk. 2, Nov 1950, Unit Hist., HQ, 89th Med. Tank Bn., p. 3.
9. 25th Inf. Div. Hist., Bk. 2, Nov 1950, Narr., Task Force Dolvin, p. 2; IX Corps WD, Bk. 1, 24 Nov 50, and G-3, Msg. No. 1479, Annex 2, Vol. 6; Brig. Gen. George B. Barth, CG 25th Div. Arty., "Tropic Lightning and Taro Leaf in Korea" (Mimeographed MS with sketch maps [n.d., but apparently written in 1951], copy in author's possession), pp. 40–41; Eighth Army WD, Sec. 2, 24 Nov 50, G-3 Jnl. entry No. 1, and msg. at 1710, Box 1130; I Corps WD, G-3 POR, 24 Nov 50, Box 1500.
10. ATIS, Enemy Documents, Korean Operations, Issue 29, No. 202051, p. 117, Item 36. Apparently the interrogation was conducted by a North Korean. The document said there were 452 American prisoners in the stockade and that, in the period 5–25 Nov, three of them had died.
11. IX Corps WD, Vol. 2, G-2 Spot Rpt., 24 Nov 50, Box 1769. One of the released

prisoners, a Sgt. Klechner, said that Pyoktong, on the south bank of the Yalu, was bounded by the river on three sides and was guarded by about two companies of North Koreans and few Chinese. He said the town was heavily bombed and burned on 19 Nov, and many civilians killed. He added that there were about 30 Americans in the camp who had been wounded so badly they could not walk and that nine needed amputations. He estimated there were about 320 American prisoners there who had not been wounded. The Counterintelligence Corps (CIC) at the 7th Cav. Regt. HQ made the Klechner interrogation. See 1st Cav. Div. WD, Nov 1950.

12. Col. Robert K. Sawyer, letter to author, 14 June 74; 25th Div. WD, Bk. 9, Annex 10, 25th Recon. Co., 24 Nov 50, Box 3765.

13. IX Corps WD, 24 Nov 50, Box 1767.

14. 38th Inf. Comd. Rpt., Summ., 24 Nov 50, Box 2473.

15. The discussion is based primarily on Cameron, "Lost Corps," pp. 9–18. Cameron's is the best account I know of what happened to the ROK II Corps in the vicinity of Tokchon in the last days of Nov 1950. But there are also many references to the ROK action in the Eighth Army, IX Corps, and 2nd Inf. Div. WDs, and in the FEC DIS for the period. Many of these references are cited in later parts of the narrative. There are virtually no South Korean Army records for the first part of the Korean War. Most of the extant information about ROK actions is to be found in KMAG advisor reports to the US Chief of KMAG, Eighth Army. These are normally included in the Eighth Army WD for the day. The Republic of Korea's Army chief of staff subsequently requested permission from the Department of the Army and from me to translate *South to the Naktong, North to the Yalu* into Korean and publish it for their use and reference because it had more information, they said, about their own army's military action in 1950 than their own existing military records possessed.

16. The 12-in-1 ration consisted of the following items: biscuits (600 gm.); two cans of two different kinds of fish – mackerel, mackerel-pike, sardines, herring, sukesotara, or Alaskan pollack (200 gm.) – or canned tuna flakes (200 gm.), dried prunes (30 gm.), roasted soybeans (30 gm.), roasted peas (40 gm.), hard candy (60 gm.), salt (10 gm.), red pepper (10 gm.), green tea (8 gm.), chewing gum (15 gm.). See *QM Review*, Sept–Oct 1951, p. 121.

17. Eighth Army WD, 23 Nov 50, G-3 Sec.; IX Corps WD, Vol. 4, G-3 Spot Rpt., 24 Nov 50, Box 1770.

18. Cameron, "Lost Corps."

19. 25th Inf. Div. WD, Ord. Off. Rpt., 24 Nov 50, Box 3769; 1st Cav. Div. WD, 24 Nov 50, Box 4446; Eighth Army WD, Summ., Sec. 1, Nov 1950.

20. GHQ FEC Communiqué No. 11, 6 Nov 50.

21. "Msg. CINCFE to JCS, NR: 68572, 9 Nov 50," in Joint Senate and House Hearings, *Pertinent Papers on the Korean Situation* (8 vols.), II, 341.

22. Eighth Army WD, 24 Nov 50, *EUSAK Daily News Bulletin*.

23. Reginald William Thompson, *Cry Korea* (London: MacDonald & Co., 1951), p. 236.

24. Eighth Army WD, 24 Nov 50, G-3 Sec.; IX Corps WD, Bk. 1, 24 Nov 50; I Corps WD, Nov 1950, p. 31; Gen. Milburn, statement to author, in *South to the Naktong, North to the Yalu*, p. 776; Brig. Gen. Edwin K. Wright (a member of MacArthur's party), interview with author, 7 Jan 54; Maj. Gen. Garrison H. Davidson (asst. div. com., 24th Inf. Div., Nov 1950), interview with author, 28 Jan 54. Davidson said in this interview that he and most of the division staff thought that Eighth Army should have stopped at the Chongchon River.

25. Brig. Gens. Edwin K. Wright and Garrison H. Davidson (ranks in Nov 1950), in interviews with the author (7 and 28 Jan 1954, respectively), asserted that they heard General MacArthur's comments and that they were as reported here. See *New York Her-*

ald Tribune, 25 Nov 50, p. 3, col. 1; *New York Times*, 29 Nov 50, p. 4, col. 4, for MacArthur's claim that he was misquoted.

26. MacArthur, *Reminiscences*, p. 373. Courtney Whitney, one of MacArthur's party from Tokyo on this trip, has also written about this flight over the Yalu on 24 Nov 50. He confirmed that the party could see no sign of activity on the snow-covered roads. See Maj. Gen. Courtney Whitney, *MacArthur: His Rendezvous with History* (New York: Alfred A. Knopf, 1956), pp. 416–17.

27. "From CINCUNC Tokyo, Japan, sgd MacArthur to DEPTAR for JCS, NR Radio C 69808, CM in 14393, 25 Nov 1950," in *Pertinent Papers on the Korean Situation*, II, 347–49; Schnabel, *Policy and Direction*, pp. 270–71, paraphrases much of this long message. MacArthur contended in his message to the JCS (1) that the UN and US had repeatedly stated a policy that saw "destroying all en forces south of Korea's boundary as essential to the restoration of unity and peace to all of Korea" and (2) that such a statement implied a policy of carrying the war to the border. MacArthur's contention cannot be supported.

28. *Military Situation in the Far East: Hearings before the Committee on Armed Services and the Committee on Foreign Relations, United States Senate, Eighty-second Congress, First Session*, to Conduct an Inquiry into the Military Situation in the Far East and the Facts Surrounding the Relief of General of the Army Douglas MacArthur from His Assignments in That Area, 5 vols. (Washington, D.C.: GPO, 1951), III, 1834, citing MacArthur's communiqué (hereafter cited as MacArthur Hearings); Appleman, *South to the Naktong, North to the Yalu*, pp. 764–65.

Chapter 5

1. Eighth Army WD, Nov 1950, Summ., Sec. 1, 25 Nov; I Corps WD, 25 Nov, Box 1496; 21st Inf. WD, G-3 Jnl., 25 Nov 50, Box 3538; 24th Div. WD, 25 Nov 50, Box 3512.

2. 24th Div. WD, Nov 1950, QM WD Summ., Box 3512.

3. 5th RCT WD, 25 Nov 50, Box 4691; 24th Inf. Div. WD, 25 Nov 50.

4. Lui Ping Chang's name is spelled variously in the FEC Intelligence records, but the name Chang or Lui Ping Chang is given in most of them. They agree that he was S-3, or operations officer, of the 590th Regt. and was a captain. See ATIS Interrogation Reports (Enemy Forces), Issue 20, No. 2577, 7 Dec 50, p. 176; Issue 23, No. 2758, 27 Dec 50, p. 49; Issue 24, No. 2842, 12 Jan 51, p. 130, and No. 2843, 12 Jan 51, p. 136; 24th Inf. Div. WD, Bk. 1, 25 Nov 50.

5. 24th Div. WD, Nov 1950, Box 3512; 25th Div. WD, Nov 1950; Col. Henry K. Fisher, interview with author, 5 Jan 52.

6. 25th Inf. Div. WD, Bk. 9, Annex 10, 25th Recon. Co. Unit Rpt., 25 Nov 50, Box 3765.

7. TF Dolvin Opn. Overlay Map No. 6, 23 Nov 50, 1:50,000-scale map of Korea; 25th Inf. Div. WD, 25th Recon. Co., Unit Rpt., Annex 10; FEC DIS No. 3000, 26 Nov 50, Box 99; 89th Med. Tank Bn., Unit Rpt., Nov 1950, in 25th Inf. Div. WD, Nov 1950, Box 3769. Dolvin's overlay map gave objectives of the task force. Hill 205, seized by the Ranger Company, was Objective 8.

8. Barth, "Tropic Lightning and Taro Leaf," p. 41; Col. John T. Corley (CO 24th Inf. Regt., Nov 1950), interviews with author, 6–7 Nov 1951; S. L. A. Marshall, *The River and the Gauntlet: Defeat of the Eighth Army by the Chinese Communist Forces, November 1950, in the Battle of the Chongchon River* (New York: William Morrow & Co., 1953), pp. 215–17. This book is based largely on interviews Marshall conducted in Dec 1950 and Jan 1951 with surviving members of the 25th and 2nd infantry divisions, which

were engaged in the battles along the Chongchon River in late Nov and early Dec 1950. The book is spotty and uneven in coverage but often makes available details of action not found in any other source. It has to be used judiciously and in conjunction with other sources and the official records.

9. Col. John T. Corley, interviews with author, 6–7 Nov 51; 3rd Bn., 24th Inf. Regt. WD, 25 Nov 50, in regimental command report, Nov 1950; 2nd Bn., 24th Inf. Comd. Rpt., in 25th Div. WD, 25 Nov 50, Box 3764.

10. Eighth Army WD, Summ., Sec. 1, 25 Nov 50, Box 1122.

11. Eighth Army GO No. 221, 19 Apr 51, Distinguished Service Cross to 1st Lt. Wynn, and GO No. 235, 25 Apr 51, Distinguished Service Cross to Capt. Wallace, 2nd Inf. Div. WD, Nov 1950, Narr. Summ., p. 30; Marshall, *River and Gauntlet,* pp. 19–34. Marshall interviewed surviving members of B Co. and gives many details of this fight.

12. Marshall, *River and Gauntlet,* p. 42; Col. Walker R. Goodrich, S-3, 2nd Div. Arty., letter to author and "Recollections," 25 Mar 80. Marshall's locations of the artillery are accurate, except for the distance of the four battalions in battery firing positions south of Kujang-dong.

13. 23rd Inf. Comd. Rpt., in 2nd Div. WD, 25 Nov 50, Box 2472; 2nd Div. WD, Ord. Rpt., Box 2435; Maj. Sam Radow and 1st Lt. William J. Majors, 1st Bn., 23rd Inf., 1952, interviews with Capt. Russell A. Gugeler, as given in Gugeler typescript MS, "Rearguard Action at Kunu-ri, A Company, 23rd Infantry, 2nd Division" (hereafter cited as Gugeler, MS), loaned to me in 1977 for use in this work. Marshall, *River and Gauntlet,* pp. 42–44, adds useful information.

14. Maj. Gen. George B. Peploe, USA (Ret.), review comments on "Disaster in Korea" MS (hereafter cited as Peploe, MS), with letter to author, 10 Dec 79.

15. IX Corps WD, Vol. 3, G-2 Spot Rpts., 25 Nov 50, Box 1769; ibid., IX Corps G-3 Activ. Rpt., 24 Nov 50; ibid., G-2, PIR No. 60, 25 Nov 50 (2nd Div. PIRs, 26–28 Nov 50, are missing from the official file).

16. Peploe, MS.

17. 38th Inf. Comd. Rpt., 2nd Div. WD, 25 Nov 50, Box 2473; Marshall, *River and Gauntlet,* pp. 97–104. Marshall tells the story of the patrol based on interviews with its surviving members. It is difficult to be sure of many events in the story of the 38th Inf.'s action in the Chongchon River battles, and later on, to the middle of Feb 1951. The regimental and the 2nd and 3rd Bn. S-2 and S-3 journals were lost in the withdrawal from Kunu-ri on 30 Nov 50, and the 1st Bn. records were lost at Hoengsong on 12 Feb 51. Maj. J. C. Bruck, inf. adj., in a memo dated 28 Mar 51, at the head of the Nov 1950 Comd. Rpt., states that, because of the losses of records, the Nov report was compiled from interviews with surviving members who had served in the periods covered.

18. Map of Korea, 1951, 1:50,000 scale; Marshall, *River and Gauntlet,* pp. 115–16.

19. Eighth Army WD, Summ., Sec. 1, 25 Nov 50, Box 1122; Map of Korea, Kujang-dong Sheet, 1951, 1:50,000 scale. Only this large-scale map can provide detail needed to understand this terrain.

20. FEC DIS No. 3000, 26 Nov 50, 1-h.

21. Eighth Army HQ GO No. 355, 26 May 51, awarding the Distinguished Service Cross, Posthumously, to Cpl. Joe R. Baldonado, B Co., 187th Airborne Inf. Regt.

Chapter 7

1. IX Corps HQ, Intelligence Bulletin No. 1, 18 Dec 50; Cameron, "Lost Corps," pp. 11–13.

2. IX Corps, PIR No. 53, Annex, Summ. POW Interrogations (also extract in I

Corps WD, PIR No. 71), 25 Nov 50, Box 1500; Eighth Army WD, Sec. 2, 25–27 Nov 50 and PIR No. 136, 25 Nov 50, Box 1131; FEC DIS No. 3000, 26 Nov 50, Box 99.

3. Cameron, "Lost Corps," pp. 14–15; Lt. Col. Thomas E. Bennett (major in Nov 1950), KMAG advisor to ROK 7th Regt., 6th Div., interview with author, 11 Dec 53; Lt. Col. Willard G. Pearson, KMAG advisor to ROK 6th Div., interview with author, 1 Aug 51; Cameron, "Lost Corps," sketch map, fig. 3, p. 15, shows situation on the ROK II Corps front as of noon 26 Nov 50.

4. Eighth Army WD, Sec. 2, G-3 Sec., 26 Nov 50, Box 1131; IX Corps WD, PIR No. 61, 26 Nov 50, Box 1769.

5. IX Corps WD, G-2 Spot Rpts., Vol. 3, 26 Nov 50, Box 1769.

6. Eighth Army WD, Sec. 2, G-3 Jnl. file, msgs. at 1515, 1820, 1830, 26 Nov 50; Lt. Col. Willard G. Pearson, interview with author, 1 Aug 51; IX Corps WD, Vol. 3, G-2 Spot Rpts., 26 Nov 50, report from 2nd Inf. Div. at 261900, Box 1769. (Note that here and subsequently, reference to a specific time may also include the day of the month. Thus "261900" refers to a report given on the 26th, at 7:00 P.M.)

7. Cameron, "Lost Corps," pp. 14–16.

8. IX Corps WD, Vol. 3, G-2 Spot Rpts., 26 Nov 50, Box 1769.

9. IX Corps WD, Bk. 1, 26 Nov 50; 1st Cav. Div. WD, 26 Nov 50; Eighth Army WD, Narr., Dec 1950.

10. Cameron, "Lost Corps," pp. 16–17.

11. IX Corps WD, G-2 Spot Rpts., 3 Dec 50, Box 1775; Eighth Army WD, Sec. 2, G-3 Jnl. File, 27 Nov 50, Box 1131; Cameron, "Lost Corps," pp. 17–18. Lt. Col. Robert E. Cameron had combat experience in World War II before serving as a ROK advisor in the Korean War. He had served with the 37th Inf. Div. in the Aleutian Islands and with the 71st Inf. Div. in Europe. In Korea he was the senior KMAG advisor to the ROK 10th Regt. and subsequently was advisor to the ROK 8th Div. His article in the *Military Review* is, to my knowledge, the most informative source on the CCF attack that routed the ROK II Corps on 25–27 Nov 50. Cameron was on the scene with the ROK 10th Regt., ROK 8th Div.

12. IX Corps WD, Vol. 4, G-3 Spot Rpts., 27 Nov (Amido, KMAG advisor with ROK II Corps, msg. to G-3, IX Corps 271930); Eighth Army WD, Summ., Sec. 1, 27 Nov 50.

13. 1st Cav. Div. WD, G-3 Jnl., 27 Nov 50, and PIR No. 127, 27 Nov 50, Box 4416; Eighth Army WD, Summ., Sec. 1, 27 Nov 50, Box 1122.

14. Maj. Gen. Doyle Hickey, GHQ, FEC, and Col. Landrum, Eighth Army, telephone conversation, 1225, 27 Nov 50. By "little friends," Landrum was referring to the ROK II Corps.

15. Eighth Army WD, Sec. 2, PIR No. 13, and G-3 POR 417, 28 Nov 50, Box 1131; IX Corps WD, PIR No. 63, and Vol. 3, G-2 Spot Rpts., 28 Nov 50, Box 1769; FEC DIS No. 3003, 29 Nov 50, Box 99.

16. Eighth Army WD, Summ., Sec. 1, 28 Nov 50, Box 1122.

17. FEC DIS No. 3003, 29 Nov 50, Box 99; see also FEC DIS No. 3002, 28 Nov 50, for a misleading and erroneous analysis of "2) Counter-Offensive Operations in Present Areas: a) Flank Operations Along Boundary 8 Army/X Corps."

18. Appleman, *South to the Naktong, North to the Yalu*, p. 68; 25th Div. Comd. Rpt., Jan 1951, p. 54; 25th Div. WD, Summ., Nov 1950.

19. Turkish Brigade private who participated in its first action in Korea, interview with author, Washington, D.C., 1976 (private's name is missing from author's notes, but the man was employed in a Turkish rug company). He said that he was wounded at Wawon and killed a Chinese soldier there with his sword when the Chinese, thinking he was dead, started to search him for valuables.

20. Harry Gordon, "The Turks Were There," in Bartlett, *With the Australians in Korea*,

pp. 210–14; Lt. Francis G. Nordstrom (D Co., 89th Tank Bn.), interview with author, 31 Aug 51. Nordstrom was liaison officer from the 25th Inf. Div. with the Turkish Brigade.

21. Eighth Army WD, Sec. 2, G-3 Jnl. file, 26 Nov 50, and G-3 Jnl. file, 27 Nov 50, Narr. Summ., 26–28 Nov 50, p. 32; IX Corps WD, Bk. 1, Nov 1950, 26 Nov 50, and Sec. 4, Operations, 26–27 Nov 50.

22. Brig. Gen. George B. Peploe, CO, 38th Inf. Regt., at time of incident, interview with author, 12 Aug 51; IX Corps WD, Vol. 3, G-2 Spot Rpts., 28 Nov 50, Box 1769; Marshall, *River and Gauntlet*, pp. 170–72; Map of Korea, 1:50,000 scale, area of Kunu-ri and Tokchon.

23. Eighth Army WD, Sec. 2, G-3 Jnl. file, entry at 1500, 27 Nov 50, Box 1131; IX Corps WD, Vol. 4, G-3 Spot Rpts., entry at 1310, 27 Nov 50, Box 1770; Marshall, *River and Gauntlet*, p. 171.

24. Peploe, interview with author, 12 Aug. 51. In Nov 1950 Peploe commanded the 38th Inf. Regt. on the left (northwest) flank of the Turks. The Eighth Army and IX Corps records for 28 Nov seem to be recording delayed messages, since they report actions and events relating to the Turks as taking place on the morning of 28 Nov, when they almost certainly took place on 27 Nov (Eighth Army WD, Sec. 2, G-3 Jnl. file, 28 Nov, and G-2 PIR No. 139, 28 Nov 50; IX Corps WD, 28 Nov 50).

25. IX Corps WD, Vol. 4, G-3 Spot Rpts., 28 Nov 50, Box 1770; IX Corps WD, Vol. 3, 28 Nov 50, and POR 191, 28 Nov 50, Box 1769; FEC DIS No. 3004, 30 Nov 50, Box 99 (covers period from 29 Nov up to 2 A.M., 30 Nov, but actually reports situation as relayed to it from Eighth Army as of about 9 A.M., 29 Nov). The Kaechon referred to in this narrative is shown as Pongmyong-ni on most maps, and they also show Kaechon as being where Kunu-ri was located on the early 1950 maps. Unless this is understood, there is endless confusion and misunderstanding of the Kunu-ri action.

26. Peploe, interview with author at IX Corps HQ in Korea, 12 Aug 51; Col. John C. Coughlin, interview with author at Army War College, Carlisle Barracks, Pa., 13 Dec 51; IX Corps WD, Vol. 4, G-3 Spot Rpts., 291510 Nov 50, Box 1770.

27. Eighth Army Comd. Rpt., G-3 Jnl., 29 Nov 50, Box 1132; ibid., WD, Sec. 2, G-3 Jnl. file, Box 1132; ibid., G-3 POR Mp 420, 29 Nov 50.

28. 2nd Inf. Div. WD, G-3 Jnl. entries, 29 Nov 50, Box 2435.

29. Maj. William J. Fox, "History of the Korean War" (Mimeographed report, copy in US Army Military History Center, Washington, D.C.), Vol. 3, Pt. 2, Sec. B, pp. 62–63.

30. Ridgway Papers, Box 17, S-3, Public Information Officer (PIO) News Account, Eighth Army, 13 Dec 50, US Military History Research Center (USMHRC), Carlisle Barracks, Pa.

31. 1st Cav. Div. WD, G-3 Jnl. msgs. 271745, 271945, 27 Nov 50; ibid., PIR No. 127, 27 Nov 50; IX Corps WD, Narr., Nov 1950, Box 1767.

32. 1st Cav. Div. WD, 30 Nov 50, pp. 28–29, Box 4416; IX Corps WD, Bk. 1, Sec. 4, Operations, Annex 2, Vol. 7, Box 1769.

33. IX Corps WD, POR No. 191, 28 Nov 50, Box 1769. The 1st Cav. Div. WD and the 5th Cav. WD have different stories of what happened to the 2nd Bn. at the end of the Samso-ri fight. The former says the 1st Bn., 5th Cav., relieved the 2nd Bn. at 1 P.M., 29 Nov. The WD for 5th Cav., 28 Nov, says it gave up the fight, bypassed the roadblock, and made its way to Sunchon, as stated in the narrative. I have followed 5th Cav.'s account, since it would know firsthand what it did.

34. Gen. Harold K. Johnson (Army chief of staff), interview with author, 24 Apr 54. (Johnson was colonel and CO, 5th Cav. Regt., in Nov 1950.)

35. 1st Cav. Div. WD, 30 Nov 50, Box 4417. The 7th Cav. Regt., defending on the road to Sinchang-ni, captured on 30 Nov eight Chinese prisoners, who identified their unit as the 374th Regt., 125th Div., 42nd Army.

36. 1st Cav. Div. WD, 29 Nov 50, Box 4416.

37. Ibid., and 7th Cav. Regt. Hist. Rpt., and PIR No. 130, 29 Nov 50, Box 4416; IX Corps WD, Vol. 4, G-3 Spot Rpts., Box 1770. From reports on hand on 29 Nov, IX Corps estimated that the ROK II Corps had 1,200 men of the ROK 7th Regt., 1,500 men of the ROK 19th Regt., and 1,000 stragglers of the ROK 2nd Regt. left in its control.

38. Maj. Bennett, memo to CG, 1st Cav. Div., 16 Jan 51, no subject, attached to letter from Senior Adv., KMAG 6th ROK Div. to CG, 1st Cav. Div., 16 Jan 51, no subject, in 1st Cav. Div. WD, Nov 1950. (Lt. Col. Willard G. Pearson was the senior KMAG advisor to the ROK 6th Div.)

39. Col. William A. Harris, letter to CG, 1st Cav. Div., 6 Feb 51, Kujang-ni Incident, Enclosure 3, in 1st Cav. Div. WD, Nov 1950. Concerning this incident, Lt. Col. Willard G. Pearson (then exec. off., 21st Inf. Regt., 24th Inf. Div.), in an interview with the author, 1 Aug. 51, maintained that the 7th Cav. was responsible for many ROKs being killed and wounded, because the ROK 6th Div. was kept outside its lines on the morning of 29 Nov 50. He also alleged that the 1st Cav. Div., under General Gay, antagonized Korean civilians, ROKs, and adjacent units, shot too many civilian refugees, and ran them off the road. I know of incidents where the 1st Cav. Div. did stop refugee movement by fire to prevent enemy infiltration into its lines, but only after ample warning to the refugees and after their refusal to heed the warnings.

40. 1st Cav. Div. Comd. Rpt., 29-30 Nov 50, G-3 Jnl. file, msgs. at 290900, No. 18, and at 291530, No. 52, and Enclosure 3, rpt. of ROK 6th Div. withdrawal through 7th Cav. position at Kujang-ni, Box 4416; Eighth Army WD, G-3 Jnl. file, 29 Nov 50, Box 1132.

41. 1st Cav. Div. WD, 29-30 Nov 50; and ibid., G-3 Jnl. file, 29-30 Nov 50, Msg. No. 77, 292340, Box 4416.

42. HQ, Eighth Army GO No. 220, 19 Apr 51, awarding the Distinguished Service Cross, Posthumously, to M. Sgt. Richard R. Beard, C Co., 70th Tank Bn. (Heavy) for action during the night of 29 Nov 50 near Sinchang-ni; ATIS Interrogation Rpts. (Enemy Forces), Issue 22, No. 2706, p. 17, 14 Dec 50, reporting testimony of Capt. Gordon Sumner, Jr., 77th FA Bn., on action approximately two miles east of Sinchang-ni, 30 Nov 50. See also 1st Cav. Div. WD, 30 Nov 50, Box 4416.

43. 1st Cav. Div. WD, 30 Nov 50, and G-3 Jnl. file, 29-30 Nov 50, Msg. No. 77 at 292340 and Msg. No. 26 at 301945, Box 4416.

44. Eighth Army, Combat Information Bulletin No. 13, 13 Mar 51, 7 pp., reproducing extracts from a captured document issued by "The 38th Chinese Peoples Volunteer Army," entitled, "Experiences Gained in Three Battles Since Entering Korea."

Chapter 8

1. The document "Primary Conclusions of Battle Experience at UNSAN" was printed by the Chinese People's Volunteer Army Headquarters, 66th Army, 20 Nov 50, and captured by the ROK 1st Div. on 26 Nov 50. The Eighth Army translated, reproduced, and widely distributed this document among its officers and men. I have used the document as reproduced in the X Corps, G-3 Sec. "Combat Notes," 30 Dec 50.

2. 25th Div. Operation Order No. 6 and Overlay, 23 Nov 50; Topographic map of Korea, Unsan Sheet, scale 1:50,000. Ipsok is shown in some later 1:250,000-scale maps as Sondol. See Barth, "Tropic Lightning and Taro Leaf," p. 41. Yongbyon is known as the Walled City to many American soldiers who passed through it. It had extensive medieval fortified walls on all sides, enclosing a steep-sided oval and relatively flat area.

3. IX Corps WD, 26 Nov 50, POR No. 184, 26 Nov 50, Box 1769; 89th Med.

Tank Bn. WD, S-3 Jnl. file, 26 Nov 50, Msg. 0255, Box 3765; Eighth Army WD, Sec. 2, G-3 Jnl. file, 26 Nov 50, Box 1131; Col. Robert K. Sawyer, USA, Ret., letter to author, 14 June 74 (Sawyer was plat. leader, 3rd Plat., 25th Recon. Co., as a part of TF Dolvin, Nov 1950, and was well acquainted with the Ranger Co. and its officers); Marshall, *River and Gauntlet,* pp. 195–96; Barth, "Tropic Lightning and Taro Leaf," p. 41.

4. 25th Inf. Div. WD, 89th Tank Bn., G-3 Jnl. file, msg. at 2215, 25 Nov 50, Box 3765; Marshall, *River and Gauntlet,* pp. 188–92. Marshall interviewed surviving members of E Co., 27th Inf., in late Dec 1950 or early Jan 1951.

5. 25th Inf. Div. WD, 25–26 Nov 50, including Unit Hist., HQ 89th Tank Bn., p. 4, and S-3 Jnl. file; Marshall, *River and Gauntlet,* pp. 190–91, 194–96. Careful study of the 1:50,000-scale map of the Unsan Sheet is necessary to fix the 1st Plat.'s route as described in the narrative.

6. 25th Inf. Div. WD, including Narr., 89th Med. Tank Bn., 25–26 Nov 50, Box 3769.

7. Sawyer, letter to author, 14 June 74. Sawyer was wounded north of Ipsok on 27 Nov 50 while trying to help rescue wounded from a knocked-out tank, and he was rescued by his own men.

8. IX Corps WD, POR No. 184, 25 Nov 50, Box 1769; 25th Div. WD, 2nd Bn., 27th Inf. Unit Rpt., 25 Nov 50, Box 3764; Marshall, *River and Gauntlet,* pp. 215–16. The 2nd Bn., 27th Inf., Unit Rpt. cited above gives the 2nd Bn. as being within 500 yards of TF Dolvin's CP and 1,500 yards south of the front line. A measurement on the 1:50,000-scale map of the Unsan Sheet indicates that the distances were greater and approximated the distances I have given in the narrative.

9. Thompson, *Cry Korea,* p. 243.

10. Eighth Army WD, Summ., Sec. 1, 26 Nov 50.

11. 89th Med. Tank Bn., Bk. 9, Unit Rpt., 26 Nov 50, Box 3765. It should be remembered that the 89th Tank Bn. kept the official records of TF Dolvin; its commander was also the TF commander, and his Tank Bn. staff was also the staff of TF Dolvin.

12. 25th Inf. Div. WD, 89th Tank Bn., Unit Rpt., 26 Nov 50; ibid., Bk. 9, Annex 10, 25th Recon. Co. Unit Rpt., 26 Nov 50. Lt. Sawyer, 3rd Plat. leader, 25th Recon. Co., has said that a large lagoon bulge in the Kuryong River, shown on the 1:50,000-scale map at the point where his 3rd Plat. took position on 26 Nov did not in fact exist.

13. 25th Inf. Div. Hist., Bk. 2, Nov 1950, Narr., TF Dolvin, p. 5; ibid., Unit Hist., HQ 89th Med. Tank Bn., p. 4, Nov 1950.

14. 25th Inf. Div. WD, Bk. 9, Nov 1950, including Unit Hist., 89th Med. Tank Bn., 26 Nov 50, Box 3765.

15. Sawyer, letter to author, 14 June 74.

16. 25th Inf. Div. WD, 26–27 Nov 50; 89th Med. Tank Bn., Unit Rpt., Nov 1950, and S-3 Jnl. file, 26–27 Nov 50, Box 3769; FEC GO No. 58, 2 Aug 51, awarding the Medal of Honor, Posthumously, to Capt. Reginald B. Desiderio, E Co., 27th Inf., for action 27 Nov 50; see Marshall, *River and Gauntlet,* pp. 200–209, for details of this action.

17. 25th Inf. Div. WD, Bk. 9, 27 Nov 50; Sawyer, letter to author, 14 June 74, and Sawyer, interview with author, 23 June 74.

18. 25th Inf. Div. WD, including Unit Rpt., 89th Med. Tank Bn., 27 Nov 50, Box 3769; ibid., Bk. 2, Unit Hist., HQ 89th Med. Tank Bn.; Marshall, *River and Gauntlet,* p. 210.

19. *New York Times,* 29 Nov 50, p. 3, col. 1.

20. The account of Murch's 2nd Bn. action, the night of 26–27 Nov 50, is based on 2nd Bn., 27th Inf., Unit Hist., 26–27 Nov 50, 25th Inf. Div. WD, Nov 1950, Box 3764; and Marshall, *River and Gauntlet,* pp. 216–19.

21. Barth, "Tropic Lightning and Taro Leaf," p. 42; 25th Inf. Div. WD, Bk. 10, Unit Rpt., 8th FA Bn., 26–27 Nov 50, Box 3769; 64th FA Bn., Summ. Rpt., Nov 1950,

25th Inf. Div. WD, Bk. 9, and 90th FA Bn. WD, 27 Nov 50, Unit Rpts., Box 3769; 25th Inf. Div. WD, 89th Tank Bn., Unit Rpt., 26-27 Nov 50, Box 3765; Marshall, *River and Gauntlet,* pp. 250-60; Map of Korea, Unsan Sheet, 1:50,000 scale, shows the topography around Ipsok and the terrain of the 8th FA Bn. positions.

22. Sawyer, interview with author, 23 June 74; Sawyer, letter to author, 14 June 74.

23. Sawyer, letter to author, 14 June 74; 25th Inf. Div. WD, Nov 1950, Bk. 9, Annex 10, Unit Rpt., 25th Recon. Co., 27 Nov 50, Box 3765.

24. 25th Inf. Div. WD, Bk. 9, 89th Med. Tank Bn., Unit Rpt., 27 Nov 50, Box 3765; Marshall, *River and Gauntlet,* pp. 231-33.

25. IX Corps WD, PIR No. 62 and POR No. 190, 27 Nov 50, Box 1769; 25th Inf. Div. WD, Bk. 2, HQ 89th Med. Tank Bn., p. 5, Box 3769, and 89th Tank Bn., S-3 Jnl. file, 27 Nov 50, Box 3765; 25th Inf. Div. WD, 2nd Bn., 27th Inf., Unit Rpt., 27 Nov 50, Box 3764; Marshall, *River and Gauntlet,* p. 234.

26. Robert F. Futrell, *The United States Air Force in Korea, 1950-1953* (New York: Duell, Sloan, and Pearce, 1961), p. 237; 25th Inf. Div. WD, Nov 1950, Unit Rpt., 2nd Bn., 27th Inf., 27-28 Nov 50, Box 3764; 25th Inf. Div. WD, Nov 1950, Unit Hist., HQ 89th Med. Tank Bn., p. 5; Marshall, *River and Gauntlet,* pp. 243-45.

27. 25th Inf. Div. WD, Nov 1950, Bk. 9, Annex 10, Unit Rpt., 25th Recon. Co., Box 3769.

28. The account of the 25th Div. withdrawal on 28 Nov is based on the following sources: IX Corps WD, Bk. 1, 28 Nov 50, and Annex 2, Vol. 6, G-3 Msg. No. 1938; 25th Div. WD, Bk. 1, 28 Nov 50, and 25th Div. WD, PIR No. 133, 28 Nov 50, and POR No. 73, 29 Nov 50, and PLR No. 135, 29 Nov 50, Box 3763; IX Corps WD, Vol. 4, G-3 Sec. Spot Rpts., 28 Nov 50, Box 1770; I Corps WD, Summ., 28 Nov 50, Box 1496; 25th Inf. Div. WD, Nov 1950, Bk. 2, including 89th Med. Tank Bn. Unit Rpt., 28 Nov 50, and Bk. 9, Unit Rpts., Box 3769. Overlay showing positions and movements of the 25th Div., 28-29 Nov 50, is in author's possession.

29. Overlay of 25th Div. regiments and its own CP positions, 28-29 Nov 50, in author's possession; IX Corps WD, Vol. 4, G-3 Spot Rpts., 29 Nov 50, Box 1770; 25th Inf. Div. WD, 2nd Bn., 27th Inf. Unit Rpt., 29 Nov, and 3rd Bn., 27th Inf. Unit Rpts., 29 Nov 50, Box 3764; 25th Inf. Div. WD, Nov 1950, 25th Recon. Co. Unit Rpt., 29 Nov 50, Box 3769; 25th Inf. Div. WD, Nov 1950, Bk. 9, Box 3769.

30. 25th Inf. Div. WD, Summ., 26 Nov 50; Col. Henry K. Fisher, interview with author, 5 Jan 52; Lt. Hoyt, 2nd Bn., 35th Inf., interview with author, 4 Sept 51; Eighth Army WD, Sec. 2, G-3 Jnl. file, 26 Nov 50; 3rd Bn. S-3 Jnl. entry, 35th Inf. Unit Rpt., in 25th Inf. Div. WD, 26 Nov 50, and 35th Inf. Narr., 26 Nov 50, in 25th Inf. Div. WD, 26 Nov 50. The 3rd Bn. and the 35th Inf. Unit Rpts. tell about the CCF penetration of L Co. and the capture of five American prisoners.

31. Barth, "Tropic Lightning and Taro Leaf," p. 42; 3rd Bn., 35th Inf. Narr., and S-3 Jnl. file, 25th Div. WD, 26-27 Nov 50, Box 3764; 35th Inf. Narr., 25th Inf. Div. WD, 27 Nov 50, Box 3764; IX Corps WD, Vol. 4, 27 Nov 50, Box 1770; ibid., Vol. 3, G-2 Spot Rpts., 27 Nov 50, Box 1769, and IX Corps, PIR No. 62, 27 Nov 50, Box 1769; Eighth Army WD, Sec. 2, G-2 PIR No. 138, 27 Nov 50, Box 1131.

32. 25th Inf. Div. WD, 35th Inf. Narr., 27 Nov 50, Box 3764; 1st, 2nd and 3rd Bns., 35th Inf. Narrs., 27 Nov 50, all in 25th Inf. Div. WD, Box 3764; IX Corps WD, POR, 27 Nov 50, Box 1769; Eighth Army WD, Sec. 2, G-3 Jnl. file, 27 Nov 50, Box 1131; Marshall, *River and Gauntlet,* pp. 210-11.

33. 2nd Bn., 35th Inf. WD, 25th Inf. Div. WD, 27-28 Nov 50 (the records in the National Archives for this battalion are missing those for 27-28 Nov 50; the narrative presented here reflects only a general account prepared later from recollections); 1st Bn., 35th Inf. Narr., 27-28 Nov, 25th Inf. Div. WD, Nov 1950; 3rd Bn., S-3 Jnl. file, 28 Nov 50, 35th Inf., in 25th Inf. Div. WD, Nov 1950. (All foregoing bn. records are in

Box 3764.) 89th Med. Tank Bn. Unit Rpt., in 25th Inf. Div. WD, 28 Nov 50, Box 3769; 35th Inf. Narr. in 25th Inf. Div. WD, 27–28 Nov 50; IX Corps POR No. 190, 27 Nov 50; IX Corps WD, Vol. 3, 28 Nov 50, Box 1769; Barth, "Tropic Lightning and Taro Leaf," p. 43.

34. Records of the 1st, 2nd, and 3rd Bns., 35th Inf., for 28 Nov 50, and 35th Inf., as cited above; Barth, "Tropic Lightning and Taro Leaf," p. 43.

35. IX Corps WD, Nov 1950, PIR No. 62, 27 Nov 50, Box 1769; I Corps WD, Nov 1950, PIR No. 74, 28 Nov 50, Box 1501.

36. See Appleman, *South to the Naktong, North to the Yalu*, for the combat record of the 24th Inf. in the earlier phases of the Korean War. Black infantry units were integrated into white infantry units in the fall of 1951, and segregated infantry units then ceased to exist in the US Army.

37. 2nd Bn., 24th Inf. Unit Rpt., in 25th Inf. Div. WD, 25 Nov 50, Box 3764; 24th Inf. Comd. Rpt. 25 Nov 50; 3rd Bn., 24th Inf. Unit Rpt., 25 Nov 50, in 25th Inf. Div. WD, Nov 1950, Box 3764; 25th Inf. Div. WD, Bk. 9, Nov 1950, Box 3769.

38. 2nd Bn., 24th Inf., Unit Rpt., in 25th Inf. Div. WD, 26 Nov 50, and 24th Inf. Unit Rpt., 25th Div. WD, 27 Nov 50, Box 3764; 25th Inf. Div. WD, Summ., 26 Nov 50; IX Corps WD, PIR No. 61, 26 Nov 50, and POR No. 185, 26 Nov 50, Box 1769; IX Corps WD, Vol. 4, G-3 Spot Rpts., 26 Nov 50, Box 1770; Eighth Army WD, Sec. 2, G-3 Jnl. file, 26 Nov 50, Box 1131; Barth, "Tropic Lightning and Taro Leaf," p. 41.

39. 1st Bn., 24th Inf. Unit Rpt., in 25th Inf. Div. WD, 26–27 Nov 50, and 24th Inf. Comd. Rpt., in 25th Div. WD, 26 Nov 50, both in Box 3764; Corley, interviews with author, 6–7 Nov 51; Marshall, *River and Gauntlet*, p. 213.

40. 3rd Bn., 24th Inf. Unit Rpt., in 25th Inf. Div. WD, 26 Nov 50; IX Corps WD, 26 Nov 50; 3rd Bn., 27th Inf. Unit Rpt., in 25th Div. WD, 26–27 Nov 50, and 27th Inf. Narr., in 25th Inf. Div. WD, both in Box 3764.

41. 2nd Bn., 24th Inf. Unit Rpt., 27 Nov 50, in 25th Inf. Div. WD, Nov 1950; 24th Inf. Comd. Rpt., 25th Div. WD, 27 Nov 50, Box 3764. This 24th Inf. Comd. Rpt. has no further daily reports for the month of Nov 1950 in the official records at the National Archives.

42. 3rd Bn., 24th Inf. Unit Rpt., in 25th Div. WD, 27 Nov 50, Box 3764; 89th Med. Tank Bn. Unit Rpt., 27–28 Nov 50, in 25th Inf. Div. WD, Nov 1950; Corley, interviews with author, 6–7 Nov 51; Barth, "Tropic Lightning and Taro Leaf," p. 43.

43. HQ 89th Med. Tank Bn. Unit Hist., in 25th Inf. Div. WD, Bk. 2, 28 Nov 50; 1st Bn., 24th Inf. Unit Rpt., 28 Nov 50; 2nd Bn., 24th Inf. Unit Rpt., 28 Nov 50; 3rd Bn., Unit Rpt., 28 Nov 50; 24th Inf. Comd. Rpt., 28 Nov 50; 3rd Bn., 27th Inf. Unit Rpt., all in 25th Inf. Div. WD, Box 3764; IX Corps WD, Vol. 4, G-3 Spot Rpts., 28 Nov 50, Box 1770. Overlay of troop unit positions of 25th and 2nd Inf. Div. in Kunu-ri area, 1:250,000 scale, in author's possession.

44. Corley, interviews with author, 6–7 Nov 51.

Chapter 9

1. 19th Inf. Regt. Unit Rpt., in 24th Inf. Div. WD, 26 Nov 50, Box 3534; 24th Inf. Div. WD, 25–26 Nov 50, Box 3512; I Corps WD, 26 Nov 50, Box 1496; Eighth Army WD, Sec. 2, G-3 Sec., and PIR No. 137, 26 Nov 50, Box 1131.

2. 24th Inf. Div. WD, Bk. 1, 26 Nov 50.

3. 24th Inf. Div. WD, 27 Nov 50, Box 3512; 21st Inf. Regt. Unit Rpt., and S-3 Jnl. file, in 24th Inf. Div. WD, 27 Nov 50, Box 3538; I Corps WD, Summ., 27 Nov 50, Box 1496; Eighth Army WD, Sec. 2, G-3 Jnl. file, 27 Nov 50, Box 1131.

4. 5th RCT Unit Rpt., 27–28 Nov 50, Box 4691; 24th Inf. Div. WD, 28 Nov 50,

and 24th Inf. Div. PIR No. 139, 28 Nov 50, Box 3512; I Corps WD, Summ., and PIR No. 74, 28 Nov 50, Boxes 1496 and 1501.

5. 21st Inf. Regt. Unit Rpt. 143, 28 Nov 50, in 24th Inf. Div. WD, Nov 1950, Box 3538.

6. 24th Inf. Div. WD, Bk. 1, 28 Nov 50, Box 3512; I Corps WD, Nov 1950.

7. I Corps WD, 28 Nov 50, p. 38; 24th Inf. Div. WD, Bk. 1, 28 Nov 50.

8. 21st Inf. Regt., S-3 Jnl. file, 29 Nov 50, and 21st Inf. Unit Rpt., 29 Nov 50, in 24th Inf. Div. WD, 29 Nov 50, Box 3538; I Corps WD, 29 Nov 50, pp. 39–40.

9. 5th RCT Unit Rpt. Nos. 108 and 109, 29 Nov 50, Box 4691.

10. Capt. William F. Brown, Arty., "Chongchon Withdrawal," *Antiaircraft Journal* 94, no. 2 (Mar–Apr 1951): 18–20.

11. IX Corps WD, 25 Nov 50, Box 1496; IX Corps WD, Vol. 4, G-3 Spot Rpts., 25 Nov, Box 1770.

12. I Corps WD, Summ., 26 Nov 50, Box 1496; Eighth Army WD, Sec. 2, G-3 Jnl. file, 26 Nov 50, Box 1131; FEC DIS Nos. 3001 and 3002, 27–28 Nov 50, Box 99; Eighth Army WD, Summ., Sec. 1, Nov 1950.

13. Brown, "Chongchon Withdrawal," p. 19.

14. I Corps WD, Summ., 27 Nov 50, Box 1496; IX Corps WD, Vol. 4, G-3 Spot Rpts., 27 Nov 50, Box 1770; Eighth Army WD, Sec. 2, G-2 PIR No. 138, and Intelligence Summ. No. 3002 for Combined G-2/G-3 Situation Map, 28 Nov 50.

15. I Corps WD Summ., 28 Nov 50, Box 1496; IX Corps WD, Vol. 3, 28 Nov 50, and Vol. 4, G-3 Spot Rpts., 28 Nov 50, Boxes 1769 and 1770, respectively; 24th Inf. Div. WD, 28 Nov 50, Box 3512; FEC DIS No. 3003, 29 Nov 50, Box 99; Eighth Army WD, Summ., Sec. 1, 28 Nov 50, Box 1122; Brown, "Chongchon Withdrawal," pp. 19–20; Eighth Army WD, Intelligence Summ. Nos. 2002 and 2003, Situation Maps, 28–29 Nov 50, Box 99.

16. Brown, "Chongchon Withdrawal," p. 20; Eighth Army WD, G-3 Jnl. file, 29 Nov 50, Box 1132, and Eighth Army WD, Summ., Sec. 1, 29 Nov 50, Box 1122.

17. 25th Med. Bn. Unit Rpt., Nov 1950, Box 3769.

18. See Roy E. Appleman, *East of Chosin: Entrapment and Breakout in Korea, 1950* (College Station: Texas A&M University Press, 1987), pp. 301–302.

Chapter 10

1. Peploe, MS.

2. Eighth Army WD, Sec. 2, G-2 Interrogation of POWs Annex, interrogation of Capt. Chang Han-chung, captured 25 Nov 50, by 23rd Inf. at Chinaman's Hat, Box 1131; IX Corps WD, PIR No. 61, Annex 2, 26 Nov 50, POW Rpt., 359th Regt., Box 1769; ATIS Interrogation Rpts. (Enemy Forces), Issue 23, No. 2791, 3 Jan 51, p. 161, reporting interrogation of Cultural Officer We Yu Shu, Hvy. Weapons Co., 2nd Bn., 359th Regt., 120th Div., 40th Army, captured 26 Nov 50 at Chinaman's Hat.

3. Map of Korea, Kujang Sheet, 1950, scale 1:50,000; 2nd Inf. Div. WD, 1–30 Nov 50, Narr. Summ., p. 50, Box 2435; Marshall, *River and Gauntlet*, pp. 58–63.

4. ATIS Interrogation Rpts. (Enemy Forces), Issue 22, No. 2705, 13 Dec 50, p. 15.

5. Map of Korea, Kujang Sheet, 1950, scale 1:50,000; Marshall, *River and Gauntlet*, pp. 64–75; 2nd Inf. Div. WD, Summ., 25–26 Nov 50, Box 2345.

6. Eighth Army Gen. Ord. No. 139, 13 Mar 51, awarding the Silver Star to Cpl. Walter K. Crawford, Jr., B Co., 9th Inf.; 9th Inf. Comd. Rpt., Narr. Hist., 25–26 Nov 50, Box 2471; Marshall, *River and Gauntlet*, pp. 29–40. Marshall interviewed many B Co. survivors of the Hill 219 action. Records of the 9th Inf. and of its battalions and companies are almost nonexistent for the period 25–26 Nov 50. No doubt many offi-

cers and enlisted men of B Co. deserved awards for combat performance on 25–26 Nov 50 at Hill 219 who never received recognition. The same can be said about many combat episodes.

7. Marshall states in his account that the personnel of A Co., 23rd Inf., whom he interviewed gave the time as about dusk. Official American unit reports of the Chinese crossings vary from 10 P.M. to 11 P.M. I believe this period of time is about correct. Dusk would be far too early, since that puts the crossings at 5 P.M. or a little later.

8. 1st Cav. Div. WD, 26 Nov 50; 23rd Inf. Comd. Rpt., 25 Nov 50, Box 2472; Eighth Army WD, Sec. 2, G-3 Sec., 26 Nov 50, Box 1131; Marshall, *River and Gauntlet*, pp. 47–48; Radow, 1st Bn., 23rd Inf., and Majors, A Co., 23rd Inf., interviews with Gugeler, 25 Nov–1 Dec 52, in Gugeler, MS. See also Capt. Edward C. Williamson, "Action at Kunu-ri" (Mimeographed copy in files, Office Chief of Military History, DA), which tells the story of the 17th FA Bn. from 24 Nov through 1 Dec 50. This battalion's 8-inch howitzers were in firing position at Kujang-dong at the time of the Chinese attack.

9. Marshall (*River and Gauntlet*, p. 44) gives the time as about 6:30 P.M. The 23rd Inf. WD gives it as 10 P.M. The 1st Cav. Div. WD, which reported for the 61st FA Bn., gives the time of the attack on the 61st FA Bn. as 11 P.M. The 61st FA Bn. returned to its parent organization, the 1st Cav. Div., on 27 Nov. The Gugeler MS, based on interviews with 1st Lt. Majors and Maj. Radow, gives the time of the CCF crossing as being about 10 P.M. I accept that time as being approximately correct.

10. Gugeler, MS.

11. Details of the 1st and 3rd plats., A Co., action are based on Marshall, *River and Gauntlet*, pp. 46–49, and Gugeler, MS. See also IX Corps WD, Vol. 3, Nov 1950, Box 1769; 23rd Inf. Comd. Rpt., 25–26 Nov 50, Box 2472, which gives 10:30 P.M. as the time for the CCF crossing of the Chongchon. The 2nd Inf. Div. WD, 25 Nov, G-2 Rpt., Box 2435, gives the time of the enemy attack as 10 P.M.

12. Gugeler, MS; 23rd Inf. Comd. Rpt. 25–26 Nov 50, Box 2472; 2nd Div. WD, 25–26 Nov 50, Box 2435; Marshall, *River and Gauntlet*, pp. 50–54. Marshall says that there were 410 Chinese dead counted in front of the 23rd Inf. and 111 CCF prisoners taken during the night.

13. 38th Inf. Comd. Rpt., Summ., 25–26 Nov 50, Box 2473; Marshall, *River and Gauntlet*, p. 104; Peploe, MS.

14. 38th Inf. Comd. Rpt., Summ., 25–26 Nov 50, Box 2473; Map of Korea, Kujang Sheet, Nov 1950, scale 1:50,000; Eighth Army, Intelligence Summ. No. 3001 for Combined G-2/G-3 Situation Map, 270200 Nov 50, Box 99.

15. Capt. William E. Manning (S-3, 3rd Bn., 38th Inf.), interview with author, 20 Aug 51. Lowery related his experiences in this episode to Manning in Aug 1951.

16. 38th Inf. Comd. Rpt., Summ., 25–26 Nov 50, Box 2473.

17. Ibid., 25–26 Nov 50; Marshall, *River and Gauntlet*, pp. 148–49.

18. Manning, interview with author, 20 Aug 51; Marshall, *River and Gauntlet*, pp. 116–33.

19. 38th Inf. Comd. Rpt., in 2nd Div. WD, 26 Nov 50, Box 2473. This document in the S-2 and S-3 Jnls., Item 43, reports that Lt. Hollingsworth had 60 men with him when he arrived at the 2nd Bn. CP.

20. Peploe, MS.

21. Ibid.; Manning, interview with author, 20 Aug 51; 38th Inf. Comd. Rpt., in 2nd Div. WD, 26 Nov 50, Box 2473; IX Corps WD, Vol. 4, G-3 Spot Rpts., 26 Nov 50, Box 1770; Marshall, *River and Gauntlet*, pp. 134–51; Eighth Army WD, Sec. 2, G-3 Jnl. file, 26 Nov 50, Box 1131; FEC GO No. 223, 2 Sept 51, awarding Distinguished Service Cross to Capt. Nicholas N. Gombos (F Co., 38th Inf.) for command competence and personal bravery, 26–27 Nov 50.

22. HQ Eighth Army, GO No. 138, 13 Mar 51, awarding Distinguished Service Cross to Cpl. James L. Brown, then private first class, E Co., 9th Inf.
23. HQ Eighth Army, GO No. 631, 11 Aug. 51, awarding Distinguished Service Cross to 2nd Lt. Robert Gallardo, E Co., 9th Inf.
24. HQ Eighth Army, GO No. 139, 13 Mar 51, awarding Distinguished Service Cross to Pfc. Andrew J. Gasquet, Jr., G Co., 9th Inf., for action 26 Nov 50.
25. 2nd Inf. Div. WD, 1–30 Nov 50, Narr. Summ.; *New York Herald Tribune,* 28 Nov 50, p. 1, cols. 6 and 8; IX Corps WD, Vol. 4, G-3 Spot Rpts., 27 Nov 50, Box 1770; IX Corps WD, POR No. 186, Box 1769. This last source stated that the 2nd Bn., 9th Inf., occupied Hill 148 on the east side of the Chongchon after it crossed. See also Eighth Army WD, Sec. 2, G-3 Jnl., 27 Nov 50; 9th Inf. Regt. Comd. Rpt., Narr. Hist., 26–27 Nov 50, Box 2471; 23rd Inf. Comd. Rpt., 27 Nov 50, Box 2472; IX Corps WD, PORs No. 186 and 188, 26 and 27 Nov 50; HQ IX Corps, Intelligence Bulletin No. 1, 18 Dec 50, "CCF Activities on U.S. IX Corps Front," p. 3.
26. 1st Cav. Div. WD, 26 Nov 50; ATIS Interrogation Rpts. (Enemy Forces), Issue 23, No. 2791, 3 Jan 51, p. 161; IX Corps WD, Vol. 3, 26 Nov 50, Box 1769; Eighth Army PIR No. 137, 26 Nov 50 gives an incomplete count of CCF prisoners captured on 26 Nov 50, Box 1131.
27. HQ Eighth Army, GO No. 330, 23 May 51, awarding Distinguished Service Cross to Capt. Emerson, CO G Co., 23rd Inf.; 23rd Inf. Comd. Rpt., 26 Nov 50, Box 2472; IX Corps WD, POR No. 186, 26 Nov 50, Box 1769.
28. DA, GO No. 39, 4 June 51, awarding the Medal of Honor to Sgt. John A. Pittman (also in *Medal of Honor Awards, 1863–1963,* 88th Cong., 2nd sess. [Washington: D.C.: GPO, 1964]), p. 285.
29. 23rd Inf. Comd. Rpt., 27 Nov 50.
30. Peploe, MS.
31. 2nd Inf. Div. WD, G-2 Sec., 6 Dec 50, Box 2439. This information is contained in a G-2 document, as delayed, dated 26 Nov 50, and inserted in the G-2 material for 6 Dec 50.
32. 38th Inf. S-4 Jnl., 26–27 Nov 50, Box 2473; 2nd Inf. Div. Ord. Sec. Rpt., Box 2435.
33. 38th Inf. Comd. Rpt., Summ., 26 Nov 50, Box 2473; 2nd Div. WD, 1–30 Nov (26–27), Narr. Summ., pp. 31–32; IX Corps WD, Vol. 4, G-3 Spot Rpts., 26 Nov 50, Box 2473; IX Corps WD, PIR No. 62, 27 Nov 50, Box 1769; Marshall, *River and Gauntlet,* pp. 171–73.
34. HQ Eighth Army GO No. 329, 23 May 51, awarding the Distinguished Service Cross, Posthumously, to Cpl. Robert K. Imrie, F Co., 38th Inf.; Peploe, MS.
35. Peploe, MS; 38th Inf. Regt. Comd. Rpt., Summ., 27 Nov 50, Box 2473.
36. 2nd Inf. Div. WD, Summ., 27 Nov 50, Box 2435; IX Corps WD, PORs No. 189 and 190, 27 Nov 50, Box 1769; 38th Inf. Regt. Comd. Rpt., Summ., 27 Nov 50; Marshall, *River and Gauntlet,* pp. 177–80; Peploe, MS.

Chapter 11

1. 38th Inf. Comd. Rpt. Summ., 27 Nov 50; IX Corps WD, Vol. 4, G-3 Spot Rpts., 27 Nov 50; Eighth Army WD, Sec. 1 and Sec. 2, 27 Nov 50, Box 1131; Peploe (then chief of staff, IX Corps), interview with author, 12 Aug 51.
2. Lt. Col. Edgar Bell, letter to Maj. Gen. E. F. Bullene, chief chemical officer, US Army, 16 Dec 50, in Capt. John G. Westover, *Combat Support in Korea* (Washington, D.C.: Combat Forces Press, 1955), pp. 78–79; IX Corps WD, PIR No. 63, 28 Nov 50.
3. IX Corps WD, POR No. 191, 28 Nov 50; IX Corps WD, G-3 Spot Rpts., 28

Nov 50, Box 1770; and IX Corps WD, Narr., 28 Nov 50, Box 1767; Eighth Army WD, Sec. 2, POR No. 417, 28 Nov 50, Box 1131.

4. 9th Inf. Comd. Rpt., Narr. Hist., 28–29 Nov 50, Box 2471.
5. IX Corps WD, POR No. 191, 28 Nov 50, Box 1769.
6. 2nd Inf. Div. WD, 27–30 Nov 50, Narr. Summ.
7. Col. Walker R. Goodrich, G-3, 2nd Inf. Div. Arty. review comments on "Disaster in Korea" MS, 25 Mar 80 (hereafter cited as Goodrich, Comments), and Goodrich, "Recollections 2nd Div. Arty., 26 Nov–1 Dec 1950," with letter to author 25 Mar 80 (hereafter cited as Goodrich, "Recollections"); 2nd Inf. Div. WD, G-3 Operations Order No. 011, Box 2435.
8. Goodrich, letter to author, 25 Mar 80; Goodrich, "Recollections."
9. The account of the 38th Inf.'s breakout west along the road to Kujang-dong in the pre-dawn hours of 28 November is based on a variety of sources: Peploe, MS; Manning, S-3, 3rd Bn., 38th Inf., interview with author, 20 Aug 51; 2nd Inf. Div. WD, 1–30 Nov 50, Narr. Summ., p. 32; Futrell, *U.S. Air Force in Korea*, p. 237; 38th Inf. Comd. Rpt., 28 Nov 50, Box 2473; IX Corps WD, Vol. 3, G-2 Spot Rpts., 28 Nov 50, Box 1769; ORO-R-1 (Office of Research Operations), "The Employment of Armor in Korea," 1, no. 13, 8 Apr 51.
10. Goodrich, Comments, and "Recollections," for author; Peploe, MS.
11. Futrell, *U.S. Air Force in Korea*, pp. 237–38; 38th Inf. Comd. Rpt., Summ., 28 Nov 50, Box 2473.
12. 23rd Inf. Comd. Rpt., 28 Nov 50, Box 2472; Gugeler, MS.
13. Goodrich, "Recollections," and letter to author, 25 Mar 80.
14. Gugeler, MS.
15. 23rd Inf. Comd. Rpt., 28 Nov 50, Box 2472; 2nd Inf. WD, 28 Nov 50, Box 2435; IX Corps WD, Vol. 4, G-3 Spot Rpts., Box 1770; Gugeler, MS. Gugeler says that A Co., 23rd Inf., did not arrive at Won-ni until 2 A.M. on 29 Nov.
16. 2nd Inf. Div. WD, 28 Nov 50, Narr. Summ., p. 33; HQ IX Corps, "CCF Activities on U.S. IX Corps Front," 18 Dec 50, p. 3; Gugeler, MS; 2nd Div. WD, G-1 Rpt., 28 Nov 50, Box 2435.
17. Homer Bigart dispatch, *New York Herald Tribune*, 30 Nov 50, p. 3, col. 1 (datelined 28 Nov. delayed).
18. Thompson, *Cry Korea*, pp. 240–41, 247; IX Corps WD, G-3 Activities, 27 Nov 50, Box 1767; Eighth Army WD, Summ., Sec. 1, 27 Nov 50, Box 1122; *New York Herald Tribune*, 27 Nov 50, p. 7, col. 1.
19. Ronald Monson, "The Great Retreat," in Bartlett, *With the Australians in Korea*, p. 200; Linklater, *Our Men in Korea*, p. 29; 1st Cav. Div. WD, 27 Nov 50, Box 4416.
20. Monson, "Great Retreat," pp. 201–202.
21. Linklater, *Our Men in Korea*, pp. 29–30; IX Corps WD, POR No. 196, 29 Nov 50, Box 1769. The tanks were attached at 6 A.M. on 29 Nov 50.
22. Eighth Army WD, Summ., Sec. 1 and Sec. 2, 29 Nov 50, Box 1122.
23. Eighth Army WD, 29 Nov 50.
24. IX Corps WD, Bk. 1, 29 Nov 50; IX Corps WD, POR No. 196, 29 Nov 50; 2nd Inf. Div. WD, chief of staff Jnl., 28 Nov 50, Box 2435; Pfc. Arthur Cohen, HQ Co., 2nd Inf. Div., "Diary of a Week, 23 Nov–1 Dec 1950" (Typescript copy in author's possession; hereafter cited as Cohen, Diary). It appears from Cohen's diary that the main 2nd Div. CP remained near Kunu-ri from the beginning of the Eighth Army offensive that began on 24 Nov, until it moved in the pre-dawn hours of 28 Nov. The advance party of the 2nd Div. CP moved on 26 Nov about 20 miles north of Kunu-ri on the river road. It returned to Kunu-ri the next afternoon, 27 Nov, when it became apparent that the enemy was making big inroads into the division front lines. The CP main party arrived at the new CP six miles south of Kunu-ri before dawn on 29 Nov.

25. I Corps WD, 29 Nov 50, msg. from CG, Eighth Army to corps and division CGs, Box 1501.

26. These comments are based on the Map of Korea, Yongbyon Sheet, 1950, 2nd ed., scale 1:50,000.

27. 9th Inf. WD, Hist. Narr., 29 Nov 50, Box 2471; Eighth Army WD, Sec. 2, G-2 PIR No. 140, 29 Nov 50, and G-3 Jnl. file, 29 Nov 50, Box 1132; 23rd Inf. Comd. Rpt., 29 Nov 50, Box 2472; IX Corps WD, Vol. 3, 29 Nov 50, Box 1769.

28. IX Corps WD, Vol. 3, G-2 Spot Rpts., 29 Nov 50, Box 1769; Eighth Army WD, Sec. 2, G-2 PIR No. 140, 29 Nov 50, Box 1132.

29. 9th Inf. WD, Hist. Narr., 29 Nov 50, Box 2471.

30. 38th Inf. Comd. Rpt., Summ., 29 Nov 50, Box 2473; 2nd Inf. Div. WD, 29 Nov 50, Box 2435; Peploe, MS.

31. 38th Inf. Comd. Rpt., Summ., 29 Nov 50, Box 2473; 2nd Inf. Div. WD, 29 Nov 50, Box 2435; IX Corps WD, Vol. 3, 29 Nov 50, Box 1769.

32. Peploe, interview with author, 12 Aug 51; 2nd Div. WD, 29 Nov 50, and 2nd Div. G-3 Jnl., entry No. 65, same date; IX Corps WD., Vol. 3, 29 Nov 50, G-2 Jnl. entries at 1030 and 2200, 29 Nov 50.

33. IX Corps WD, Vol. 4, G-3 Spot Rpts. and G-3 Jnl. file, Msg. No. 20149, received by Maj. Rice; Eighth Army WD, G-3 Jnl. entries at 1810, 29 Nov 50, Box 1132.

34. Peploe, MS.

35. 38th Inf. Comd. Rpt., 29–30 Nov 50, Box 2473; 2nd Div. WD, G-3 Jnl., 29 Nov 50, Box 2435; Manning, interview with author, 20 Aug 51.

36. Manning, interview with author, 20 Aug 51.

37. 38th Inf. Comd. Rpt., 29–30 Nov 50, Box 2473; 2nd Inf. Div. WD, G-3 Jnl., 29 Nov 50, Box 2435; Manning, interview with author, 20 Aug 51.

38. Maj. Gen. William F. Marquat, "Automatic Artillery in Korea," *Antiaircraft Journal* 94, no. 1 (Jan–Feb 1951): 7–10.

39. Peploe, MS; 38th Inf. Comd. Rpt., Summ., 30 Nov 50, Box 2473.

40. 1st Lt. William H. Harr (in Nov 1950, a plat. leader with the 25th Recon Co., accompanying the 24th Inf. unit), interview with author, Sept 1951; Gugeler, MS; 23rd Inf Comd. Rpt., 29 Nov 50, Box 2472; Map of Korea, Yongbyon Sheet, 1950, scale 1:50,000. Detailed study of this map is needed to understand what hills and terrain were involved in the confused but important American and Chinese troop movements at Kunu-ri.

41. Maj. Sam Radow (CO 1st Bn., 23rd Inf. in Aug 1951), interview with author, 16 Aug 51; Manning, interview with author, 20 Aug 51; Peploe, interview with author, 12 Aug 51; 38th Inf. Comd. Rpt., 29–30 Nov 50, Box 2473; 23rd Inf. Comd. Rpt., Sec. 3, Operations, 29–30 Nov 50, Box 2472; Gugeler, MS.

Chapter 12

1. Futrell, *US Air Force in Korea*, pp. 230–32. MiG is a sort of acronym for Arlem Ivanovich Mikoyan and M. I. Gurevich, their initials M and G being joined by the Russian conjunction *i*. The two men began collaborating on the design for the MiG-1 jet in 1939. When the MiG-15 first appeared at the Korean border in Nov 1950, it was superior to anything the Americans could send against it. But its superiority did not last long. The United States soon had F-86 Sabre jets in Korea. They proved to be better than the MiG-15, and the Americans again ruled the air over Korea.

2. *New York Times*, 29 Nov 50, article datelined Washington, D.C., 28 Nov 50.

3. "NR: C69953, 28 Nov 50, from CINCFE TOKYO JAPAN SGD MACARTHUR

TO: JCS WASH.DC INF: DEPT AR WASH DC CM IN 14957 28 Nov 50," printed in full in *Pertinent Papers on Korean Situation*, II, 345.

4. Ridgway, Memo of Record, 28 Nov 50, in Ridgway Papers (USMHRC).

5. Eighth Army WD, 29 Nov 50, *EUSAK Daily News*, Summ., giving text of the communiqué; *New York Times*, 29 Nov 50, p. 1, col. 6, including text of the communiqué. This communiqué was published in part or in whole throughout the press of the United States and in many parts of the world. Some press observers in Tokyo believed the added paragraph was an appeal for permission to bomb the bases of the communists in Manchuria. The FEC DIS No. 3004, 290200-300200, 1950 (Box 99) accepted Chinese strength in Korea on 29 Nov as being 127,200 and another 66,000 as tentatively accepted, for a total of 193,200 men.

6. Maj. Gen Edward M. Almond, Diary, 28 Nov 50, in Almond Papers, US Military History Research Center, Carlisle Barracks, Pa. (cited hereafter as Almond Diary). We know so many details of General Almond's movements during the Korean War because one of his aides, either Maj. Ladd, senior aide for a time, or Capt. Alexander M. Haig, Jr., his junior aide—whoever accompanied him on a particular day—had the task of preparing a diary of General Almond's movements and meetings but not a brief of discussions and decisions. Because Capt. Haig accompanied Almond on 28 Nov until he left for Tokyo, it is believed that Haig kept the diary for the day, with additions covering the Tokyo trip supplied by Gen. Almond or Maj. Ladd. Gen. Almond always reviewed the diary for each day and approved it for inclusion in the historical record of X Corps.

7. Whitney, *MacArthur*, pp. 423-24. Whitney has a discussion of the substance of the meeting and lists the persons named here as being present. In an interview with the author (28-29 Apr 77), Lt. Gen. Almond, USA Ret., confirmed the attendance of the meeting and the comments about his and Walker's views given to MacArthur in the conference. Whitney erroneously gives the date of the conference as the night of 1 Dec 50.

8. Whitney, *MacArthur*, pp. 423-24; Schnabel, *Policy and Direction*, pp. 278-79 and n. 22; Almond, interview with author, 28-29 Apr 77.

9. Schnabel, *Policy and Direction*, p. 279, and n. 22; Whitney, *MacArthur*, pp. 423-24; Futrell, *U.S. Air Force in Korea*, pp. 224-25; Roy E. Appleman, "Escaping the Trap: The X Corps in Northeast Korea," MS. Futrell seems to rely on Whitney for most of his comments on the conference.

10. Almond, Diary, 29 Nov 50; Lt. Gen. William J. McCaffrey, USA, Ret., interviews and correspondence with author, 1976-79; Almond interview with author, 28 Apr 1977.

11. Maj. Gen. Leven C. Allen, USA, Ret., interview with author, 15 Dec 53. After the issuance of these orders, the Eighth Army everywhere hurriedly completed its withdrawal south of the Chongchon River on 30 Nov and moved south toward Pyongyang.

12. I Corps WD, 29 Nov 50, msg., CG EUSAK to Units I, IX Corps, 187th Airborne, Box 1501.

13. "Msg. from JCS to: CINCFE TOKYO JAPAN NR: JCS 97592 29 Nov 50," in *Pertinent Papers on Korean Situation*, II, 354. On 22 May 51, Sen. Fulbright entered into a rather detailed examination of Gen. Omar Bradley, chairman of the Joint Chiefs of Staff, regarding Gen. MacArthur's radio message of 28 Nov 50 to the JCS, and their reply of 29 Nov (MacArthur Hearings, pt. 2, pp. 972-76).

14. "Msg. from: CINCUNC TOKYO JAPAN SGD MACARTHUR TO: DEPT AR WASH DC FOR JCS NR: C50021, 29 Nov 50," in *Pertinent Papers on Korean Situation*, II. Generalissimo Chiang Kai-shek had offered at the beginning of the war, through aide memoirs from the Chinese Embassy in Washington to the secretary of state on 27 and 30 June 50, to send 33,000 seasoned Chinese troops from Formosa (Taiwan) for op-

erations in Korea, in response to a resolution of the UN Security Council on 27 June 1950.

15. "Radio Msg., TO CINCFE TOKYO JAPAN FROM JCS NR JCS 97594 29 Nov 50," in *Pertinent Papers on Korean Situation*, II, 355; Whitney, *MacArthur*, pp. 422-23.

16. Thompson, *Cry Korea*, pp. 252-53.

17. *New York Herald Tribune*, 30 Nov 50, p. 8, col. 4, AP dispatch from US Eighth Army HQ, 29 Nov 50; Eighth Army WD, Summ., Sec. 1, Nov 1950, pp. 113-14, gives the text of the press release. We have no reliable information concerning what the CCF intention was, or what it would have done, had not Eighth Army and X Corps attacked toward the border in late Nov 1950.

Chapter 13

1. 24th Inf. Div. WD, Bk. 1, 30 Nov 50; 21st Inf. WD, 30 Nov 50, Box 3538; Eighth Army WD, 30 Nov 50, Summ., Sec. 1, Box 1122.

2. I Corps WD, POR No. 237, 30 Nov 50, Box 1501; I Corps WD, Summ., 30 Nov 50, Box 1496; I Corps Comd. Rpt., 1 Dec 50 states that the east bridge was destroyed at 5:15 P.M. and the west bridge at 6:30 P.M.

3. *New York Herald Tribune*, 1 Dec 50, p. 1, col. 4, Homer Bigart dispatch from US I Corps in Korea, 30 Nov 50.

4. Eighth Army WD, 30 Nov 50, G-2 Staff Rpt., Box 1132; IX Corps WD, Vol. 4, 30 Nov 50, Box 1770; Lt. Col. Clarence E. Stuart, CO 555th FA Bn., interview with author, 9 Aug 51.

5. 35th Inf., 25th Div. WD, 30 Nov 50, Box 3764; I Corps WD, Summ., 30 Nov 50, Box 1496.

6. 24th Inf., 25th Div. WD, 30 Nov 50, Box 3764; 3rd Bn., 24th Inf. WD, 30 Nov 50, Box 3764; 1st Lt. Francis G. Nordstrom, D Co., 89th Tank Bn., interview with author, 31 Aug 51; Col. John T. Corley, interview with author, 1 Nov 51. Corley said that he found Lt. Col. Blair in a state of shock, suffering from combat fatigue.

7. 25th Inf. Div. WD, Bk. 1, Narr. Rpt., Nov 1950; 3rd Bn., 24th Inf. WD, 30 Nov 50, and 3rd Bn., 23rd Inf., S-3 Jnl., 30 Nov 50, Box 3764; 23rd Inf. Comd. Rpt., 2nd Div. WD, 30 Nov 50, Box 2472; HQ., 89th Tank Bn., Unit Hist., p. 5, in 25th Inf. Div. Hist., Bk. 2, Nov 1950. The 25th Inf. Div. had 1,313 battle casualties in Nov 1950.

8. IX Corps WD, Bk. 1, G-3 Msg. No. 2059, Vol. 6, Annex 2, 30 Nov 50; Eighth Army WD, G-3 Jnl., 30 Nov 50, Box 1132. The IX Corps POR No. 197, 30 Nov 50, says the corps CP opened at Pyongyang at 2 P.M.

9. Eighth Army WD, G-2 Staff Rpt., 30 Nov 50, Box 1132.

10. 24th Inf. Div. WD, G-4 Daily Summ., 30 Nov 50, Box 3512. Lt. Col. Dale D. Dixon, G-4 of the 24th Inf. Div., left perhaps the best record of logistic and supply subjects by any G-4 in Eighth Army to be found in the official records. I Corps WD., Summ., 30 Nov 50, Box 1496; I Corps WD, 29 Nov 50, Box 1501.

11. I Corps WD, Ord. Staff Sec. Rpt., 30 Nov 50, Box 1501; 2nd Inf. Div. WD, G-4 Activ. Rpt., 30 Nov 50, Box 2435; Eighth Army WD, G-4 Jnl., 30 Nov 50, Box 1132.

12. IX Corps WD, G-3 Rpt. and PIR No. 65, 30 Nov 50, Box 1767; I Corps WD, POR No. 237, PIR No. 76, and G-3 Staff Sec. Rpt., 30 Nov 50, Box 1501; Eighth Army WD, G-3 Jnl., entry at 11:30 A.M., Box 1132; IX Corps WD, G-3 Sec., 29 Nov. 50, Box 1767.

13. Eighth Army WD, Summ., Sec. 1, 30 Nov 50.

Chapter 14

1. Lt. Col. Maurice C. Holden, G-3, 2nd Inf. Div. (Nov–Dec 1950) letter to author, 26 Feb 52. Lt. Col. Frank Sinsel, 2nd Div. G-4 (maj. in Nov 1950), and Lt. Col. Robert Schwartz, asst. G-3, 2nd Div., in 1950, reviewed the facts in this letter before it was sent. Lt. Col. Holden forwarded the letter through Maj. Gen. Joseph S. Bradley (brig. gen. and asst. div. comm., 2nd Inf. Div., in Nov 1950), deputy director for strategic plans, Joints Chiefs of Staff, Washington, D.C., who sent it to me with a covering letter. Lt. Col. Holden's lengthy letter and Gen. Bradley's letter are important documents concerning the 2nd Div. and other command headquarters mentioned in the events of 30 Nov–1 Dec 50 south of Kunu-ri. This source will henceforth be cited as Holden, Letter, except where Gen. Bradley's covering letter is quoted concerning Col. Freeman's withdrawal of the 23rd Inf. on the Kunu-ri–Anju road. As operations officer for the 2nd Inf. Div. in the period discussed in this chapter, Lt. Col. Holden was in a position to know decisions and events at the 2nd Div. HQ.

2. Holden, Letter, and Holden, interview with author, n.d.; Peploe, interview with author, 12 Aug 51.

3. IX Corps WD, Vol. 4, G-3 Spot Rpts., 29 Nov 50, Box 1770.

4. Holden, Letter; Marshall, *River and Gauntlet*, pp. 261–62.

5. 1st Cav. Div. G-3 Jnl., 29 Nov 50, Box 4416; Eighth Army Combined G-2/G-3 Intelligence Summ., in FEC DIS No. 3004 and map, Box 99; Marshall, *River and Gauntlet*, pp. 261–62.

6. Goodrich, "Recollections," pp. 4–5.

7. 25th Inf. Div. WD, Ord. Sec., 29 Nov 50, Box 3769; 24th Div. WD, PIR No. 140, 29 Nov 50, Box 3512; 1st Cav. Div. WD, G-3 Jnl., 29 Nov 50, Box 4416.

8. 24th Div. WD, 19th Inf. Unit Rpt., 29 Nov 50, Box 3534; 24th Div. WD, 29 Nov 50, Box 3512; I Corps WD, POR No. 234; and PIR No. 75, 29 Nov 50, Box 1501; 19th Inf. WD, 30 Nov 50; Combined G-2/G-3 Situation Map for Intelligence Summ. No. 3005, in Eighth Army WD, 010200 Dec 50. There is confusion in the map coordinates in various records cited for the location of the enemy fireblocks, and in the names of towns and villages near them. Some of this is due to the early 1:50,000-scale maps, which contained many revisions. I have tried to reconcile these difficulties, using as a basic map the Anju Sheet, 6332 IV, Series L751, 2nd ed., 1950, scale 1:50,000, which normally would be the map used by the army units involved in giving coordinates in their records at the time.

9. Maj. Gen. George B. Peploe, USA, Ret., letter to author, 2 Feb 80. Col. (then Capt.) Hodges, 38th Regt. S-3, confirms Peploe's comments; Holden, Letter; IX Corps WD, Vol. 4, G-3 Spot Rpts., 29 Nov 50, Box 1776; Peploe, interview with author, 12 Aug 51; Peploe, MS.

10. Holden, Letter.

11. Ibid.; 2nd Inf. Div. WD, Narr. Summ., pp. 33–36, Box 2435; 9th Inf. WD, Hist. Narr., 30 Nov 50, Box 2471. While all contemporary testimony of participants, including officers of the 9th Inf., is to the effect that Col. Sloane had only about 400 effectives for his attack on the roadblock, the 9th Inf. WD, S-1 Narr. Hist. (Box 7471) gives the 2nd Bn. as having a strength of 13 officers and 257 enlisted men, and the 3rd Bn. a strength of 11 officers and 239 enlisted men for 30 Nov 50, a total of 520 men, not counting the 9th Regt. HQ personnel.

12. Holden, Letter.

13. Cohen, Diary; Holden, Letter; 2nd Inf. Div. WD, G-2 Activ. Rpt., 1–30 Nov 50.

14. 2nd Inf. Div. WD, Narr. Summ., 1–30 Nov 50, pp. 33–36, Box 2435; Holden, Letter; there are minor discrepancies among various sources as to the march order.

15. Holden, Letter; Goodrich, "Recollections," p. 6.

16. Col. Epley, review comments on "Disaster in Korea" MS, 30 Oct 79 (hereafter cited as Epley, Comments).

17. My study of march order as actually followed by units making the run through the enemy fireblock and roadblock south on the Sunchon road; Col. Joseph H. Buys, exec. off., 2nd Div. Arty., review comments on "Disaster in Korea" MS, 13 Mar 80 (hereafter cited as Buys, Comments), and letter to author, 13 Mar 80.

18. Col. Walker E. Goodrich, telephone conversation and interview with author, 6 Apr 80; Goodrich, "Recollections," and letter to author, 25 Mar 80.

19. Goodrich, Comments, with sketch map of artillery locations. Also, Buys, Comments.

20. Lt. Col. Walter Killilae, "Operation Roadblock," *Antiaircraft Journal* 94, no. 2 (Mar–Apr 1951): 15. I added the infantry identifications.

21. Buys, Comments; Holden, Letter; Marshall, *River and Gauntlet*, pp. 264–65.

22. Holden, Letter. The location of the 2nd Div. CP as described is based on a study of the 1:50,000-scale map in use at the time, and a sketch by the 17th FA Bn. of its route on 30 Nov 50. The high ground immediately south of the 2nd Div. CP carries no elevation in hill number meters, but according to terrain contours, its two knobs rose about 300 feet above the valley and the CP site at their northern bases.

23. Peploe, MS. Marshall, in *River and Gauntlet* (pp. 267-68), has some of the artillery north of the Kaechon River at this time and vulnerable to CCF attack. He was mistaken; all the artillery had crossed to the south side of the river and were in firing positions south of the 23rd RCT.

24. 23rd Inf. Comd. Rpt., 30 Nov 50, in 2nd Inf. WD, 30 Nov 50, Box 2472; Gugeler, MS; Maj. Sam Radow, CO 1st Bn., 23rd Inf., interview with author, 16 Aug 51.

25. Marshall, *River and Gauntlet*, pp. 277–79. Marshall based his account of the ROK attack on interviews with eyewitness American officers, including Lt. Col. McMains (CO, 3rd Bn., 9th Inf.), Lt. Col. Skeldon (CO 2nd Bn., 38th Inf.), and Lt. Heath (38th Inf.); 9th Inf. WD, Hist. Narr., 30 Nov 50, Box 2471; Peploe, MS.

26. IX Corps WD, Bk. 1, 26 Nov 50, and Vol. 6, Annex 2, G-3 Msg. No. 1786; Brig. C. N. Barclay, *The First Commonwealth Division: The Story of British Land Forces in Korea 1950-1953* (N.p.: Aldershot, Gale, and Polden, 1954), p. 34; Eighth Army WD, G-3 Sec., 3, 6, 9, and 24 Nov 50, and Transportation Sec., 24 Nov 50; 2nd Logistical Comd. Hist. Rpt., G-3 Sec., Nov 1950; Lt. Col. G. I. Malcolm, *The Argylls in Korea* (London: Thomas Nelson & Sons, 1952), pp. 58–59.

27. Barclay, *First Commonwealth Division*, p. 25; IX Corps WD, Vol. 4, G-3 Spot Rpts., 29 Nov 50, Box 1770; 1st Cav. Div. WD, G-3 Jnl., 29 Nov 50.

28. IX Corps WD, Vol. 4, G-3 Spot Rpts., 30 Nov 50, Box 1770.

29. Holden, Letter.

30. 38th Inf. Comd. Rpt., Summ., 29–30 Nov 50, Box 2473; Manning, interview with author, 20 Aug 51; Peploe, MS.

31. Peploe, interview with author, 12 Aug 51; Peploe, MS; Manning, interview with author, 20 Aug 51; 38th Inf. Comd. Rpt., Summ., 30 Nov 50, Box 2473.

32. IX Corps WD, Vol. 4, G-3 Spot Rpts., 30 Nov 50, Box 1770.

33. Peploe, interview with author, 12 Aug 51, on beginning of the tank movement at head of the 2nd Bn., 38th Inf. Also, Peploe, MS. The account of Lt. Mace's run through the enemy fireblock is based partially on Marshall, *River and Gauntlet*, pp. 281–86. Marshall interviewed Lt. Heath and others in the party in late Dec 1950.

34. 9th Inf. WD, Hist. Summ., S-3 Narr. Diary, 30 Nov 50, Box 2471; Sgt. Richard H. Shriver, combat correspondent assigned to 9th Inf. Regt., "Personal Experiences with 9th Inf. HQ Company at Kunu-ri and in Fireblock," 11 pp. (Typescript MS, 16 Aug 51, prepared at the author's request, copy in his possession).

35. Maj. Gen. George B. Peploe, USA, Ret., letter to author, 8 Dec 79.
36. The account of Manning's and Peploe's travel through the enemy fireblock and arrival at the Middlesex Battalion position is based largely on Manning, interview with author, 20 Aug 51, and Peploe, letter to author, 8 Dec 79. During the interview Manning frequently consulted a map of the area and his contemporary notes in giving the map coordinate readings that have been included here. Regarding the movement of the 38th Inf. Regt. through the enemy fireblock, see also 38th Inf. Comd. Rpt., Summ., 30 Nov 50, Box 2437. The British Centurion tanks were too large for the Sunchon-Kunu-ri road north of where they stopped on the night of 29–30 Nov. They probably would have blocked the road at some points to southbound traffic if they had tried to travel north on it. But the American medium tanks attached to the Middlesex Battalion could have negotiated the road. Many from the 72nd Tank Bn. with the 2nd Div. did.
37. Goodrich, letter to author, 25 Mar 80, and idem, Comments.
38. Peploe, letter to author, 8 Dec 79. Peploe, in his MS, states that he conferred with Gen. Keiser at the 2nd Div. CP at Sunchon during the evening of 30 Nov 50.
39. Marshall, *River and Gauntlet*, p. 297, based on his interviews with survivors.
40. Ibid., pp. 303–306.
41. Ibid., pp. 321–23, apparently based on an interview with Turner.
42. 38th Inf. Comd. Rpt., Summ., 30 Nov 50; IX Corps WD, PORs No. 197 and 198, 29–30 Nov 50, Box 1769; IX Corps WD, Bk. 1, 30 Nov 50.
43. Manning, interview with author, 20 Aug 51.
44. Peploe (in MS) again emphasized the misleading combat intelligence Gen. Keiser and he had at noon on 30 Nov 50, when his regiment started south into the enemy fireblock.
45. Manning, interview with author, 20 Aug 51.
46. Epley, Comments.
47. Cohen, Diary; Homer Bigart in *New York Herald Tribune*, 2 Dec 50.
48. Cohen, Diary. Col. Epley's journal memorandum for 30 Nov states that he left the CP at 1:30 P.M. and arrived at Sunchon at 8:40 P.M. (Box 2435).
49. Cohen, Diary; 2nd Div. WD, Summ., 30 Nov 50, Box 2435; Holden, Letter.
50. Cohen, Diary; Homer Bigart dispatch, datelined 1 Dec 50, with 2nd Div., to *New York Herald Tribune*, 2 Dec 50, p. 1, col. 6.
51. Col. Albert K. Stebbins, interview with author, 4 Dec 53.
52. Col. Gerald Epley, USA, Ret., letter to author, 6 Dec 79.
53. Goodrich, "Recollections," pp. 8–9.
54. Epley, Comments; Epley, letter to author, 6 Dec 79; 2nd Inf. Div. WD, Capt. Richard S. Johnston, CO, 2nd Mil. Pol. Co., Rpt., 30 Nov 50 (hereafter cited as Johnston, Rpt.).
55. Epley, Comments, pp. 4–5.
56. Johnston, Rpt.
57. Epley, letter to author, 6 Dec 79, p. 4.
58. IX Corps WD, Vol. 4, G-3 Spot Rpts., msg. 301930, Holden to Kunzig, 30 Nov 50, Box 1770; Buys, Comments.
59. IX Corps WD, Vol. 4, G-3 Spot Rpts., and G-3 Summ., 30 Nov 50, Box 1770.
60. Capt. Edward C. Williamson, after-action interviews. See his report, "Kunu-ri: Support of the 2nd US Inf Div Rearguard by Battery A, 17th FA Bn (8-in how) During a Retrograde Movement 24 Nov–1 Dec 50," No. BA 64 (Mimeographed, in Office Chief of Military History, Washington, D.C.); Capt. Russell A. Gugeler, "Artillery at Kunu-ri," in *Combat Actions in Korea* (Washington, D.C.: Association of the US Army, 1954), chap. 6. Gugeler used Williamson's report and his own interview with Lt. Col. Harrelson, and other sources. See also Goodrich, Comments.
61. Williamson, "Kunu-ri."

62. Ibid.; Gugeler, "Artillery at Kunu-ri"; Marshall, *River and Gauntlet,* pp. 235–36. Gugeler says the weapon sent forward to fire on the enemy machine gun was a dual-40. Marshall gives it as a quad-50. There is often confusion in interview comments referring to these two potent antiaircraft weapons carriers. One distinction, aside from their armament, is the half-track character of the M16 quad-50 and the full-track character of the M19 dual-40.

63. Williamson, "Kunu-ri"; Gugeler, "Artillery at Kunu-ri"; Holden, Letter; Goodrich, Comments.

64. Goodrich, "Recollections," pp. 8–9. In light of Goodrich's comment about the FDC operations sergeant's description of the bypass when he came through it, its condition then (which became worse as time passed) more accurately explains why the bypass was closed to vehicular traffic. We also know that many of the soldiers in the last two serials (6 and 7 on the Sunchon road) abandoned their vehicles and artillery in the fireblock area, long before they reached the bypass, and walked out over the hills.

65. Marshall, *River and Gauntlet,* pp. 339–40, quoting Lt. Col. William Kelleher, CO, 1st Bn., 38th Inf.

66. Ibid., pp. 337–38; Johnston, Rpt.; Epley, Comments.

67. 23rd Inf. Regt. Comd. Rpt., 30 Nov 50, Box 2472; Holden, Letter, and previous text and citations.

68. Col. Paul L. Freeman, interview with author, 17 Apr 52; Col. Gerald G. Epley, interview with author, 13 Dec 51; Buys, Comments, 13 Mar 80; Peploe, MS.

69. 23rd Inf. Comd. Rpt., Operations Sec. 3, 30 Nov 50, Box 2472; Freeman, interview with author, 17 Apr 52.

70. 24th Inf. WD in 25th Div. WD, 30 Nov 50, Box 3764; Maj. Sam Radow, CO 1st Bn., 23rd Inf., interview with author, 17 Aug 51; Capt. Ordie Taylor, liaison officer, 24th Inf. with 23rd Regt. at Kunu-ri, interview with author, Aug 1951.

71. Col. Paul L. Freeman, CO 23rd Inf., "Withdrawal of the 23rd Infantry from Kunu-ri" (Memorandum for record, per conversation with Gen. Keiser, addressed to CG, 2nd Inf. Div., 9 Dec 50, copy in author's possession; hereafter cited as Freeman, Memorandum); Freeman, interview with author, 17 Apr 52.

72. See references in n. 71. Col. Epley told me on 13 Dec 51 that Gen. Bradley had come part way back from the Pass area to where Col. Sloane was at that time and that Gen. Keiser was at the Pass.

73. Goodrich, "Recollections," pp. 8–9.

74. Marshall, *River and Gauntlet,* p. 328.

75. Maj. Gen. J. S. Bradley, deputy director for strategic plans, Joint Chiefs of Staff, Washington, D.C., letter to Maj. Roy E. Appleman, 2 Apr 52 (signed by D. Kaplan, secy. to Gen. Bradley, for him). Kaplan said that Gen. Bradley was in Walter Reed Hospital at that time and had asked him to send the letter to me.

76. Freeman, Memorandum; idem, interview with author, 17 Apr 52.

77. Freeman, interview with author, 17 Apr 52; Marshall, *River and Gauntlet,* p. 329.

78. Radow, interview with author, 16 Aug 51; Freeman, Memorandum.

79. Freeman, Memorandum; idem, interview with author, 17 Apr 52; Lt. Col. George H. Williams, Jr., letter to author, 28 Nov 52 (Williams rode in the lead jeep behind the section of tanks at the head of the column); 23rd Inf. Comd. Rpt., 30 Nov 50, Box 2472; 2nd Inf. Div. WD, 30 Nov 50, Box 2435; Gugeler, MS; Maj. Frank Meszar, exec. off., 23rd Inf., interview with author, 15 May 53.

80. IX Corps WD, Vol. 4, G-3 Jnl., Spot Rpts., 30 Nov 50, Box 1770; Radow, 16 Aug 51 (Lt. Col. Claire E. Hutchins, Jr., was CO of the 1st Bn. in Nov–Dec 1950); Gugeler, MS; Freeman, interview with author, 17 Apr 52; 1st Lt. Clark C. Monroe, interview with author, 1951; 23rd Inf. Comd. Rpt., Sec. 3, Operations, 30 Nov 50, Box 2472.

81. Freeman, Memorandum.
82. My interview with Col. Freeman grew out of the latter's desire to obtain a copy of Gen. Bradley's letter to me. Although I did not know it at the time, Col. Freeman was a student at the National War College at Fort McNair, Washington, D.C. In some manner, Freeman had learned that Bradley had written to me on the subject of Freeman's authority to use the Anju road for the 23rd Inf. RCT at Kunu-ri. Freeman telephoned Maj. Gen. Orlando Ward, my superior officer, then chief of the Office of Military History, and asked him to have me send a copy of Bradley's letter to him. Gen. Ward declined to issue such an order, saying that I, the recipient of the letter, should decide whether to comply with the request. Gen. Ward then informed me of Col. Freeman's request and told me to handle the request in my own way. I telephoned Col. Freeman at the National War College and discussed the request, arranging to meet Freeman the following day. In the ensuing conversation I found Col. Freeman intensely interested in having a copy of Gen. Bradley's letter to me of 2 Apr 52. That letter was the only existing written record that showed authority for Freeman's action. I provided Col. Freeman with a copy of the correspondence from Gen. Bradley, and he seemed much relieved at receiving it. Col. Freeman seemed nervous about the continuing criticism of his actions on 30 Nov 50 and fearful that it might result in some official action that would adversely affect his military career. With a copy of Gen. Bradley's letter in his possession, he felt more secure.

In a conversation at a reception at Fort McNair the evening of 11 Apr 52, S. L. A. Marshall told me that Gen. Bradley wanted Col. Freeman court-martialed after Kunu-ri and that he (Bradley) had denied Freeman authority to move out by the Anju road. Marshall said that Freeman's authority to do so was from Gen. Keiser over Col. Sloane's 9th Inf. radio at the north end of the enemy fireblock. This statement is incorrect. How Marshall's mixup in this matter could have taken place I do not know. His view, however, became known to many officers in the army. That condemnation of Col. Freeman's action was widespread in Korea was well known to me in the Eighth Army in 1951.

83. Marshall, *River and Gauntlet,* pp. 350–51, quoting Fralish, whom he apparently had interviewed; Capt. Perry Davis, public information officer (PIO), 2nd Div., interview with author, 17 Aug 51. Regarding Maj. Lavell's death, see *U.S. Military Academy Register of Graduates* (West Point, N.Y.: Association of Graduates, USMA, 1975), p. 460, Item 11651.

84. Marshall, *River and Gauntlet,* pp. 357–58.

85. The 9th Inf. Comd. Rpt., Narr., in 2nd Div. WD, Dec 1950 (Box 2471) gives a good account of a large group of men from the rear of the 2nd Div. withdrawal, apparently including the Fralish-Grinnell group of artillerymen, who escaped on foot over the hills from the vicinity of the Pass area to the Sunchon road some miles southward and were guided on into Sunchon by liaison airplane messages dropped to them.

86. Goodrich, "Recollections."

87. Lt. Col. Robert J. O'Donnell, letter to the editors, *Combat Forces Journal* 3, no. 12 (July 1953): 2.

88. Holden, Letter, includes the comment that Col. Goodrich, S-3 of the 2nd Div. Arty. in 1950, gave him the information on the 155-mm howitzer blocking the bypass.

89. Goodrich, "Recollections," p. 9, and letter to author, 25 Mar 80.

90. Killilae, "Operation Roadblock," pp. 15–16.

91. Sgt. Richard H. Shriver, HQ Co., 9th Inf., "What I Know of the Battles near Kunu-ri," 11 pp. (Typed MS, 16 Aug 51, prepared for and copy in possession of the author; hereafter cited as Shriver, MS). See also 9th Inf. WD, Hist., Summ., 30 Nov 50, Box 2471.

92. Shriver, MS; 9th Inf. Comd. Rpt., Narr., in 2nd Div. WD, 1 Dec 50, Box 2471.

93. See references in n. 92, above.

94. Shriver, MS.
95. 2nd Div. WD, G-1 Personnel Periodic Rpt., No. 12, 15-30 Nov 50, Box 2435.
96. Epley, letter to author, 6 Dec 79.
97. 2nd Inf. Div. WD, Narr. Summ., 1-30 Nov 50, p. 36; ibid., G-4 Narr. Rpt., p. 3, Box 2435; Col. Pascal N. Strong, (Eighth Army Engineer in 1950) "Army Engineers in Korea," *Military Engineer* 44, no. 302 (Nov-Dec 1952): 405-10; Maj. Lawrence B. Farnum, letter to the editors, *Combat Forces Journal* 3, no. 12 (July 1953): 4.
98. 2nd Inf. Div. PIR No. 71, 5 Dec 50, in 2nd Div. Comd. Rpt., G-2 Sec., Box 2439; 2nd Inf. Div. Comd. Rpt., G-2 Sec., 29-30 Nov and Dec 1950, PIR No. 71, 5 Dec 50, Box 2439, for estimate of enemy forces and dispositions.
99. Futrell, *US Air Force in Korea*, pp. 237-38; IX Corps WD, Vol. 3, G-2 Spot Rpts., 30 Nov 50, Box 1769; Field, *Naval Operations*, pp. 267-68. Rear Adm. E. C. Ewen, commanding the Fast Carrier Task Force, informed the commander of the 5th Fleet at 10:30 P.M., 30 Nov 50, that two-thirds of their effort to aid Eighth Army had been wasted because they could not find controllers.
100. Epley, Comments; Goodrich, Comments.
101. Capt. John T. Dunphy, I Corps historian, letter to author, 1 Dec 51, citing I Corps G-3 Jnl. Serial 559, 291915. But Maj. Odum of I Corps, G-3 Plans, who was in the I Corps, G-3 Sec., on 30 Nov 50, told Dunphy that all requests of that nature were approved.
102. Maj. Lucas M. Prescott HQ, IX Corps, letter to author, 26 Dec 51. Prescott wrote: "Have made every check on all available sources of information in regard to the request of the 2nd Infantry Division for authority to use the Kunu-ri-Anju road. In so far as written journal entries I have not been able to locate any . . . Lt. Col. Rice and Capt. Kovar who were on duty in IX Corps G-3 Section during the night of 29 November 1950 state that request was received from the 2nd Division and cleared with I Corps and transmitted to the Division." The IX Corps WD, Vol. 4, G-3 Spot Rpts. for 29 Nov, states that it received a radio request from the 2nd Div., G-3 Sec., for a report on the Kunu-ri-Anju road and then south, and information on the 25th Div. movement. This source states that IX Corps G-3 Sec. gave the 2nd Div. G-3 Sec. information on the road and secured permission for the division to use the Anju road but that from Anju to Sukchon the road was crowded and it would have to work into the traffic as best it could—that the 25th Inf. Div. was doing the same. This message apparently was sent at 7:50 P.M. on 29 Nov. Another reference to the subject in the 2nd Div. Activ. Rpt. for 29 Nov says a request was made through IX Corps to use the Anju road, but does not state what response, if any, resulted from the request. See IX Corps WD, Vol. 4, G-3 Spot Rpts., Jnl. entry No. 2542 (or 2140?) 291950, 29 Nov 50, Box 1770; 2nd Div. WD, G-3 Activ. Rpts., 29 Nov 50, Box 2435.
103. Epley, interview with author, 13 Dec 51; Lt. Gen. Frank M. Milburn (I Corps CG, Nov-Dec 1950), interview with author, 4 Jan 52; Buys, Comments.
104. Holden, Letter.
105. Marquat, "Automatic Artillery in Korea"; 5th Cav. Regt. WD, Nov 1950; 1st Cav. Div. WD, Nov 1950, Box 4416; 1st Cav. Div., G-4 Jnl., 30 Nov 50, Box 4417; Buys, Comments.
106. 2nd Div. WD, G-1, Personnel Rpt. No. 12, 15-30 Nov 50, dated 1 Dec 50, and Enclosure 2, Box 2435; and G-1 Rpt., 2nd Div., Lt. Col. James D. Tanner, G-1, 7 Dec 50, Box 2435.
107. The figures relating to the 9th Inf. Regt. are taken from the 9th Inf. WD, Narr. Hist., S-1 Narr. Diary, Nov. 1950, Box 2471.
108. Eighth Army WD, Sec. 1, Summ., 30 Nov 50, Box 1122; 2nd Inf. Div. WD, Dec 1950.
109. 25th Inf. Div. WD, Summ., Nov 1950, Boxes 3764 and 3765.

110. 2nd Div. Comd. Rpt., G-l Sec., Dec 1950, Box 2436.
111. 2nd Inf. Div. Comd. Rpt., Dec. 1950, Narr. Summ., Appendix D-la, and G-3 Jnl., 1 Dec 50.
112. "Report on Status of the 2nd Infantry Division, 5 Dec 1950," four-page memorandum from Lt. Col. A. E. Lancaster, Eighth Army G-3 Sec., to Col. Dabney, Eighth Army G-3, in Eighth Army Comd. Rpt., G-3 Sec., 5 Dec 50, Box 1136 (hereafter cited as Lancaster, Report); Lt. Col. Holden, Report, 2nd Div. G-3 Rpt. with 2nd Div. POR, 5 Dec 50, Box 1136 (hereafter cited as Holden, Report).
113. Killilae, "Operation Roadblock," p. 15; Marquat, "Automatic Artillery in Korea," p. 7.
114. Lancaster, Report; Holden, Report.
115. Eighth Army Comd. Rpt., Narr., Dec 1950, Box 1134.
116. The depth of Gen. Keiser's feelings about Kunu-ri may be sensed from the fact that, when Gen. Matthew B. Ridgway later wrote to Gen. Keiser (they were both in the West Point class of 1917) for information as to what happened at Kunu-ri, Keiser never answered (Ridgway's statement to author).
117. Epley, Comments.
118. 2nd Inf. Div. Comd. Rpt., chief of staff Jnl., 5 Dec 50, Box 2436.
119. Eighth Army Comd. Rpt., G-3 Sec., 5 Dec 50, Box 1136; 2nd Div. Comd. Rpt., Dec 1950, for 7 Dec.
120. Maj. Gen. Leven C. Allen, interview with author, 15 Dec 53; Mrs. Edward M. (Margaret) Almond, conversation with author, 28 Apr 77. Mrs. Almond told me that Gen. Keiser told her on or about 15 Dec 50 in her home in Tokyo that Gen. Allen had come to Yongdong-po and relayed to him Gen. Walker's order relieving him of command.
121. "Testing of Gen. Keiser; A Soldier Remembered," three columns, in a clipping unidentified as to date or name of newspaper, copy provided by Maj. Gen. George B. Peploe, USA, Ret., in letter to author, 3 Feb 80. Keiser's physical disabilities led to his retirement from the Army in 1954. He died 20 Oct 69 in San Francisco.
122. Mrs. Margaret Almond, conversation with author, 28 Apr 77. At the time of this conversation, Gen. Almond, who was present, would not comment on the incident. He said he was not present when it occurred (he was in northeastern Korea with the X Corps), and he preferred that his wife tell the story as she remembered it.
123. Epley, interview with author, 13 Dec 51. Brig. Gen. Bradley had come down with a bad cold also, and he was sent to Japan for hospitalization soon afterward. He had insisted that he would go only if returned to his position in the division. It turned out, however, that he returned to Korea as assistant division commander of the 25th Inf. Div. Subsequently, he became the division commander. In 1951 Gen. Keiser was given command of the 5th Inf. Div. It did not serve in the Korean War. See *Register of Graduates*, p. 338, Item 5719.
124. Epley, letter to author, 6 Dec 79.
125. Gen. Matthew B. Ridgway, letter to author, 12 Oct 79, and also in conversation with author.

Chapter 15

1. 2nd Logistical Command (C), Monthly Activ. Rpts., Nov 1950, Transportation, Water Div.
2. "Msgs. CINCUNC Tokyo, sgd MacArthur to DEPTAR Wash., DC for JCS, NR: C-50107, 30 Nov 50; and CINCUNC Tokyo, Sgd. MacArthur to DEPTAR Wash., D.C. for JCS, 30 Nov 50, NR: C 50095," in *Pertinent Papers on Korean Situation*, II, 356–57.

3. "Msg. JCS to CINCUNC Tokyo, 30 Nov 50, NR: JCS 97772, in *Pertinent Papers on Korean Situation*, II, 356.

4. *New York Herald Tribune*, 2 Dec 50, p. 2, col. 7, citing MacArthur interview for *U.S. News and World Report*.

5. The brief discussion of the atomic bomb issue and British distrust of American policy in the Korean War is based on Schnabel, *Policy and Direction*, pp. 288–93. For Defense Minister Shin's statement, see *New York Herald Tribune*, 4 Dec 50, p. 1, col. 4, UP dispatch from Seoul, 3 Dec 50.

6. Gen. Charles L. Bolte, AC/S-G3, DA (deputy chief of staff for administration) for Gen. Ridgway, memorandum, US Army Capabilities, 1 Dec 50, in Ridgway Papers.

7. Eighth Army WD, Summ., Sec. 1, 30 Nov 50.

8. Eighth Army WD, G-3 Sec., 1 Dec 50, Box 1136.

9. 38th Inf. Comd. Rpt., Narr., 1–2 Dec 50, Box 2474; Bartlett, *With the Australians in Korea*, p. 49.

10. Bartlett, *With the Australians in Korea*, p. 55.

11. Malcolm, *Argylls in Korea*, pp. 61–67; Linklater, *Our Men in Korea*, p. 29; Barclay, *First Commonwealth Division*, p. 34.

12. Eighth Army Comd. Rpt. G-2, PIRs No. 142, 143, 1–2 Dec 50, Box 1135; ibid., G-3 Sec., 1 Dec. 50, Box 1136; 1st Cav. Div. Comd. Rpt., Narr., 1–2 Dec 50, Box 4419.

13. Eighth Army Comd. Rpt., Narr., pp. 44–45, 2 Dec 50, Box 1134; ibid., G-2, PIR No. 143, Box 1135; ibid., G-3 Jnl. file, 2 Dec 50, and Briefing for CG, Eighth Army, 3 Dec. 50 (covering period 020001–030800), Box 1136; Gen. Harold K. Johnson (Army chief of staff), CO 5th Cav. Regt., Nov–Dec 1950, interview with author, 28 Apr 54.

14. *New York Herald Tribune*, 2 Dec 50, p. 3, col. 3, AP dispatch, datelined US 1st Cav. Div. CP, 1 Dec; 7th Cav. Regt. Comd. Rpt., Narr., 2 Dec 50, Box 4431.

15. 1st Cav. Div. Comd. Rpt., Narr., 2 Dec 50, Box 4419; Eighth Army Comd. Rpt., G-2 PIR No. 143, 2 Dec 50, Box 1135, and G-3 POR 431, 3 Dec 50 (covering action on 2 Dec), Box 1136.

16. Eighth Army Comd. Rpt., G-2 PIR No. 144, 3 Dec 50, Box 1135.

17. Eighth Army Comd. Rpt., G-3 Jnl. file, G-3 POR No. 427, and G-3 Air Briefing Rpt., 1 Dec 50, Box 1136.

18. IX Corps WD, PIR No. 66, 1 Dec 50, Box 1767; FEC DIS No. 3006, 1–2 Dec 50, Box 99.

19. Radow, interview with author, 16 Aug 51.

20. Lt. Col. Edward McMaken, 24th Inf. Div., G-3 Air Officer, 5 Aug 50–3 Jan 51, Debriefing Rept., No. 45, 13 Dec 51, Dept. of Training Publ. and Aids, Artillery School, Fort Sill, Okla.; 25th Div. WD, Bk. 1, G-4 Action Rpt., 30 Nov 50; I Corps WD, Ord. Off. Rpt., 30 Nov 50; Lt. Col. John W. MacIndoe and Capt. Andrew I. Wessling, Jr., G-3 Sec., I Corps, interviews with author, 27 July 51.

21. I Corps WD, Ord. Off. Rpt., 30 Nov 50, Box 1501.

22. 24th Div. WD, Lt. Col. S. D. Cocheu (24th Div. QM), Summ. Rpt., Nov 1950, Box 3513; 24th Inf. Div. WD, Bk. 1, Operational Highlights, 1–30 Nov 50, Box 3513. Col. Cocheu's Quartermaster reports in the 24th Div. records are the best and most revealing Quartermaster reports of any in Eighth Army for this period.

23. B. C. Mossman and Harry J. Middleton, "Logistical Problems and Their Solutions (EUSAK)," June 1952, pp. 91–92 (reproduced, Office Chief of Military History, DA).

24. Futrell, *U.S. Air Force in Korea*, p. 232.

25. James W. Spellman, exec. off., QMC, memorandum to G-4, 24th Inf. Div., 2 Dec 50, and included as enclosure in 24th Div. WD, G-4 Summ., Box 3512 (hereafter cited as Spellman, Memorandum).

26. Ibid.; 24th Div. QM Sec. Rpt., 1 Dec 50; 24th Inf. Div. WD, Bk. 1, Operational

Highlights, 1-30 Nov 50, and 24th Div. QM Summ., Bk. 1, p. 254, Boxes 3512 and 3513.

27. Futrell, *U.S. Air Force in Korea,* p. 248.

28. Col. Henry Fisher, CO 35th Inf. Regt., review comments on "South to the Naktong, North to the Yalu" MS, 7 Nov 57 (hereafter cited as Fisher, Comments).

29. I Corps Comd. Rpt., Dec. 1950, pp. 5-6; Lt. Col. MacIndoe, G-3, I Corps, and Capt. Dunphy, I Corps historian, interviews with author, 25 July 51.

30. Lt. Col. Clarence E. Stuart, CO 555th FA Bn., interview with author, 9 Aug 51.

31. *New York Times,* 6 Dec 50, p. 1, col. 6, dispatch from Seoul, 5 Dec 50.

32. Lt. Col. Barton O. Baker, ord. off., 25th Inf. Div., "Division Ordnance Work," in Westover, *Combat Support in Korea,* pp. 127-28.

33. Eighth Army WD, Narr., Logistics Sec., 2 Dec 50, Box 1134; IX Corps Comd. Rpt., 2 Dec 50, Box 1505.

34. Eighth Army Comd. Rpt., G-3 Jnl. file, POR No. 430, and G-3 Briefing for CG, 2 Dec 50, Box 1136; 24th Div. Comd. Rpt., Narr., 2 Dec 50, Box 3522.

35. Eighth Army Comd. Rpt., G-3 Air Rpt., 3 Dec 50, covering action on 2 Dec, Box 1136.

36. FEC DIS No. 3007, i-g, 2-3 Dec 50, Box 99.

37. 5th RCT, 24th Div. Comd. Rpt., 2-7 Dec 50, Box 4691.

38. 1st Cav. Div. Comd. Rpt., Narr., 3-5 Dec 50, Box 4419.

39. 24th Inf. Div. Comd. Rpt., Narr., 3-5 Dec 50, Box 3522; Eighth Army Comd. Rpt., G-3 Sec., 3 Dec 50, Box 1136.

40. 3rd Bn., 35th Inf. Exec. Off. Jnl., 3 Dec 50, in 35th Inf. Comd. Rpt., 3 Dec 50.

41. 9th Inf. Comd. Rpt., in 2nd Div. WD, 3-7 Dec 50, Box 2471.

42. Eighth Army Comd. Rpt., G-3 Sec., G-3 Jnl. file, 3 Dec 50, Box 1136. The G-3 Daily Briefings for Gen. Walker, covering the actions for the previous day and up to 8 A.M. of the morning of the briefing, usually had excellent summaries. They also revealed that the Eighth Army had good information on what had happened in X Corps for the same period, and thus showed good radio and liaison communication between the two commands.

43. Eighth Army Comd. Rpt., Narr., 3 Dec 50, Box 1134; *Far East Air Force Operations History,* Vol. 2, 1 Nov 50-28 Feb 51, p. 84.

Chapter 16

1. Col. Albert K. Stebbins, Eighth Army G-4, was a close and loyal friend of Gen. Walker. In an interview on 4 Dec 53, he told me that Gen. Walker personally made the decision to abandon Pyongyang—that it was not ordered by Gen. MacArthur. After he made the decision, Gen. Walker informed MacArthur of it, saying he could not hold the city (also, Maj. Gen. Leven C. Allen, interview with author, 15 Dec 53).

2. Stebbins, interview with author, 4 Dec 53.

3. Ibid.

4. Col. Richard W. Stephens, interview with author, 8 Oct 51.

5. Barclay, *First Commonwealth Division in Korea,* p. 35; Linklater, *Our Men in Korea,* p. 3, "The Retreat Southward." The 8th Royal Irish Hussars, an armored unit, included two squadrons of Centurion tanks, the largest tanks used in Korea. They were wider than the other tanks, of a low profile, and carried 20-pounder guns. The Hussars also had a reconnaissance troop of light tanks, and C Squadron of the 7th Tank Regt.

6. *New York Herald Tribune,* 4 Dec 50, p. 3, dispatch from Tokyo, 4 Dec 50.

7. The reverse side of the Map of Korea, 1952 Chinnampo Sheet, scale 1:25,000, has a good outline map of Pyongyang and its main military facilities. Pyongyang is said to be the oldest city in Korea and for a long time was its capital. Probably no other Ko-

rean city has been so prominently identified with the ancient culture of Korea and its arts, developed over nearly 3,000 years. Pyongyang throughout most of its history was known as Heijo. As the course of history passed over this land in 1950, the United States was fated to control this ancient place for a brief period of about six weeks but left no permanent marks on the city.

8. I Corps Comd. Rpt., 5 Dec 50, Box 1502; Eighth Army Comd. Rpt., 5 Dec 50, Box 1134; FEC DIS No. 3009, 5 Dec 50, covering events on 4 Dec, Box 99; 24th Div. Comd. Rpt., Narr., 5 Dec 50, Box 3522; *Antiaircraft Journal* 94, no. 1 (Jan-Feb 1951): 6, 24; Map of Pyongyang, reverse side of Map of Korea, Chinnampo Sheet, Aug 1952 ed., scale 1:25,000 (approx.).

9. Col. Emerson C. Ischner, "Engineers in Operation Bug-Out," *Military Engineer* 43, no. 294 (July-Aug 1951): 255ff. Most of the narrative covering Engineer demolitions in and near Pyongyang is based on this source, unless otherwise noted.

10. Ibid.

11. This picture was printed in many newspapers and magazines in the United States at the time. The picture was first published, I believe, in *Life* magazine, 18 Dec 50. *Newsweek* republished it as late as 11 Sept 72 to illustrate the desperation of the Korean people trying to flee south on 3-4 Dec 50.

12. *New York Herald Tribune*, 4 Dec 50, p. 1, col. 8, Homer Bigart dispatch from Pyongyang, 4 Dec 50; ibid., 5 Dec 50, p. 1, col. 6, Bigart dispatch from Pyongyang, 4 Dec 50. Bigart was generally considered one of the most enterprising and reliable war correspondents in Korea.

13. Capt. B. C. Mossman, "Problems in Railroad Operation," in Westover, *Combat Support in Korea*, pp. 62-65; Capt. Max N. Brown, "Railroading in Korea," in ibid., pp. 65-66. For more detailed information on the Mukden cable, Korea's key telephone and telegraph system, see ibid., pp. 94-97.

14. Col Thomas A. Pitcher, "Signal Operations in Korea," in Westover, *Combat Support in Korea*, p. 97.

15. 35th Inf. Regt. Comd. Rpt., Narr., 4 Dec 50, Box 3771; 24th Inf. Regt. Comd. Rpt., Narr., Box 3766.

16. Eighth Army Comd. Rpt., G-2 PIR No. 145, 4 Dec 50, Box 1135; and Eighth Army, G-3 Sec., Jnl. file, G-3 Air Rpt., 4-5 Dec 50, Box 1136; 5th RCT, 1st Cav. Div. Comd. Rpt., Narr., 4 Dec 50, Box 4430.

17. 24th Inf., S-3 Jnl., 4 Dec 50, Box 3766; Maj. Gen. Basil A. Coad, "The Land Campaign in Korea," *Journal of the Royal United Service Institution* 97, no. 585 (Feb 1952).

18. 2nd Inf. Div. Comd. Rpt., Narr., 2-7 Dec 50, pp. 3-4, Box 2436; Capt. Fred Myers, 2nd Div. historian, Diary, 2-7 Dec 50 (used by me at 2nd Inf. Div. CP in Korea, 14 Aug 51). Myers wrote the data in his diary for 2-7 Dec during the train trip from Pyongyang to Yongdong-po, as a member of the 2nd Div. Rear. Most of the details are from his diary.

19. *New York Times*, 2 Dec 50, p. 5, col. 2, UP dispatch from Pyongyang, 1 Dec 50.

20. Eighth Army Comd. Rpt., G-3 Sec., Jnl. file, and POR No. 436, 4 Dec 50, Box 1136.

21. Eighth Army Comd. Rpt., G-4 Sec., and G-3 Jnl. file, 4-6 Dec 50, Box 1138, and Eighth Army Comd. Rpt., G-3 and G-3 Jnl. file, with enclosed "Report of Liaison Visit to Turkish Brigade 5 Dec 50, to G-3 and Chief of Staff, Eighth Army," Box 1136. The liaison report copy I found in the Army official files in the National Archives was unsigned, but I believe it was written by Lt. Col. Frank to Col. John A. Dabney, G-3, Eighth Army.

22. Eighth Army Comd. Rpt., G-4 Sec., G-4 Jnl. file, entry No. 26, at 1700, 6 Dec 50; ibid., G-4 Jnl. file entry no. 10, 2155, 7 Dec 50, Box 1138.

23. "Division Supply Operations," in Westover, *Combat Support in Korea*, pp. 141-50.

24. 1st Lt. Francis G. Nordstrom, D Co., 89th Tank Bn., attached to 25th Div., interview with author, 31 Aug 51.
25. Eighth Army Comd. Rpt., G-3 Sec., G-3 Jnl. 5 Dec 50, Box 1136; 25th Div. Comd. Rpt., 24th Inf. S-3 Jnl. msg. from 3rd Bn., 8th Cav. Regt., 5 Dec 50, Box 3766.
26. Nordstrom, interview with author, 31 Aug 51.
27. Futrell, *U.S. Air Force in Korea*, p. 248.
28. Mossman and Middleton, "Logistical Problems and Their Solutions (EUSAK) June 1952," p. 93.
29. Capt. Edward C. Williamson, "Evacuation of the 44th Ordnance Company from Pyongyang 30 Nov–4 Dec 50," No. BA73 (Mimeographed MS, in Office Chief of Military History, DA). Williamson's MS is based on interviews with Capt. Robert M. Elser, exec. off., 44th Ord. Co., and with other officers and noncommissioned officers of the company in Oct 1951, in Korea.
30. Ibid.; Capt. Edward C. Williamson, interview with Capt. Gentle J. Banks, No. BA-69 (MS copy in Office Chief of Military History); "Attempted Tank Evacuation," in Westover, *Combat Support in Korea*, pp. 132–35.
31. Williamson, "Evacuation"; Capt. Elser and Sfc. John H. Wright, interviews with author, 5 Oct 51.
32. The account of the 57th Ord. Recovery Co. to evacuate 17 disabled tanks from Pyongyang is based on Capt. Edward C. Williamson, "Attempted Evacuation of Disabled Tanks by Rail by 57th Ordnance Recovery Company During the CCF Offensive 29 Nov–6 Dec 1950," No. BA-69 (Mimeographed copy MS, in Office Chief of Military History, DA). Williamson held extensive interviews on this subject with Lt. Col. Herbert W. Wurtzler, I Corps ord. off., 5 Sept 51; with Capt. Gentle J. Banks, 57th Ord. Recovery Co., 4 and 6 Sept 51; and with 1st Lt. LeRoy Ingram, 4 Sept 51, and several noncommissioned officers of the 57th Ord. Recovery Co., including M. Sgt. William T. Wilson, Sgt. Richard L. White, and Cpl. Earl M. Friday. A partial account of this episode is given in "Attempted Tank Evacuation," in Westover, *Combat Support in Korea*, pp. 132–35. It differs in some details from that given in the narrative. I have followed Williamson's MS wherever there are discrepancies.
33. Eighth Army Comd. Rpt., Narr. 45, 3–4 Dec 50, and G-4 Logistics Narr., 4–5 Dec 50, Box 1134; Map of Pyongyang and vicinity, 1952 Chinnampo Sheet, scale 1:25,000. This map shows the two principal airfields at the northeast edge of Pyongyang and east of the Taedong River.
34. "Msg. NR: C-50371, 4 Dec 50, From CINCFE (signed Collins) Tokyo, Japan: to DEPTAR for JCS for Haislip," in *Pertinent Papers on the Korean Situation*, II, 373; Eighth Army Comd. Rpt., 5 Dec 50, reporting on Gen. Collins's meeting with Walker on 4 Dec 50, Box 1134; Schnabel, *Policy and Direction*, pp. 282–83. Maj. Gen. Doyle Hickey, MacArthur's acting chief of staff, FEC, had given Gen. Collins on 4 Dec 50 a memorandum outlining Gen. MacArthur's view that Pyongyang could not be held and that Eighth Army would have to fall back to Seoul-Inchon (copy in Ridgway Papers, USMHRC).
35. Gen. Collins reported to the JCS on his Korean visit in a memorandum for the Joint Chiefs of Staff, 8 Dec. 50. See Schnabel, *Policy and Direction*, pp. 283–84.
36. I Corps Comd. Rpt., Engineering Sec., 4–5 Dec 50, Box 1503; Marquat, "Automatic Artillery in Korea," p. 6.
37. Eighth Army Comd. Rpt., G-3 Jnl. file, 5 Dec 50, Box 1136.
38. Eighth Army Comd. Rpt., Narr. 5 Dec 50, Box 1134; Eleventh Report of the United States Command in Korea to the Security Council, United Nations, 31 Jan 51, Dept. of State Publication 4108, p. 4.
39. Eighth Army Comd. Rpt., Narr., 5 Dec 50, Box 1134; Field, *Naval Operations*, pp. 271–74. Most of the account of the evacuation of Chinnampo is based on Field.
40. Lt. Col. Ralph L. Foster, letter to author, 11 May 54.

41. Appleman, *South to the Naktong, North to the Yalu,* pp. 649–53; Cpl. Randle M. Hurst, "The History of the 502nd Reconnaissance Platoon in Japan and Korea, 1950," 99 pp. (Typescript MS, Aug 1977, copy in author's possession; hereafter cited as Hurst, MS). Hurst, a guard at Gen. Walker's CP in Pyongyang and often posted inside or outside Gen. Walker's office, said Stalin's picture was still in the room when he left the building on the morning of 4 Dec 50. There is a picture of the North Korean capitol building on p. 651 in *South to the Naktong, North to the Yalu,* and on p. 653 is a picture of Kim Il Sung's room (and Gen. Walker's office while his CP was at Pyongyang) with Stalin's photograph on the wall.

42. Hurst, MS. Hurst has a schematic drawing of the second floor of the North Korean capitol building and Walker's CP office in Pyongyang, in binder 1, p. 57. I learned in 1977 in correspondence with Hurst that he had been a member of Gen. Walker's personal guard detail in Korea and knew the details of the general's death. I urged Hurst, then long a civilian living in Fresno, California, to write all he could remember of his experiences in Korea. Blessed with a retentive memory and using a series of letters to relatives he had written from Korea, often on the same day as some important event, Hurst produced a fascinating and extremely readable account of experiences in Korea that differs widely from those of the ordinary soldier. It becomes clear in Hurst's often modest and deprecatory narrative that he was an extremely good soldier and an expert with the weapons he might be called on to use: the M-3 submachine gun, the M-1 rifle, the BAR, the .45-caliber pistol, and the .30- and .50-caliber machine guns. In addition to his 99-page typescript MS covering the period up to the end of 1950, there are a number of letters written to me that supplement his MS on such matters as Gen. Walker's death, the general's habits of command, and the nature of guard duty at Eighth Army Headquarters at Taegu, Seoul, and Pyongyang. Hurst subsequently wrote another 100-page MS covering the period of Gen. Ridgway's command and part of Gen. Van Fleet's in 1951. I have these manuscripts in my possession.

43. Hurst, MS, binder 1, pp. 66–67. Hurst is confused in his MS as to dates in early December. But tying in his sequence of events with the big explosions he heard about midnight or later the last night he was in the North Korean capitol building, and associating these explosions with the burning and destruction of the British ASP 16 near the K-23 airfield on the night of 3-4 Dec, I place the date of Hurst being relieved of guard duty at Gen. Walker's residence in Pyongyang as about noon on 3 Dec. I have edited the excerpt from Hurst's MS only to reflect what I believe are the correct dates. Hurst's 30 Nov becomes 3 Dec, and 1 Dec becomes 4 Dec. One of Hurst's letters to his family confirms the dates I have used in the narrative (letter to his "Aunt Nettie," 11 Dec. 50; see n. 44).

44. Hurst, MS, binder 1, pp. 68–75. Hurst wrote a letter on 11 Dec 50 from Seoul to his "Aunt Nettie," in Pasadena, California, in which he said, "We got into Pyongyang on the 12th of November. Left there about the 4th or 5th of this month." He was correct in that letter in that he did leave Pyongyang on the fourth.

45. Eighth Army Comd. Rpt. G-2 PIR No. 146, citing Air Observer Rpts., 5 Dec 50, Box 1135; FEC DIS No. 3011, 6–7 Dec 50, covering 4 Dec, Box 99; I Corps Comd. Rpt., 5 Dec 50, Box 1502; Eighth Army Comd. Rpt., Narr., 5 Dec 50, Box 1134.

46. Eighth Army Comd. Rpt., G-2 PIR No. 146, 6 Dec 50, Box 1135.

47. Eighth Army Comd. Rpt., G-3 Jnl. file, 5 Dec 50, Box 1136.

Chapter 17

1. JANIS, *Study of Korea;* Brief, Apr 1945.
2. Based on my study of maps of Korea.

3. Lt. Gen. William J. McCaffrey, USA, Ret., letter to author, n.d., but received Jan 1977.
4. FEC, "RR and Hwy Transport in NK and Their Impact on Enemy Logistics," Intelligence Digest, Vol. 1, no. 13, 16–30 June 1953, pp. 25–45.
5. Ibid.
6. *New York Herald Tribune*, 6 Dec 50 (Homer Bigart dispatch filed at Seoul, 5 Dec 50), p. 1, col. 7.
7. Dean Acheson, letter to the Hon. Harry S Truman, 25 July 55, in Acheson, *Among Friends: Personal Letters of Dean Acheson*, ed. David S. McLallan and David C. Acheson (New York: Dodd Mead, 1980), pp. 99–107. For the decision of 29 Sept 50, see p. 102.
8. Ibid., p. 103.
9. "JCS to CINCUNC, Tokyo, NR JCS 97772," *Pertinent Papers on the Korean Situation*, II, 356.
10. Schnabel, *Policy and Direction*, pp. 279–82, gives the substance of the messages exchanged between Tokyo and Washington on holding at the waist of Korea.
11. Eighth Army WD, Summ., Sec. 1, 22–24 Nov 50, Box 1122; FEC DIS No. 2999, 25 Nov (covering 23 Nov 50), and No. 3000 (covering 24 Nov 50), Box 99.
12. Eighth Army WD, Summ., Sec. 1, 25 Nov 50, Box 1122.
13. Eighth Army WD, Sec. 2, G-3 Sec., 26 Nov 50, Box 1131; FEC DIS No. 3001, 27 Nov 50 (covering 26 Nov), Box 99. This latter source included a map entitled, "Guerrilla Activities, Chongpong-ni–Kapyong–Chonchon–Chorwon–Yonchon Quadrangle."
14. Eighth Army WD, Sec. 2, G-3 Staff Section, 29 Nov 50, and G-2 PIR No. 140, with attached memo, "Current Guerrilla Activities," 29 Nov 50, Boxes 1131 and 1132.
15. 187th Airborne RCT WD, 1–30 Nov 50, Summ. for 30 Nov 50; IX Corps WD, PIR No. 65, 30 Nov 50, Box 1767; Eighth Army Comd. Rpt., G-2 Sec., Dec 1950, Box 1135.
16. Eighth Army Comd. Rpt., Narr., 1 Dec 50, p. 19, and Plate 9 following, Box 1134; IX Corps WD, 1 Dec 50, PIR No. 66, and Annex 1 on Chorwon guerrillas, Box 1767.
17. FEC DIS No. 3015, 11 Dec 50, Box 99; 5th RCT WD, Unit Rpt., 10 Dec. 50, Box 4691. On 7 Dec the FEC estimated there were 23,000 guerrillas in the UN rear area; on 11 Dec it estimated the number at 40,000.
18. 5th RCT Comd. Rpt., and Unit Rpt., 13–14 Dec 50, Box 4691; Eighth Army HQ Gen. Orders No. 132, 11 Mar 51, awarding the Distinguished Service Cross, Posthumously, to Sgt. 1st Class Neal M. Morris, A Btry., 26th AAA Bn., 24th Inf. Div.
19. 2nd Div. Comd. Rpt., G-2 Sec. and Annex 1 to G-2 PIR No. 155, and POR No. 369, 11 Dec 50, Box 2439.
20. FEC, *History of the North Korean Army*, pp. 58–59, 31 June 52, Box 707.
21. Eighth Army, G-4 Sec., Vol. 4, Comd. Rpt., June 1951, Lt. Col. Charles I. Davies, exec. off., G-4 Sec., "Notes on Anniversary of the Korean Conflict," looks back at the events of Nov and Dec 1950 in the light of a calmer period (Box 1210).
22. Eighth Army WD, 14 Nov 50, G-2 Sec., PW Inter's ADVATIS, FWD Rpt. No. 0213, 14 Nov 50 (Liu Piao Wu, captured 9 Nov near Kaechon).
23. FEC, Weekly Intelligence Rpt., No. 96, 22 Dec 50, p. 22.

Chapter 18

1. Eighth Army Comd. Rpt., G-2 PIR No. 159, and G-2 Sec., Narr. Rpt., 9–13, 18 Dec 50, Box 1135; FEC DIS No. 3012, 7–8 Dec 50, Box 99.
2. I Corps Comd. Rpt., 6–7 Dec 50, Box 1505; ibid., Narr., 6 Dec 50, Box 1502; Eighth Army Comd. Rpt., G-2 PIRs No. 146, 147, 5–6 Dec 50, Box 1135.

3. I Corps Comd. Rpt., 9 Dec 50; FEC DIS No. 3013, 9 Dec 50, Box 99; *New York Herald Tribune,* 7 Dec 50, p. 13, col. 1, AP dispatch filed northwest front, Korea, 6 Dec. 50.
4. *New York Times,* 6 Dec 50, p. 4, col. 3.
5. I Corps Comd. Rpt., 9–19 Dec 50; Eighth Army Comd. Rpt., G-4 Sec. and Jnl. file, 8–10 Dec 50, Box 1138.
6. 1st Cav. Div. Comd. Rpt., Narr., 11–16 Dec 50, Box 4419; 5th Cav. Regt., Narr. Rpt., 11–14 Dec 50, Box 4430; 24th Div. Comd. Rpt., 8–13 Dec 50, Box 3522; Eighth Army Comd. Rpt., Narr., 13 Dec 50, Box 1134.
7. Eighth Army Comd. Rpt., Narr., 3–11 Dec 50, pp. 8–11, Box 1134.
8. Eighth Army Comd. Rpt., Narr., 11 Dec 50, Box 1134; *New York Herald Tribune,* 12 Dec 50, p. 1, col. 8, and p. 2, col. 5, gives the text of MacArthur's statement.
9. Eighth Army Comd. Rpt., G-3 Sec., G-3 Jnl. file, 15 Dec 50, Box 1136.
10. 25th Div. Comd. Rpt., G-3 Jnl. file, and CG and Chief of Staff Sec. Rpt., 13, 16, and 19 Dec 50, Box 3766; Eighth Army Comd. Rpt., G-3 Sec., Jnl. file, 13 Dec 50, Box 1136.
11. 25th Div. Comd. Rpt., 13–14 Dec 50, Box 3766; 19th Inf., 25th Div., Comd. Rpt., 13 Dec 50, Box 3523; I Corps Comd. Rpt., Narr., 18 Dec 50, Box 1502; Eighth Army Comd. Rpt., G-3 Sec., Jnl. file, 15, 17 Dec 50, Box 1136.
12. Eighth Army Comd. Rpt., Narr., 20–22 Dec 50, pp. 74–75, Box 1134; 24th Div. Comd. Rpt., Narr., 15–21 Dec 50, Box 3522; 21st Inf. Comd. Rpt., Narr., 20 Dec 50, Box 3523; I Corps Comd. Rpt., Narr., 18–19 Dec 50, Box 1502.
13. Field, *Naval Operations,* pp. 307–309.
14. Gen. Leven C. Allen, interview with author, 15 Dec 53.
15. Col. Pascal Strong, Eighth Army Engineer, interview with author, 17 Sept 51. Lt. Col. Wilder, assistant chief engineer, Eighth Army, participated in this interview at Taegu, Korea. When I asked Gen. Ridgway later if he knew of the prevailing army demolition policy at the time he took command, he replied that he did not.
16. There is little in the records about opposition within Eighth Army to Gen. Walker's demolition policy in the withdrawal from North Korea in late 1950 and its continuation for a period in early 1951. One has to learn from interviews with responsible officers present at the time that the policy was in force. The comments in the narrative are specific to officers named below, in addition to the interview, cited above, with Col. Strong and Lt. Col. Wilder. The officers interviewed by me were: Col. Harold K. Johnson, 4 Jan 52; Brig. Gen. James Brittingham, 29 July 51; Capt. Bodkin, Aug 1951. Many other officers whom I talked with in Korea in 1951, and later in the United States, voiced similar opinions. Most felt that the wholesale destruction was being carried out because the Army was on its way out of Korea.
17. Futrell, *US Air Force in Korea,* pp. 230–35; *New York Times,* 18 Dec 50, p. 1, col. 6.
18. Futrell, *US Air Force in Korea,* pp. 235–36.
19. *New York Times,* 8 May 51, sec. C, p. 16, col. 5; 9 May 51, p. 21, col. 3; and 12 May 51, p. 6, col. 5. In the MacArthur Hearings, Gen. Marshall testified that the State Department on 13 Dec 50 presented the matter to the UN Allies who had troops in Korea. It is clear, therefore, that UN allies effectively vetoed the hot pursuit desired by the United States.
20. Futrell, *US Air Force in Korea,* p. 244.
21. Gen. Marshall, testimony in MacArthur Hearings before the Senate Committee on Armed Services and the Committee on Foreign Relations, 7 May 51, as reported in the *New York Times,* 8 May 51, p. 18, cols. 6–7; Futrell, *US Air Force in Korea,* p. 245.
22. Futrell, *US Air Force in Korea,* pp. 149–50.
23. Ibid., p. 243. In his book Futrell frequently refers to Lin Piao, commander of

the CCF Fourth Field Army, as if he were in command of the CCF forces in front of Eighth Army in Korea. His book was published in 1961, yet he and its editors, like Eighth Army and American and UN intelligence during the war, seem not to have known that Lin Piao was not in Korea in charge of any troops during the Korean War.

24. FEC DIS No. 3191, 7 June 51, OB-4, Box 469.
25. ATIS Research Supplement, Interrogation Rpts. No. 99, 49.
26. FEC DIS No. 3012, 7-8 Dec 50, 1-f, Box 99; HQ FEC, *History of the North Korean Army*, July 1952, p. 84.
27. ATIS Interrogation Rpts. (Enemy Forces), Issue 23, No. 2768, p. 95, interrogation of 2nd Lt. Lee Son Kuk, NK 4th Div. HQ; FEC DIS No. 3014, 9 Dec 50, 1-e, Box 99; Eighth Army Comd. Rpt., Narr., 9-10 Dec 50, pp. 56-58, Box 1134.
28. FEC DIS No. 3024, 20 Dec 50, 3-3a, Box 99.
29. *New York Herald Tribune*, 13 Dec 50, p. 3, col. 3.
30. FEC DIS No. 3016, 12 Dec 50, 1-g, Box 99; ATIS Interrogation Rpts. (Enemy Forces), Issue 22, No. 2744, p. 140, interrogation of Jr. Lt. Cho Yang Su, and Issue 2775, p. 124, interrogation of Cpl. Kang Cho Hyun, both captured 13 Dec 50.
31. Eighth Army Comd. Rpt., Narr., 13-14 Dec 50, pp. 63-64, Box 1134.
32. 2nd Inf. Div. Comd. Rpt., Narr. Summ., 14-15 Dec 50, p. 7.
33. 2nd Inf. Div. Comd. Rpt., G-2 Sec., Jnl. Summ., 16 Dec for 14-19 Dec 50.
34. Eighth Army Comd. Rpt., Narr., 17 Dec 50, Box 1134; FEC DIS No. 3022, 18 Dec 50, Box 99.
35. FEC DIS Nos. 3025 and 3026, 21, 23 Dec 50, Box 99.
36. Eighth Army Comd. Rpt., Narr., 21 Dec 50, Box 1134, and Eighth Army Comd. Rpt., G-3 Sec., 21-23 Dec 50, Box 1136; FEC DIS No. 3026 and No. 3027, 22-23 Dec 50, Box 99.
37. Maj. Eldon B. Anderson, KMAG, 10 Nov 50-14 Dec 51, Arty. Advisor to ROK 9th Div., Artillery School, Debriefing Rpt. No. 76, Fort Sill, Okla., 6 Mar 52, p. 3.
38. Gen. Collins's Memorandum for the Joint Chiefs of Staff, 8 Dec 50, in Ridgway Papers (USMHRC); Eighth Army Comd. Rpt., Narr., Dec 1950, pp. 12-13, 60-61, Box 1134.
39. Eighth Army Comd. Rpt., Narr., 18-19 Dec 50, Box 1134; ibid., 14-20 Dec 50, Box 1136; X Corps Comd. Rpt., 11 Dec 50, Opn. Order No. 10, Task Organization, Annex A.
40. Eighth Army Comd. Rpt., Narr., Dec 1950.
41. 2nd Logistical Comd. Rpt., Dec 1950, p. 9, 18 Dec 50, US Department of State, 11th Rpt. to the Security Council, 31 Jan 51, p. 3; "Tropiques: Revue des Troupes Coloniaux," No. 345 (Paris: Les Ministères de la Defense Nationale et des Colonies, Aug-Sept 1952); Bartlett, *With the Australians in Korea*, p. 69; Lt. Col. Herbert Fairlee Wood, *Strange Battleground: Official History of the Canadian Army in Korea* (Ottawa: Ministry of National Defense, Roger Duhamel [Queen's Printer], 1966), p. 49. The 16th Field Regt., New Zealand Artillery, arrived at Pusan on the last day of Dec 1950 but is not included in the narrative discussion.
42. Eighth Army Comd. Rpt., Narr., Dec 1950, p. 58; 2nd Inf. Div. Comd. Rpt., Narr. Summ., Dec 1950, p. 6 and Appendix D-2, and POR 112400, Dec 1950; 23rd Inf. Comd. Rpt., 15 Dec 50, Box 2473; 38th Inf. Comd. Rpt., Narr., 13 Dec 50, Box 2474.
43. 2nd Inf. Div. Comd. Rpt., Narr. Summ., 7-8 Dec 50, and Chief of Staff Jnl., 7 Dec 50, Box 2436; ibid., POR No. 360, Appendix D-2, 8 Dec 50, p. 5 of Narr. Summ., Capt. Fred Myers, 2nd Inf. Div. historian, interview with author, 14 Aug. 51.
44. Maj. James A. Huston, "Time and Space" (MS, Office Chief of Military History, Washington, D.C.), pt. 4, pp. 162-65; Schnabel, *Policy and Direction*, p. 297. List of items

is selective and only partial. The two authorities cited differ on some details; Huston is more detailed, and I have followed him where there are discrepancies.

45. Eighth Army Comd. Rpt., G-3 Sec. Jnl., 12 Dec 50, including report of Liaison Visit to 2nd Div., Box 1136; 2nd Div., 9th Inf. Comd. Rpt., 3–14 Dec 50, Box 2471; 2nd Div., 23rd Inf. Comd. Rpt., Narr., 7 Dec 50, Box 2473; 25th Div. Comd. Rpt., 9 Dec 50, Box 3766.

46. Eighth Army Comd. Rpt., Narr. Summ., 6–9 Dec, and 2nd Inf. Div. Comd. Rpt., Narr., 13–23 Dec 50, Box 2436; ibid., 38th Inf. Comd. Rpt., Narr., 22–23 Dec 50, Box 2474; ibid., 9th Inf. Comd. Rpt. Narr., 22–24 Dec 50, Box 2471; 23rd Inf. Comd. Rpt., Narr., 22–23 Dec 50, Box 2473.

47. 2nd Inf. Div. Comd. Rpt., G-3 Sec., Dec 1950, Box 2436; ibid., G-4 Staff Sec. Rpt., Dec 1950.

48. Lt. Gen. Edward M. Almond, interview with author, 28 Apr 77.

49. Eighth Army Comd. Rpt., Narr., 16–20 Dec 50, Box 1134; Schnabel, *Policy and Direction*, pp. 300–301; Maj. Gen. David G. Barr, CG, 7th Inf. Div., interview with author, 1 Feb 54.

50. Eighth Army Comd. Rpt., Narr., 18 Dec 50, Box 1134; ibid., Eighth Army Logistics Narr., 5–20 Dec 50, pp. 98–99, Box 1134; Field, *Naval Operations*, p. 298; I Corps, Comd. Rpt., G-4 Sec., June 1951, map showing Korean War zone, Anju-Yongdong-po area of I Corps, ports and railroad net supporting I Corps to 22 June 51, giving dates of opening and closing ASPs, Box 1542.

51. 24th Inf. Div. Comd. Rpt., Nar., 13–22 Dec 50, Box 3522.

52. Eighth Army Comd. Rpt., Narr., 10 Dec 50, Box 1134.

53. Eighth Army Comd. Rpt., Narr., 10 Dec 50, and Eighth Army Opn. Plan 12, map of defensive lines, and order to 2nd Logistical Comd., 11 Dec 50, Box 1134; ibid., G-3 Sec. and G-3 Jnl. files, 11 Dec 50, with enclosures, including map of four defensive lines, Box 1136; Maj. Gen. Garrison H. Davidson, interview with author, 28 Jan 54. I saw work in progress on the Davidson Line in July 1951.

54. 2nd Logistical Comd., Comd. Rpt., Dec 1950, p. 3.

55. Eighth Army Comd. Rpt., G-3 Sec., Situation Maps, 20–31 Dec 50, Box 1134; ibid., G-3 Sec., 20 Dec 50, Box 1136; *Operations in Korea (25 June 1950 to 1 April 1951)* (West Point, N.Y.: Dept. of Military Art and Engineering, US Military Academy, 1951), Maps 9 and 10; Map of Korea, 1950, scale 1:250,000.

56. 35th Inf. Regt. Comd. Rpt., 25th Div., Narr., 14–22 Dec 50, Box 3771; I Corps Comd. Rpt., Dec 1950, p. 36.

57. Eighth Army Comd. Rpt., G-2 Sec., 17–22 Dec 50, Box 1135.

58. 2nd Inf. Div. Comd. Rpt., G-2 Jnl., 14 Dec 50; FEC DIS No. 3019, 14 Dec 50, and No. 3024, 19 Dec 50, G-2 conclusions, Box 99.

59. Futrell, *US Air Force in Korea*, p. 252.

60. FEC DIS No. 3028, 24 Dec 50, Box 99; I Corps Comd. Rpt., Narr., 19–23 Dec 50, Box 1502.

61. Eighth Army Comd. Rpt., G-2 Sec., PIRs No. 165, Enclosure No. 2, 24 Dec 50, and No. 170, Enclosure No. 2, 29 Dec 50, Box 1135.

62. Maj. Gen. Edwin K. Wright (FEC G-3 during Korean War), interview with author, 7 Jan 54.

63. 25th Inf. Div. Comd. Rpt., G-4 Sec., G-4 Daily Act. Rpt., 6 Dec 50, Box 3766. Lt. Gen. William J. McCaffrey, USA, Ret., told me that while he was deputy chief of staff, X Corps, and CO of the 31st Inf. Regt., 7th Inf. Div., on the central front of Korea in early 1951, "Wrong-way Ridgway" was a phrase often heard.

64. Lt. Gen. W. B. Palmer, "Commanders Must Know Logistics," *Army Information Digest*, Apr 1953, p. 11.

65. I Corps Comd. Rpt., Engr. Sec., 15 Dec 50, Box 1503.

66. 1st Lt. Robert J. Teitelbaum, in Debriefing Rpt., No. 47, 14 Dec 51, and Capt. Paul R. Kaster, Debriefing Rpt., No. 33, 1 Nov 51, Dept. of Training Publications and Aids, Artillery School, Fort Sill, Okla.

67. Maj. Harry E. Apgar, Jr., Asst. G-1, 25th Inf. Div., interview with author, 4 Sept 51; Maj. Joe B. Lamb, CO 2nd Bn., 35th Inf., 25th Div., and Lts. Snell and Hoyt of 2nd Bn., 35th Inf., interviews with author, 4 Aug 51; Col. Robert G. Ferguson, Eighth Army G-2, Combat Intelligence, interview with author, 7 Oct 53; Mossman and Middleton, "Logistical Problems and Their Solutions," p. 91; Col. Robert Halleck, CO 24th Div. Arty., interview with author, 7 Aug 51.

68. *New York Herald Tribune*, 3 Dec 50, p. 10, col. 1, AP dispatch, 2 Dec 50, US Eighth Army HQ.

69. Coad, "Land Campaign in Korea," p. 9. Gen. Coad had led the 27th British Brigade in Dec 1950 in Korea. His remark about the withdrawal is rather smug, since the brigade had not been engaged in any heavy combat in the CCF 2nd Phase Offensive; nevertheless, there is truth in the remark about Eighth Army being overly intimidated about the danger of being cut off by the G-2 red-marked maps showing enemy forces.

70. Barclay, *The First Commonwealth Division in Korea*, p. 48. Cyril Falls, the English military historian, discusses the Eighth Army retreat in "Theory and Practice in Korea," *Illustrated London News*, 27 Jan 51.

71. Col. David M. Butler, DSO, letter to author, 5 Sept 72. Butler was an officer in the Australian Battalion in Korea in 1950.

72. Gen. Milburn, Col. Harold K. Johnson, Col. Charles B. Smith, and Col. Henry G. Fisher, interviews with author. In Korea in 1951 I heard countless uses of the term "bugout" among all ranks in Eighth Army.

73. Col. Emerson C. Itschner, I Corps Engr. officer, "Engineers in Operation Bug-Out," *Military Engineer* 43, no. 294 (July-Aug 1951): 255.

74. Schnabel, *Policy and Direction*, p. 94; Gen. Matthew B. Ridgway, letter to author and review comments on "Disaster in Korea" MS, 10 Mar 80.

75. Schnabel, *Policy and Direction*, pp. 295-96.

76. Adm. Sherman died on 22 July 51 and was replaced by Adm. William M. Fechteler as chief of naval operations and member of the Joint Chiefs of Staff.

77. MacArthur Hearings, I, 341-42.

78. "NR: CX-50635, 7 Dec 1950," in *Pertinent Papers on Korean Situation*, II, 376.

79. MacArthur, *Reminiscences*, pp. 369-70. If I had known of this alleged incident at the time I interviewed Gen. Hickey in Tokyo on two occasions in 1951 in the Dai-Ichi Building, I would have sought to obtain his recollections of the event.

80. Andrew Boyle, *The Fourth Man: The Definitive Account of Kim Philby, Guy Burgess, and Donald MacLean and Who Recruited Them to Spy for Russia* (New York: Dial Press, 1979), p. 359. This book was first published in England in 1979 under the title, *The Climate of Treason: Five Who Spied for Russia*. MacLean's Soviet control official to whom he reported while he was in the United States and to whom he delivered his espionage material was a member of the Soviet consular office in New York City. The "Fourth Man" was Sir Anthony Blunt, for many years Surveyor of the Queen's Pictures. Although Blunt confessed his part in the espionage ring to Britain's M15 counterespionage service in 1964, it was not generally known to the public until Queen Elizabeth stripped him of his knighthood on 15 Nov 79, after Prime Minister Margaret Thatcher told the British Parliament that Blunt had been a Soviet spy. Blunt told M15 that he had been recruited at Cambridge University by Guy Burgess for the espionage work.

Burgess died in Moscow in 1963. His cremated remains were sent to England and buried near his father's grave in Hampshire. Donald MacLean died 11 Mar 83 in a Moscow hospital (or, as some reported, alone in his apartment), reportedly of cancer. (See *Time* magazine, 21 Mar 83, p. 69, and other periodicals and newspapers of the time for notices and comments on his death.) Anthony Blunt, age 75, died in London on 26 Mar 83. (See *Newsweek,* 7 Apr 80 and US press coverage on 26 Mar 83 for comments on Blunt in his last years.) Harold ("Kim") Philby died in Moscow on 12 May 88. A strange angle of the British espionage ring became known in 1983 when a prominent American, Michael Whitney Straight, published a book entitled, *After a Long Silence,* in which he confessed that he had been a member of the British espionage ring, telling how Blunt had recruited him in 1935 in Cambridge University in England. Blunt ordered Straight to return to the United States in 1937 and work as a Soviet "mole." Straight went to the FBI in 1963, the year Philby fled to Moscow from Beirut, and told his story. Richard Grenier's review of Straight's book for the *Wall Street Journal,* 24 Mar 83, considers the British spies and Straight's espionage work in relation to the Korean War and MacArthur's charges. See also *Time* magazine, 21 Mar 83, pp. 79, 81.

81. Schnabel, *Policy and Direction,* pp. 299–300; *New York Times,* 16 Dec 50, p. 1, col. 8, and 17 Dec 50, p. 1, col. 8

Chapter 19

1. Maj. Gen. John B. Coulter (CG of HQ at Uijongbu and of IX Corps at the time of the accident), interview with author, 3 Apr 53; Bartlett, *With the Australians in Korea,* p. 58; Barclay, *The First Commonwealth Division in Korea,* pp. 39–40; Eighth Army Comd. Rpt., Narr., Dec 1950, Box 1134.

2. Coulter, interview with author, 3 Apr 53.

3. Hurst, MS, binder 1, pp. 25–37. Hurst often rode behind the .50-caliber machine gun in Jeep No. 2. He was expert with the machine gun and also with the M-1 rifle.

4. Randle M. Hurst, letters to author, 17 May and 13 June 77; Hurst, letter to Mr. and Mrs. Irvin Hurst, 25 Dec 50; Hurst, MS, binder 1, pp. 84–85. Maj. Gen. Edward M. Almond came to Seoul on 27 Dec 50 to meet Gen. Ridgway and later flew to Eighth Army Main HQ at Taegu, where he had dinner at the commander's mess with Maj. Gen. Leven Allen, Col. Landrum, and others. In his diary entries for the day he wrote, "Col. Landrum stated that he felt Gen. Walker's death was primarily the result of reckless driving with excessive speed on the part of the vehicle. He said that General Walker's jeep was struck by a 3/4 ton truck travelling in the opposite direction which caught the rear of his vehicle and caused it to roll over twice . . ." (Almond Diary, 27 Dec 50, entry at 8:30 P.M.). In his letter to his parents on 25 Dec 50, Hurst wrote that Cpl. Reenan suffered a broken leg, the most minor injury sustained among the four men in the lead jeep.

5. Gen. Chang Chang Kuk, interview with author, in the Korean Embassy, Washington, D.C., 14 Oct. 53. Gen. Chang was then a member of the embassy staff. Gen. Chang drew a sketch of the road at the scene and the relative travel courses of the two cars involved in the accident. I had heard stories from American sources that the ROK Army executed the driver of the jeep. I asked General Chang if this was true. Gen. Chang replied, "No, but the driver was punished." I asked him the nature of the punishment, but he would not comment further.

6. Hurst, letter to Mr. and Mrs. Irvin Hurst, 25 Dec 50. Hurst said that he thought this letter was published in the *Oklahoman and Times* in Jan 1951. A Christmas card from Hurst to me, 19 Dec 78, comments further on this event, in which he praised the performance of the South Korean band.

7. Letter from Asst. Secy. to Gen. Staff to Gen. Hickey FEC, 28 Jan 51, Box 16, in Ridgway Papers (USMHRC); *Hearings, Subcommittee to Investigate Administration of the Internal Security Act and Other Internal Security Laws of the Committee on the Judiciary, United States Senate,* 83rd Cong., 2nd sess., Testimony, 29 Sept 54, p. 2026.

8. Eighth Army Comd. Rpt., Narr., 23 Dec 50, Box 1134, nd G-3 Sec., 23 Dec 50, Box 1136; 24th Div., Comd. Rpt. Narr., Box 3766.

9. FEC DIS No. 3031, 27 Dec 50, Box 99, covering situation of 24 Dec 50 in Korea; Eighth Army Comd. Rpt., G-3 Sec., 24 Dec 50, Box 1136; I Corps Comd. Rpt., 24 Dec 50, 1502; IX Corps Comd. Rpt., Narr. 24 Dec 50, Box 1772.

10. FEC DIS No. 3029, 25 Dec 50, Box 99; Eighth Army Comd. Rpt. Summ., 24–25 Dec 50, Box 1134.

11. FEC DIS No. 3029, 25 Dec 50, Box 99; Eighth Army Comd. Rpt., Summ., 25 Dec 50, Box 1134.

12. 2nd Inf. Div. Comd. Rpt., Narr. Summ., Dec 1950, pp. 10–11, and Appendix D-1f, J-5, G-3 Jnl., 23–25 Dec 50.

13. FEC DIS No. 3030, 26 Dec 50 (covering 25 Dec), Box 99.

14. FEC DIS No. 3031, 27 Dec 50, pp. 3–8, Box 99.

Bibliographical Note

Only two or three published works, listed here, relate closely to the subject of this volume. The most important is perhaps S. L. A. Marshall, *The River and the Gauntlet: Defeat of the Eighth Army by the Chinese Communist Forces, November 1950, in the Battle of the Chongchon River* (New York: William Morrow, 1953). It is a work of uneven proportions, a disconnected series of narratives about small-unit actions of the US 25th and 2nd infantry divisions in the late November 1950 battles between Chinese and American forces along the Chongchon River. Colonel Marshall went to Korea in December 1950 as an analyst for an organization that had a contract with the US Army to study and report on its actions. In this capacity he extensively interviewed platoons and companies of the two infantry divisions on a selective basis to cover many of their more significant actions. In these interviews he obtained detailed accounts of many of the actions. His book is in no sense a connected narrative of the Eighth Army's conduct of the campaign, and it must be used with discretion. If used in that manner, it can supply detail about certain aspects of the operations that are nowhere else available. The book does have occasional errors, a few of them major. One such error is his statement that General Keiser, commander of the 2nd Infantry Division, gave Colonel Freeman of the 23rd Infantry Regiment the authority to leave his station as rear guard of the withdrawing division at Kunu-ri and take the Anju road out of the battle area. General Keiser did not give Freeman that authority; it was given by the assistant division commander, Maj. Gen. Joseph S. Bradley, as the latter has stated in a letter to me that described the event. This authorization to Colonel Freeman was a very controversial action. I have used Marshall's book extensively for certain details of action, but always with discretion and in comparison with the other information in official records, from interviews, and from correspondence with participants.

A second book that relates to the action is Capt. Russell A. Gugeler's *Combat Actions in Korea: Infantry, Artillery, and Armor* (Washington, D.C.: Combat Forces Press, Association of the US Army, 1954). This book discusses a series of small-unit actions. The information is all based on interviews conducted in 1951 and later by Captain Gugeler and the nine officers who were members of historical detachments attached to the major commands in the US Army in Korea. A few of the accounts relate to the series of actions along the Chongchon River in November 1950. This is a generally reliable work, although some of its accounts are incomplete.

Eric Linklater, an Englishman, published *Our Men in Korea* (London: Her Majesty's Stationery Office, 1952), a small book that recounts the highlights of the British 27th Brigade, which was sent to Korea in 1950 as a United Nations force. Under the command of Brig. Basil Coad, it consisted of the 1st Battalion of the Middlesex Regiment and the 1st Battalion of the Argyll and Sutherland Highlanders Regiment. The 45th Field Artillery Regiment, Royal Artillery, was also a part of the brigade. A battalion of Australian volunteers was added to the brigade during the autumn of 1950. These UN troops saw limited action in the battles along the Chongchon and the subsequent retreat.

The only other publication used extensively in the writing of this volume was an article entitled "The Lost Corps," by Lt. Col. Robert E. Cameron, in *Military Review* 33, no. 2, (May 1953). Colonel Cameron had been senior advisor to the ROK 10th Regiment, ROK 8th Division, in November 1950 and was subsequently advisor to the ROK 8th Division, ROK II Corps. He was present in the Tokchon area with the ROK 10th Regiment when the Chinese attacked and almost immediately overran the ROK II Corps on the right flank of Eighth Army in the battles of the Chongchon, leaving the army line exposed in the center. Cameron's article is invaluable in reconstructing what happened in this disaster at the very beginning of the Chinese counterattack against Eighth Army. I have based my account of the destruction of the ROK II Corps on it. There is no other comparable source.

Other than these four publications, the sources used are the war diaries, command reports, and the special action reports of the units of Eighth Army, supplemented by numerous interviews and much correspondence with survivors. The narrative is thoroughly documented with notes.

All units of battalion strength or higher were required to prepare and submit for the adjutant general's records monthly reports of their activities. Independent units of battalion strength also submitted such reports. Sometimes units also prepared special action reports. The accumulated reports of companies, battalions, regiments, divisions, corps, army, and the independent battalions, together with the mass of intelligence material and the S-1, S-2, S-3, S-4, G-1, G-2, G-3, and G-4 section reports and the G-2 and G-3 journals and journal message files combined, represent a mountain of material that was read and sifted for relevant information.

But only by studying all this information and plotting actions on overlay maps, usually on 1:50,000-scale tactical maps of the area concerned, can one understand the events of actual combat and their importance. Nearly all the books published on the Korean War have confined themselves to generalities or repetitions of previous publications of the same kind or have been based on contemporary newspapers or periodical reports of war correspondents and on the writing of armchair analysts who never saw the inside of an operations journal or message file. I know of at least one widely distributed work that is little more than a plagiarized version of official Department of the Army publications, with no credit given either to the authors or to the Army.

All the unit reports of the Eighth Army engaged in ground combat in Korea are preserved in the National Archives, Federal Records Center, in Records Group 407, in Federal Building 1, 4205 Suitland Road, Suitland, Maryland, 20409. To avoid needless repetition in the notes, I have eliminated "Records Group 407" and used only the box number in which documents are located.

Index

(Italicized page numbers refer to photographs.)

A Co., 38th Inf. Regt., 70–71, 177–79
A Co., 23rd Inf. Regt., 171, 200
abbreviations, xv, 398
Acheson, Dean G., 297, 346
Ackert, Lt. Col. Thomas W., 149
Acosta, Cpl. Renaldo, 70, 177
Acosta, M. Sgt. Felix, 181, 183–84
Adams, Capt. Robert, 289
Adams, Pfc. John, 67
ADs: sorties of, 282
air control, 282
Air Force, US, 50, 53, 225, 362–65
airlifts, 32, 60, 225
air sorties: 192, 202, 225–26, 304, 310, 371
air strikes, 203, 340; at Hill 943, 192; on horse cavalry, 144, 150; on members of G Co., 38th Inf. Regt., 183; night-time, 129, 225; on open ground, 193, 267, 304; and retreat, 127, 153, 193, 224, 242, 254
airstrip, Tokchon, 81
air support: at Kunu-ri, 282
AKAs: and Chinnampo, 333
Allen, Maj. Gen. Leven C., 81, 218, 291, 313
Almond, Maj. Gen. Edward M., 21, 27, 214–15, 216–17, 375, 436n.4
ammunition, 43, 65; abandoned or destroyed, 190, 225, 306, 365; dumps, 190, 365; enemy, 43, 190, 365; shortage of, 65, 119, 183
Ammunition Supply Point 16 (British), 331

Anderson, Maj. Eldon B., 369–70
Anderson, William, 126
animals, pack, 86, 368. *See also* horse cavalry
An Jong Sup, 181–82, 183
Anju, 57, 147, 222; road to, 233–34, 267–71, 283–84, 424n.102
Antung, 212
Apa-ri, 301
APAs: at Chinnampo, 333
Argyll Bn., 201–202, 301–302
Arnold, Maj. Thomas A., 149
arsenal, North Korean, 354–55, 365
artillery: 43, 66–67, 149, 288–89. *See also* weapons
artillery firepower. *See* firepower, artillery
Ascom City: as main supply center, 375
Aspinwall, Sgt. Theodore A., 172
Atlee, Clement: on atomic bomb use, 297–98
atomic bomb: use of, discussed, 296–98, 332
attack plan, Chinese, 73, 77–79
Australian Bn., 37, 88, 201–202, 300–302

B Bty., 82nd AAA Bn., 269
B Bty., 503 FA Bn., 272
B Co., 89th Tank Bn., 52
B Co., 9th Inf. Regt., 186; at Hill 219, 64–65, 165–68
B Co., 72nd Tank Bn.: at Chinaman's Hat, 175

B Co., 35th Inf. Regt., 51, 111, 120
B Co., 24th Inf. Regt., 113–14
B-29s, 23, 364
B-26s, 129
Bach, Capt. L. V., 363
Baker, Capt. Willard, 329
Baker Line. *See* Line Baker
Baldonado, Cpl. Joe R., 73
Baldwin, Hanson, 355
Banks, Lt. Gentle S., 329
Barberis, Maj. Cesibes V., 165, 187–88, 242
Barns, Cpl., 336–37
Barsanti, Lt. Col. Olinto, 344
Barth, Brig. Gen. George, 52, 106
batteries: 2nd Inf. Div. commanders of, 289
Baturalp, Maj. Recai, 87
Bayliss, Capt. J. C., 118
bayonet, 90
Beard, M. Sgt. Richard, 98–99, 408n.42
Becker, Lt. Col. Henry C., 227, 233, 238, 258–59, 265–66
Bed Check Charlie, 306, 307, 322
Beishline, Col. John R., 213
Belgium, 38
Bell, Lt. Col. Edgar V. H., 193–95
Bell, Lt. James H., 335
Belton, M. Sgt. George, 336, 391–92
Bennett, Maj., 97
Benton, Capt. Benjamin J., 158, 160
Bigart, Homer, 200, 345
Bishop, 1st Lt. Raymond, 96
blacks, 51, 137, 384
Blackwell, Capt. John L., 176
Blair, Clay, 10
Blair, Lt. Col. Melvin R., 138, 141, 142, 223
Blunt, Sir Anthony, 435–36n.80
Bolte, Maj. Gen. Charles L., 298–99, 384–85
Bomber Command, US, 364
bonfires, 83, 161–62, 163
boundaries: of IX and I corps, 203; CCF attacks on, 100–101; coordination at regimental, 185
Bradley, Gen. Omar N., 24, 25, 26
Bradley, Maj. Gen. Joseph S., 292, 419n.1, 425n.123; and 23rd RCT withdrawal on Anju road, 266, 268, 269, 423n.82

bridges, 28, 317, 356–58; Bailey, 361; blown, south of the Pass, 263–65; Chongchon River, 222; floating, 203, *204,* 379; Imjin River, 379; railroad, 316–18, 365; Taedong River, 203, 218, 300–301, 310–11, 315–16, 316–18; Yalu River, 24, *25,* 47–48
British 29th Brigade, 55, 244, 245, 302, 315–18, 321
British 27th Brigade, 42–43, 201–202, 207, 243–44, 300–302, 303, 315
Brittingham, Brig. Gen. James, 362
Brodie, Brig. Thomas, 315
Bronze Star, 92
Brown, Henry, 197
Brown, Lt. Robert L., 329
Brown, Lt. Russell, 21
Brown, Pfc. James L., 186–87, 414n.22
Brown, Pfc. Lawrence, 159
Bryers, Sfc. Maynard K., 110
bugles, 117, 118, 123
"bugout": Eighth Army retreat as, 381–84; origin of term, 383–84
Bullock, Lt. Col., 314
Bunn, Lt. Charlie, 107
Burch, Lt. J. C., 107–109, 117
Burgess, Guy, 387–88, 435–36n.80
Burns, Col., 81
Buys, Col. Joseph H., 236, 238, 266
bypass: on 2nd Inf. Div. withdrawal route, 275–76, 281, 422n.64

C Co., 72nd Tank Battalion, 229
C Co., 38th Inf. Regt., 181, 229
C Co., 24th Inf. Regt., 139
camels, 368
Camel's Head: of Kuryong River, 106
Cameron, Lt. Col. Robert E., 406n.11
camouflage: Chinese use of, 14, 394
Campbell, Lt. Col. Clark, 82
campfires: decoy, 139
cannibalization, vehicle, 309, 326, 328
Carle, Col. (2nd Inf. Div. surgeon), 290
Carne, Lt. Col. J. P., 315
Carr, Lt. William, 231
Carson, Lt. Col. R. J. H., 315
Casey, Capt. Edgar L., 289
casualties, battle (enemy), 133, 144, 149, 152, 175, 193; from air attacks, 151, 364
casualties, battle (UN), 22, 153, 286–

casualties, battle (*cont.*)
 87, 289; abandoned, 264; of B Co., 9th Inf. Regt., 168; in 8th FA Bn., 124; from friendly fire, 241; of 2nd Bn., 5th Cav. Regt., 92, 93; in 2nd Engineer Combat Bn., 278; in 2nd Inf. Div., 175, 285–88, 289; of 7th Cav. Regt., 99; in Turkish Brigade, 92. *See also* wounded
casualties, nonbattle, 187, 303
Catalogy, Capt. Ismail, 324
"Cavalry Canter": Argyll Bn. and, 302
caves: in Honey Comb Hill, 54
Centurion tanks, *302*, 419n.36, 427n.5
Chaney, Sgt. Lewis F., 289
Chang, Capt. *See* Lui Ping Chang, Capt.
Chang, Col.: and ROK 3rd Regt. action, 242–43
Chang, Gen. (commander, ROK 6th Inf. Div.): and Kujang-ni incident, 94–95, 96–97
Chang Chang Kuk, Gen., 392, 436n.5
Chang Han-chung, Capt., 156
chanting: of Chinese to F Co., 27th Inf. Regt., 121
Charnetski, 1st Lt. Peter F., 174
Chasan, 203
Chemical Mortar Bn., 2nd: C Co. of, destroyed, 193
Ch'en Yi (commander, Third Field Army), 15
Chiang Kai-shek, 417–18n.14
China, Communist. *See* People's Republic of China
Chinaman's Hat, 65–69, 165, 169–71, 171–72, 174, 175, 188–89
Chinnampo, 28, 306, 333–35, 355
Chipyong-ni, 353
Chongchon bridgehead line, 145, 146
Chongchon River, 32–33, 37; Chinese crossings of, 169, 174; Eighth Army and, 21, 131, 220; and environs described, 45–48; road through valley of, 204–205
Chongju, 60
Chorwon, 347, 348
Chosin Reservoir, 19
Chotong-gang, 204, 205
Chou En-lai, 7, 8
Chungju, 374
Church, Maj. Gen. John H., *41,* 57

Chusong-dong, 92–93
Chu Teh (commander in chief, People's Liberation Army), 15
civilians, Korean: CCF disguised as, 94, 134; conscription of, 395; as guides for CCF, 79; report CCF movements, 14, 60, 81, 82, 98, 190, 230, 231. *See also* refugees
Claridge, Lt. (FO for 38th FA Bn.), 178
Clark, Sgt. Charles, 161
Clausewitz, Karl von: military theories of, 74, 389
Clayton, Maj. George A., 138, 139
Clearing Stations, 153
clothing, winter, 33, 55, 60, 191, 308
Coad, Brig. Gen. Basil A., 201, 383, 435n.69
Cocheu, Lt. Col., 307
Cohen, Pfc. Arthur J., 37, 255–56
Collier, Col. William A., 34, 335, 336
Collins, Gen. Joseph Lawton, 214, 298, 331–32, 384
combat capability: of ROK troops assessed, 43
combat fatigue, 142
communication: between X Corps and Eighth Army, 29–30, 427n.42; breakdowns in, 80, 138, 181, 186, 245; Chinese systems of, 5, 17, 156, 345; and transport network, 31, 320
communiqués: No. 11, 56; No. 12, 56; No. 14, 214, 417n.5
Communists, Chinese, 5. *See also* People's Republic of China; troops, Chinese Communist
conference, commanders', 215–17
confidence: of US command, 22, 23
Congressional Medal of Honor. *See* Medal of Honor
conscription, 18, 355, 395
Constellation airplane, 56, 57, 393
construction: of bridges, 317; of Eighth Army defense lines, 377
Cook, Sgt. John H., 256–57
Coontz, Maj. John B., 149
Cooper, Lt. Col. Marcus E., 325
Corley, Col. John T., 51, 116, 137, 141, 142, 223
corridors of advance, enemy, 378
Corsairs, 212, 282
Coughlin, Col. John C., 90

Coulter, Maj. Gen. John B., *36, 37, 38,* 85, 203, 284–85, 292, 293, 335, 390–91
Counterintelligence Corps, 335
Cox, M. Sgt. William D., 109–11, 117
Craften, 1st Sgt. Larry, 277
Crawford, Cpl. Walter K., 166–68
Crockett, Lt. John O., 71
Crombez, Col. Marcel G., 356
Curcio, Cpl. James C., Jr., 166–67

D Bty., 865th AAA AW Bn., 332
Dabney, Col., 391
Davidson, Maj. Gen. Garrison H.: on Eighth Army advance, 376, 403n.24
Davidson, Sgt., 391
Davidson line, 376–77
Davis, Capt. Perry, 290
daylight attacks, enemy, 151, 253
daylight movements, enemy, 100, 147, 203, 364
DeCorrevont, Sfc. Floyd, 125–26
Defense Department, 297
defense lines, Eighth Army, 25–26, 31, 146, 152, 311, 314, 375–79
defilade, 110, 250–51, 259
defile. *See* Pass
Delotaba, Sgt., 119
demolition policy: Eighth Army, 317, 360–62; enemy, 361. *See also* "scorched-earth" policy
demolitions: of Chinnampo installations, 334; in Pyongyang, 316–18
Denham, Sgt., 209
deserter, Chinese, 61–62
Deshoen, Pfc. Harvey M., 172
Desiderio, Capt. Reginald B., 107, 109, 116–19
destroyers: at Chinnampo, 334
Deuce-Four. *See* 24th Inf. Regt.
Dick, Col., 199
Dickson, Lt., 9, 113
Dill, Sgt. Bobby F., 289
Dingeman, Capt. Robert E., 123
discipline: of Chinese troops, 75, 179; in Eighth Army, 64–65, 111, 134, 137, 382; of ROK troops, 77–79, 84
Distinguished Service Cross, 65, 187, 408n.42, 413n.21, 414nn.22, 23, 24, 27, 34
documents, captured, 100–101, 102–104, 150, 232, 349–50

Dolvin, Lt. Col. Weldon G., 51, 107, 111, 116–19
Dolvin, Task Force. *See* Task Force Dolvin
Donlin, Sgt. Eugene, 392
Dora, Col. Celal, 87
Dry Creek, 158–60
dual-40s, 209, 259, 260, 273, 289, 422n.62
Duckworth, Lt. George, 336–37

E Co., 24th Inf. Regt., 64
E Co., 27th Inf. Regt., 5, 107–109, 116–19, 186
E Co., 23rd Inf. Regt., 186
East of Chosin: Entrapment and Breakout in Korea, 1950, xiv
Echard, Pfc. Robert L., 173
Eddington, Capt., 122–23
Edwards, Lt. Col. James W., 188, 246–47
Eighth Army (US), 292, 353; command decisions and management, 113, 146, 147, 232–33, 246, 333, 360; CP location, 34; defensive moves of, 21, 130, 299–300, 313, 356, 359, 375–79; after 1st Phase Offensive, 13, 21; Headquarters, 335, 336, 360; order of battle, 24 November, 37–44; records of, xiv; strength and situation of, 40, 71–72, 113, 299
Eighth Army Operational Plan, 32
Eighth Army Ranger Co.. *See* Ranger Co., 8213th
8th Cav. Regt.: 20, 52, 62, 156, 310
8th FA Bn., 122, 123–24
Eighth Kings Royal Irish Hussars, *302,* 427n.5
89th Medium Tank Bn., 106–107, 116, 409n.11
82nd AAA AW Bn., 285
82nd Airborne, 384–85
82nd FA Bn., 114–15
8213th Ranger Co.. *See* Ranger Co., 8213th
11th Regt., ROK 1st Inf. Div., 61
Elser, Capt. Robert M., 327–28, 328–29
Emerson, Capt. John E., Jr., 188–89, 414n.27
enfilading fire, 127, 250, 252
Engineer Aviation Bn., 822nd, 326–27

Engineer Combat Bn., 8th, 304
Engineer Combat Bn., 2nd, 240, 277, 278–80, 286
Engineer Combat Bn., 65th, 120, 124–25
Engineers, I Corps, 332
engineers: reconnoitering by, 300
enveloping movements, 17, 98, 100–101, 162, 220, 226, 231, 358
Epley, Col. Gerald G., 91, 207, 236, 257, 258–59, 266–67, 279, 282–83, 292
equipment, military: losses of, 141, 224–25, 288–89, 305–10; resupply of, 372–73; salvaging of, 97
Erekson, Lt. Comdr. Henry J., 333
espionage, 386–89, 435n.80, 435–36n.82
Evans, Lt. Dell G., 117
Evers, Capt., 168
Ewen, Rear Adm. E. C., 424n.99

F Co., 38th Inf. Regt., 70, 185
F Co., 27th Inf. Regt., 121–22
F-80s, 21, 256, 330
F-80C, 212
F-84E Thunderjets, 362
F-86A Sabre Wing, 362
F-51s, 249, 330
F9F. *See* Pantherjets
Faith, Lt. Col. Don C. Faith, Jr., 215
Far East Command, 8, 14, 56–59, 72–73, 212, 310, 331, 360–61, 381, 397
Farnum, Maj. Lawrence, 279–80
Farrell, Brig. Gen. Francis W., 81, 97
Fast Carrier Task Force, 424n.99
Fast Carrier Task Force 77, 282
Ferguson, Lt. Col., 202
field army, Chinese: organization of, 18
15th FA Bn., 267, 269
Fifth Air Force, 29, 202, 282, 304, 364, 371, 380
5th Cav. Regt., 92–93, 232
fifth column, 319
5th RCT, 144, 146, 271, 310, 349, 350
50th Army (Chinese): 74, 144–45, 394
fireblocks, enemy, 227, 231–33, 238, 260, 280–82

firepower, relative, 43; formula for, 401n.9
1st Bn., 65th Inf. Regt., 30–31
1st Bn., 24th Inf. Regt., 63, 116, 138–39
1st Bn., 23rd Inf. Regt., 198–200, 240–41
1st Cav. Inf. Div., 20, 83, 85, 92–99, 196, 244, 285–86, 302–304, 310, 408n.39
1st Marine Inf. Div., 358, 375
Fisher, Lt. Col. Henry K., 37, 49, 51, 132–37, 308
503rd FA Bn., 265, 271–76
flanking movements, Chinese, 26, 28, 63, 220, 244, 313
Fleming, Maj. Harry, 19
Fletcher, Pfc., 109
Flicker, Lt., 330
flutes: played by Chinese at Hill 291, 182
food, 36–37; Turkish, 87. *See also* rations
footgear, Chinese, 352
Force, Lt. Clyde, 127
ford. *See* bypass
40th Army (Chinese), 155–56, 281
42nd Army (Chinese), 93–94, 310, 394
Foster, Lt. Col. K. O. N., 315
Foster, Lt. Col. Ralph L., 334–35
Fourth Field Army (Chinese), 11–12
4th NK Inf. Div., 350
4th Platoon, B Co., 9th Inf. Regt., 166
Fralish, Maj. John C., 272–74
Freeman, Col. Paul L., Jr., 68–69, 155, 172, 175, 199–200, 257–58, 266–71, 423n.82
French Bn., 300, 371
friendly fire, 241, 265
frontal attack: Chinese use of, 17, 28, 74
Frost, Pfc., 167
Fusen Reservoir, 19

G Co., 38th Inf. Regt., 71, 180–85
G Co., 24th Inf. Regt., 64
G Co., 27th Inf. Regt., 121–22
Gallagher, Lt., 127
Gallardo, 2nd Lt. Robert, 187, 414n.23

Index

Gandy, 2nd Lt. John, 173
gap. *See* separation of commands
gasoline: used as cooking fuel, 60
Gasquet, Pfc. Andrew J., Jr., 187, 414n.24
gauntlet: from Kunu-ri to Sunchon, 75
Gay, Maj. Gen. Hobart R., 92, 94, 96–97
Genung, Maj. Joel M., 123
Gillette, Col., 82
Giudici, Pfc. Louis, 158–59
Glass, Lt. Col., 215, 217–18
Gombos, Capt. Nicholas, 185–86, 208, 413n.21
Goodrich, Col. Walker R., 196–97, 199, 251, 258, 263–64, 274
Goolsby, Maj., 114
Gough, Capt., 121, 126, 127
grassfires, 121, 177
Great Britain: and MacArthur's plan to attack in Manchuria, 387
Greek Bn., 371
Green, Lt., 139
Grinnell, Lt. Douglas D., 272–74
Grunby, Col., 91, 207
guerrilla army: Chinese troops as, 17
guerrillas, North Korean, 30, 31, 55, 73, 313, 346–50
Gunnell, Capt., 171

Haig, Capt. Alexander M., Jr., 417n.6
Haislip, Lt. Gen. Wade H., 214
Hanpo-ri: bridge at, 320
Han River: Eighth Army defense line at, 294
Han Xianchu, Gen., 11
Happacham: IX Corps CP at, 203. *See also* Unhung-ni
harassing, 306. *See also* Bed Check Charlie
Harper, Lt., 229
Harrelson, Lt. Col. Elmer H., 236, 261
Harriman, Averell, 297
Harrington, Capt. Robert H., 125
Harrington, Maj. Bill, 256
Harris, Col. William A., 94, 96
Hathaway, 1st Lt. C. T., 289
Hayden, Col. John, 238
Haynes, Brig. Gen. Loyal M., 236, 237, 261, 292

Haywood, Lt., 188
Heath, Lt. Charles S., 243, 248–49
Hector, Lt. Col. John R., 236
Hennig, Col. W. H., 149
Henry, Sgt. Joel, 161
Hewette, Maj., 95
Hickey, Maj. Gen. Doyle O., 85, 313
highway: in Chongchon valley, 47
highway crossings. *See* bridges
Hill 82, 93
Hill 107, 208
Hill 127, 246, 251
Hill 153, 64, 187–88
Hill 167, 93
Hill 171, 73
Hill 180, 64, 164–65, 187
Hill 182, 208
Hill 192, 60
Hill 201, 128–29, 240–41
Hill 205, 63, 104, 106–107, 111, 113
Hill 206, 109–10
Hill 207, 104, 107–109
Hill 208, 140
Hill 216, 115, 121–22, 126–27, 128, 359
Hill 219, 64–65, 154, 165–68
Hill 222, 106, 116–20
Hill 227, 144
Hill 234, 104, 111, 120
Hill 273, 138–39, 232
Hill 291, 71, 180–85
Hill 298, 240
Hill 329. *See* Chinaman's Hat
Hill 335, 303
Hill 356, 160–64
Hill 358, 150
Hill 383, 180, 185, 186, 191–92
Hill 387, 134
Hill 404, 192
Hill 453, 70–71, 176, 178
Hill 526, 178
Hill 625, 176
Hill 659, 150
Hill 750, 150
Hill 782, 150
Hill 943, 192
Hill 1229, 53, 69–71, 155
Hinewood, Lt.: in fistfight with Chinese soldier, 133
Hinton, Capt. Reginald J., 248, 252–53
Hinton, Lt. Col. Bruce H., 363

Holden, Lt. Col. Maurice C., 227, 233, 238, 275, 284, 419n.1
Hollingsworth, 2nd Lt., 181, 183–84
Honey Comb Hill, 54
horse cavalry, 82, 86, 99, 144, 151
"hot pursuit," 17, 24–25, 212, 363–64
Howard, Pvt. John, 166
howitzers, 43; 8-inch, 66; of 503rd FA Bn., 273, 274–75
Hue, Gen. (ROK II Corps commander), 80, 82
Hughes, Capt., 133
Hungnam, 28
Hurst, Cpl. Randle M., 335–40, 392–93, 430nn.42,43
Hutchins, Lt. Col. Claire E., Jr., 68, 155, 172, 199, 210, 241
Hwachon Dam, 349
Hyangjok-san (mountain mass), 147, 149–50

I Co., 3rd Bn., 38th Inf. Regt., 42
I Corps, 34; operational directives of, 145, 146; in order of battle, 39, 45; and 2nd Phase Offensive, 50, 143; withdrawal of, 153, 222, 283–85
Ichon, 348
Imjin River, 294, 394
Imrie, Cpl. Robert K., 191–92, 414n.34
Inchon, 3
Indian Field Ambulance Unit, 321–22
information: lack of, in Turkish Brigade action, 89
Ingram, Lt. LeRoy, 329
intelligence, combat (US), 60, 63, 82, 216, 243, 310; of enemy activity near Pyongyang, 326, 340, 349; poor condition of, 13–14, 230, 233, 254, 300, 358, 395–97; of 3rd Phase Offensive preparations, 380, 395
interdiction fire, 110, 153, 168, 175, 185, 196, 225–26, 261
Interdiction Plan No. 4, 365
interrogations, prisoner, 349–50, 365–66
Ipsok, 52, 122, 129
Iron Triangle, 349–50; activity in, 313, 366; extent of, 347; North Korean guerrillas in, 299, 313, 360, 366

Itschner, Col. Emerson C., 317, 318, 384

Jackson, 1st Lt. Clinton, 162–63, 164
jets: first battle between, 21
Johnson, Col. Harold, 356, 361–62
Johnson, Cpl. Kenneth F., 181
Johnston, Capt. Richard S., 259
Joint Chiefs of Staff, 24–25, 218, 331, 341; and Gen. MacArthur, 23–25, 58, 213–14, 296, 311, 346; members of, 385; and proposals to end war, 23–25, 297; and use of Nationalist Chinese troops, 219, 298
Jomini, Antoine Henri: military theories of, xiii, 74
Judd, Lt. Donald D., 263

K Co., 9th Inf. Regt., 158–60
K Co., 35th Inf. Regt., 37, 133–34
K-29 airfield, 153, 307
K-23 airfield, 316
Kaechon, 91, 325, 407n.25. See also Kunu-ri
Kaesong, 324, 325
Kallimuki, Capt. Wayne, 327–28
Kangdong, 220–22, 348
Kanggye, 346–47, 366
Kanghwa-do, 358–59
Karhyon, 246, 273–74, 281
KATUSA, 49. See also specific ROK units; troops, ROK
Kavanaugh, Lt. Martin, 188
Kean, Maj. Gen. William B. Kean, 37, 39, 50–51, 90, 106, 112, 393
Keiser, Maj. Gen. Laurence B. ("Dutch"), 42, 290, 425n.121; in Eighth Army advance, 37, 90, 190, 191; and Kunu-ri situation, 208; in 2nd Inf. Div. withdrawal, 226, 234, 241–42, 246, 282, 284–85, 289–92; and 23rd RCT, 266
Keith, Lt. Col. John W., Jr., 236, 269–70
Kelleher, Lt. Col. William, 69–71, 197–98, 264–65
Keller, Maj., 80
Kelly, Capt. S. G., 333, 334
Khrushchev, Nikita, 7, 8–9, 11
Killilae, Lt. Col. Walter, 236, 237–38, 275–76
Kim, Col., 95
Kim Chaek, Gen., 367

Kim Chaek Inf. Div. *See* 4th NK Inf. Div.
Kim Il Sung, 8–9, 11, 367
Kim Pac Il, Maj. Gen., 370
Kim Paek, Gen., 348
King, 2nd Lt. Elster, 181, 183
King, Sfc. Lionel, 162–63
Kings Royal Irish Hussars, Eighth, 302, 427n.5
Klechner, Sgt., 402–403n.11
Knoeller, Capt. Frank O., 139
Koksan, 348
Kopischkie, Maj. Carl, 272, 274
Korangpo, 394
Korea, waist of. *See* waist of Korea
Kreuger, Lt., 160
Kryloff, Maj. Eugene, 335
Kujang-dong, 189, 190, 196–99; strategic importance of, 190–91
Kujang-ni: incident at, 94–97
Kumhwa, 347, 348
Kumhwa-Uijongbu axis, 397
Kunu-ri, 34–36, 48, 199, 203, 204–205, 230–31, 407n.25
Kunu-ri–Anju road, 210, 211. *See also* Anju
Kunu-ri–Sunchon road. *See* Sunchon–Kunu-ri road
Kuryong River, 47, 50–51, 136, 147–48, 151–52
Kydland, Capt., 227–29

L Co., 9th Inf. Regt., 160–64
L Co., 35th Inf. Regt., 133
L Co., 23rd Inf. Regt., 211, 270–71
Ladd, Maj., 215, 217–18, 417n.6
Lancaster, Lt. Col. A. E., 288
Land, Lt., 122–23
Landrum, Col. Eugene M., 85–86, 336
Lavell, Maj. Geoffrey, 236, 272–73
leadership, 111, 134, 136
Leaphart, Sfc. Tillman B., 173
Leckie, Robert, 27
Lefler, Sgt., 117, 119
Line Baker, 377–78
Lin Piao, Gen., 10, 16–17
Lin Po-cheng, 15
Lock, 2nd Lt. J. M., 244
Logistical Command, 2nd, 376–77
logistics and supply, 27–28, 32–33, 45, 314. *See also* supplies

Long March: Chinese veterans of, 15
looting, 323
Lowery, Capt. Leonard, 70, 176, 178–79
LSTs. *See* tank loading ships
Lui Ping Chang, Capt., 61–62
Lynch, Lt. Col. James H., 97

M19s. *See* dual-40s
M16s. *See* quad-50s
MacArthur, Gen. Douglas A., 4, 38, 56–59, 214, 381, 389; confers with commanders, 217, 358; and Eighth Army advance and retreat, 87, 358, 381; and Joint Chiefs of Staff, 213, 296, 332, 346, 384, 386; military judgments of, 14, 24, 33, 59, 212, 382; and separation of commands, 27, 400n.4; on waist of Korea, 311, 345–46
MacArthur hearings: testimony in, 26
McCaffrey, Lt. Col. William J., 215, 217–18, 344
McClure, Maj. Gen. Robert B., 290–91, 372
Mace, Lt. James, 248–49
machine guns, coaxial, 112
McKnight, Cpl. Jack, 178
McLaughlin, Sgt. Elijah, 66
MacLean, Col. Allan D., 215
MacLean, Donald, 387–88, 435–36n.80
McMain, Lt. Col. D. M., 242
MacMillan, Cpl., 81
Maengjung-dong, 149
Maengsan, 84
Mahoney, Lt., 127
mail: burned in Pyongyang, 323
main supply road, 43, 192, 206, 210
Maixner, Lt. Col. Harold V., 69–71, 208
Major, 1st Lt. William J., 172, 174, 199
Manchuria, 296, 347
Mann, Cpl. Eugene, 159–60
Manning, Capt. William E., 246, 250–51, 290
Manto, 1st Lt. Joseph, 186, 188
Mao Anying, 10–11
Mao Tse-tung, 8–9
march capability: of Chinese, 14
march order. *See* order of march

Marquat, Maj. Gen. William F., 332
Marshall, Gen. George C., 25, 297, 346, 363, 385–86
Marshall, S. L. A., 269, 279–80, 291
matériel: of American forces, 352. *See also* equipment, military; ordnance
Mays, Pfc., 108
Medal of Honor: to Capt. R. B. Desiderio, Posthumously, 119; to Sgt. J. A. Pittman, 414n.28
medical care: lack of, 176
Medical Clearing Co., 25th: patients at, 226
Medical Co., 2nd Inf. Div., 286, 287
medical supplies, 225
Melzer, Pfc., 108
Memoirs of a Chinese Marshal, 9–11
Messinger, Col. Edward J., 238, 311
Meyer, Lt. Col. John C., 363
Mezar, Maj., 246
Michaelis, Col. John H. ("Mike"), 51, 140
Michaely, Capt. Jack, 121
Middlesex Bn., 201–202, 207–208, 229, 243–46, 249, 251
MiG-15s, 21, 212–13, 362, 363, 416n.1
Milburn, Maj. Gen. Frank W., 57, 234, 284–85, 390
military campaigns, classical: Chinese campaigns compared to, 14
military history: great errors in, 59
Military Police Co., 2nd, 265
military positions: need for study of, xiv
military records, 148, 283–84, 323, 390, 400n.1, 403n.15
military tactics, Chinese, 137, 156; changed, 86, 118; chanting used in, 121; compared to classical military tactics, 14, 74; described, 14–15, 17–18, 28–29, 74–75, 100–101, 102–104; feigning death in, 310; suicide in, 120
military theory, xiii, 14, 74, 79, 389
military weakness, Chinese, 352
military weaknesses, American: as perceived by CCF, 102–104, 150; lack of ground reconnaissance as, 311
Miller, Lt. Col. Gerald G., 137–38
Millet, Capt. Lewis, 123
mines, 32, 127, 334

mine shaft: air strikes trap enemy in, 282
minesweepers, 32
misjudgments, 56, 87, 285
mismanagement, 246
mistaken identity, 89, 98, 111, 122, 355
Mobile Army Surgical Hospital (MASH): 8076th, *195*; 8063rd, 226, 287
morale, 64–65, 309, 363, 382–83
Morand, Maj. Leon F., Jr., 114, 119–20
Morris, Sfc. Neal M., 349, 431n.18
Mosier, Cpl., 127
Mosquitos, 80, 81, 224, 270, 282, 321
motor transport, Chinese: assessed, 43
MSR. *See* main supply road
Muksi-dong. *See* Unhung
Mulsil-san (mountain mass), 147, 149–50
Mupyong-ni, 216–17
Murch, Lt. Col. Gordon E., 106, 112–13, 126–29
Mustangs: compared with MiG-15s, 212
Myers, Col. Gilbert, 308
myths: about Korean War, xiii–xiv, 26

Naechong-jong, 144
Napchong-dong. *See* Naechong-jong
Nationalists, Chinese. *See* troops, Nationalist Chinese
National Security Council, 25
Navy, US, 360
Netherlands Bn., 55, 300, 371
news media, 57, 88–89
New York Herald Tribune, 57, 200, 219
New York Times, 57, 213, 355
night fighting, xiii, 102
night marches, 62
19th Inf. Regt., 144, 232, 310–11
IX Army Group, 12–13, 22, 380, 397
IX Corps, 36, 39–40, 40–42, 224, 245, 246, 283–85
9th Inf. Regt., 72, 154, 189, 193–95, 205–206, 276–78; casualties in, 168, 286–87; at Hill 219, 64–65; at Sunchon road fireblock, 241–43; and 38th Inf. Regt., 185
NK II Corps, 348. *See also* troops, North Korean

no-man's-land: from Pyongyang to Imjin River, 379
Nordstrom, 1st Lt. Francis, 326
Northern Taebaek Mountains: roadway through, 343
North Korean Army, 348, 365–68. *See also* troops, North Korean
Northumberland Fusiliers, 348
Norum, Lt. Col., 262

objectives, military: of Task Force Dolvin, 104–106
Obong-san (mountain), 148
O'Donnell, Lt. Col. Robert J., 155, 236, 269, 272–73, 274, 279
187th Airborne, Regt., 73
159th FA Bn., 138
113th Div., 38th Army (Chinese), 177, 280
112th Div., 38th Army (Chinese), 79–81
120th Div., 40th Army (Chinese), 174, 177
125th Div., 42nd Army, 21–22
operational directives, 145, 146
operational plans, 43–44, 356, 376, 377
operation orders, 104, 218, 312
optimism: of commanders, 216–17
order of march, 25th Inf. Div., 309
orders of battle: Chinese: 44–45, 62, 401–402n.14; Eighth Army, 37–44
ordnance, 231, 372–73. *See also* matériel
ordnance companies: 44th, 327–29; 724th, 307; 25th Inf. Div., 309
Ordnance Recovery Co., 57th, 329–31
Osterhout, Lt., 307
Otomo, Lt. William, 107, 119
Overmeyer, Capt., 307

Paengyong River, 69–71
Paik Sun Yup, Brig. Gen., 20, 135, 143, 152
Pakchon, 152
Palmer, Lt. Gen. W. B., 382
panic: of B Co., 23rd Inf. Regt., 173
Panikkar, Sardar K. M., 7
Pantherjets, 212
Partridge, Gen., 312, 362, 380
Pass, 205, 246, 250–53, 256–57, 281, 283
patrols, Chinese, 37, 68–69

Pearson, Lt. Col. Willard, 81, 96–99
Pecoraro, Capt. Anthony, 120
Peng Te-huai, Gen., 9–11, 15–16
peninsula: tactical significance of, 341
People's Liberation Army (PLA), 99–101, 352, 353. *See also* troops, Chinese Communist
People's Republic of China: and reasons for Korean intervention by, 7–11
Peploe, Col. George B., 41–42, 69–71, 91, 186, 190, 191; at Kunu-ri, 206–209; and 2nd Inf. Div. breakout, 247, 250, 252, 254
Pertree, Sgt. Henry, 109
Peterson, Capt. Ivar, 231
Peterson, Lt., 171
petroleum products: shortage of, 33
Phase Offensives (Chinese), 5; 1st, 6, 19–22, 44, 102–104, 150, 156; 2nd, 6, 11, 12–13, 26, 74–75, 99–101, 145, 150, 154, 174, 183–85, 282, 347; 3rd, 6, 11, 350, 381, 393; 4th 6; 5th, 6
Philby, Harold ("Kim"), 387–88, 435–36n.80
Philippines, 38
Phillips, Lt. Col. J. W., 315
photography, aerial, 15
Pitcher, Col. Thomas A., 321
Pittman, Sgt. John A., 189, 414n.28
planning: and defense of Pyongyang, 326, 350–53
policy: of Far East Command and Joint Chiefs of Staff, 384–86
Pong-dong, 131
Pongmyong-ni, 206, 407n.25
power plants: at Korean border, 44, 401n.11
press. *See* news media
Princess Patricia Canadian Light Inf. Regt., 371
prisoners, American, 51–52, 132, 139, 160, 224
prisoners, Chinese, 12, 60, 61, 77–79, 380–81; intelligence from, 14, 84, 99, 128, 149, 156, 165, 188
prisoners, North Korean, 60, 69
propaganda, 219
Puckett, 1st Lt. Ralph, 106, 107, 110
Pugwon. *See* Won-ni
Pukchang-ni, 86
Pusan, 294–96, 332

Putnam, Capt. Darrell, 222
Pyoktong, 52, 402–403n.11
Pyonggang, 347
Pyongyang: airstrip at, bombed, 309; bridges blown at, 310–11; Chinese recapture of, 340; described, 306, 316, 427–28n.7; Eighth Army and, 34, 216, 224, 256, 296, 326, 332; fires in, 321
Pyongyang-Seoul highway, 299
Pyongyang-Wonsan road, 344–45

quad-50s, 65, 209, 259, 260, 273, 289, 422n.62
Quartermaster Co., 15th, 325–26
Quartermaster Co., 24th Inf. Div., 306–307
Quartermaster Corps, 33
quartermaster dump, 261

Racin, 364
Radow, Maj. Sam, 305
rail equipment, 305–306
railroads, 28, 31, 47, 307, 320–23, 343–44, 345
rail transportation: and abandonment of supplies, 225
Ranger Co., 8213th, 51, 63, 104–106, 106–109, 114, 359; renamed, 373
Ranger hill. *See* Hill 206
Raskin, 2nd Lt. Al, 159–60
rationalization: of Eighth Army advance, 87
rations, 55, 60. *See also* food
Raybould, Lt. Lynn R., 162
rear areas, UN: NK guerrilla action in, 73
rear-guard action: A Co., 23rd Inf. Regt., in exemplary, 200. *See also* 23rd RCT
reconnaissance: aerial, 29, 86, 203, 380; Chinese, for unit boundaries, 79; lack of ground, 311
"reconnaissance in force": as rationalization of Eighth Army advance, 86–87
Reconnaissance Platoon, 502nd, 392–93
Reconnaissance Platoon, ROK 7th Regt., 19
reconnoitering, 300
records, military. *See* military records

Reeder, Maj. Gen. William O., 385
Reenan, Cpl. Francis S., 392, 436n.4
refugees, Korean, *301;* at Chinnampo, 333, 334, 355; conscription of, 355, 395; fired on, by UN troops, 358–59, 408n.39; flight by, 218, 224, 323; at Pyongyang, 311, 318–19, *319.* *See also* civilians, Korean
Reifers, Staff Sgt. Raymond N., 125–26
reinforcements, UN, 49, 298–99, 371–74
Remagen Bridge: and Taedong River bridges situation, compared, 317
Remillard, M. Sgt. Roger W., 172–73
Repose (hospital ship), 32
RFP. *See* firepower, relative
Rhee Chong Chan, Brig. Gen., 370
Ridgway, Lt. Gen. Matthew B., 97, 214, 292, 298–99, 385, 395, 397
River and the Gauntlet, The, 269, 279–80, 404–405n.8
Rivet, 1st Lt. Robert H., 71, 180–82, 183
roadblocks, enemy, 52, 80; of exploding ammunition, 130; on 38th Inf. Regt. route, 80–81, 196–98; on 35th Inf. Regt. route, 134, 135; on Sunchon road, 248, 249, 252; on 24th Inf. Regt. route, 64, 141
roadnets, 31, 48, 64, 204–205, 211, 316
roads: condition of, 30, 49, 60; strategic, 48
rocket launcher, 190
Rodarm, Capt. Jack W., 70–71, 176, 178
ROK Army: lack of military documentation in, 148; NK attacks on, 394–95; reorganization of, 368–71
ROK 8th Inf. Div., 83, 312, 368
ROK 11th Regt., 149–50, 152
ROK 15th Regt., 152
ROK 1st Inf. Div., 71, 134–35, 150; captures CCF captain, 61–62; composition of, 143; in Eighth Army actions, 136, 148–53, 368–69; in first UN battle with CCF, 20; retreats, 152–53, 222
ROK II Corps, 40–42; action of, 20, 45, 53–55; in attack north, 72, 82, 101; in order of battle, 40; after 2nd

ROK II Corps (*cont.*)
 Phase Offensive, 312, 348; 38th
 Army divisions attack, 77–81
ROK 2nd Inf. Div., *322;* North Korean guerrillas attack, 347
ROK 17th Regt., 347
ROK 7th Inf. Div., 80
ROK 16th Regt., 82
ROK 6th Inf. Div., 86, 94–97, 101, 349
ROK 10th Inf. Div., 349
ROK III Corps, 366
ROK 3rd Regt., 7th Inf. Div., 84, 101, 190, 208, 209, 240, 242–43
Royal Ulster Bn.: as last British unit out of Pyongyang, 332
Ruffner, Maj. Gen. Clark L., 218

Sabres, 362–63
Sadon Station, 329–30
Sahyoncham, 262
Sainjang, 304
Samso-ri, 93, 205
Sangdong-Aechang road, 82
satchel charges, 120, 125, 127
Savage, Cpl., 119
Sawyer, 1st Lt. Robert K., 52–53, 112, 115–16, 120, 124–25, 125–26
Schnabel, Cpl. Jacob, 249
"scorched-earth" policy: issued, 309; rescinded, 356. *See also* demolition policy
screening forces, American: lack of, 352
screening forces, Chinese, 52, 62–63, 71, 104, 107, 155
2nd Bn., 5th Cav. Regt., 92–93
2nd Bn., 9th Inf. Regt., 164–65
2nd Bn., 10th ROK Regt., 30–31
2nd Bn., 24th Inf. Regt., 141–42
2nd Bn., 27th Inf. Regt., 136; and Task Force Wilson, 115, 121–24, 126–29
2nd Inf. Div., 53, 64–65, 99, 154, 168, 191, 203, 260; air support of, 282; artillery of, 237; casualties in, 285–88, 289; at Chinaman's Hat, 65–69; and combat intelligence, 233; and fireblock on Sunchon road, 227, 246–54, 254–61; at Kunu-ri, 36, 288–89, 415n.24; and Middlesex Bn., 245; in Pyongyang withdrawal, 322; after 2nd Phase, 372–73, 374–

2nd Inf. Div. (*cont.*)
 75, 378–79; threat to, 91, 220; withdrawal of, 189, 196, 226, 230, 235–38, 283–85
2nd Inf. Div. Operational Order No. 13, 374
2nd Inf. Div. Operational Plan No. 1, 373–74
2nd Plat., B Co., 187th Airborne, 73
2nd Plat., G Co., 38th Inf. Regt., 183–84
2nd Plat., L Co., 9th Inf. Regt., 163–64
Secton, 1st Lt. Leon D., 258–59
security: in Eighth Army Headquarters, 336, 338
Seegar, M. Sgt. Herbert, 166
segregation, racial. *See* blacks
Seoul: plans for evacuation of, 376
separation of commands, 26–31, 87, 296, 346, 351, 388
serials: of 2nd Inf. Div. withdrawal, 237–38
17th FA Bn. (8-inch howitzers), 189, 261–64; uniqueness of, 66
7th Cav. Regt., 94–97, 98–99
Seventh Fleet, 8, 12
7th Marine Regt., 1st Marine Inf. Div., 19, 21
7th Regt., ROK 6th Inf. Div.: at Kunu-ri, 55
78th AAA Gun Bn., 151
72nd Tank Bn., 269
77th FA Bn., 63, 99, 107, 111–12, 114, 123
Sheehan, 1st Lt. John E., 94
Shin Sung Mo, 297
shoepacs: shortage of, 33. *See also* clothing, winter
"Shoo-Fly" bridges, 320. *See also* bridges
Shriver, Sgt. Richard H., 276, 278
Signal Service, 321
Silver Star, 92
Sinanju, 56–57, 153
Sinchangcham, 262
Sinchang-ni, 98–99
Sinnim-ni, 206
Sinuiju, 21
606th Squadron (B-26s), 308
61st FA Bn., 169–71
64th FA Bn., 134

66th Army (Chinese), 61–62, 102–104, 145, 150, 394
Skeldon, Lt. Col. James H., 69–71, 176, 183, 186, 208, 247
Sloane, Col. Charles C., Jr., 64–65, 139, 165, 206, 241–43, 266, 311
Smith, Maj. Gen. Oliver P., 26, 215
Smith, Pfc. Lawrence E., 65
Smith, 2nd Lt., 270–71
Snow, Edgar: and interview with Chou En-lai, 8
Sochang-ni, 86
Sok To Island, 32
Soloway, Sgt., 123
Somin-dong, 180, 185, 192
Songchon, 55, 98, 303
Song Yo Chan, Brig. Gen., 370
Sosa-ri, 324
South Korea: planned date of invasion of, 11
South to the Naktong, North to the Yalu, xiv
Soviet Union, 8–9, 364, 386–89
spare parts: shortage of, 33. *See also* cannibalization, vehicle
Spellman, Maj. James W., 307–308
Stai, Capt. Melvin, 68, 171, 172–74
Stalin, Joseph, 8–9
Stanley, Capt. Milford W., 139
State Department, 297
Stebbins, Col. Albert K., 49–50, 313, 314, 427n.1
Stephens, Col. Richard W., 315
Stevens, Capt. Simon J., 273, 289
Storrs, 1st Lt. Barrie E., 199
Story, Lt. Col. Anthony F. ("Toney"), 57
stragglers: counting of, 287
Strahorn, Sgt. Robert, 172
Straight, Michael Whitney, 436n.82
Stratemeyer, Gen., 56, 312
Strong, Col. Pascal N., 279, 360–61
Stuart, Lt. Col. Clarence E., 222, 308–309
suicide: as Chinese military tactic, 120
Sukchon, 305, 307
Sullivan, Sgt. Emerson A., 392
Sumner, Capt. Gordon, Jr., 99
Sunchon, 147
Sunchon road, 227–94, *passim*; described, 261, 278; fireblocks on, 280–82

supplies, Chinese, 30, 147
supplies, Eighth Army, 28, 32, 83, 160–61, 165, 224–25, 305–10, 324, 375–76. *See also* demolition policy; logistics and supply; "scorched-earth" policy
swords, sidearm, 88
Syngman Rhee, 8, 97, 360, 392

tactical air control, 80, 282
tactical errors: of Gen. MacArthur, 26, 31, 388–89; of Eighth Army, 314, 354
tactical plan, Chinese: against Eighth Army, 45
Taebaek Range: roadway through, 343; and separation of commands, 27–28
Taechon, 50, 61, 90, 145
Taedong River, 32, 47, 93, 202, 304, 310–11, 316
Taegwan-ni, 349
Taeryong River, 47, 147–48, 151–52
Taiwan, 8, 11. *See also* Chiang Kai-shek; troops, Nationalist Chinese
Takahashi, Lt. Gene, 162, 163, 164
tank landing ships (LSTs), 32, 294–96
tanks: CCF infantry assault on, 197–98; fire among ROKs, 213; in fireblock, 249–50, 252, 265–66; at Hill 222, 117–18, 119; secret equipment on, 329–30; with Turkish Brigade, 88
Tanner, Lt. Col. Howard N., Jr., 234
Tanner, Lt. Col. James, 286
Task Force Dolvin: composition of, 51; mission of, 51–53; northernmost location of, 63; in order of battle, 40; progress of, 63, 72; renamed, 114; in 25th Inf. Div. attack, 104–106. *See also* Task Force Wilson
Task Force Indianhead, 335
Task Force Wilson, 114; attacked, 115; CP of, attacked, 119–20; cut off, 123; dissolved, 130; fights back to Ipsok, 128; withdraws, 126–30. *See also* Task Force Dolvin
Taylor, Sfc., 129
10th AAA Group, 149, 153
X Corps, 5, 21, 31, 193, 351, 358, 360
terminology, military: comments on, xv–xvi

terrain, 45–48, 54, 55. *See also* topography
Terry, Capt. Leslie C., Jr., 138–39
Terry, Lt. Col. A. T., 123
Thackeray, Adm.: ordered to remove supplies from Inchon, 360
Thailand 10th Expeditionary Force, 38, 300
3rd Bn., 9th Inf. Regt., 64, 156
3rd Bn., 35th Inf. Regt., 135
3rd Bn., 31st Inf. Regt., 7th Inf. Div., 21
3rd Bn., 24th Inf. Regt., 25th Inf. Div., 223–24
Third Field Army (Chinese), 12
3rd Plat., B Co., 9th Inf. Regt., 65
XIII Army Group (Chinese), 12, 22, 352
38th Army (Chinese), 77–79, 93–94, 99–101, 281, 394
38th FA Bn., 24th Inf. Div., 267, 271–76
38th Inf. Regt.: in advance north, 42, 53, 72, 83; CCF attacks on, 155, 177, 190–92; in fireblock, 248–54; movements of, in early December, 300; and 2nd Inf. Div. breakout, 247–49; survivors of, 253; and Turkish Brigade's battle, 91; withdrawal of, to Kunu-ri, 196–98, 199, 211
38th Parallel, 11, 294, 323
35th Inf. Regt., 62, 124, 129; and Unsan, 132–37
39th Army (Chinese), 102, 128, 394
39th Parallel: and waist of Korea, 343
37th FA Bn., 187, 262, 267
359th Regt. (Chinese): strategy of, 156
Throckmorton, Lt. Col., 144
Tidwell, Pfc. Ernest, 67
Timberlake, Maj. Gen. Edward J., 364
Tohoe-ri, 232
Tokchon, 53–55, 80–81
Tokchon–Pukchang-ni road, 84
Tongchang, 190
Tongjukkyo River, 88
topography, 27–29, 164, 344. *See also* terrain
torpedoes, bangalore, 61
traffic, military, 307, 321, 325
training: of reinforcements, 374
transport, military: Chinese methods of, 17; lack of, north of Pyongyang,

transport, military (*cont.*) 306; and road-rail conditions north of Wonsan-Chinnampo, 31; in 2nd Inf. Div. withdrawal, 191. *See also* APAs
troops, Chinese Communist: American perceptions of, 351; assist British soldiers, 315; at Kaechon, 91; leaders of, 15–17; numbers of, 13, 45, 399n.11; orders of battle for, 44–45; prefer to fight Americans, 367; and Pyongyang, 354, 379–80; in rear areas, 184, 232; synonyms for, 5. *See also* People's Liberation Army; discipline; military tactics, Chinese
troops, Nationalist Chinese: and American prisoners, 253; MacArthur's plan to employ, 218–19, 298
troops, North Korean: activity of, behind Eighth Army, 346–50; as guerrillas, 45; occupy Pyongyang, 354. *See also* guerrillas; North Korean Army
troops, ROK: CCF disguised as, 198; discipline of, 84; and Iron Triangle, 350; and lack of technical knowledge, 370; Turks accidentally attack, 89
trucks, 55, 82, 252, 307. *See also* transport, military
Truman, Harry S, 23, 297–98, 346, 389
tunnels: enemy ammo and billets in, 190
Turkish Brigade, 87–92, 190; attacks ROK troops, 88–89; Eighth Army command decisions on, 34, 49, 83, 90, 196, 359; equipment losses of, 289; leaves Pyongyang, 312; problems of, 233, 323–25; and refugees at Kanghwa-do, 358–59; and Sunchon road fireblock, 227, 229–30, 255; and 38th Inf. Regt. near Kunu-ri, 206–208
Turner, Lt. Tom, 253
turning movements, 74, 83. *See also* flanking movements
Turtle's Head: of Kuryong River, 106
Turun, Maj. Faik, 87
25th Inf. Div., 34, 50, 130, 147, 199, 222–23, 287
25th Recon. Co., 124, 125–26
21st Inf. Regt., 24th Inf. Div., 144–45, 146

24th Inf. Div., 143, 145, 147, 152, 220-22, 306-307
24th Inf. Regt., 25th Inf. Div., 131, 137-42, 402n.7: advances toward enemy territory, 63-64; composition of, 51; effectiveness of, 142
24th Recon Co., 145
27th Inf. Regt., 25th Inf. Div., 131, 140
26th Regt., ROK 3rd Inf. Div., 19
23rd Inf. Regt., 2nd Inf. Div.: at Chinaman's Hat, 68-69, 189; and Chongchon River crossing, 223; as rear guard, 210-11; saves K and L cos., 24th Inf. Div., 267
23rd RCT, 237, 266-71
23rd Tank Co., 171
Tyner, Lt. Col. Joseph, 391-92

Uijongbu, 390
Unhung, 137
Unhung-ni, 36, 57
uniforms, enemy, 81, 86, 169-71, 198, 304
Union of Soviet Socialist Republics. *See* Soviet Union
United Nations, 59, 371
University of Seoul: Eighth Army CP at, 392
Unsan, 20, 132; campaign at, 102-104

Vail, Capt. Maxwell M., 160, 161, 162, 164
Vandenberg, Gen. Hoyt, 362
Van Duskirk, Lt. Col. Kryder E., *195*
Vaun, Capt. J. P., 373
vehicles, 82, 252. *See also* cannibalization, vehicle; transport, military
vehicular road. *See* highway
Viveiros, Sgt. Manuel P., 124
Volunteers, Chinese. *See* troops, Chinese Communist

Wadley, Lt. Jack, 231
Wadong, 250
waist of Korea, 26, 311, 341-43, 344
Walker, Lt. Gen. Walton H., *4, 39;* at commanders' conference, 215; death of, 390-93; and Eighth Army advance, 34, 50, 85, 219; and Eighth Army withdrawal, 217, 284, 292, 341, 381-82; and Gen. Collins, 332;

Walker, Lt. Gen. Walton H. (*cont.*) and Gen. MacArthur, 57, 358, 381-82; and Kujang-ni incident, 97; and Pyongyang, 203-204, 217, 294, 312, 313-15, 335; relieves Gen. Keiser of command, 291; "scorched-earth" policy of, 361; whereabouts of, 34, 293
Wallace, Capt. William C., 64-65
Walled City. *See* Yongbyon
warfare, aerial, 21
Warneke, Lt., 273
war of movement: in Korea, to mid-1951, 5
war of position: in Korea, after mid-1951, 5
Warren, Sfc. Jack W., 199
Waters, Donald, 392
Wawon, 88-89
weapons, American: Eighth Army artillery support, 43; jamming of, 173, 184; use of, by Chinese, 17
weapons, Chinese, 17-18, 61; ancient, xiii
weapons, North Korean: Soviet-made, 366
weapons, Turkish: sidearm sword, 88
weather, 49, 60, 82, 83, 112, 119, 188, 205, 355
Weathered, Lt., 167, 168
Weaver, Lt. Col., 89
Weikel, M. Sgt. Thomas E., 177
Wei Wei: on Chinese appointment of commander, 10
We Yu Shu, 156, 188
Whitney, Gen. Courtney, 56
Wichon River, 129, 130, 137
Williams, Lt. George, 159
Willoughby, Maj. Gen. Charles, 45, 56
Wilson, Brig. Gen. Vennard, 114, 126, 128, 224, 359
Wise, Lt. Jim, 276
Wolbong-san, 89
Wolff, Lt. Col., 165
Wolfhound Regiment. *See* 27th Inf. Regt.
Wolpo-ri, 94, 95-96
Won-ni, 210, 270
Wonsan, 28
wounded: convoy of, ambushed, 122; desperation of, 264-65; evacuations of, 153, 226, 287; at Hill 153, 188. *See also* casualties, battle (UN)

Wray, Capt. Lincoln, 277
Wright, Brig. Gen. Edwin K., 56, 313, 375, 381
Wright, Sfc. John H., 329
Wurtzler, Lt. Col. Herbert W., 330
Wynn, Lt. Ellison C., 65, 166, 167

Yalu River: described, 47; importance of, 23–26, 43–44. *See also* bridges
Yangnim Range, 27–28
Yangwon-ni, 230
Yazici, Brig. Gen. Tahzin, 87, 90–91, 92, 207

Yesong River, 320
Yonchon, 348
Yonchon-Seoul axis, 397
Yongbong-ni, 231, 232
Yongbyon, 408n.2
Yongpo-dong, 129
Yongsan-dong, 134, 135, 151, 152
Yongwon-Maengsan road, 83
Young, Lt. Col. M. F., 315
Younger, Maj. A. E., 315
Yu-li, 310

Zabilski, Lt., 307